The Powered Paragliding Bible⁶

Jeff Goin

www.FootFlyer.com

Powered Paragliding Bible⁶

Copyright © 2020 Jeff Goin All Rights Reserved
Published by
Airhead Creations dba FootFlyer.com

Sixth Edition
1st edition printed 2005
2nd edition printed 2008
3rd edition printed 2012
4th edition printed 2015
5th edition printed 2018

ISBN: 978-0-977096640
Library of Congress Control Number: 2019918987

Edited by
Tim Kaiser
George Hawkins
Julian Cates

Polk City, Florida, USA

Email: info@FootFlyer.com

Photographs: Jeff Goin or Tim Kaiser except where noted.
Illustrations: Jeff Goin except where noted
Cover Photo: Jeff Goin (photographer) and Marty Hathaway

For related materials,
please visit **www.FootFlyer.com**.

The information is accurate to the best of our knowledge but errors may occur. This material is protected by U.S. and International copyright laws. No part may be reproduced or transmitted in any form or by any means, electronic or mechanical, without written permission from the publisher.

The reader acknowledges that powered paragliding, paramotors, wing handling, and related activities carry significant risk including dismemberment and death. You take this risk completely of your own volition and understand that the creators of this book assume no liability in connection with its contents.

Printed in Canada

Table of Contents

Is it Risky? vi
How to Use This Book vi
Companion Web Site vi

Section I: First Flight

Ratings 2
What it Takes Physically 2
After Training 2
Finding an Instructor 3

1 The Training Process 3
   Choosing a School 4
   Different Methods of Instructing 5
   Instructor Certification 5
   Training Aids 7
   Choosing Equipment 9
   Preparatory Physical Exercise 10
   Getting to that First Flight 10
   Progression 11
   Instructor Score Sheet 12
   The Wing 13

2 Gearing Up 13
   Risers 17
   Harness 18
   Thrust Spreader 19
   Frame & Motor 21
   Instruments 22

3 Handling the Wing 25
   Deflating the Wing 26
   Brake Positions/Pressures 26
   Preparing To Practice 26
   Calm or Light Winds (Forward Inflation) 27
   Forward Inflation: Setup 28
   Reverse Inflation: Setup 32
   Wind Over 6 mph (Reverse Inflation) 33
   Cleaning the Wing 37
   Storing the Wing 38
   Adjusting the Motor 41

4 Preparing for First Flight 41
   Fueling 42
   Preflight Inspection 43
   Putting it On 45
   Starting the Motor 45
   Have a Plan: Patterns and Altitudes 46
   Taking Instructions via Radio 47
   Handling Emergencies 47
   Launch 55

5 First Flight 55
   Climbout 61
   Basic Control 62
   Flying Around 63

Reflex Wings 65
Landing 66
After Landing 68

6 Adding Wheels 69
   Wheel Types 70
   Setup 70
   Launch 71
   On Balance 72
   Flying 73
   Landing 73
   Risk Comparison 74

Section II: Spreading Your Wings

Fitness 77
Performance 77

7 Weather & Performance 77
   Weather For the Perfect Day 78
   Thermals & the Daily Cycle 79
   Indications of Turbulence 79
   Thunderstorms 80
   Mountains 81
   Beaches 81
   Whenever There's Wind 81
   Lift & Sink 83
   Acquiring Aviation Weather 83
   Best Weather Apps & Websites 84
   Context, Wx Guides, and Luck 84
   Following the Crowd 84

8 Common Sense & the Law 85
   Regulations 86
   Trespass 87
   Who Owns the Air? 88
   Case Law & Other Issues 88
   Commercial Use 89
   If I Violate the Rules? 90
   Exemptions 90
   Airspace Types & Classes 91

9 Airspace 91
   Airspace Classes: the ABC's 92
   More on Reading The Charts 97
   Avoiding Aircraft Flight Paths 98
   Other Uses For the Charts 99
   Things Look Different out West 100

10 Flying From Anywhere 101
   Choosing the Site 102
   Site Permission 104
   High Elevation Fields 104
   Flying at or near Airports 104
   Finding Sites 108
   Telling Wind Direction from Flight Path 108

11 Flying from Controlled Airports 109
Telephone 109
Towered Airport Talk 110
Letter of Agreement 114

12 Setup & Maintenance 115
Harness & Frame Setup 115
Motor.. 120
Deferring Maintenance 121
Reduction Drive 121
Clutch... 122
Propeller 122
Balancing Act 123
Propeller Repair 125
The Wing 126
Emergency Tool Kit.. 129
Reserves 130

13 Flying Cross Country 133
Basic Tips 133
Fuel & Range 134
Getting Lost 134
Navigation 135
Pilotage 137
Altitudes 139
Using a GPS 140
Deep Cross Country 140

14 Flying with Others 141
Courtesy 141
Risks 142
Rescuing a Pilot 143
Communications 144
Formation Flying 144

Section III: Mastering the Sport

15 Advanced Ground Handling 147
Upside Down Kiting to Clean out Cells 147
Kiting Without a Harness. 148
High Wind Techniques 150
Light Wind Techniques...................................... 155
Inflation Issues.. 157

16 Precision Flying... 159
Brakes—The Feel Position 159
Straight Lines—Pendular Precision 160
Finessing the Climb 162
Balance of Power.. 163
Low Flying 164
Catching Suspended Targets............................. 165
Formation.. 165
Active Flying in Turbulence.............................. 166
The Perfect Touchdown 168

17 Challenging Sites...................................... 171
The Horror of Hot, High, and Humid 171
Tight Spaces: Takeoff 173
Tight Spaces: Spot Landing............................... 175

18 Advanced Maneuvers 179
Weight Shift Turns 180
Speedbar Usage 181
Maneuvers Course (SIV) 181
Descent Techniques 182
Wing Anomalies 184
Pendular Control 186
Tip (Stabilo) Line Pull 188
Pressure, not Position.. 188

19 Risk & Safety.. 189
Probability and Severity 189
Energy and Injury... 189
Getting Away With It 190
Where the Risk Is 191
Adding Safety Equipment 196
Combining Risks 197
Handling Situational Emergencies................... 197
Launch Risks 204
Risk To Others 204
It's Not *That* Bad.. 204

20 Competition.. 205
How Good Do I Need To Be? 206
Equipment Selection.. 206
Ground Precision & Pylon Racing 206
Flight Precision (Navigation)............................ 209
Fuel Limited Tasks 209
Endurance 209
Kiting.. 210
Unsupported Races 210
Demonstration Competitions 210

21 Free Flight Transition 211
Transition to Thrust: Becoming a Power Pilot........... 211
Transition to Free Flight: Gone Soaring................... 214

Section IV: Theory & Understanding

22 Aerodynamics & Performance 221
Balance of Forces.. 221
Static and Dynamic Stability 223
Glide & Drag 223
Center of Lift and Drag 224
Sink Rate 224
Speed 225
Efficiency Under Power 225
Wing... 225
Angle of the Dangle 227
Downwind Flying 229
Performance Curves 230

23 Motor & Propeller..................................... 231
Thrust & Horsepower.. 231
2 And 4-Stroke Motors 232
Propeller & Reduction Drives.......................... 236
Balance & Paramotor Geometry...................... 239
Twisting Forces At Work 240
Electric Propulsion 243

24 Weather & Wind 245
Using Forecasts 245
Principles 245
Standard Atmosphere 247
Daily Cycles 247
Yearly Cycle 249
All About Thermals 249
Clouds 250
Fronts 252
Highs and Lows 252
Getting Weather Info 253
Turbulence from Wind 253

25 Roots: Our History 255
Parasailing 255
Hang Gliding & Ultralighting 255
Sport Parachuting 256
Lost Lineage 256
Powered Parachutes 258
Performance Improvements Over Time 258

Section V: Choosing Gear

26 The Wing 261
Ease of Launch 261
Size (Wing Loading) 262
Reflex 262
Steering Options 263
Glide and Sink Rate 264
Stability as Collapse Resistance 264
Handling 264
Speed 264
Mini & Speedflying Wings 265
Certification 266
Kiting-Only Wing 266
Advanced Risers 267

27 The Motor Unit 269
Weight 269
Comfort 270
Thrust 270
Quality 271
Powerplant Considerations 271
Ease of Launch 273
Ease of Maintenance 274
Fuel Storage 274
Propeller Size and Style 274
Attachment Points & Spreader Bars 275
Weight Shift 276
Transportability 277
Support—Parts and Expertise 277
Paramotor Safety 278

28 Accessories 279
Reserve 279
Adding Wheels 280
Helmet, Hearing & Communications 281
Engine Indicating 282
EGT, CHT 282
Wind Indicators 282
Airspeed Indicator 282
Multifunction Meters 282
GPS 283
Emergency Kit 283
Cold Weather Gear 284
Phone Apps as Accessories 284

29 Home Building 285
Non-Welding Choices 286
Building Your Own Design 286
Building From Plans (Scratch) 287
Building From A Kit 287
Testing & Changes 288

Section VI: Getting the Most out of PPG

30 Other Uses 291
Using PPG for Transportation 291
Flags & Banners 292
Cattle Herding 293
Search and Rescue 294
Finding Model Aircraft 294
Public Relations & Exhibition 294
Motor Madness 294

31 Traveling with Gear 295
Shipping 295
Freight Carriers 297
Transporting via Road 299
Customs & Declarations 300

32 Photography 297
Still Photography Basics 297
Video 300

Appendix & Other Goodies 303
Fuel/Oil Mix Chart 304
Repair 304
Instruction 304
Welding 304

Foreword

Easy travel has given me access to our sport's greatest pilots and teachers. They all share at least one thing: a desire for excellence. This is a culmination of that extraordinary wealth of knowledge. And paramotor instructors remain our greatest resource.

No book can instill a skill. We'll show how to do a task, what kind of *practice* will turn it into a skill, and more importantly, how to minimize risk in the process. You can't learn kinematic "feel" from reading, but knowing what to practice, and what success looks like, will certainly help.

Is it Risky?

No Risk, No Reward. Know Risk, Know Reward.

Flight always involves risk. Our limited statistics suggest that risk is about the same as flying small airplanes or ultralights, but we're likely to have more minor injuries. Being a slow, stable craft helps, but other risks, covered in this book, apply.

For complete safety, watch others live life on YouTube. From a bunker. As Wilbur Wright observed: "If you are looking for perfect safety, you will do well to sit on a fence and watch the birds."

We make no quality judgment on risk choices, but rather strive to point out where risk is. When we say "don't do this or that" it pertains to risk avoidance.

How to Use This Book

Don't use this book for self-training!

Absolutely nothing here should be tried without getting *good* instruction first—it's the best money you will spend. It's cheaper than hospitals, funerals, and repairs. Our craft is a wonder of simplicity—graceful and capable aloft, but ungainly and challenging on the ground. And there are some dark corners. Skilled pilots make it look easy, but skilled sword swallowers make *their* endeavor look easy, too.

1. **Section I** takes you from initial training through the first few flights, including terminology. "From first sight to first flight" either on foot or wheels. Later sections will be more meaningful as you progress. It assumes that your instructor will take responsibility for determining appropriate gear, conditions, location, legalities, and other minutia. We do offer guidelines to help understand and evaluate the instructor's choices.

    It avoids academics, like aerodynamics and regulations, because they're not relevant to the physical skills required. That material *is* covered quite fully in later sections.

2. **Section II** provides the basic knowledge needed to head out on your own. Use your instructor and fellow pilots, whenever possible, to make it more relevant to your location and situation. For example, if you live near a big city, ask about charts and airspace. If you live in mountainous terrain, learn more about mountain weather.

3. **Section III** is for mastering the finer points: there are many. Precision control is available to those who are willing to work at it.

4. **Section IV** is for the curious. It offers a more complete understanding of what's going on, especially regarding aerodynamics, while dispelling many stubborn myths.

5. **Section V** is for pilots buying their *second* wing or motor. New pilots should choose an instructor rather than gear, but there is benefit to understanding the trade-offs, especially to avoid shysters who would try to fit their square-pegged gear into your round-holed needs.

6. **Section VI** offers suggestions on "what now?" Some are just plain fun, but that's what this sport is about.

Companion Web Site

Updated and supplemental information to this book can be found on **www.FootFlyer.com**, under "*Educational By Chapter*" using the book's chapter structure (QR code at right points there). Videos and other material are included. Where possible, QR codes will point to relevant pages for convenience.

Section I

First Flight

Laurence Bertin
by Franck Simonnet

Section I
First Flight

For most pilots, powered paragliding is the ultimate in personal flight, providing unprecedented freedom, simplicity, controllable safety, and low cost. There is no runway, no radio, no trailer—just pull up, preflight, and go.

Learning is relatively quick. A dedicated student, under competent instruction, can solo in as little as two days, although 3 to 5 is more common. He can become reasonably independent in a couple weeks, and a confident pilot after a year of regular flying. This section is aimed at those first few weeks.

Ratings

Paramotoring in the U.S. does not require a license or rating unless you're flying tandems (two-seaters) and even that changes periodically. See Foot-Flyer.com for the latest. A rating may be required for insurance, or to fly some sites or events.

Even if a rating is *not* required, it helps ensure that you get thorough training and skills for independence.

What it Takes Physically

Physical requirements are minimal for carts, and average for foot-launching, but some prep will grease the skids. See "Preparatory Physical Exercise" on page 10 for more.

Fortunately, as skills improve, it gets *much* easier. Even after just a few sessions, newly recruited muscles *will* adapt to their strange use as brute force gives way to finesse. A skilled "kiter," for example, can go for over an hour with minimal exertion, whereas a neophyte will be winded in a few minutes.

Even after the recommended exercises, expect some muscles to ache for a few days. It's well-earned soreness to be relished.

After Training

After training, try hooking up with a community which is especially handy for finding sites ("Finding Sites" on page 108). Section II is for pilots setting out on their own.

by Angie Bateman

The Training Process

CHAPTER 1

No, a license is not required, but skill certainly is.

Paramotoring may epitomize aerial simplicity, but without proper training, it can be an arduous, vexing, and probably painful pursuit. Quality instruction takes you through important milestones while making the process safer and more enjoyable.

With proper care and appropriate gear, mature children can learn paramotoring.

Skimping on good instruction can easily cost more in equipment repair and/or medical expense than any saving gained.

Plus, flying in anyone's national airspace system is not trivial. Given societal fears, heading aloft without knowing the rules is at best irresponsible. Fortunately you've taken a huge step by using this book—let your instructor bring it to life.

Finding an Instructor

We do this because it's fun—so, too, should be the training. Find an instructor you get along with, who is thorough, known for *safe*, quality teaching, has the necessary tools, including training aids, and has access to good flying sites.

Instruction is a lot of work for both of you. Don't expect to be pampered, but do expect to be treated with respect. Become immersed and you'll probably get along with anyone. Most instructors teach because they love making pilots. They are the sport's national treasure.

Start with the "Instructor Score Sheet" on page 12, which includes getting advice from respected pilots, especially those with nothing to sell. Try to visit potential schools, talk with the instructor(s), and watch them train to learn their demeanor and style.

For certification, make sure they use a respected organization that's focused on paramotoring, if available. Instructor certification is not required in many countries (except for tandem), but it shows that they meet the organization's knowledge and skill minimums, and have access to its resources. In the U.S., that's the U.S. Powered Paragliding Association (USPPA).

Fig 1-1 Go tandem in *something* before soloing—something you get to control. The closer to what you'll be flying the better. There *are* those who react poorly to piloting.

Wheeled tandems are ideal but rules can make it difficult depending on the country and may require more formal certification. In the U.S., powered paraglider tandems are allowed under non-governmental exemptions granted to organizations such as the USPPA. Regulations may differ between wheel and footlaunch tandems. Current information is at the QR link below.

 Fig 1-2 USPPA schools and Tandem certification status can be found at footflyer.com/training-status/

Be careful choosing instructors with only a year of flying themselves—they won't have a depth of experience or know the intricacies of student issues. If they are inexperienced, find out how they got certified.

They should use the national organization's current syllabus to help ensure important information is covered. Not all do, even if they're certified. An old syllabus won't include the latest improvements. Favor those who are actively giving ratings, which suggests they're current with best practices.

Don't worry so much about equipment and be leery of pushy sales pitches. The "legends in their own mind" types are among the worst teachers.

Like all aviation, expect trade-offs. Gear must match your size, weight, and intended take-off elevation (high elevations impose different choices). A reputable instructor will do this matching within the gear he sells. Success has *far* more to do with your **attitude** and **instructor choice** than gear.

Choosing a School

The person who actually does your training is the most important factor in choosing where to learn, but there are other considerations.

- A large school isn't necessarily a better school just because it's bigger. It is, however, more likely to be full-time which makes scheduling easier. You'll be able to train on consecutive days which hastens progression. Travel can be a drawback and support will be handled remotely.

- Fewer students per instructor is desirable during more intense instructional phases, namely kiting and first flights—it's safer and better for learning.

- Smaller schools, even just one-person, part-time affairs, can offer equally good training, but it may be spread out over more time. Being local likely means better support for equipment, places to fly, advanced training, and probably a ready community of other pilots. If you have a qualified local instructor, be thankful.

- Some instructors will come to you, but find out what expenses you'll be covering—it may be less of a value. Also, consider how you'll get service after they leave. Can they do tandems? One benefit is that they may help find local sites, identify local weather patterns, and cover your particular airspace issues.

- Location, location, location. They need access to a sufficiently open area to fly.

- They should have appropriate training aids (Fig 1-8, Fig 1-13) and examples of what they sell. It's common to have only a few types of wings and motors since they've figured out how to train on them and provide support.

- Ideally, the school *provides* equipment, including an easy-to-launch "school" glider in the right size ("Choosing Equipment" on page 9). That's less money *and* safer, plus they have more vested in your success. You will obviously be responsible for damage, and can expect a significant deposit.

- If you need insurance, or want to fly anywhere that requires ratings, make sure the instructor is *actively* offering them. Of course, you must pass a skills test—the actual rating is not a given.

- Make sure they use best practices to minimize risk. See "Training" on page 191.

A tandem introductory flight lets you try paramotoring before diving in wallet-first. It takes around 50 solo flights before most pilots start to feel independent. After only 10 flights you're nowhere near ready to set out on your own. Be super leery of any instructor that suggests otherwise.

Different Methods of Instructing

One size does *not* fit all: some instructors are laid back, some are intense, some are more aggressive, and some are conservative. Disciplined drill sergeant types with a serious demeanor can be *very* effective if you have thick skin.

Schools in mountainous areas tend to teach free-flying first. That's fun in its own right and has some advantages. Plus you learn a different type of flying. But it can be more limiting since weather must fit a narrower window. You will learn "para*waiting*."

Flatland schools tend to teach motor flying only. Better schools incorporate tow or tandem flights. A few don't offer either one—your first flight will be your first solo which is not ideal. Under strong guidance, very good kiting skills, proper practice on the simulator, reliable communications, and a huge open field, it *can* be done with acceptable safety. Using a stable, wheeled platform improves your chances for early success even more (Chapter 6 on page 69).

The best instructors adapt to each learning style, but some adapting on your part is needed, too.

Fig 1-3 Free flight paragliding

Seek balance in pacing. For example, if you or the instructor pushes too hard, you'll skip necessary information or rehearsals. On the other hand, going too slowly means re-learning prior lessons. Don't let ambitious scheduling encourage shortcuts or extra risk. For example, needing to be on tomorrow's flight home isn't worth taking on today's nasty air.

Good instructors have tools that allow working in the broadest conditions. For example, they'll have smaller wings to allow higher-wind ground handling practice.

We love the leeway of our minimal regulation, but it's up to us to become informed, responsible citizens of the sky. Like all freedoms, paramotor flying requires responsibility—we either accept that responsibility or lose the freedom.

Fig 1-4 One on One

Instructor Certification

Certification is a good, qualifying start.

Anyone can hang out a shingle, but not everyone can demonstrate the skills and knowledge. There may be good uncertified instructors, but the onus is on you to determine competence and thoroughness. Expect that any instructor who downplays certification may well skimp on other areas.

Fig 1-5 Tandem Wheel-launch

Certification requirements vary dramatically by organization. What minimums apply? What skills have to be shown to become rated? An instructor can hardly teach skills they don't possess. Do they get recurrent training themselves? The USPPA has a thorough program but, even then there is variety in who is good at teaching.

Just because someone can fly well, and even pass a certification course, doesn't make them a great teacher. That requires patience, dedication, discipline, and a desire to see someone succeed. Effective teaching of paramotor is a completely different skill than precision control of a paramotor.

Fig 1-6 Towing

No ratings program is perfect, either. They all rely on imperfect humans, and regardless of organization, there will be variety. It's a flaw that bedevils even government certification programs.

Towing For Training

Towing is valuable for training but is terribly unforgiving of carelessness. Best practices include a proper towline, a "tow-assist" type split bridle with release mechanism, line tension control, a way to cut the line (like a hook knife), and a weak link that breaks before overstressing the glider. Tow operators should be certified for towing and use best practices as listed by their certifying org (USPPA.org or USHPA.org in the U.S.) Towing is safer with a dedicated, skilled tow operator *in addition* to the instructor.

Special procedures and gear make towing safer, including reliable radio communications. Pilot response usually comes from kicking the legs fore and aft for "yes" or waving them left and right for "no." Below are the most common tow types.

1 Stationary winch towing uses a powered drum to reel in tow line fast enough to fly the connected pilot. Tow operators (techs) control reel-in speed with a throttle.

2 A Turn-Around Pulley lets the instructor be next to you during launch, but it adds risk since you are going *away* from him. It's harder to see how much distance remains to the pulley, and flying past the pulley can be disastrous. Low tows, less than 10 feet high, are *somewhat* safer.

3 Truck or Boat towing uses a pay*out* winch to reach higher altitudes, commonly over 2000 feet. It requires a longer run to allow paying out more line. Boat tows, which get the highest, are used for special maneuvers clinics (page 181).

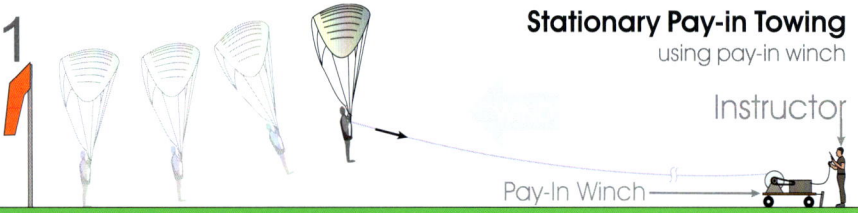

Stationary Pay-in Towing using pay-in winch

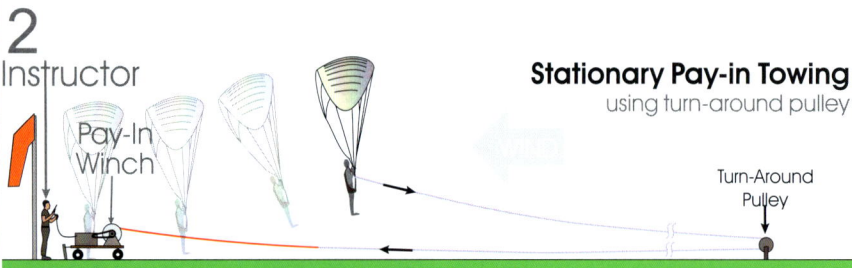

Stationary Pay-in Towing using turn-around pulley

The truck (or boat) starts moving, paying out line and pulling the pilot with a controlled tension. It may be moving 30 mph but line is paying out at 10 mph for an effective pull of 20 mph. Line length quickly increases. The operator controls how fast the line pays out by controlling drum resistance (tension). Once the pilot releases, a motor winds the line in.

4 Some instructors use low power vehicles (quads) and short lines which is inherently riskier. Towing like this by untrained people is horribly dangerous.

In any towing, more wind means more altitude, just like if you were pulling a kite. Line tension is metered to prevent dangerously steep climbs, overstressed gear, or other maladies. Weak links are especially important on pay-out systems since, if the drum stops, line suddenly starts moving at the vehicle's speed, imposing immense loads on the glider.

Pay-out Towing using pay-out winch

Truck speed: **30 mph**
Payout speed: **10 mph**
Pilot speed: **20 mph** (over the ground)

Boat towing gets the highest so it's used for maneuvers clinics or acrobatic (acro) practice. Extra precautions are needed, namely flotation for the pilot. Boat tows can be a bit bumpier in rough water since wave action gets transferred through the line.

Static-Line Towing using low-power vehicle

Extremely dangerous! Requires a *highly* skilled operator, and a low-power quad to reduce inherent risk.

ATV speed: **20 mph**
Pilot speed: **20 mph** (over the ground)

More on towing: footflyer.com/paraglider-towing-for-training

Fig 1-7 Tow line may be color coded so the operator knows how much line is left. Seeing red means the tow must end shortly. Reaching the end of the drum would be ugly.

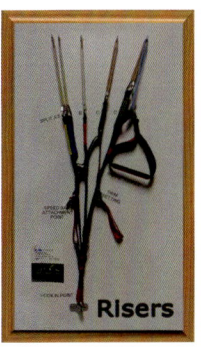  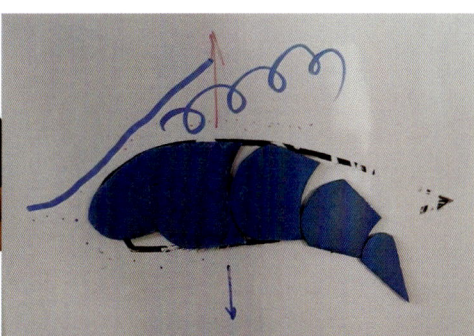

Fig 1-8 Visual Aids
Better schools will have training aids that make quick work of learning certain concepts. There's not much—this is mostly a physical endeavor—but what's there is important.

Training Aids

Training aids like these (Fig 1-8) are surprisingly helpful, but the most essential tool is a quality simulator (more on page 8). Plus, schools need a way to get students airborne and in control of *something* before their first powered solo. That reduces first-flight jitters, and may reveal a dangerous reaction to being airborne in the open. If your school does not offer a way to do this (towing, hill launch or tandem), get at least one dual training flight in whatever craft is available—a powered parachute or other open ultralight where you can control it. The fewer sensory firsts on your solo flight, the better.

Towing

Towing provides experience controlling the craft through launch, climb, glide, and landing, before adding thrust. Increasing skill allows for higher flights, although a few instructors do high tows from the start.

Towing is also used to get free flyers high enough to catch rising air currents (thermals) and soar without power. Payout winching is more common for that because it gets pilots over 2000 feet (600 meters) high. In the right conditions, soaring pilots can then fly for hours—a skill that requires handling more turbulent conditions but provides different sensory rewards.

Low tows, less than 10 feet, have some safety benefits but still require extreme care since you're continuously close to the ground.

With some minimum breeze (5-10 mph), hand towing is possible using appropriate precautions. It gives some minimal feel for the wing, flying, and landing flare, but treat it with respect—the puller must know exactly what he's doing to prevent injury.

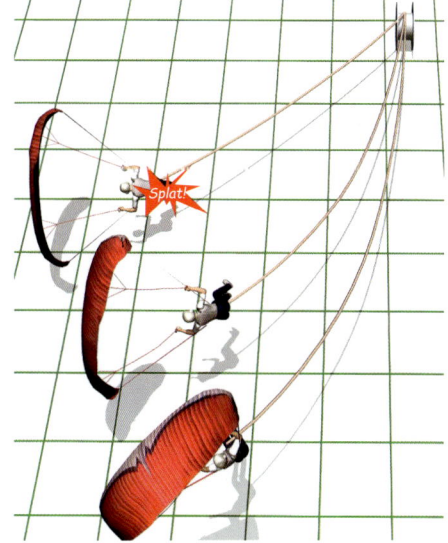

Fig 1-9 Lockout
During tow, if the pilot gets off-heading, the towline's pull makes him want to go off-heading more—and into an even steeper bank. If allowed to continue, it will exceed his ability to correct: that's lockout.

It's more likely 1) with low-time pilots or tow operators, or 2) while using a turn-around pulley (opposite page #2). It's easy to avoid by the tow operator reducing tow tension if a pilot gets off-heading, but it can happen fast, especially when using a turn-around pulley because the line is getting shorter as the pilot is getting farther away (harder to see).

Fig 1-10 (Top) Tandem foot-launching requires the instructor to wield a motor powerful enough for both occupants. Tandem on wheeled craft is safer, especially in very light wind. Some of the most experienced tandem pilots won't do tandem foot-launch in winds under about 3 mph.

Fig 1-11 Wheels are easier, especially in calm winds, and have slightly less chance for damage during training. They are also less likely to incur prop-related injuries.

> **Caution!**
>
> *Learning* paramotor is one of the riskiest parts of the sport. Don't skimp on training. Any school who doesn't use a national syllabus, or use beginner wings in their weight range, or doesn't do appropriate simulation exercises is adding immense risk to your life. Choose wisely.

Hills

Bunny hills are small slopes that allow ground-skimming free flight. You can practice launching, flying briefly, and landing before ever strapping on a motor. Lightweight harnesses make trudging up the hill easier. This is how most students learn to paraglide—launching from shallow hills at first then progressing up to bigger hills where soaring flights are possible.

Ideal slopes drop about 1 foot for every 4 feet forward, enough to get cleanly away from the hill after launch. Flight time (and height) can be metered by how far up the hill you start. Winds must be just right but most schools in hilly areas have several sites to choose from.

Tandems

Tandems get you airborne with an experienced pilot at the helm, granting a basic understanding of handling while gauging your reactions to being aloft.

A *major* benefit is getting to experience and practice handling the craft's pendular swinging behavior. While a tandem does swing different than a solo craft (each swing takes longer), the concept is identical. A good instructor will ensure you have mastered pendular control before sending you up solo.

Control feel on tandem rigs is heavier, and performance is sluggish, but the principles and directions are the same.

The legal status of tandems varies by country as covered in Fig 1-2 with a web link.

Wheels

Starting on wheels with a highly stable cart is another good method to learn. Some schools have students solo on wheels before moving on to foot-launching. It will still take as much time to achieve the requisite skills, especially wing handling, but there's less chance for equipment damage early on. Foot-launching is, of course, quite different from wheel launching (see Chapter 6).

Simulator

A quality simulator (Fig 1-13) is *hugely* important. You'll learn and rehearse critical responses to situations while sitting in your motor unit, hanging by its own hook-ins. Simple straps around a tree limb may work, but more accurate devices with brake lines, bungees, and special riser spreaders are far better.

Key aspects of flying will be learned from this simple setup. Besides certain routine flight drills, you will rehearse emergencies in which solutions are not always obvious and must be practiced. **Rehearsal is the only way to ensure proper responses!**

You will learn to react to instructor directives on the radio while coping with a flood of strange sensations. On that first flight, you'll be glad you paid attention in the simulator.

Throttle Simulator

Handling the wing is challenging enough—adding a throttle to the mix can make it feel like you're starting over. A throttle simulator helps.

It's a regular throttle, preferably with cable, start and kill switches that feels just like the real thing. You get used to handling the wing while working this throttle. It's

Fig 1-12 **Throttle simulator.** If your school doesn't provide one, consider building it yourself. See "Fig 3-6 Throttle Simulator" on page 27.

helpful since adding power is already a difficult transition. A good instructor will also have you practice killing the motor when things go awry.

More advanced versions have a kill switch that beeps when pressed so the instructor knows you're pressing it—a critical reaction to learn. But even just practicing while holding a throttle-sized stick can help acclimate to the extra complication.

Weighted Frame

You may use a motor frame (no motor) for early training then progressively add weight as you improve. This great technique lets you learn kiting with the bulky frame and harness but without the full burden of the motor's weight.

Multimedia

There are some highly useful videos: Powered Paragliding Essentials, Risk and Reward, Instability II, and the Master Powered Paragliding series, among others. Airspace and Law for Ultralights clarifies this difficult topic with live action and motion graphics. These tools, though, cannot begin to replace thorough instruction.

Radios

Being a solo craft makes communication critical. Good radios allow the instructor to give directions while you learn launching, flying, and landing. If something goes wrong, or conditions change, the instructor can provide guidance. You'll either have to purchase or be provided with a helmet that works with the radio or comm system that your instructor uses. A few allow two way, hands-free communications.

Choosing Equipment

You must first survive. These tips will help.

If possible, use instructor-provided gear as covered in "Choosing a School" on page 4, or at least use what the instructor teaches on since he'll be familiar. Choices for *after* training are covered in Fig 26-6 on page 262.

Training success has little to do with brand as long as your instructor is familiar with it. If you bring your own gear, then there may be a learning curve while the instructor learns its nuances. If you bring unacceptable gear (too heavy, too little power, dangerous, etc.) the instructor may wisely opt out of training on it.

Wing

A wing for *learning* has very specific requirements.

Avoid the dangerous trap of skipping a "beginner" wing because you don't want to have to buy another after training. A good pilot, even on that wing, will do amazing things. It's easy to barrel roll a tiny wing, rolling a school wing requires finesse and mastery of energy management.

A first wing should minimize your chance of getting into roll oscillations and be forgiving of excessive brake—common, consequential student errors. Highly capable humans have come to grief because they bypassed "beginner" gear and chose something "hotter," usually smaller than what was recommended.

The wing should be 1) EN-A rated, 2) configured essentially as it came from the factory, and 3) flown within its weight range. That means your weight, the motor's weight with fuel, and the wing's weight.

Motor

Chapter 27 covers motor choices for an experienced pilot.

When learning, excess power is *not* your friend—it contributes to pitch oscillations and unwanted twisting. The chart in Fig 27-3 shows ideal thrust for new pilots, but it's common to learn with more.

Fig 1-13 Simulators

1. Don't expect this in your training, but it's out there. Rob Catto's Virtual FootFlyer is an immersive experience that lets students learn and correct for the unusual pendular behavior of a paramotor. Version 2 of its flight code is far more realistic and even allows limited aerobatics.

2. This simulator lets you practice taking radio directions while experiencing the noise, vibration, distraction and feeling of full power. It helps ensure responses are swift and correct when it really counts.

3. The most effective simulators allow manipulation of risers, brakes, and throttle. A practice reserve can also be added.

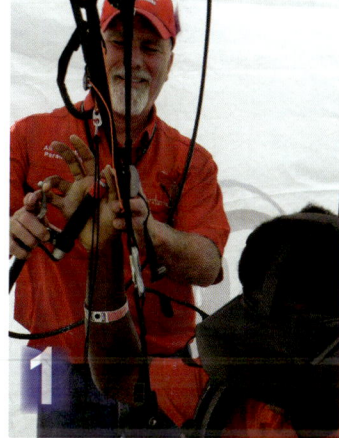

Here is the latest on paraglider and paramotor simulators: footflyer.com/paraglider-simulator/

Fig 1-14 Exercise

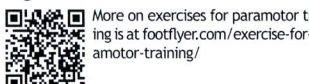
More on exercises for paramotor training is at footflyer.com/exercise-for-paramotor-training/

Fig 1-15 Risk & Reward

A must-see video is the classic "Risk & Reward." Watch it with your instructor and ask about anything that's not clear.

William Shatner, who appears several times, had 12 flights of instruction in California then, several years later, asked for help flying into a Chicagoland charity event. As a certified airplane pilot he knew the importance of training, recency of experience, and personal limitations.

Below is Mr. Shatner flying East over the Northern Illinois landscape, accompanied by Nick Scholtes (on the right), myself (shooting the picture), and several other Illinois pilots. The mission was a success. Score one for the Federation.

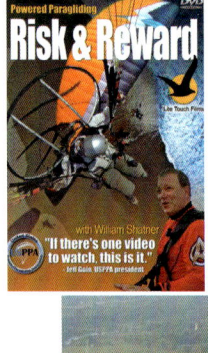

Preparatory Physical Exercise

You don't need to be an athlete, but footlaunch students will benefit from certain exercises—mostly for kiting, but also for managing the motor. Footflyer has more (see the QR link in Fig 1-14) but here are some basics.

- Cardio: anything that gets you breathing hard for at least 20 minutes helps with endurance, especially running. It's valuable for kiting—the skill that best predicts success in paramotor (or paraglider) launching. Interval training is ideal.

- Squats and leg exercises. Good kiting technique involves moving with bent knees which is most closely matched by these exercises. Leg lifts and "core" exercises help with getting into the seat and carrying the motor.

- High repetitions of lightweight dumbbell lifts and lat pull-downs will help with arm endurance while kiting. Choose a weight that you can lift at least 10 times.

Getting to that First Flight

An open-minded attitude drives success, enjoyment, and safety. Listening intently and reacting properly is key, and it's not always easy: new pilots struggle to process instructions amidst the cacophony of sensory overload. Listen closely. The instructor must be confident you'll respond.

Be prepared to work. Even if the training seems harsh at times, or slow, it's due to progressing in a metered, orderly fashion. Many students cement a relationship with their instructor that's enjoyed for years.

How Long Will It Take?

Training time will vary a lot depending on weather, equipment, location, and personal ability. If flyable conditions prevail, expect to solo in 2-5 days of solid training. A solo flight, with assistance, can be done quite early when extra precautions are taken.

Under rare circumstances, you may get an assisted solo on the first day, possibly using wheels. It's a bit riskier since you wouldn't be prepared for emergencies.

Training time depends on your stamina, too. Being able to ground handle the wing (kiting) is the seminal skill for launching—and it takes practice. Newly minted muscles will make their presence known after day one.

Learning is way more demanding than flying. Once equipped with the necessary skills, you'll only bear the motor's weight for a few minutes before launch transforms it into your magic chair. Expect at least 20 hours of "kiting" to get good enough—an investment that will return years of benefit.

Getting to the pilot level (PPG2 in the U.S.), where you can reasonably go out on your own, will nearly always take at least 8 days of training and 25 flights. If you only get a few days, you're not ready to be alone yet. Either fly with experienced pilots willing to be mentors or find another instructor.

Dependent

We love flying in still air, but it's not so great for early training where you want a 6 to 12 mph wind. Gusty winds, common at mid-day, are as bad for learning as they are for flying. Beaches usually serve up sweet sea breezes almost every warm afternoon. That's perfect for learning ground handling of the wing.

Winter weather can be fun if you can stand the cold. Low sun typically leaves smoother winds which is good for kiting, plus it's mellow for more of the day.

Progression

If you must travel to a distant school, try scheduling at least 5 consecutive days at a time. A full week improves your chance of having enough acceptable weather which can be tough. Count yourself lucky if the school is within daily driving range but be prepared to be canceled due to weather—call first.

Arriving on day one, you'll likely be introduced to the people, the school, and yes, the paperwork. Have a full pen and strong glasses—the forms are many and the print is fine. Of course there's risk (see Chapter 19) but don't be put off by the dreadful waivers—our sport has proven safer than they would lead you to believe.

Depending on what the school provides, expect to buy a few things. This book and the videos mentioned earlier were hopefully among them (kudos to your instructor). A kiting harness and helmet are common. Avoid buying gear in advance unless requested by the school—instructors have reasons for their choices beyond profit margins. Most motors and wings are just as good for flying as they are for training—so your best bet is to purchase the gear on which you learn. Then, after gaining a year or so of experience, you can better judge other brands.

Fig 1-16 Kiting

A top-notch instructor will help you become good at ground handling, or *kiting*. It is the foundation of successful launching—by far, the most difficult thing to learn.

This student is learning to kite on a practice glider which is smaller than a regular wing to allow practice in stronger winds.

Expect to be handling the wing (kiting) in the first hour of your training *if* conditions cooperate—a big if. You'll need to practice this essential skill on your own but get rudimentary training first to avoid picking up bad habits. Since mid-day conditions are usually too rough for flying, expect to use that time for simulator or other ground work.

At some point, while gaining proficiency at wing handling (15 - 25 hours is considered ideal), you'll add a throttle simulator. Then the motor (not running). You may do more practice in the simulator with the instructor on radio, possibly with the motor running.

The big day for your first flight will probably include some dress rehearsal and review of emergency procedures before actually going aloft. The solo may be "assisted," which can get you airborne earlier but in a less-prepared state. There is nothing wrong with that as long as you remain committed to further training.

For those able to do training in stages, learning to kite during an early visit is valuable so that you can go home and practice. Mind the cautions given by your instructor—life-changing dangers lurk whenever you're hooked into the wing.

Fig 1-17

A skilled skydiver can expend his excess swooping energy over many meters after a long dive. But trying this on a paraglider is way different in potentially deadly ways. Respect the limitations and dark corners as you would any life and death pursuit.

One common frustration is when you seem to reach a learning plateau or, worse yet, go backward. It happens. One day everything is great, and the next day you're all fumbles. Maddening, but normal. Keep at it; success will come.

Previous Experience

So you're an airline pilot? Or helicopter pilot? Or fighter pilot? Cool. That *will* provide some academic knowledge, but won't help with physical skills. It would be like a sailor thinking he can surf.

Completely new muscle memory must be learned. It's not difficult, but deserves the same respect as your first "V1 cuts" (or auto-rotations or spot landings or hydraulic failures, etc.).

Skydivers must be particularly careful. While there is similarity, there are also deadly differences. Some few skydiver moves can cause catastrophe under a paraglider. *Flying* may indeed be easier, but unlearning those behaviors will be harder. Pay super close attention to the limits of brake pull, riser pull, and steep maneuvering—give the craft special respect.

Don't short-change training based on perceived capability—an arrogance that has proven most unforgiving.

Instructor Score Sheet

An instructor is your most important choice. This tool will help better apportion your own priorities.

- __7__ 10 points. Can he fly to the level you're seeking? For new students that just means consistently launching, landing, *solid* ground handling, and maneuvering.
- __7__ 10 points. Does the instructor have recommendations and a reputation for thorough, quality instruction? And a bevy of capable former students?
- __7__ 10 points. Does he teach and emphasize ground handling skill?
- __0__ 10 points. Does the school provide gear (wing, motor, etc.)? Starting with a correctly-sized, forgiving beginner wing is *much* safer. Plus, this better aligns their primary motivation to yours: successful flying with no damage.
- __8__ 10 points. If you're moving on to precision flying, handling high winds, competition, or acro, the instructor must have those skills. Not all do.
- __8__ 10 points. Can he teach? This involves demeanor, personality, and the ability to convey ideas clearly. The best test is watching him train.
- __4__ 8 points. Do your schedules match? It's a practical but important concern since you must connect with high frequency, especially in the early stages.
- __6__ 8 points. Does the instructor emphasize quality and thoroughness? If he's about being cheap and quick, then don't expect much.
- __5__ 6 points. Does he use the syllabus from a respected national organization or licensing body? This helps ensure you cover what's considered necessary.
- __2__ 5 points. Is he seasoned? Has he flown a wide variety of equipment, conditions, and locations? One year is not much depending on what was *done* in that year.
- __3__ 5 points. Can he support you with spare parts and know-how?
- __5__ 5 points. Is he professional (certified, responsible, reliable, prompt, etc.)?
- __3__ 3 points. Is he efficient? For example, does he have students practice when conditions are good and do ground work when they're not? If they could be kiting but aren't, or he's flying while he should be training, he's wasting time.
- __3__ 3 points. Can he issue a license or ratings? This is more if you want insurance or plan to fly at sites/events that require them.
- __3__ 3 points. Does he have an adequate place to fly? Kite (steady winds)? That can be a big problem and your safety is proportional to the size of the training field.
- __0__ 3 points. Does he have appropriate training aids? At least a simulator with working brakes and riser system, and a throttle simulator for kiting practice.
- __2__ 3 points. Can he get you airborne using either hill, towing, or tandem flights? If he does towing, is he certified? Towing is weirdly dangerous, especially in the hands of marginally trained tow operators (called tow techs).
- __2__ 2 points. Will he test-fly your gear? It's important that he knows what you face.
- __2__ 2 points. How much? The importance of cost obviously depends on your finances, but skimping on training rarely turns out to save money in the long run.
- __2__ points. Will the training site reflect where you'll fly? If you'll be flying in Denver (high elevation), learning in Florida (sea level) may be less ideal.
- __2__ 2 points. What success rate does he have? In the U.S., you can see how many ratings an instructor has issued at USPPA.org. But the best measure of success, by far, is seeing competent prodigy out there mastering their craft.
- __2__ 2 points. What kind of gear will you train on? Lighter is better, but you need *enough* thrust (see "Appropriate Thrust" on page 270). Too much thrust is just as bad or worse. Some choices make it harder to learn on.

Your instructor may well become a friend and resource for your entire journey through this incredible endeavor. Choose wisely.

Gearing Up

CHAPTER 2

If only the Wright Brothers could see our stuff now. This chapter covers the typical gear that gets us up. Later chapters have more on choices and maintenance.

The Wing

The paraglider is your most important piece. It can suffer numerous individual failures and still fly, but it degrades with time and use, especially if not cared for.

During flight, the wing's airfoil shape and arc are maintained through tension. Air goes into the leading edge (front) openings, spreads through internal holes, and maintains a very slight internal pressure. That helps keep the shape along with line tension—front to back and tip to tip.

We share essentially identical technology with soaring (free flight) pilots who launch from hills or get towed up. Purpose-built motoring wings may sacrifice some efficiency for speed and load-bearing capability.

A "collapse" is where part of the wing folds down, usually from a downward gust, and quickly pops out. It's rare and easily managed in the conditions we fly in.

Standard and Reflex Gliders

The term *Reflex* (Fig 2-10) refers to an airfoil shape where the aft portion angles upward for safer flight at higher airspeeds. Standard paragliders have minimal, if any reflex, while many motoring wings have a lot, sometimes only at faster settings.

Fabric

Most modern gliders use a nearly airtight (*low porosity*) ripstop nylon with stouter fabric on top. The upper surface gets more UV exposure and ground wear. Lightweight fabric on the bottom and internal structure lowers weight, which improves inflation. Extra lightweight wings may only have a single surface for all or part of their area: they're easier to inflate but less efficient. With care, a wing will last 300-600 hours but abuse or neglect could halve that.

Wings don't like heat, ultraviolet light (UV from the sun), dampness, harsh chemi-

Fig 2-1 Paramotor

Not all motors have all features, but these (above) are common.

Most manufacturers have at least one model like this, with moderately low hook-in points (Fig 2-21) and pivoting S-arms.

Webbing is another name for large load-bearing straps.

Why So Expensive?

Mostly it's because they're individually hand-made. A highly automated car plant might crank out 500 units in a *day*, the most prolific paramotor maker averages 5 in a day. Labor is the biggest cost and building a paramotor or wing is time consuming. Wings may be cut with a laser but the sewing is still labor intensive.

Engines cost up to half the price of a new paramotor because they, too, are largely hand-built, even if many parts are made by CNC machines.

Wing, Line & Risers Overview

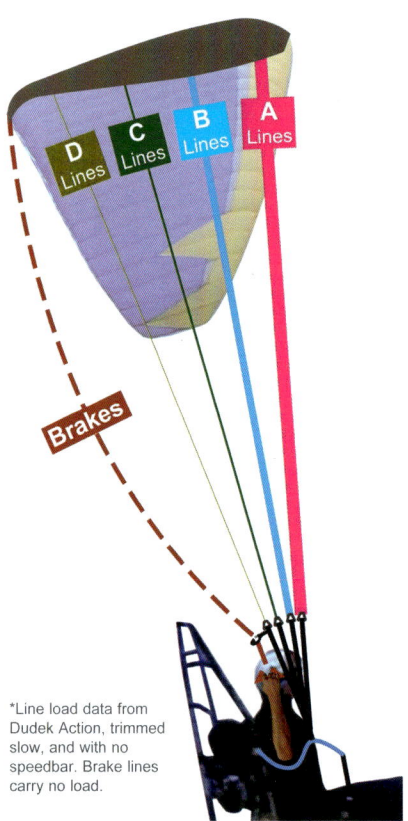

*Line load data from Dudek Action, trimmed slow, and with no speedbar. Brake lines carry no load.

Fig 2-2 Lines Overview

The above side view shows a 4-line paraglider where relative thickness represents load*. It reveals that most load is on the A's and B's.

Also, 3-line versions are common, especially on more advanced models.

Below is a front view of one line cascade.

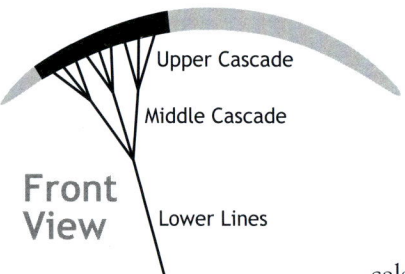

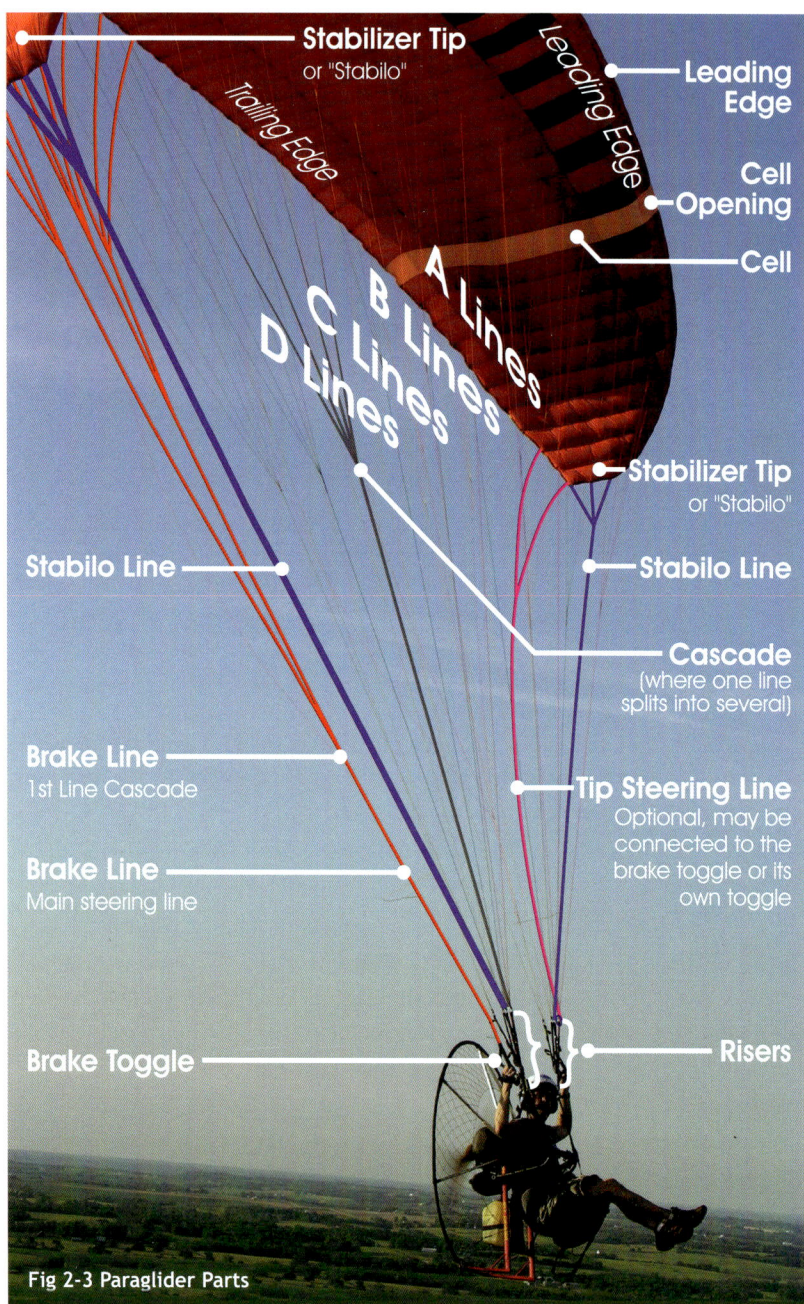

Fig 2-3 Paraglider Parts

cals, sharp objects, gnawing insects, or snagging on things. "Ripstop" just means that tears don't spread *easily*.

Nearly invisible degradation weakens the fabric and makes it porous. Some manufacturers consider 300 hours of direct UV the maximum lifetime exposure. Thankfully, limiting sun time to early morning or late afternoon lowers total UV, so it may last much longer.

Suspension Lines

Three or four rows of suspension lines, lettered A through D (or C), carry the load. They *also* form the wing's primary airfoil shape as set by the risers (Fig 2-7). If the rear lines ("D's" in gliders shown here) shrink, for example, they pull the rear wing down. As Fig 2-2 shows, front lines carry most of the burden.

Risers Detail

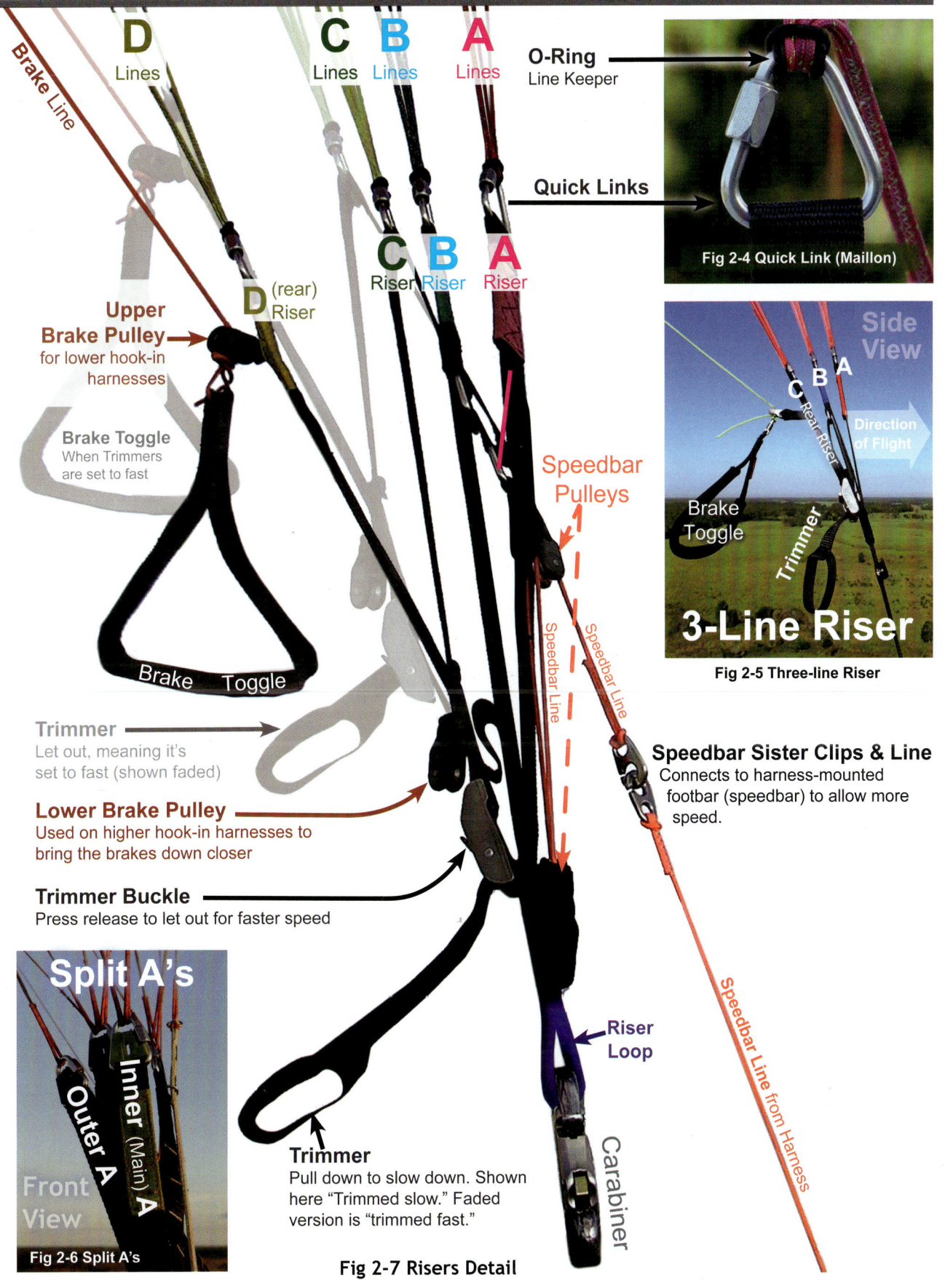

Fig 2-7 Risers Detail

Fig 2-8 Speed Control

Trimmers and speedbar are different approaches to speed control. Speedbar lowers the leading edge while trimmers raise the trailing edge. They may also deform the airfoil in different ways. Neutral trim is usually considered whatever puts the quick links straight across (#1).

Trimmers are set using a tab on the rear risers while speedbar must be held out with your feet using 10+ pounds of push. #1 shows the trimmers set to slow, #2 shows it set to fast. #3 is "trimmed fast" and on full speedbar. In this example, fast trim changes the airfoil to be more reflexed.

Soaring wings tend to only have speedbar while motor wings tend to have both.

Sister Clips (*Brummel Hooks* or *Inglefield Clips*) connect the harness's speedbar to the wing.

Here is how to attach a standard looped line to one sister clip, then connect the clips together before flight:

Fig 2-9 Sister Clips (Brummel Hooks)

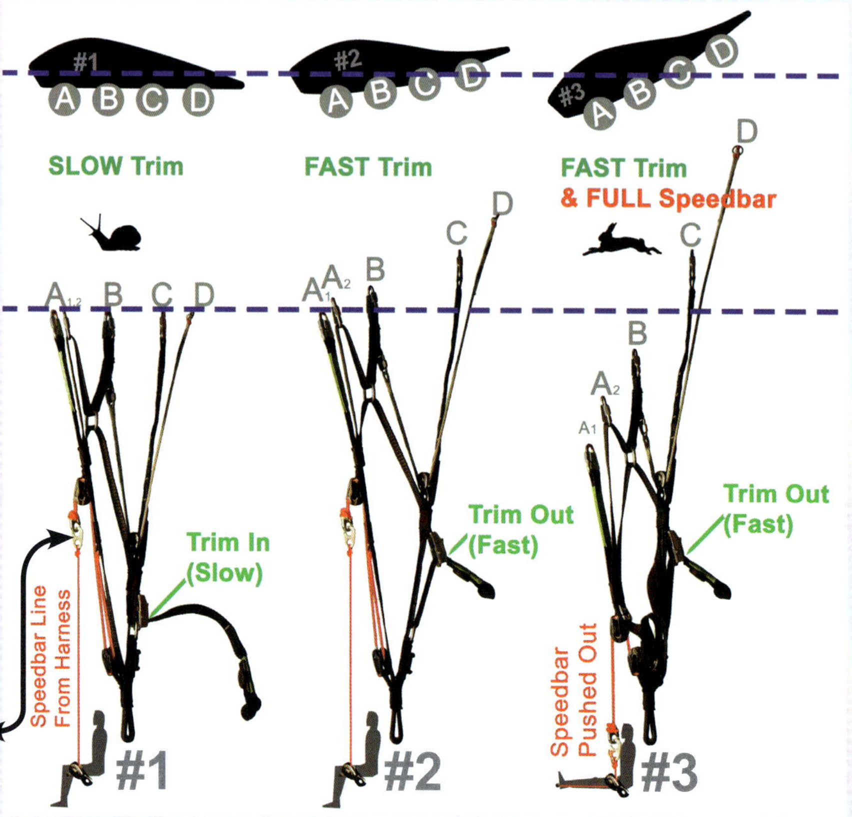

Super high-end competition soaring wings may have only 2 rows of lines.

Line cascades reduce the total number of lines and therefore drag. While each line individually carries relatively little weight, it must be able to handle sudden "pops" from re-inflation after a fold.

Most gliders have small loops sewn into the wing where the lines attach for easy line replacement. A very few models, mostly older ones, have lines sewn right into the wing—not good when individual lines need to be replaced.

Suspension lines (not brake lines) are made with a strong bundle of finely spun Aramid material like Kevlar and are usually sheathed in a thin protective outer weave. They're very strong in the stretch direction (high tensile strength), but degrade if exposed to UV, bent sharply, heated excessively, or put away wet. Don't walk on them or tug hard on snagged lines.

Fig 2-10 *Reflex* cross section

Reflex cross sections (*airfoil shapes*) are used by wing makers to allow higher speed with greater safety. Specific steering methods must be followed at those higher speeds.

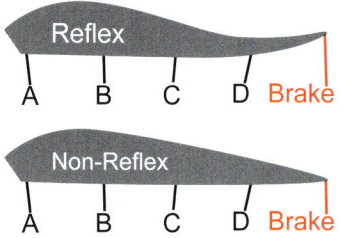

Brake and Tip Steering Lines:

Brake (steering) lines run from the trailing edge (back of wing), down through a brake pulley into toggles held by the pilot, enabling the magic of control. Brake lines are more flexible to better tolerate constant bending at the pulley, but have less tensile strength since they carry no flight load.

Brakes pull one side of the trailing edge down, causing drag that slows that side down. The pilot swings opposite which is what causes the bank.

Some gliders, especially reflex models, have tip steering that can cause a turn without affecting the main airfoil shape. If tip steering is connected to the main brake handle it's called "2D steering" (see "Steering Options" on page 263).

Risers

Our cool, variable geometry wings are mostly managed through *risers* (Fig 2-7) that spread load from the harness's carabiners to suspension lines. Each left or right riser has individual risers, lettered A through D (or A - C for 3 riser systems) that hold corresponding rows of lines lettered A through D. Colors are not standard. The most aft riser (D on a 4-line setup) is called the rear riser.

Quick links, or *maillons* (Fig 2-4), connect lines to risers.

Changing the length of a riser changes the shape of the airfoil and "tilt" (front up or down) of the wing. Wings and risers are certified together, so they're *not* interchangeable. In rare cases, pilots will put motor risers on a free flight wing to get trimmers and/or to accommodate higher hook-ins. We'll cover those shortly.

Weight Ranges in Paraglider Specs

Weight ranges for paragliders may use several terms. Since nearly all gliders are made in metric system (SI) countries, they're in Kilograms (2.2 lbs per kg).

All-up weight: 🚶, ⊕, ⌒. You, your motor with fuel, and wing, ready for launch. This is the most common value and means you must add in the glider's weight (usually close to 5 Kg). It may also be called "In-flight" or "takeoff" weight.

Clip-in weight: 🚶, ⊕, You and your motor with fuel, ready for launch.

Naked pilot wt: 🚶. You (in all your glory). The wing maker hopefully includes a note about how much extra weight is assigned, but 20 kg (44 lbs) is common. Unfortunately, that's for free flight kit, so ask for clarification. This is rarely used.

Trimmers

Most motor wings have trimmers (Fig 2-8) that, when extended in flight, increase airspeed by 10% to 35%. The biggest speed increase is on reflex models. But going faster requires more power, or a higher sink rate when gliding power off.

Reflex wings usually have a longer trimmer range.

Split A's

Some wings have Split A's (Fig 2-6 & Fig 2-12), where the outer A line has its own riser. Among other things, it's easier to reach up and pull down just those lines for a descent maneuver. See "Big Ears" on page 182.

Quick Links

Maillons or Quick Links (Fig 2-4) connect riser fabric to lines to reduce wear and make changes easier. A rubber O-ring usually keeps the lines together so they can't wrap around the Maillon's bottom.

Speed System

Most wings have a speed system that connects to harness-mounted speedbar lines. It's not used during training, and most pilots rarely even hook it up. Competition pilots nearly always do, as do many cross-country pilots. There are two parts: what comes on the risers, and what comes with the harness. On each riser, two pulleys act like block and tackle to give mechanical leverage, which takes more speedbar travel but is easier to push.

Not all harnesses come with proper attachments, but the requisite pulleys are easy to add (see "Speedbar Setup" on page 117). When everything is connected, a foot-activated speedbar is pushed out to tilt the wing down and fly faster. It may also change the airfoil shape (Fig 2-8).

Speedbar is typically more effective than trimmers, and can be released immediately by letting off the considerable foot pressure, whereas trimmers stay set. So speedbar

Fig 2-12 Risers with Split A's & Trimmers

Caution!

Lines on many gliders have an outer protective sheathing that protects their inner Aramid (like Kevlar) core. A break can go undetected as shown below. To check, run the line through your fingers feeling for a "lip" where the Aramid core has separated. If you find one, the line won't hold any significant load and must be changed. Brake lines use a single, flexible material.

Higher performance gliders have unsheathed lines, especially in the upper lines, to reduce drag. They do tend to tangle more.

Fig 2-11 Line Core Break

is more for temporary speed changes, especially when brake input will be needed.

On some gliders, pulling brakes while on speedbar can cause collapses or make them more likely. On a few models, the manufacturer says their wings may be *more* collapse resistant on speedbar *if* controlled using only special "tip steering." Always, *always* consult the wing's manual.

Harness

A harness supports you and your motor in flight, so it's just as critical as the wing. Harnesses are usually mated to a specific motor frame and have at least a seat with leg loops, waist strap, and a way to connect to the motor and wing. But there is a lot more than meets the eye. Some harness models are used on many different frames.

Wheeled craft (carts) frequently have just a seat and belt, although they will have other critical balance adjustments (see "Wheel Types" on page 70.)

Harnesses seem overbuilt, with webbing capable of supporting many times their rated loads, but steep turns or turbulence can push those limits. UV exposure, extreme heat, chafing, chemical, or other damage can reduce margins further, although harness failures are still extremely rare. Frame elements are more likely to fail.

During launch, the wing first lifts the motor's weight, then your weight by the harness's leg loops. Once safely in a climb, you lift your legs into a seated posture which pulls the seat into position so you can scooch back into a comfy posture. Reverse the process for landing.

Harness adjustments are critical for more than comfort—for example, it must not block leg circulation which could leave you numb for landing (*suspension trauma*).

Adjustments accommodate various sizes and weights, so expect your instructor to spend some time on them (Chapter 12). Among other things, they determine how your motor will hang, how it will handle torque, where the brakes will be, and how to best get into the seat (not always a simple matter). Failure to do this could yield a dangerous or unflyable machine.

On at least one brand, you don the harness first, then the motor.

Diagonal Anti-Torque Strap

Propeller torque causes numerous turning evils, so some harnesses add a strap that transfers pull from one side to the other to help alleviate it (Fig 2-14).

On machines that allow much weight shift (shifting one riser up and the other down to help turn), this strap should be loosened after takeoff.

Fig 2-13 Seat Board

#1 shows the seat board up against the frame for walking, launching and landing.

#2 shows the seat board in flight (blue). But when the landing gear (legs) are down it stows against the frame as shown in green.

It also shows how the speedbar is deployed. Before takeoff it is stowed under the seat using at least two double Velcro strips. You won't have this hooked up during training.

Fig 2-14 Anti-Torque Strap

Tighten for takeoff and landing but leave loose for general flying.

Fig 2-15 Fixed Harness

Fixed harnesses take several minutes to detach from the frame.

Fig 2-16 Detachable Harnesses

Detachable harnesses are made to come off the frame quickly for kiting practice and easy transport.

Ground Handling & Sternum Straps

Ground handling, or carry straps, help carry the motor on the ground. They bear no flying loads. Many harnesses include a chest (sternum) strap to keep the motor from sliding off your shoulders. Loosening it once airborne may improve comfort and inflight turning.

High or Low Hook-ins

Footlaunch paramotors have essentially **high** and **low** hook-ins based on where the carabiner's bottom is *in flight*. If it's above the pilot's collar bone, it's a high hook-in, if it's below, it's low. S-arm systems are low hook-in.

Some instructors feel that high hook-in machines are slightly easier to learn on, but there seems to be no difference in safety.

Thrust Spreader

Nearly all paramotors have some type of spreader system to keep the motor from squeezing you against the harness's front webbing (Fig 2-23). If the carabiner hooks to a bar there is a safety strap connecting the carabiner and harness together. That keeps a bar failure from being catastrophic.

Pivoting S-Arm or Gooseneck

Pivoting S-Arm, or "gooseneck" bars (Fig 2-21) are common. They keep the pivoting points (magenta circles in illustration) mostly even with the thrust line. Arms move up and down around the "motor pivot" point.

Over-Shoulder J-Bars

High hook-in systems that use over-shoulder bars (Fig 2-18) impart less wing motion to the pilot, which feels smoother in turbulence. There is no difference in actual collapse resistance but it feels better.

Other variations use pivoting or floating J-bars (Fig 2-17) that allow enough movement to feel the wing's motion and enable limited weight shift. They keep the pilot hanging in the same way as regular over-shoulder J-bars but without being as stiff.

Underarm or "Comfort" Bars

Underarm bars (Fig 2-24) are another approach. Like J-bars, they transfer force to the forward harness straps. The bars may swivel up and down to provide some weight shift steering. In Fig 2-24, the carabiners are above the pilot's collar bone, so it's clearly a high hook-in system. Some models may allow the arms to swivel outward for easier ingress and egress, but they must never be allowed to swivel *inward*—they could come together and cause dramatic twisting under power.

Fig 2-22 Why a Spreader?

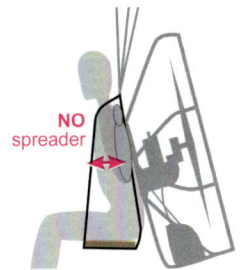
Fig 2-23 No Spreader

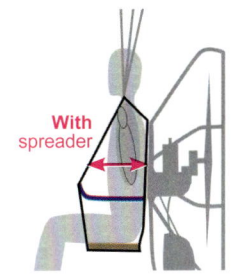
Fig 2-24 Underarm Bar

Some early low-power systems had no spreaders and it worked. But as thrust increased, the pilot would get pushed against his front straps. Various methods shown here solved the problem, although the most popular, by far, is the Pivoting S-Arm.

Harness Styles & Spreader Systems

Spreaders transfer the motor's thrust forward to keep the pilot from being squeezed between the backrest and front harness webbing.

High Hook-in

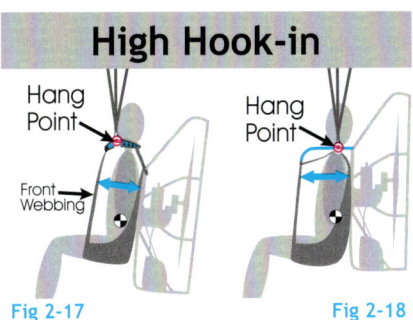

Fig 2-17 Floating J Bar

Fig 2-18 Over-Shoulder J-Bar

Low Hook-in

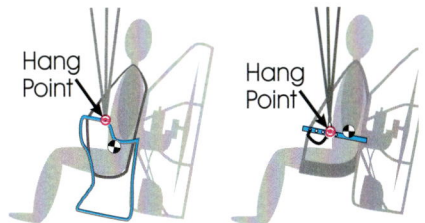

Fig 2-19 Frame Spreader

Fig 2-20 Swing Arm

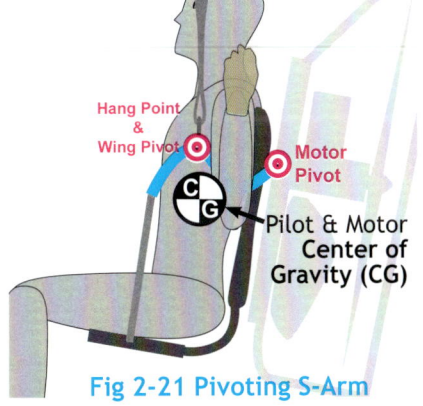

Fig 2-21 Pivoting S-Arm

Fig 2-25 Low & Fixed

Buckle Up

Fig 2-26 Single Point Buckle
Five-point buckles offer quick exit, but must prevent accidental release since that would undo *both* legs. Below is a Velcro release lever.

Fig 2-27 Quick-Release vs Others
Buckles should be quick release to allow for quick egress in case of fire, ditching (water landing), or other reason. Simple rectangle buckles are *not* quick release.

Fig 2-28 Safety Leg Straps
This reduces the chance of hooking in without any leg straps. If the chest strap is hooked up, at least one leg strap is, too. Forgetting both leg straps can be catastrophic.

Fig 2-29 Direct Drive Motor
In the early days these loud, underpowered, but simple direct-drive machines could fly lightweight pilots on larger wings.

On some low hook-in systems, straighter pivoting bars make the attachment even lower. These are intended to more closely mimic free flight harnesses and to mate better with soaring wings that typically have longer risers.

Machines like Fig 2-25 do *not* have pivoting bars and will have less weight shift than those that do. Hip motion tilts the entire frame left/right. Tilting left, for example, lowers the left riser, causing a shallow left turn.

No-Spreader Harness

Only the simplest harnesses, mostly on older, direct drive units like Fig 2-29, don't use separating (spreader) bars at all. These would only be suitable for smaller pilots.

Harness Buckles

Most harnesses have quick release buckles (Fig 2-27 top) with pinch buttons on the side. They are not designed to be released while under tension.

Avoid old-style simple rectangular buckles like in Fig 2-27 bottom. They're plenty strong but would be treacherously difficult to disconnect in an emergency.

Get in the habit of fastening your leg loops first—it may be a life-saver if you start free flying (no motor) where launching without those is usually fatal. On a motor, that may just be embarrassing unless you try to take off. At least buckle one leg loop, even when you're just wearing the motor, to avoid accidentally taking off with both leg loops unbuckled.

Make sure the buckles are properly fastened too—try to pull them apart. If they're not solidly fastened you could fall out after liftoff. The chest strap keeps the motor from falling off backward during launch or abort.

Some harnesses help prevent forgetting the leg straps. These "diaper" styles (Fig 2-28) make the chest strap fasten into a center piece that comes up from between your legs. If the chest portion is fastened then at least one leg is fastened too. Some may also use a central connection point (Fig 2-26) where all the straps come together and fasten with one action. On those, make sure there is no way to accidentally unbuckle since you would fall out when getting out of the seat for landing. Their advantage is rapid escape in case of emergency (water, fire, or other egress woe).

Frame & Motor

The frame is what everything attaches to: the engine, gas tank (or battery), and harness/suspension system. On some machines, the harness can be detached easily enough to use for kiting practice (Fig 2-16). Harnesses are usually matched to a particular frame but some work on many models.

Any good school will match the pilot to a motor based on his size, weight, fitness, and expected launch elevation. Chapter 27 has details on options. Expect a 2-stroke engine with 80 to 280 cc's (cubic centimeters of piston displacement).

Throttle

The most common throttle is #1 in Fig 2-30 although hopefully you *don't* have "cruise control" (throttle lock)—a major source of prop injuries. It can accidentally get set to a high power before engine start.

Carabiners

Carabiners provide the connection from wing to motor or harness. They're like mountain climbing hardware but with a locking gate to prevent accidental opening, which could catch lines or other elements.

Ideally they allow one-handed operation even with gloves since requiring two hands makes it harder to hook in while holding a throttle.

They don't typically allow releasing under tension like sport parachute systems. They must be deliberately unclipped and must obviously stay connected in flight which is more important than a quick disconnect. Even after a reserve deployment, we don't "cut away" from the paraglider. There *is* a "quick-out" carabiner model (Fig 2-33) that can release under tension, but it's rare.

The strongest carabiners are made of steel, but lighter aluminum versions have proven sufficient if not abused. Strength is rated by how many kilonewtons (kNs) they can bear without deforming while the gate is closed. One kN is about 225 pounds. 18 to 22 kN is typical for aluminum, whereas steel carabiners go up to 28 kN. They may list an open-gate strength rating but should never be flown that way.

Carabiners must occasionally support many times their average load due to turbulence or recovery from upsets. They degrade from nearly invisible scratches, cracks, and metal fatigue. Aluminum is the most common, but steel is recommended for higher loads like tandems. There have been failures, so follow manufacturer guidelines on replacement, generally after any physical damage, 5 years, or 1500 hours.

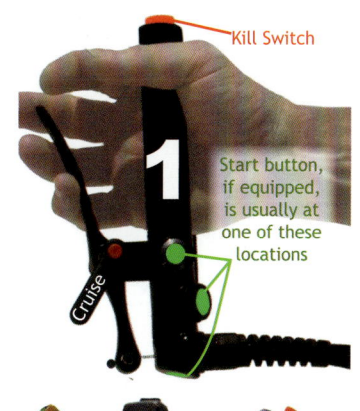
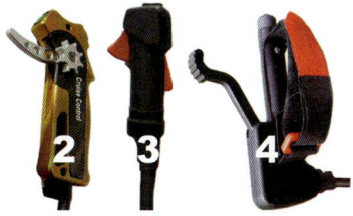

Fig 2-30 Throttles

#1 Standard lever with top kill switch and common e-start locations.

#2 Trigger-style with screw-in cruise control.

#3 Trigger-style with safety switch. A mechanical interlock prevents the throttle from engaging unless a hand is holding its stem.

#4 Standard lever setup for a pull-start only machine.

#5 Finger throttle. This uncommon setup uses the index finger as an actuator. On some models it is difficult to get to the kill switch quickly.

Carabiners & Connections

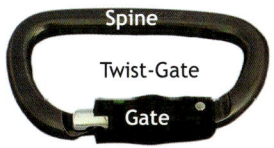
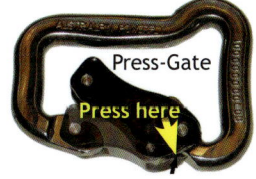
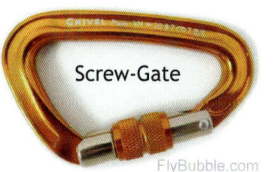

Fig 2-31 (above) Conventional Locking Carabiners

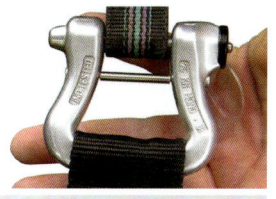

Fig 2-32 Non-Locking **Fig 2-33 "Quick-Out"** **Fig 2-34 "Pin Lock"**

Fig 2-35 Soft Shackle

A backup option for carabiners or other connections is some form of soft shackle, also called soft links. They're extremely lightweight and generally stronger than metal but are not as convenient.

You will not likely see these in a training environment.

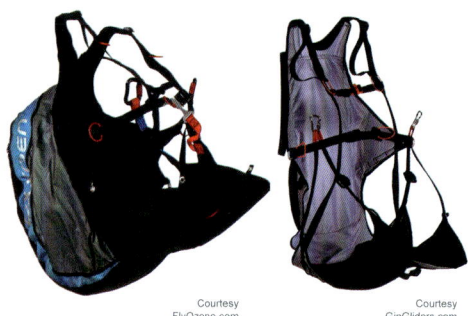

Fig 2-36 Purpose Built: Kiting is different from flying so you'll be most comfortable in a purpose-built kiting harness. Favor those with at least an option for low hook-in points. Use flight-rated (or at least strong) carabiners: you may get lifted in a gust and they must hold.

Fig 2-37 Free flight Harnesses work, especially lightweight models. They're less comfortable than the best kiting harnesses because they tend to scoop your feet out in stronger winds. They're best if you're also planning to do free flight (flying without a motor).

Fig 2-38 Other Harnesses, like those for mountain climbing and utility work, can be used. Try to have separate attachment points about 4 inches above your waistline.

Paramotor Kiting Harnesses

Kiting Harness

Don't skimp on a kiting harness—you'll rightfully spend a lot of time in it so get one that's portable, convenient, and comfy.

Some motors have easily removed harnesses for kiting practice—otherwise, it's not worth the hassle. Harnesses with only high hook-in points will cause back strain after a short time.

Instruments

Simplicity is the sport's hallmark but a few basic instruments are worth their minor added complexity. See "Engine Indicating" on page 282 for more.

CHT, EGT & RPM

The most common engine instruments are Cylinder Head Temperature (CHT) and tachometer for engine speed in revolutions per minute (RPM). Since prop pitch is fixed, RPM is a good indication of power. An engine that's making its rated RPM with the correct prop is making full power. CHT can reveal overheating that suggests a pending engine failure. Its probe is easy to install since it just replaces the existing spark plug washer.

Fig 2-39 A tachometer for motor RPM and a mirror to see how cool you look flying this thing. It shows fuel level too.

Exhaust gas temperature (EGT) reads temperature from a probe in the hottest part of the exhaust stream. Probe life is harder, so they don't always last as long. Plus, the hole introduces a failure point on an already failure-prone part. But EGT is valuable because it's so immediate, whereas CHT ramps up with the metal—it's slower to reveal changes. If the piston gets too hot, it can either get a hole or weld itself to the cylinder walls with dollar signs.

Altimeter

Most altimeters report altitude using atmospheric pressure (also called barometric pressure) since air pressure decreases as you go up. They can show altitude above mean sea level (MSL) or, if set to zero before launch, display height above ground level (AGL) during flight.

Fig 2-40 Temperature and RPM gauges keep track of engine performance.

Cylinder Head Temperature (CHT) and RPM probes are easily mounted. Exhaust Gas Temperature (EGT) requires tapping into the exhaust.

Altimeter watches are generally accurate to within 20 feet if they're set to launch elevation before flight. An altimeter is essential near restricted or controlled airspace.

Altitude from GPS devices is less accurate, although they don't have to be set. A GPS with 20 feet of lateral error will likely have a 100 foot vertical error.

Accessories

Remember: if you bring it, you've got to launch with it, muck with it in flight, and keep it out of the prop. Chapter 28, page 279 has more on accessories, including phone apps.

Flotation

If water landing is a possibility (like flying at a beach), auto-deploying flotation is a must, whether training or not. Students have died from going into water without it. Choices abound and are covered at "Flotation" on page 283.

Water is deceptively dangerous. Before auto-inflating devices became commonplace, drowning was the leading cause of death in paramotoring. It still happens, but now almost exclusively to those who don't bother with flotation.

Reserve

Reserve (or rescue) parachutes offer a last-chance option for major wing malfunctions, midairs, or structural failures. But without proper installation and understanding, it can add more risk than benefit due to the possibility of accidental or improper deployment. See "Reserve" on page 279 for more on choices, "Reserves" on page 130 for installation, and "Reserve Deployment" on page 52.

Reserves go in a pouch attached to the motor's frame. Bridles then attach to the paramotor harness in such a way as to avoid entanglement during deployment. The bridles connect near the paramotor's regular carabiners to ensure sufficient strength to endure opening shock while providing proper hang angle (tilt-back of the motor). Some motor harnesses have special reserve attachments, usually above the main carabiner hook-in. The reserve's pouch has a handle with pins that must be installed and inspected to prevent accidental deployment, a dire situation (see "Reserves" on page 130).

Most schools don't use them during initial training because of the extra weight and accidental deployment risk (see "Accidental Reserve Deployment" on page 203). Schools that teach free flight first *do* frequently use reserve-equipped harnesses if students will be flying high enough for them to work.

Fig 2-41 Built-in Reserve Container
This unit has a built in-reserve container under the seat. It *can* make launching a bit harder because the seat is forced away from the frame.

Fig 2-42 Steerable reserves
These trade steerability for some expense in complexity and cost. On initial opening, they descend vertically until the pilot releases steering lines, then they glide about 2 feet forward for every foot down.

Fig 2-43 Round Reserve
This *pull down apex* is the most common type of reserve. It's made to open quickly, reliably, and have a relatively slow descent for its size.

Fig 2-44 Best Apps and Sites

A number of apps and websites add fun factor while improving safety. Weather, charting and navigation capabilities are especially helpful for cross country flying or exploring. The QR code below points to a Footflyer list of good ones as a base to start searching.

footflyer.com/best-apps-and-websites-for-paramotor-pilots/

Navigation

You might think it's hard to get lost at 25 mph, but think about how many people get lost at 3 mph (walking). Things look different from above, and many areas have few distinct landmarks. Plus, it's easy to get completely engrossed in the experience and find yourself over unfamiliar terrain after only 5 minutes.

GPS navigation options abound. Chapter 28 has more hardware suggestions, with usage tips in Chapter 13 along with visual navigation methods.

Helmet / Hearing Protection

Most schools wisely require a helmet for both flight *and* ground handling (kiting). It's especially valuable for kiting because, if the wind shifts or picks up, you can get dragged. Full face helmets provide protection in a "face plant"—the unflattering result of falling forward—but they restrict head motion, limiting vision, and are rarely used.

PPG helmets usually have decent hearing protection with audio and a microphone. The quietest designs avoid having a chin strap go through the ear cups. Most have a push-to-talk (PTT) switch on an ear cup or, rarely, on a coil that goes out to your hand. See "Helmet Types" on page 281.

Communications

There are many choices but, unfortunately, no standards. Expect to have radio communications with your instructor during training, but after that, it's mostly dependent on the people you fly with.

Aviation radios are typically only used at airports. See "Fig 28-6 Aviation Radio Setup" on page 281 for more. If your instruction is at an airport, usually the instructor deals with it. Outside the U.S. regulations may require a special license. Frequencies depend on location and purpose; check FAA AC 90-50D for frequency allocation.

Check with your instructor about helmets and radios since they rarely play well together. Schools may have a specific model they use for communications and will usually provide it.

Sometimes 2-meter radios are used for their better range and less frequency congestion. They require an amateur (HAM) license, which means passing a multiple-choice test (no Morse code) and periodic use of call signs among other rules.

Special business-band radios may be used in the U.S., mostly by schools that also teach free flight. Pilots must pass a *really* simple test and be members of the free flight organization (visit USHPA.org).

Footwear

Boots generally help reduce ankle injuries while kiting, launching, or landing. Even more so on rough surfaces. Free flyers benefit the most since sites are frequently strewn with nature's rocky randomness.

Choose comfy boots that allow easy running and don't have lace hooks which can snag paraglider lines during inflation—a really dumb reason to have to abort.

If you'll be training in dewy grass, go with something that's waterproof. Otherwise, bring a change of socks to each outing.

Hook Knife

A hook knife, carried on some accessible part of the harness, allows for quickly cutting harness webbing, risers, or lines in an emergency. It's mostly for the unlikely case of getting dragged or dipped (in water). Practice pulling it out without looking since the action must be automatic if you want to count on it.

Handling the Wing

CHAPTER 3

A Kiting War puts kiting skills to the test against other pilots as each one tries to be the last one up.

"But officer, I'm just flying my kite."

Ground handling the glider, or *kiting*, is getting the wing overhead and controlling it in a breeze. Fortunately, it's fun, since capable ground handling is the seminal skill of successful launching. It's also the most challenging aspect to master.

The initial goal is to keep the glider overhead while standing mostly in one place, then ultimately, to make it go where you want with the least amount of effort. Besides reliable launching, kiting capability will make you look good, and spare much costly aggravation.

Finesse and higher-wind skills come with practice which, thankfully, can be done in any open area having a smooth, steady breeze. But it's surprisingly risky without proper instruction. Chapter 15 at page 150 has more on the subject.

Your site should be big, free of fabric-tearing, line-snagging protrusions, and be upwind of buildings or other obstructions that would cause turbulence (a wind shadow). You also want smooth terrain downwind—space you're willing to get dragged through if the wind picks up. A wing's powerful pull in a gust can easily be overpowering.

Use your instructor. He can save enormous frustration with sometimes important and seemingly trivial tips. Once the basics are down and you understand the limitations of when to kite, doing it on your own will hasten the training process *dramatically*. Repetition greases the wheels of progress.

Few students will want to attempt kiting in more than about a 10-12 mph breeze, but it takes at least 7 mph to practice effectively. As skill develops, you should be able to handle winds as light as 5 mph and as much as 14 mph.

A small kiting wing expands the allowable winds.

One thing: in even moderate conditions, be ready to handle the wing, with helmet on, *before* hooking in. A sudden gust can cause a nasty fall.

Fig 3-1 Rear Riser Pull

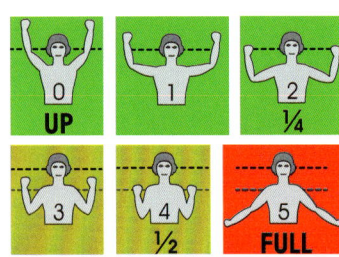

Fig 3-2 Wing is de-powered

Fig 3-3 Brake Positions/Pressures

Learn to equate these positions to brake pressures rather than position. If it takes 5 pounds of pressure to get position 3, remember the 5 pounds.

Gliders vary: one glider's position 2 may do very little, while on another it's highly responsive. Smaller gliders tend to require more pressure but are more responsive.

Think of 0-2 as the green zone, 3-4 the yellow (caution) zone, and beyond 4 the red (danger) zone.

Generally 3 is considered maximum brake for everything except landing.

The bottom numbers (up, ¼, ½, full) are common terms used for brake positions.

Later in your flying career, position 1 will be significant for precision flying as covered in "Brakes—The Feel Position" on page 159.

Deflating the Wing

A wing in a wind has a mighty pull. Before learning to control it, first learn how to depower/disable it. Here are some techniques.

- The brake pull method works well in winds up to 10 mph. Pull both brakes hard until the wing comes down (Fig 3-28 on page 38). But first, reduce brake pull so that it surges overhead, then immediately pull hard so it comes quickly down through the power band (highest pull force).

- Use the rear riser pull in winds over 10 mph. Reach up and pull both rear risers as far as possible (Fig 3-1). Hold them. Since they're hard to find while being dragged, rehearse this under benign conditions. Rear risers are what the brake pulleys connect to. B's or C's can also be used (Fig 3-29 on page 38) but don't keep the glider down as well, and never use the A's—after the leading edge tucks under initially, it will re-inflate with vigor.

- As a last resort, let go of one brake and pull the other brake hand-over-hand until you're holding tip fabric. The wing will flip over and swirl around, twisting the lines, but keep pulling. You'll be happy to be wearing decent gloves.

If the wing is pulling hard, try walking or running towards it to reduce the relative wind. Your goal is to grab tip fabric, then keep pulling it, hand-over-hand by the upper surface, until regaining control.

Brake Positions/Pressures

We refer to brake positions using a fractional position or a number from 0 to 5. Zero is hands up so brake handles are at their pulleys, and five is the maximum brake pull possible without stalling the wing (flying stops, dropping begins). Note that forearms remain essentially vertical through 4.

Every wing is different: lower hook-in motors (most common) tend to have lower hand positions than higher hook-ins. Either way, brakes should be adjusted so the following positions work to ensure the most brake travel.

- **Position 0:** Hands up. There's no brake pull, toggles are stowed or at the pulley, and the trailing edge has NO deflection.

- **Position 1:** Starting to feel brake pressure, around ½ pound.

- **Position 2:** Quarter brake. About the weight of your arms. An extended thumb would be near ear height, but see where it is by relaxing your arms.

- **Position 3:** Intermediate. The most brake generally *held* for normal flight.

- **Position 4:** Half brake. About shoulder height. Your forearm doesn't go beyond vertical. Use with great care, especially if holding for more than 5 seconds.

- **Position 5:** Anything beyond position 4 should only be used for landing flare, managing strong turbulence, or advanced maneuvering. Use with extreme care. Holding this for more than a couple seconds will likely cause a stall.

Gliders differ, but they should be adjusted so these positions work. Our physical reach doesn't change with glider brand. And beware that a glider can stall **well before reaching position 5** under some conditions.

Preparing To Practice

You've got a wing, harness, helmet, and gloves—it's time to practice. If there's more than about a 6 mph wind, do a reverse inflation (Fig 3-4); otherwise, do a forward inflation where you run with the wing coming up behind. Forwards are much harder, especially as the wind nears calm. That's where we'll start.

Don a helmet before clipping in; kiting is one of the most likely times to need it. Pilots have been seriously hurt after getting caught by a gust. "Helmet on before hooking in."

If possible, have (or make) something to simulate a throttle (practice throttle). After learning basic kiting, start using it in whatever hand your motor uses. It will grease the transition to motor launching, but sadly, not all instructors use them.

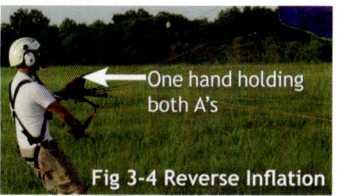

Fig 3-4 Reverse Inflation

Calm or Light Winds (Forward Inflation)

Calm winds are great for *flying* but a challenge for *launching*. Unless you're at a beach, most early flights will probably be in light or calm winds. That means lots of forward launch practice, a skill you'll be thankful to have.

The basic technique is similar to what free flyers use and can be practiced at home with no motor, preferably with a throttle simulator (Fig 3-6).

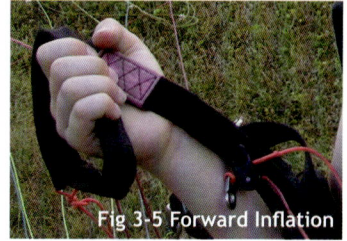

Fig 3-5 Forward Inflation

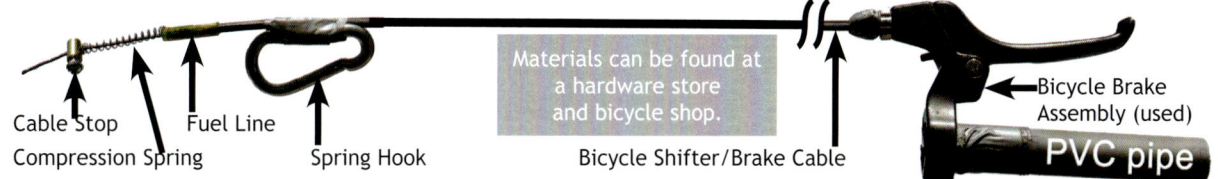

Fig 3-6 Throttle Simulator

Untangling Lines: Preventing the Dips and Loops

Fig 3-7 Riser Stowing — Inner A

Prevention is easier than untangling. Keep steering toggles on their keepers, put risers together (as shown at left) or in a riser bag, and keep risers from going into the lines when finished.

Tangles still happen, these tips may help.

Don't disconnect anything!

1. Find a clear, open area to lay out the wing like a forward launch, kiting it between steps, if possible. That frequently reveals a solution.

2. Snap the brakes into their retainers and separate the risers. Using brake line (not toggle), pull the trailing edge as far as possible and shake to clear the easy stuff.

3. Make sure there are no line overs where a line goes over the leading edge. If so, bring the rogue line(s) back underneath (pulling the wing through if necessary).

4. Untwist the riser. It might be difficult to tell which way to do this early on, but keep making sure they're untwisted as you proceed. Shake the riser and try teasing lines apart as you go.

5. Remove sticks and ensure nothing is caught in the riser pulleys or brake handles.

6. Pull apart any rats nests as much as possible. Look for and remove loops. Clearing one loop (dip) can depuzzle the whole mess.

7. While holding the risers up and outstretched, tension them slightly while sliding them back and forth so the lines rub on each other.

8. Hold the cleared A's up with some tension to help sort out remaining tangles. Then try tensioning and separating the individual B, C, and D risers.

9. If it's still tangled, start from the wing. Pick a riser and pull the innermost A until the riser is hanging by that A line (as shown above with "Inner A") and let everything else drop below.

Orient the A riser properly and, while holding some tension to the wing, it will be more obvious what needs to be done. You'll probably have to put the riser loops through some of the outstretched lines. It may require twisting the risers around to sort things out.

Pull loops through — Rats Nest. Rubbing the risers back and forth. See step 7.

Line Over - see step 3.

Line overs can be difficult to see, check from behind.

Forward Inflation: Setup

Fig 3-8 Pictorial Guide

This step-by-step guide unravels the potentially confusing setup for a forward inflation. But always follow your instructor's guidance since he may have a different twist on it.

Doing it in the right order is important.

1. Start with a good layout. Spread the wing out properly, lines clear, and on smooth ground. This reduces the chance it will come up crooked or not at all.

A slight inverted "V" pattern is helpful, but too much "V" slows inflation.

2. Clear the A's. Nothing can be draped over the A riser and lines out to the wing.

3. Clear the brakes to ensure they're not caught on anything. Don't deform the wing: pull just enough to see the trailing edge move an inch or so.

Move out towards the tip as he is doing, to provide for an even pull on the trailing edge, and make sure all the brake lines are free.

4. Lay the risers down the same way every time. It's surprisingly easy to get it wrong while picking them up. Make sure the A stays pointed upward/forward to avoid confusion.

5. As you bring the riser up, keep the A's and speedbar pulley facing forward (or outward depending on harness). Clip into the carabiner then let it hang down.

6. Now the brake is pointed forward or outward and there are no lines draped over the connected brake. Repeat for the other riser.

7. (opposite page) Strap on your practice throttle. If you were wearing a motor, this is when you would strap on the real throttle.

While keeping the riser flat, run your hand down it, over the trimmer, and pull each brake off its keeper. Spread your arms out to reveal a triangle, formed by your arm, risers, and brake line, that should look like this. The Brake Check ensures no lines are hanging over the brakes and that the risers are on properly.

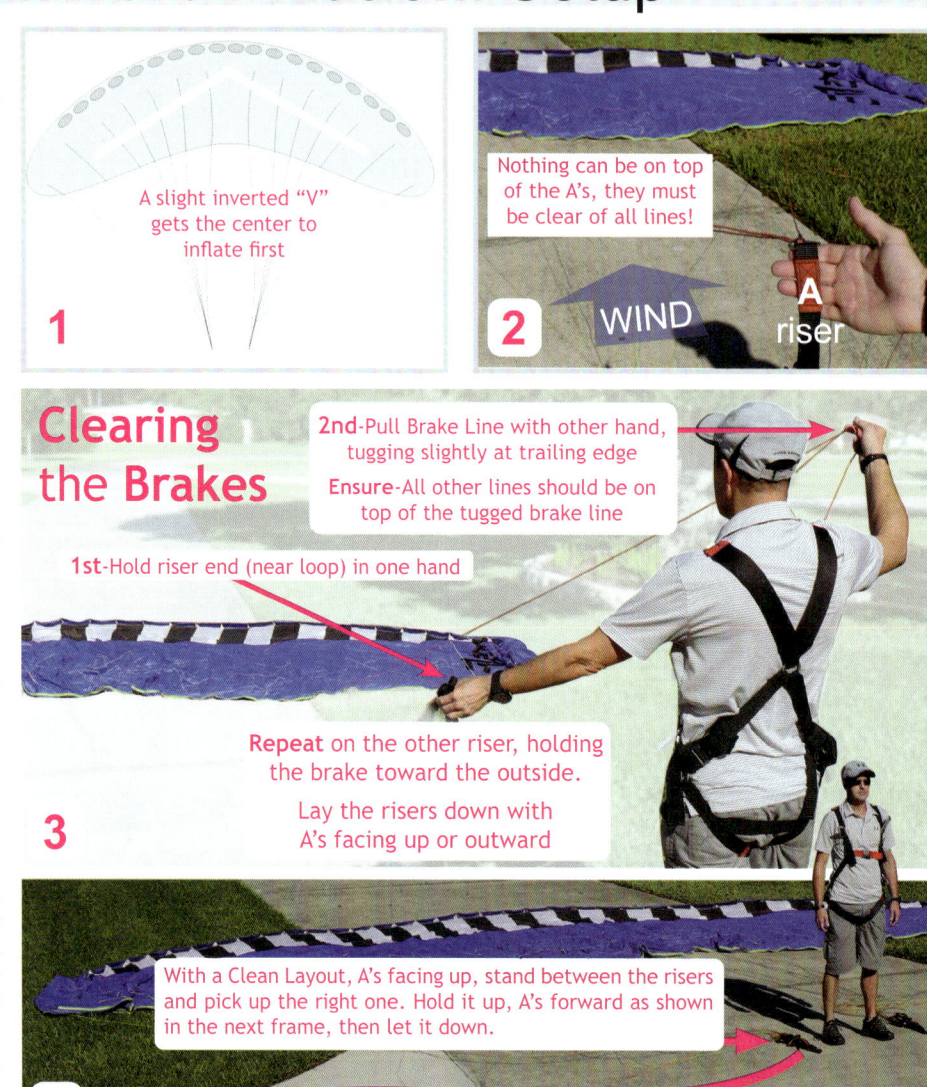

Chapter 3: Handling the Wing — Page 29

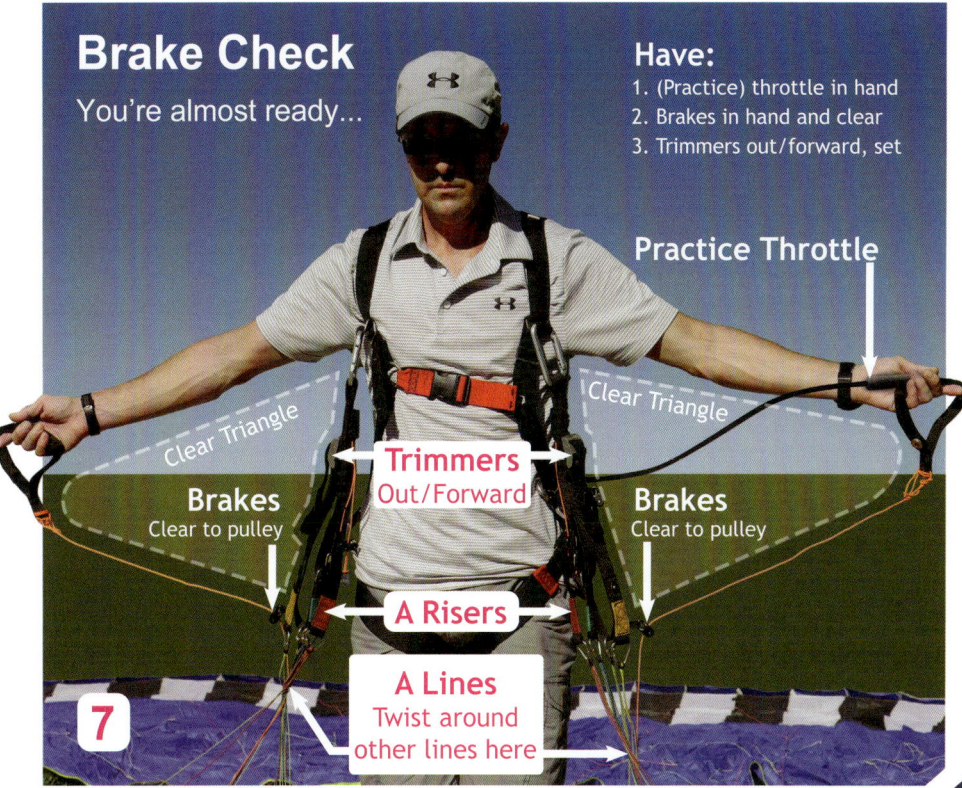

Brake Check
You're almost ready...

Have:
1. (Practice) throttle in hand
2. Brakes in hand and clear
3. Trimmers out/forward, set

Practice Throttle

Clear Triangle — Clear Triangle

Brakes — Clear to pulley
Trimmers Out/Forward
Brakes — Clear to pulley
A Risers
A Lines — Twist around other lines here

7

8 Gunslinger A-Grab

Ready?

Trimmers are facing up. If this gets confusing, imagine how it will look when the wing comes up.

A riser

A Risers — Should be forward of, or on top of, throttle. It's this feel that makes using a practice throttle so helpful.

Brake Toggles

Other Risers & Lines will be draped *behind* and *over* your arms. ONLY the A risers (inner A on some) are held.

Throttle cable is in front of arm.

A Lines — Must be clear to the wing with no other lines draped over.

9

8a
8b
8c

8a-8c. These steps simplify the process of getting the "A" riser in your palm properly.

Order is important.

Get the throttle, then the brakes (7), then the A's. If your glider has split A's, use only the inner (center) A's if it's easy to do so.

Grab the A's from the *inside*. Notice that the other risers are *outside* or over your arm.

9. When done correctly it should look this.

Be centered and aimed at a target object ahead that's exactly perpendicular to the wing. You'll run towards it. See Fig 3-12.

Fig 3-9 Centering & Clearing

Once setup, step forward until you *just* feel some tension without pulling the leading edge over.

Look down the A's. They should be "clean" to the wing with no lines draped over. Nothing.

Move left and right to make sure you're centered. That slight line tension should feel equal.

Most wings don't require grasping the A's, rather they will slide through your open palm (below). Larger or more sluggish wings may require a firmer grip like that shown at right.

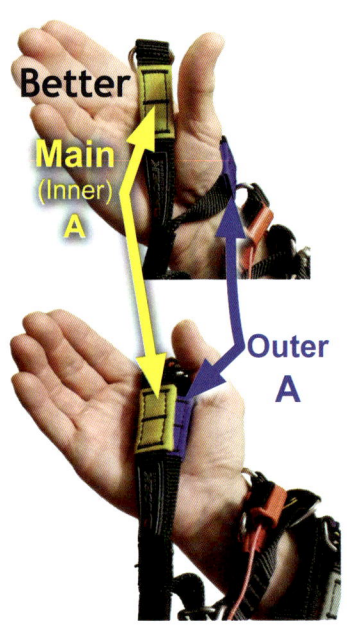

Fig 3-10 Split A's

With split A's, it's usually better to hold only the center (inner) A like the top pic. It's sometimes easier to put your fingers through the split so the outer A drapes behind your hand/arm.

Avoid forward launches in stronger winds. The breeze may yank you backward as the wing inflates, unceremoniously dropping you into the "turtle" position (left).

The Run

You're standing there centered, holding the brakes, a throttle simulator, the A's, and carefully facing a target object. A light crosswind, up to 30°, is OK if it's less than about 2 mph. Don't accept *any* tailwind.

The instructor is invaluable here and will help with the many nuances.

Take one step backward toward the wing and plan the direction you'll start to run. It should be directly away from the wing. Find a distant object to look at and plan your run towards (Fig 3-12). Here we go.

1. **Inflation. When you go for it, go hard.** Lunge away from the wing, arms back, leading with your chest to quickly tension the lines, and pulling a *bit* of A's. Once it takes shape, **then** pull more A's as necessary. It initially inflates quickly but then imposes enormous resistance. Keep driving, and **now** pull the requisite A's—usually only an inch or two.

2. **Rise.** Drive hard through the resistance, with just enough A pressure to keep the wing coming up. Too much A pull will cause a *front tuck* (leading edge folds downward). Not enough A's will allow the wing to fall back. Your instructor will let you know. Consider using open palms to let the A's slide up, thereby limiting how much you can pull.

   On some wings, especially older or larger models, or in completely still air, you may need to hold the A's for quite a while, until you've gathered some speed and you're moving briskly with the wing fully overhead. Wings that take more A-pull are less likely to overfly and front tuck.

   Bigger wings take longer to come up and probably need more A-pull.

3. **Damping.** Keep forging forward with your body—speed is life. As the wing nears overhead, let go of the A's and pull some brake pressure so the wing doesn't overfly. If it's coming up quickly you'll need to let off on the A's and pull brakes sooner. That's called "*checking*" or "*damping*" the wing. If it's hanging back you'll need to stay on the A's longer, waiting until it's fully overhead and you're moving quickly.

4. **Control.** You're running with the wing overhead. Speed is life, but this will get tiring *very* quickly if there's no wind. You will use all your 1 person power to generate the full 6 mph or so to keep it flying.

   If the wing leans right, run right just enough to get under it while pulling a little left brake—"less brake is best brake." It's easy to pull too much and have the wing fall back.

5. **Finish.** After some seconds of running you'll be done, but pull some brakes during the last couple steps. Turn around, walk backward (if it's safe to do so), and hold brakes so the wing lands more neatly on its trailing edge.

In very light or no wind, you may not be able to turn around fast enough. Still pull brakes while moving forward to avoid getting draped in line spaghetti.

While running, you will learn to detect a subtle pull, left or right, from the tensioning lines. If the wing starts pulling left, go left just enough to keep under it. If you have enough speed, pull *slight* right brake. Speed is life. Speed is control. Looking back at the wing can slow you down. Consider turning your head (but not torso) left or right, looking at the tip instead of looking straight up.

Later on, with a motor, you'll be upright—almost leaning back—letting the thrust push. For now, though, you'll need to lean forward to get enough oomph. In completely calm wind, the initial run will feel like you're pulling a limp rag with little resistance. Keep driving forward: speed=success.

With even a couple mph breeze, the wing will snap to attention much faster than in a dead calm. It will try to stop your forward momentum, then come up quickly and want to overfly; be ready to dampen it with brakes ("checking" the wing) while getting speed, then reduce brakes quickly. Most blown forward inflations stem from insufficient speed, releasing the A's too early, or checking with too much brake. Even slightly crooked inflations can be managed if you get enough speed and get under the wing. Use *minimum* corrective brake pull lest the wing fall back.

Move Under the Wing

This is unnatural, but essential: you must move under the wing while running or forward kiting. If it goes right, you must move right. In calm wind, don't pull any brake while gathering speed; then, once moving with the wing nicely overhead, use just enough brake pressure to steer and keep it from overflying. This won't come easy. Fight the instinct to pull against the wing—it always wins.

Through inflation you'll keep the A's in your hand, pushing them up and forward to help the wing come overhead. On some models, you must stay on the A's (keep applying pressure) until it is fully overhead and your body is moving nicely forward. Then let off on the A's and pull just enough brakes to keep the wing from overflying you.

Speed (airflow over the wing) is key to having brake control. If the wing goes left or right, move with it, but only as much as needed. Turning your body too much can thrust you into the start of a zig-zag oscillation that worsens. For example, you run right and the wing goes left in a series

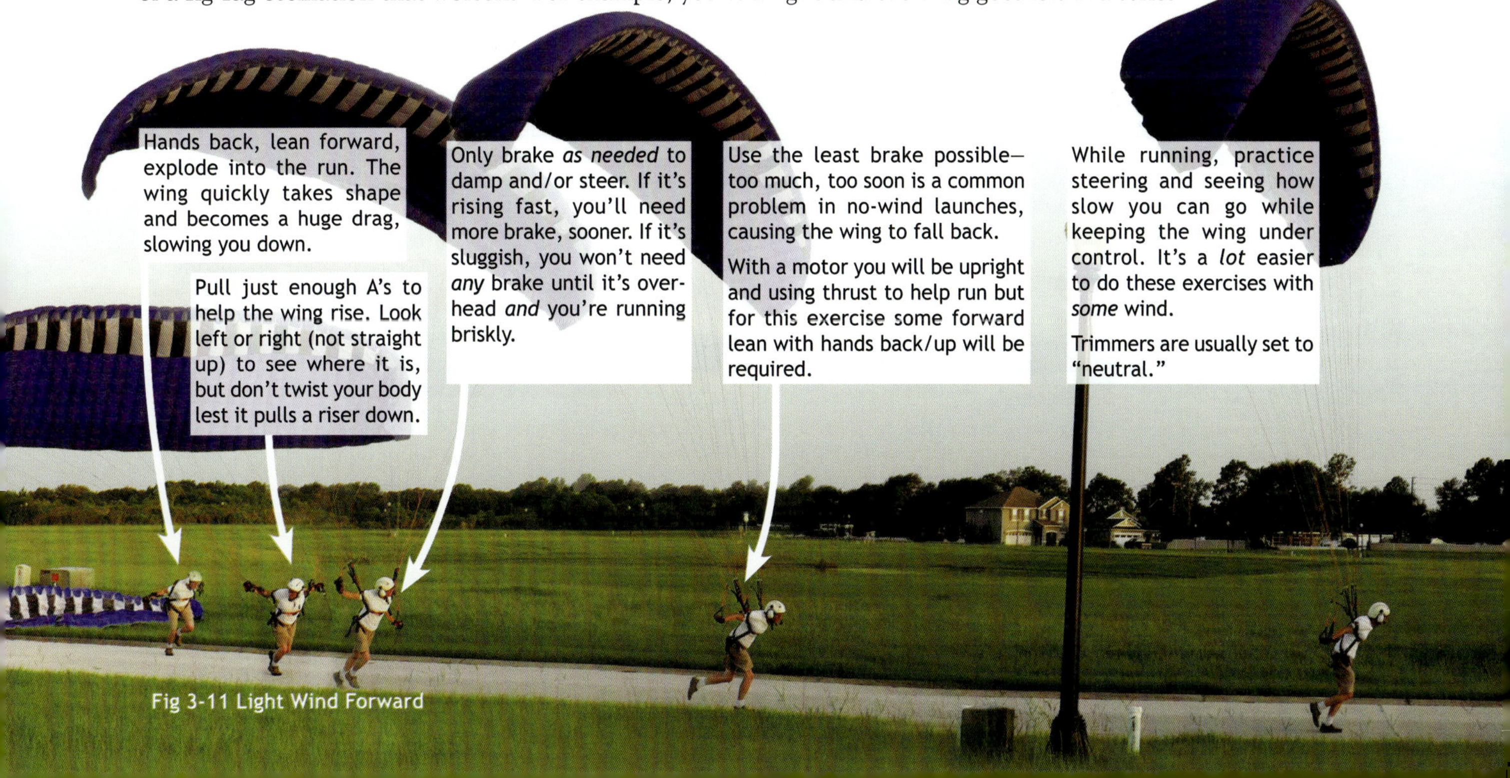

Fig 3-12 Look Here

Start the inflation by running towards an object that's exactly perpendicular to the wing.

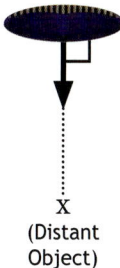

(Distant Object)

Hands back, lean forward, explode into the run. The wing quickly takes shape and becomes a huge drag, slowing you down.

Pull just enough A's to help the wing rise. Look left or right (not straight up) to see where it is, but don't twist your body lest it pulls a riser down.

Only brake *as needed* to damp and/or steer. If it's rising fast, you'll need more brake, sooner. If it's sluggish, you won't need *any* brake until it's overhead *and* you're running briskly.

Use the least brake possible—too much, too soon is a common problem in no-wind launches, causing the wing to fall back.

With a motor you will be upright and using thrust to help run but for this exercise some forward lean with hands back/up will be required.

While running, practice steering and seeing how slow you can go while keeping the wing under control. It's a *lot* easier to do these exercises with *some* wind.

Trimmers are usually set to "neutral."

Fig 3-11 Light Wind Forward

Red=Left
Green=Right

Reverse Inflation: Setup

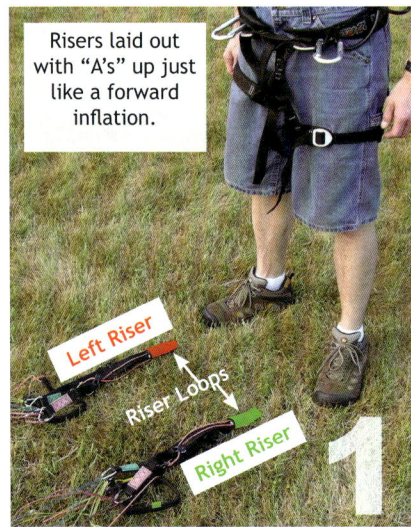

1. Risers laid out with "A's" up just like a forward inflation.
   Left Riser — Riser Loops — Right Riser

2. Put the risers together and turn them over. If you turn around to the left, turn them over to the left (counter clockwise as shown).

3. Trimmers facing up. A's and speedbar pulleys facing down.

4. Keep the riser loops level while clipping them into the carabiners they're closest to.

5.

6. Grab the brakes and pull apart. No lines should be in the "V" created by doing this. You'll grab the A's from the *inside* next.

7. While holding the brakes, reach inside to grab the A's and bring them up. It should look like this.

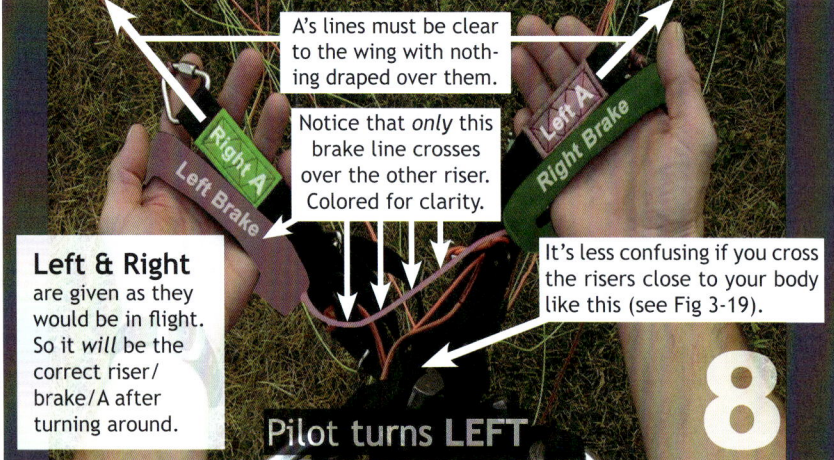

8. A's lines must be clear to the wing with nothing draped over them.
   Notice that *only* this brake line crosses over the other riser. Colored for clarity.
   It's less confusing if you cross the risers close to your body like this (see Fig 3-19).
   Left & Right are given as they would be in flight. So it *will* be the correct riser/brake/A after turning around.
   Pilot turns LEFT

Fig 3-13 This **free flight style reverse** hook-In uses one hand per A. Notice there's no mention of a practice throttle—that's because this method is *not suitable for motoring*. If the throttle gets caught in a line during inflation you could suddenly go to full power—an unexpected 100 pound push from behind that rarely ends well.

For motoring, the best technique is to hold **both A's in one hand** and the throttle in your other hand (Fig 3-17). It's the same through step 6, then in step 7, instead of grabbing one A per hand, you grab and hold both A's with your non-throttle hand.

If your instructor *does* have you use the above method with power, definitely use a throttle simulator to get used to it.

If your motor has a left hand throttle, plan on turning around to the right. Fig 3-15 shows the rationale for choosing a turn-around direction.

For kiting, especially in light and/or variable winds, the one-A-per-hand method shown above offers a bit more control. It will come in handy later if you choose to advance beyond ground handling basics.

of increasing oscillations that could end in a fall. Use small direction changes with minimal brake inputs to ease back into balance. It's a delicate dance that requires practice, but it's oh so fun when mastered.

But remember, with a motor, after inflation you'll need to stand up straight and let the motor push.

Forward Kiting

Most wings need at least a 6 mph breeze to become controllable, and more is better, up to about 12 mph. The value of some breeze becomes painfully apparent after a few tries dragging 20+ square meters of wing overhead. It's good that you can (and should) practice this in no wind, but it's a lot of work.

Forward kiting reveals a critical behavior of the wing—if you move your body left, the wing goes right, and will continue to the ground. It reinforces why staying centered under the wing is so important. It also means that you can make the wing go right by first moving slightly left then following the wing as it goes right. That'll be important later on when we explore advanced ground handling.

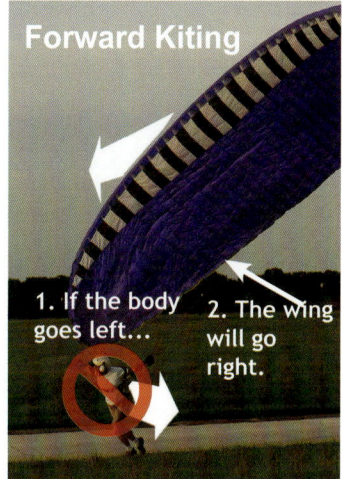

Fig 3-14 Body motion

Wind Over 6 mph (Reverse Inflation)

Much early learning will involve reverse kiting in 7 to 12 mph wind, less if using a lightweight wing. Some schools teach the useful skill of riser kiting "Kiting Without a Harness" on page 148.

Hooking In Reversed

Some free flyers hook in forward then turn around while lifting one riser over their head. That's tough with a cage, so we use other techniques. There are several ways to hook in reversed, but we cover the most common (Fig 3-13).

It seems complicated, but when you pull the wing to life and turn around (you'll turn left using these instructions), it all sorts out magically. The correct hand will already be in the correct brake.

At Fig 3-13 step 6 grab the brakes. Don't let go of the brakes. For anything. And notice those "**V**"s? There can be *nothing* going through them.

On wings with split A's you may be holding four risers although it's usually best just to hold the inners (Fig 3-10).

Repetition fixes the inevitable confusion. There are many ways to teach this—go with what your instructor is most familiar. You're now ready to build a "wall."

Construction: Building a Wall

Having the wing partially inflated while on the ground is "building a wall." It improves launch success rate and is a good wing handling exercise. Plus it:

- Ensures being properly hooked in and positioned to bring the wing up centered.
- Quickly spreads out the wing and exposes tangles or snags.
- Lets you get a feel for the wind strength and direction.
- Needs about 10 mph (16 kph) wind to work well.

To build a wall, spread out the wing and hook in, holding the brakes like Fig 3-18. You should be holding the brakes with an "A" in each hand.

Be prepared to pull brakes immediately if the wing tries to billow up before you're ready. In a stronger wind it will want to snap to attention and come up.

Get some tension on the risers with your body, step forward once then lurch backward

Fig 3-15 Turn Around Direction?

Plan to turn around opposite of your throttle hand. If your machine has a right hand throttle (as shown), plan to turn to the left. This is so, in light-wind reverses where you're walking backward, you can hold the A's longer while turning around as shown above.

Fig 3-16 Alternative Hook-in for Reverses

1. This starts like a forward launch except you stand *beside* the risers, facing into the launch direction. It's shown for those with a right hand throttle who will turn left after inflation. With a left hand throttle, stand to the right of the risers and bring them up over your left shoulder.

2. Pick up both risers while facing forward and lift them over your right shoulder. Hook the left riser (red) to the left carabiner then the right riser to the right carabiner. Don't twist anything but do envision how they will as the wing comes up. Grab the throttle (if not already in hand).

3. Once clipped in with risers and lines draped around your right side, turn right to face the wing—you're ready.

Fig 3-17 Both A's in One Hand: With practice throttle in right hand, grab the brakes, *then* the A's. It's awkward at first.

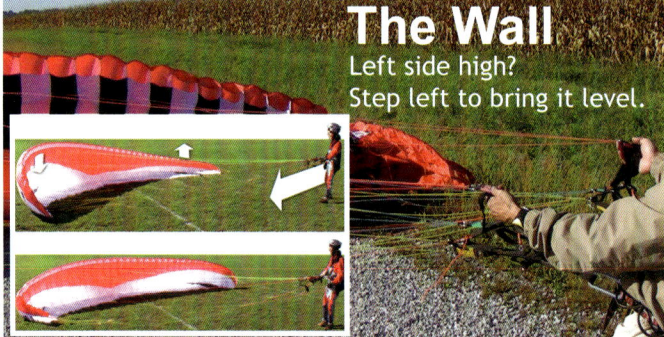

Fig 3-18 Building a Wall: With enough wind it's helpful to "build a wall" to make inflation easier and more predictable.

Fig 3-19 Crossing the Risers

It can be confusing, but try this.

Use your left hand to cross the risers close to your body as shown (this is for a left turn-around). Then grab the right A with your right hand as shown, followed by the left A with your left hand.

Make sure there are no lines on top of the A's from your hand out to the wing. Not one.

while applying some upward pressure on the A's. If there's enough wind, the wing will start to come up. Right before it leaves the ground, let go of the A's and pull *just* enough brakes to bring it back down. Not hard—you want to leave the wing standing there "at attention" like in Fig 3-18.

Simply *finding* the two A risers quickly is tough, but practice really pays off. It feels like work for a while. Those A risers are easier to figure out if you cross the risers like in Fig 3-19. That makes it more obvious where the A's are going.

Once the wall is up, modulate how tall it stands by stepping towards or away from it. Leveling the wall is done by stepping sideways toward the higher side. The wing must see fairly even pressure on the lines before this works well.

Get used to going for the A's, pulling the wing up mostly with your body, and then bringing it back down using brakes. Timing is a challenge; you want it to come just off the ground and then bring it right back down again—the trailing edge should never get more than a few feet high and come down *gently*. Fast *and* gentle are tough. With experience, you'll do it without the trailing edge even leaving the ground.

Don't bother with a wall unless you have a steady 8-10 mph. It's just frustrating.

Use your body more than the A's. After the wing billows out, *then* modulate A-pull. If the leading edge deforms, you're pulling too much. On some wings, you don't need any A-pull.

Once you've mastered the basics, practice doing it while holding both A's in one hand and a throttle simulator in the other to help prep for power.

See more "Controlling the Wall" on page 151.

Riser-Only Inflation

Kiting a wing without hooking into a harness (riser kiting) has value beyond just looking cool. More detail is found on page 148. Far from a waste of time, it:

- is an easy way to reposition the glider,
- is useful for quickly inspecting lines and fabric,
- is a good way to feel wind strength, direction, gustiness, and
- helps improve wing-handling skill.

Reverse Inflation

Time to bring the wing up.

Fig 3-20 Riser-only Inflating with the A's and Rears

If there's enough wind for a wall, lower it slightly then lurch backward, knees bent, pulling from your waist, not the A's. If there's too little wind for a wall, take several steps backward, letting your body pull on the risers as your hands (or hand if using one hand) pull on the A's. Think more fast snatch than a walk. Otherwise, you end up just dragging the wing around. Use your *body*, not just the A's.

As the wing comes up, keep some A pressure until it's nearly overhead, then let off. Walk backward, if necessary. If the wing is coming up quickly, you'll get off the A's early and "check" it with liberal brake pull. Then *reduce* pull so it doesn't fall back.

If it's lumbering up limply, stay on the A's nearly all the way up, waiting until it's almost overhead before using any brakes. You may need to be walking backward to keep it rising and under control. That increases airflow and therefore brake authority. It also increases the risk of tripping; be on a smooth surface.

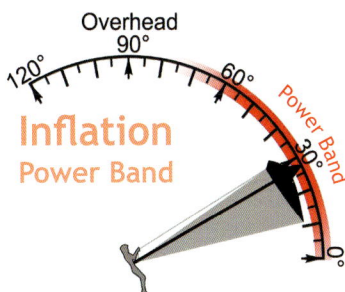

Fig 3-21 During inflation, wing pull is strongest while rising through the *Power Band*. If it's rising slowly, stay on the A's. If it's rising quickly, let off early and be ready to damp it.

In a stronger wind, it will dart up quickly, possibly dragging you downwind with it—be prepared. Shortly after it starts up, you may not be able to avoid getting pulled for several feet. Let yourself slide and be ready to check the overshoot (where it flies past your head) with brakes. If you start getting lifted, *reduce* brakes until you get turned back around to face the wing, then bring it down; hopefully you've rehearsed this. These conditions are clearly too strong.

Reverse Kiting

Once the wing is happily overhead you want to use the **least amount** of input necessary to keep it there. We'll refine this more later, but for now, that means:

- Stay under the wing's center cell. If it moves left, you move under it *then go another foot more*. The extra foot is because the wing's momentum will carry it a bit farther.

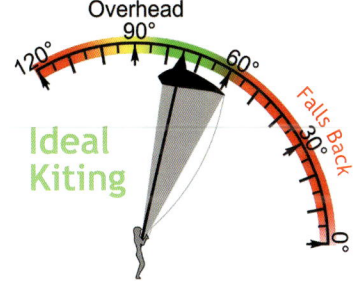

Fig 3-22 Ideal kiting position is around 75°. More overhead makes the leading edge want to tuck under (front tuck), less than about 65° makes it want to fall back.

- Keep good posture and stay loose, almost relaxed, with knees bent, and leaned back as needed by the wing's pull. If everything is well-adjusted, your hands will be in front like a boxer protecting his face. This is the *neutral position*. Periodically reduce brake pressure to make sure you're not tensed up or pulling too hard.

- If the wing goes left, move left, pull the brake in your left hand (yes, *left* hand— the risers are crossed) and lower your left hip (does some weight shift). Vice-versa if it goes right. Respond only to what's needed. A little motion now will prevent the need for big motion in a few seconds. Lead it; stop responding *before* the wing approaches the desired spot.

- Be light on the brakes to **1)** avoid over-correcting, **2)** avoid the wing falling back down, and **3)** work less. If the wing keeps falling back, use less brake pull, walk backward faster to increase airflow, and/or set the trims faster.

- Take a few steps backward whenever the wind dies and controls feel soft.

Fig 3-23 Move with the wing and react as shown. If it tries to overfly you, pull both brakes.

If it wants to fall back, let up the brakes and walk backward to give it more airflow.

Always be moving towards the center cell until you're good enough to keep the wing overhead with*out* moving your body.

Another good exercise is kiting with **ONLY** body motion.

Fig 3-24 Straight Riser Kiting

This is rarely used, and almost never beyond the first day, since you must learn crossed-riser kiting to launch.

The goal is to stand in one place, using the least amount of control input, especially motion, to kite it overhead. Move your body as needed, of course, but work towards being able to just stand there, kiting, without over controlling. That's because later you may find yourself in a tricky launch area where there's little room to move. This skill comes in handy.

Another benefit of having minimum brake pull is that you're less likely to get lifted. If the wing is hanging back and you're heavy in the brakes, you're vulnerable to being lifted.

In a light wind you may need to walk backward to improve airflow over the wing. If it isn't responding enough, walk backward to improve control. As much as we love easy-to-inflate wings, they do tend to front tuck more.

Practice kiting until it's second nature. Mastering wing handling is mastering launching. It will determine what conditions you can handle, especially in light or strong winds. More advanced techniques are covered later.

Alternative Training-Only Method: Straight Risers

Standard reversed kiting can be confusing at first, so a very few instructors use this method (Fig 3-24) to quickly get the student kiting. The standard method must eventually be learned, so use this only briefly if at all.

The risers go straight out to the wing without crossing or twisting. The drawback is that brake input is backward from what you'll eventually learn. It is quicker to get some basic feel for the wing and how to stay centered.

Hook in without crossing the risers, A's facing up. Grab the brake closest to each hand from the outside; there should be nothing crossed. With the brakes in your hands, reach up to hold the A's and inflate the wing like with crossed-risers.

As it comes overhead, pull enough brakes so it doesn't overfly. Then modulate the brakes to keep the wing there just like the other methods. In light winds you'll have almost no brake pulled most of the time. If it wants to fall back, walk backward to increase the wing's airflow and reduce brakes. If it starts falling left, step left and pull some brake with the right hand and vice versa if it falls right then let up. Only left/right steering is opposite to the normal method.

Whether kiting with crossed (standard) or straight risers, watch the trailing edge move and visualize that side slowing down which is exactly what's happening. This will make the wing's behavior and response more clear.

The Turn *and Move*

Once you are reliably kiting the wing overhead, next up is turning around—a common failure point in lighter wind reverse launches.

You'll turn left if hooked in as described here. The key is to ensure the wing is moving forward, turn around quickly, and *immediately* start moving forward.

While keeping the wing centered overhead, take a step backward to get the wing moving, turn around quickly and move forward. Forward motion improves control authority, especially in lighter winds. Lean forward as needed, but remember that with a motor on, you will stand up straight and power up to keep moving. Just before starting to turn, have the wing slightly left (while reversed), so you're turning towards it (assuming a left turn-around).

The key is to turn *and move*—to get airflow over the wing for brake effectiveness. This is a common failure point because pilots tend to ponder their navels instead of moving forward. The wing sees this indifference, feels no love from the air, and falls back or sideways.

Fig 3-25 Even in light wind, practice the "turn and move." Bring the wing up; then, just as it reaches overhead, back up, turn to face forward and start walking or running. You'll need to generate more speed in less wind. While running, keep your hands back and up to avoid pulling too much brake.

Your goal is to use the least amount of brake and body movement to maintain control.

Practice turning back around to face the wing and setting it back down neatly.

Once the wing is happily under control, you're now just doing forward kiting.

More on Bringing the Wing Down

The following tips add to "Deflating the Wing" on page 26. You could just let it flop down in a heap, but that's not classy. Instead, let it down gently, with the leading-edge up, and level. Besides being easier to re-inflate or put away, you'll look awesome.

After forward kiting, turn right to face the wing, walking backward slowly if needed to keep it powered (loaded on the risers). The risers will be crossed like you started. You can turn the other way, but it's easier to habitually use the same direction so you can re-inflate in the familiar manner.

Once you're facing the wing, pull enough brakes so that it falls back evenly. Just before it touches down, let off the brakes some and step towards it. The leading edge lays back nicely.

Windy conditions can make it hard to bring the wing down at all. Without muscle memory, mere advice won't survive the fog of flailing. Strong winds are lethally dangerous, especially for newer pilots, so build reactions first in a controlled environment—see "High Wind Techniques" on page 150.

The best deflation to practice is the Rear Riser Pull (Fig 3-1 and Fig 3-30). You can also use the B or C risers (B's or C's), but they are harder to find, and some wings "snake" around if their B's or C's are pulled (Fig 3-29).

Fig 3-26 Tip Openings
Some wings have Velcro openings in the last cell's trailing edge to help get that last bit of debris out.

Cleaning the Wing

Sand, grass clippings, bugs, wedding rings, and field debris collect in the trailing edge and other areas. Besides weighing down inflation, they can abrade the fabric, causing wear and hurting porosity. Kiting the wing upside down (page 147) gets some material out, but stubborn remnants may require going through each cell in succession, especially on leading edge shapes like shark noses.

Cleaning with Water

Most experts suggest never washing with more than a cloth rag dampened with clean water, or at most a mild soap (like Woolite).

Fig 3-27 Debris Removal
If you have two people, lay your wing out on the ground with the leading edge *downwind* and the top up (line side down).

With one person on each end, pick up the trailing edge and walk it into the wind. Shaking in a coordinated fashion as shown.

With one person, do it stages, shaking one part of the trailing edge then moving down until finished.

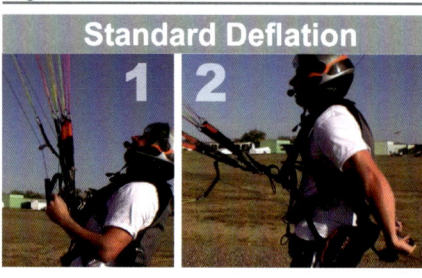   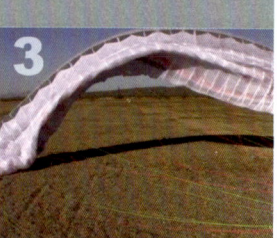

Fig 3-28 Standard Deflation

The standard deflation is pulling full brakes which is easy since they're already in your hands.

Finesse tip: Just before the wing touches down, reduce brake pull halfway to ease its impact. You look like a hero and the wing says "ahhh."

Fig 3-29 C-Line Deflation

On 4-line gliders (D riser is the rear riser), a C Line Deflation is another way to depower. But some wings tend to "snake" like in (3).

Generally the Rear Riser pull shown below, and in Fig 3-1 is better.

Fig 3-30 Rear Riser Pull Overhand

Here is another example of the rear-riser pull shown in Fig 3-1. He's using an overhand grip which is slightly more effective.

Rear risers are convenient in that they're farthest away *and* have the brake pulleys for easy identification.

Caution!

Never put the wing in a washing machine or dryer. The stress and heat would be destructive.

Gliders hate moisture, so If it does get wet, dry it immediately in an open area, preferably out of direct sunlight.

Drenching or submerging a wing can be damaging, mostly from improper handling or drying. Pulling on fabric that has water in pockets can quickly be damaging. Any kind of fabric rubbing, even with itself, will increase porosity. Soap is taboo, although some techniques used for cleaning may be beneficial, especially given that dirt imposes its own wear. Consult with your wing's manufacturer or rep.

Lines will shrink when they dry. The loaded lines (A's mostly, and B's some) will stretch back during flight but less loaded lines (rears) will not, causing a deformation of the airfoil that hampers inflation and affects handling. You should stretch the rear lines before flight ("Fig 12-36 Line Stretching" on page 129).

If the wing gets in salt water, It *should* be soaked in fresh water then *carefully* (slowly) removed and dried using techniques recommended by the wing maker. Techniques may vary based on material used for lines and surfaces. The upper surface material, for example, is usually different than the lower.

While drying, avoid having lines dry with sharp bends.

Storing the Wing

Stow the wing as recommended by its manufacturer. Absent that, a loose fold or rosette (Fig 3-32) is generally OK. Most wings have nylon rods in their leading edge that need to be protected from sharp bends. For that some form of accordion fold works best (Fig 3-31).

Get it out of the sun quickly. The 300-hour average lifetime is measured mostly in UV exposure, so a $3000+ price tag, degrading in sunshine, costs about $10 per hour.

Before putting the wing away, try to make sure there are no bugs inside or on it—primarily by getting it into its bag right away. Critters that get trapped inside will make a hole one way or another, either by chewing to freedom or by leaving their acidic little carcasses to cause carnage.

If you notice crawling things already inside, find a reasonably bugless place and shake the trailing edge so that they fall out the leading edge openings. This can be done indoors but you'll be amazed at how big even a small wing is. Leave half of it folded while you attend to the other half. Ribs have big holes in them for air flow, but they also make fine bug highways.

Before putting the wing away, clip the riser ends together with a small carabiner or other clip. As you put it away, don't let the riser ends go through any lines. Keep them well separated to reduce the likelihood of tangles when pulling it out again. That's the purpose of a riser pouch if you have one.

Rosette

Follow the guide in Fig 3-32. It's generally a convenient way to carry the wing, but if there's a wind, turn around once so the fabric doesn't billow. **Don't let the riser ends go through any lines**.

Stuffing

Stuffing the wing into a wide-opening stuff sack is quick and easy. Put it away the same way each time, with risers pointed down from the wing's center, so when you get it out again, you'll know which way it goes. A riser pouch is great, if available, or you can clip them to the sack's carry handle. Most importantly, make sure the risers are situated so that no lines will get mixed in.

Stuffing isn't better or worse than folding, although stuffing will leave more wrinkles. Newer wings with special leading edge rib reinforcements benefit from an accordion (or concertina) fold where the leading edge cells are all kept flat.

Folding—Accordion

Most modern wings have leading edge rods that don't react well to bending so they need a bit of extra care. A loose stuff works well enough but the method at right, one of many, is more compact and reduces wrinkles.

Minimize dragging the fabric. Starting from a rosetted (mushroom) shape helps.

Fold techniques go by several names: *pro-pack*, *concertina* or *accordion*. There are many variations and some good videos as pointed to in Fig 3-31, but stick with your wing maker's suggestions since requirements vary based on construction.

The goal is keeping all the leading edges ribs together and flat. On higher performance gliders, the rods go farther back towards the trailing edge. Some gliders may also have rods in the trailing edge.

Fig 3-31 Accordion Fold

This process is made easier with a Concertina Bag (sometimes called a Saucisse bag).

Bring the leading edge nose ribs together so they're flat against each other. A strap is frequently used to keep them together, but that can also be done with proper folding. The QR link goes to suggested videos on Footflyer.com.

 Footflyer.com/best-way-to-stow-a-paraglider/

Fig 3-32 A Rosette is convenient for short carries.

Folding—Halves

Folding takes a bit more time than rosetting but gives a much smaller package and leaves fewer wrinkles. Methods abound, but the one below is quick and easy, even if you're alone, although it's a bit quicker with two.

First off, be loose. Tight folding stresses the stitching and weakens the seams if done repeatedly. Don't drag the fabric over anything, including itself. Avoid sharp bends of the leading edge rods (older gliders may have mylar rib reinforcements) so they stay shapely for better performance. These stiffeners help keep the cells open during light-wind inflations and hasten recovery from in-flight deflations (collapses).

Lay the wing out flat with the lines laid in the same position as for a forward launch (without any "V" of course). Pull the riser loops away from the trailing edge and lay them, A's up, on the ground, then fold it as shown in Fig 3-34.

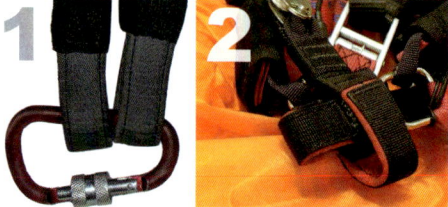

Fig 3-33 Riser Loop Keepers

Keeping risers together prevents many tangles. Method #1 causes the least wear, but method #2 requires no hardware.

Then put the risers in a small bag.

Fig 3-34 Folding in Halves:

1. Lay out like a forward and clear the lines.
2. Stow the risers (Fig 3-33), if desired, and have them sticking out from the trailing edge to keep them separate. Walk the tip to the wing's center. It's a bit quicker with two people as shown above.
3. Keep folding the tips to the center until it's about 1 foot wide then push the air out from the trailing edge. Air can only flow out of the forward openings.
4. Roll or fold *loosely* from the trailing edge, avoiding bending leading edge rods or mylar reinforcements (older wings). Many manufacturers recommend an accordion fold (Fig 3-31), check the owners manual. Don't stress seams.

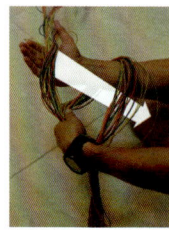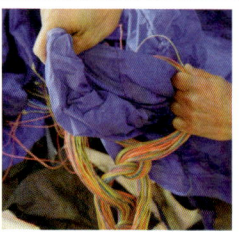

Fig 3-35 Daisy Chain / Braiding

You may come across "daisy chain" line stowing. It's used for skydiving canopies, and is NOT recommended by paraglider makers due to the increased likelihood of overly sharp line bends.

Plus it can leave an impressive tangle if not done perfectly.

Preparing for First Flight

CHAPTER 4

First flights can provide one of life's most memorable experiences. There's a lot going on, though, and we will help it be a *good* memory.

Given how intensely engrossing the experience is, sensory overload is possible. A disciplined instructor, following best practices, and having your full attention makes success far more likely.

We'll assume you're good at wing-handling by now. The material here, and in Chapter 5, will build on that to help you become an aircraft under control. Expect it to feel awkward at first, and tiring, but everything *does* come together.

Adjusting the Motor

You'll do a simulator hang check to get the motor and harness set up for flight (Fig 12-2 in Chapter 12). That ensures you can get seated easily, reach all the controls, and hang at the correct angle. The harness must be comfortable with no straps, bars or frame parts pushing uncomfortably on any body part. If there's a kick-in strap to help get into the seat, you must be able to reach it. The motor should not force your legs out front excessively as it lifts ("Scooping").

The hang check can be done anywhere, like a tree branch or rafter. It's just for adjustment and doesn't need all the features of a training simulator.

Getting seated is surprisingly critical. Harness leg straps are not designed to hang from for more than a few minutes which could lead to blackout or numb legs from *harness hang syndrome*. Not good for landing.

Practice getting into the seat while in the simulator, and if your equipment requires using a hand to do so, don't forget to let go of and stow the brakes—a potentially fatal ommision. Ideally, you can get in the seat just by lifting your legs and sliding back while wiggling. The second best method is using a kick-in strap, which should be heavy enough to hang down in the slipstream.

Fig 4-1 Simulation & Reactions

Learning to react to instructions is *critical* to success. Quality simulator rehearsal is highly effective with minimal risk. It is one of many *best practices* that your instructor hopefully employs. See more at the link below.

See best practices for paramotor instruction at Footflyer.com/ best-practices-for-paramotor-instruction/

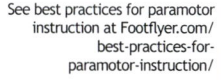

Fig 4-2 Siphoning Fuel

Siphon hoses use gravity to pull fuel from an elevated gas can into the paramotor tank which must be lower. Once started, fuel will flow until the source pickup is sucking air.

Here are two ways to start the siphon.

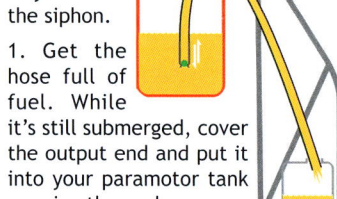

1. Get the hose full of fuel. While it's still submerged, cover the output end and put it into your paramotor tank opening then release.

2. Use a "Jiggle pump" as shown above. Submerse the pump end into your gas can and the other end into your paramotor tank. Wiggle the pump up and down until fuel starts to flow.

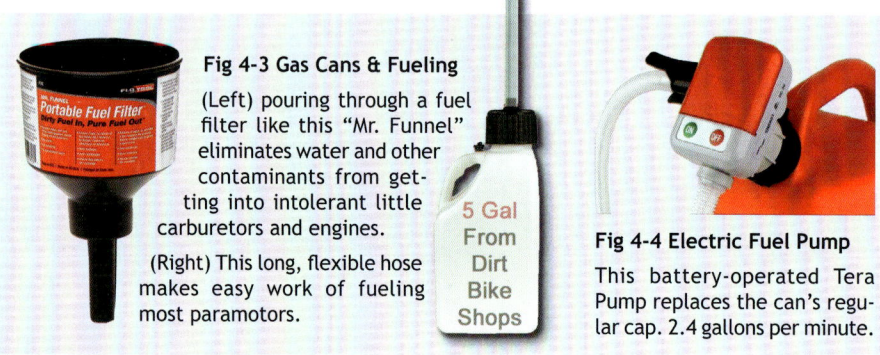

Fig 4-3 Gas Cans & Fueling

(Left) pouring through a fuel filter like this "Mr. Funnel" eliminates water and other contaminants from getting into intolerant little carburetors and engines.

(Right) This long, flexible hose makes easy work of fueling most paramotors.

5 Gal From Dirt Bike Shops

Fig 4-4 Electric Fuel Pump

This battery-operated Tera Pump replaces the can's regular cap. 2.4 gallons per minute.

Fueling

Most paramotors use two-stroke engines that consume a proper mix of gasoline and 2-stroke oil. It can be mixed in the fuel tank, but most pilots use a different container for convenience, and to ensure only mixed gas goes in the motor's tank—that's really important! If mixing in the paramotor, put the gas in first.

When filling gas cans at the pump, always put your can on the ground first.

Running a 2-stroke on unmixed (no oil) gas will cause overheating and seizure within minutes.

Do your preflight inspection *after* refueling to catch the common and dangerous mistake of forgetting the paramotor's fuel cap.

Don't over fuel since you have to lift it and launch it; mixed fuel weighs 6.2 lbs per gallon. When pouring premix (mixed fuel and oil) into your motor, a long skinny funnel, like a transmission funnel, or a siphon hose is handy (Fig 4-2).

Fuel Selection and Storage

Fuel that's left exposed to air for over a couple weeks may degrade and cause motor problems. If stored in an airtight container (it hisses when you open the lid), fuel may last several months, although some engine gurus recommend fresh fuel regardless of storage.

Use what the manufacturer recommends but, absent that, use mid or higher grade auto gas, preferably with no Ethanol. Higher octane ratings reduce knocking, a premature rapid combustion that puts holes in pistons. Gas stations that sell pure gas can be found on websites like pure-gas.org.

Aviation fuel (avgas) is preferred by some makers, but it leaves lead deposits. The common 100 "low lead" (100LL) is actually heavily leaded by modern standards. Avgas formulations are more consistent throughout the year (auto gas varies), plus it doesn't stink. Avgas can be purchased at small airports' Fixed Base Operators (FBO's) for about 30% more than auto gas. Tell them it's for your ultralight.

Efforts are underway to replace 100LL with 100UL (Unleaded).

Mixtures

Two mixtures get discussed: **fuel/oil** mixture is how much oil goes into a gallon of gas, and fuel/air mixture is how much fuel is mixed with air in the carburetor. **Fuel/air** mixture is managed through carburetor jets, orifices, and needle valves. When you hear the term *lean*, it means too little fuel in the fuel/air mix, which can cause overheating.

Oil Selection & Mixing

2-stroke motors get lubrication from oil mixed into the gas in proper proportion, typically around 50 parts gas to 1 part oil (50 to 1 mix ratio). Lower ratios (more oil) may be specified for new engine break-in. There's a mix chart in the Appendix, plus, most 2-cycle oil bottles also have a chart on the container.

You'll hear nearly religious fervor when seeking advice on oil selection and ratio—go with the manufacturer's recommendation, if available. Otherwise, make your selection based on the following priorities by order of importance:

- Use 2-cycle oil, never 4-cycle oil (like for cars).
- Use oil made for *air-cooled* motors. Marine varieties are made for cooler running outboards (water cooled), and may break down at our hotter temperatures.
- Use oils that meet the JASO FD or ISO-L-EGD standards. TC-W3 is for marine engines so it may be OK, but may not be ideal.
- Use synthetics which are commonly recognized as having better characteristics at higher RPMs and hotter temperatures. They also leave fewer deposits.
- Use oil that is dyed so that you can tell whether a particular batch of fuel is mixed. If using clear oil, develop a fool-proof way to track what fuel is already mixed. The phrase "I thought it was mixed" follows many a piston seizure.

Avoid mixing synthetics and mineral oils. A very few brands may not mix well and could form gel-type clumps in the tank. This was more common years ago.

Preflight Inspection

A preflight inspection is done before each flight. It should be (1) consistent—start from the same place (carabiners) and do it the same way each time, (2) thorough—don't skip items; touch each one as you check it, and (3) without interruptions. If you are interrupted, start over at the carabiners.

Motor

There's little reason to skimp—preflighting a paramotor takes less than a minute on most machines. Resist the temptation to crank & go, and ***never,*** start without checking the throttle-carburetor linkage (Fig 4-5) and having access to the kill switch.

Start the preflight by pulling at the carabiners. That will bring out harness webbing to expose potential problems and allow inspection of the critical carabiners and harness. Check the webbing, fabric, straps, and any attached connection hardware. They must be free of excessive fading, tears, cuts, badly worn sections, or other damage that could affect integrity. Here are other items to check:

- Look for small cracks in the carabiners. They could propagate to a catastrophic in-flight failure, especially on some aluminum models.
- Make sure any "cruise control" (throttle lock) is off, and SafeStart, if equipped, is on. Then **do a throttle check** as shown in Fig 4-5. These steps avoid sudden, unexpected power-up on start, our most common cause of serious injury.
- Walk around the machine, checking parts for security, and looking for loose bolts or other parts. A loose prop bolt can set up a vibration that tears the prop completely off its mount, possibly taking the engine with it. Torque marker paint (Fig 4-6) makes loose parts more obvious.
- Mufflers cause many problems. Look for cracks, loose or broken mountings, fiberglass packing inside, missing rivets/screws, and general security. Put safety wire, or other restraint, on anything of consequence that can loosen.
- Check redrive belts for proper tension and position.
- Check motor mounts and reduction drive bolts for security.
- Check spark plugs & wires for security, especially on inverted engines.

Fig 4-5 Throttle Linkage Check

The most important preflight action is to move the throttle while observing that the carburetor linkage returns to idle.

Float bowl carburetors hide the throttle mechanism inside a housing. Just make sure the trigger moves freely to max and idle, listening for the "clunk" of a stop.

When you first acquire a motor, and know everything is working, cycle the throttle several times. Watch what happens at the carb. Listen. This becomes what you check during preflight.

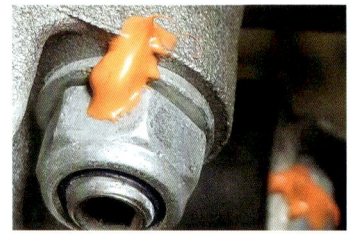

Fig 4-6 Torque Marker
This makes preflight quicker since loose parts are immediately obvious. See also Fig 12-15.

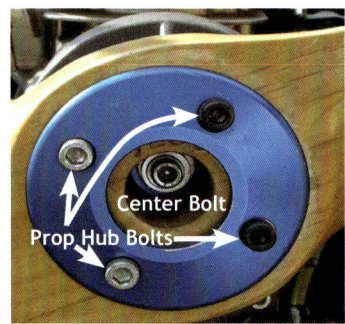

Fig 4-7 Prop with Center Bolt (2)
This style of prop mount has a center bolt. If there is any play in the prop (wiggling a tip fore and aft), this bolt may be loose.

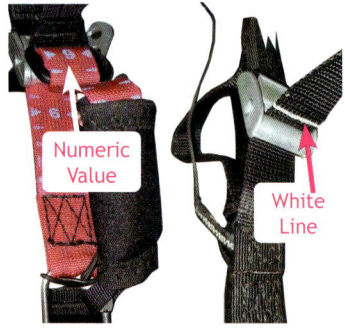

Fig 4-8 Setting Trimmers
Trimmers must be set for takeoff. Most wings have a recommended position, either a number or sewn line, frequently called the *neutral* setting.

If they're pulled in too far (set slow) the wing is sluggish to come overhead. If they're let out too far (set fast) the wing requires more damping brake, is more prone to front tuck, requires more running, and more brake to lift off.

- Verify fuel system integrity, including cap and a clear vent to allow air in. Check for tank security and turn on the appropriate valves, as installed. Some have an off valve for the vent—it must be open (on). With a blocked vent, the engine will run until diminishing fuel lowers tank pressure, possibly collapsing the tank. Eventually, the fuel pump can't suck hard enough and the motor quits.

- Check the propeller for condition. Small nicks are generally OK, but long splits must be repaired. Fortunately, many prop maladies can be repaired in the field without removal (page 125). Ensure hub and center bolts (if equipped) are tight.

- Align the prop vertically then push the top tip fore and aft. It should have less than about 1/16th inch (1.5 millimeters) of play. Check the motor mounts when doing this to see that they flex but have no cracks or excessive looseness.

- If the prop has been removed since its last flight, check that it's not on backward. This embarrassing mistake will be felt when the motor produces about half of its normal thrust. The curvy surface faces forward, in the direction of flight. Another way to remember is that the fatter part of the prop, the leading edge, is more forward.

- Check the cage for security and complete assembly. If the motor has a clutch (prop spins freely), spin the prop around to ensure sufficient clearance from the hoop and cage parts. Moving a belt-driven prop through an engine compression stroke *could* cause it to start.

- Ensure that accessories are secure and straps are out of harm's way. Nothing should be able to touch the exhaust or get into any moving parts. Close any zippered compartments.

- If equipped with a reserve, ensure its bridle routing remains unobstructed, attached, and the reserve pins are secured properly without being pushed all the way through (Fig 12-38).

Wing

With a breeze of at least 6 mph, checking the wing is easier: kite it up for a look. Always check that:

- Lines are connected, kink-free, and sheathed (outer covering intact).

- The fabric has no structural tears or holes.

- Risers have no visible damage, quick links are closed and tight, trimmers are set for takeoff, all toggles are in their holders, and the speedbar system is free. Brake lines must go straight through their pulleys, which must be free spinning. A frozen pulley will wear the brake line quickly to failure.

- Speedbar Trimmer Interconnect (page 265), if installed, is set properly.

A more thorough inspection is warranted every few months, depending on wear, but especially after rough handling. Lay the wing flat in a calm location then:

- Do a field-strength test. Find the most faded areas of fabric, usually on the top surface. Pull the fabric taut with your hands about 3 inches apart, then push your flat thumb into the spread as if trying to poke a hole. It should hold with about 3-5 pounds of pressure.

- Run each sheathed line between your fingers from the quick-link to the first cascade. Feel for thin spots which would reveal broken Kevlar inside, rendering the line unusable (Fig 2-11). One broken line may not seem like a big deal, and usually isn't, but it stresses the remaining lines. A lines are most critical (Fig 2-2).

- Check overall condition of the risers, quick links, and brakes. Try to pull the

the Rope Trick

Fig 4-9 Rope Trick (Prop Stopper)

On clutched machines this prevents the prop from spinning during start.

1. Use a sufficiently stout 4-foot rope or strap with a loop in one end.

2. Before starting, wrap it around the prop, then try to move the prop to make sure it doesn't slip off.

4. Start the motor and strap in.

5. Before runup, pull the rope's free end and stow in a safe place (can't get into the prop).

risers apart at the stitching with about 20 pounds of pull.

If you leave something for later, it's likely to be forgotten—maybe not this time, but eventually. Take the fuel cap, for example. If you leave the machine, even for a moment, secure the cap. Before walking away from your motor, try to leave it in an airworthy condition. If unable, use a reminder, like a wrench on the seat. Interruptions of routine contribute to aviation accidents of all kinds.

Putting it On

Heavy motors can be hard to stand up with, especially for smaller people, but the tips in Fig 4-10 may help. Specific technique depends on your body type, and a good-fitting harness keeps the motor from sliding around.

Kneel or sit, sliding your arms through, then grab the throttle (not shown).

Lean forward with the motor, then push with your arm(s) to help stand up.

For some body types, especially taller people, it may be easier to push off the ground while using your legs like in a & b. Experiment. Donning the motor while it's up on a stand is always much easier.

Fig 4-10 Getting in / Strapping on

Starting the Motor

Wait for your instructor to demonstrate proper starting, especially how to avoid propeller injuries. Treat every start like it will go to high power—cages only protect *lines* from the prop, not people, although having a safety ring (Fig 4-11) helps. Advise bystanders to stand clear and away from the propeller arc. **Check that the throttle is at idle** and shout "CLEAR PROP." Never, ever start without a cage—its minimal protection is still way better than nothing.

A motor that's not starting easily has proven to be particularly dangerous as pilots stop treating it with respect, taking more chances like holding the throttle open.

An electric starter *can* be safer if it allows starting on your back. The least desirable method is to start an unsecured machine by yourself while standing in front it.

Fig 4-11 Safety Ring

Surviving Starting

These tips reduce the immense prop danger while starting. Imagine your motor's full rated thrust suddenly pushing from its prop hub on *every* start.

- Always do a throttle check (Fig 4-5), even if you've done the preflight.
- Have the motor **well secured** on a rack (best option), on your back, or positioned in front of something that would hold it in place at full thrust.
- If able, start the motor choked to limit thrust, then shut down. Restart just before launch when it's on your back.
- On pull-starts units, have someone else pull while you control the throttle and kill switch.
- Don't remove an idling motor from its secure place until you have the throttle *and* kill switch in hand.
- If the machine has a clutch, consider using the "rope trick" (Fig 4-9).
- Have and use the best built-in protections available (Fig 27-23 on page 278).

Starting & Runup

Any gas motor requires fuel, air, spark, and spin. An electric starter makes the spin easy but needs some extra care. Specific details of priming, choking, master switches, cruise control, and fuel/air valves depend on model and should be described by your instructor or seller. If there's an owner's manual, be thankful and read it thoroughly. See "Troubleshooting" on page 119 for fixing some motor problems.

Make sure the ground area is clear of loose objects that could get sucked into the prop. They *love* props. Loose straps or cords must not reach the prop or exhaust. And be mindful of where the prop blast is going—even at idle it can disturb things nearby, especially paraglider wings.

Don't let the motor idle for too long, carbon builds up on the spark plug, cylinder head and other parts (called loading up). After idling for more than a few minutes, run it up to 50% power for about 10 seconds to "clear" the motor.

Sometime before takeoff, do a runup where you ensure the motor can make climb power, respond properly to throttle, and stop with the kill switch.

Have a Plan: Patterns and Altitudes

Before soloing, you need a plan, including signals, in case of radio failure (page 48). Your instructor's signals may differ from those shown here. You will fly a rectangular pattern (Fig 5-23) that helps judge landings, provides a known path that other pilots can easily search, and gives a way to describe your location.

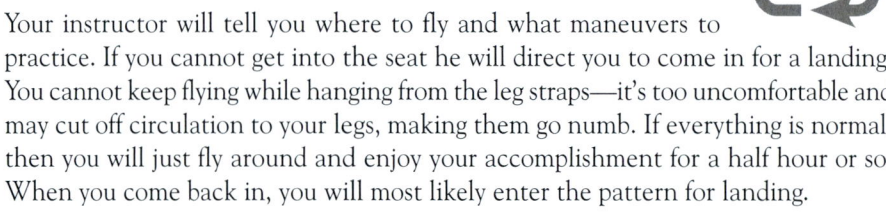

Takeoff and landing is always into the wind to reduce groundspeed. After reaching a safe altitude and getting seated, you will turn crosswind and continue climbing. The next turn is downwind and positions you for landing back at the launch site in case of a motor-out. Even if you're not landing right away, fly this path before departing the area. As a new solo student you will likely continue climbing so as to stay within gliding distance of the launch area.

Your instructor will tell you where to fly and what maneuvers to practice. If you cannot get into the seat he will direct you to come in for a landing. You cannot keep flying while hanging from the leg straps—it's too uncomfortable and may cut off circulation to your legs, making them go numb. If everything is normal, then you will just fly around and enjoy your accomplishment for a half hour or so. When you come back in, you will most likely enter the pattern for landing.

Caution!

Propellers are the #1 source for serious paramotor injuries.

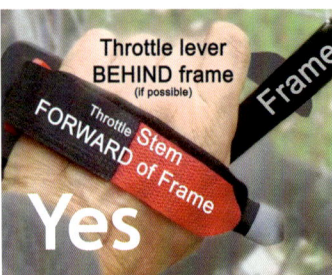

Fig 4-12 Surviving a Pull Start

If you *must* start it this way:

1. Keep access to the kill button.
2. Make sure the throttle can't be pushed accidentally.
3. Hold it strongly, and in a way that would keep control at the motor's full rated thrust.
4. Use the "Rope Trick" (Fig 4-9).

Taking Instructions via Radio

You'll be up there alone but with instructor guidance—filling in blanks or insisting on immediate responses. New sensations make concentrating difficult but concentrate you must. This is why simulator practice is so valuable, especially with the motor running and controls in hand. Some instructors may not run the motor in their simulator (which involves some risk of its own) but should still have you go through the drills while causing other distractions. It could save your life: prior rehearsal is critical!

You will be required to pull brakes, add power, reduce power, and kick your legs in response to radio instructions. Front/back kicking means "yes" and left/right scissor motion means "no." Follow instructor commands explicitly. You may not know why, but he will. Responding right away will reduce how dramatic the response needs to be.

Reaction and Overcontrol

Because you hang below the center of roll, your instinctive reaction to swings is *exactly opposite* to what it should be. Plus, it is common for new pilots to pull too much brake. This combination can result in an increasing oscillation, especially on non-beginner wings. You must use deliberate, smooth inputs and hold them for at least 3 seconds, resisting the urge to correct each swing. Listen and respond intently to the instructor: your life depends on it. We have more details next chapter.

Rehearsing

If you have to think about a response, don't count on it. Reactions must be rehearsed and automatic. For example, the reaction to a forward surging wing is applying some brake for a couple seconds then letting up. The reaction to a wing falling back is to immediately reduce power and reduce brakes while preparing to "catch" the impending surge with brake pull. Throwing a reserve is another action that must be rehearsed—if it's needed, you won't be calmly contemplating your navel.

Any good instructor will have you rehearse, in a simulator, what you'll do in flight, preferably some of it with the motor running. Rehearsal is key to ensuring necessary reactions. You must get to the point of responding to commands instinctively in the simulator.

You must rehearse taking instructions, especially for those early flights. Then, as experience is gained, add other situations. When hell is breaking loose, rehearsed reactions win the day.

Handling Emergencies

These must be rehearsed in a simulator. Some are best done with the motor running or other artificial distractions since the flight environment is loud and foreign at first. Simulator practice makes it less so.

Distraction and reaction can be worse than its cause or consequence. So when something does go pop, take a deep breath and deal with it methodically.

Situational emergencies, where the pilot has more time, are covered in Chapter 19 and include thought processes and options to be considered.

Above All

Following your instructor's radio commands is paramount, but a few common priorities apply to all emergencies:

- **Maintain Control.** Regardless of what happens, keep flying the craft. Use "reduce power, reduce brake, then steer" in uncertain situations, but in turbulence, follow the advice in "Turbulence" on page 49. Steer essentially straight with the least control input possible, avoiding large movements. Preparation keeps panic at bay, and reason in play.

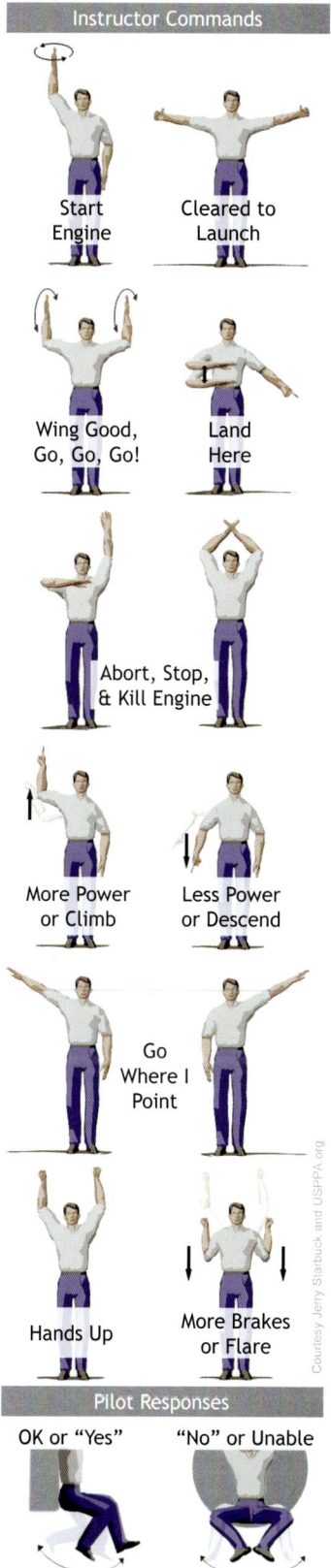

Fig 4-13 Visual Signals

These are common instructor hand signals. They supplement radio communications and can be useful in emergencies or comm failure.

> **Caution!**
>
> Not sure what's happening? "Reduce power, reduce brake, then steer."
>
> Be smooth, be ready to dampen any surge, and be measured: too much brake is the most common cause of in-flight control-related paramotor mishaps.
>
> Don't abruptly dump the power, reduce it by half *and hold*.
>
> After reducing brake pull, go back to, and hold, position/pressure 2 for a good feel of the wing. Do this unless you know a different action is correct.

Fig 4-14 Rear Riser Steering

Pulling a rear riser (D in this case) is one way to turn after a brake line failure. This wing uses a 4-riser set designed for motoring. A soaring wing will have longer risers and may require a longer reach to grab the quick-link—just grab as high as you can. On a 3-riser set, you would be pulling the C's.

It takes a lot of pull for even a small turn.

Situations needing immediate action are rare. They exist, and reactions should be rehearsed, but the most likely new pilot sin is over-reacting.

- Be smooth and hold inputs for 2 - 3 seconds to avoid oscillations.
- Establish a safe course and altitude. When something unexpected happens, *look* towards a safe course, *steer* that way, and climb slowly if appropriate.
- Avoid the natural tendency to unconsciously reduce power while dealing with a problem. Periodically check your hold on the throttle and increase as necessary to maintain a shallow climb. Altitude is usually your friend.
- Only once control and flight path are established, deal with the problem. Consider what you've got. Loud noises are usually a good reason to power off and land (if it's safe to do so) rather than "limping" home.

Aborting Launch

If something doesn't feel right, or your instructor calls an abort: 1) **Release** the throttle, 2) **press and hold** the kill switch (for most gas motors), and 3) carefully **stop running** then turn around to face the wing unless it overflies you.

Whenever shutting the motor off, be deliberate about "**press and hold.**"

Aborting Landing (Go-Around)

If something feels amiss with your landing, go around and climb back up using two steps. (1) throttle to half power as you ease up the brakes, wait 3 seconds to swing out, then (2) smoothly throttle up to climb power.

Throttle Cable Caught

After launch, while bringing your hand up from getting seated, the throttle cable snags. It works, but your hand is stuck and you can't reach up for the brake.

Maintain control. This is a non-event *unless* you do something rash, like yanking it really hard or letting go which throttles to idle. Keep climbing. Use normal input of the other hand for shallow turns and accept some torque turn if able.

At a safe height and flight path, move the throttle back, away from the motor and up. Make turns to stay near the launch site. It will probably be a simple matter of looking down to see the obvious solution then executing it.

If it remains snagged, get over the landing area with plenty of height and shut off the motor. Pull your hand out of the throttle, grab the brake, and enjoy a nice, quiet, power-off landing.

Radio Failure

Your instructor's input is important, but radios quit—have a plan. Usually that's to continue around the pattern, climb out above the field to get some feel for the machine, then come in for a normal landing near center-field. You should have rehearsed this in the simulator, reciting back a detailed description of climbing up, getting into the seat, pattern, killing the motor, and landing.

Maneuver gently to see your instructor's signaling and respond accordingly.

Brake Line Failure or Tangle

A brake line can break, come untied, get cut off by the prop, tangle, or become disconnected, but there is plenty of steering authority in the rear risers. As with all emergency situations, fly the aircraft first. Use available control to steer while climbing to a safe altitude.

Most likely it's a loop of brake line fouling the pulley. You may be able to undo this in flight but climb to at least 300' first. Remember, if the brake is stuck in its pulley, it will still pull that rear riser which will cause a turn.

Don't be rash, it's normally benign. Once at altitude, get into the seat (if able) and establish level or slightly climbing flight. Then deal with the problem.

It's usually easy to see what needs to be done—reach up and do that. Mind the flight path. You can safely land without the brakes, but it's obviously better to regain their use.

If a brake line is just stuck, you may be able to activate it from *above* the pulley, especially if you have shorter risers and/or a low hook-in machine.

If it *stays* stuck, plan on using the rear risers for steering and flare (Fig 4-14). Don't use one brake and one rear riser, use both rear risers.

Do some practice turns and flares to get a feel for how much pull is needed, it's a lot of pressure but not a lot of movement. They're not nearly as effective, so allow for a longer, straight-in approach.

At the point where you would normally use the brakes to flare, pull harder on both rear risers and be ready for a firm touchdown. Landing power-off is generally preferable to avoid prop/cage damage but a fall is still more likely without use of the brakes. With experience, you can land power-on, which allows a softer, but still fast, touchdown at some increased risk to your gear.

Don't pull the rears while at high power to reduce possibility of parachutal stall, where the wing descends vertically (see "Parachutal Stall/Spin" on page 53).

Engine Failure

Engine failure is a non-event unless you've gone beyond gliding range of a safe landing spot. Our naturally slow landing speed leaves us options from all phases of flight. Keep track of wind direction.

Quick reactions to a failure are only required if it happens during initial climb or while flying low (under 20 feet). Steeper climbs beget stronger surges (wing darting forward) and need more aggressive responses. See Fig 4-16.

After the initial surge is controlled, and altitude permitting, ease your hands up to accelerate for a normal flare. If it happens while cruising below about 10 feet (you won't be doing that on first flights), the brakes should just be held with a flare at the normal height. There won't be much brake left for flare, but it beats coming off the brakes and diving into the ground.

A motor failure from over 100 feet—less with experience—gives time to turn into the wind for a normal landing. Other *landing priorities* must be considered ("Motor Failure and Landing Priorities" on page 201).

If you have enough altitude (about 200 feet), get established in a landing pattern, then try to restart. Fly the craft before dealing with the motor. Try different throttle settings. If you do get it started, maintain the same power setting until reaching a point where a normal power-off landing pattern can be made. Plan the landing with no power even if you let the motor idle.

Concentrate on the landing once you're below 200 feet.

Turbulence

On most wings, if it gets bumpy, set trimmers to slow and increase brake pressure to between 2 and 3. Pressure is key. If a brake handle yanks upward, let it, while maintaining the same pressure. Likewise, if a toggle goes limp, let it go down. When throttling off, increase brake pressure slightly, closer to 3. At low power settings, slowing down is generally better, but be careful—too much brake can be more dangerous than not enough.

You'll be swinging around some, but don't try to correct for individual swings as a new

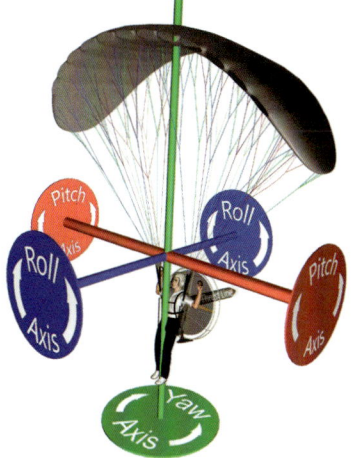

Fig 4-15 Axis Simplified

The craft moves around these 3 axes. Banking is around the *Roll* axis.

Pitching is around the *Pitch* axis. Throttling up, for example will make you "pitch up" into a climb and a sudden power loss will cause the wing to surge forward or "Pitch down."

Twisting left/right is done around the *Yaw* Axis.

There's more to it at Fig 22-4.

**Demo:
Embarrassment Avoided**

Right after liftoff, during an impromptu demo flight for some police who showed up, I discovered the right brake was stuck (bad preflight). Not wanting to look bad in front of our new observers, I came back around and landed using the rear risers to flare. They had no idea that anything was amiss and I wasn't about to tell them.

"Wasn't that cool?" I asked while quietly fixing my brake. "Here, I'll go again." And I took off uneventfully this time.

They probably wondered why that flight was so much longer.

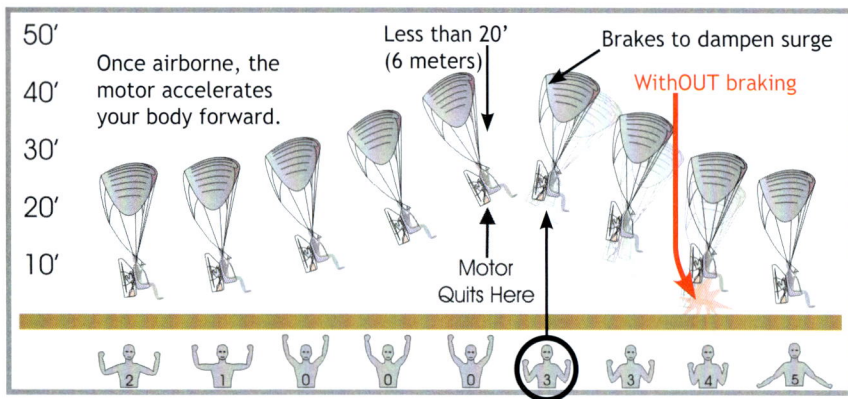

Fig 4-16 Motor Failure during Takeoff or at Low Altitude

A motor failure just after takeoff requires damping the surge, as shown above, to prevent an excessive dive. How much and how quick depends mostly on climb angle, height at failure, and wing.

Above about 30 feet (9 meters), establish a brief glide and do a normal landing.

Smaller (faster) wings require a bit more height to establish a glide.

This is easy and valuable to practice up high after getting some flights in.

The Spectator Question

You'll hear this a lot: "What do you do when the engine quits?"

For best effect, answer "plummet and die." But the real answer is actually quite mundane: "Not much," at least if you're above 200 feet.

> **Caution!**
>
> In any unusual situation, never accept an increasingly steep turn. After initially reducing brake pressure, use whatever input it takes to prevent a spiral dive.

pilot. If you need to turn, *hold* some brake input for at least 5 seconds, and turn slowly. This avoids inducing roll oscillations, which newer pilots usually make worse. If you *do* start oscillating, ease up pressure, hold both hands steady or put them on your helmet, and ride it out.

Keep a good posture (Fig 5-18) with elbows in to further minimize over-controlling.

These actions reduce the chance of various wing maladies where the leading edge tucks under, causing a brief but rapid descent and possibly a severe turn. This is *not* "active flying" (page 166), which at this point in your learning, will make matters worse due to our craft's pendular weirdness.

A few reflex models may recommend setting the trimmers to fast and not giving any brake input during turbulence encounters. Consult the manual.

Small Asymmetric Wing Folds

Small folds (collapses) happen occasionally in turbulence, and the wing usually snaps back before being noticed. Following the advice above will both reduce the odds and hasten recovery.

Small collapses that don't come out immediately can usually be cured with normal steering inputs—keep flying straight and it pops out soon enough. A stronger, quick pull of brake on the folded side may also work, but don't overdo it.

Large Asymmetric Wing Fold

A big fold (see "Asymmetric Collapse" on page 185), where over half of the wing tucks under, is rare enough that most motor pilots have never experienced it. Unfortunately, the motor does add complexity which is why "big air" (strong turbulence) should be avoided.

Simple folds up to 60% are still controllable. But if the fabric bunches up, it creates a powerful turning force. Smoothly reduce power, reduce brake pressure (but not completely), then steer. Go about as fast as you say those words to avoid over controlling. Then add brake pressure 3 and steer for straight ahead with brakes and weight shift. **Do what it takes to prevent a steepening bank**, which may be a lot more steering input, and be ready to let the collapsed-side brake come back up as its pressure builds.

Many collapse-related paramotor incidents are from, or aggravated by, excessive pilot response. But, if you're low to the ground or near an obstruction, do whatever it takes to steer clear, even if that means a nearly immediate turn input.

Cravat

Cravats are when part of the wingtip folds into the lines, causing a turn. More fabric, more turn. A small cravat, like in Fig 4-19, isn't bad—if you can steer easily, just come around to land. Sometimes a quick brake pump to pressure 3 will clear it. Act immediately if a turn develops or worsens. Use minimum brakes at first, but do what it takes to fly straight (or as straight as you can).

If you have enough time, consider pulling the stabilo (tip) line on the cravatted side. It may free the fabric. Stabilo lines can be hard to find, though, with so much going on. Practice finding and pulling them while kiting.

Large cravats are a *much* bigger deal ("Cravat" on page 185).

Riser Twist

If you feel yourself twisting as the wing starts to lift on launch, abort. Before trying again, figure out why it happened and find a cure (page 240).

If a twist starts *after* launch, immediately, *smoothly*, reduce power, reduce brake pressure, then steer (Fig 4-20). Reducing power removes the twisting force. Reducing brake pull avoids going into a full twist while trapping pulled brakes in the twist.

With reduced thrust, you should swing back around and resume forward flight. The glider flies just fine regardless of your body's heading as long as you relax power and brakes. Once facing forward, throttle up just enough to fly. If terrain allows, landing right away may be your best option.

Riser twist almost always happens on launch. Trying to continue at full power can spin you around into a crash. Even without going all the way around, if your body points left, thrust will push you left, which causes a right bank (motor-induced lock out). The only solution is reducing power—trying to stop the twist with brakes can lead to spinning and dropping.

Kill Switch or Throttle Failure

Your run-up (page 46) should have tested the kill switch, but if it fails in flight, it won't be noticed until landing. If you've rehearsed alternative shutdown methods, use one, otherwise make a normal landing at idle. After touchdown, carefully turn around, bring the wing down to keep lines out of the prop, and have your instructor shut it off using other means. You could run it out of gas, but that will take time and require a power-off landing (which isn't a big deal).

Getting the throttle cable chopped in the prop could lead to having no kill switch, *and* being at high power. That situation is addressed in "Motor Stuck at Full or Partial Power" on page 199, which also lists some alternative kill methods.

Unfastened Leg Straps (Loops)

In free flight paragliding, launching with forgotten leg straps is usually catastrophic. It can be equally dangerous for motor pilots *if* they try to hang on and "take care of it in the air." Plus, many motor pilots eventually wind up free flying. So get into the habit of always buckling your legs first and unbuckling them last. Use the checklist

Fig 4-17 Pilot-induced 50% fold
While this was easily controlled, mother nature can dole out much worse: don't be fooled.

Fig 4-18 Accelerated Fold
This happened on speedbar (accelerated flight) but he was able to continue steering straight as the fold came out on its own.

Fig 4-19 Small Cravat
In this case, the cravat had little effect, but if it cups the air in certain ways, it can cause a turn that *must* be stopped.

Fig 4-20 Riser Twist and Torque

This shows a belt-driven machine which yaws (twists) the pilot left, meaning that motor thrust pushes him left and causing a right bank.

Geared drives go the other way.

1. Lifting off he feels his body start to twist left. It's worse if the wing was slightly right at liftoff due to *loaded riser twist* (see "Twisting Forces At Work" on page 240)

2. Forces quickly conspire to make it a pronounced left pilot yaw.

3. Once twisted, thrust now pushes his body left and the wing into a right bank. This is an odd feeling—your body is pointed left but the wing is right, and you're *turning* right, but not climbing much. Thrust is being wasted on pushing your body left instead of climbing.

4. Pulling excessive left brake in an effort to stop turning may cause a spin and rapid descent as shown.

5. The only solution is to **reduce power, reduce brake, then steer.**

in the Appendix every time to prevent this problem.

If you do forget one (or both) leg straps, you'll feel it quickly on launch as the motor tries to lift off without you. If that happens, **abort!** Swallow your pride and quietly buckle up before another try.

Reserve Deployment

Reserve deployments in motoring are rare, but there have been "saves," usually following botched aerobatics, midair collisions, strong thermal turbulence, or huge wind shifts. Free flyers are more likely to "toss" in strong lift or aerobatic exuberance.

Situations that warrant throwing must involve developing spiral dives, or impending loss of control—some malady that won't likely recover. In spirals, act fast. G-forces build quickly, and may soon prevent deploying at all. Follow these steps deliberately to get the reserve out within 3 seconds.

1. **Kill** the motor, holding the switch (or as needed by the motor) so it doesn't restart. We don't want our "last chance" getting chopped by the prop.

2. **Look** at the reserve handle to avoid wasting time reaching endlessly for a handle that's not there. At least one pilot hit the ground while grasping wildly for the reserve handle on his right side—it was on the left.

3. **Pull** the handle out in a forceful "Z" pattern to help pull both pins positively. The reserve sits at the end of a foot-long line. It can be difficult if you've never rehearsed it in a moving simulator. Let go of the brake before pulling to avoid throwing it into the brake line. Some instructors suggest putting both brakes in one hand before tossing with the other hand.

4. **Clear.** Find a clear direction that is free of wing lines and paramotor. Be deliberate but quick.

5. **Throw** towards clear air, down, and outward of any turn, in one motion. It will be like tossing a 5 pound rock at the end of a foot-long cord. Yank on the bridle to help open the parachute if it doesn't deploy immediately.

These actions must be rehearsed, automatic, and performed with purpose. Commit this to muscle memory: "Kill, Look, Pull, Clear, and Throw."

Once the reserve opens, your glider may reinflate and begin *downplaning,* where it's flying straight down and pulling the reserve sideways, reducing its effectiveness. It's generally best to disable the glider, possibly by pulling hard on the "B" lines so it cannot degrade your descent. Be aware that, while pulling lines, it can yank powerfully out of your hands, causing burns.

If everything is stable, and you're not very high, consider leaving it alone to prepare for landing.

Approaching earth, look at the horizon and prepare for a Parachute Landing Fall (PLF) as shown in Fig 4-23. It's an established method for absorbing high impact that primarily says to keep your legs together with knees slightly bent.

You'll hit hard, like jumping off a 4 to 6 foot platform (Fig 28-1 "Jump Height Equivalent"), but try orienting yourself to roll left or right. Think "feet, knee, hip, then shoulder," ending in a rolling motion. Use the motor to absorb some impact if the frame is below you. Protect your spine at all costs. Pulling your legs up to hit on the motor's frame may reduce the chance for leg injuries at the expense of your spine. Use the frame (lift your legs) only if you *know* it will give sufficient protection.

Parachutal Stall/Spin

A wing goes parachutal when it stops flying forward and starts descending vertically like an old round parachute. The wing, which remains fully inflated, may seem to fall back a bit as forward airspeed slows.

It usually involves some combination of factors: large, old and/or porous wing, too much brake, turbulence, and engine thrust. It may devolve into a spin, where the glider rotates due to one side having slightly more drag (from brakes or turbulence).

Fig 4-21 Motor Reserve Clinic
This pilot was surprised by how little his first "toss" moved the reserve. By the third try (pictured), he succeeded at getting it out with good force.

Throwing a reserve is much like throwing a 5-pound weight from the end of a foot-long cord.

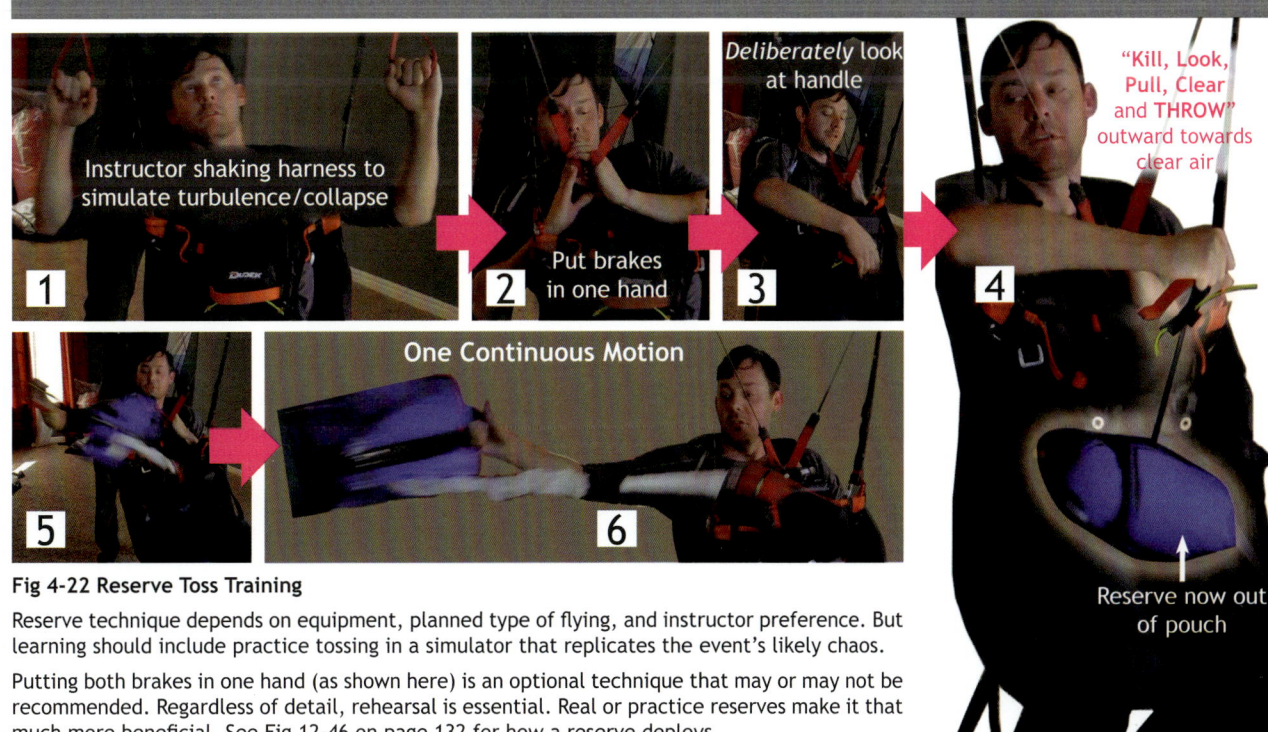

Fig 4-22 Reserve Toss Training
Reserve technique depends on equipment, planned type of flying, and instructor preference. But learning should include practice tossing in a simulator that replicates the event's likely chaos.

Putting both brakes in one hand (as shown here) is an optional technique that may or may not be recommended. Regardless of detail, rehearsal is essential. Real or practice reserves make it that much more beneficial. See Fig 12-46 on page 132 for how a reserve deploys.

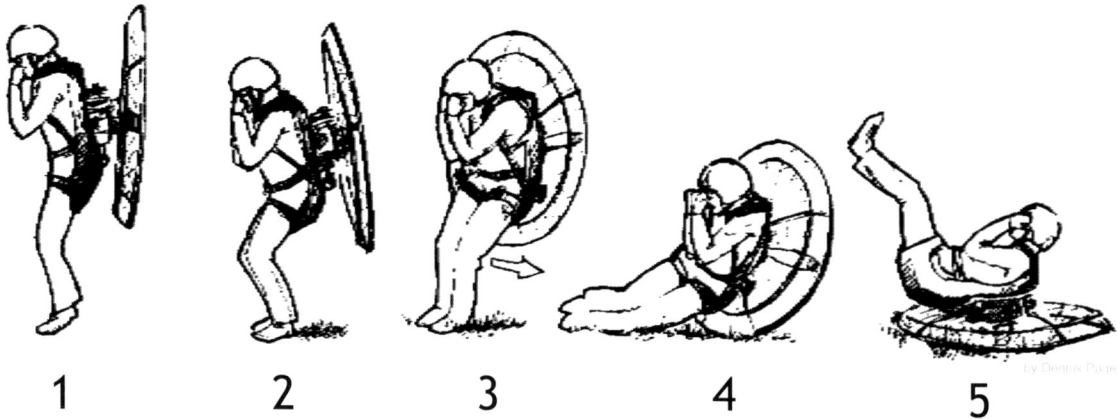

Fig 4-23 Parachute Landing Fall

Landing under a reserve can cause injury, especially on smaller reserves (see Fig 28-1 for descent rates).

Many years ago, military paratroopers devised a way to get their soldiers down with fewer injuries—the Parachute Landing Fall (PLF). It works for any anticipated hard landing.

The idea is to transfer vertical energy into horizontal energy. For a motor pilot, the frame may intervene which is good. Some instructors advocate lifting your legs to let the frame take the impact, but that risks serious back injury if the motor deforms poorly or is not in a position to protect the spine.

Once you recognize the need for a PLF, put your **legs together** with **toes angled down** slightly, and **knees slightly bent**. At touchdown, **roll** in whatever direction is natural, absorbing some with the knees, then hips then the frame.

Parachutal stalls are quite different than full stalls (on page 185) or aircraft type stalls.

While thrust alone won't cause it, they're far more common under power because thrust keeps the paraglider stalled where it would otherwise recover on its own. Most parachutal PPG accidents involve the pilot impacting at full power under a fully inflated wing and frequently spinning or starting to spin. It *can* be caused by simply pulling too much brake, such as when slowing down to make a landing spot.

Recovery is simple but must be done immediately and fully upon feeling the wing slow down or the airflow stop. Thankfully, the default emergency reaction will normally work: **"Reduce Power, Reduce Brakes, Then Steer."** In this case, reduce all power, let completely up on the brakes and be prepared to dampen a big surge when the wing recovers into flight.

In the extremely unlikely chance that it's still not flying, and you're well above 100 feet, then: reach for the A's, palms forward, thumbs down, grab and twist the A's down about 2 inches. This is called tweaking the A's. If you happen to have your feet on the speedbar (not likely), then push it. Letting out the trimmers could also work if you've become a Samurai Trim Releaser.

At recovery the wing may surge *violently* forward, followed by you swinging below it. With too little altitude, that might be worse than landing from the parachutal stall. It may be better to hold the controls stable and ride it down, ready for a PLF.

First Flight

CHAPTER 5

Time to fly.

Your first flight may not be some momentous event, but rather a converging of skills and conditions that make it the right time. You will have already learned kiting, rehearsed the flight, and know what to expect. You've been practicing, waiting for conditions that have now arrived.

This flight adds major new sensations and adrenaline. Don't underestimate them. It's why practice is so critical: **in the face of kinematic newness, only rehearsed reactions survive.** We're not good at thinking things through in such conditions. Like airline trainers, good PPG instructors understand this and use repetitive practice to avoid drama.

Launch

Variations in technique exist to accommodate different equipment, conditions, experience, and simple preference. Do what you've learned to minimize surprises. Listen intently to your instructor. Be prepared to abort quickly and nothing gets fed to the prop.

Unlike other forms of flight, takeoff is literally and figuratively the biggest hurdle. You'll spend more time learning launch than all other areas combined.

After preflight, secure the motor and ensure its throttle is at idle *and* free moving. Say "clear prop," wait a second, carefully start, warm it up, then shut down.

Lay out your wing carefully into any hint of wind and clear the lines. This is especially critical to success in near-calm conditions.

Don the motor, fasten *all* the harness straps, starting with the legs since forgetting those have more consequence. Get the throttle situated comfortably in your hand then hook into the wing. With everything now connected, do a pre-launch checklist from memory to cover the basics (see back cover).

Fig 5-1 Checklists

Airlines use checklists for good reason: they work. Skipping the checklist for expediency or omitting items has proven deadly.

In comparison to a Boeing 737, our checklist is mercifully brief, but is no less critical. An easy-to-use set of checklists is in back of the book.

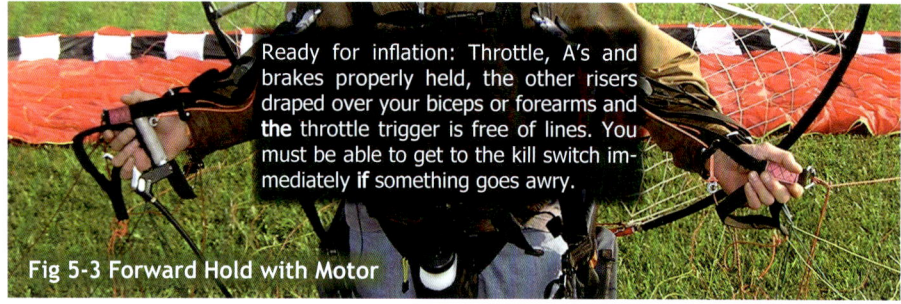
Fig 5-3 Forward Hold with Motor

Ready for inflation: Throttle, A's and brakes properly held, the other risers draped over your biceps or forearms and **the** throttle trigger is free of lines. You must be able to get to the kill switch immediately **if** something goes awry.

Fig 5-2 Launch Posture

Posture is important. Lean too much, or with arms forward, pulling too much A's, and the leading edge folds down (front tucks). That's what's happening at the arrows.

Start with hands more back. Then, when the A's are released, hands must be near the brake pulleys to avoid pulling brake.

Some forward lean is needed to start, but then, as power is applied, the hips must come forward while chanting "power up, hips out."

Excessive forward lean causes:
1. Looking down too much, making it harder to see the wing.
2. Thrust to push you down.
3. The seat to come out, which instinctively encourages trying to sit down too early.
4. Too much A-riser or brake pull since "up" hands are forward (like in the image).
5. Difficulty in getting one leg in front of the other for a good run.

Start the motor. On some gear you may have to start before putting the motor on—follow "Surviving Starting" on page 46.

Do as you've rehearsed, but now with the motor's throttle, thrust, and weight. It will feel different, but prior practice with a throttle simulator helps.

Just before launch, determine the wind direction. Feeling it on your face is ideal if the prop isn't spinning (clutched machines), otherwise, use whatever wind indicators are available (Fig 7-15). If the wind has turned significantly, you'll either need to wait or move. When it's light and variable (better known as "light and miserable"), waiting may be better. As morning wears on, thermals increasingly change the wind direction from minute to minute. About the time you get it laid out into a new direction, a thermal comes by, changing it again.

Rehearse the abort: "**Release** the throttle, **press** and **hold** the kill switch."

Inflation—Light or Nil Wind

Launching in zero wind is our most demanding task. The following are two techniques and a variation, but they all start with a good layout and posture.

Tension the lines slightly with*out* curling the leading edge, get centered, be perpendicular to the glider, and pick a target to run towards. Now take *one* step back. If the A's are split, use the inners, if they're easily reachable.

Start the run with arms back, leading with your chest and minimal A-pull. Once the glider takes shape, *then* pull appropriate A's. Some gliders require more, some less, and some glider/motor combinations require holding your arms up more. A good instructor will know. And he will earn his entire keep in these moments. Bigger gliders take longer to come up because of longer lines.

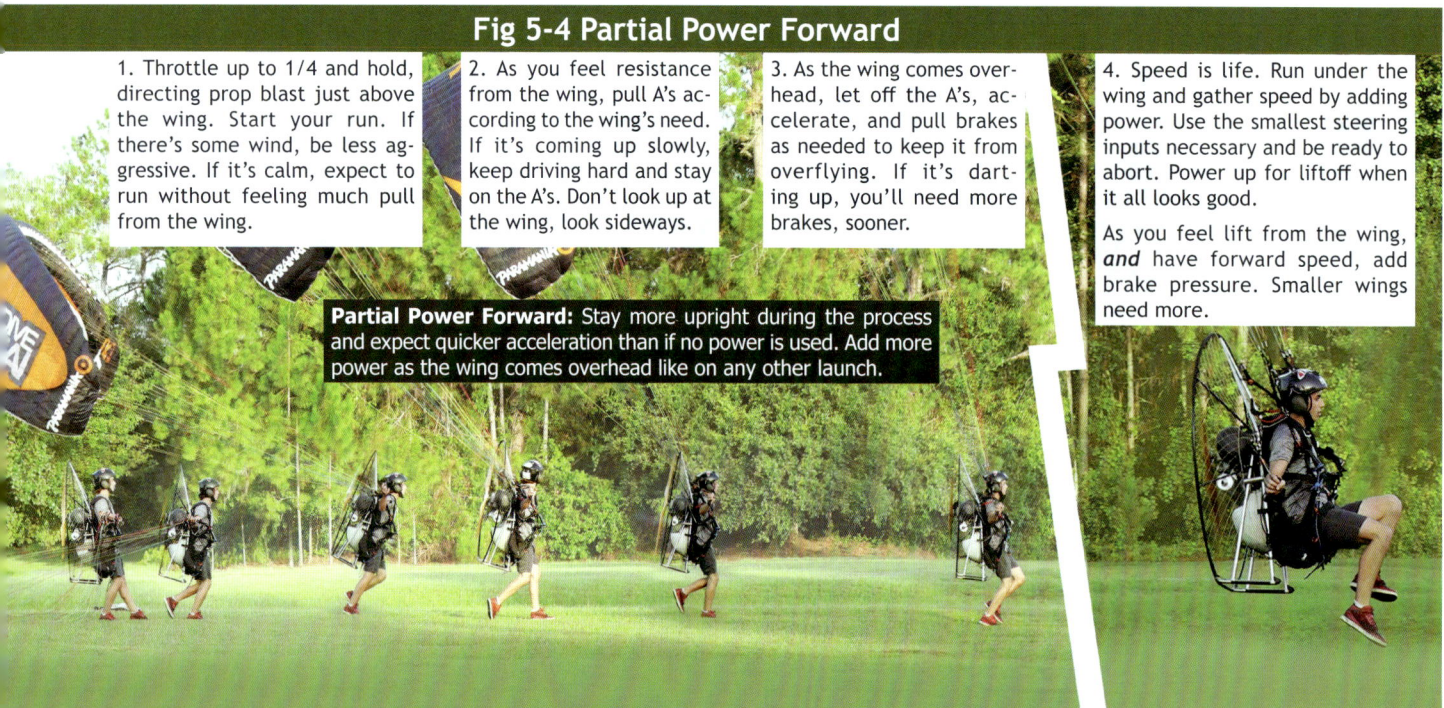

Fig 5-4 Partial Power Forward

1. Throttle up to 1/4 and hold, directing prop blast just above the wing. Start your run. If there's some wind, be less aggressive. If it's calm, expect to run without feeling much pull from the wing.

2. As you feel resistance from the wing, pull A's according to the wing's need. If it's coming up slowly, keep driving hard and stay on the A's. Don't look up at the wing, look sideways.

3. As the wing comes overhead, let off the A's, accelerate, and pull brakes as needed to keep it from overflying. If it's darting up, you'll need more brakes, sooner.

4. Speed is life. Run under the wing and gather speed by adding power. Use the smallest steering inputs necessary and be ready to abort. Power up for liftoff when it all looks good.

As you feel lift from the wing, *and* have forward speed, add brake pressure. Smaller wings need more.

Partial Power Forward: Stay more upright during the process and expect quicker acceleration than if no power is used. Add more power as the wing comes overhead like on any other launch.

1. Partial Power Forward.

This is a reliable launch method, but is not good for all machines, especially larger pilots on bigger wings and/or with powerful motors. For those, use a no power forward (shown next.)

Using too much power, too early, can pull the lines and cage back enough to hit the prop. Or it can make the wing dart overhead too fast, allowing sudden acceleration that pushes you onto your face. Partial power means: *before* starting the run, establish steady thrust at about 25%, *then* go for it—holding power steady through inflation. See below for a description.

2. No-Power Inflation

On a no-power inflation, it's all you getting the wing up past about 60°. This is more difficult with large wings due to their higher air resistance while coming up. It's even more difficult with even the tiniest tailwind up at 15 ft (5 meters).

You'll start just like you did in Fig 3-8, leading with your chest, arms back, *then* arms pulling A's as needed by the wing. The challenge is adding power just as the wing passes about 60° so lines are clearing the cage. This is a vulnerable time; with too little speed the wing is likely to fall back or sideways.

2a. No Power Inflation – Variation

A variation is to throttle up to 50% or so before starting your run. Let it stabilize then lunge forward, but *just* before reaching full line extension, throttle off. This way the motor propels you quickly into inflation without too much risk to the cage. It's good for small wings and may prevent lines from catching on some cages. Then it's just like a regular no-power Inflation.

On All Launches

Every inflation morphs into a powered, controlled run. If the wing is darting up, damp with brakes, accelerate your body, then reduce brake so it doesn't fall back. Add only enough power to stay in a controlled run. Speed is life, speed is control, but **don't try to fly before you're stable**. Don't try to jump in the air—keep running until your feet are churning air. On lower powered motors, some instructors may have you go to *full* power as the wing nears overhead.

Once in a **controlled run** with the **wing overhead**, **tracking** in a safe direction and **in control**: throttle up for takeoff. Think of takeoff as the reward for good control.

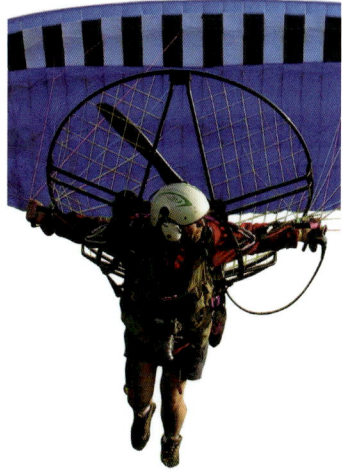

Fig 5-6 Looking at the Wing

During inflation, if you need to look at the wing, look to the side. As it comes overhead, looking up tends to slow you down. In calm or light wind, concentrate on getting speed quickly. Speed is life!

Older gliders, or those with shrunken rear lines, or trimmers set to slow, may not come up all the way or will tend to fall back. If so, try setting the trimmers faster (see "Troubleshooting Forward Launch Problems" on page 58).

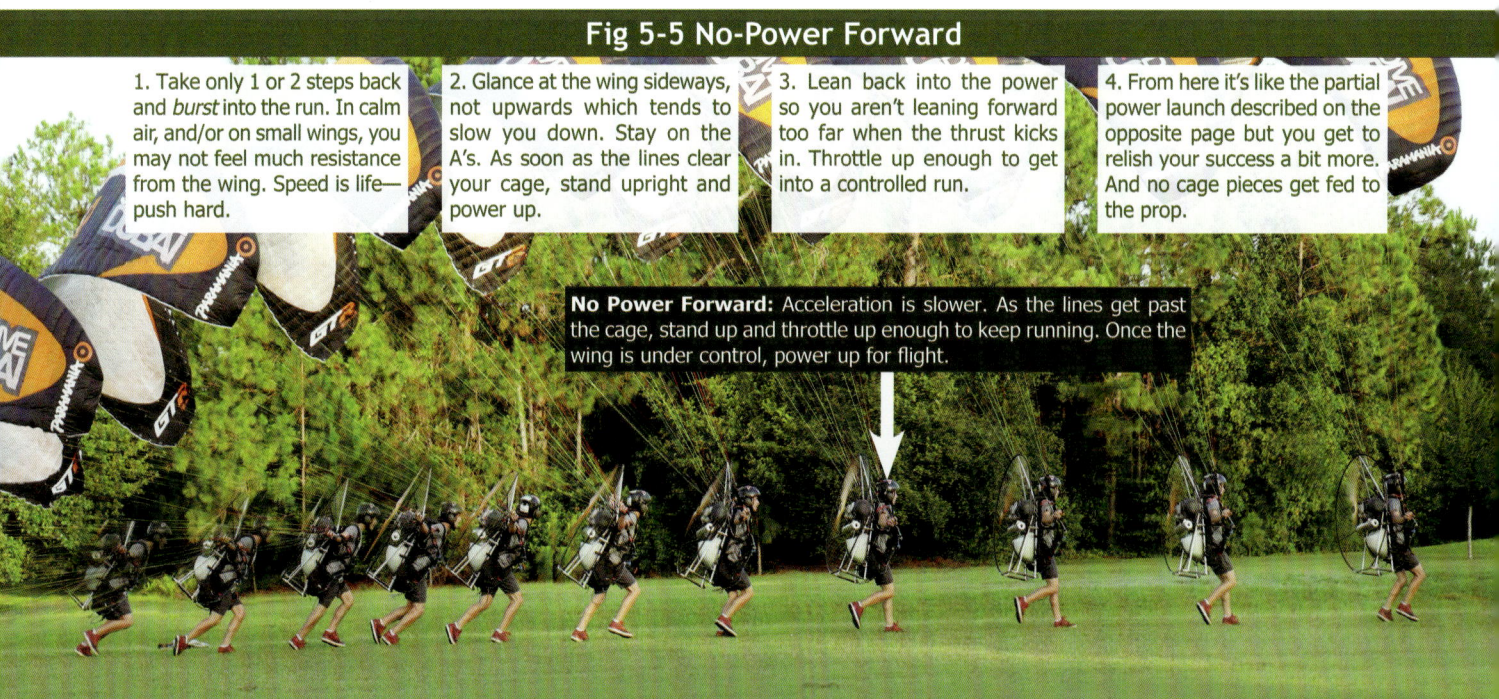

Fig 5-5 No-Power Forward

1. Take only 1 or 2 steps back and *burst* into the run. In calm air, and/or on small wings, you may not feel much resistance from the wing. Speed is life— push hard.

2. Glance at the wing sideways, not upwards which tends to slow you down. Stay on the A's. As soon as the lines clear your cage, stand upright and power up.

3. Lean back into the power so you aren't leaning forward too far when the thrust kicks in. Throttle up enough to get into a controlled run.

4. From here it's like the partial power launch described on the opposite page but you get to relish your success a bit more. And no cage pieces get fed to the prop.

No Power Forward: Acceleration is slower. As the lines get past the cage, stand up and throttle up enough to keep running. Once the wing is under control, power up for flight.

Troubleshooting Forward Launch Problems

Some of these are contradictory because they address different problems. Follow your instructor's advice since he *sees* what's happening.

Symptom 1: Wing comes up crooked.

1. You're not starting the initial run exactly centered and perpendicular to the wing.
2. If the wing always comes up to the left, stand an inch to the right, and/or point your body (and run) slightly to the right.
3. Start from a clean surface with enough V shaped layout, and be pointed exactly into whatever whiff of wind is present.
4. Be more aggressive to build speed faster. Speed improves control. This is easier with a relatively small wing.
5. You're pulling too much A's or pulling them unevenly. Lead with your chest (arms back), then A's, then power.
6. Lines are catching on the cage (right). Install smooth tubing around the offending cage hoop and ensure there is nothing to snag on. Don't use line holders for foot-launching. Holding your arms up higher or wiggling doesn't help since it's the rear lines that catch.
7. A brake is tied too short, or there's something caught in the lines.
8. Use the center A's if they're split.

Fig 5-8 Lines catching on the cage.

Symptom 2: The wing doesn't come all the way overhead, especially when there's no wind.

1. Stay on the A's longer and delay going to the brakes. Some wings, especially older gliders, require lots of A pull during inflation and acceleration. Gather good forward speed *before* applying any brakes.
2. Make sure you're not pulling brakes inadvertently. After letting go of the A's, touch the brake pulleys before pulling any brake.
3. You're pulling *too much* A's, curling the leading edge (Fig 5-2 on page 56). Start with arms back *then* apply A pressure.
4. Not enough power or not throttling up early enough.
5. Your initial run needs to be more aggressive. It's common to slow down when looking back up at the wing.
6. Don't look *up* at the wing; look *sideways* while continuing to drive forward.
7. Set trimmers to a faster setting. This requires a slightly faster launch run and/or more brake pressure to lift off.
8. Some pilots *may* benefit from looking up at the wing as they throttle up *if* it forces a more correct upright posture.
9. The brakes are tied too short or the rear lines have shrunk. See Fig 12-36 "Line Stretching"
10. That museum-piece wing needs to be retired. Newer models employ improvements to help inflate in zero wind.

Symptom 3: The wing tends to over-fly then collapse, especially with some wind.

1. Get off the A's earlier and damp with brakes earlier. Then accelerate right away to get in front of the wing.
2. Set trimmers to a slower setting (pulled in).
3. If using power, use less. Prop blast aggravates the problem.
4. Use a reverse inflation.

Symptom 4: Can't lift off despite running fast.

1. After initial inflation, stand up straight while easing into full power. Concentrate on letting the motor push you as fast as your legs will go, with long strides before adding more brake. You may need brake to take off but then reduce to climb ("Hands up to go up").
2. Set the trimmers to a slower setting.
3. Make sure your motor is producing full RPM and you're into the wind. If the motor is making full RPM, but it's not pushing hard enough, make sure the prop is mounted forwards.
4. Adjust your harness for the least amount of tilt-back possible so the wing's lift doesn't force you to run while tilted back.
5. If it's calm, try going the other way. It's possible the wind at wing height is slightly tailwind.

Symptom 5: I tend to go side to side before lifting off and almost fall.

1. Once you get the wing up overhead and moving, use just enough power to keep moving, steer the wing overhead straight, *then* grab full power. Never take off with the wing off-center—it must be almost exactly overhead before throttling up.
2. Don't change running direction. Only correct *half* as much as you think or not at all.
3. Master forward kiting through an obstacle course—steering the wing then following it. You'll need to master leading it.
4. Stand straight up early in the launch run. If you're leaning forward, then the wing lifts you into an upright run; precession will impart a twist. Consider using less power for initial climb.
5. Adjust your harness to minimize torque effects (Fig 12-7).
6. Make sure the wing is either exactly overhead or slightly left (right for geared machines) just before lift off to prevent *loaded riser twist*.

Symptom 6: I tend to sink back down to the ground and land on my butt.

1. Keep running until you are churning air. Don't get in the seat until well clear of the ground and established in a climb.
2. Don't let off the brakes too quickly after liftoff. *Ease* them up slowly to accelerate into a climb.
3. Adjust the harness to prevent the seat from kicking you into the air too early. Be less tilted back.

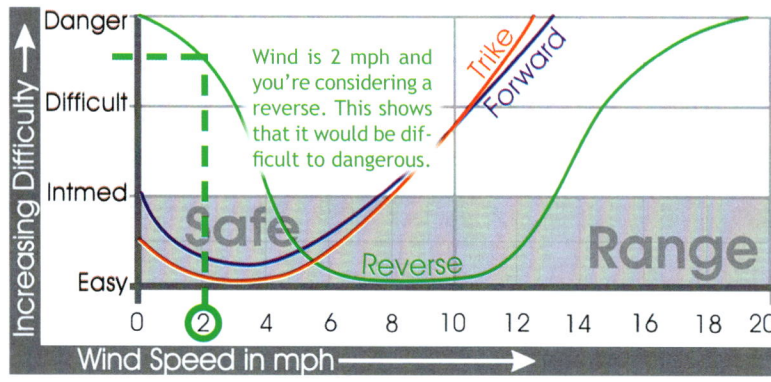

Fig 5-7 Choosing Inflation Type

This chart relates inflation type to wind speed and difficulty. For example, a reverse inflation (green line) is easiest and safest in winds between 5 and 13 mph. Forwards are safest in calm to 5 mph.

The Trike (cart) line assumes forward inflations. Reverse cart inflations are possible ("Cart Reverse Launch" on page 154). Carts are easier and safer in a dead calm.

    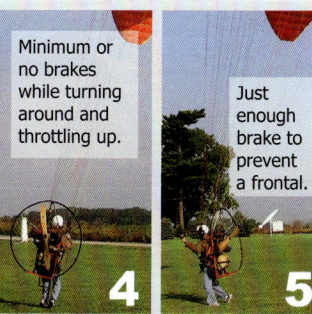

Fig 5-9 Building a wall is best, but there's not always enough wind. Wing layout must put your back square to the wind.

Fig 5-10 Snap back hard with your body, applying pressure to the A's as necessary. Walk backward as needed.

Fig 5-11 Use no brakes as the wing comes up unless needed to slow it. Move left or right with the wing. Pull the A's as necessary.

Fig 5-12 Turn and *move*. Get airspeed over the wing quickly: 1) to prevent it from overflying, 2) to keep it from falling back, and 3) to get immediate directional control.

Reverse Inflation

Troubleshooting Reverse Launch Problems

The reverse launch can vary from easy to frustrating depending on conditions. These may help fix your foibles.

Symptom 1: Wing doesn't come up even when the wind should be strong enough.

1. Take one step toward the wing before moving backward to build momentum when you back up.
2. Pull more/less A's as needed, but pull primarily use your body. Too much A's can be a problem, too, so vary it up.
3. If there is enough wind, building a "wall" helps make sure it comes up straight and quickly.
4. You need to be moving backward faster or are trying in too little wind.
5. Set the trimmers to a faster setting and ensure no brake is being pulled, especially by the hand holding the A's.

Symptom 2: The wing falls back when I turn around.

1. With the wing overhead, step backward to get it moving, go hands UP, turn around and start moving forward immediately.
2. Throttle up during the turn so there is less delay in getting forward momentum.
3. Try to turn around only when the wing has forward momentum (into the wind).
4. Do a forward inflation instead.

Symptom 3: The wing falls over sideways when I turn around.

1. Ensure the brakes are up when you turn, and the wing is tracking straight in the same direction as your movement.
2. Avoid stepping significantly sideways as you turn. If you step left, the wing will fall to the right.
3. Get the wing leaning slightly in your turn direction before starting the turn.

Don't dawdle–that has its own problems—but stabbing at the throttle of a powerful machine can provoke a riser twist. Be smooth. Stand upright and let the power push.

A lot is going on during these early flights, and this level of control will be tough. It's one reason high thrust is not always best, and why becoming adept at ground handling, especially with a practice throttle, is so helpful.

Be primed to abort. If anything starts to go wonky, *immediately* release the throttle and *hold* the kill switch so nothing gets fed to the prop.

Reverse Inflation—Stronger Conditions

Anytime you can stand there and kite the wing, do a reverse inflation as shown starting in Fig 5-9. With enough wind, build a wall as described on page 34.

You'll be facing the wing holding everything as shown in Fig 5-13 with A's in one hand and throttle in the other. Lean a bit towards the wing, with your A-holding arm fully extended but the A's taut. When ready, snap back using your *body* to pull the wing up with just a bit of pull on the A's. Get it stable overhead and moving into the wind (walking backward) before turning around. You want the wing to have some forward momentum before turning around. The *moment* you're facing forward, move. Throttle up slightly in the turn to help keep forward motion.

Your instructor may have you hold off throttling up until you're walking forward with the wing stable. It lessens the chance of having the wing overfly and collapse into the prop, but is more difficult in other ways. As soon as you've verified that the wing is under control, add *some* throttle and move.

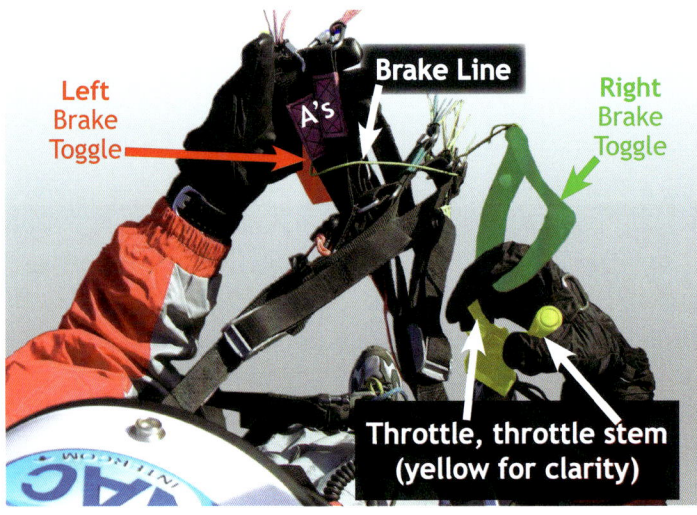
Fig 5-13 Two A's, 1 Hand Reverse Hold (for pilot turning left)

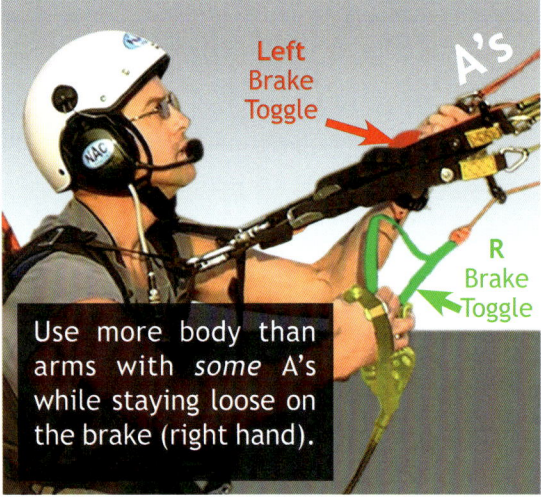
Fig 5-14 Two A's, 1 Hand Inflation

Another approach is to go strictly by feel: turn around and throttle up while looking forward and moving, responding to the small left or right tugs from the wing. Obviously this takes practice and won't likely be recommended on first flights.

If the wing tends to fall back, you're applying too much brake and/or not moving enough. More airflow means more control: keep moving. As it nears overhead, brake just enough to prevent it from overflying. If it's coming up fast, check it with brakes, then ease up, turn, and move.

During the turnaround, your hands should go mostly up to avoid engaging any brake. Move forward *immediately* after turning around, even without looking at the wing. Get moving *then* look and react. Once moving with good control, it's just like a forward launch.

As with forwards, be quick to abort if it goes awry. If everything looks good, you're running in the right direction with the wing overhead and tracking straight, throttle up and hold it. **Stand up straight**, letting the motor push while taking increasingly longer strides. Sideways glances at the wing are OK but concentrate on running and steering. If it tries to pull right, steer it back with *just* enough brake.

As the wing lifts, but while you're still running, steer it slightly left (right for geared machines) to reduce torque twisting effects (Loaded Riser Twist).

Approaching your fastest run, add brake pressure. After liftoff, ease back up on the brakes. A very few instructors may not have you pull brake before liftoff. That may work with slower training wings but not on faster, smaller rides.

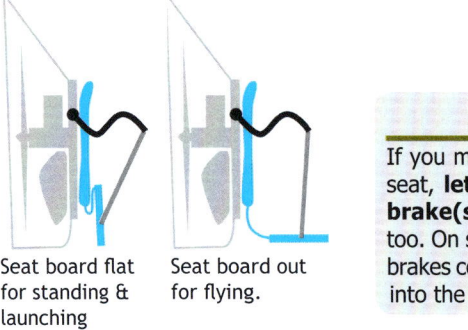

Seat board flat for standing & launching

Seat board out for flying.

Caution!
If you must reach down for the seat, **let go of and stow the brake(s) first!** Do it slowly, too. On some configurations the brakes could flail catastrophically into the prop.

Fig 5-15 Seatboard Mechanics

Climbout

Use minimum brake while climbing out, thinking "Hands up to go up." And when you *do* use brake for turning, pull *and hold* for at least 4 seconds. This piece of advice may save your life—it prevents getting into pilot-induced oscillations.

Nearly all motors torque, which causes a turn. Use minimal brake to counteract it, accepting a turn in the direction it wants to go. If you feel yourself twisting in the risers, reduce power by half even if your climb rate suffers. If you *must* turn against the torque, do so gingerly. Too much brake will cause a spin ("Parachutal Stall/Spin" on page 53).

If your body starts twisting one way, but the wing is banking the other way, you are entering a motor-induced lockout: reduce power immediately.

Climb up to at least 300 feet AGL while keeping your landing area within gliding range. Avoid long-term use of full power whenever possible, for the motor's sake. Altitude is your friend; it provides options and avoids obstacles. After reaching a safe altitude, reduce power to level off and stay there.

Getting into the Seat

This act is surprisingly critical. After liftoff, you'll be hanging uncomfortably by the leg straps. If you cannot get into the seat easily, without letting go of the brakes, keep climbing, but know that you must land within about 5 minutes. Otherwise, you risk numb legs, or worse, passing out from *Suspension Trauma*.

If it's easy to get seated without letting go of the brakes (may require a kick-in strap), do so once above 50 feet and established in a climb. Some machines require just lifting the legs and wiggling to become seated. That's ideal.

If you have to reach down for the seat, be ready for a motor out; new pilots sometimes hit the kill switch or get the throttle chopped off when it loops back towards the prop.

If the harness is not set up properly, especially if the leg straps are too loose, it may be impossible to get into the seat. You must land shortly.

Machines equipped with a kick-in strap or bar let you keep the brakes in your hands while kicking in. If the bar is hard to reach with just a foot, carefully stow the non-throttle brake toggle and reach down to position the strap for your foot.

The next best way to get seated is by using one hand to push down on the back of the seatboard. ***First***, carefully stow your non-throttle brake toggle, or put it in your throttle hand, then reach down with your free hand.

The least desirable way is using both hands. If that's required, carefully stow the brakes in their keepers then, reach down. Make it two distinct steps: release & stow the brakes so they can't go in the prop, then go for the seat. Using your thumbs, grasp the outer part of the seatboard (where the front strap attaches), pushing down and forward. On some motors, it's easier to push down on the back part of the seatboard to pop it "under center." Be careful not to press the kill switch.

Tightening the leg straps usually makes it easier to get into the seat but more difficult to run. Tighten them all the way, then loosen a couple inches. Setting it up properly may let you just wiggle in. Get several successful launches under your belt before trying the wiggle, though, since its contortions can result in killing the motor or pulling unwanted brake.

Rehearse getting into the seat while hanging in a simulator, preferably with the motor running for realism. Do it until the action is automatic.

Fig 5-16 The "Bump Scale:"
This helps relate "bumpiness" to other pilots:

0. Completely smooth
1. Getting jostled, no real change in flight path.
2. Causes small changes in flight path. The most that new pilots should fly in.
3. Causes body swings of around 3 feet with no control input.
4. Causes moderate changes in flight path and body movements of around 5 ft. Significant surging & retreating with small tip collapses on high performance wings.

5-6. Very active air. Causes small tip collapses even on uncorrected beginner wings.

7. Causes 50% collapses even on uncorrected beginner wings.

8-10. Increasing levels of dangerous air where 10 is completely uncontrollable.

Basic Control

Some unusual dynamics result from swinging around like a pendulum, namely *Pilot Induced Oscillations*—dangerous amplifications of those swings. Thankfully, there are ways to reduce it, the easiest of which is using smallish control inputs that are held for at *least* 3 seconds. **Control and hold!** You'll swing a bit but won't make it worse. Also, become really good at ground handling, a skill that directly counters many of these tendencies.

This is also why you need to be on a right-sized school glider and motor (see "Choosing Equipment" on page 9). In the beginning, even a budding star can get askew of control inputs. Forgiving gear helps keep it from becoming a slam fest.

Turning

A proper turn is **look, lean, pull,** and **power**. Look where you're about to turn, weight shift in that direction, pull and hold that brake, then add a touch of power to avoid descending. You'll first swing out initially then settle into a constant turn after a couple left-right swings.

Always raise the opposite hand when turning to avoid progressively pulling more brake. Or raise both hands slightly before starting the turn. Every now and then, ease

Fig 5-17 Basic Pendular Control

Just Brakes Pitch Demo (at right): Keep the power constant throughout and pull brakes to pressure 3. Your body swings forward a bit (pitches up), causing a slight climb. After about 3 seconds the wing arcs forward and into a slight dive. This repeats in decreasing amounts, as you settle into level flight at a slower speed, maybe descending slowly if a lot of brake is pulled.

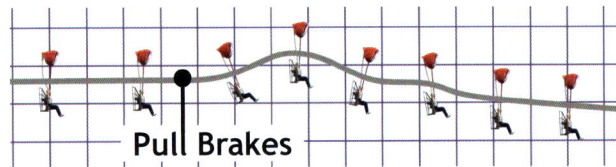

Just Brakes Turning Demo (at left): Pull *and hold* right brake. It takes about 3 seconds to swing out to a maximum bank. You'll then shallow out and steepen in decreasing amounts until stabilized in a shallow right turn. It's important to *hold* the input.

Your instructor *may* teach a two-step process where you pull some brake, wait 2 seconds then pull more. As you pull the first bit of brake, say "one thousand one, two one thousand two, pull" and pull a bit more brake."

Larger wings have longer swing times from one size to the other (the *Pendular Period*)

Simple Throttle-up

Height Control with Hold (at right): Throttle up and hold it. You'll swing out front, pitch up into a relatively steep climb, then swing back to a shallow climb, finally settling into a steady climb.

The same goes for descending. Throttle back to idle. The wing goes forward (*surges*) into a dive, levels out a bit, then settles into a steady descent.

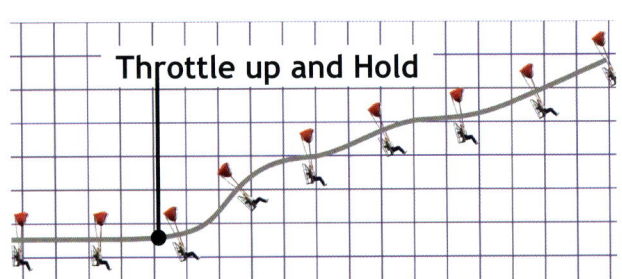

Two-Stage Throttle-up

Height Control in 2 stages (at left): Your instructor *may* teach a two-step throttle application where you increase by half, wait two seconds, then ease into full power. Done properly there will be minimal oscillation.

Do the same for descending. Reduce power to half of what you've got, wait two seconds then ease it to idle.

Hopefully you get to practice this in a well-secured simulator.

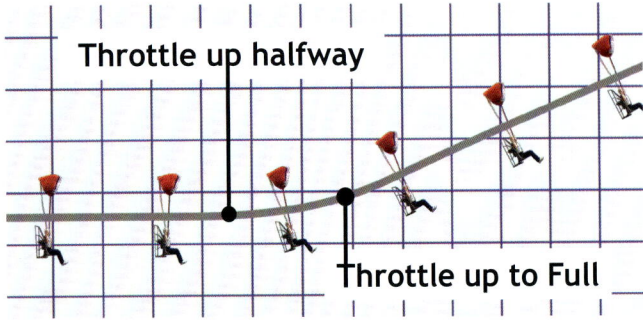

up both hands intentionally then return to the feel pressure (covered below). *Weight shift* is hip or leg motion to lower the riser in your turn direction. You may also use two-stage control input as shown in Fig 5-17 to reduce swinging.

Speed Control

Pulling both brakes slows the wing down and causes a brief climb (or reduced descent rate). You'll swing out in front then back in decreasing amounts.

Height Control

The same is true for throttling up or down. Increasing power makes you swing out into a climb (or slowed descent), then you settle into a stable flight path after a few swings. Swinging out forward like this is called "pitching up," and diving is "pitching down."

Brakes Feel Position

You'll continuously have about brake pressure 1 to improve "feel" and control response. It's a bit less than just hanging your arms from the brakes. How many inches that is depends on your wing's model and size.

Flying Around

Now the reward: You're flying! Once up at altitude, everything gets easier—relax and enjoy the view. Your instructor may have you try a few things, but most early flights last no more than a half-hour to ensure you have no numb or tired parts.

Having an Out

Your first flights will be a sensory flood, drowning out many normal thought processes. That's why rehearsal, and an instructor on the radio, is so beneficial—but there are still some things you must think about.

1. Where would I land if the motor quit? Allow enough altitude to get back and set up a pattern. 500 ft is generally about right. Always have an out; the engine will eventually quit.

2. What is the wind doing? Where are the wind shadows and rotors (see Chapter 7)? Winds may change during your flight, possibly even reversing, and you must always plan on landing into it.

3. How much fuel/time do I have left? Noting your launch time and knowing your endurance is one way to avoid running out of gas. But it's also good to check the fuel level using a visual means such as a mirror. Even if you started with enough fuel, it is possible for a leak to dramatically reduce your flying time.

Posture in Flight

Keeping good posture (Fig 5-18) does more than make you look good—it helps avoid over-controlling. Don't hold the risers unless instructed to. It's like grabbing the dash on a car—it may feel good but doesn't do much for control.

Accelerated Flight

On later flights, you may use the wing's speed system—speedbar and/or trimmers, but rehearse it first in the simulator. Working a trimmer with the throttle in hand may accidentally kill the engine. Consider reaching over with your non-throttle hand. Release trimmers in short increments on each side to avoid too much turning.

Speedbar should be applied slowly and preferably while under power. Certain combinations of speedbar, brakes, and trimmer use can cause a front tuck.

On some reflex models, when accelerated, they have different steering requirements, usually with some kind of tip steering or rear risers—consult the wing's manual. See also "Steering Options" on page 263.

Yes, your airspeed is slow, but it's still faster than the bugs. Keep your mouth closed.

Fig 5-18 Posture

Elbows in, head back or upright, legs together. It helps with control even when the motor is angled too far back like this.

More on Turns

We covered "Look, Lean, Pull, then Power." Part of that is to signal others about your intentions, which is why looking should be deliberate. Start with a shallow turn, then look up and down in the direction of turn, and finally, turn.

Start with position/pressure 1. Learn how much pressure it takes to get there and use that feeling (pressure). Don't try to counteract swings, and don't try to damp oscillations yet either; just use measured, steady pressure and wait for the turn to develop as shown in Fig 5-17. Too much brake will spin the glider.

To level out of a turn, let up the brake slower than the glider's natural swing rate (pendular period). Good posture—elbows in and forearm vertical—will naturally help prevent over-braking.

Wake Turbulence

> **Caution!**
> Look at your desired flight path, **not** nearby obstructions! Numerous accidents stem from *target fixation*, where a pilot looks at an obstruction, fixates on it, then flies into it.

Planes and paragliders fly by pushing air down as they move through it. They spin off powerful little tip vortices along the way that spread slowly, drifting with the wind, and settling about 300 feet per minute (Fig 5-19).

Turning more than about 180° may result in flying through your own wake, a potentially startling ripple in your universe. It's not prop blast either, which is a disorganized burble of minimal effect.

Altitudes

Altitude means options. You stay above obstacles, have time to handle unhappy engines, and stay within reach of more landing sites.

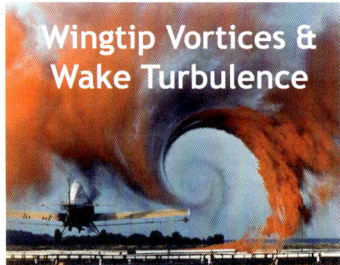

Fig 5-19 Wake Turbulence

Pattern altitude is 200-300 ft (about 90 meters), high enough to make it back to the landing site and land into the wind while avoiding obstacles.

Cruise between 200 and 500 ft, which is below *most* other aircraft yet above most obstructions. If you're flying near an airport, learn about airplane patterns and altitudes (Chapter 10); avoiding them is legally our obligation. 200 feet is down there with drones, but they should be able to see and avoid *you*.

At higher altitudes more visibility is required (see Chapter 9) but we we're never allowed to fly with less than 1 mile visibility.

Glide Ratio & Wind

As part of always having a safe place to land, you must know how far you can glide. This *glide ratio* is how far you'll travel per unit of altitude lost. For us, that's about a 6:1 glide ratio (pronounced "six to one"), meaning that you go 6 feet forward for every foot down.

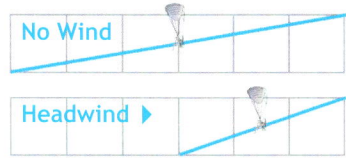

Fig 5-20 Glide Ratio & Wind

A headwind shortens our power-off glide distance. With a headwind that's half your airspeed, glide ratio drops by half.

In the no-wind condition, glide is 6 units forward for every foot dropped.

In the Headwind condition, it's 3 units forward for every foot dropped.

Wind affects glide a lot (Fig 5-20). With an airspeed of 20 mph, it only takes a 10 mph headwind to cut glide in half. That same 10 mph wind from behind yields 30 mph over the ground while still dropping at the same rate, yielding a glide ratio of 9:1 (9 units forward for every foot down).

Think of your landing options as a cone spreading out below you (see "Motor Failure and Landing Priorities" on page 201). Wind will move the cone of options downwind. As you go higher, the available area gets bigger since you can glide farther. Allow room for maneuvering and unexpected sink, too.

Ground Track

You may get up and notice that you're flying sideways, especially after turning crosswind. That's wind blowing you "downstream." The wing is still flying through the air like always, but the air is moving over the ground, carrying you with it.

Ground track (Fig 5-22) is the line that your flight path draws over the ground. If

Troubleshooting Landing Problems

Landing is a given; style points are up for grabs. These tips will help improve the second most demanding task of our sport. The point of flaring is to have your body swing forward, making the wing grab more air, reduce descent, and slow down.

Symptom 1: My landings are hard, making it difficult to stay on my feet.
1. You have too much brake during the last 30 ft. Have your hands nearly full up (no brakes) before starting to flare.
2. If you consistently flare then drop to the ground, you're flaring too early.
3. Do a two-part flare from a hands-up condition: pull some pressure at 5 to 10 ft, swing forward, then get full brake by 1 to 2 ft (Fig 5-23). As headwind increases, you can start the flare later since you don't have to slow as much.

Symptom 2: My landings are fast and hard.
1. You need to start the flare earlier, and with enough pull to swing out in front of the wing before touchdown. Make it a two-step process, where you pull some brake, swing forward, *then* pull more brake, ending with full deflection at touchdown.
2. Make sure you're exactly into the wind with no turn.
3. Make sure you're landing with the trimmers in (set slow) or neutral.
4. You're not landing into the wind. What seems like calm wind may be a slight tailwind which, on landing, becomes significant.

Symptom 3: I swing left/right a lot on final approach.
1. Unless you have *mastered* dampening these oscillations, do *not* try to correct them below about 50 ft. For *steering*, brake and hold.
2. Practice oscillation dampening at altitude; see Chapter 16.

Symptom 4: Sometimes I land drifting sideways.
1. Be lined up into the wind on final. For example, if you're drifting right, turn left gradually but be level by touchdown.
2. Avoid steering inputs below 20 feet.

Symptom 5: I don't land where I want.
1. Look where you *want* to land not where you want to *avoid*. *Target fixation* is looking at the obstruction and subconsciously steering that way.
2. Practice landing on a target *every* landing ("Tight Spaces: Spot Landing" on page 175). Be careful, though, trying too hard is unusually risky.
3. Plan the final approach to start from around 100 ft (30 m). As skill builds, lower this to 50 ft (15 m).

you want to be flying directly into the wind, as you will on landing, then turn into the "current." If you're drifting right (sliding sideways to the right), gently turn left. Don't just pull the brake and release it, but hold the gentle turn until drifting stops. Practice this input when you're up high so it doesn't surprise you on landing. You'll want to minimize sideways drift on landing.

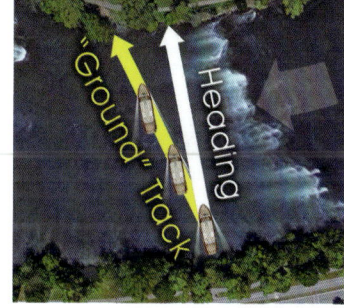

Fig 5-22 Ground Track

Picture yourself in a glass-bottomed boat pointed (heading) straight across the river but drifting downstream.

If water is air and the river bottom is ground, imagine this drift as seen from a glass-bottom boat. Water flow is a crosswind.

Ground track is the yellow line, and white is which way you're pointed. Lots more about this starting on page 135 in Chapter 13.

Reflex Wings

If first flights will be on a reflex wing, start with trimmers securely in their launch position, or as directed by the manual, and *leave* them. Consider using tape to prevent slippage. Control is similar to any other glider at this setting. When trimmed fast, and/or with speedbar applied, these gliders are usually flown using a tip steering system instead of main brakes. Your first few flights won't involve accelerated flight; later on you'll probably use the trimmers.

Get at least a dozen flights before trying trimmers. Practice using the glider's tip steering (as equipped) first. When comfortable, grab the tip steering then stow the brakes (if necessary), and carefully let the trims up, maybe an inch. Trimmer buckles slip, so be deliberate.

Reflex Wings usually have long trimmer travel to manage their wider speed range. Follow the pilot's manual carefully due to control differences when accelerated (trim or speedbar). Inflation tends to be sluggish in the slowest settings.

Since tip steering does little for pitch (fore/aft) control, reset to normal trim and handling before landing.

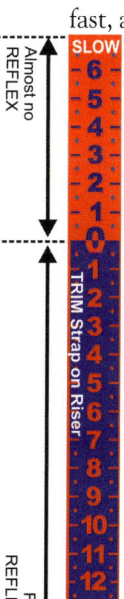

Fig 5-21 Reflex Wing Trim

Trimmer from highly reflexed wing. Takeoff is normally done at the 0 or neutral setting. Some wings just have a white line to mark neutral.

Landing

Beyond the mechanics and concepts, landing can't be simulated well. That's why tow, hill, or tandem training is so beneficial. Every landing should be basically level, into the wind, and end with a good flare—enough for swing-out before touchdown (see also "Motor Failure and Landing Priorities" on page 201). The instructor will help with timing to get consistently smooth, stand-up landings.

Always have a spot to aim for. Initially, it will be huge. By flight 25, you should be getting within 100 feet of a target, and with **lots** more practice, you'll be landing on a Frisbee ("Spot Landing" on page 177). Don't try too hard, though, it's easy to stall or spin.

The Pattern

Patterns provide an orderly traffic flow and easier assessment of height, wind, field condition, and obstructions. Plus, one-way traffic offers better collision avoidance. Initial segments are named by their relationship to the wind as shown in Fig 5-23.

AGL = Above Ground Level

Fig 5-23 Landing Pattern

Here are the basic legs of an aircraft style landing pattern. This is a right pattern because turns are to the right.

With more wind, "S" turns on final work, but be straightened out and into the wind by 50 ft. Don't turn completely away from the field.

Leave the motor idling until reaching 50 ft or so in case a go-around is needed (page 48).

Patterns are right or left according to the turn direction. "Standard" patterns are to the left since airplane pilots sit on the left. But for us, direction is driven more by wind and terrain. If possible, in a crosswind, base leg should be *into* it (see Fig 10-4 on page 103).

Enter on the downwind leg at about 300 ft AGL. Pass beside the desired landing point (abeam) and continue until it's about 45° behind you, then ease off the power and turn onto base leg.

Now judge whether you are high or low. If it looks like you're low, and might not make the spot, turn towards it some. Of course there's throttle, but you're trying to learn this without relying on that.

If you're high, angle away from it to lose altitude before lining back up. **Never turn completely away from the spot**—it's easy to quickly get too low or not make it back directly into the wind. Plus, losing eye contact with the spot can be disorienting.

Final Approach

Turn final and point yourself towards the landing spot; then extend your legs so you're hanging by the leg loops. That should fold the seat back up against the frame. Make *small* corrections to keep aimed at the spot. Hold the inputs for at least 3 seconds, then ease up.

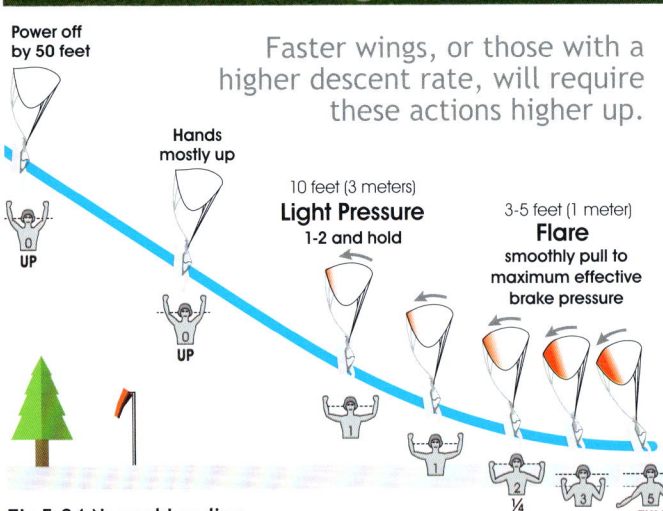

Fig 5-24 Normal Landing

Don't try to correct oscillations below 50 feet, and avoid steering inputs below 20 feet. On the first few dozen flights, such inputs are usually wrong, especially in the flare.

Once you've got the field made (no overshoot or undershoot), press and hold the kill switch until the motor stops completely. If you release it early, the motor may restart. Get the prop stopped no later than 50 ft.

Be mindful of drift. If you're drifting left it means a wind from the right is pushing you. Ease in, *and hold* just enough right brake to correct right until the drift is almost stopped, then ease off the brake. Check the wind streamers but rely more on your sight picture. Stop making drift corrections below 20 feet to concentrate on flare.

Controlling Glide

During initial training, your instructor will guide you through these glide maneuvers, but you'll want to learn them.

When trying to stretch glide, have your hands up and legs together in a way to minimize drag. In a headwind fly faster (trimmers out). In a tailwind, fly at minimum sink speed—normally trimmers slow and very slight brake pressure.

If you're getting low, the spot will be rising in your field of view. You've been doing this in a horizontal direction for years: the stationary spot in your windshield or visual field is where you're headed; everything else slides by your periphery.

As covered in Fig 5-20, glide is steeper (worse) when flying into a headwind and shallower with a tailwind. In a headwind you can steepen the descent by slowing down, but don't overdo it. Pull no more than about position/pressure 2 until you're very familiar with the wing. If you do slow down, reaching 50 feet, ease up the brakes back up to have enough speed for an effective flare. Sink rate momentarily increases while regaining speed.

You can also do small S-turns to lose altitude and effectively shorten a glide. But keep them shallow, and again, get yourself steadily back into the wind, hands mostly up, by 50 feet.

Flare & Touchdown (Below 100 Feet)

Below about 100 ft, forget the spot and concentrate on landing level and into the wind for a good touchdown. Use minimum brakes. Below 50 ft, you should be out of the seat, motor off, and with hands nearly full up. Being hands up makes the flare more effective. As you gain skill, you'll lower these heights.

If you feel left/right swinging (like a pendulum) **do nothing!** Slight directional adjustments are OK down to about 20, then ensure the brakes are almost completely up. This may be the only time to hold the risers (briefly) *if* you've rehearsed doing so, and your instructor says to. The goal is to prevent subconscious brake input.

Pendular oscillations are such that, attempting to stop them at this skill level, will almost certainly **make matters worse**. It's better to accept a small pendulum than to try correcting. Later on, reactions will be automatic. Not yet.

Flaring is pulling brake to reduce speed and sink rate just before touchdown as shown in Fig 5-24. Start from a nearly hands-up posture at about 10 ft. It's not the pulled trailing edge—it's the *forward swing* that does most of the work, angling the wing up to momentarily add lift. The effect is fleeting, too—after swinging out and slowing down, if you're not on the ground, a high sink rate develops. Timing is important.

By 3-5 ft, have one foot forward, knees bent, ready to take the weight and run. This posture reduces the chance of going to a knee on firmer landings. That happens periodically during early training.

With some wind you can flare a bit later and less aggressively. Specifics vary by wing model and conditions.

A two-stage flare works best. If you notice some drift while flaring, resist the temptation to hold out your downwind hand as if you're falling—it's exactly the wrong input. Being in the flare is too late for steering inputs.

After touchdown and a few steps of running, turn around and pull both brakes to quickly bring the wing down. If it's windy, bring it down using one of the techniques covered in "Deflating the Wing" on page 26. Ideally it lands on the upper surface with the trailing edge towards you. That makes you look good and prepares the wing for easy rosetting.

On Glide

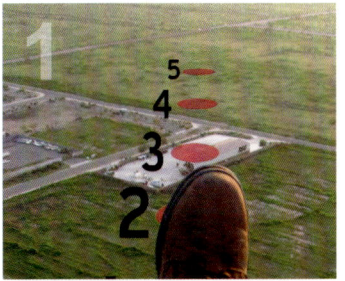

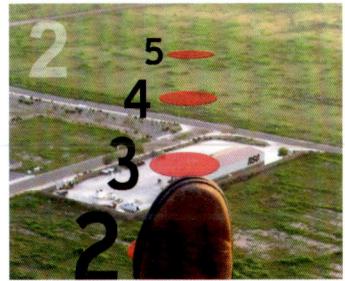

Fig 5-25 Gliding for the Spot

Gliding for spot 3, put your shoe up to the spot. If the spot stays in that relative position, you're on target. If you're foot sinks below it you will land short. If you foot starts covering it, you will land long.

With a calm or steady wind, the spot that you're going to hit will not be changing angle, just getting bigger. That is your "aim line" and hopefully it's also your target.

Fig 5-26 Transporting Gear On Boat

Stowing equipment properly can be extremely important in some settings!

Custom-made frame mounts are great for your para-barge while regular platforms and modified bike racks work for cars. See Fig 31-5 for mounting ideas.

After Landing

Run out the landing enough to keep the wing from overflying you. Getting the wing on its back makes folding or stowing easier and reduces tangles. Plus, it keeps lines off of the motor.

Unclip quickly to avoid catching a gust. Wearing a motor makes this both more likely and more expensive.

Postflight

Get the wing covered to reduce its UV exposure, even with clouds. Then either fold, bundle, or put it in the shade, away from sandy, buggy, dusty, or gravel areas.

Check out the motor and harness as you would during a preflight inspection. Discovering problems now will let you can fix them before your next session. Even if it was running fine when you landed, parts loosen, props get nicked, and gremlins gnaw on flexible stuff.

Cleaning

Clean the machine afterwards to notice cracks, crankcase leaks, and other dollar-sucking precursors to catastrophe. They hide in the grime. For example, if you see a large increase in black goo squirting onto the prop, suspect problems; that's hard to detect with a dirty machine.

Gasoline, WD-40, and mineral spirits are good for wiping down motor parts. Carburetor cleaner is great on unpainted surfaces but brutal on paint. Avoid getting citrus-based cleaners on aluminum. Fabric sprays that offer other protection work well and help preserve the gear but don't use them on wing fabric. If possible, cover the motor during transport to prevent UV damage to the harness; it fades pretty quickly when exposed to sunlight. Don't let wood props get wet.

Clean the wing as described in "Cleaning the Wing" on page 37 if needed.

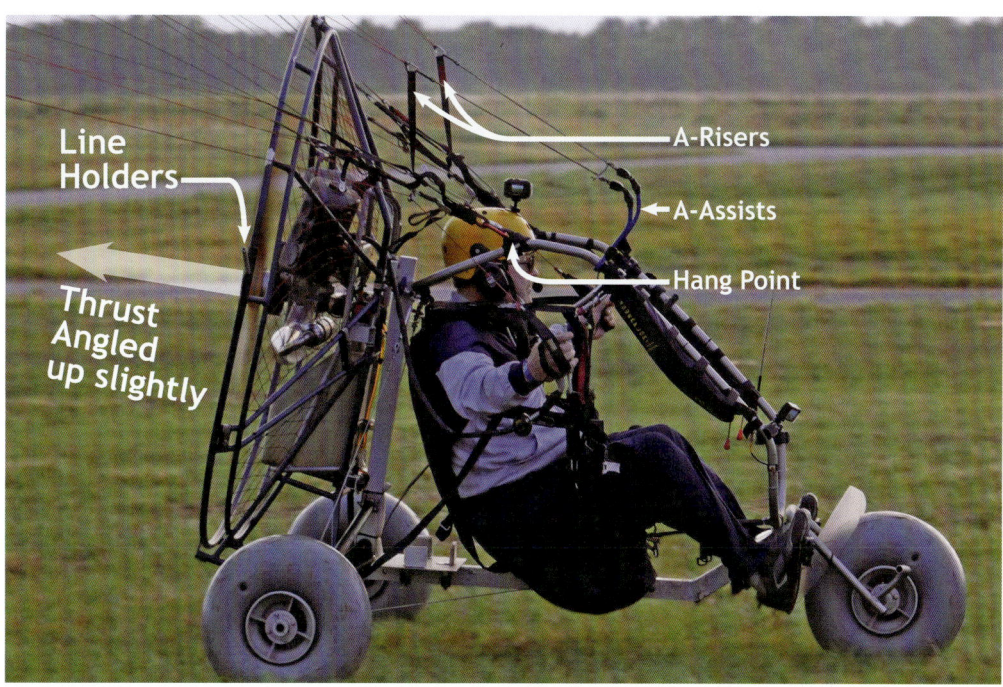

Adding Wheels

CHAPTER 6

Wheels add a new dimension to paramotoring. Besides skipping the run, they allow carrying more stuff, more fuel, and/or more power. Plus, no-wind inflations, the bane of foot-launchers, become almost trivially easy.

Carts can be anything from mere accessories ("Adding Wheels" on page 280) to hulking, purpose-built machines with integrated motor and seat. Those considered powered parachutes (PPC's) are usually foot-controlled. We address only craft that are hand-controlled.

Since pilots don't have to run with all the weight, they tend to fly heavier on the wing, making cruise speeds higher, reducing climb, and burning more fuel than foot-launched craft.

Wheels do impose limitations; mostly on uneven ground or strong winds. They're more difficult in some ways—you can't step sideways during launch—but are easier in nil winds and/or high elevations where groundspeed is higher.

Just like foot-launching, more skill means more capabilities. A good wheel pilot can handle nearly as much wind as a good foot-launcher—it mostly depends on wing-handling skill. The practical wind limit for most cart pilots is 8-10 mph without mastering reverse inflation on carts ("Cart Reverse Launch" on page 154).

Tandem operations (Fig 8-11 on page 89) on wheels are *much* easier and *much* safer. Whereas foot-launched tandems require the student to keep running at liftoff, wheels don't. They let students take it all in while only getting as involved as the instructor sees fit.

Large, soft, and slippery wheels are preferred since they act as shock absorbers, and roll better on rough or soft surfaces. Being able to slide helps reduce the chance of flipping over since they don't grab in a sideways drift. Thinner, large diameter wheels work OK on hard-packed surfaces. A wide wheelbase, having four vs three wheels, lower center of gravity (CG), and lower hook-in points reduce the chance of flipping over. But nothing reduces it more than thorough training and skill building.

Fig 6-1 Cart Launching

The pilot above is launching a trike with A-Assists, meaning he doesn't have to hold the A's—they're too high up on this model.

Thrust is angled up to avoid ruffling a laid-out wing while the motor idles.

Foot steering uses pegs that are connected directly to the axle, so pushing the right peg makes the cart go left (like shown below). That's opposite to airplanes, but airplane pilots need not worry, it's a quick transition. Fig 28-5 on page 280 has more on steering.

Wheel brakes are rare due to our low speeds; but be careful, there is more mass than you think—it's just masked by the wheels.

Fig 6-2 Hybrid. It's heavy and powerful like a PPC, but with hand controls and an elliptical wing like PPG's.

Fig 6-3 A strap-on trike that uses the paramotor's seat but provides support.

Fig 6-4 Cable-braced trike with separate seat that's highly portable. Cables allow folding. Uses detachable paramotor

Fig 6-5 Four-stroke generator engine trike that's heavy and swings a huge prop, but has readily available parts and doesn't require mixing fuel.

Fig 6-6 PPG Quad with its own harnesses that uses detachable paramotor for tandems. See Fig 8-11 for more on their legality.

Fig 6-7 Compact quad with integral seat that uses detachable paramotor.

Fig 6-8 Low-slung style trike with integral seat that uses detachable paramotor.

Fig 6-9 The "Timber Trike" may be the cheapest way to roll but you still better know what you're doing.

Wheel Types

Powered parachutes (PPC's) are typically high-powered craft with parachute style, squarish wings that trade efficiency for ease of operation. High control forces necessitate foot steering—a primary difference from PPG's. PPC wings generally have very long risers.

The distinction between PPC's and wheeled PPG's have blurred, but if it's hand-flown using brake toggles and a hand throttle, techniques in this chapter apply.

Hybrids are PPC's with hand controls and sometimes a hand throttle. They may have multiple-line wing attachments that don't unclip quickly. Standard wheeled PPG's use foot-launchable paramotor engines, and paragliders.

Wheeled PPG's have other distinctions such as the number of wheels. 3-wheel trikes are popular for simplicity, while 4-wheels (quads) are more stable. Buggies derive their name from kite buggies—low slung carts propelled by a kite, and provide their own seat. Collapsible cable-braced carts are highly portable via a fold-up structure.

Carts have been built that are jettisonable, but that's risky to others and the cart.

Hook-in position, high or low, is another difference. High hook-in lessens in-flight wobbling of the cart, while low hook-in resists tipping on the ground but feels "busier" in the air.

Setup

Before flying, do a hang check to make sure the rear wheels are slightly lower than the nosewheel—a 5 to 15° nose-up angle is ideal. If the nosewheel hangs below the rear wheels it will wheelbarrow on takeoff or landing, making a rollover far more likely. As fuel burns during flight it will tilt progressively more nose-down.

Adjusting clip-in position must be done for each different pilot weight to assure proper balance. A heavy pilot will be nose heavy (very bad), and a light pilot will tend to be tipped back (not as bad). All tandem and most solo carts allow moving the attachment points to get a proper hang angle.

Set the motor angle so that, on the ground, thrust blows just above the wing to minimize ruffling the wing. It also lets the cart start rolling before inflation. If the wing inflates before you get moving, it can cause a tug-of-war where thrust pushes against the wing, which pulls back on the cart and nothing moves.

Hook up the A-assists (A-helpers), if installed, like in Fig 6-14. They pull the A's during the wing's initial upward arc, then become slack.

Launch

Nearly all cart launches use forward inflations, and they excel in calm winds.

Lay out like a forward foot launch. Wing and cart must be centered and directly into the wind with lines draped over the line holders (Fig 6-12), if installed, and clear of the rear wheels.

Before engine start, roll the cart forward, *barely* tensioning the lines to ensure everything is centered with*out* curling the leading edge. A slight tension keeps lines from getting sucked into the prop. Some instructors will roll it back a few feet to build speed before inflation, but not if the prop is likely to suck in lines.

Here are the steps for launching a cart.

1. Get the motor idling if your machine doesn't disturb the paraglider, get in, grab the throttle, then the brakes, then the A's (if not using A-assists). Go through your pre-launch checklist.

    If it has electric start, get situated first as described above, then start the motor. A little wing ruffling is OK as long as it doesn't ruin your layout.

    If thrust really disturbs the wing, you'll need to have everything situated, then start and throttle up almost immediately. It's a bad design.

2. Look around to be sure it's clear, put your feet on the pegs, and throttle up. How much throttle depends on the gear. Powerful units on smooth surfaces, especially with small or easy inflating gliders, do better with partial power.

    How much A's you hold (if no A-helpers) depends on the wing. Some require a lot. Some carts don't allow getting a good hold of the A's.

> **Caution!**
>
> Never accelerate for takeoff in an oscillation. The wing must be **overhead, stable, and tracking with the cart** before committing to flight. Be quick to abort!

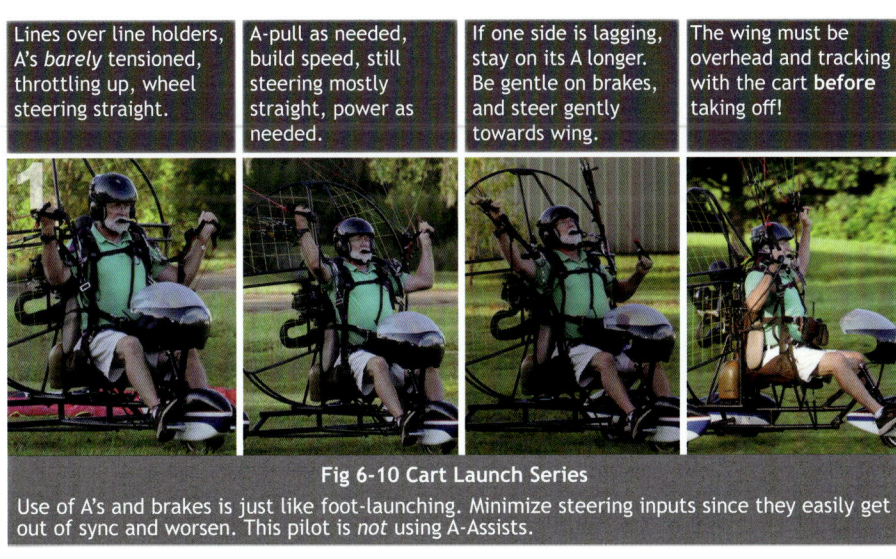

Fig 6-10 Cart Launch Series
Use of A's and brakes is just like foot-launching. Minimize steering inputs since they easily get out of sync and worsen. This pilot is *not* using A-Assists.

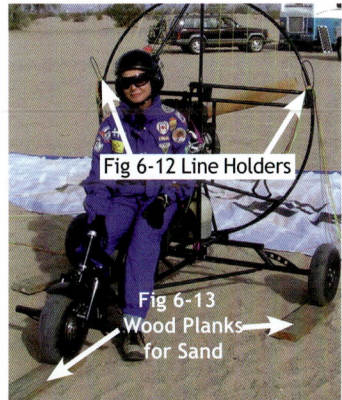

Fig 6-12 Line Holders

Fig 6-13 Wood Planks for Sand

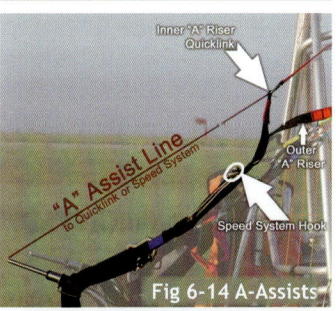

Fig 6-14 A-Assists

Fig 6-15 Wing Mirror

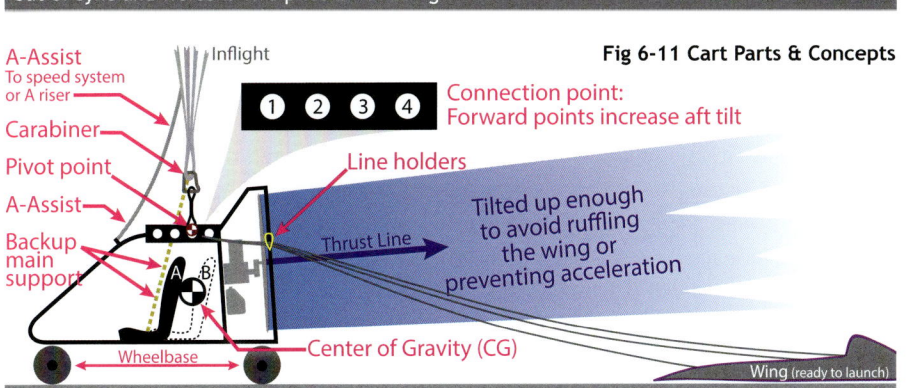

Fig 6-11 Cart Parts & Concepts

On Balance

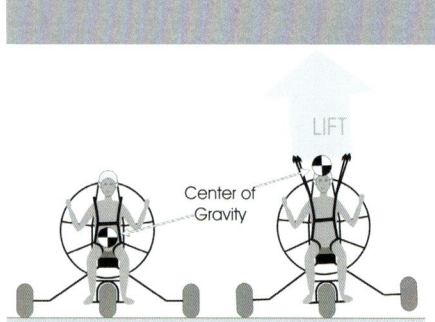

Fig 6-16 Cart Center of Gravity (CG)

Wing lift makes the cart act like it has a higher center of gravity (CG), making it more tippy. Combined with a crooked wing, toppling gets surprisingly easy, and turning *away* from the tilt makes matters worse.

Always be turning slightly *towards* the wing to reduce tip-over tendency.

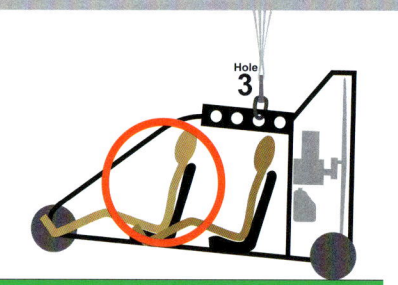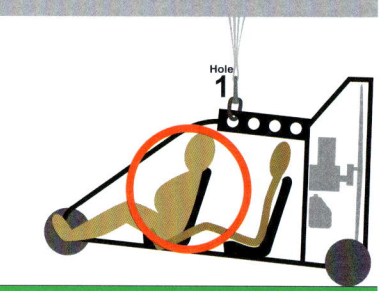

Fig 6-17 Cart CG Adjustments

Use a hang check to adjust hook-in points so the nosewheel lifts off first. For tandems, a heavier front passenger will require using a more forward hole. Consider setting up a chart that shows what weight range works for each hole. Or put the nosewheel on a scale after determining what weight works for what holes using a hang check.

To make the nosewheel(s) ride higher on a cart like this, do any of these: 1) increase fuel weight, 2) decrease front occupant weight, 3) move the attachment point forward, 4) move either seat aft. Fuel burn makes the nosewheel ride lower on landing than at takeoff.

Fig 6-18 Tipping Over?

Extending a hand towards the fall is an instinctual reaction that makes matters worse.

If you start to roll over, do these *immediately*:

1. **Steer** towards the wing.
2. **Throttle idle.** While an experienced pilot may be able to recover, it's safer and cheaper to abort.
3. **Reduce brake pressure**. More brakes = more pull, ergo more tipping force. This may also overcome the intense (and wrong) reaction of putting a hand out as if to brace against a fall.

To build correct automatic reaction, practice taxiing where you get the wing slightly right or left then steering towards it.

3. Look left or right to monitor the wing's inflation, or use a mirror (Fig 6-15). As the wing comes overhead, let off the A's and be ready to check the wing. Stay on the power a few seconds after damping. Reducing early, or not damping enough may cause the wing to overfly and dive into the prop.

   If the wing *rockets* upwards, get off the A's, damping sooner and harder. Stay on the power though—when the wing comes up quickly it usually stops the cart. Be just as quick to *reduce* brake as the wing comes overhead.

   If it's hanging back or coming up slowly, stay on the A's longer. Once the cart has accelerated to a good kiting speed, throttle back enough to prevent further acceleration. Don't take off yet.

   If the wing comes overhead crooked, minimize brake pressure, keep up enough speed to kite, and turn slightly towards it. Too much turn will start an oscillation. If the wing gets more than about 20° off-center, abort. As you build finesse—lots of finesse—you can redeem surprisingly crooked inflations.

4. Taxi the cart/wing combo mostly by steering the cart straight and controlling the wing overhead. Steer the wing first, *then* follow with the cart. Airflow (rolling speed) over the wing is key. **The wing must be tracking with the cart, centered, and stable before liftoff!**

5. Once you and the wing are tracking together with no oscillations, smoothly throttle up for liftoff. Use minimum brake input, respecting that if the wing gets very far off, abort.

On thick grass or other soft surface you may need brake pressure to lift off the ground, but once airborne, *slowly* reduce brakes to accelerate. Climb rate is almost always better with less brake. At high density altitudes you may be un*able* to climb if holding excessive brakes.

Never lift off in an oscillation. **If you feel the wing going side-to-side, slow down, straighten it out, or abort**. Cart dynamics make it worse; as the wing careens overhead in an oscillation, it unloads the cart, which then accelerates rapidly to the other side, pulling the wing even more powerfully into a bank the other way. Getting airborne like this can be disastrous.

The skill of anticipating control inputs—leading the wing— is what you must learn through practice. It is what will give you *command* over launch.

Crosswind Takeoff

Taking off in a crosswind (illustration at right) should be avoided until you've mastered steering the wing during taxi. It's tricky and increases rollover risk, but can allow flying from sites like beaches, runways, or roads.

1-3. Inflate into whatever wind there is, if possible.

4-5. Once the wing is overhead, you've damped it, and are moving nicely, turn the wing towards the runway then steer yourself under it.

6. Now keep the wing exactly overhead. It will be pointed somewhat upwind (crabbing) but just do what it takes to track down the runway. More crosswind will take more wing crab.

Before liftoff, gather speed and reduce brakes to stay solidly on the ground. Accelerate hands mostly up then, just as the nosewheel comes off, quickly apply enough brake to liftoff solidly, gaining a few feet right away. This avoids having the cart—now angled upwind— settling back down to the ground crabbed sideways. Don't overdo the brakes though, it could cause settling.

The technique under "Handling Crosswinds" on page 158 also works for cart launching just as well as foot-launching.

Flying

The main differences in cart flying are 1) a slightly higher airspeed, 2) somewhat heavier control inputs, and 3) lower climb rates if using typical foot-launch motors. Carts bobble around more due to higher mass that's spread out more. Torque is less noticeable because the center of gravity is lower and the motor is usually more vertical (not tilted back much, if at all).

Low altitude maneuvering must be done with care and planning if you have a lower climb rate. Visibility is frequently slightly restricted by framework, so you may have to move your head around a bit to watch for traffic. Skimming the ground is fun since your eyeballs are so low, but don't do it over water for rather obvious lethal reasons. Going into water may result in floating upside down even with flotation.

Landing

Wheel landings are easier than foot landings since you don't have to run it out. A little more speed or a little heavier machine is no big deal.

Fly a normal pattern then, if room permits, add some power to shallow the descent during the last 50 feet and hold the power steady to a touchdown. Use brakes like a normal landing then shut off the power. As always, if a left/right oscillation develops on final, ease up both brakes and do not try to correct it.

A power-off landing is the same as on foot but your eyeballs will be a bit closer to the ground. Glide will be slightly faster and steeper due to the extra weight and drag. Land into the wind to avoid a sideways touchdown which could flip you over.

While rolling out after landing, slow down, then get the wing to fall over sideways, avoiding hot engine parts. Turn slightly towards it to unload lines and avoid dragging fabric. In breezy conditions, use minimal brake input as the wing comes down. You may need to pull one brake in, hand-over-hand, to disable it. If the wing falls straight back, you may get pulled backward and end up flipping or tipping onto the cage and rear wheels—a turtle (Fig 6-21). After landing with much wind, be ready to unbuckle, get out, and secure the wing.

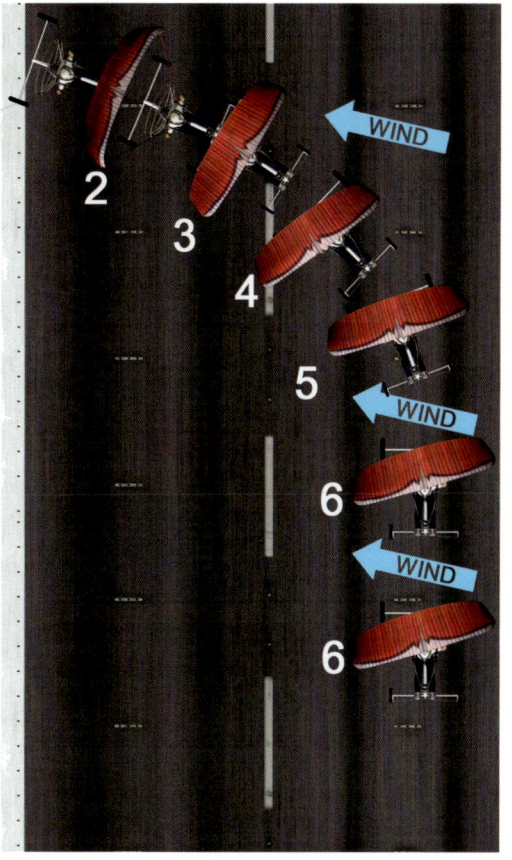

Fig 6-19 Crosswind Launch

1-3. Inflate into the wind.

4. Get the *wing* turning to parallel the runway.

5. Follow with the cart.

6. When stabilized, the wing will be angled (crabbed) into the wind as you're rolling down the runway.

Fig 6-20 Wheeled Regulations

In many countries, wheeled craft are more regulated, especially for tandems. See "Instructing" on page 89. Some countries consider them regular aircraft. In the U.S. they're ultralights just like footlaunch as long as they only carry one occupant. Tandem units may be allowed for training via tandem exemptions issued to organizations like the U.S. Powered Paragliding Association (USPPA.org).

Fig 6-21 Cart Turtling

Carts can be turtled too, usually in a breeze. It happens either during initial inflation or just after landing as the wing inflates or deflates. Lower attachment points reduce the possibility. Thankfully, if you get to the kill switch quickly, nothing gets damaged.

Risk Comparison

Cart flying is about the same risk as foot-launching with one exception: prop injury—carts are *much* safer. The motor is on a more stable platform during start and hands stay farther away from the prop.

Other risk differences are, carts tend to:

- roll over instead of you falling. This only breaks limbs that get extended as an unfortunate reaction to imminent ground contact (Fig 6-18). Keep those things in unless instructed differently (there *are* exceptions for slow speed rollovers).
- takeoff in left-right oscillations and hit the ground.
- get lines in the prop slightly more often during initial inflation.
- have fewer leg injuries, although such injuries are surprisingly rare for foot flyers, too.

The worst cart accidents happen when pilot optimism exceeds actual climb rate, and they fly into something (water, trees, power lines, buildings, etc.) Water is equally lethal if flotation is not used.

The safest carts have rollover resistance (quads or a wide wheelbase), rollover protection, and enough shock absorption to handle vertical impacts. Other safety concerns are identical to foot-launching. One plus for wheels is that it's easier to carry a reserve parachute since you don't have to heft it.

Tandem operations are *much* safer on wheels but may not be legal (check your country's regulations). Tandem footlaunch includes the significant risk of the student/passenger sitting down early, imposing more weight than the pilot, who's still running, can bear. That usually means a face plant for the student and equipment damage. Thankfully, injuries are rare.

Legal Status

In the U.S., single place wheeled craft are still ultralights as long as they meet ultralight standards. If it uses a motor that's also used on footlaunch units, it almost certainly qualifies. In some countries, adding wheels turns it into a more regulated aircraft.

Walk or Roll

Besides making easy work of calm conditions and improving tandem training, wheels extend the number of pilots who can fly and for how long. Although at least one foot-launcher went well past 80 years old, carts will help us *all* roll on.

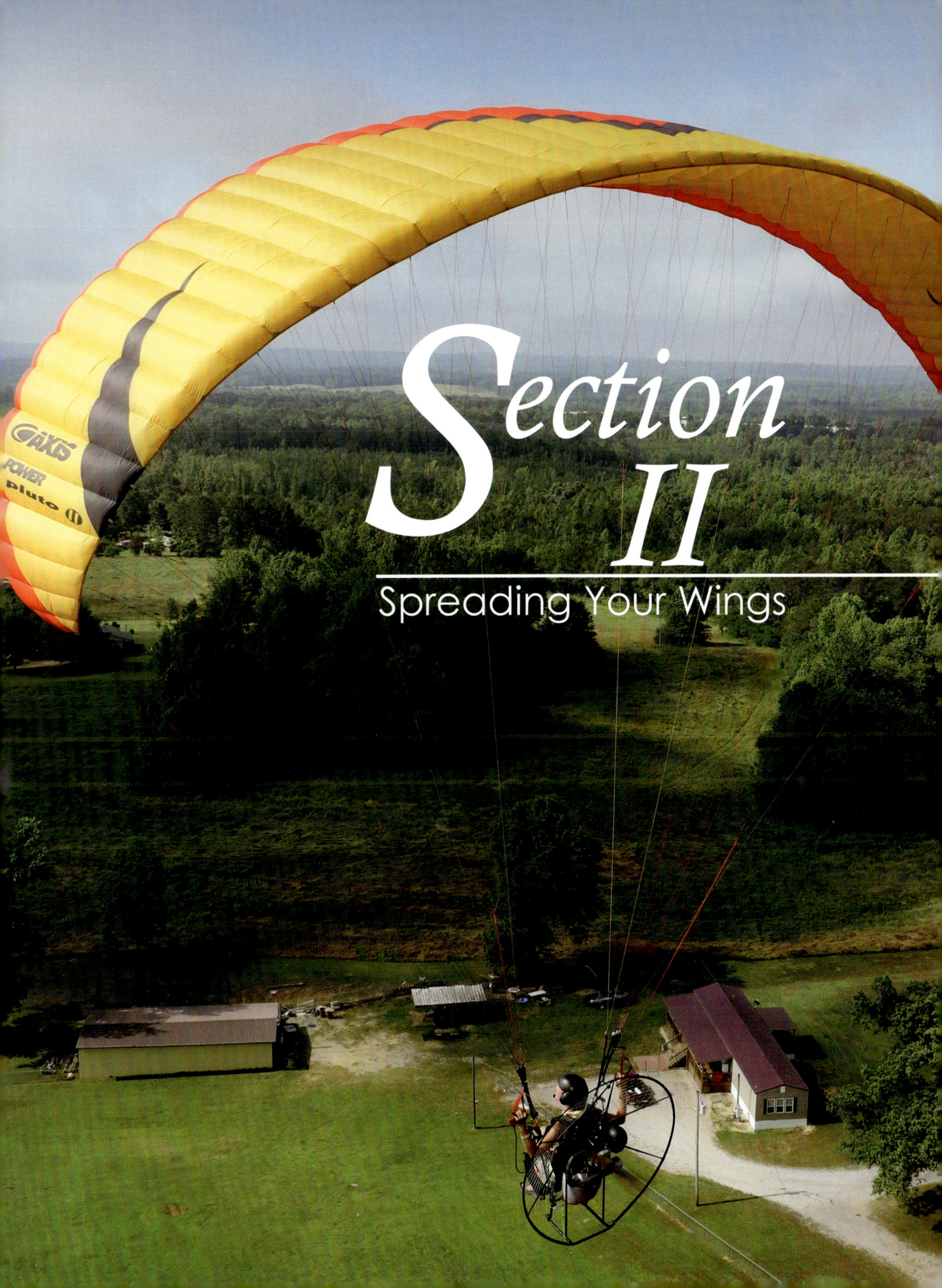

Section II
Spreading Your Wings

Section II
Spreading Your Wings

You've left training and have a world to explore. Learning is far from over.

Work with your instructor and other knowledgeable pilots to improve understanding and carefully build skill. A willingness to learn from others beats prideful distance. But be careful—some input will be useful, some will be use*less*, and some may even be harmful. If advice sounds fishy, ask your instructor or a trusted pilot before acting on it.

Ideally, you will practice on your own for a while, then visit a respected instructor to vanquish any acquired bad habits and refresh skills. It's also an opportunity to delve into new skills, more advanced techniques, and refinements to continue improving.

If ground schools or ratings clinics are held in your area, these are great ways to further your growth in the sport too. And if you haven't seen USPPA's "Risk & Reward," try to. It may help avoid calamity and does so in an entertaining, easy-to-understand format.

Weather & Performance

CHAPTER 7

This chapter will help with the all-important go/no-go decision. One that must consider pilot fitness, aircraft performance, site, skills, and of course, weather.

We take a practical approach since most of what's needed can be gleaned from apps, websites, or TV reports and forecasts. More depth is plumbed in Chapter 24, page 245, and even more in Dennis Pagen's *Understanding the Sky*. A valuable source of knowledge will be nearby ultralight pilots familiar with local weather patterns.

Put social media to work. Form or join a local group to share wisdom about sites and conditions.

It was good that he didn't fly. Soon after this picture was taken, a gust front blew through with 25+ mph winds.

Fitness for flight is another important consideration for launch. The link below points to an article on finding medications that would be disqualifying to FAA certified pilots.

 http://www.footflyer.com/medications-approved-for-paramotor/

Fitness

Aeromedical is the fancy term for relating medical fitness to flight. It's simple in practice: don't fly impaired. For example, ear blockage that's merely inconvenient on the ground can be horrible in flight. You would be fine while climbing, but be in agony on the way down—that's when nasal passages are most likely to plug, potentially perforating an eardrum. Talk about distracting.

Alcohol and recreational drugs don't mix with flight since they impact judgment and reaction time. You'll *feel* just fine—that's why it's so insidious.

Many medications have unwanted effects, both on and off label. Don't use anything that warns against operating machinery. The QR link at right points to an article on "FAA accepted medication." Compliance is not legally required, but neither is surviving.

Performance

Before every launch, ask yourself, "are my skills, and this gear, up to these conditions?" Will I clear the fence? The trees? Is the uphill too steep? Etc. Launching from higher, hotter, or smaller areas makes it harder to be confident. Same with rough surfaces, twitchy winds, and more. See "The Horror of Hot, High, and Humid" on page 171.

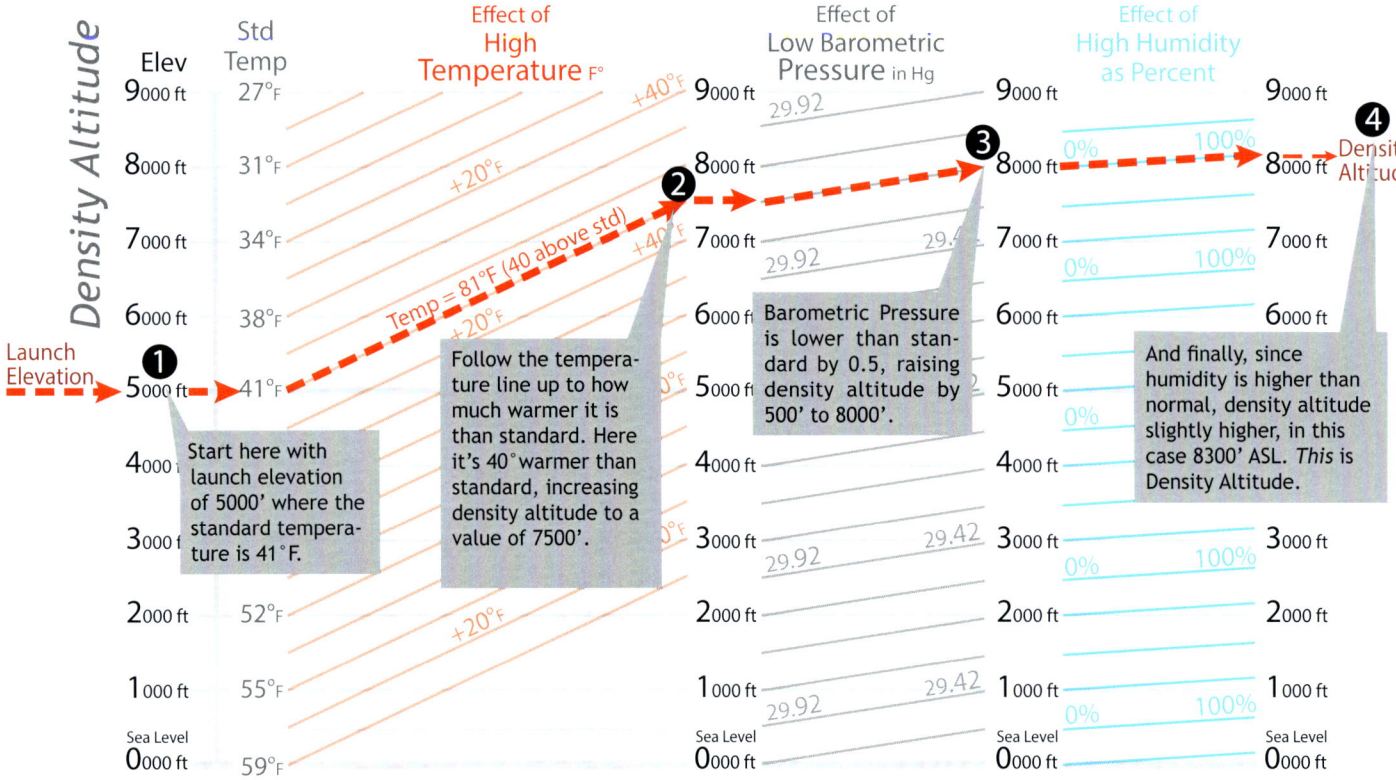

Fig 7-1 Charting Altitude Feel

This details downside of high elevation, high temperature, low barometric pressure and high humidity. Humidity is unique in that it doesn't do much to performance, but it hurts our body's ability to cool, making us less able to exert as much.

See Fig 24-6 on page 247 for details on the "Standard Atmosphere."

Details on Altimetry are on page 283 for the curious.

Density Altitude

All you really need to know about *density altitude* is that at higher elevations and hotter temperatures, performance suffers: the engine has less power, the wing has less lift, you'll need to run faster, and climb rate will be less.

More specifically, density altitude is actual altitude adjusted for factors as shown above. Launch elevation has the biggest effect, of course, followed by temperature (+/- 3000'), barometric pressure (+/- 500'), and humidity (+/- 100').

Weather For the Perfect Day

For motor flying, most of us want calm to light winds. If we have an open area, steady wind up to 10 mph is OK. We *don't* want to see a forecast with much wind shift outside of normal daily cycles. For inland flyers, that leaves mornings and evenings as ideal flying. Fronts and unusual forecast changes in temperature, winds, or clouds are cause for concern.

Beaches are commonly flown all day but have their own risks. Be especially careful as the chance for offshore flow increase (winds blowing out to sea).

Rain is always bad. It's uncomfortable, hard on vision, degrades the wing's collapse recovery ability, and makes parachutal stall more likely (see "Rain" on page 200). Rain *showers* are worse yet. They come from bigger cumulus clouds, which can cause dangerous gusts. The next time you're out and feel a gratuitous gust, think how it would have felt while flying. Be a student of windly wanderings.

Pay attention to the wind forecast because abnormal changes there mean something is amiss. A forecast for morning calm, followed by 5 to 10 mph in the afternoon, and then calm in the evening is a perfect inland forecast. If a change *is* forecast, wait until after the change has actually happened to know how bad it will be. If the wind doesn't change, they don't know what's going on—be leery.

As you fly more from an area, you'll learn its idiosyncrasies.

Thermals & the Daily Cycle

Every day, Sol arises and starts heating the ground, warming up the overlying air with rising air currents that gather strength. These are thermals. They get stronger until early afternoon, and cloud base increases through late afternoon. Expect turbulence when airborne, and gusts while on the ground. Big gusts on the ground mean big turbulence aloft. Thermals can be separated by 15 to 30 minutes so don't be fooled by a few minutes of calm while standing in the field.

Soaring pilots use them to stay up for hours but the turbulence *is* commonly dangerous. How much depends on strength, pilot skill, gear, and other factors. Thankfully, we can avoid it by flying early or late or on some cloudy days.

Clouds don't *stop* the daily cycle but they sure do dampen its power. Sometimes, a sunny afternoon will sprout *cumulus clouds* (fluffy white with a piled-up look) that mark thermal tops. Other days they build and spread out, becoming overcast.

Occasionally, on calm mornings, there can be strong wind just a few hundred feet up (Fig 7-3). It may be perfectly smooth, but you find yourself stopped when flying into the wind. Don't stay up for long—when thermals mix with this fast-moving air, it could be a nasty cauldron down low.

Fig 7-2 Dust Devil

Sometimes conditions can make thermal turbulence linger much later. It pays to heed unusual clouds or winds for the time of day.

Indications of Turbulence

Turbulence lurks in many places; fortunately, with a little knowledge, it can usually be predicted. Clouds are one important clue but dangerous atmospheric shenanigans happen in the clear, too.

Cumulus

Cumulus clouds—typical of warm, summer days—indicate a tumultuous atmosphere. Soaring pilots use them to mark rising air currents to stay aloft. More vertical development begets stronger turbulence.

Dust Devils

Dust devils (Fig 7-2) are miniature tornadoes swirling near the surface—the visible evidence of very dangerous air. While some are wide, slow, and soft, most are quickly rotating funnels that dine on paragliders. Being a byproduct of strong thermals, they're worse in dryer climates. You don't even want to be clipped into a wing, let alone flying when one of these churns through.

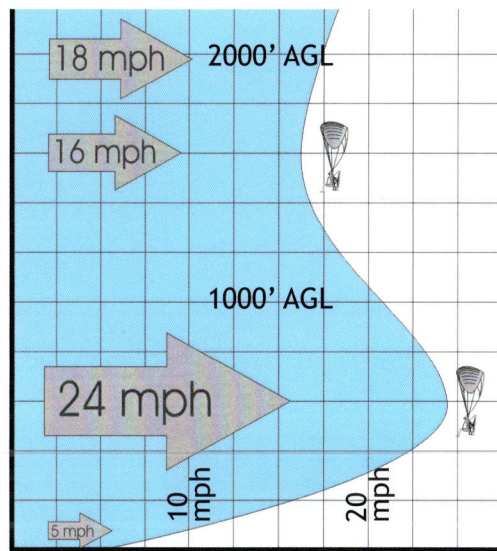

Fig 7-3 A low-Level "Jet"

Heat Sources

Fires generate potentially immense thermal turbulence depending on their sources. But any heat source that can warm the air around it will likely spawn thermals. Power plants, refineries, and many other human-made heat producers should be given a wide berth, especially if you're a bit downwind.

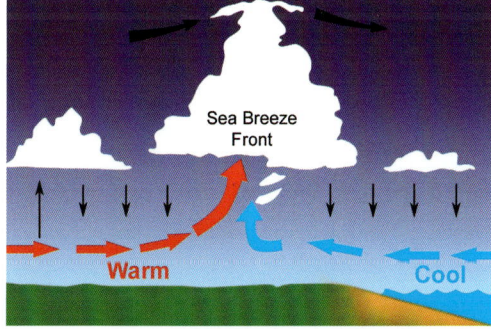

Fig 7-4 Sea Breeze with Cumulus Clouds

Testing conditions

If you have any doubt about conditions, spend at least 15 minutes at launch feeling the winds for changes. Sudden shifts in direction or speed mean a bumpy ride aloft.

Another tool for testing is kiting the wing. You can use a harness or just your hands (one reason the technique can be beneficial). Only clip into a harness if you're confident the conditions will remain benign. If you can

Fig 7-5 Heat Sources

Fig 7-6 Bigger mountain, bigger turbulence. Fig 7-7 Cumulus clouds Fig 7-8 Cumulus clouds gone bad (Cumulonimbus).

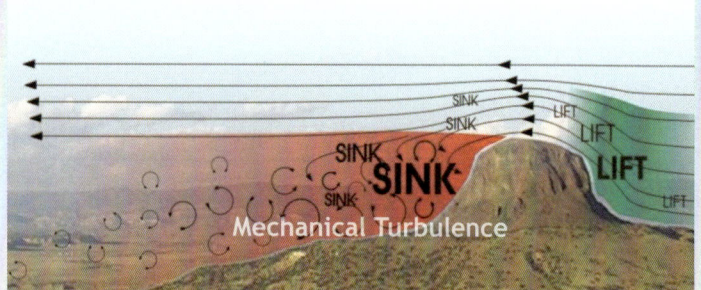

Fig 7-9 Mechanical Turbulence and Sink.

Fig 7-10 Mechanical Turbulence from Buildings.

Where the Bad Air Lurks

Fig 7-11 Wind Turbine Turbulence

These big turbines seem so benign until the atmosphere exposes their secret. It's easy to see why flying in their lee can be a bad idea.

easily and steadily kite the wing, or there isn't enough wind to kite it, that suggests acceptable conditions.

Be careful though. It can still be bumpy even when the surface air seems mellow, so don't use this test alone. It may be that gusts are simply farther apart than a 15 minute wait would reveal. Like dust devils that are sparsely spaced, you could be out there all day and never feel one. That's why we typically avoid mid-day.

Thunderstorms

Thunderstorms are nature's most violent offering and must not be trifled with. Flying anywhere near them has proven deadly, both from turbulence and from getting sucked into their freezing heights. Even small storms exceed 30,000 feet where temperatures fall below -40°F (also -40°C), and turbulence exceeds even an airliner's capability, let alone a paraglider.

They can produce gust fronts up to 20 miles ahead of the storm that can be both violent, and impossible to outrun. Microbursts are another evil output that manifest as short-lived, but fierce gusts from down-rushing cold air.

Don't be tempted to fly immediately after storms pass either. It seems innocuous at times—nastiness rages through, followed by a quiet calm and benign-looking clouds. Don't fall for it. Let some time pass, enough for the wind to shift, and see what upwind stations are experiencing to ensure there are no surprises. A localized, individual cell that's not associated with a front *may* leave flyable conditions, but give it an hour.

If there is severe weather behind one set of storms, even if it's many miles behind, don't fly. While it *may* remain mellow enough to fly, it's hard to tell.

Mountains

Wind in the mountains means turbulence in their lee (downwind). It can be nearly calm at your launch site because of a wind shadow, but just overhead it's a nasty swirl. Local knowledge and looking up forecast winds aloft can help avoid that.

For example, if you're launching at 4000 ft in an area surrounded by mountains, and the winds aloft at 6000 feet are forecast to be over 20 knots, expect strong turbulence. If the winds are forecast to be westerly (out of the west) then make sure you're flying on the west (windward) side. If possible, get to the hilltop to check winds.

Mountainous areas also have unique local conditions because of cool air flowing downhill, and warm air wicking up the sides during daily heating. Even gradually sloping terrain will have local daily flow cycles from this effect.

Beaches

Beach air is the best. On typical, sunny days, heated land sucks in a smooth sea breeze, lasting past sunset. Unfettered by thermal heating, this sea breeze (from sea to land) is normally steady and consistent—perfect for flying. But if the forecast calls for wind blowing off-shore, look out: that's a dangerous condition.

Check inland stations to see if there is off-shore flow (from land to sea). If so, and it's on-shore at the beach, that could be trouble. At some point these winds meet to form a convergence zone. At best it will produce uncomfortable turbulence; at worst, the outflow (away from land) could take over, blowing you out to sea. This is hard to forecast and can quickly go from benign to bad, let alone the whole blown out to sea bit.

Whenever conditions diverge from normal, or from the forecast—winds seem different, clouds are forming too early, temperatures are unseasonal, etc.—be suspicious.

Fig 7-12 Sea Breezes blow inland during daylight due to warm air rising inland. If the prevailing wind is otherwise out to sea then the two air currents meet in a *convergence zone*. Expect turbulence and rising air.

A stable sea breeze is ideal for paramotor.

Fig 7-13 Clouds show how air flows around a mountain like water around a boat's bow. Notice the rising portions of airflow well away from the source mountain, along with areas of turbulence.

Whenever There's Wind

From the air, use flags, smoke, trees, and other vegetation to reveal when the wind has picked up. Crops can be used to tell direction along with other methods shown at right and covered on the next page. Here are some common, significant phenomena that show up whenever the wind blows.

Mechanical Turbulence and Rotor

Just like a rock in a stream, whenever air blows past an obstruction it becomes turbulent (bumpy) downstream. More wind or bigger obstructions mean worse turbulence extending farther, and even above. Rotor, wind shadow, and mechanical turbulence, all have specific meanings (Fig 24-20 on page 253), but commonly get lumped into the term "rotor." Thankfully, most pilots know what's meant.

Wind Gradient

Friction slows airflow as it rubs against the ground. In the morning, when cool air sits at the surface, it can be calm while only a few hundred feet above it's blowing 20 MPH. As the ground heats up in the morning, that fast-moving air aloft mixes with the still air below, and a bumpy surface wind develops—be ready or be landed.

Fig 7-14 Windsocks can be confusing. To land into the wind, think "**Eat the Carrot**"

Fig 7-15 Wind indicators. More is better, but have them work in really light winds, too.

Fig 7-16 Reading Flags. Big flags take more wind to wave. It took 15 mph to ripple this monster.

Fig 7-17 A Mylar Balloon can be tell wind direction up at wing height in nearly calm conditions.

Fig 7-18 Water for Wind Direction
It will be calmer next to the shore on the upwind side.

Wind Shear

A dramatic change in wind speed/direction from one area to another is wind shear (image at right). The *shear zone* can be quite turbulent, and when associated with thunderstorms, has brought down airliners.

Forecast winds aloft give some indication of a shear's presence as do clouds moving in different directions at different altitudes. Frequently shears can be gradual and smooth, other times they're nasty and dangerous. On days with thunderstorms, wind shear can occur in many directions, even without storms nearby.

Pilots experience wind shear most often during climb; passing through some altitude you get strongly bounced around (hopefully that's all) and then notice that you're now drifting over the ground in a different direction, possibly even going backward. Look for this when it has cooled a lot from the previous day's high temperature and the forecast winds aloft are strong (over about 15 mph).

Telling Wind Direction

Besides a windsock, have light-wind streamers for near-calm conditions. If possible, have it 15 feet up to expose any slight breezes at wing height even though it's calm at the surface. "Portable Anemometers" on page 282 has some handheld gadgets, but the following are visible from aloft since winds may change while you're flying.

Fig 7-19 Smoke for Wind Direction

Smoke, steam, and blowing dust are great wind indicators. But if you see blowing dust, be ready for a wild ride! Avoid rising smoke plumes which can harbor horrendous turbulence depending on their source.

In this image, smoke shows *very* light air movement. The initial vertical rise suggests that it's calm at the surface. Lateral spreading suggests only slow movement in depicted directions—this would be great conditions.

- Lakes are calmer on the upwind side. Bigger waves mean more wind; whitecaps start at about 12 mph. Boats anchored off shore will be pointing into the wind.

- Flags flap downwind of their pole, but be careful; big flags require a big wind to wave. What looks light on a big flag may be quite strong.

- Smoke is the most sensitive indicator. Plus it shows direction at different heights, but never, *ever*, fly in the updraft from a large fire—it can spew extreme turbulence several thousand feet up.

- Crops and vegetation can show direction, intensity, and gusts. It's interesting to watch a gust form on crops then spread across the field.

- Moving cloud shadows tell the wind at cloud height.

- In desert areas, blowing sand and tumbleweeds show wind. Visible blowing sand suggests a strong, bumpy cauldron.

- Ground track can reveal the wind speed and direction at your altitude (see Chapter 10) as can some phone applications.

- Helium balloons (Fig 7-17) with lightweight streamers for *very* light breezes.

Lift & Sink

When air flows up over an obstruction it produces lift in front of the obstruction and sink behind it (lee side) along with rotor and turbulence. The strength of each depends on the shape of the obstruction and strength of the wind. Soaring pilots make use of this lift (called ridge or Orographic lift) to stay airborne, but it must be given great respect—any lift powerful enough to keep a pilot aloft can also produce deadly turbulence if you end up in the wrong place.

Acquiring Aviation Weather

There is value in *aviation* forecasts. Terminal Forecasts estimate cloud heights, coverage, winds, precipitation, frontal passage times, wind shifts, and other useful info. Winds Aloft give wind direction, speed, and temperature in 3000 foot increments.

Flight Service Station (FSS) Briefing

In the U.S., Flight Service Stations (FSS) are the official source for aviation weather and other information, including temporary flight restrictions (TFR's). Ultralight pilots have no *requirement* to use it but are allowed access.

Phone briefings are available at 800-WX-BRIEF and they *want* to hear from you—it helps justify staffing. An online briefing is also available at 800wxBrief.com after setting up a free account. If calling, have the following info on hand:

1. Launch location relative to an airport or VOR (Fig 9-18) since those are charted. For example, if you're 10 miles south of your city's airport, tell them that.

2. Approximate launch time and flight duration. They use worldwide standard time, Universal Coordinated Time (UTC), but can translate to local; just be sure to say "local" when you give the time.

3. Your planned max altitude above mean sea level (MSL). You can say height above ground level (AGL) but tell them so ("I'll be less than 500' AGL").

Don't trust forecasts that are wrong for what's happening right now. For example, if a south wind at 5 is forecast for the current time period, but it's actually northwest at 12, they don't have a handle on things. Also, see what's coming by checking upstream stations where the weather is coming from. That's true of any forecast, but is easier with aviation forecasts since they give times.

While on the phone, ask the "VAD" (Velocity Azimuth Display) winds report. Data comes from radar that uses airborne particles to determine winds aloft over a wide area. They're actual winds (not forecast) given in thousand-foot increments; other winds are in 3000' increments. You do have to ask because they're typically only used by balloon pilots, and of course, us.

 Use the QR link for a sample briefing.

Fig 7-20 Numeric Wind Direction

Aviation information reports wind as the direction it is *from* using the 360 degrees of a compass rose relative to true north. Magnetic north is where a compass points, and true north is what lines on a map are drawn with.

So a south wind would be given as 180° and a West wind would be 270°.

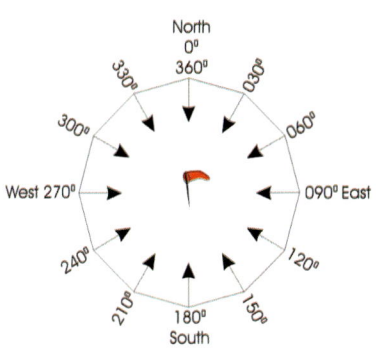

Fig 7-21 Universal Time: Converting to Zulu

Aviation uses *Coordinated Universal Time*, abbreviated UTC and known as *Zulu Time*. It's the time in Greenwich, England and does not recognize Daylight Saving Time (DST) so the conversion may be different in summer and winter. Standard Time (ST) is unadjusted.

In the U.S., DST runs from the second Sunday of March to the first Sunday in November. In Europe it's called Summer Time, going from the last Sunday in March to the Last Sunday in October. Convert to Zulu time by adding the following hours to your local time (USA).

Zulu is:	Pacific	Mountain	Central	Eastern
In Summer (DST)	Local+7	Local+6	Local+5	Local+4
In Winter (ST)	Local+8	Local+7	Local+6	Local+5

Fig 7-22 Apps Web Link The latest, best apps and sites can be found on the Footflyer page at this QR link.

Fig 7-23 Air flows over the cool, wet ocean, gathering water vapor. It condenses into tiny particles, becoming visible as a low cloud layer. Daily airflow pushes all that wetness inland where it has no new source for water vapor.

By the time it gets a few miles in, spreading has depleted the moisture until liquid cloud droplets evaporate back to invisible vapor.

Mountains that force air up, accelerate the process since rising air cools and cool air can hold less invisible moisture (vapor). Clouds thicken. Descending air on the mountain's back side reverses the process, warming the air enough so return moisture into vapor.

Weather Apps & Websites

There are great apps and websites for weather. Some are made for other wind-sensitive sports like ballooning or sailing—they outnumber us, after all. Free flight (soaring) apps abound, and these are useful, even if to point out that, when it's good for inland soaring, it's gonna be bumpy.

Apps that show your location are particularly useful to make sure you're looking in the right place. Some concentrate on showing what's going on now while others focus on forecasts. Great apps abound for other things, too, like navigation, charts, instrumentation, etc.

Compare forecasts though. If one calls for a big change in winds and another does not, someone has old information or change may be afoot. Be suspicious.

One cool feature of some inflight apps is the ability to calculate winds at your altitude. Accuracy improves if you do a constant rate 360° turn.

Context, Wx Guides, and Luck

It's difficult to make generalizations on weather guidelines because they depend on location, time of day, land formations, and big-system machinations. A rule that works well inland may be dangerously permissive on a hill-shrouded riverbank. Seek out local knowledge, especially before you've gained a deep understanding of the underlying forces. Be careful, though, atmospheric curveballs sometimes whiz by, surprising even the experts. Don't blindly follow *any* advice that suggests something more aggressive than you're comfy with.

Building weather rules *will* help avoid buffoonery. For example, in a tree-lined area, look up at the branches. Are they swaying, or is it just the leaves rustling? A good rule is: **"If the branches are swayin', on the ground I'm a stayin' "**.

Similar guides can be built for other conditions. They may be based on winds, lightning strike proximity, pressure changes on the other side a mountain range, and so on. Ask around.

A useful guide for inland sites is to avoid launching when the winds change more than 5 mph in 5 seconds. Pick specific limits and stick to your guns. Tell others: "if it gusts over 13 mph (or whatever you choose) I'm gonna pass on flying."

If you're launching in a confined area, surrounded by tall stuff, be it hills, trees or buildings, reduce your acceptable max. More wind suggests a churning cauldron overhead. Thermally conditions nearly always impose extra risk.

As covered in Chapter 19's "Getting Away With It" on page 190, just because you succeeded at something sketchy, doesn't mean it was safe. It could have been luck.

Following the Crowd

During a major paramotor gathering, clues appeared of a gust front. Many anxious pilots ignored them while others stayed put. One even offered to call Flight Service for a weather briefing and was rebuffed—the clouds just didn't look that bad. Quite a few pilots launched.

Sure enough, ten minutes later, a strong gust front came through with associated turbulence. A few suffered minor injuries in the high-wind fracas that followed, and many couldn't make it back to the field.

By skipping that call to Flight Service, they missed learning of a newly formed and very local cold front. A revised forecast indeed cautioned about a 20 knot wind shift. Yup, it was right.

by Tim Kaiser

Common Sense & the Law

CHAPTER 8

We operate at the pleasure of the people—annoy enough of them and we won't fly anymore. Enacted laws range from noise to disturbing animals. Even where no prohibition exists, annoy enough of the right people, and a law *will* be added. That's not surprising—if a neighbor started running his chainsaw at 3 a.m., *you* would want a law.

Aggravating people is rarely good—there are more of them (non-flyers) than us. We must play nice, police ourselves, and encourage others to do the same. At least one entire state's worth of beaches was put off-limits due to the inconsiderate actions of one pilot and his groupies. Don't be that pilot.

Keeping a Low Profile

Avoid over-using *any* one area if there are neighbors, even if you have permission. Launch and leave using noise abatement procedures (see below). And if confronted, try to make arrangements without flaunting our sport's crown jewel—its minimal regulation.

Animals have people and vice versa. Annoying either can be expensive. For example, if you spook someone's million-dollar horse into an injurious rampage, expect a visit from the riled owner or his lawyer; losing the flying site may be your least concern.

Don't take the approach "It's my land; I'll do what I want." That's only true to a point. Neighbors don't always need to be right next door to cause problems—they just have to convince the right people that you're violating some existing law, or get a new one enacted. Numerous laws have blossomed for exactly this reason.

Noise Abatement

Fly quietly. Stay high, use minimal thrust in noise sensitive areas, and quiet your machine—air intake silencers, mufflers, and big props help. Fly a *noise abatement* profile (Fig 8-2). The quietest motors, at cruise RPM, are almost hard to hear beyond about 500 feet. High power is a *lot* noisier. Smaller props at higher RPM make even more objectionable noise.

Like any human interaction, treat law enforcement with respect for best results. You may be legal, but if they dislike your presence they'll find a way to make it difficult.

The FAA (Federal Aviation Administration) governs U.S. airspace, but locals govern local launch sites. Many municipalities have laws that prohibit launching *any* type of human-carrying flying machine outside of airports. Just as often, very few people are aware of those laws. Don't force their hand.

Fig 8-1 Airspace & Law Video

This uses live action and animation to help clarify airspace and the gloriously brief, but sometimes vague US Ultralight Regulations.

Fig 8-2 Noise Abatement
This is your noise "footprint," where red is loud, and white is quiet. Consider taking off at reduced power, flying away from the noise sensitive areas, then throttling up once past.

Fig 8-3 Congested?
Provided you stay within the park boundaries, and don't fly over people or their pets, you're legal to fly here. It's tight, and permission is required by park authorities.

Fig 8-4 Yellow On Charts
This is the park from Fig 8-3. Yellow areas approximate city lights for aircraft pilots flying at night—they have nothing to do with what constitutes congested areas. Plenty of green areas on charts contain clusters of houses or small towns that would be considered congested.

Fig 8-5 FAR 103 Web Page
This FootFlyer page has FAR 103, AC-103, and FAR 103's Preamble.

http://www.footflyer.com/ultralight-regulations-far-part-103/

Regulations

In the U.S., we follow Federal Aviation Regulation (FAR) Part 103 which covers all ultralights—powered single-occupant aircraft ("vehicles") weighing under 254 pounds (Fig 8-5). It protects *others*, not participants. So every interpretation of your flying must conclude that you weren't endangering anyone else. Advisory Circular AC 103-7 explains the rule's intent.

The absence of training requirements is no excuse for ignorance of the law. Flying in any country's national airspace system is a privilege to be taken seriously. What a travesty for someone to buy gear, train enough to get airborne, then crash into an airliner. Besides *that* tragedy, public pressure would mount to shut us down. We must learn the rules and follow them, then help our fellow flyers do the same.

Perception is important: *looking* like you're doing something dangerous will draw unwanted attention. Besides your own safety, the *appearance* of safety gets reported less than "Showing off." So while we *can* fly close to people and their property, we must do so with discretion.

One common misconception is that we must maintain 500 ft away from anything on the ground. That may be advisable at times, but is not the law (as it is for many aircraft). Being able to legally fly down a fence row at 5 feet is a freedom worth preserving.

Night Flying

We can't fly at night, at least in the U.S., but we *can* fly in the 30 minutes before sunrise to 30 minutes after sunset if we: 1) use a strobe visible for 3 miles, 2) and stay within class G airspace. Thankfully, most of the country is covered with G airspace (Fig 9-3).

Right of Way

All certified aircraft have the right of way over all ultralights. That means if we see an airplane or helicopter, we have to stay clear or move, even if we're unpowered (or on fire for that matter). We should know where airplanes are likely to be and steer clear. Since we usually stay below their altitudes, that's easy except near airports.

Among ultralights, powered craft must give way to unpowered ones, but there are some common-sense guidelines.

- If approaching head-on, steer to the right—just like driving. Reverse that in left-drive countries.

- Overtake on the right. Free flight "ridge rules" (Fig 21-8) modify this.

- Landing pilots have the right of way. But at crowded sites, let launchers go if they're standing there with an idling motor waiting to take off.

- The craft to your right has the right-of-way.
- Give way to anyone who can't (or just doesn't) see you, that especially includes a pilot who is *below*.

What is Congested?

This million dollar question does not have a clear answer. In the U.S., FAR 103.15 tells us "No person may operate an ultralight vehicle over **any congested area of a city, town, or settlement, or over any open-air assembly of persons.**" There is no minimum altitude and no definition of congested—it's intentionally left up to the enforcer. Some regional FAA offices consider even one house to be "congested," while others have no set number.

The simple but broad wording, especially of the term, **congested area**, has many possible meanings. The following comes from experience, court cases, and interpretation. Your FAA inspector may think otherwise, so fly conservatively. With caveats covered, here goes. A congested area is:

1. Any group of occupied buildings where there would not be enough room to easily launch or land. Remember, this defines the level of congestion, not the operational conduct. It should not be construed as suggesting flight over a congested area just because you have a good landing option nearby. You can never fly over a congested area at any altitude. But, if you couldn't easily land there, it's probably too congested to fly over.

2. An open-air assembly of people is any gathering of two or more people. That includes golfers, beachgoers, sporting events, parties, and spectators (even at fly-ins!) Again, flying high makes you less likely to be complained about.

3. One interesting situation is roads. Precedence suggests that overflight of roads is *usually* OK. For example, there are airfields with FAA-approved ultralight flight patterns that go over major roads, even busy divided ones like the OSH example in Fig 8-6. In that case they specify a minimum altitude (300 feet is common).

At paramotor fly-ins there are ultralight flight patterns that go over well-traveled roads as well. But be reasonable; distracting a motorist may be seen as "Hazardous Operations" (FAR 103.9).

If there is enough traffic that something falling off your machine would likely damage a car, it's even more likely to be called congested. Your best bet is to climb to *at least* 300 feet AGL before crossing roads, and don't disturb the groundlings or their lawyers.

Trespass

Crossing fences, trespassing signs, or damaging property or crops is enough to get arrested in some areas. That seldom happens in reality, but an irate property owner may help make it happen. Rules vary immensely from country to country and even within jurisdictions in the same country.

The FAA doesn't care where you launch from, but locals sure do. It's always best to ask permission, but generally, if there's no signage, US law gives you one chance to leave when the property owner asks you to. If you come back again, you can be arrested. Use the phrase "flying my kite" and be polite if confronted.

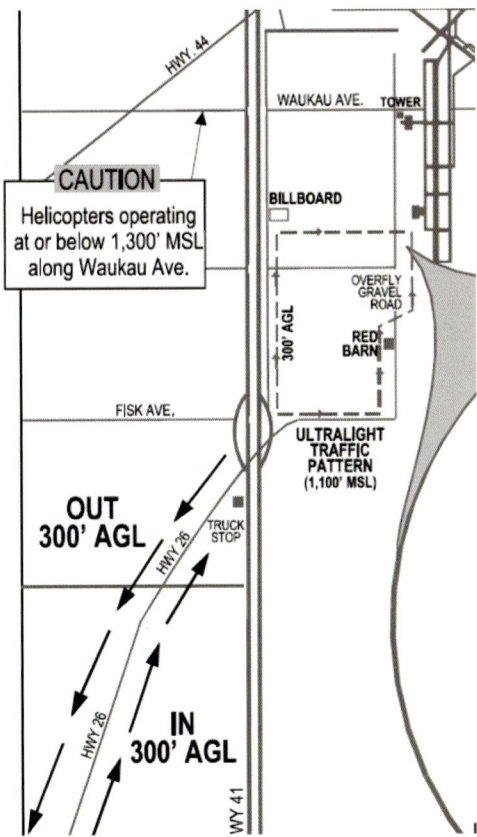

Fig 8-6 (Top) Oshkosh Congested

This is the ultralight departure/arrival corridor for the world's largest airshow in Oshkosh, WI. It's an FAA approved procedure that clearly goes over roads, including the busy Highway 41. Beware, though, pilots *have* been violated for flying over roads that were considered "congested."

Fly high: It's frequently not whether you *are* violating the law, but whether you *look* like you're violating the law.

Fig 8-7 Is this Flying "Over?"

It *looks* like he's over Chicago because of zoom; he's actually over water. This is one way that people get falsely accused of flying "over" congested areas. A GPS track can set the record straight, but never offer it up voluntarily.

Fig 8-8 Local Restrictions
Prohibition of flying won't *ever* be this obvious. You'll get ticketed over the motorized vehicle rule or some obscure municipal restriction that's not on any sign.

Fig 8-9 Dropping Objects
You can drop things provided they don't endanger property or people on the surface.

Advisory Circulars

FAA Advisory Circular **AC 103-7** spells out many details under which FAR 103 was concocted and gives some interesting background. It reveals the why of the regulation's restrictive stance. See Fig 8-5.

Who Owns the Air?

Jurisdiction over airspace can be contentious. In the U.S. it's *federally* regulated but that doesn't stop municipalities from trying. They can certainly restrict launching but likely don't have jurisdiction over the airspace above. They sometimes do this with local parks. They may also use noise ordinances to skirt the issue.

Even if you would win a challenge to their rule, a "ticket" (violation) means that you still have to defend yourself in court.

Case Law & Other Issues

Verdicts handed down to pilots who ran afoul of the law warrant study. Even though U.S. flyers abide by Part 103, cases involving violations of other air regulations have been used as precedence for ultralight pilots—used to impose fines (or other sanctions) by virtue of their definitions.

In one case, a definition of congested was given by saying that: "30 to 40 homes, located on relatively small and adjoining lots, constitutes a 'congested area' within the meaning of the regulation." Unfortunately, no dimensions were given, but little is needed; there's no doubting that most suburban developments would qualify.

Another case is even less encouraging. It is a bit more complicated because it involved an agricultural airplane that operates under different regulations but is not allowed over congested areas. The judge labeled the following as congested: An area 0.6 miles long and 0.3 miles wide (about 115 acres) with 60 houses—at nearly 2 acres per lot that's pretty sparse by most definitions. This definition was used to say a PPG pilot was flying over a congested area.

An FAA web site offers some relief regarding the definition of congested. It says that an operation (this was given for aerobatic pilots) can be done over an area as small as an acre, even if surrounded by houses. That means flying along a right of way, beside railroad tracks, or a path that keeps you away from buildings would be allowable. Just don't fly over nearby houses and avoid flying in ways that make people complain. It is worth reading and heeding these rules; each violation carries a fine of $1000 or more and can get your equipment confiscated.

Endangerment & Dropping Objects

You can't endanger another person or their property. FAR 103.9(a), a catch-all regulation that says don't operate "in a manner that creates a hazard to other persons or property." Nearly every country has similar verbiage and it will be used in an accident.

FAR 103.9(b) uses similar language, prohibiting dropping anything if it "creates a hazard to other persons or property." That's why bean-bag dropping contests are legal.

What is "Flying Over?"

When are you "over" a prohibited area? How far horizontally away do you need to be? By one measure you must be directly over it. But if an observer thinks you are too close, you will be seen (accused) as "flying over." For example, houses may be well to your right, but to an observer on your left, you may appear to be over them.

So here's a measure for keeping visibly clear of congested areas: Use the distance traveled in 5 seconds of flying time. 20 mph is about 30 feet per second. So in 5 seconds, that's 150 ft. Higher up, (300 ft) increase it to maybe 10 seconds. For example, while down low, flying alongside a road that's busy enough to worry about, stay at least 150 feet horizontally away.

Like so many aspects of life, attitude can be the difference between a lip lashing and enforcement action. If local authorities question your operation, be respectful and explain how you were following pertinent air regulations. They won't likely know what those are now but can certainly look them up later. And don't come off as arrogant—they *may* be knowledgeable. Offer to avoid the area, and if it seems appropriate, ask where a good alternative launch site might be.

Have the regs, an altimeter, an air map on your phone (or printed chart), and know how to use it all. If confronted, and it feels appropriate, show how you were staying within the law. It may be enough.

If you end up being investigated, or have to answer a letter of investigation, be prompt, be honest, but be minimal! It's quite possible that your response ***is the best they have***. Most FAA folks are not "out to get" pilots, but are just trying to do their job with the least effort. They would probably rather wrap it up quickly unless your attitude motivates them otherwise.

Commercial Use

Commercial use is prohibited in Part 103 but not directly.

Fig 8-10 Wing Advertising

It's that our activity must *only* be for recreation or sport—a broad stroke that's difficult to avoid. Don't confuse it with other rules, like those prohibiting private pilots from commercial activities—our rule is far more limiting since it defines what we *can* do. Flying for movies or photography missions is questionable even if no payment is made for the flying. A law judge must only find that your flight was not for recreation or sport.

Regulators figured that, with no license given, there is little accountability and few safeguards to the public, so ultralight flying would not be appropriate for commercial, or even practical use.

Where the payment issue comes into play is when defending the "sport or recreational" nature of a flight. Getting paid makes it difficult to justify that purpose.

The most common question is about aerial photography, although drones are taking a lot of that. The temptation is to say that you're not getting paid to *fly* but rather are selling a service and just happened to have pictures from your PPG.

If you were out flying for fun, taking pictures, and later discovered a really cool shot, it would technically be valid to sell it. If you flew solely to get pictures, then it's not even the selling that's illegal, it's that the flight's purpose is not allowed. If asked, your flight was for fun and the pictures just add to it. I've had lots of those.

Fig 8-11 Tandem Operations

Tandem flying in the U.S. is only for teaching. Wheeled tandems may have more restrictive rules, and they change periodically. This link shows tandem's legal status in the U.S. and elsewhere.

The people most likely to report your activity are those who do aerial photography, aerial advertisers, and the like, who use expensive certified aircraft and pilots. They have a lot to lose if someone drains away their business with inexpensive, unregulated capabilities, and may already be sensitive about competition from drones. Commercial drone operators may even be sensitive about it.

Instructing

The only way to get paid to fly is by giving tandem instruction, if allowed to do so in your country. Experienced pilots can go through an approved program that allows them to fly students using two-seat craft. Such flights are done under a special exemption for instruction only. In the U.S., approved programs are run by member organizations such as the U.S. Powered Paragliding Association (USPPA.org), and do not fall under the far more-involved Sport Pilot regulation.

Tandem craft can also get certified as powered parachutes under either *Light Sport Aircraft* or *Experimental Amateur Built*. But then an FAA pilot license and aircraft certification is required.

You can also get paid to teach PPG from the ground—there is no restriction on that. Of course there are many pitfalls to instructing, which is why going through a thorough certification process is important. It's what our book, *Paraglider & Paramotor Instructor*, was developed for.

by Eric Farewell

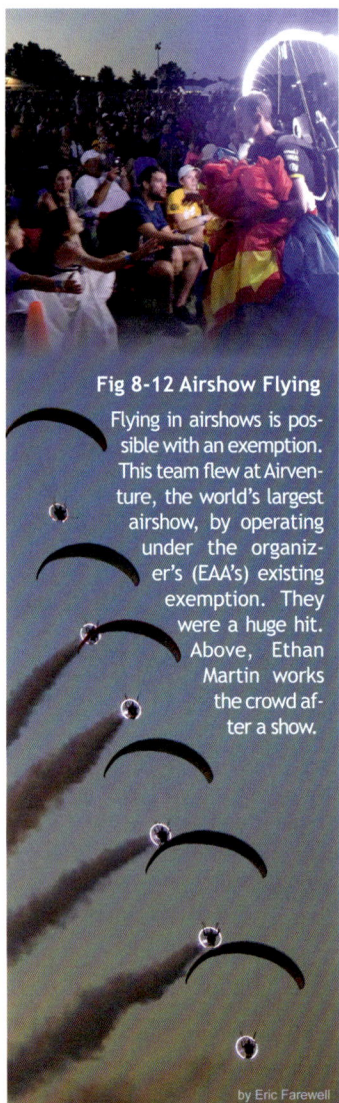

Fig 8-12 Airshow Flying

Flying in airshows is possible with an exemption. This team flew at Airventure, the world's largest airshow, by operating under the organizer's (EAA's) existing exemption. They were a huge hit. Above, Ethan Martin works the crowd after a show.

Fig 8-13 Hollywood

TV and movie produces have used paramotors. They work with FAA FSDO (Flight Service District Office) officials to get an exemption from the "Sport or recreation" limitation. That also allows for paying the pilot.

Getting Someone Else to Pay

While you can't get paid for solo flying, you *can* offset costs by having a company buy your wing, even with their logo and text emblazoned on it (Fig 8-10). But they can't tell you when or where to fly it. If you're thinking that would be hard to enforce, you're right. Don't do something blatant to bring on scrutiny, especially offering services.

Consider banner towing. If you're getting paid it would be very difficult to convince a judge that your flight was *only* for sport or recreation. You might argue that you would have been flying anyway but it would be a tough sell. Besides, AC 103-7 makes it clear that this is a violation, even if the banner is for a charity.

If I Violate the Rules?

Professional pilots have the most to lose: FAA officials will go after their certificates because it's easy and effective. A good aviation attorney is a must there.

Generally, the FAA is obliged to investigate any complaint, and once that train has left the station, it's hard to stop. However, if handled amicably, the event may be settled with minimum fuss.

Your first indication is usually the police showing up and taking a report. They don't always contact aviation authorities but will be more motivated if you're belligerent. They *may* know our rules, but more likely will accuse you of violating rules that don't apply, which can work in your favor later. Be polite, you'd rather avoid having a "later."

This is where having the regulations and air map handy may help show that you're trying to be responsible. Only offer the rules if the official is being reasonable and it feels they will help. Some officers recoil at "being schooled," and you'll only make matters worse. Be observant.

Protecting Yourself

Consider recording your ground track with a GPS. That's easy on most phones: make sure the GPS is on, download an app (Fig 2-44 on page 24), and turn on its recorder. Now, if you get accused of a violation, the track could exonerate you. But as mentioned before, ***never offer it up*** unless forced to legally. Many phones are already recording location.

Exemptions

It is *possible* to get exemptions from FAR 103 providing equivalent safety is maintained. For example, airshows commonly let pilots fly in ways that would otherwise be illegal but do so with a waiver. It adds guidelines aimed at protecting the public. The airshow organization is trusted with setting rules to that end.

Any hope for success hinges on providing evidence for how the public interest is served while maintaining equivalent safety.

UNITED STATES OF AMERICA
NATIONAL TRANSPORTATION SAFETY BOARD
WASHINGTON, D.C.

Adopted by the NATIONAL TRANSPORTATION SAFETY BOARD at its office in Washington, D. C. on the 6th day of February 1980.

LANGHORNE M. BOND, Administrator, Federal Aviation Administration, Complainant,

vs.

OTHA W. WINSETT Respondent.

Docket No. SE-4066

OPINION AND ORDER

The Administrator has appealed from the initial decision [1/] of Administrative Law Judge Thomas W. Reilly, issued orally at the conclusion of a full evidentiary hearing held August 2, 1979. The law judge concluded that a violation of section 91.9 of the Federal Aviation Regulations (FAR) occurred during the flight of a manned free

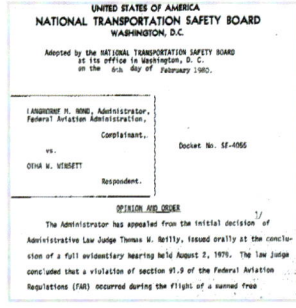

Fig 8-14 Court Case Lost

Our freedom is a double-edged sword that can cut deeply.

When one PPG pilot ran afoul of local law, police contacted FAA officials. The case went all the way to trial, and FAA lawyers used prior rulings (left) to prosecute the pilot. Even though those judgments weren't directly about FAR 103, they did include a reference to "congested."

The pilot was fined over $1000 and had to pay his legal fees. There is, unfortunately, little recourse in such cases and one avenue, the National Transportation Safety Board (NTSB), is not likely to help.

Airspace

"Can I launch here?" Assuming you have landowner permission, probably.

Sectional Aeronautical Charts (Fig 9-1) describe airspace for aviators. For simplicity we skip verbiage like "up to but not including." In almost the entire U.S., you can launch and fly from the ground up to 1200' above ground level (AGL) with as little as 1 mile visibility while staying Clear of Clouds (CoC). You can climb higher but need more cloud clearance and visibility.

Airspace Types & Classes

There are different types of airspace, but the most discussed are **Air Traffic Classes A through G**. We launch and fly in G airspace—the most permissive class. Think "G for ground", and "G for goodness." E overlays G *almost* Everywhere (Fig 9-2). We fly in E, too.

In G, we only need to stay **C**lear-**o**f-**C**louds and have **1** mile visibility, abbreviated as "**CoC & 1.**" In the U.S., Class F is not used, so think "F for Forgotten."

Most G airspace goes from the ground up to 1200' or 700' AGL where E starts. Near airports, G only goes up to 700' AGL. A very few places have no G, rather E starts right at the surface. Just remember this: in most of the U.S., "We launch in G, and climb into E at 1200 or 700 feet AGL." Got that? You're halfway there.

Security airspace (starts on page 95) includes Temporary Flight Restrictions (TFR's), Prohibited, Restricted, and Alert areas. Most are charted but TFR information may only appear in Notices to Airmen (NOTAMs).

Wilderness airspace (starts on page 95) includes national parks and other public areas, which may have altitude minimums for overflight. Regardless of air rules, disturbing wildlife may run afoul of park rules. The FAA governs airspace in the U.S., but they don't define "disturbing" as it relates to animals.

Other: Special airspace restrictions can pop into being for a variety of reasons, including tethered balloons, high powered rocket launches, drones flying, and disaster areas.

Fig 9-1 Sectional Charts
Current Sectional Aeronautical Charts are available online (SkyVector.com). Paper versions are available from a decreasing number of local airports or online shops. Phone apps are helpful because they show your location relative to airspace boundaries. Charts are updated every 6 months.

500' 500 **feet**
AGL **A**bove **G**round **L**evel
MSL **M**ean **S**ea **L**evel

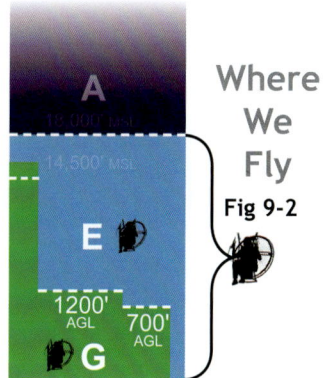

Where We Fly
Fig 9-2

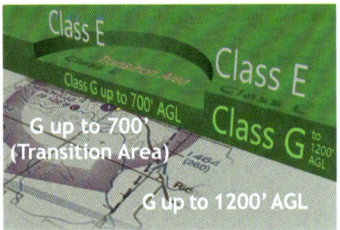

Fig 9-3 We Fly In G & E Airspace

Pick a random spot in the U.S. and it's almost certainly G airspace up to 1200' or 700'. The lower value is near airports like depicted above. We can fly in both the G and the E above.

Fig 9-4 Alphabet Airspace

❷ & ❿ are both over 10,000' and have identical cloud clearance minimums even though 10 is in G. ❻, & ❽ have the lower G minimums, being below 1200' AGL.

You *can* fly below B and C airspace (❶ and ❼). You'll launch in G and climb into E airspace, staying below the shelves.

At ❾ you need only a mile visibility but still need more cloud clearance. Position ❿, being above 10,000', requires much higher visibility. Position ❻ is above a *transition area* where the floor of E drops from 1200' to 700'.

Airspace Classes: the ABC's

Hopefully it's clear that we fly primarily in G and E airspace, starting with G at the ground. This mostly 1200' thick blanket of G covers nearly the whole country, with E immediately above, then A airspace way above that.

Where G airspace only goes up to 700' is a *transition area* (Fig 9-3). As with nearly all G, we need Clear of Clouds and 1 mile to launch (**CoC & 1**). Up in the E airspace we need 3 miles visibility and more cloud clearance (Fig 9-5).

Mid-sized or bigger airports tend to have control-towers (D airspace) which means controller permission is needed. We cover these in Chapter 11.

You've got the basics now—launch in G, climb into E—but here is the rest of the story. Definitions are recognized worldwide as shown in Fig 9-4 with **A** being the most restrictive and G the most permissive. Details vary by country.

Class A

Class A airspace is everything over 18,000' MSL (above Mean Sea Level). You need special equipment, pilot certifications, and must be on an instrument flight plan. It extends 12 nautical miles (nm) beyond shore and is *not* depicted on charts. Think "A for Above."

Class B

Class B airspace surrounds the biggest airports. Layered like an upside down wedding cake, it's marked with solid blue lines and tops out around 10,000' MSL. We can fly below the layers (shelves), but so too can everyone else—expect a lot of traffic and fly well below the bottoms. Think "B for Big & Blue."

Permission is definitely required and will be difficult to get. You must maintain Clear of Clouds (CoC) and 3 miles visibility.

You *can* fly above it, but jets will be commonly be accelerating past 300 mph.

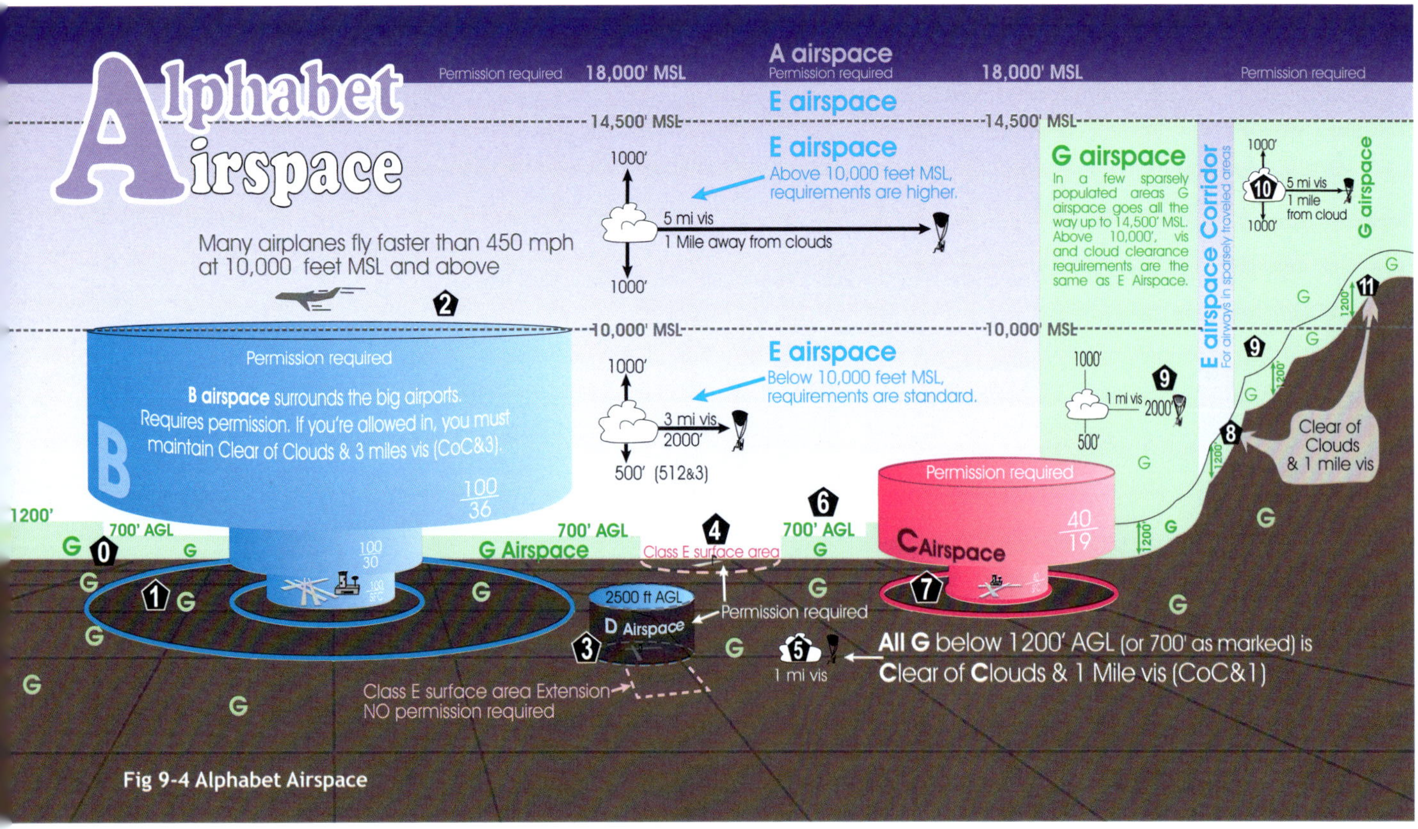

Fig 9-4 Alphabet Airspace

Class C ⊙

C airspace is a mini version of B with less traffic. There is still plenty of airline, business, and private airplane flying. It's marked on charts with solid magenta lines.

It typically extends 10 nautical miles (nm) from the airport and goes up about 4000' AGL. Think "C for Commuter Airlines."

Permission is required and will be hard to get. It requires **512 & 3** (Fig 9-5).

Class D ◌

D airspace surrounds virtually all airports with an operating control tower, typically extending 4 nm out and rising 2500 feet above the airport's center. If the control tower is not operating then it usually reverts to G Airspace.

Permission is required but can be had relatively easy and *may* be possible using a phone call without having an aircraft radio.

Class E

Class E airspace is everything else. It sits on top of G nearly everywhere. Think "E is everywhere," which is mostly true—the vast volume of available airspace is Class E, and no permission is required. The floor of E normally starts at 1200' AGL, dropping to 700' near bigger airports as a *Transition Area* (▮ Fig 9-3). In a few places, E drops to the surface (Fig 9-10), which we'll cover shortly.

Minimums are 512 & 3 (Fig 9-5).

Class G

As we've covered, Class G airspace goes from the ground up to some overlying airspace, usually Class E at 1200' (or 700') AGL. It is the least restrictive and only requires CoC & 1. It's also the only airspace where we can fly before sunrise or after sunset (see Fig 8-4).

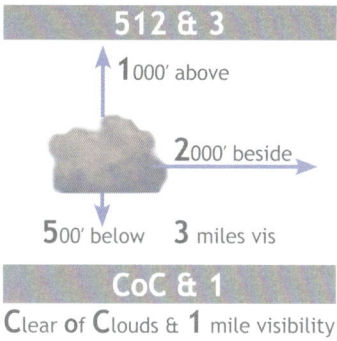

Fig 9-5 Clouds & Visibility

Atlanta Example Airspace

Fig 9-6 Class G airspace starts at the ground over most of this map—all but the red areas in Fig 9-7. Class E airspace is above that. Vignetted lines (highlighted here) show where E drops from 1200' to 700' AGL. There *are* places out west where G goes up to 14,500' MSL.

Fig 9-7 Even around Atlanta's **B airspace** we can launch from anywhere but the red areas, provided we mind other FARs like avoiding congested areas. We've added red: 1) where B drops to the surface, 2) D airspace, and 3) one airport where E goes to the surface.

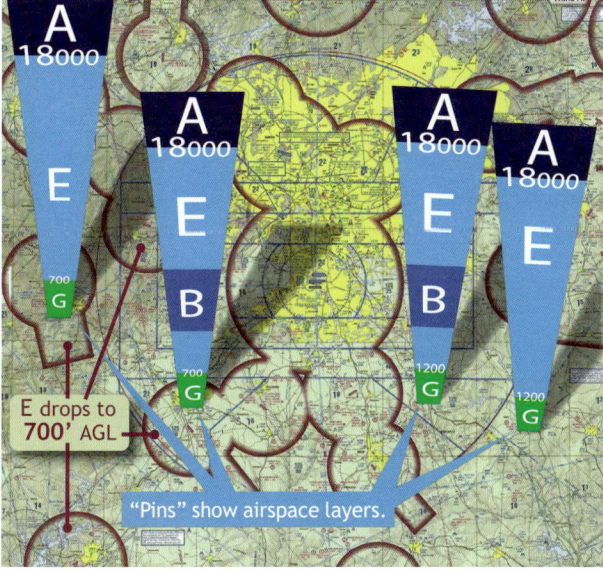

Fig 9-6 Atlanta Terminal Area Chart (TAC)

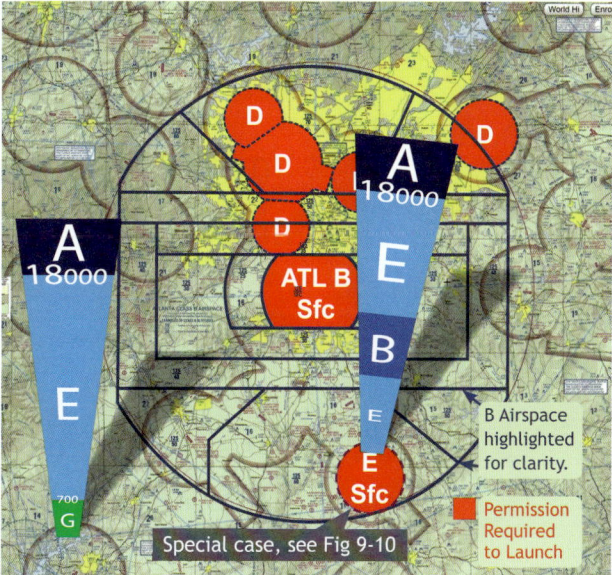

Fig 9-7 Class E Floor and airspace requiring permission (red)

Fig 9-8 3D Chicagoland B & C

O'Hare International (ORD) is Chicago's big airport with runways outlined in blue. Its rings of Class B airspace radiate outward with increasingly higher bottoms as shown in this cutaway. We can't fly within the center ring but *can* legally fly below the outer layers, or *shelves*. Finding enough uncongested area will be a far bigger problem.

Midway (MDW), Chicago's 2nd busiest airport, sports the smaller Class C airspace. Like O'Hare, you can't launch in the center, but you can launch under the outer ring. It happens to be the same floor as O'Hare's first ring, 1900' MSL.

However, these areas will be extremely congested with air traffic operating below the main airspace. If you do find a field, stay less than 500 feet AGL to avoid most air traffic (expect helicopters).

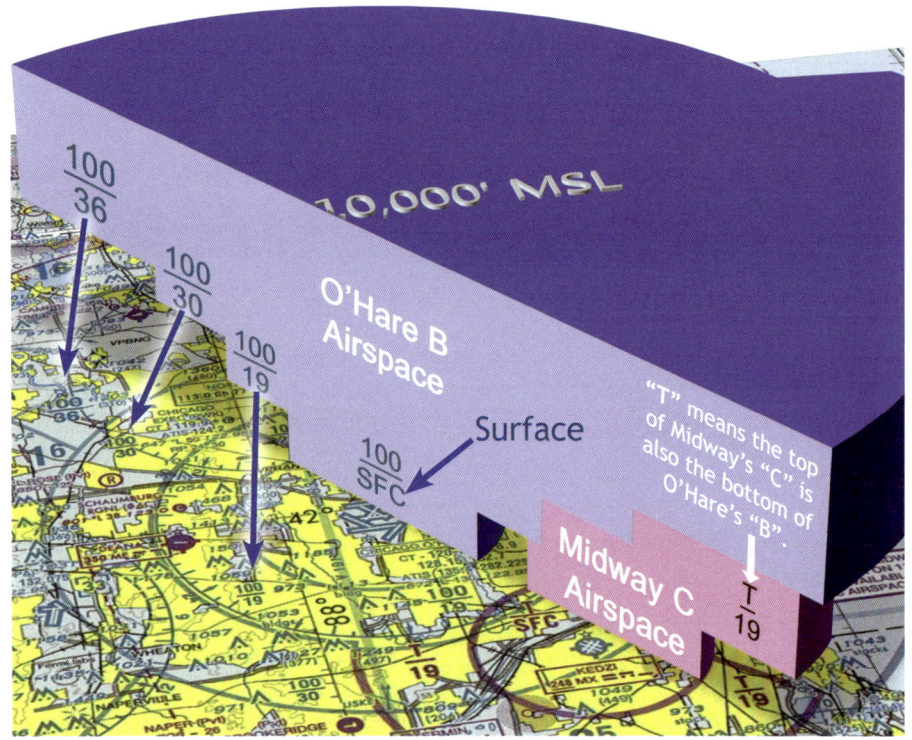

Class E Surface Area

A few moderately busy airports have no G airspace, but rather class E starts right from the surface. These are FAR 103.17's "Surface area of Class E Airspace *Designated for an Airport*" (Fig 9-10). Another surface area is *Designated as an Extension* (Fig 9-11), usually extending from control tower airports. We only need permission to fly in the airport version (Fig 9-10) but ***not*** the extensions (Fig 9-11).

Visibility and cloud clearance minimums are the same as other Class E: 512 & 3.

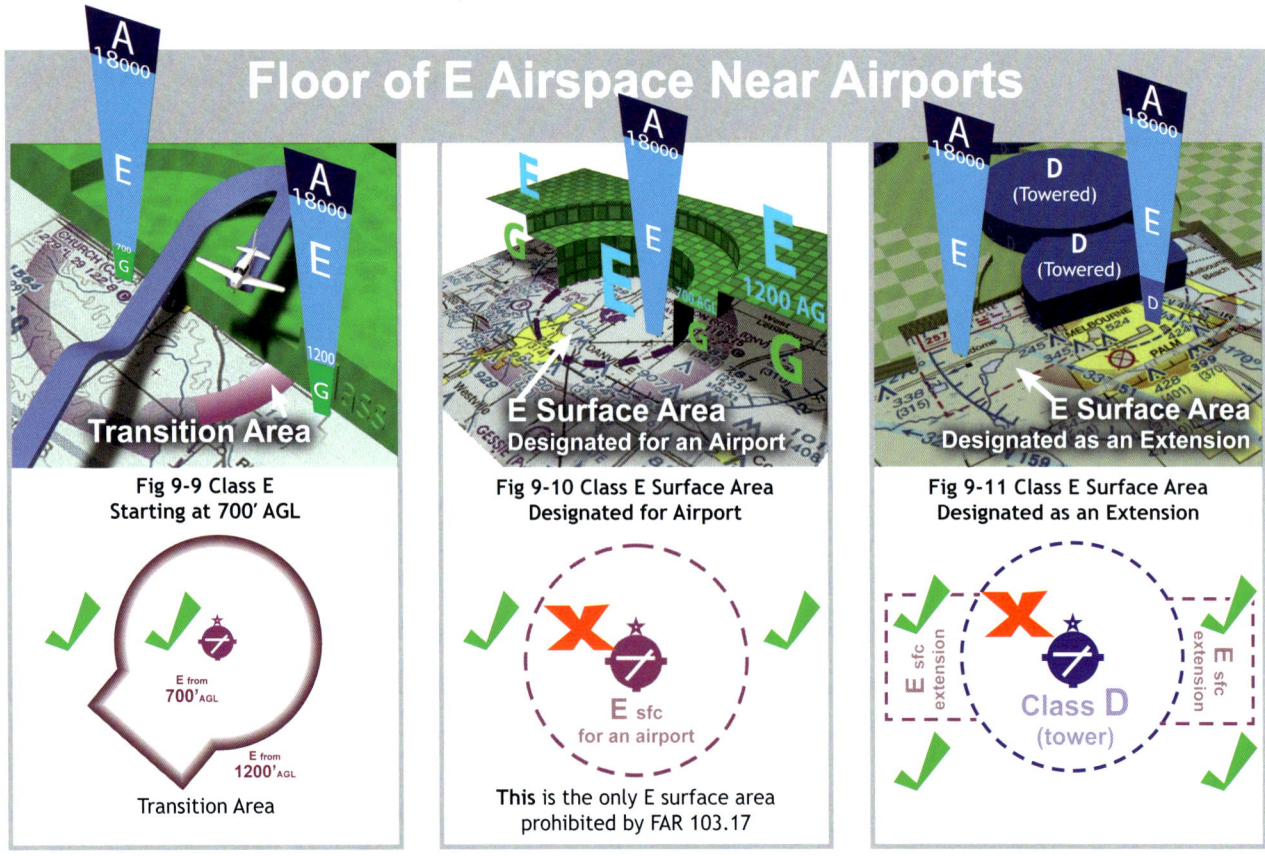

Fig 9-9 Class E Starting at 700' AGL

Fig 9-10 Class E Surface Area Designated for Airport

Fig 9-11 Class E Surface Area Designated as an Extension

Security Airspace

Most military airspace is off-limits to us while it's active. There is frequently a limited time or altitude range. Some of it doesn't *exclude* us, but warns of "incompatible" activity.

Air Defense Identification Zones (ADIZ) and Flight Restricted Zones (FRZ) protect national borders, capital cities (including the U.S.), and a few other extremely sensitive sites. Penetrating one could get you shot at.

Visual and Instrument military routes (VR and IR) depict courses the military uses for practice and transit. We should minimize our time in them. Military aircraft have no speed limit, and their radar isn't optimized to pick up paramotorists.

Prohibited and **Restricted** areas keep airspace closed during certain published times as depicted on sectional charts. Times vary but you can call Flight Service to find out their "hot" (active) times.

Alert areas, **Controlled Firing areas,** and **MOA's** do not *prohibit* flight; rather they serve as a warning about military operations. Pilots should "look out." Some military training involves low-altitude "nap-of-the-earth" flying where they follow the terrain, staying below a couple hundred feet AGL. And where do we fly? Yeah, a good area to avoid.

Temporary Flight Restrictions (TFRs) are put up anywhere government agencies deem them necessary. Some have been up for years while others pop up whenever the president or his people appear and may appear with no warning. More on notification about these events (NOTAMs) shortly.

Large Public Events

Regulations and TFR's prohibit flying near large gatherings like sporting events, conventions, and others. Some facilities that might be considered terrorist targets are off limits. Even when there are no specific restrictions, charted notes may admonishes pilots not to "loiter" at sensitive sites. Doing so may garner a special reception, possibly by helicopter, at your return.

Knowing the rules is important, but so is common sense. If an area looks like it might be considered sensitive from a security perspective, either find out first or avoid it altogether. Put yourself in the protector's shoes.

Wilderness Areas

Many public parks, like the Grand Canyon, have areas preserved for their natural, quiet separation from civilization. Some are protected by special rules prohibiting launch and even overflight. In most cases, these areas are not strictly prohibited but pilots are "requested" to stay at least 2000' above anything within 1000' of the flight path.

Flying in national parks is prohibited and it's a pretty big deal—violations could land you in jail with big fines and confiscated gear.

Wilderness areas are indicated by a blue dotted line. Some, like the Grand Canyon, have special restrictions outlined in Special Federal Aviation Regulations (SFARs). Others are covered in Notices To Airman (NOTAMs). Before flying a popular park or famous site, contact the FSS and ask if they know of any restrictions. There may also be local restrictions—check with Park administrators. Ask about overflight rules too.

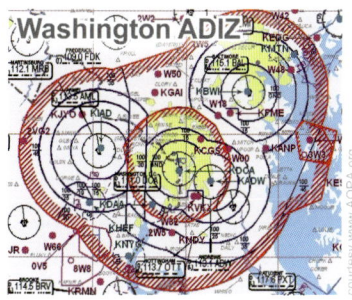

Fig 9-12 Getting TFR's
Several websites offer Temporary Flight Restrictions (TFRs) maps. But the most reliable source is a "Flight Service Station (FSS) Briefing" on page 83. An added benefit is that you're on record as having checked.

Fig 9-13 Wilderness & Restricted
Ocotillo Airport (magenta arrow) is in a charted wilderness area (dotted blue line) which means the 2000' AGL minimum "request" applies there. Don't take this lightly, they can issue expensive fines for violating noise ordinances or disturbing habitat.

Restricted (no fly) areas are just a few miles Southeast. R-2510A covers both north and south areas, going from the surface to 15,000' MSL. R-2510B sits atop the northern half of R-2510A, going from 15,000' up to 40,000—not a factor.

The magenta Kane West MOA outlines a Military Operating Area that we can fly in but at elevated risk.

Details are in the LAX chart margin.

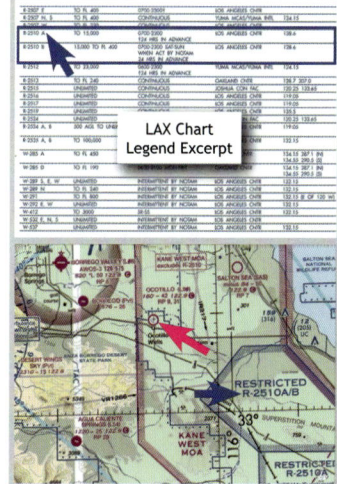

The Nautical Mile (nm)

Aviation's standard measure of distance is the nautical mile (nm). It is 1 minute of one degree of the earth's 360° circumference. There are 60 minutes in 1 degree.

Nautical miles are the tic marks on Sectional Chart's vertical lines (of longitude). Charts also have a scale at the bottom (online versions have this as well). For reference, 1 nm = 1.15 statute (regular) miles.

Fig 9-14 Radials

The concept of radials, or degrees from a point, is central to aviation—providing both course and location information. In the compass rose at right, 3 means 30° relative to magnetic North, 6 is 60° and so on. The 43° radial is depicted in red. When combined with distance, a point can be marked on charts.

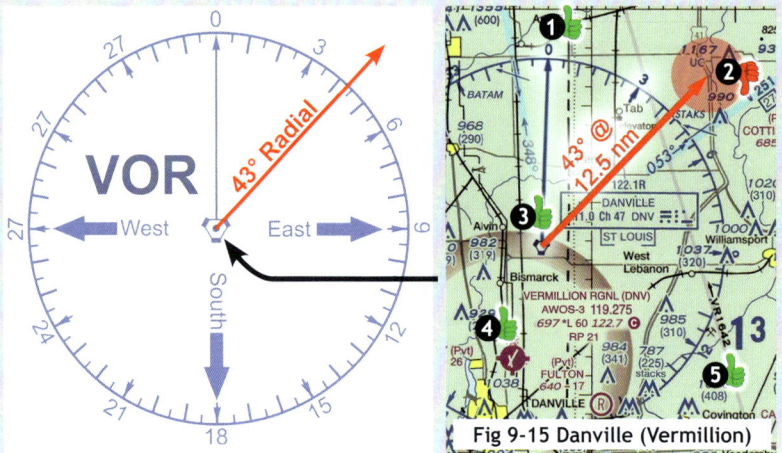

Fig 9-15 Danville (Vermillion)

Fig 9-16 Special FAR Airspace

In order to fly in this white airspace area you must comply with the charted instructions. Only the areas that start from the surface are off limits for launching.

Transponder

Nearly all aircraft use an *ADS-B transponder* which is required above 10,000' MSL and within 30 nm of big airports. It reports location, identification, and altitude for collision avoidance.

The page at this link shows possible portable transponders for paramotor pilots.

NOTAMs

When airspace is closed for dignitaries, disasters, military needs, rocket launches, etc., the FAA issues Notices to Airmen (NOTAMs) with Temporary Flight Restrictions. It could be for a small area or the entire country.

Locations are usually defined by the distance and direction (radial, see Fig 9-14) from some navigation aid (navaids). Radius describes how big the area is. Get NOTAM's from FSS like a weather briefing ("Flight Service Station (FSS) Briefing" on page 83). If not offered, ask for any pertinent NOTAMs in the area.

For example, a fuel truck explodes on the highway northeast of Danville, IL (Fig 9-15). FAA officials close the overlying airspace by issuing a NOTAM—prohibiting overflight below 2000 ft and within 2nm of the DNV 043 at 12.5nm. The closed TFR area is shaded red for clarity. It is expected that once receiving this NOTAM, you will get your chart (or computer or phone) and plot it out.

NOTAMs also alert pilots about unusual activity, usually near airports, including paramotor events. Event organizers should file a NOTAM if their gathering is at or near airports. The QR linked page shows how to file.

Special FAR Airspace

Some areas of the country have airspace that doesn't fall into regular Classes, so they use special FAR's like Fig 9-16. It's structured much like Class B airspace in that there are altitude layers or shelves. Check any special inset instructions.

Like with Class B, only parts of it goes to the surface, elsewhere you can fly below it.

Visibility & Cloud Clearance

Remember, we *always* need to maintain at least clear of clouds and 1 mile visibility (CoC & 1). We may need more, but never less. That low minimum is primarily in G airspace below 1200' AGL (see Fig 9-3). Up higher it's more, which makes sense given that fast airplanes are eating 440 feet *every second*. At a half-mile away, that's 6 seconds to impact—precious little time to recognize the threat and actually get out of the way in time. Realistically, it's too late. Better visibility allows more time for you or the airplane pilot to see and avoid.

Fig 9-17 Don't be the Bug

Jets commonly cover 400+ feet in 1 second. From 800 feet away you're a pretty small target *if* they're even looking. They'd have 2 seconds to recognize a threat, determine an action, and react—not likely.

Chapter 9: Airspace Page 97

Below 10,000 feet MSL, airplanes are limited to 288 mph but have no limit above that. No wonder minimums are higher yet up there. Jets commonly exceed 400 mph, and they punch right through those nice looking cumulus clouds. That's why the *horizontal* cloud clearance is a mile, and visibility required is 5 miles. Even with that, a jet popping out of a cloud from a full mile away is only 9 seconds from impact.

More on Reading The Charts

Charts depict our world. A legend panel shows the basics, but full detail lives in the downloadable *Aeronautical Chart User's Guide*.

G and E Airspace on Sectionals

Reference Fig 9-15. In this exercise we consider launching near Danville Airport—DNV. Its details are in the Digital Chart Supplements (formally the Airport Facilities Directory). There is a TFR, created by NOTAM, restricting flight for the firefighting situation mentioned under NOTAMs (previous page).

All the spots ❶ are in G airspace up to 1200' AGL except ❹, which is inside Vermillion's transition area, so it's G up to 700' with E above. Only spot ❷ can*not* be launched from since it's in the TFR. The TFR is defined off the Danville VOR as the 43°radial at 12.5 nm.

Fig 9-21 shows what the airplane pattern would look like if planes were using runway 3 (taking off and landing to the NE). Visualizing these patterns helps us steer clear.

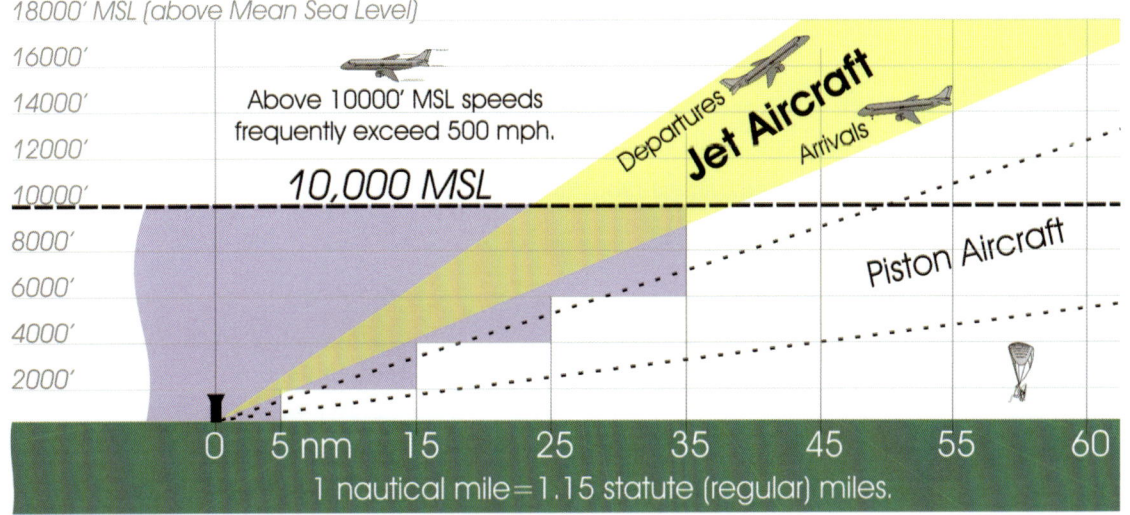

Fig 9-19 Airplane Vertical Paths

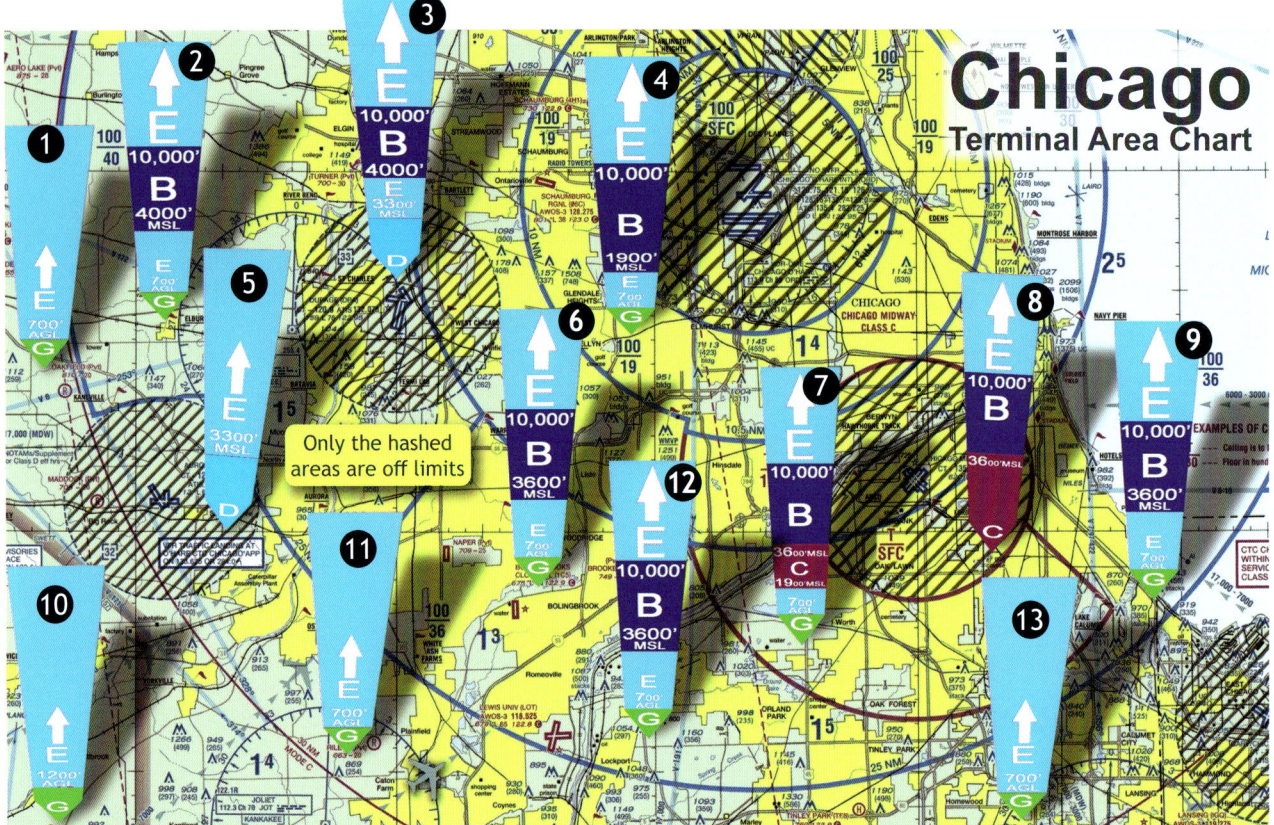

Fig 9-20 Chicago: Can I Fly Here?

It's surprising how much of the *airspace* is available for launching: only the hashed areas (added) are off limits.

Markers show what airspace you'd be launching in, and what's above. As expected, you mostly launch in G and climb into E above. In fact, except near ❿, where E starts at 1200′ AGL, the entire area is G up to only 700′ AGL.

❸ & ❺ are inside Class D airspace—airports with towers. Even if you have a radio, the airport must be reporting 3 miles visibility. If the rotating beacon is on and its daylight, it means the visibility is too low. The field is "IFR" (requires Instrument Flight Rules).

Airspace-wise you could fly above the Class D's (tops are 3200′ MSL at ARR and 3000′ at DPA) without talking to anybody but that might violate FAR 103.13b by creating a collision hazard. Then there's surviving. Above DPA (❸) you must remain below ORD's class B at 4000′.

❹ It's *legal* to fly here if you find a big-enough park to stay within, and stay below 1900′ MSL, but talk about traffic. Lots of northbound airplanes are skirting O'Hare's B airspace here.

❻ This is prime flying and ultralights do fly at that little airport.

❼ You're good up to 1900′ MSL which starts Midway's C airspace.

❽ You'd be launching in MDW airport's C airspace (permission will be hard to get). The "T" in T/SFC means the top of Midway's C airspace is the base of ORD's B.

❾ & ⓬ You're good up to ORD's B at 3600′ MSL.

⓫ & ⓭ You're good up to 18,000′ MSL. These are just inside the "Mode C" ring (*veil*) which doesn't apply to us. It's also just north of the Joliet VOR and a published arrival route (✈).

Avoiding Aircraft Flight Paths

Air traffic gets concentrated around predictable vertical and horizontal paths (Fig 9-19). Jets depart steeply but arrive shallow—about 300 feet per mile from the airport or about 3 miles per 1000′ of altitude loss, shallower for piston-powered planes.

So 10 miles out, jets are roughly 3000′ above airport elevation. Fast aircraft spend more time at 10,000′ MSL since they must slow down before going lower. Controllers can vary these values dramatically.

Airports with paved runways show the approximate runway layout so you can visualize traffic patterns. By default, pattern turns are to the left (as shown), but if "RP 3" appears below the airport it means right turns (Right Pattern) are used for runway 3 (Fig 9-21). See also "Flying at or near Airports" on page 104.

If you're up where airplanes fly, consider that jet pilots may only have 7 seconds to notice you, recognize that you're a threat, figure out what to do, do it, and have the aircraft react. And pilots are definitely *not* always looking outside.

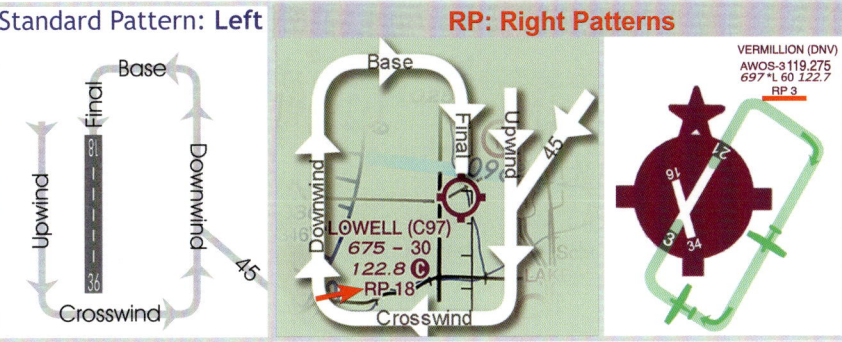

Fig 9-21 Left or Right Pattern?
The first illustration is a standard left pattern. Overlay it on the chart runway to visualize airplane traffic. Like us, they prefer landing into the wind. Left patterns are standard because most airplane pilots sit in the left seat.

The next two illustrations show right patterns like Lowell airport (middle). The open circle means its runway is not paved. RP 18 means a right pattern is used for runway 18.

Other Uses For the Charts

Charts show more than airspace. Here are some of the better bits that have proven useful, including some that might help find flying sites.

Topographical

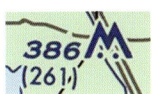

You can get elevation for airports and obstruction tops. When obstructions list AGL in parenthesis like at left, that can be subtracted to get elevation at the base. In this case, a pair of towers top out at 386' MSL and is 261' AGL. So the base is 386-262 or 125' elevation.

Contours give elevations in 500 foot (sometimes 250) increments—not terribly precise but good for general knowledge. You can generally estimate your height visually to within a couple hundred feet. Of course, if you used GPS to locate yourself on the chart, then it should also show your altitude within a few feet. The terrain feature of Google Maps can serve a similar purpose.

Finding Sites

Ultralight strips and *some* soaring schools will usually tolerate us. Small, and/or private airports may be welcoming, too, so it's worth asking. Same with sky diving airports which are used to seeing canopies, although they don't usually go back up. Skydiving airports are marked by a ▽, while sailplane, hang glider, and ultralight sites have a symbol with a letter. They use G for regular gliders (sailplanes), H for hang gliders, and U for ultralight strips. Sadly, there's no paraglider symbol.

Airports that accept federal Airport Improvement funds include "grant assurances," which among other things, obligate them to welcome *all* aviation. But there are loopholes. See "Grant Assurance Airports" on page 105.

Fig 9-22 South Mountain
Reporting point: this concentrates airplane traffic nearby.

B airspace goes from 5000' to 9000' MSL

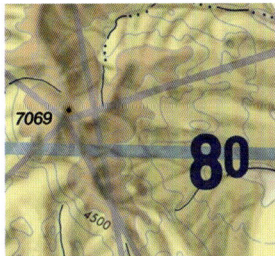

Fig 9-23 Elevation Contours
Contour lines can be useful for knowing what the terrain is like. They're usually in 500' increments. The 80 is a maximum elevation figure for the area (8000' MSL) and peaks are sometimes shown.

Fig 9-24 Mine
This old copper mine doesn't look like much on the chart, but it's a gaping hole in real life. Using online mapping tools can help relate chart features with reality, but that may diminish the fun of individual discovery.

Not all seemingly obvious features are marked on charts, and some charted features are nearly indistinguishable from the air. Plus, accuracy is well below 100% since ground features change faster than charting gnomes can update.

Things Look Different out West

Refer to Fig 9-26. Notice the brown colors. Those depict higher elevations as per the chart at right, not surface appearance.

You'll also find some rare G airspace poking above 1200' AGL, up to its maximum of 14,500' MSL (blue vignetted line around ❶). You still need a mile and clear of clouds to launch but can legally (albeit unwisely) have that visibility up to 10,000' MSL. Cloud clearances remain 5,1,2 (Fig 9-5).

❷ is another rare area where the G goes above 1200' AGL, in this case to 12,000' MSL. But this type of airspace has mostly vanished, and is no longer found at the sites shown. Instead, G goes up to 1200' AGL like over most of the country.

❸ is the surface area of E designated for an airport as indicated by the dashed magenta lines (Fig 9-10). You need permission to launch here and must have 5,1,2 & 3.

❹'s are in the transition area (Fig 9-9) where G goes up to only 700' AGL.

❺ is a rare case of G all the way up to 14,500' MSL. As with everywhere else on this excerpt, E goes from there up to the A above at 18,000' MSL.

You can launch almost anywhere here without airspace permission and need only a mile visibility to start. This allows visualization of the boundary between G and E. We need a mile and clear of clouds in G, with more when climbing into E just like everywhere else.

Chart colors are different out here to reflect the terrain, too. See Fig 9-25. Each chart has its own scale. If you look at charts online (SkyVector.com) they have a seamless product where you don't even see boundaries, although the stitching process can cover up needed text. In that case, select the individual charts.

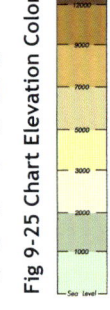

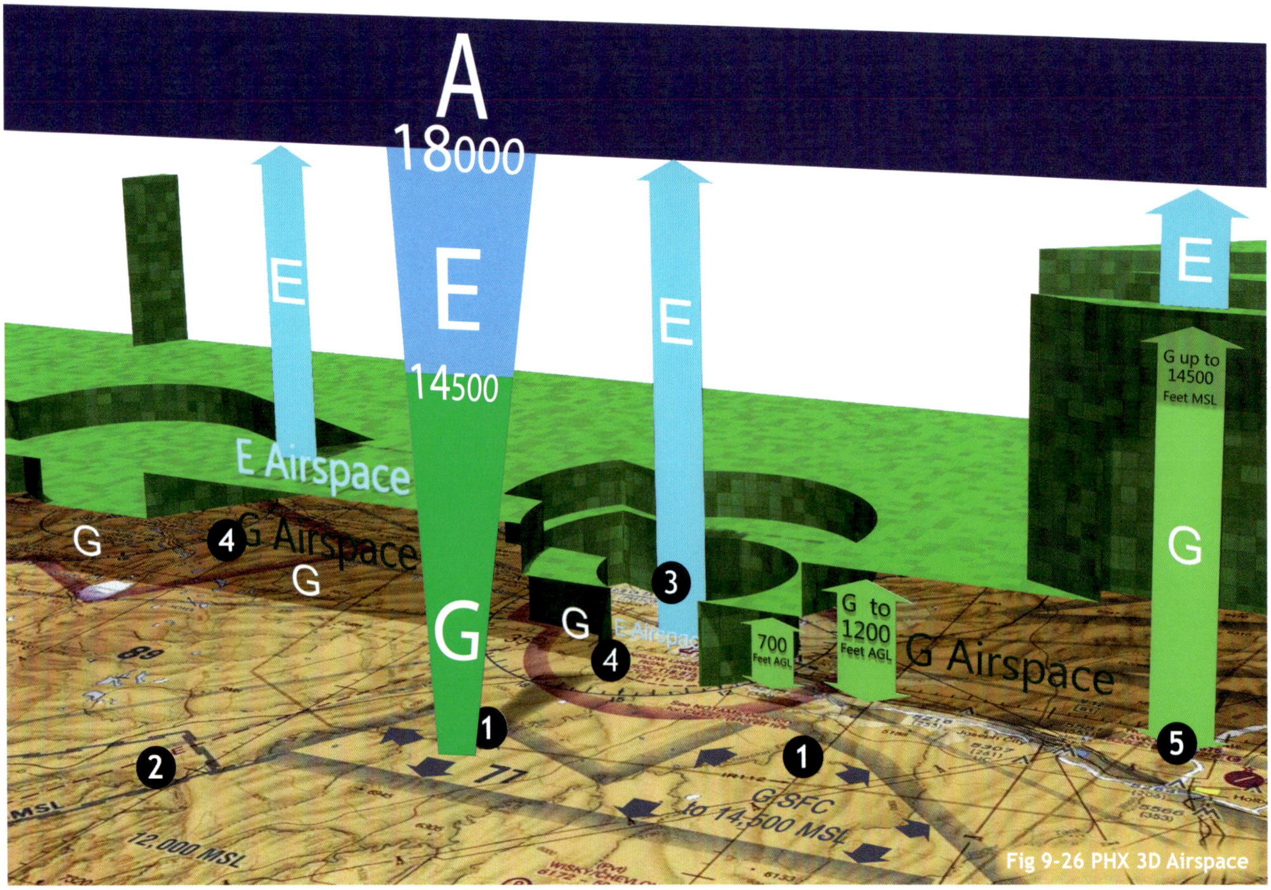

Fig 9-25 Chart Elevation Colors

Airspace and rules are always changing, for the latest, to Footflyer.com Chapter 9.

Fig 9-26 PHX 3D Airspace

Flying From Anywhere

CHAPTER 10

What a treat—running aloft from such unlikely locales, then setting off for parts unseen. This awesome capability does add some challenge and risk.

Being *able* to launch from anywhere doesn't mean that you *should*. Both safety and permission can be showstoppers. There's nothing worse than being all suited up, motor idling, A's in hand, only to have someone come up shaking their finger at you.

These basic tips are intended to help improve success and prevent catastrophe.

Any prospective site should 1) be in legal airspace, 2) match your skill, and 3) be legal to launch from. Don't trample crops, climb fences, or ignore "No Trespassing" signs. Public property, especially state or federal lands, usually prohibit any kind of flying. Parks are notoriously difficult because they frequently have specific prohibitions and the staff to enforce them.

Needing to maintain an emergency landing option puts many forested and swampy areas out of reach. Even there, though, if you can find a sufficient clearing, it's fun to launch and circle up high to check things out. Many otherwise boring views expand into gorgeous panoramas with a bit of altitude.

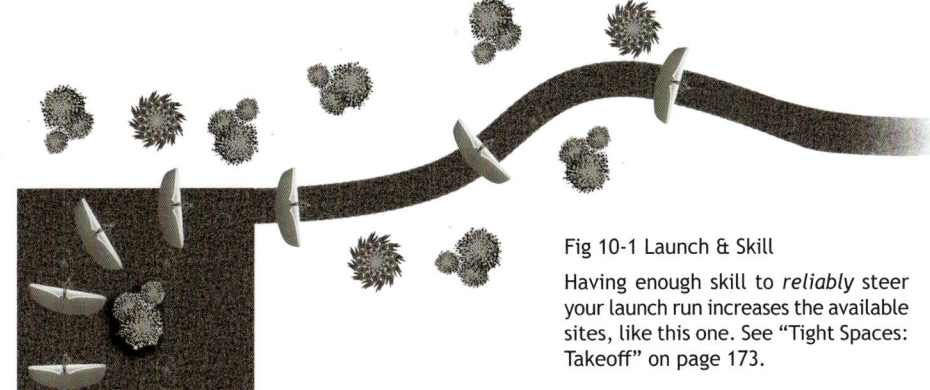

Fig 10-1 Launch & Skill

Having enough skill to *reliably* steer your launch run increases the available sites, like this one. See "Tight Spaces: Takeoff" on page 173.

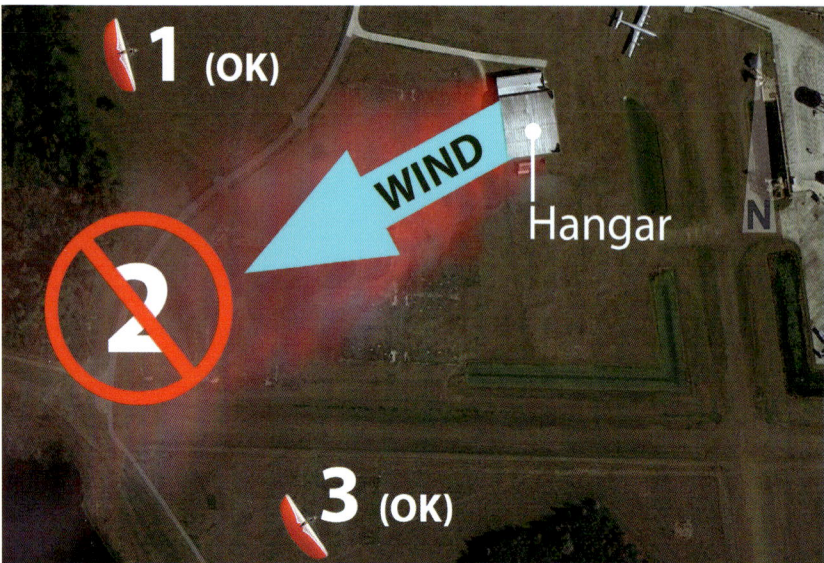

Fig 10-2 Appropriate Sites

If we could see the wind it might look like this. Air burbles over buildings and upwind of obstructions in ways that make launching difficult at best. Besides having enough room for your skill level, avoid areas like this. Consider what the winds will be like on your return. Use Google Earth's measuring tool to determine dimensions.

As skills improve enough to accurately and consistently steer the launch, options open way up. For example, you can consider long, narrow spaces like in Fig 10-1.

Fig 10-3 Surface & Size

Surfaces can be deceiving. Walk the launch area to make sure there is traction and support. This surface (above) hid quicksand.

This green patch looked good from the ground but the pilot nearly impaled himself on a fence post. Pace it off, then be conservative.

Choosing the Site

A top indicator of success and survival is choosing appropriate sites to fly from.

Size Matters

Bigger is, in fact, always better. Depending on your skills and conditions, a congested site with trees or wires can be deadly. Those early, unsupervised flights require *much* more space. For one thing, you probably have little experience telling field size, knowing climb angle, etc. Another factor is climb technique—newer pilots should only accept fields that allow a straight-out climb for the first 100 feet of altitude.

A smooth, flat 500' x 500' takeoff area, inside an obstruction-free 1200' x 1200' area, is generally good for newer pilots. If there's water nearby, make sure your paramotor has automatic flotation.

That seems large, but in still air, distance goes by *quickly*. Past incidents have shown that new pilots need more than they think. And don't be fooled by training experiences where you got airborne in a hundred feet—launch distances can triple under hot, high (altitude), or calm conditions, and it's easy to underestimate requirements.

One way to size up a field is to pace it off. Find your stride's length by walking a known distance then dividing that by your footsteps. Even easier is using the mileage ruler in Google Earth, which also allows seeing the surrounding terrain, and in some areas, obstructions.

Don't guess—wires, trees, and buildings are unforgiving, and distance is hard to judge. When in doubt, pace it out.

A small field is OK *if* the obstructions are soft enough to plow through when things go awry (beans, wheat, tall grass, etc.) As directional control skill improves, you can decrease field sizes, especially width, to the point where launching on a road, even in a crosswind, is doable. Even with good control, though, be leery of mechanical turbulence, mentioned below.

A skilled pilot can launch from anywhere that's long enough to get airborne and circle over. That will also be big enough to land in if the motor quits. Beware that wind can render small, obstructed sites dangerous at *any* skill level.

Mechanical Turbulence and Obstructions

Airflow around obstructions creates mechanical turbulence downstream.

Some locations work well for some wind directions. In Fig 10-2, launching at 1 or 3 is OK but not 2. With less than about 5 mph wind, the turbulence will be present but probably manageable. But if the wind picks up, as it tends to after sunrise, it could get nasty. Consider the forecast for your return.

As wind increases, turbulence will extend many times the obstruction's height. At 10 MPH, for example, it extends at least 4 to 10 times the obstruction's height depending on shape.

Mechanical turbulence has caused large collapses or altitude loss at the worst possible time (while flying low). Wind shadow, the calm area just behind an obstruction, must also be avoided. Here's more: "Mechanical Turbulence and Rotor" on page 81.

On Patterns

By default, use whatever pattern you're most familiar with (Fig 5-23 on page 66 for the basics), but other factors come into play at unfamiliar sites.

- Favor a headwind on base leg (Fig 10-4) to make judging the turn to final easier. It also decreases the amount of turn, and the chance of pulling too much brake.

- Be extra vigilant for wires, including a before-launch check, and don't fly a pattern that requires overflight at lowish altitudes. Wires feed on paramotor pilots and prefer them slightly singed.

- Unless you're coming in power-off, don't fly near people or houses.

Slope and Surface

In still air, launching downhill is always best. You can run faster *and* will have more lift from upward relative airflow. Downhill *landings* aren't so good since the ground falling away makes you go long. But landing *up*hill is worse, with the potential for a hard impact due to both the upslope and sinking air if wind is coming down the hill. In either case, consider landing cross-hill (and crosswind) instead.

Smooth surfaces are better than rough ones. In fact, tall grass, soft sand, or a rutted surface can add so much leg drag as to prevent a launch (see "Leg Drag" on page 172). They also make tripping and falling more likely.

Fig 10-5 Takeoff Distance

Learn your takeoff distance by setting out four cones, 50 foot apart, in your launch direction. Then see how far it takes you to liftoff in nil wind.

Learn your circle radius by flying to a soccer field of known dimensions (they're not all the same) and seeing how far out of it you fly when circling. Google Earth is a good way to measure the soccer field size.

Fig 10-6 Climbout Angle

Know your climbout distance, too, if there are obstructions to climb over. 5 feet of gain per 100' of distance is a rough average for lower power motors.

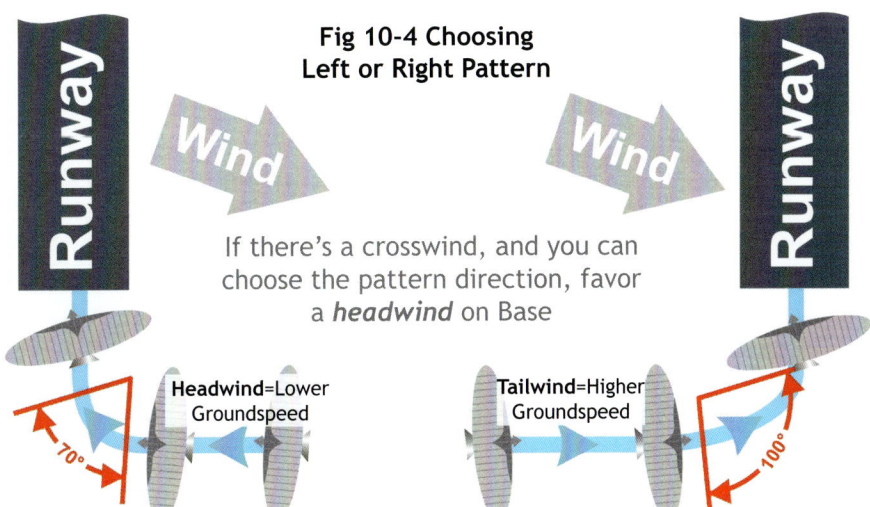

Fig 10-4 Choosing Left or Right Pattern

If there's a crosswind, and you can choose the pattern direction, favor a *headwind* on Base

Headwind=Lower Groundspeed

Tailwind=Higher Groundspeed

Fig 10-7 Roads

It doesn't look like much, but this dirt road got us airborne. We planned it so as to turn well before the highway. This entire area is landable leaving plentiful engine-out options.

Obviously, roads must be nearly abandoned, have no wires, and the pilot must be capable of steering during his run. That is an advanced skill that is well worth mastering.

Fig 10-8 Developments as Launch

Incomplete residential or commercial areas can be great sites. Play nice with neighbors and nobody gets chased away.

Site Permission

"It's better to beg forgiveness than to ask for permission" is a well-worn adage that gets us in trouble—permission is always preferable. Even if you think a particular site is OK, at least mind these guidelines:

- Never climb a fence or cross "No Trespassing" signs to get there.
- Never do any property damage, especially crops—damaging crops will upset the owner and his brother, the sheriff.
- If somebody lives on the property or has a presence, you must ask.
- Never use a park or other facility where known rules prohibit flying. Almost all state and federal parks prohibit launching aircraft and ultralights except at airports. You can probably use the airport. Parks have a minimum altitude to fly over. Don't quibble over who controls the airspace (probably another agency) since they can always get you for disturbing the animals.
- Don't linger. Launch and leave to minimize attention from neighbors and fly quietly (see *"Noise Abatement" on page 85*). Use low power to get away from people, then power up once clear of the area.
- Seek a local pilot or group. Learn their sites' rules and be courteous. Pilots tend to be protective of sites until they know you will respect the rules. We cover this more at "Finding Sites" on page 108.
- Check hunting times. If it's gun season then you risk encountering a "stray" bullet after disturbing someone's target. Hunters and paramotor pilots frequently like the same times of day. This is another reason for talking with locals.

High Elevation Fields

High elevation fields require longer runs and better climbout options. See "The Horror of Hot, High, and Humid" on page 171 for details and techniques.

Always have an "out" that allows for unexpectedly shallow climb, and doesn't require clearing obstructions or hills, especially wires.

Unless there is a decent wind, the launch surface must be pretty smooth. Ruts, tall growth, soft sand, or deep snow can keep you from generating the requisite speed. Roads out in the boondocks are good as long they don't have power lines or barbed wire fences. The barbs have proven particularly hard on canopies, and don't do much for skin, either. It's obviously bad form to leave your vehicle sticking out on the road.

Flying at or near Airports

Uncontrolled airports (no control tower) can be great sites if the airport manager is a normal human. Airports with control towers are usually too busy but *can* be used with the right equipment (see Chapter 11 on page 111).

General aviation (non-airline) uncontrolled airports normally sit in G airspace with E airspace 700 feet above. Functionally, that means you only need CoC & 1 (Fig 9-5).

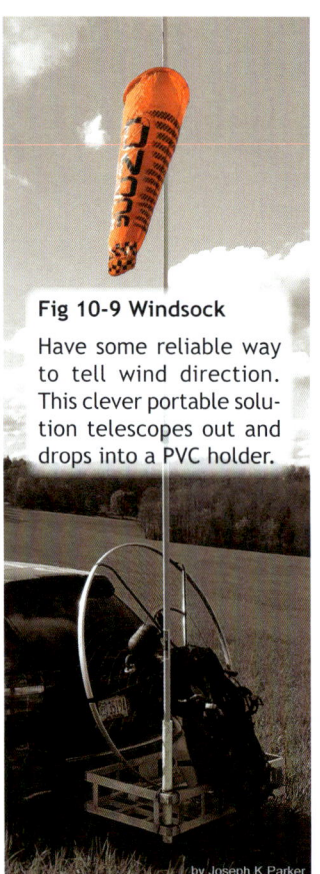

Fig 10-9 Windsock

Have some reliable way to tell wind direction. This clever portable solution telescopes out and drops into a PVC holder.

Grant Assurance Airports

A popular misconception is that airports accepting federal grant funds *have* to let us fly (Airport Grant Assurance #22). That's *almost* true. They can, and frequently do, prohibit us based on perceived safety issues even though that determination must come from FAA officials, *not* airport management. Still, they can impede access so much as to make it impractical for us. It pays to get along.

Many licensed pilots and airport managers are quick to condemn having us mix with their traffic. That's too bad since a conscientious PPG pilot (you, since you're taking the time to read this) adds less risk than a general aviation aircraft: we're slow, highly visible, and don't use their patterns. Another reason for the occasional cold-shoulder (and probably a big one) is our lack of financial contribution. Airplanes need airport hangars to rent and expensive fuel. Paramotor pilots, even if they do buy fuel, contribute almost nothing.

So it's hugely beneficial to get along with management and other users to show how easily we fit, and how our flying can have minimal impact on other operations. Explain our capabilities (to those willing to listen), then follow through with consistently responsible flying. Launch away from airplane traffic and remain clear of their patterns.

Don't become a collision hazard. Don't *look* like you're a collision hazard—if you must tear it up (full power turns, foot drags, acro, etc.), leave the airport area. Beyond complying with local and FAA rules, we must not annoy people, create a hazard, or even have the appearance of such. We can *fly* almost anywhere, launch sites are much harder to come by.

When planning regular operations from an airport, contact the airport manager to find out the best places to operate. Explain how you plan to avoid conflicts with existing users. Ask about gates, codes, areas to avoid, noise sensitive areas, and other location-specific needs, then comply with those requirements. You may be asked to rent a hangar or pay a fee to gain regular access.

Fig 10-10 Airport Patterns

It's best to avoid runways altogether, more for *perceived* risk to airplane operators than actual safety. But if crossing is needed, fly over the middle, a bit closer to the beginning, at 400' AGL like the depicted PPG. He takes off into the wind and climbs in a left turn before heading across.

Airplanes will typically be around 300 feet high for every mile away from the runway. Airport managers may (unwisely) ask us to be above pattern altitude before crossing the runways. They don't understand that doing so increases our exposure to other traffic by putting us up where more planes are.

Watch out for aircraft wakes that descend at about 500 feet per minute (fpm) and can linger up to 2 minutes.

Check out FAA Advisory Circular AC 90-66 for more on this. It explains that, among other things, ultralights should stay at least 500' below the published traffic pattern altitude which is normally 1000' AGL.

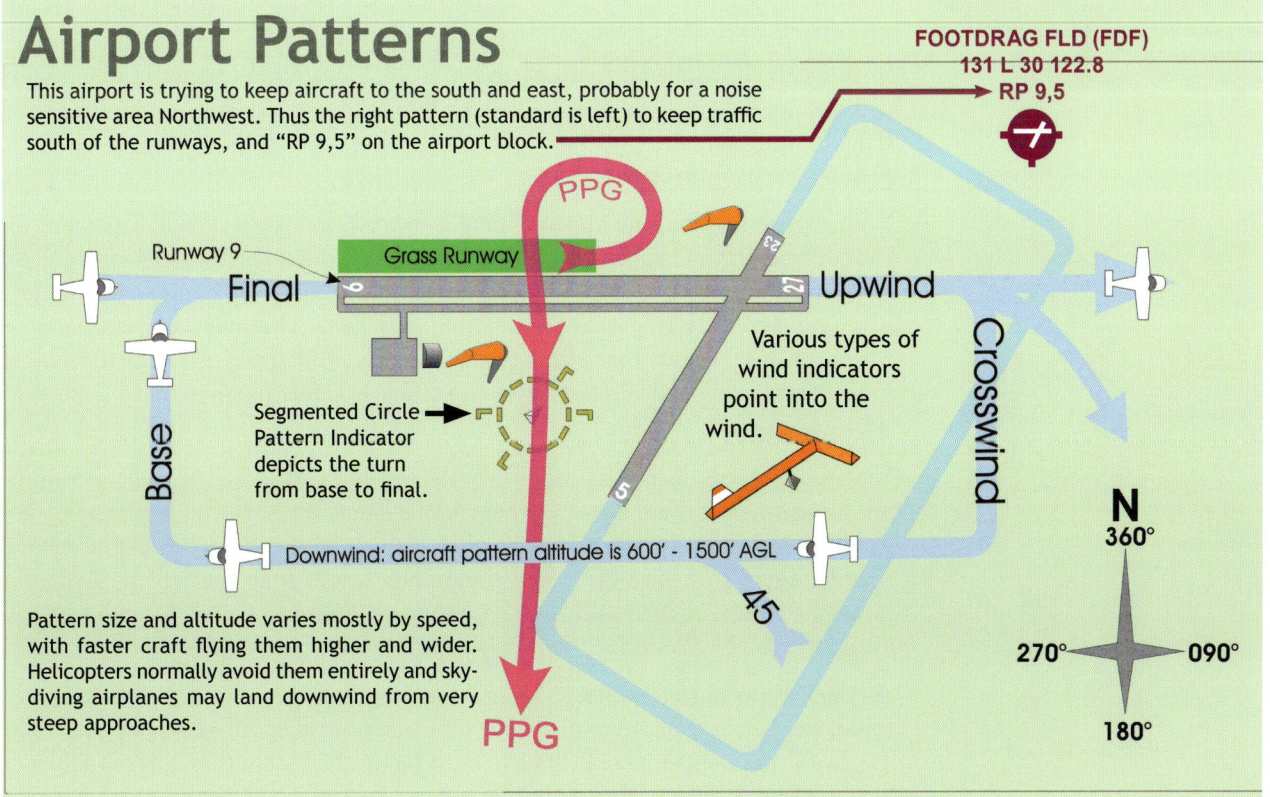

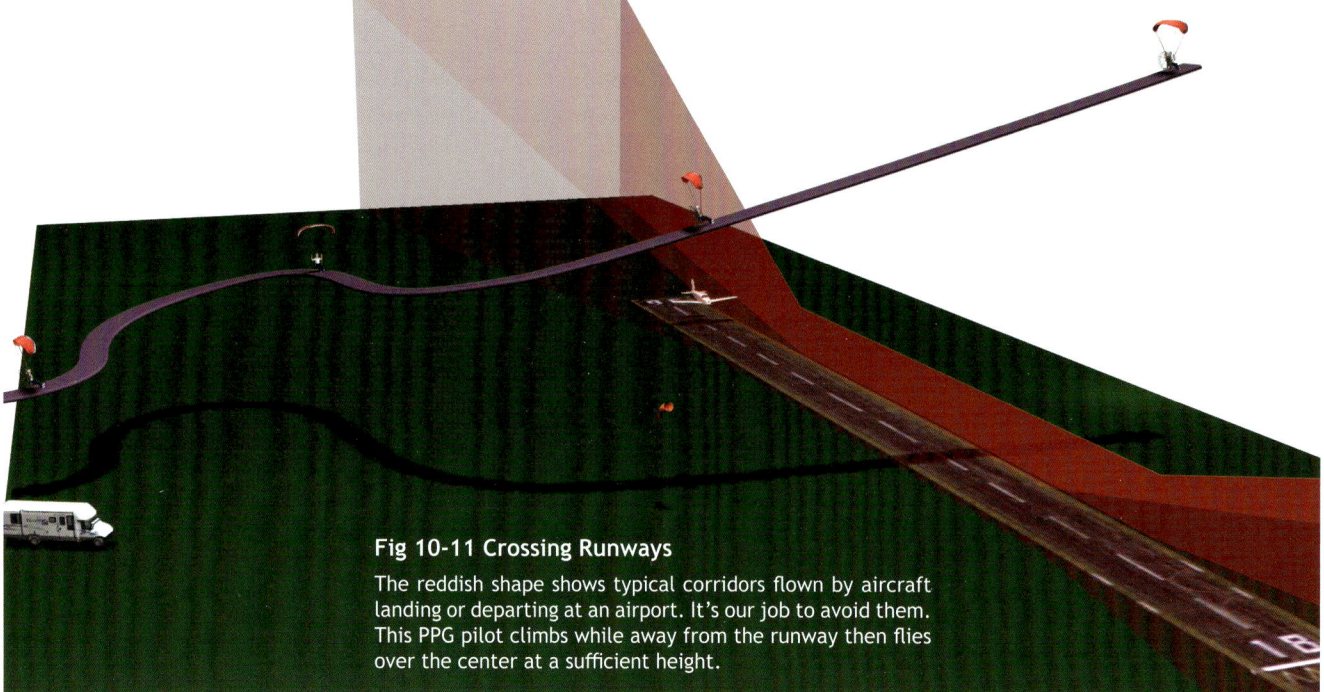

Fig 10-11 Crossing Runways
The reddish shape shows typical corridors flown by aircraft landing or departing at an airport. It's our job to avoid them. This PPG pilot climbs while away from the runway then flies over the center at a sufficient height.

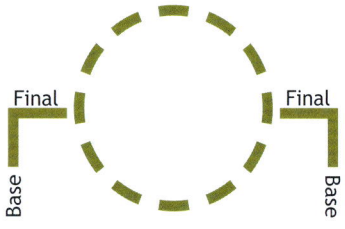

Fig 10-12 Segmented Circle
This airport has an east/west runway like in Fig 10-13. Downwind leg is south of the field.

About Runways & Patterns

Know where air traffic is in order to stay clear. Patterns are well defined but rarely get followed precisely.

Understand runway numbers—they indicate magnetic heading for aircraft taking off or landing with the ending "0" removed. So north is 360 (runway 36), east is 090 (runway 9), and so on. If the runway were aligned east/west, and winds were out of the west, aircraft would be taking off to the west (just like us) on runway 27. See Fig 10-13.

Standard traffic patterns are to the left—meaning turns are made to the left. Runway 27 in Fig 10-10 uses a left pattern and runway 9 uses a right pattern. When right patterns are used like the ones depicted, airports frequently have a *segmented circle* (Fig 10-12) to show the turn from base to final on each runway. If no indicator is present, left patterns apply.

Normal pattern altitude for airplanes ranges from 600 to 1500 feet AGL depending on aircraft type; jets and larger twins use the higher altitudes. Pattern size varies greatly based mostly on aircraft speed, with faster aircraft flying larger, higher patterns. Jets may fly downwind leg 2+ miles away from the runway while slower aircraft may be within a half-mile and other ultralights even closer. PPG patterns will be the closest to the runway (around 300 feet away and 200 to 400 feet high).

Airport Status

You must know the airport's status—whether portions are closed, special operations are going on, or if there are any other unique situations. Ask the airport manager if there is anything you should be aware of. If that's not possible, call Flight Service (See Chapter 7 on page 83). Tell them your name, that you will be flying an ultralight at airport such-and-such, your launch time and duration, and that you would like the NOTAMS.

Airplane pilots normally choose the runway based on wind but not always. Sometimes they'll do a long, straight-in final approach to a different runway even if it has a tailwind (for convenience). PPGers must be on the lookout for this—5 knots of tailwind isn't as big a deal to an airplane on a long runway.

How to Mesh

Now that you have the airport information and know where the patterns are, it's easy to stay out of the way.

Launch away from the runways and their departure/arrival corridors. Plan your flight path to avoid runways, their extended centerlines, and any buildings.

Be vigilant about noise sensitive areas. Noise complaints called in to airport management could shorten your welcome. Staying clear of congested areas (required anyway) will frequently suffice.

Unfortunately, some airport managers will unwisely ask you to fly around the end of the runway instead of crossing over (if needed). He's unwittingly putting you and air traffic at more risk, but if that happens, fly *well* away from its end, recognizing that airplanes on approach will be about 300 to 500 feet high for every mile from runway's end.

Wake Turbulence

All aircraft produce wake turbulence like in Fig 10-14, but it can be severe when generated by an airplane, or even worse, a slow-flying helicopter. A helicopter in cruise throws about the same wake as an airplane but, as it slows down, the wake turbulence worsens.

Plan your flight path to be above, or well beside, another aircraft. If you're following a ground track, be upwind since the turbulence sinks, spreads out, and drifts with the wind. It lasts up to two minutes, lingering longer in smooth air which is when we like to fly.

After Takeoff

When leaving the airport, it's best to stay well below aircraft traffic patterns. Four hundred feet below should suffice, but balance the need to keep a safe landing option open and avoiding wake turbulence. If overflying a runway is absolutely necessary, go over the center, slightly closer to the beginning (downwind end) at 400 feet AGL as shown in Fig 10-11. There is less likelihood an airplane will be flying there.

If climbout near the airport is necessary, do so away from any pattern in use. But realize that airplanes may overfly the airport from any direction, usually from pattern altitude, up to 500 feet above it. They do this to check things out before landing, a fairly common practice.

See and Be Seen

If you see an airplane that you suspect does not see you, turn. Not only will motion make you more visible, but the changing aspect on your wing will help as well. If you need to escape, the only thing a paramotor can do quickly is descend.

Keep a look out, especially when you're flying up where other air traffic may be. We have the best view in the world with nothing but a pair of risers between us and the visible planet—use it wisely.

Be Heard

If possible, have an aviation radio that can transmit and receive on the airport's frequency—Unicom or Common Traffic Advisory Frequency (CTAF). Even a receive-only radio would reveal where other radio-using traffic is. The airport frequency is on sectional charts like that pictured left. For Wickenburg airport, it's 123.0.

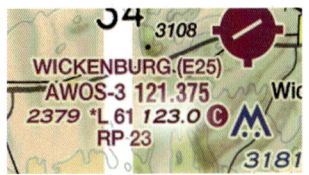

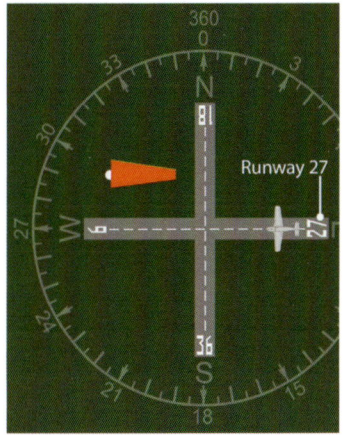

Fig 10-13 Runway Numbers

Runway numbers represent the heading on takeoff or landing. So taking off runway 27, as depicted here, means heading 270.

Fig 10-14 Wingtip Vortices

Wingtip vortices are dangerous little tornadoes spinning off aircraft that's producing lift. They are worse following heavy, slow, aerodynamically clean airplanes.

Between the vortices is sinking air.

Their full horror story is at "Tip Tornadoes" on page 226.

Fig 10-15 Facebook Group

This is a well-managed international online paramotor group. Discussions vary widely, but volunteers keep things pretty civil.

facebook.com/groups/paramotor

Keep any talk to a minimum but be listening for other traffic. When you're ready to go (if able to transmit), announce your intentions, "Powered Paraglider 1, just south of runway 5 approach, launching northeast then turning south, remaining south of the airport."

Represent Us Well

We are ambassadors—make us look good. Future access and continued welcome depend on it.

Finding Sites

It's strange that you sometimes have to go near cities to find launch sites. We don't want to be in the city, but near its perimeter, the humans are frequently building things. Before they build, they clear—opening up land that is frequently usable. Many industrial areas have a long way to go before build-out, and in the meantime, they tend to keep it nicely mowed for potential customers, which is perfect for us.

Private farms with a co-located home can be good too, given their frequently launchable grass areas and agreeable owners.

Finding Others

By far, the best way to find sites is to get with a local group who may already be there. What we do is so unique it's easy to make friends who share the passion.

Start by asking your instructor who may know a local in your area. Go online to see if there's a local group. Facebook groups is one source—search for the nearest big city. If there's a group, ask there. If not, go onto a broader group (see the QR link).

You'll get better results by pointing out that you respect sites, follow local rules, and work with people on preserving sites. If they worry that you'll be a loose cannon, they'll be less likely to share. You would be protective of your personal site, too.

Most of us are pretty trusting, but that trust can be erased through bad behavior. Buzz a site's annoyable neighbor and don't expect to be invited back.

PPG Schools are another resource. They obviously have sites where they train, and may allow others to fly there provided those others respect the site and its surroundings. Not surprisingly, these schools may require a membership, or some form of payment from those who didn't train with them.

It seems like every site has at least one unhappy, fun-stomping, noise-hating neighbor. Never mind the busy railroad tracks along their back yard—they'll still call the cops on *you*. Steer clear for the sake of the site's regulars.

Telling Wind Direction from Flight Path

If you choose to land somewhere that has no wind indicators, you'll need to know wind direction. "Telling Wind Direction" on page 82 has tips on using ground features, but in the absence of those, here is one method to use while you're aloft. Descend to about 200 feet and do a slow 360° turn while watching the ground (or look at your GPS groundspeed). When you're moving the slowest over the ground, you're going directly into the wind. If there's much wind at all, you'll notice drift. If you're drifting left, the wind is from your right—turn into it until the drift stops, that's the wind direction.

There are phone apps that can do this also (Chapter 28 on page 283), and they, too, benefit from a slow, steady 360. Wind at the surface may be different, but this is a good start. In thermally conditions, *expect* surface winds to be variable and turbulent.

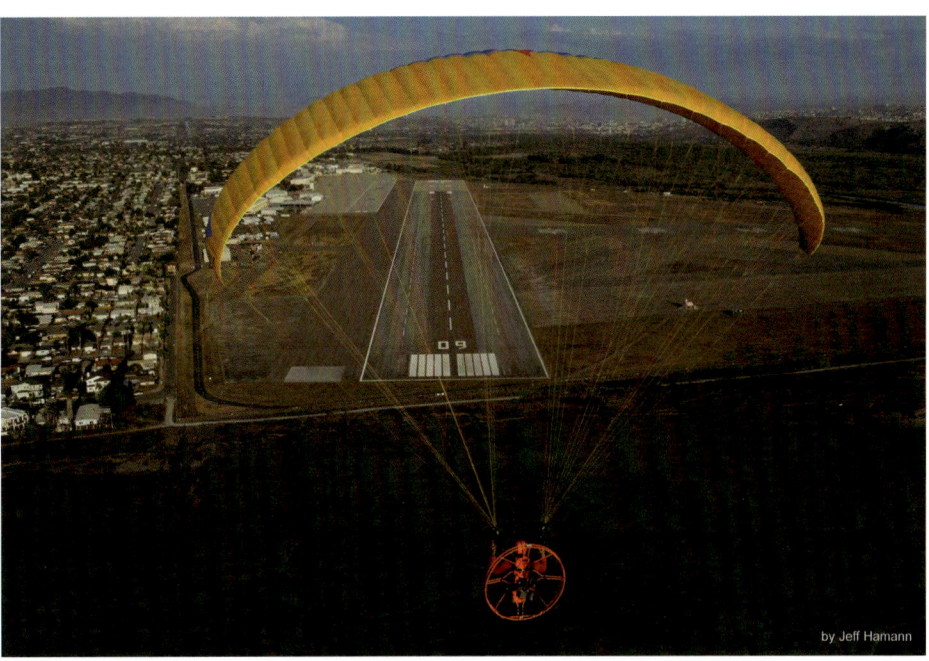

Flying from Controlled Airports

CHAPTER 11

There have been ultralight clubs flying from controlled airports, mixing it up splendidly with others, for years. Foot-launching adds another dimension but can certainly be done safely.

As learned in Chapter 9, airports with control towers have class D airspace around them for air traffic control (ATC) and, therefore, require permission. It's not hard to get, but it's easier if you have an aircraft radio. Most towered airports will require it. See Chapter 10 on flying from airports.

Flying into any control tower airport is made easier by phoning the tower in advance.

Telephone

If your launch site is within class D airspace, but not on the airport, you may be able to get permission via telephone. Even if you're using an aircraft radio, phoning first lets you explain your plans, your unusual craft, and accommodate any special needs they may have.

Before calling, figure out where you'll launch relative to the airport. Using a sectional chart or phone app, plot out a bearing and distance in nautical miles. Google Earth can be a great resource too, by using its ruler function. If there is a VOR (see Chapter 9) nearby, you can plot out a radial and distance from that. Know the airport's elevation, where the runways are, and their traffic patterns. ATC will try to keep you away from known air traffic. Have a route that will let you exit and re-enter their airspace quickly (as much as we do "quickly").

Tower numbers can be hard to find. Try Acukwik.com although you may have to register. Or try searching Department of Transportation, FAA Control tower, airport name. For U.S. airports search using the airport identifier preceded by the letter "K". That's the international code. So ARR is known internationally as KARR. Failing those, call Flight Service (800 WX-BRIEF) and explain that you need to talk with the "local controller" or "tower cab" for flight permission.

Ask for the Tower Chief. Arrange this a few days in advance because if you can't reach him and have no aircraft radio, it may not work. Explain that you:

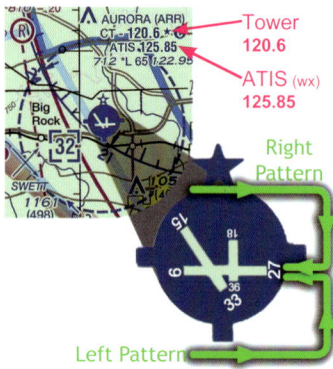

Fig 11-1 ARR Traffic Patterns

Three of us flew into this Class D airport while one talked on the radio and the others followed.

We were told to make "Right Closed Traffic" for the grass North of runway 27 and remain east of runway 33. So we followed the *right pattern,* as depicted above, making turns being to the right. Airplanes were using the a left pattern which is standard unless otherwise marked (Fig 10-10).

Being instructed to remain East of 33 kept us away from aircraft using that runway.

Airplane wakes ("Tip Tornadoes" on page 226), just like ours, settle and drift with the wind but is way stronger—truly worth avoiding!

Fig 11-2 Visibility Requirement

You can sometimes get permission to fly into control tower airports but only if the airport is reporting at least 3 miles visibility.

1. Would like to launch your "ultralight, a powered paraglider" (that may take some explanation) from location x.
2. Will stay below 500 feet AGL (or some acceptable altitude) as you exit or enter their class D airspace.
3. Have (or don't have) an aircraft transceiver and a transponder (used by radar controllers to identify specific aircraft.)
4. Will be flying between certain times.

Ask if they have any special requests. Permission is much better than forgiveness in this case, especially for certified pilots.

If you do have a radio then tell them you'll call on the tower frequency once airborne. Even if the airport has radar service, they will still probably want you on tower frequency, but ask to be sure.

Towered Airport Talk

If you fly from the towered field itself then have an altimeter that can be set to field elevation and an aircraft radio—Chapter 28 has more on the hardware. Also, have a working knowledge of runways, how they're numbered, airport markings, and traffic patterns. Chapter 10 can help, especially before talking with the airport manager about access and launch space.

When talking with airport management in person, have pictures or a video to show. On the phone, describe yourself as a "foot-launched powered parachute." They'll get the idea.

Call Signs

Make up a descriptive call sign for use on aviation radios; there is no need to register it with anyone. Make it easily understood, brief, and descriptive so it's easily picked out from other aircraft and conveys immediately that you're a low speed craft. "Ultralight Papa Gulf" is one example.

Rules for aviation transceivers vary by country and may require a license but not in the U.S. Generally, if the equipment is used as intended, nobody will ask questions.

ATIS

Most controlled airports have a continuously repeating weather recording—Automatic Terminal Information Service, or ATIS, that gets updated every hour. It includes airport weather, runways in use, and other relevant bits. To ensure pilots have the latest information, each update is labeled with a different letter. So the first hour's recording may be information "Alpha" (A) and the second hour's would be "information Bravo" (B) and so on. The tower wants to know that you've listened to this and will expect you to let them know on initial call.

The ATIS frequency is on sectional charts under the airport's name and control tower frequency (CT). See Fig. 11-15. Listen to this broadcast first then contact the tower via radio and mention it to them "…information Bravo" (if it's B).

Tower Talk: Launch

Communications are taken seriously, for good reason—when you're transmitting, it ties up the frequency. Nobody wants to deal with slow, uncertain transmissions. Plan your words, press the transmit button, then speak clearly and succinctly. Rehearse a few times.

Your initial call to the tower should include the facility name, your call sign, the letter of the ATIS recording (if one is broadcast), and your request. When you're ready to launch, motor running, A's in hand, then call the tower, saying that you're ready for launch. They will give you the winds, special instructions, and clear you to launch. They will probably tell you to "proceed as requested" or "at your own risk" since technically you're not on any clearance and aren't using a runway.

Complete your launch and comply with any instructions. If you delay more than a half-minute or so they will probably cancel the authorization and ask you to call them back when you're ready. If the launch doesn't work out, explain that you needed to abort and will call back when ready.

After you've launched and flown a few miles away, the tower may offer a frequency change; just respond with your call sign and "roger." You are not required to ask for a frequency change nor are they obligated to give you one once you leave their airspace.

Tower Talk: Landing

Before returning to land, listen to the airport's ATIS and note the letter (Alpha for A, Bravo for B, etc.).

Call the tower by saying its name and that you "have information such and such (ATIS letter)" followed by your request for a landing. They will issue instructions regarding patterns and runways. If you're coming into the airport you will need to tell them exactly where on the field you want to land.

Example Communications

Here is a sample communication for a paramotor pilot flying from Aurora airport near Chicago, IL. It's in Class D airspace at 600 ft MSL elevation (above mean sea level). Ideally you will have already talked with the tower by phone, so they know about the craft and where on the field you will launch from. Have a name for the place such as "in front of GF Aviation" (Fig 11-5). Make sure you understand the airport's runway and taxiway layout along with its typical patterns.

Your transmissions are in blue and ATC transmissions are in red.

Dial in the ATIS frequency:

"Aurora Tower information Charlie, time one four five three Zulu weather, wind 040 at 5, visibility 6 haze, scattered 35 hundred, temperature 24, dew point 18, runway 9 in use, runway 33/15 closed, caution for crane operating 600 feet east of the tower up to 150 feet, taxiway Charlie closed, tower and ground combined on 120.6, advise on initial contact you have information Charlie"

The above tells you that the wind is from the northeast at 5 knots and runway 9 is in use (airplanes will be taking off and landing towards the east). The weather observation was made at 1453 Zulu (see Chapter 7).

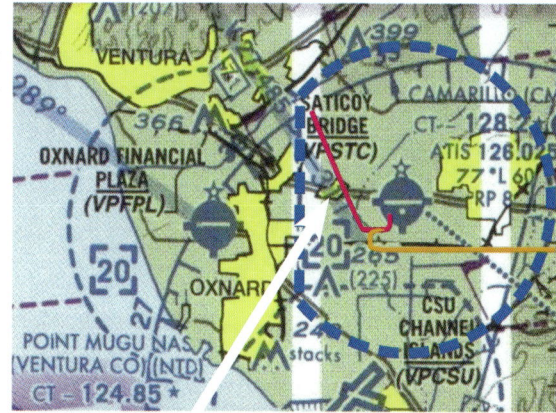

Fig 11-4 Ultralights Playing Well Together

Here is an example of ultralights playing well with aircraft. The tower controllers, airport management, and club operators have agreed on this arrangement. It allows a very active ultralight pattern to be flown right next to the airport runway. Aviation radios are required but the ultralights aren't expected to mix with the regular traffic.

Fig 11-3 Tip: AWOS

Some non-tower airports also have Aviation Weather Observation Systems (AWOS). These feed weather for various sources, and broadcast continuously on the aviation frequency depicted, in this case 132.175 Mhz. Search for "Current Aviation Weather Reports" or "METARs".

As an aside, notice the RP 23 (boxed in yellow here): aircraft will be flying a *right* pattern for runway 23. Otherwise, they'd fly a left pattern. See Fig 10-10 on page 105 for more on this.

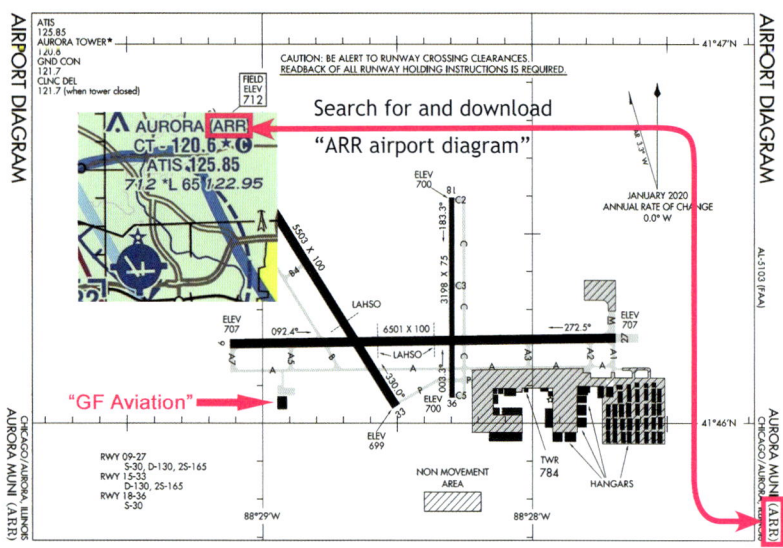

You are set up in the grass south of runway 9 near the GF Aviation building (Fig 11-5), planning to head south. Call the tower when ready to inflate.

"Aurora Tower, Ultralight Papa Golf by GF Aviation is ready to launch, would like a south departure."

"Ultralight Papa Golf, remain clear of runway 9, southbound departure approved, proceed as requested, launch is at your own risk."

"Ultralight Papa Golf, will remain clear of runway 9 and head south."

After launch, turn south and head out. If the tower knows about traffic in your vicinity, they may call it out. Positions are given relative to your ground track using clock directions where 9 o'clock is off your left, 12 o'clock is in front of your flight path, and 3 o'clock is to the right of it.

Fig 11-5 Aurora Airport Diagram
This for Aurora Muni, identified as ARR. GF Aviation is a fictitious paramotor-friendly business we've added for our examples.

"Ultralight Papa Golf, you have traffic at your 11 o'clock and a mile, westbound at 1500 feet, he's on right downwind for runway 9"

Look for the traffic; it is given relative to sea level (not airport elevation) so 1500 feet means he's 900 feet above the ground. Your altimeter should be set so that it reads airport elevation at launch for this reason.

Stay below about 500 feet or as instructed and respond accordingly.

"Ultralight Papa Golf, traffic in sight" or, if you don't see it, *"Ultralight Papa Golf, negative contact."*

After you've flown out of the tower's airspace you are legal to change frequencies (no permission required). They may, however, offer the change.

"Ultralight Papa Golf, clear of my area, frequency change approved."

"Ultralight Papa Golf, roger."

When returning to land, listen to the ATIS again (note the letter—X in this case) to make sure there are no changes. Call the tower with your position and request. Since this is an initial request, use the facility name.

"Aurora Tower, Ultralight Papa Golf is 6 miles south, southeast, landing with X-Ray (the ATIS letter)."

"Ultralight Papa Golf, approach the field from due south, remain below 1200 feet, call 2 miles out."

When reaching 2 miles out, report your position.

"Ultralight Papa Golf is 2 miles out."

If there's no traffic, it's fun to do a "touch and go" on a runway. If it's not being used, you may be able to get permission.

"Ultralight Papa Golf, if traffic permits, request touch and go on runway 36."

"Ultralight Papa Golf, roger, can you keep your pattern south of runway 27?"

Airport Codes

There are 3 primary types of airport identifiers. Bigger airports usually get the same basic 3-letter code. Not every airport has a code from every international organization.

1. The FAA (U.S.) uses 3-letter codes, like ARR, for most airports and 4-letter/number combinations for small and private airports like FA08 for Orlampa, better known as Fantasy of Flight in Polk City, Florida.

2. The International Civil Aviation Authority (ICAO) uses 4-letter codes that start with a unique country ID. For the U.S. that's "K", so ARR is KARR. Smaller countries have two-letter ID's and only the last two letters are unique. EB is Belgium, for example, so Brussels is EBBR.

3. International Air Transport Association (IATA) uses 3 letter / number codes mostly to be more obvious for airline passengers. Brussels, for example, is BRU. It's not perfect, though, Aurora, IL is AUZ.

If you're *absolutely* certain that you *can* safely comply, respond with "affirmative." Otherwise, say "negative." For this exercise we'll assume there is plenty of room.

"Ultralight Papa Golf, affirmative."

"Ultralight Papa Golf, keep your pattern south of runway 27, make right traffic for runway 36, report abeam the tanks on downwind."

When abeam the tanks (they pass by perpendicular to your flight path), report.

"Ultralight Papa Golf is abeam the tanks."

"Ultralight Papa Golf, cleared for the option runway 36, then make right traffic, remain south of runway 27."

This means you are cleared to land and stop, do a touch and go, or do a flyby of the runway. If you land and stop the clearance ends (you cannot takeoff again until cleared for takeoff), but if you touch and go, or fly by, make your pattern turns to the right while staying south of runway 27.

When you are ready to land back at your launch site:

"Ultralight Papa Golf is ready to land back in front of GF Aviation."

"Ultralight Papa Golf, remain south of runway 9, landing is at your own risk, proceed."

You will only be "cleared" to land or take off from a runway, not the adjoining grass or taxiways. Clearances, per se, are only issued when they involve the runway.

"Ultralight Papa Golf, roger."

Most instructions should be repeated (read back) to ensure you understand and will comply. All clearances relating to runways and taxiways must be read back. If you're only told to "proceed" then a full read back isn't really necessary; a simple "roger" will do. If you are asked to maintain an altitude it will be MSL so have a reasonably accurate altimeter available—most wrist altimeters work.

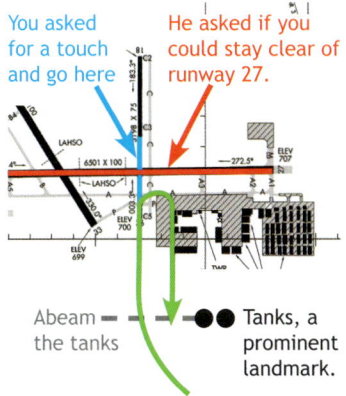

Fig 11-7 ATC Expectation

The green line is what he expects you to fly coming from the southeast with the instruction "keep your pattern south of runway 27, make right traffic for runway 36."

The black arrow is "abeam the tanks."

Letter of Agreement

If you fly frequently from a site within D airspace, you may be able to get a letter of agreement from the controlling facility, usually a control tower.

Set up an appointment with the tower chief (or his appointed minion) and have a map that shows where you fly along with a picture of your craft. If approved, you will be issued a letter specifying boundaries, altitudes, and times where you can fly without contacting them. It can work for a club, too.

Digging Deeper: *Phonetic Alphabet*

Aviation radios aren't known for clarity, so a special alphabet was developed to help, especially with B's, C's, D's, T's, etc.

A	Alpha	K	Kilo	V	Victor	
B	Bravo	L	Lima	W	Whiskey (strange choice?)	
C	Charlie	M	Mike	X	X-Ray	
D	Delta	N	November	Y	Yankee	
E	Echo	O	Oscar	Z	Zulu	
F	Foxtrot	P	Papa			
G	Golf	Q	Quebec			
H	Hotel	R	Romeo			
I	India	S	Sierra			
J	Juliet (See R; someone had a sense of humor)	T	Tango			
		U	Uniform			

These numbers pronunciations prevent confusion in some languages:

3 Tree
5 Fife
9 Niner

A flight of five paramotorists flew right off the end of this airline runway. Sometimes all you have to do is ask.

Another person on the ground monitored air traffic control via aviation radio and stayed in contact with the PPG pilots. Wake turbulence is always a concern.

by Wesley Woo

Setup & Maintenance

CHAPTER 12

"You're not a paramotor pilot, you're a mechanic who gets to test your work."

Unfortunately, reliability is not our machine's strongest suit. They look simple, and in many ways they are, but some dark corners lurk. Proper setup and maintenance is critical beyond appearances. Follow manufacturer guidance, when available, then your instructor or dealer who is experienced with the brand. Improper adjustments, especially to the harness, can render a paramotor unflyable or dangerous.

Harness & Frame Setup

A harness includes the critical liftweb (Light Blue in Fig 12-1)—structural elements that connect you to the wing, frame, motor, and provide a seat. They include key adjustments for hang angle, torque management, comfort, and others. Metal parts don't like moisture, and fabric parts don't like rays, moisture, extreme heat, cuts, critters, and harmful chemicals.

Riser Spread

The harness and frame should provide a riser separation of around 17 inches (42 cm) to keep most wings within certification. Measure from the base of the carabiners. These types of limitations are part of paraglider certification guidelines (EN926-2).

Be especially careful to avoid *less* than minimum separation which would accentuate riser twist, where the pilot spins around under the wing. Having too *much* separation can hurt glider structural integrity and handling.

Setup

Setup must be done while hanging from the carabiners. Simulators obviously work (see Fig 1-13 on page 9), but for this, anything to get your feet off the ground is OK. Work with someone who is familiar with the harness.

You want it tilted back between 5° and 15° (see Fig 12.5). More tilt may be more comfortable but it makes takeoff and landing more difficult. Sitting bolt upright is less comfortable but minimizes the twisting effect of torque and makes launch easier.

Fig 12-1 Common Swing-Arm Setup

This common low hook-in style connects carabiners to the S-arms (blue tint) and, in case of S-arm failure, has a backup strap (dashed blue) that goes to the fabric harness. The solid blue line is structural webbing that continues across and under the seat.

Ground handling straps are adjusted for walking around and motor height. Being "hiked up" higher on the pilot's back generally makes a machine easier to wield.

Ground handling straps (yellow)

Fig 12-2 Harness Adjustments
For more on paramotor geometry, see Chapter 27

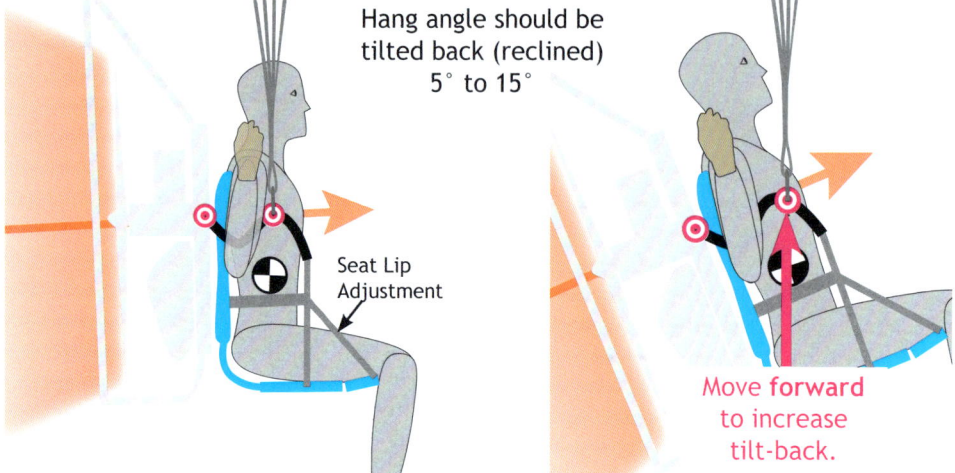

Fig 12-3 Low Hook-in Adjustment
Moving the hang point forward makes the motor hang back farther. Motors with no carry straps are usually launched with the main strap (over-shoulder) tight; then it's loosened in flight for comfort.

Fig 12-4 Attachment
A set screw clamps this placeholder on the S-arm.

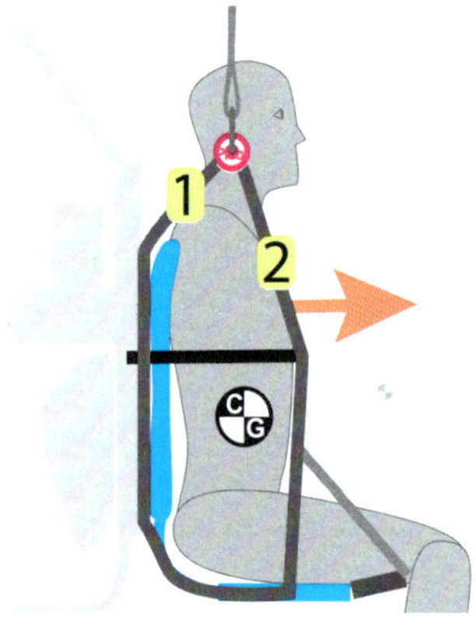

Fig 12-5 High Hook-in Adjustment
Lengthen yellow #1 to increase lean-back. Shorten yellow #2 to lower attachment point and slightly increase lean-back.

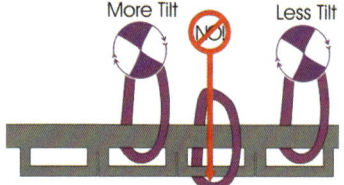

Fig 12-6 Bar Attachment
If the attachment is to a bar of some sort, make sure it's through the appropriate holes. Having it outside the hole will allow a severe tilt-back with likely riser twist and crash.

Adjust the hang angle by moving the carabiner hook-in point.

On low hook-in setups, that's done by moving the carabiner loop as shown in Fig 12-3. On all units we've seen, only the aftmost 2 or 3 positions are used. Many S-arm systems use a loop and retainer system as shown in Fig 12-4.

On high hook-in units, there are usually two parts of the harness web that can be adjusted (Fig 12-5). You should feel little or no harness pressure on your body. J-bars of some sort, either overhead or underarm, prevent that by transferring motor thrust to the forward harness straps and carabiners.

If the carabiners clip into a bar or frame, selecting the appropriate hole or position is critical. Moving the carabiner forward increases tilt-back. Lightweight pilots typically use the most aft positions (nearer the motor) to counteract the motor's weight. It's opposite if the *motor* clips into a bar (which is rare)—holes farther back make the motor tilt back farther.

Leg straps should be snugged up tightly then let out a couple inches. If they're too tight, it's hard to run, and on most machines, if they're too loose it's difficult to get seated. A few models, however, are designed for the leg loops to be completely loose—check with the manufacturer.

The Anti-Torque strap (Fig 2-14), if equipped, should be tightened until it's just snug but without forcing the carabiners together. This slightly reduces the effect of motor torque at some expense in weight shift. Machines made to weight shift don't usually have one.

On machines equipped with a seat lip adjustment strap (Fig 12-2 left image), it should be left loose for launch and landing. Pull it tight while hanging in the simulator to get some feel for how much tightening it takes and then let it loose again.

The front chest web keeps you from falling out forward, and prevents the risers from spreading out too far. Many machines also have a Sternum Strap to keep the shoulder straps from falling off while walking around. Over-tightening either of these might bring the risers too close together and will also reduce weight shift authority. The chest strap should be just barely snug. It should be adjusted after walking around with the motor.

Ground Handling Straps

Ground Handling straps, or carry straps (Fig 12-1, Fig 12-7) help keep the motor "hiked up" while preparing for launch. On over-the-shoulder machines they keep the bars off your shoulder and make forward launches easier by preventing the motor from wallowing around.

In flight, the ground handling straps can be loosened for comfort if needed. On harnesses where these straps pass through a buckle, tie a knot at the end so the strap can't come all the way out and find the prop. Props never hide.

A sternum strap may be used to keep various load-bearing straps together so they don't slip off your shoulders.

Machines without carry straps should have their main over-shoulder webbing cinched up reasonably tightly. You can loosen them in flight for comfort. These machines may also provide a side strap lumbar tensioner that can be tightened for launch and loosened in flight if necessary.

Kick-In Bar

A kick-in bar or rope is used to help get in the seat on some machines. It should be heavy enough (like an aluminum bar) to hang down a bit but must not interfere with walking backward (for reverse launches). Normally, it should hang a little over halfway down to your foot while sitting in the simulator.

Speedbar Setup

Unclip the speedbar from its holder. It should ride just below the seat to allow full travel. If the machine has a speedbar *and* kick-in bar/loop, the speedbar should hang closer to the seat for max travel. Some harnesses have Velcro loops to stow foot bars during takeoff (Fig 12-8).

Setup involves mimicking what the wing will be doing in flight. The speedbar line must not be so tight that it pulls the A's while stowed—that could be deadly. When fully depressed, the two A-riser pulleys should almost touch each other like Fig 12-10.

Make the line a bit longer than what the simulator suggests, then go test-fly it. While flying on a safe flight path, pull the bar up as far as possible using its line, but still get your feet on it. Mark that spot then make adjustments

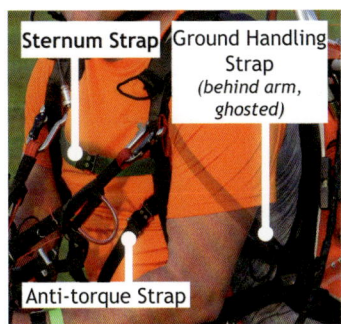

Fig 12-7 Anti-Torque, Ground Handling, and Sternum Strap
(Sternum Strap added for illustration)

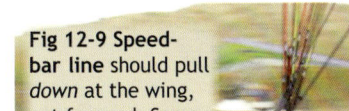

Speedbar Setup Tips

Fig 12-8 Speedbar Setup on the ground.

Hold Riser up to determine speedbar line length.

Built-in loops for pulleys

Velcro bar holders

Fig 12-9 Speedbar line should pull *down* at the wing, not forward. Some have 1 pulley, others have 2 pulleys like this one.

Fig 12-10 Speedbar Pulleys

At full speedbar, the 2 pulleys on each riser come together like this. Max speedbar is when they touch.

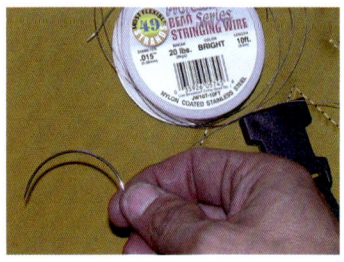

Fig 12-11 Liftweb Work

Repairs to the liftweb should be done by a certified parachute rigger or equally qualified professional. Other harness repairs can be made with any strong thread such as for leather or carpet. The hooked needle helps push it through thick straps.

after landing—that's how far the bar should hang below the seat board.

Some "speedbars" have no hard bar; they're just thick line or a strap. They may also come with another strap that attaches to the seat board for kicking out the seat.

Ladder-type speedbars have two loops for two-stage activation. Push out on the first loop to full leg extension, then go to the closer loop for yet more travel.

See also "Speedbar Usage" on page 181 for other suggestions on use and setup.

Hard Point Hook-Ins

On machines with low hook-in points, there are usually hard points that the carabiners attach to through a short strap as shown in Fig 12-4. Adjusting hang angle is a compromise between keeping the risers forward of the pilot's arms and leaning back too far. Leaning is more comfortable but causes stronger torque effects and can make landing more difficult.

If carabiners attach to a bar instead of the harness webbing, they use a safety strap that goes from the riser loop to the harness. That avoids a loose metal-to-metal contact point, which is slightly more susceptible to fatigue failure.

Reducing Torque & Twisting

The spinning prop inflicts two forces: riser shift (weight shift) and yaw (left/right twisting of the motor). Yaw is worse since it redirects thrust, which then pushes you sideways and into a bank. It can easily overpower your turn authority.

Offset thrust is another powerful cause of twist. If it's pushing on your right shoulder, for example, your body will yaw left.

Here are some mitigations that work through adjustments. See also "Twisting Forces At Work" on page 240.

Fig 12-12 Two Parts of Torque

The prop spins one way, trying to spin its connected engine/pilot the other way. Much grief comes from this.

1. Reduce the hang-back angle. This reduces riser twist due to the horizontal component of torque, especially for smaller pilots flying powerful motors.

2. Use anti-torque aerodynamic airflow redirection, like lamels (Fig 23-32 on page 243), if available for your model.

3. Ensure left-right thrust offset counters other twisting forces. And make sure the motor can't slide left or right on the harness which would *cause* offset thrust. If you tend to twist right, (motor pushing on left shoulder) adjust the motor to push slightly on your right shoulder (Fig 23-27 on page 241). This can be done by moving the hook-in point(s) laterally left or right.

   On some motors, the redrive's output shaft (right & Fig 12-21) can be adjusted to move the thrust line by a small amount.

4. Ensure that there is sufficient riser separation, and the motor is held rigidly in place. Left-right swinging arms must never swing *inward* (outward is OK).

5. Create a differential carabiner hang height. In other words, if the motor torque tilts you to the right (pulls down the right riser), make the left carabiner lower. That will make it turn slightly left during power-off glides, fly straight at cruise power, and turn only slightly right during climb. This works best on higher hang point motors because the motor/pilot center of gravity (CG) is well below the hang points.

6. Move the hook-in point aft on one side and forward on the other side. This makes the motor hang a bit twisted. So if you move the left point aft, the motor points right a bit, that makes thrust push right, causing a left bank. Use this to counter your motor's natural yaw tendency.

Two-Cycle Motor Troubleshooting Chart

Start Here

Does the starter make the piston move? → No →

Starter Problem:
- Pull start - check pawls, looseness.
- Flash starter - check main spring.
- Electric starter - power, engagement solenoid, motor, gears.

↓ Yes

Does the motor have compression when pulled/cranked?

→ Too Much →

Remove the spark plug. If there's still too much resistance to pulling, it could be:
- Seizure (piston melts against cylinder wall).
- Bad pull or electric starter.
- Other internal problem$.

Otherwise, it could be:
- Clogged decompression hole (if equipped) - clean it out.
- Bad decompression valve (if equipped). Clean or replace.

→ No →

No/Low Compression:
- Spark plug is loose - tighten.
- The piston has a hole in it - replace.
- If it has a decompression valve this is normal but you'll hear hissing during pull.

↓ Yes

Does the motor start and continue to run?

↓ No

Does it fire at all?
Make sure it's not flooded: remove the spark plug and ground it (to prevent coil damage), pull the starter or crank it, then replace the plug. A wet plug may indicate flooding.

↓ No

Is the spark weak or absent?
Set the connected plug on the cylinder and look for a spark while pulling/cranking the motor. Don't touch!

→ Yes →

Spark is not being generated or is being shorted. It could be:
- Bad spark plug - Try a new one.
- Kill switch is shorted - disconnect it and see if it fires or verify the kill circuit is an "open" when not pushed. Some motors use the throttle sheathing to complete the circuit.
- Coil or magneto (as equipped) is bad. Most use a magnet and coil to generate the high voltage required of the spark plug.
- Spark plug boot. Black soot means a loose contact.

↓ No

Has Fuel-Air-Spark-Compression; could be:
- Excess internal carbon deposits.
- Bad ignition system (coil, plug, wire, boot). Even though you see it spark, the strength may be inadequate.
- Exhaust is bad. Tuned pipes can make engines run rough if broken or improperly made.
- Ignition timing is off, call an expert.
- Timing issue, loose/off timing mechanism
- Piston rings stuck or sticking.
- 100 other arcane possibilities. Assume the fetal position and cry, or consult an expert.

(From "Does the motor start and continue to run?" Yes branch →)

Does it develop and keep full RPM?

→ Yes →

If full RPM doesn't give full thrust, it could be:
- The prop is on backward - the curved side always faces forward (towards the motor).
- The belt or clutch (if equipped) is slipping.

↓ No

Does it go to full RPM then fade, or does the power vary without changing the throttle setting?

→ Yes → **Is it Overheating?**

- No → **Power Fade, Not Overheating:**
  - The prop is either too big or has too much pitch - "over propped."
  - Mixture may be changing as the motor heats up (even if not overheating). Tune Carb.
  - De-carbonize cylinder and piston.
  - Bad/broken tuned pipe—damage may not be visible. Try replacing the pipe if able.
  - Check for cylinder or crankcase air leaks.
  - Throttle cable allows activation of the throttle without squeezing the trigger.
  - Air leak (bubbles) in fuel line, especially at primer bulb or fuel filter, as installed.
  - Contaminants in carburetor or inline fuel filter. They compress with time.

- Possibly → **Overheating has several possibilities:**
  - Mixture is/gets too lean, possibly from air leak into cylinder from exhaust flange, base gasket, cylinder head O-ring (or gasket), or crankcase.
  - Too little oil in fuel. This should not be a problem up to 50:1 fuel/oil ratio.
  - Bearings have seized.
  - The cylinder is scored.
  - The piston ring(s) are stuck or sticking.
  - Cooling fan failure or blockage.
  - Head bolts loose.
  - Carb needs tuning ("Tuning a Membrane Carburetor" on page 234).

↓ No

Tune the carburetor, check the reed valve, get fresh fuel.

Did that solve the problem?

→ Yes → **Go Fly!**

↓ No

Is fuel getting to the carburetor?
Try spraying starter fluid in the air intake. If it pops when cranked, then a proper fuel mixture is not being delivered by the carb.

→ Yes →

Losing Proper Fuel/Air Mix:
- Air leak in a fuel line. Replace line. This can sometimes be seen as bubbles in the fuel line.
- Blocked fuel filter.
- Fuel tank air intake vent blocked. This will cause the motor to run for a while then become lean and quit.
- Old fuel - it may last only a week if unsealed.
- Improper fuel. Small motors may not like Avgas or low octane fuel.
- Pinched fuel line.

Motor

Getting into this sport means, to some degree, becoming a mechanic. Precious few shops—motocross and cart racing shops mostly—will work on our gear, and they may be reluctant once they know it's for flying (liability worries). They won't likely have parts, either, so you'll need someone who specializes in your particular brand. In all likelihood, you'll need to ship your broken unit to a shop that knows the model. But if you want it fixed quickly, you'll do it yourself. There are, fortunately, some preventive measures that can keep little problems from blossoming into big ones that require repair.

Troubleshooting

All internal combustion motors need four elements in the right proportion and at the right time: spark, fuel, air, and compression. Ensure these are present, and you'll likely solve the problem. Sometimes, just replacing the spark plug is all it takes. At other times you'll need full use of the flowchart (page 119) and more.

Start with simple and cheap, then progress to the more involved. If your dealer can't help, FootFlyer.com has a troubleshooting section (QR link). Internet discussion groups dedicated to your motor can be helpful.

Fortunately, these machines are relatively simple, fairly reliable, and easy to work on. Many "mechanically challenged" pilots, when faced with being grounded, have risen to the occasion.

Bolt Tightening and Force

Fig 12-13 Torque Wrench

A torque wrench lets you gauge how hard you are tightening something. With the model at left, you must hold it at the handle. More expensive versions use a different mechanism and it doesn't matter where on the handle you hold them.

Units of bolt tightening force, or *torque*, are about leverage; they always include a force and distance. A special torque wrench (Fig 12-13) makes this easy. Kilogram-meters and Foot-pounds are most common. If you hold a wrench way out on the handle, it doesn't take much force to tighten (or break) something. Holding the wrench 12 inches away from the bolt and applying 1 pound of force equals 12 inch-pounds of torque.

Be careful with units: one foot-pound is 12 *times* more torque than 1 inch-pound, and over-tightening is worse because it can quickly strip threads, especially in aluminum.

Bolts and other parts are always seeking escape. Aircraft safety wire is good prevention. Muffler springs, for example, should be "safetied" so broken pieces can't find the prop. In some cases, paraglider line can work—favor solutions that won't damage bystanders, the wing, cage, or wallet on their way out.

Safety wire (Fig 12-17) comes in various sizes; thicker is better given our machines' vibration. Use the thickest size your application allows. Few bolts are made to accept safety wire and must be drilled through the head. Never re-use safety wire since it loses strength in subsequent bends.

Paramotor parts break. It's what they do. Or they loosen and fall off. What happens *afterward* (like remaining captive) determines how many dollars go with them.

Preventative Maintenance

Spark Plugs may last as little as 10 hours before carbon deposit and other wear degrades performance. They should either be changed every 20 hours or at the first sign of trouble—primarily because they are so cheap and easy to change. Tighten them to manufacturer specs, typically, about 15 ft-pounds, or just enough to flatten the washer that comes with most plugs.

Fuel line hardens or forms interior gunk over time which clogs carburetors, even with a fuel filter. Replace fuel line at least every other year. Don't route it around sharp corners or against sharp objects to avoid chaffing. Bubbles in the fuel line might be from holes—the motor may run rough, lean, or not at all. Only secure fuel line with

Fig 12-14 Belt Tightening
Try to move the prop. Belt slippage should start at about 13 ft-lbs (1.8 kg-m) of torque if it's appropriately tight.

Fig 12-15 Torque Marker
After tightening a fastener, mark it with torque marker paint like "Cross Check." Fingernail polish works too.

Fig 12-16 Flash Starter
Flash starters have TWO springs, one to retract the cord, and a big one to spin the motor. They can be rather fragile.

Fig 12-17 Safety Wire
Aircraft safety wire stays strong even after being twisted. Attach it to prevent bolts or other parts from unscrewing or departing.

---

clamps or ties intended for the job (Fig 12-18).

Exhaust system bolts, rivets, and springs are always trying to vibrate off. Although a fire is still *highly* unlikely, these very-hot parts deserve close scrutiny. Exhaust components, whenever possible, should be safety wired. Spring vibration can be reduced by infusing them with heat-tolerant sealant.

Head bolts should be checked with a torque wrench, especially within 10 hours of replacement. If they work loose, air leakage may cause a lean-mixture overheat.

Deferring Maintenance

So you hear an unusual sound? How bad is it? Should you continue?

A new noise in flight usually portends a failure. Early shutdown, if it's safe to do, will keep it from becoming an expensive destruction.

Reduction Drive

Nearly all gas paramotors use a reduction drive to turn the engine's high-RPM into a propeller-friendly RPM using either a belt or gears. Electric powered machines are usually direct drive. Engines turn 8000-1000 RPM, while props ideally turn under 3000 RPM.

Gear Drive

Most gear drives bathe two gears in a grease or oil-laden aluminum housing. It's usually driven by the motor through a clutch bell (Fig 12-20).

Normal maintenance requires ensuring everything has sufficient lubricant and good bearings. They generally require very little attention, but on rare occasion, little bits of metal can foul the works. Then the case must be split open and cleaned out.

If you feel play in the prop that's *not* due to prop bolts, bearing(s) may be failing. Replacement requires splitting gearbox case which is fortunately easy. Unscrew the bolts partway then tap on their heads with something that won't do damage. Once the halves are barely separated, use a gear puller or prying tool (chisel or something wide that won't scrape the metal) to finish the separation. If the gears are damaged, you may need a gear puller. If the bearings are bad, you'll probably have to heat the case to get them out. Youtube will be your best friend during some of this work.

Belt Drive

The primary adjustment on belt-drive units is belt tension. Too loose and it slips—causing a "chirping" noise on each power stroke. Being too tight can bend the standoff or stretch the belt. All motors have some way to adjust belt tension by changing

Fig 12-18 Fuel Line Zip Ties
Don't use regular zip ties on fuel line. They dig into the rubber causing cracks and failure unless they're done like the standoff shown above. Or use specially-made fuel line ties that have a curve (above right). The QR page has more ideas.

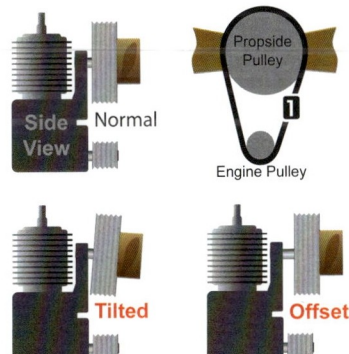
Fig 12-19 Belt Woes
Mis-alignment of the pulleys will cause dramatically higher belt wear. With proper adjustment and a light weight propeller, a belt should last at least 100 hours.

On average it should be tensioned so that there is about a 1/4" of play when pressed at spot 1 above. Or tension as shown in Fig 12-14.

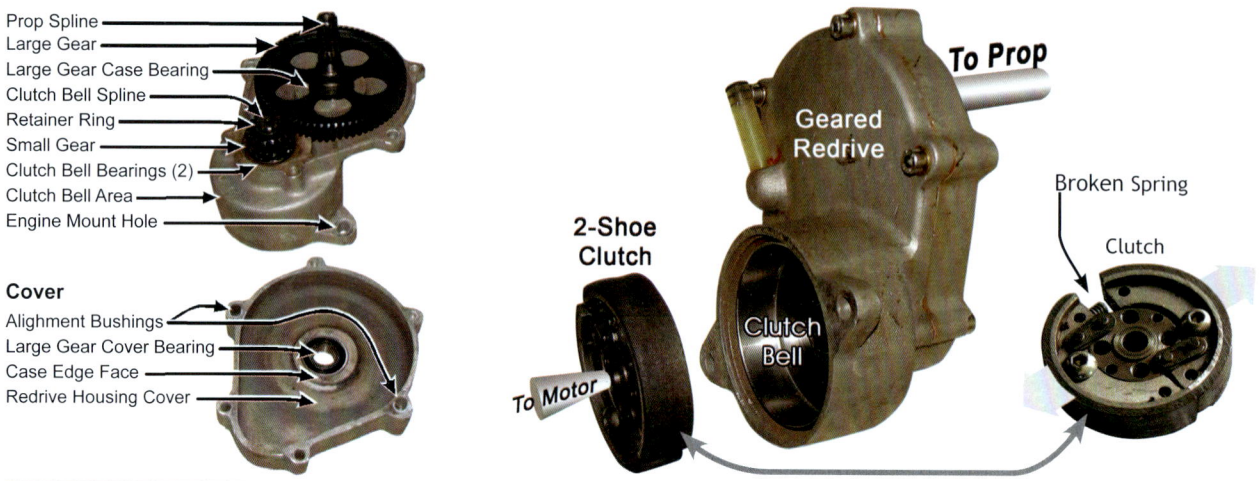

Fig 12-20 Gear Reduction Drive (Redrive) with Clutch

The motor spins the clutch fast enough for clutch shoes (aka pads) to expand into the clutch bell which is part of the redrive's small gear. That then drives the much larger prop-side gear at a lower, more prop-friendly RPM.

The clutch pictured above on the right has one broken spring. So the two shoes spread out against the clutch bell too easily, causing the clutch to engage, which makes the prop spin, even at idle. It should be stationary at idle.

Fig 12-21 Eccentric Shaft Reduction Pulley

Moving the concentric shaft can raise or lower the secondary (prop) pulley. It's a common way to tighten belts—rotate the shaft so the pulley moves farther from the engine drive pulley.

the distance between pulley (Fig 12-21). You must tighten new belts a few times since they stretch in the first few flight hours.

The two pulleys must be aligned properly (Fig 12-19) to prevent belt damage.

Besides a loose belt, a heavy propeller (especially where the mass is out towards the tips) will aggravate slipping and may shorten belt or redrive bearing life.

Clutch

Clutches allow starting and idling the motor without spinning the prop. On larger motors, clutches are paired with either flash pull starts, or electric start. Flash starters are used since the prop doesn't serve as a flywheel to get past compression.

At idle, springs hold the clutch shoes in. As you throttle up, RPM increases, throwing the clutch shoes outward and grabbing the clutch bell, which spins reduction drive gears or a belt that's attached to the prop. The prop must be free-wheeling (no rubbing) with the motor off. Worn or rusty contacting clutch parts will do damage—replace them early or face dramatically more expensive repairs.

New sounds from the redrive are usually shouts of "attend to me now *or else!*"

Propeller

The propeller is mounted with the curved side facing the direction of flight (Fig 12-22). It'll work the other way—but not well enough to fly. Bolts must be tightened evenly (see Fig 12-26) to avoid an offset that could cause an imbalance. The prop is held in place by friction with the plates, not the bolt shafts. If there is torsional stress on the bolts, such as when they're too loose, they *will* break.

Do not drill extra holes in the prop hub to fit a different bolt pattern. The weakened wood could break, causing a catastrophic failure.

Use grade 8 bolts (Fig 12-23) or better, and check tightness periodically. They should be torqued to approximately 5 foot-pounds (0.7 kg m)—secure but not deforming the wood. Tighten each bolt partway in succession, one at a time, on opposite sides, until getting to the desired torque just like a car wheel. Composite props can be torqued up to 7 foot pounds (1.0 kg m).

Rotate the prop to vertical and try to move the tip fore and aft while watching the engine mounts. A broken or nearly failed mount may allow enough flex for the prop to hit a frame/cage part and must be replaced. If the prop wiggles, check the center nut (on those motors that use it) and tighten if needed.

Balancing Act

Vibration is a paramotor's mortal enemy and props can be a big contributor. Thankfully, static balancing is an easy, effective mitigation. Less obvious, and less common, is the need to balance out various aerodynamic maladies.

Static Balance

A prop should balance exactly at the center of its hub. A special balancer (Fig 12-27) can quickly reveal if the prop is heavier either spanwise (tip to tip) or chord-wise (leading edge to trailing edge). Most balancers have a cylinder plug sized to fit snugly in the prop's center (hub) hole. The prop is then hung from, or balances on a single point right in the middle. If one blade (or side) droops, then it's heavier.

The cure is to put enough weight on the lighter side. One method is to drill a hole opposite the heavy side and melt solder into it until balanced. Drill only partway through so there's only one side to dress afterward. Cover the hole with a Super Glue (or epoxy) and baking soda mix, then sand to match the prop's contour.

Carbon Fiber props are different since they're mostly hollow. Drill a hole near the tip and add epoxy, or in more extreme cases, melted solder (usually only after a big repair on the opposite blade). Seal the solder with epoxy and sand to shape.

Minor corrections to fix an imbalance can be done by spraying clear varnish to the lighter side. Several coats will be necessary as much of the weight evaporates off.

Aerodynamic Balance

If one blade is pulling harder than the other blade, it is aerodynamically unbalanced and will cause vibration. Possible causes are:

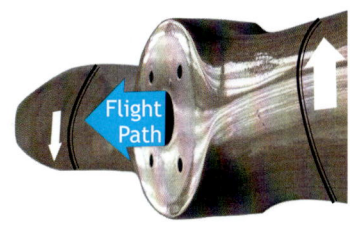

Fig 12-22 Curvy Side Forward
If you put the prop on backward it *will* produce thrust, but not enough to launch or avoid embarrassment.

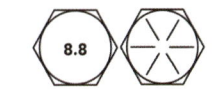

Fig 12-23 Grade 8 Bolt Markings

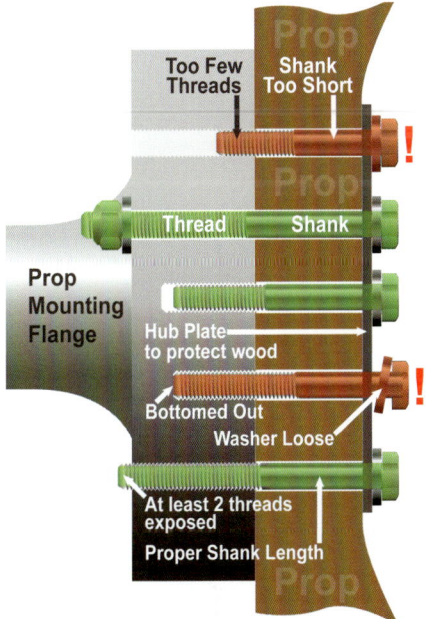

Fig 12-24 Propeller Bolts

Prop hub bolts must be used properly (in green) to avoid dangerous prop failures. If there's a center bolt holding the hub onto a spline, thrust is normally imparting a tightening torque. Letting off the thrust, however, is when that bolt would tend to come out. It may need Loctite or something similar.

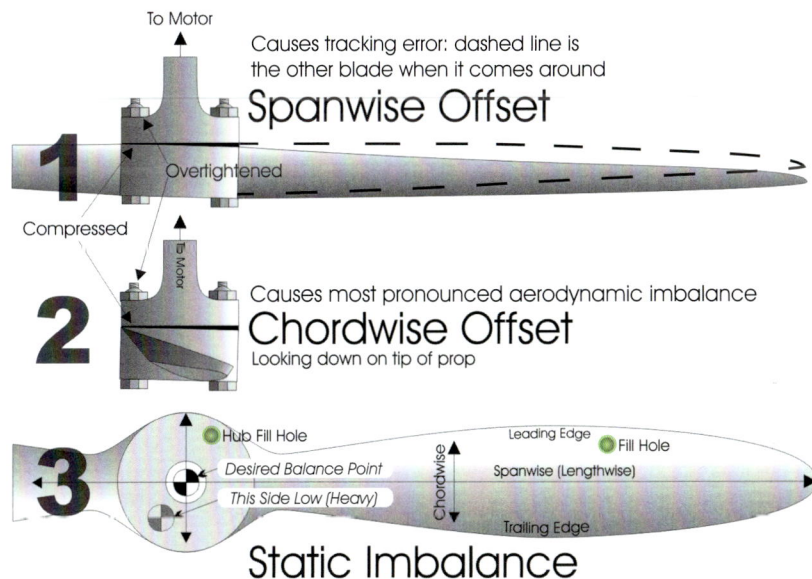

Fig 12-25 Propeller Imbalance

If a prop is not flat on its flange, the offset will cause vibration. A *chord*-wise offset (2) is worse because one blade has more pitch than the other, pulling harder as it goes around. This creates an *aerodynamic imbalance* and can happen even if *statically balanced*.

Static imbalance (3) can be fixed by drilling a shallow hole where weight is needed and melting solder into it. In the Static Imbalance example above, the prop needs weight at the "Fill Hole" to counteract being heavy low and to the left. Account for the small weight added by the varnish or paint.

Fig 12-26 Bolt Tightening Order

Finger tighten all bolts in this order then continue tightening in small increments using the same order. That prevents an offset from forming.

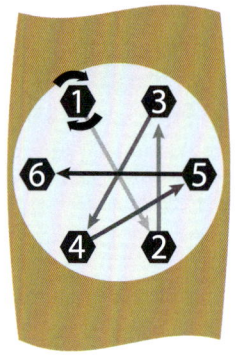

1. The propeller has a chord-wise offset, probably one or two bolts on one side are over-tightened, compressing the prop unevenly like #2 in Fig 12-25.
2. The propeller is warped. This is more likely on a wood prop, especially if it has been exposed to moisture, or after a big repair.
3. One blade is longer or fatter than the other. That's relatively easy to correct by shaving off some length. One way to tell is to set a large piece of paper on the floor, put the prop on it, and carefully outline one half. Then put the other half over the outline and see if it's close. If not, reshape the larger half to match.

You can measure the angle of each blade by first setting it on a smooth, flat floor. Go 75% out towards the tip, hold a straight edge against the prop's flat bottom and measure its angle to the floor with a protractor.

Anytime a prop is worked on or reshaped, it should be at least statically balanced.

Tracking

If one blade tip passes by the same point in space at a different spot (either fore or aft) than the other blade, its tracking is off, like #1 in Fig 12-25. Besides improper mounting, it could have an aerodynamic imbalance as described above which is harder to detect.

Tracking can be off by a ¼ inch with little effect, but more than that should be corrected unless it's not vibrating—then leave it alone.

All propeller blades flex and twist a bit when under power—causing either more or less lift (push) as they do. If one blade twists more than the other, it will cause an aerodynamic imbalance and vibration even though the prop balances statically. A vibration that worsens with higher rpm may be caused by this. Flexing happens more on poorly made, thin, or extensively repaired props.

Prop Tape

Specially-made prop tape can be applied to the prop's leading edge to protect it from minor dings. Theres a minor performance penalty, and if it's not adhering well, it can come off, causing an uncomfortable imbalance.

Thin tape is better for going around the sometimes-difficult curves and tends not to hurt performance as much. Thick tape can sometimes be coaxed to work but may require small V-cuts (Fig 12-28) or using a hair dryer to make it more malleable.

Fig 12-27 Static Prop Balancers.

These are all based on the fact that the heavy side droops down.

1. A stand balancer checks only for lengthwise imbalance which causes most vibration. Put the cylinder through the prop's center hole and place on the green stand. This one uses razor blades mounted on the stand to improve sensitivity.

2. A string balancer checks for both spanwise and chord-wise imbalance. Put the cylinder through the prop and hang from its string.

3. Inexpensive lawn mower blade balancers work OK. Steps on the cone accommodate most inside diameters.

4. Cylinder-style balancers are identical in principle to lawn mower types, allowing both lengthwise and widthwise balancing.

The cylinder goes in the prop's hub hole then sits on the pointed stand. A bubble level shows where it's heavy, in this case, lower left. Add weight at the x, and if necessary, out near the right tip.

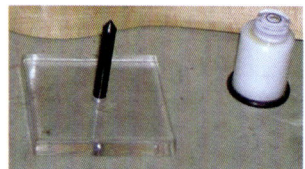

Propeller Repair

Props will be sacrificed—to cages, to lines, to departing parts, and to ground debris. Fortunately, many oopses are easy to fix. But repairs must be done correctly to avoid pieces flying off with potentially devastating consequences. If in doubt, send it out.

On all repairs, the surface should be cleaned first and sanded afterward. If two-part epoxy is used, it should be allowed to fully cure before sanding; use a hard sanding block to prevent airflow-ruining bumps. Long curing epoxy is stronger.

Repairing a Wood Prop

The quickest repair for small divots is Super Glue and powder, either baking soda or microballoons (google "microballoons filler"). Layer on the glue and sprinkle in the powder. The mix may smoke a bit but should harden quickly. Repeat until the damage is filled then sand to shape.

Somewhat bigger gouges can be filled with epoxy and powder. Use tape to follow the prop's contour in a way that you can pour the mixture into. That reduces sanding. Use an equal amount of epoxy and baking soda (by volume) to help reduce weight and make it easier to sand. The right mix of powder gets closer to wood's density.

After it is fully cured, use progressively finer sanding blocks to reshape it.

Larger repairs, up to 30% of the length or width of one blade can be done with a variety of methods, one of which is shown in Fig 12-30.

Balance the prop, getting it close but allowing for final sanding and varnish. Let it dry and repeat until you're satisfied. Then do a final balance with varnish.

Repairing Carbon Fiber Props

Carbon fiber props can be less forgiving of damage. Even after being repaired, they may harbor invisible damage that could separate later, without notice, throwing shards.

They're usually hollow with some foam elements to keep the halves spaced appropriately. They generally weigh less and are a bit more challenging to repair. Don't expect repairs to all look perfect since, on more structural repairs, impregnated fiber cloth may cover part of the outer shell.

Simple divots can still be filled using the glue-and-powder techniques mentioned above. Bigger damage should use epoxy forced into the hole then use tape to form the prop's shape while the epoxy sets. Lay it so the epoxy puddles against the tape while curing. Putty-type epoxy works, too.

More severe damage, such as when more than about an inch of tip is missing, or when the load path is compromised (Fig 12-29) requires another technique (Fig 12-31). You'll need fiber cloth and resin.

Clean and sand the area within two inches of the damage to have a good bonding surface for the resin.

Spray foam (insulating foam is sold at many hardware stores) into the tip void for support. With worse damage, embed some reinforcement material (wood or wire) into the foam such that it extends beyond the foam. It should be epoxied to the existing prop shell for strength. That piece also helps hold the repair in place. Let the repair set up overnight.

Trim the foam so it does not protrude into the repair area.

Mix the resin according to its directions—a finicky step that warrants practicing elsewhere. The mix must be just right. Cut up pieces of cloth, mix them into the resin then work the saturated pieces into the tip and around the mold. Longer pieces

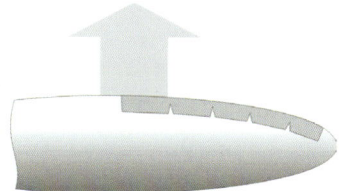

Fig 12-28 Prop Tape

Prop tape is great for beach flying. If it does not adhere well to the curves, cut V's out as depicted here.

Fig 12-29 Prop Load Path

Inboard damage (closer to hub) is more structurally significant because there's so much more mass outboard to support.

Centripetal loads increase to the square of RPM so forces skyrocket at max power. It's not just outward pull, either, the prop is also bending forward from generating thrust.

Caution!

Poorly done repairs, especially closer to the hub, can render a prop dangerously weakened.

If you're uncertain about the safety of a repair, replacement is best.

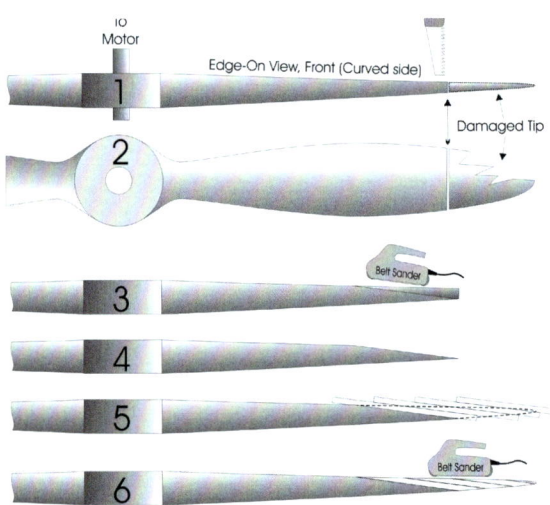

Fig 12-30 Wood Prop Tip Repair

Surprisingly large repairs can be made on wooden props if done right. A belt sander makes it easier but having a steady hand and some basic wood-working skill is a must.

Use a quality wood glue, spread evenly on 1/4" thick slabs of poplar wood (step 5). Make sure they're completely flat against each other and clamp firmly for overnight drying before sanding.

Sand to shape then varnish, sand, varnish, and balance.

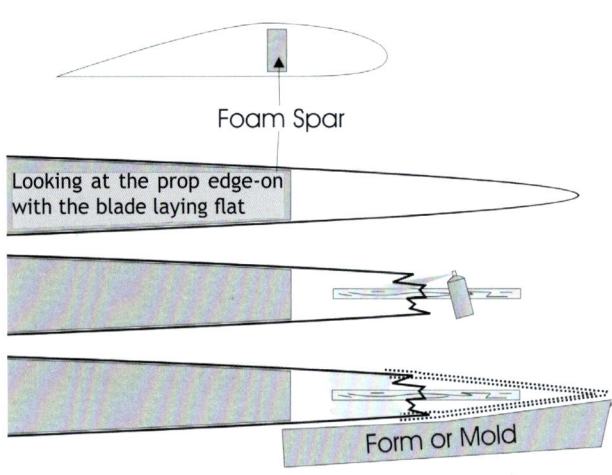

Fig 12-31 Carbon Fiber Tip Repair

Small repairs can be filled without stiffening. Anything over about an inch across or a half-inch deep needs more care. Anything over 3 inches should be repaired professionally, and most carbon fiber prop makers recommend against trying to fix their products.

Fiberglass is heavier than carbon fiber so balancing afterward is especially important.

Wear appropriate protective gear, generally a filtered mask and goggles.

---

should overlap the prop's top and bottom upper and lower surfaces for the best bond.

Once hardened completely, sand to shape. A belt sander really helps to speed up the process but don't sand away where the fiberglass overlaps the existing prop. It won't look perfect but is necessary for strength. Lightly hand-sand the overlap area to smooth it out without decreasing strength.

Balance the prop and expect to add weight in the other tip.

The Wing

Paraglider maintenance is minimal depending on use and storage, but it's even more critical than the motor.

Age and moisture tend to shrink the less-loaded rear lines while more heavily loaded A's tend to stretch. The combination of these factors change an airfoil's shape and Angle of Incidence (Fig 22-6 on page 225) which can degrade flight behavior.

Lines weakened by heat or sharp bends (especially knots) can fail early.

Fabric can tear, rot, become porous, moldy, weak, or get chewed by insects. Direct sunlight and moisture in storage are mortal enemies.

Some of these degradations are not obvious, which is why periodic professional inspections are so valuable. They're covered under "Inspection" on page 128).

Replacing Risers

Unless risers get damaged they will outlast lines and fabric. Check newly acquired wings for riser stitching and quick links. At least one wing was shipped with tack-stitched riser loops—they would likely have failed on the first flight.

Risers can be separated from the lines to have a new riser model or replacing a damaged riser. For example, some manufacturers offer motor risers for their soaring wings. Mostly that's to accommodate the higher attachment points on motors and trimmers which soaring wings don't have.

A different riser set can dramatically change the wing's flight characteristics and usually takes the wing out of certification. **Only use risers recommended by the manufacturer.** Flight behavior probably hasn't been fully tested.

You can remove risers by taking the lines off at their quick links.

Complete one side before doing the other side, starting from the A's, then proceeding back to the brakes. Put masking tape across a group of lines before detaching them and use a felt tip marker to note which side faces forward ("F" in picture at left) as well as what lines they are (A's, B's, etc.) including the split A, if equipped. Replacing the lines on one individual riser at a time is another good way to keep everything straight.

Here is one method for replacing risers. Start by marking the brake line knot location with a felt tip pen. Untie the brake toggle to pull its line through the brake pulley (or guide) then:

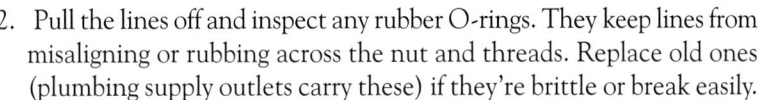

1. If you have to cut away anything (like shrink wrap plastic), always cut *away* from soft material. Don't let tools scratch the metal which weakens it.

2. Pull the lines off and inspect any rubber O-rings. They keep lines from misaligning or rubbing across the nut and threads. Replace old ones (plumbing supply outlets carry these) if they're brittle or break easily.

3. If hard plastic shrink wrap was used, replace it with something similar like electrical heat-shrink tubing (from electronics supply stores).

4. Put the heat shrink tubing on the lines (if used), put the lines on the new riser, put the O-ring on with a figure 8 pattern (as shown), and then snug up the fastener.

5. Snug to finger tight, then go an 1/8th turn more with a tool.

When completed, **kite the wing before flying** to make sure everything is in order, and it handles properly. Make sure the brake lines get adjusted before flying.

Brake Lines

Brake line length is critical; seek help from someone familiar with the procedure. **Pilots have died from incorrectly set brakes.** If they're too short, the trailing edge stays deflected, which could cause parachutal stall or a spin. Too long risks a toggle in the prop, and/or dangerously reduces steering and flare authority.

With toggles at their pulley (flying hands-off), there should be some slack in the brake line with no trailing edge deflection, even with fast trim and/or speedbar pushed out. You want some arc in the line (Fig 12-34) from its pulley up to the trailing edge. In flight, your hands should rest near position 2—that leaves enough flare authority while remaining comfortable. Having your arms hang lower may be more comfortable but sacrifices brake *travel*. Your bicep should be about horizontal when resting the weight of your arms in the brakes. A few inches can make a big difference in comfort.

Free flyers set their toggles lower since they can take wraps (wrap the excess line around their hands) for full authority. The throttle makes that difficult for motor pilots.

Some wings have adjustable brake pulleys, some have multiple pulleys—use the one that's most comfortable. Generally, with a low attachment motor, use the high pulley, and use the low pulley for high attachment motors.

Most wings come from the factory with the brakes set somewhat long to reduce the likelihood of a new pilot stalling. But that also limits control authority. To

Fig 12-32 Toggle Knots

The "8 Follow Through" puts low stress on the line and is easy to tie since, after looping through the toggle, it follows itself back through the half-hitch.

The bowline (below) works well but may be harder to get out.

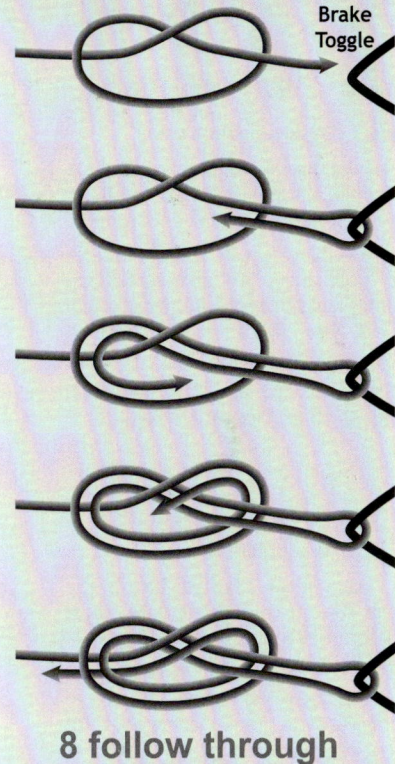

8 follow through

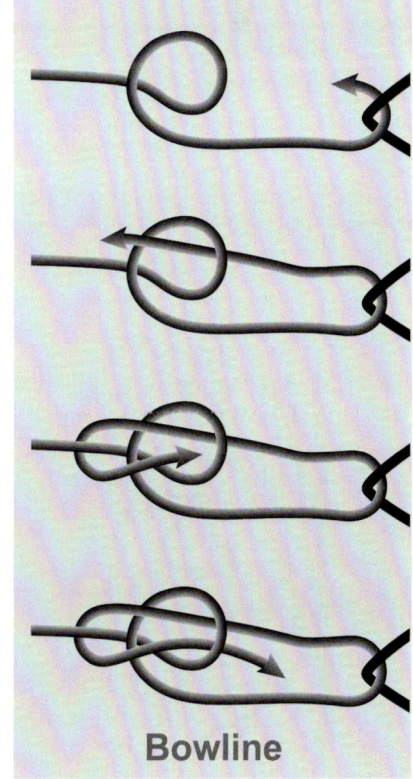

Bowline

Fig 12-33 Riser Quick Links

Triangular and D shaped quick links (maillons) use inserts, grommets, or heat shrink to keep lines positioned.

If you have to use a tool to close or open the screw connector, that link should be replaced. Over or under-tightening can cause structural failure under load.

Grommets (O-ring line keepers) should be replaced if cracked.

Fig 12-34 Brake Line Setup

For general brake setup:

1) Have about 2 feet of bow in the line so it takes some toggle travel before the trailing edge deflects.

2) If 2D steering (Fig 26-8 on page 263) is used, the tips should engage *slightly* earlier than the inboard trailing edge but always defer to the wing's manual.

3) Account for trimmer motion since the brakes are attached above the trimmer line. With the trimmers let out, can you still reach the brakes easily?

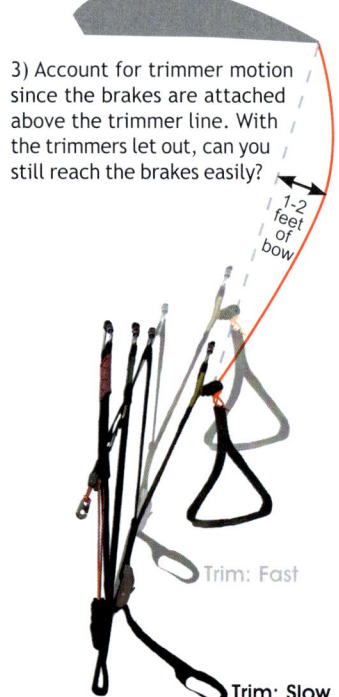

set the length, kite the wing and mark where the new knots should go. Untie the existing knot and retie it at the new location using a knot in Fig 12-32.

Repairing Wing Fabric

Tears usually come from pulling too hard on the risers and snagging the wing on sharp rocks or other protrusions. Thankfully, small tears may be field-repairable (Fig 12-35).

Professional attention is needed if the tear is structural: line attachment loops, supports, seams, most internals, or anything that changes the wing's shape.

Getting wing or lines in a spinning prop is obviously bad. Even if they just barely get wrapped around the hub, it can do invisible damage—get the wing inspected. Surprisingly extensive damage *can* sometimes be mended by qualified shops.

Rip-stop nylon tape from camping stores, available in various colors, can work in a pinch. Cut it into an oval that covers the tear with about an inch of overlap. Make one for both sides of the fabric. Stretch out the fabric, wipe it clean, dry, then press the repair tape on top. Press hard. It is best to line the pattern of little squares up with the wing material's pattern. Repeat on the other side.

Inspection

After 2 years or 100 hours of sun time on a new wing, it should be professionally inspected. After that, annual inspections are recommended for hard-core flyers and every other year for others.

Although there are many lines, a cascade failure is where one line breaks and transfers load to adjoining lines, which break in a cascade of many lines. It is rare but does happen, especially on wings that are "ridden hard and put away wet." That includes heavy maneuvering or aerobatics—such wings should see at least double the inspection frequency, much more if they're flown often.

Some wing inspectors put the brake lines back to their original specs, which may be much longer than your setting. Or they could just be too long—kite the wing before flying it! In one case the brakes were so long that the pilot couldn't turn.

Line Stretching

Don't tie a broken line together, especially the highly loaded A's: it shortens the line and halves the strength. Replace it.

Lines shrink with time, especially if they get damp, losing up to a couple inches in length. Kevlar lines shrink less than Dyneema (or Spectra). Since the A's and B's bear more load, they tend to stretch back to their proper length during flight leaving just the rear lines shrunk. That changes wing camber (curvature) and Angle of Incidence so they should be stretched back to their proper length (Fig 12-36). A wing that's getting hard to inflate may need this treatment.

If you cannot get the lines to be within a 1/4 inch of their specified length, or they stretch too far, the offending lines need to be replaced.

After an Ocean Dunking

It is universally accepted that dunking a wing in salt water is bad—finely abrasive salt crystals remain after the water evaporates, shortening the glider's life (both lines and fabric). But if you remove the salt water right away by hosing it down with fresh water, the damage can be minimized.

To rinse a wing after immersion, clip it along the trailing edge to a strong clothesline. Hoist it up high enough to get the cell openings above ground.

Spray it thoroughly with fresh water to clean out any remaining brine. Get up inside each cell opening to get it completely soaked. That should drain away or at least dilute the briny badness to a safe level. Then leave it on the line, out of direct sunlight, to dry.

Whether fresh or salt water, take care when extricating a submersed wing—it becomes extremely heavy and will tear easily if lifted with water in the cells. Pull it out slowly by the trailing edge. One method is to stuff it in a wing bag while both are in the water.

Emergency Tool Kit

A lot can be fixed in the field with a few simple tools and parts that fit in your harness. Mostly, you want to be able to tighten anything that can loosen, replace the belt (if applicable), adjust the carburetor, and replace the spark plug.

- Allen wrenches. Almost all engines use metric sizes 3, 4, 5, and 6mm.
- Screwdrivers. Make sure you can adjust the carburetor.
- Lightweight spark plug wrench. The type with just the round hex fitting and a hole is good—your screwdriver can double as the leverage.
- Small knife, small locking pliers, and a small socket set (3mm - 8mm sizes).
- Spark plug, wire ties, 2 feet of safety wire, spare fuel line, and super glue (for the prop).

Multi-tools are convenient, but having a bunch of accessories that aren't useful just adds bulk and weight.

If you're flying enough distance to need this kind of kit, think about packing a very small container of 2-stroke oil—enough to mix up one full tank's worth.

> **Caution!**
>
> Never put the wing in a washing machine or dryer. The stress and heat would be very damaging. If it gets wet or submerged, pull it out carefully by the trailing edge and dry immediately in an open area, preferably out of direct sunlight.

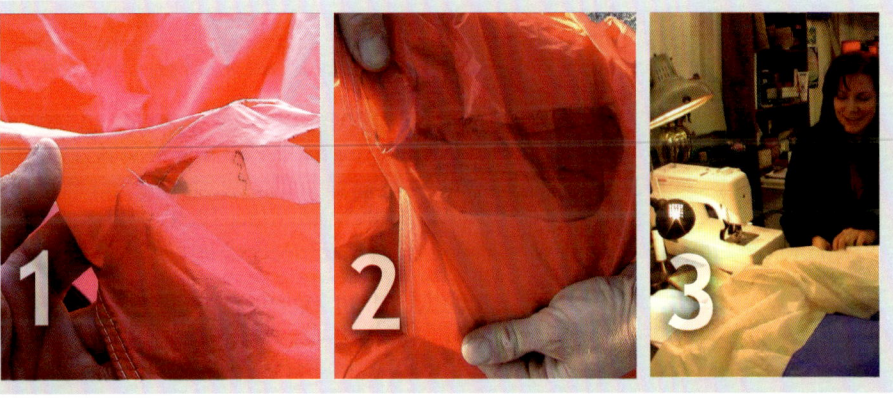

Fig 12-35 Glider Repair

1. The hole.
2. The patch.
3. The real fix. Here is a typical inspection shop where gliders are tested and repaired. A porosity meter measures how quickly air can seep through the fabric. Strength testing of lines is done with a special scale and repairs are done with various types of sewing machines. There's more to it than meets the eye.

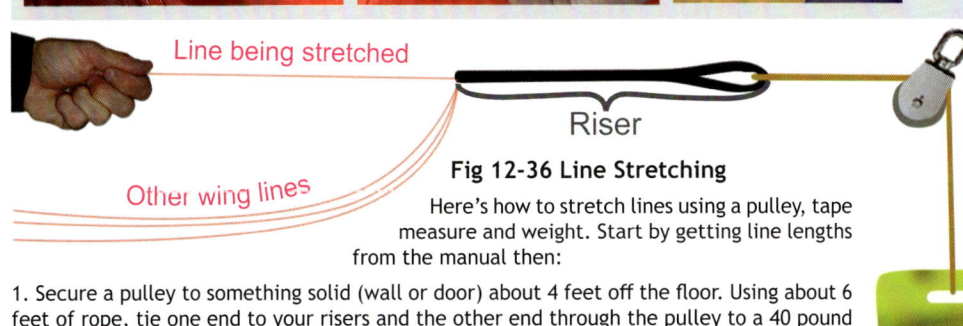

Fig 12-36 Line Stretching

Here's how to stretch lines using a pulley, tape measure and weight. Start by getting line lengths from the manual then:

1. Secure a pulley to something solid (wall or door) about 4 feet off the floor. Using about 6 feet of rope, tie one end to your risers and the other end through the pulley to a 40 pound weight.

2. Stand behind the wing fabric and grab a D line (or cascaded lines that the D connects to) where it attaches to the wing. Pull hard enough to lift the weight up and hold for 20 seconds. Compare it with the same line on the other side to see how much it stretched, then stretch that other line. Repeat for each line.

3. As you do this, measure the line length periodically to see if it's getting to the manual-prescribed length. If not, stretch again.

Reserves

Reserves generally come from the factory ready to install and deploy; most come with containers that easily clip onto your motor frame and harness, but this must be done correctly. Installing it wrong may be worse than not having it at all. For example, the bottom must be secure so that it doesn't flop outward when the handle is pulled. See "Reserve" on page 279 for more on reserve choices.

There are several places where a reserve gets mounted (Fig 12-39), each with advantages and disadvantages. For example, a side mount is reachable by only one hand, front-mounts can get in the way of egress, overhead mounts can be difficult to grab in wild air, and underseat mounts have a slightly awkward pull.

Set up with an eye on easy reach and deployment. You need enough arm travel to pull it all the way out of the container **and throw** in a clear direction. Underseat and over-head mounts are best if the paramotor was built for them. Here are some considerations for reserve mounting:

- Never require pulling a reserve with the throttle hand—the throttle will prevent full extension. Don't worry about hand dominance—rehearsal can make either hand work.

- For side mounts, the reserve's weight can *slightly* oppose the motor's torque roll (weight shift) force. For clutch machines, that means putting it on the right side.

- Research has shown that we naturally grab near our hip and initially pull up and back rather than outward. Mount accordingly.

- Portable front mount reserves can be added quickly where the reserve container clips in and its bridles go right to the carabiner—quick and easy—but must be disconnected to get in and out of the motor.

- If reserve bridles connect to the regular carabiners, use steel carabiners.

- The reserve bridle should be routed along the harness or motor frame and remain clear of throttle cable, straps, speedbar, or anything else that would get in the way during deployment. Use Velcro or a very small wire-tie that breaks loose with about 20 pounds of pull. This will prevent nuisance breaks during normal handling but allow the reserve to pull free when needed.

- Go through a deployment in your mind, imagining where the reserve will come out, catch air, and pull as it extends fully with the pilot hanging below. If possible, do a deployment while hanging in a simulator then have someone pull the reserve bridles with enough force to peel them out of any retaining system (Velcro or wire-ties). Make adjustments as necessary.

- Hook each reserve bridle to a D-ring (or other) above your regular attachment. Hang from that point in a simulator to see what the landing would be like. Imagine landing like that. There are reasons to be tilted back and let the motor hit first, and good reasons to be upright and do a proper PLF ("Fig 4-23 Parachute Landing Fall" on page 54). The latter has less chance for a broken back and more chance for a broken leg. If you have a large enough reserve, the upright option would be better.

- Connecting to the main carabiners works but offers no protection in a carabiner failure. Ideally, the harness allows for separate attachments.

- As with any reserve, follow its user manual and consult with someone who is familiar with that model's installation and use, especially on motors.

- If your harness comes equipped with reserve loops, use them—they will be designed to distribute the opening shock.

> **Caution!**
>
> Paraglider reserves are **NOT** compatible with skydiving reserves and vice-versa. Ours open quickly and theirs opens slowly, each for good reason.

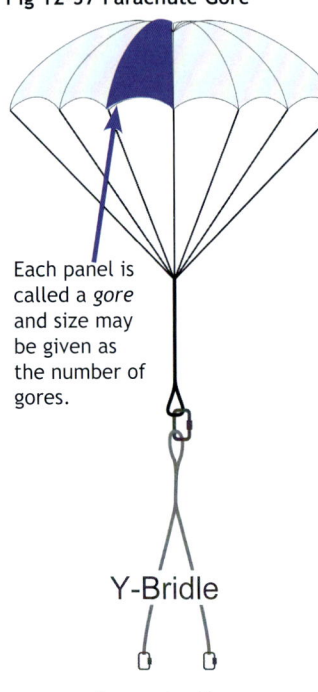

Fig 12-37 Parachute Gore

Each panel is called a *gore* and size may be given as the number of gores.

Y-Bridle

Paramotor Harness Attach Points

Reserve Care & Maintenance

Store the reserve as you would a paraglider—in a cool, dry place away from sunlight or chemicals. Of course, if it remains on your motor, be careful about where the motor goes. For example, getting the motor wet is no big deal, for the reserve it means a repack.

Reserve Repacking

Have your reserve repacked annually or biennially depending on storage and where your motor has been. Over time, fabric tightens into shapes that don't open quickly, and rubber bands degrade.

Any reputable glider shop can pack a reserve as long as they're familiar with the design. They will inspect it and replace anything that's needed. Parachute riggers, used for skydiving canopies, are a good resource if they're familiar with our rapid-opening needs.

You can do it yourself if you're certain about the procedure, and have the requisite parts. Particular techniques make it *much* easier, and while videos help, a repacking clinic lets you ask experts during the act. It's also a great time to rehearse tossing it just before starting the repack. Steerable reserves are more complicated and may warrant professional repacking.

Fig 12-38 Reserve Pins

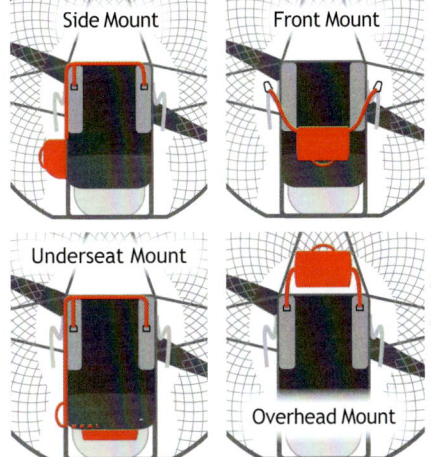

Fig 12-39 Basic Positions

Fig 12-40 Reserve Mounting Examples

Fig 12-41 Front Mount
Convenient, easy to reach, impedes egress.

Fig 12-42 Overhead
Requires lots of practice to reach quickly.

Fig 12-43 Under Seat
This harness is made to accommodate an under-seat reserve. A flatter pack will be more comfortable.
Inset: deployment pins.

Fig 12-44 Side Mount, Low Carabiners
Bridles go through the main carabiners to lower "D" rings. Landing will be more leaned back since the D-rings are more forward.

Fig 12-45 Side Mount, High Carabiners
Pilot lands more upright with these attachments. Wire-ties/tape must break at 20 pounds max pull.

Bridle attachments should be fabric to metal unless you learn when and how it's safe to use webbing-to-webbing connections (shown below in #4).

See Fig 4-22 on page 53 for deployment procedure. The illustration below explains the mechanics of deployment. Envision an angry Gorilla suddenly yanking your reserve lines with 300 pounds of pull.

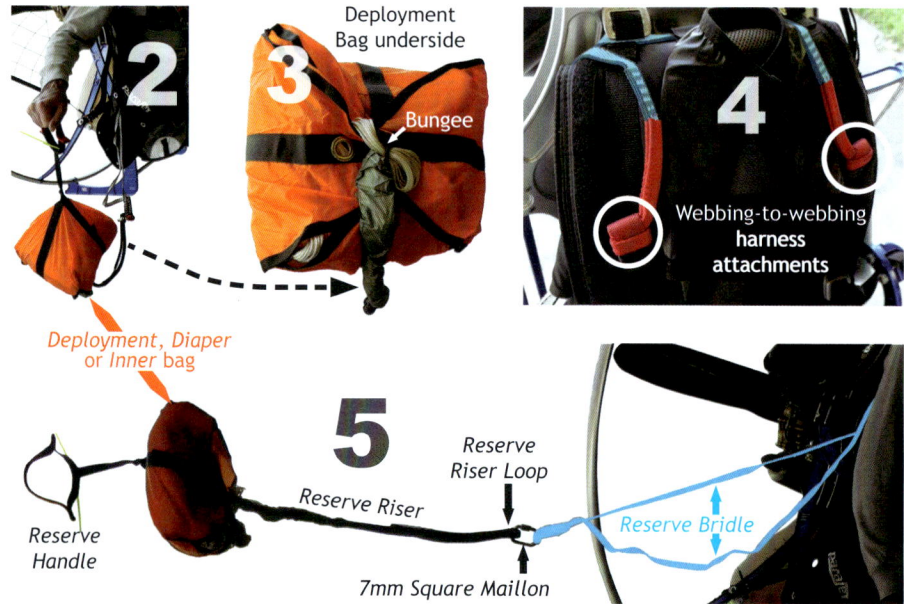

Fig 12-46 Reserve Deployment Mechanics

#1 Handle placement determines how quickly pilots will find it while being tossed around. Get near the hip which is where they naturally tend to grab.

#2 shows the handle pulled, opening the harness container and exposing the reserve-containing deployment (inner) bag.

#3 The inner bag's underside. A loop of reserve riser keeps the flaps closed until the bag hits full extension. Those loops pull out, the flaps open, and magic happens.

#4 Bridle routing must ensure nothing (throttle cable, speedbar line, bars, cameras, accessories) can interfere with reserve opening.

#5 The deployment bag opens just after this point. It and the handle fall away as sacrificial bits. On some setups they stay attached.

by Dana Denney

Flying Cross Country

CHAPTER 13

Heading out on a cross country is strangely exciting. Exploring new directions, going for miles to nowhere in particular, poking about the landscape from barely above—it's a freedom that many have only dreamt about.

Obviously there are limits. Don't plan on commuting to work, although it's been done, and beware of small changes in weather that can lay waste to plans. Don't get out and *need* to get back unless that's part of your planned adventure. Desire to return clouds sound decision making. But once armed with appropriate skills, gear, and weather knowledge, cross countries can be extremely rewarding. You launch from home, alight at some distant spot, relish the accomplishment, replenish, then head back or press on.

There are parts of the planet that show their best face when viewed from above. But not too far above. Our magic chairs are the best seats around.

Basic Tips

Whenever flying farther than you're willing to walk, these tips may help, especially as distance increases.

1. Choose days with benign weather for your whole flight and several hours afterwards. You can't see what's happening back at the departure point.

2. Let somebody know that you will be flying and take a cell phone. Better yet, take a satellite locator beacon which have become *very* affordable.

3. If the wind shifts, try changing altitudes for better groundspeed. Wind is normally stronger up high, but not always. GPS phone apps and devices are invaluable. Some even have a display that shows winds at your altitude (Fig 13-14).

4. Avoid flying low, but if you must, do it while headed *into* the wind. Staying above 200 feet AGL avoids most of humanity's many protrusions (especially wires). Do scan for towers that stick *way* up.

5. Cross power lines at their supports (poles or towers) and well above. See Fig 19-5 on page 193.

Fig 13-1 Airspace & TFRs

Is the airspace on your route legal *today*? See Fig 9-12 on page 95.

Temporary Flight Restrictions (TFR's) pop up for many reasons, including dignitaries, security, and firefighting. Check online or call Flight Service to make sure you don't blunder into one.

This was from SkyVector.com for a fire fighting area. Presidential TFR's are bigger and less forgiving. Mousing over any point in the circle shows its basic values.

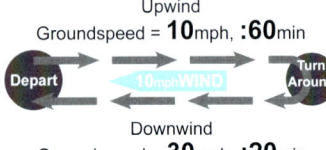

Fig 13-2 Go Upwind First

In a 20 mph craft, groundspeed gets cut in half pretty easily by a headwind.

In the above example, with just a 10 mph wind, it takes 3 times longer to go 10 miles upwind than it does to come back.

6. Download maps to your favorite map app. If you lose cell signal, you'll still have data. Consider printing a paper map to tape onto your leg.

7. Don't get squeezed into night time. Besides being illegal, finding your way *safely* to the ground gets harder. On evening flights have a small flashlight or fully charged cell phone for its light.

8. Carry basic tools. Consider having bug spray.

9. Have a simple wing bag in case of engine out.

10. Consider taking a small amount of two-stroke oil in case you wind up in someone's yard and they're willing to let you use their lawn mower gas.

As always, stay within gliding distance of safe landing areas. Consider retrieval options—can they get across that river, for example?

Fuel & Range

When choosing a route, start off *into* the wind. If you decide to come home early, the return trip will be quick. Fuel planning is easier, too: go upwind for half of your endurance and then turn around to land with some reserve.

If there is little or no wind, only fly 1/3 of your endurance before turning around just to leave some margin for error. On a many-leg flight, plan the last leg to be downwind.

Know your endurance and have an in-flight way to check fuel (like a mirror).

If you're carrying oil, sometimes it's possible to land near a gas station and refuel. It does feel funny—walking up to the pump with your bizarre-looking tank, filling it and knowing you'll be using it to run off into the sky. Strange, but amazing.

Getting Lost

In most areas of civilization, getting lost is unlikely given how ubiquitous GPS is. And then it's more of an inconvenience. Embarrassing yes, but you could land and ask for directions. The following tips should avoid that fate.

1. After takeoff, look back towards your launch area to remember what it will look like. Do this first a mile out, then a few miles out. On the way back you will better recognize it. Lighting and clouds will change appearances, but it's a good start.

2. Climb up higher. As long as airspace and clouds allow, you may get a better perspective.

3. Use roads and other prominent landmarks. Think of major roads, rivers, or railroad tracks in your area and whether you've crossed them. For example, if a major north/south highway runs west of your launch site, but you haven't yet crossed it, then you know you're east of it.

4. Use road signs. Find a nice, landable field along a road with signs and scoot down to read it. Only with a PPG! **Don't get below wire height** though, and always maintain safe landing options. This could be quite risky if you're not careful or there aren't any good "outs."

5. There's always the maps program on your phone. Even without Internet the GPS works and can show location.

6. If you will be away from civilization, follow best practices for hiking in remote areas, including what to carry.

Navigation

The following tools aren't *necessary* to enjoy cross country flight, but they can be fun to master. In fact, they underpin an entirely different skill set: dead reckoning and pilotage, skills that are still taught during airplane pilot training.

Dead reckoning is using a plotted course, calculated groundspeed, and heading to navigate and predict your future position. Using forecast winds, a map, and a compass, you can come up with the heading to fly that should keep you on course. Pilotage, covered later, is reading the map in flight and adjusting heading to stay on course. Manual navigation is a combination of these skills.

Even though we don't need all this, understanding it can be helpful. Mostly it can be a fun exercise—planning, then flying it accurately with just a map, compass, and watch. Some types of competitions score prowess in these abilities.

The purpose of all navigation is to fly a desired track over the ground and arrive at the destination at an estimated time. Using the navigation log (Fig 13-8) do the following:

1. Draw a line representing your desired ground track. Mark the line at easily identifiable checkpoints along the way (Fig 13-6 spots 2 - 7) and measure the distances between each mark. Enter these checkpoints on your PPG navlog.

2. Measure the *true course* (described below) of each straight segment, then apply variation to come up with a magnetic course for that segment.

3. Calculate the magnetic heading that corrects for wind and tells what the planned groundspeed will be (using the wind calculator in Fig 13-5).

4. Build a navigation log to be used in flight or just for reference.

5. Go fly the course using pilotage.

Plotting the Course and Heading

True course comes from measuring your course line relative to the chart's nearest line of longitude. You get to use a protractor. As an aside, lines of longitude end at the true north and south pole. From true course, add or subtract the variation as shown in Fig 13-6 on page 137 to get magnetic course. In this case, there is 12° east variation.

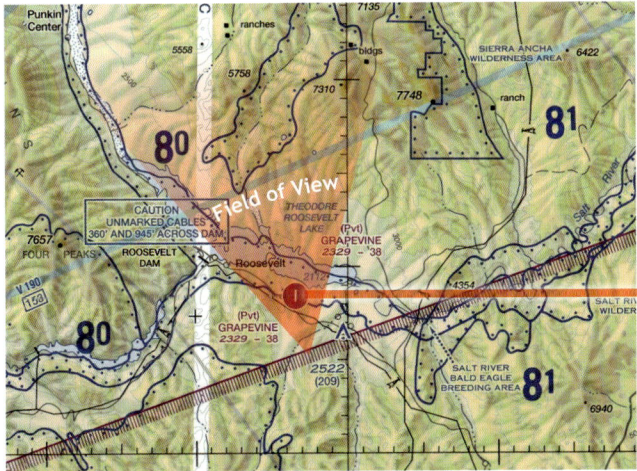

Fig 13-3 Sectional Chart Roosevelt Lake
You're departing Grapevine Airport, Northeast of Phoenix, AZ. Use SkyVector.com (or something similar) to check the airspace and see what's along the route. These charts give only a rough idea of terrain; use Google Earth to see photo-realistic accuracy from an inflight perspective.

Fig 13-4 Google Earth View
Open up Google Earth on a phone, tablet, or preferably a PC. Use the tilting, slewing, and pointing tools (look up "Google earth shortcut keys") to look in the place and direction of flight. On a computer, mousing over terrain shows the elevation and "eye alt" so you can relate it to how high you'll be flying.

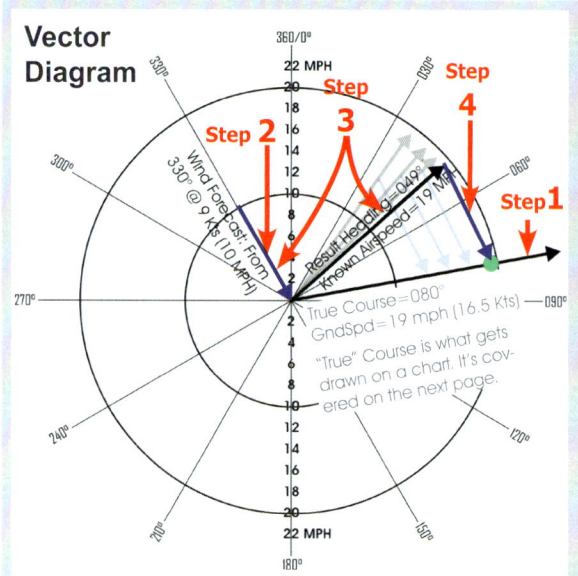

Fig 13-5 Calculating Ground Track & Groundspeed

Once you know the desired ground track (plotted course) and your airspeed you can use this to get heading and groundspeed:

Step 1. Draw your plotted course (080°) from the center outward.

Step 2. Draw your forecast wind (blue line) as the direction the wind will be from. Length is wind speed and its head is touching the center.

Step 3. You'll need two strips of paper. Mark one as a wind speed arrow (length is 10 mph) and the other as airspeed (length is 19 mph).

Step 4. Keep the wind arrow parallel with the wind direction while sliding its arrowhead along the plotted course. Keep the airspeed arrow's tail anchored at circle center, its body touching the tail of the airspeed arrow. While sliding the wind arrow, its tail will eventually be touching the head of the airspeed arrow. Stop. You've got a wind triangle. The airspeed arrow represents heading-to-fly and the wind arrow is pointing at groundspeed (the ●).

Here the plotted true course of 080°. The quartering tailwind turns out not to have any effect on groundspeed—tailwind benefit is canceled out by the slowing effect of crosswind. You will fly a 049° heading to maintain the 080° ground track if all goes as planned.

Remember this saying: "West is best; east is least." That means west variation is added to true course, and east variation is subtracted from it. So if you want to go true east, (090°), subtracting 14° from 90° gives a magnetic course (MC) of 076°. Flying 76° in no wind would yield a 090° ground track.

In Fig 13-5, the true course is 080°. With that in hand, add (for west) or subtract (for east) the variation to get a magnetic course. In this case, subtract the 14° east variation to get a magnetic course of 66°. That is the magnetic heading you would fly with no wind. We'll correct for wind next.

Choose checkpoints along the route that will be easy to identify and easy to get a time measurement on. The best ones will be usable even if you're off-course. Rivers, power lines, highways, or railroad tracks that cross perpendicular to your course are great. If they angle across your course, as in real life, it's more difficult—you must know more accurately that you're on the course line when hacking the time.

If you're writing out a navigation log, it can be filled in with the points, distances, and magnetic courses. After headings, these are the most useful bits. You're on a foot-launched craft, though, so writing on a log will be challenging. This is why competition pilots fly with clipboards Velcroed to their legs.

Wind Correction

Any wind will affect your groundspeed and track. Think of wind as a block of air in which you're drifting. When you're airborne, that motion is added to your own and must be accounted for to achieve a desired ground track. If you're trying to track due east and the wind is from the north (wind is given as the direction it's from), then you'll need to hold a heading to the left—what is called crabbing. With our slow speed, a little wind makes a lot of difference.

One way to figure this out is with a vector diagram as shown on the previous page—it represents speeds and directions visually. Vectors, in this case, are arrows, one for your in-flight speed and heading, and another for wind speed and direction. Follow the diagram's directions for "Calculating Ground Track & Groundspeed."

If you're flying a round trip that ends up back at your launch site, any wind will increase your total flying time. Also, direct crosswinds slow you down. If any wind is present, it must have some tailwind component to keep groundspeed equal to or better than airspeed.

Chapter 13: Flying Cross Country

Fig 13-6 Magnetism, Truth, & Courses

Sectionals are laid out in grids of longitude and latitude with respect to True North. Compasses, however, point to Magnetic North. The difference is *variation* (also called declination). Constant lines of variation are shown as dashed magenta *Isogonic Lines*. On this chart, the line at ▼ means that variation is 12° East. If you looked exactly North using your compass, you would be looking 12° East of True North.

To get Magnetic Course (MC), **subtract east** ("east is least") variation and **add west** variation to the true course (TC).

So, in this case, our measured TC was 81°. After subtracting 12° of variation (use the closest Isogonic Line), Magnetic Course is 69°. Fly that heading in still air and you'd stay on the plotted line.

But air is usually moving, so we must account for wind drift. The result is Magnetic Heading (MH)—the compass heading you fly to stay on course.

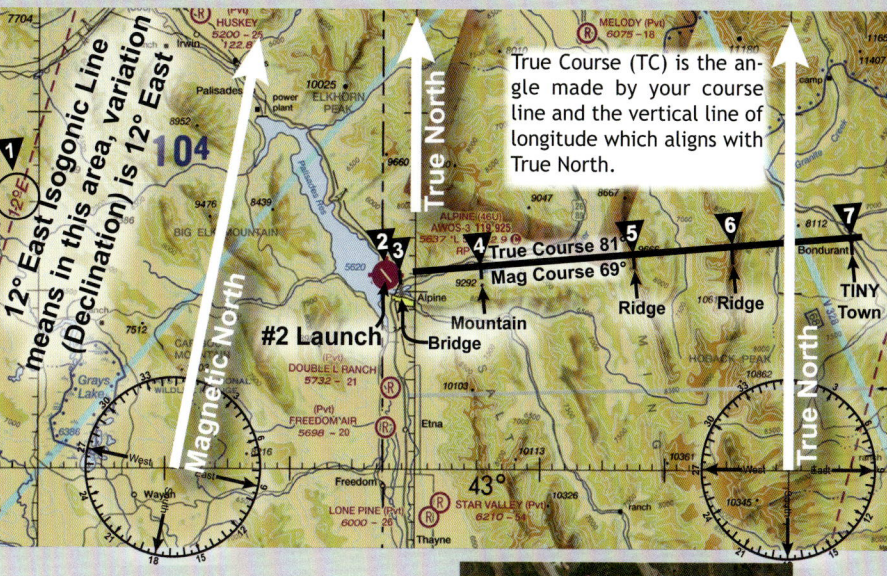

Pilotage

Pilotage is flying a course using a map, log, and visual cues. It's particularly fun and pretty easy from a paramotor, given our awesome view.

Good planning provides ground track and initial heading to account for wind. It's only as good as the wind forecast.

After launch, take up the planned heading until you can find some of the checkpoints and see what kind of correction it really takes. The goal is to maintain a desired ground track: if there's a crosswind, don't just point at the next checkpoint when it comes into view—point upwind, crabbing into the wind enough to compensate. You want a straight line over the ground. It's not necessarily intuitive since you're pointing upwind of the target, so make sure it's your ground track that is heading towards the target. The pictures below give some insight.

Reading a map and associating ground features takes practice. Sectional charts work well for an airplane moving 100+ mph but, for us, topographic maps make more sense. They are far more detailed which is why they're used for competition.

Google Earth can help visualize a route in 3D before flying. Fig 13-4 is a great example of seeing what points will look like from above.

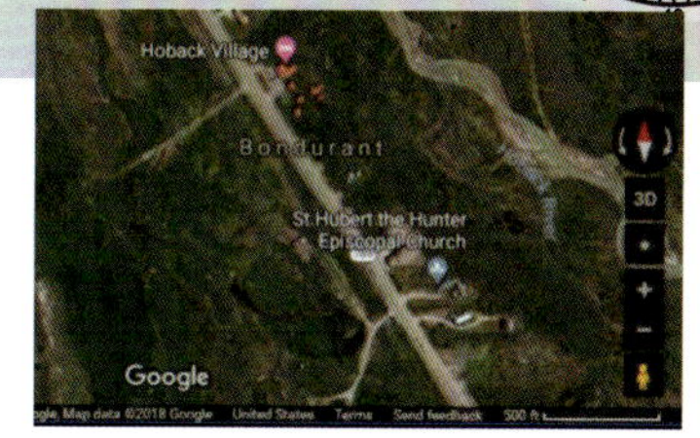

Fig 13-7 Choosing Waypoints

The destination is Bondurant, a tiny town on a road. The road should be reasonably obvious, especially since it crosses the course and has a river alongside. But the town itself would be hard to pick out.

This is a good example where looking on Google Earth or Maps (like here) is helpful even if you've driven by an area. Yes, it takes a small part out of the exploration fun—but it's a trade for reducing destination drama.

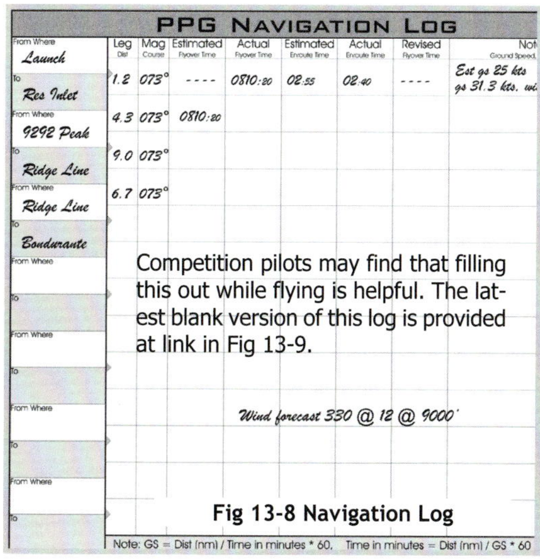

Digging Deeper: Earth's Moving Magnetic North

The Earth's magnetic north moves slowly over the years. In fact, the rate of drift is measurable and some charts show not only the current variation, but how fast it's drifting.

The Agonic Line shows where there's 0 variation between true and magnetic north (lucky compass users there). In the U.S. this line goes through Central Indiana—your compass heading is also your true heading.

The most significant difference between true and magnetic courses in the U.S. is on the northernmost coasts. Both east and west coasts have a difference of up to 20 degrees.

Fig 13-8 Navigation Log

Competition pilots may find that filling this out while flying is helpful. The latest blank version of this log is provided at link in Fig 13-9.

Fig 13-9 Navigation Tools

A number of navigation tools mentioned in this Chapter can be downloaded from FootFlyer.com at this link.

 http://www.footflyer.com/powered-paragliding-navigation-tools/

Even on detailed maps, some depictions are nearly worthless—small roads and populated areas, for example, are similar to other small roads and populated areas unless they're next to some prominent feature. Once you identify town A, it's easy to see what the town just south of it is. Yellow areas on aeronautical charts try to indicate what lighted areas look like at night and have marginal semblance to what you'll see in daylight.

Obvious features, such as highways, railroad tracks, landmarks, and the like are best. Using a long, straight feature (like railroad tracks) requires some way to tell where you are along that feature.

Telling distances is tricky too; although it's easier in areas that are conveniently laid out in a N/S and E/W grid pattern. Early settlers were thinking of us. There is no such order to other areas, especially hilly ones.

The most useful tools on a navigation log are the mileage and estimated groundspeeds. You can either fill in the actual numbers or just use the log for reference. Some navlogs (or electronic calculators) have time in minutes; they must be converted to tenths—every 6 seconds is one tenth, so 8 minutes and 12 seconds is 8.2 minutes.

Crabbing & Drift

Fig 13-10 Crabbing in Real Life

Here's the pilot's view. He's aimed (heading) right of course to maintain the desired ground track. Pick points that line up and keep them lined up.

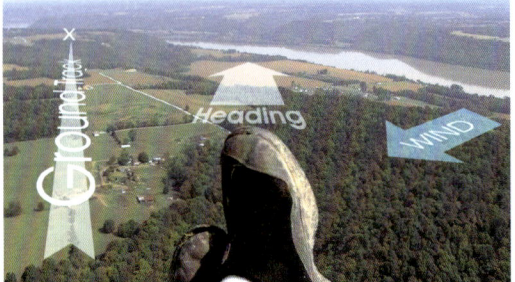

Fig 13-11 Crabbing

A. The pilot started off heading for point 3, a water tower which is due North, and suspects that there's an Easterly wind (*from* the east). He did a good job picking out easily identifiable visual waypoints in a line. Sure enough, he notices left drift by seeing the angle to point 1 (church) change and the next two points no longer lining up. Number 2 (antenna, #2) is to the right of #3.

Clearly he's drifting left.

B. This illustrates a correct crab into the wind so that everything stays in line and the least distance is flown. That's also the fastest and uses the least energy (fuel or watt-hours). He's pointed to the right like in Fig 13-10 but keeping the next waypoints in line with each other. The idea is to figure this crab angle out right away. Guess at a heading that includes some crab, pick two points ahead that are on your course and see if you're staying on course. Adjust the crab as needed. You're pointed in the "Heading" direction but looking left (in this example) down the ground track.

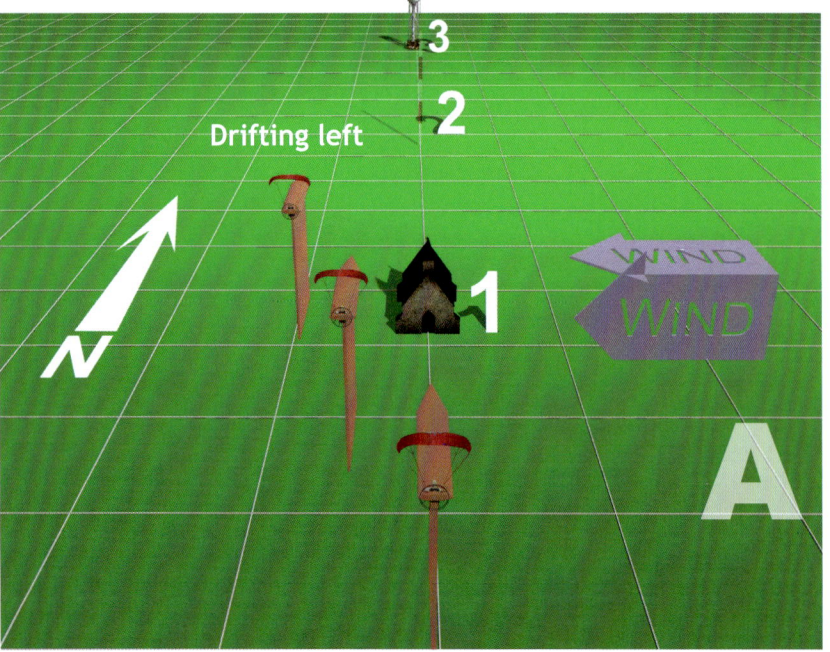
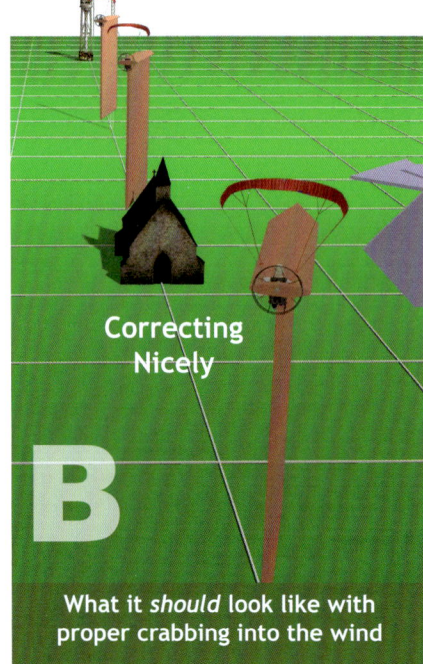

What it *should* look like with proper crabbing into the wind

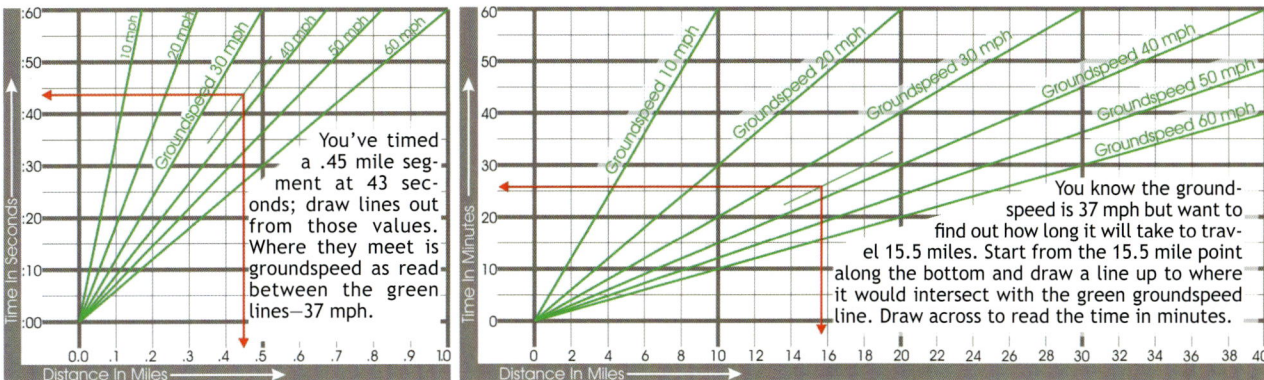

Fig 13-12 Speed, Time & Distance Charts

Full resolution versions of these charts are available on FootFlyer.com.

Mixing Units: As with all charts in this chapter, different units can be used as long as speed and distance are compatible. For example, knots are nautical miles per hour. So if distance is in nautical miles, then speed must be in knots. If distance is in regular (statute) miles, then speed must be in regular miles per hour. U.S. air maps (*sectionals*) are marked in nautical miles so knots and nautical miles are a convenient combination.

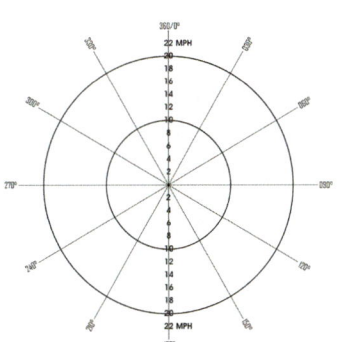

Fig 13-13 Vector Diagram

Once you know the wind at your altitude, a vector diagram can help calculate your groundspeed for an upcoming route segment. For example, you may be able to follow a road that goes due east in a northerly wind of 30 mph, but you'll make no headway trying to go due north.

Calculating Groundspeed

With a stopwatch and a map, you can calculate groundspeed. With that you can estimate your position at any time, or time at position. If you also know your heading and airspeed, you can even tell what the winds are, although that's a bit much for someone piloting a paraglider. And no, if you're already doing this manually, looking at an app for winds aloft is not sporting!

Charts included here facilitate these calculations without any electronics. The charts can be taped to the same clipboard as your navlog for easy reference. Competition or personal challenge is what these tools are about.

Altitudes

Choosing altitudes is critical for maximizing performance—climbing or descending can yield free additional groundspeed if more favorable winds are found. Start with the best possible winds aloft information from preflight to get an idea of what to expect. Then improve your mental wind-image by trying different altitudes. Generally, the higher you go, the stronger the winds blow but not always. Be quick to try different altitudes, especially if groundspeed dwindles appreciably.

Most airplanes cruise over 1000 feet AGL. Above 3000 feet they tend to fly in 500 foot increments with the eastbounders using odd altitudes (3000, 3500, 5000, 5500, etc.) and westbounders using even altitudes (4000, 4500, 6000, 6500, etc.). Knowing that may help you know where to look out for them. Eastbound is considered a magnetic course of 0° through 179°; westbound is 180° through 359°.

Lingering above 10,000 feet is risky given that jets fly their fastest speeds up there, even more so within 60 miles or so of larger cities.

Fig 13-14 Paramotor App on Phone

(Top) Screenshot that shows an app's winds feature in use.

Fig 13-15 Paramotor App on Watch

Altimeter watches commonly include GPS capability. Displays can corral useful information into one or two screens.

On many models, altitude can be based on air pressure *or* GPS. Pressure is a bit more responsive.

See more about navigation accessories under "GPS" on page 283.

Using a GPS

GPS is everywhere, and cheap navigators abound (see "GPS" on page 283). Besides moving maps, they offer groundspeed, ground track, and even derived winds aloft—helpful for inflight route changes.

If the GPS says you're tracking 120° (southeast), but you're pointed due east (090°), the winds are mostly out of the north. If it says you're only going 15 mph and your normal airspeed is 25 mph, there's a 10 mph headwind component. If your route has a northerly pointing segment coming up, you may end up with too much headwind.

The GPS time-to-destination is hugely valuable, but mostly on the last straight segment of a journey. On routes with course changes, it's good to know the winds aloft to choose ideal altitudes for each segment and building an idea of its impact on average groundspeed.

Deriving Winds Aloft

You can estimate winds aloft using GPS by doing a slow 360. Note the slowest groundspeed and heading where it occurred—that's where the wind is from. Also, note the fastest groundspeed. The difference divided by 2 is wind speed at your altitude.

So if your slowest speed was 10 mph and your fastest speed was 30 mph, the wind is blowing 10 mph (30–10=20, 20/2=10). A side effect is getting your "True" airspeed (what a GPS would measure in perfectly still air): it's slowest speed + wind speed. In this case, 20 mph.

Deep Cross Country

Most cross country flights are out-and-back, but some pilots like to go farther—out where a pickup, or even overnight camping is needed. Difficulty varies with skill, terrain, weather, ease of navigation, and how much you carry. Here are some tips.

1. Consider landing sites with an eye to re-launching at the planned time. For example, a hill with a friendly upslope wind in the evening will likely be downslope by morning. It's what cool air does—flows downhill.

2. Plan, plan, plan. Consider *lots* of contingencies for landing short, including retrieval. For example, loss of power on one side of a river, may be *dramatically* more difficult to deal with than on the other side.

3. Have a charged cell phone with extra battery capacity and/or an emergency satellite device (Fig 28-20 on page 284) and let someone know your plans.

4. Start off by underestimating your ability to cover distance. Plan flights with only about half of your normal range to ease stress, allow for changes in wind, and getting a handle on real-life limitations.

5. Plan for pee. Drink enough to stay hydrated, but don't overdo it. There are ways to use the inflight bathroom but they're not perfect.

6. Try out new gear on local flights before it's really needed. Work out the bugs while close to home and consider the safety implications of added goodies. That extra fuel bladder is a great idea, for example, until it leaks all down your pants or gets pulverized by an uncaring prop.

7. Keep it simple, savoring the adventure over the number of miles. Start with easy LZ's within 10 miles that have food. Grab a bite and fly back. Observe the logistics, weather, unforeseen issues, etc. Grow from there.

8. Don't wait for tailwinds—it gives up too many opportunities.

See also "Unsupported Races" on page 210.

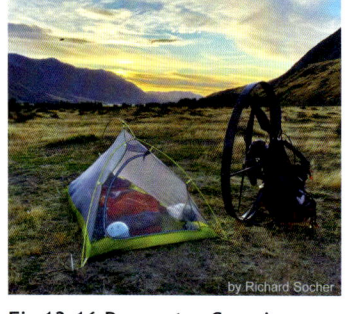

Fig 13-16 Paramotor Camping

You've got to carry everything, but for those who launch reliably, and crave adventure at some expense in uncertainty, this is tough to beat.

Flying with Others

It's fun to flock together. When done with care, using best practices, flying together can be safe and enjoyable. But it obviously complicates matters in sometimes surprising ways, adding risk and unsavory elements that this chapter aims to help minimize.

CHAPTER 14

Fig 14-1 Being on Radio

Techniques for formation flying are covered in Chapter 16. Here we concentrate on of surviving and thriving with our fellow flyers.

The pilots above are all in radio contact, which makes formation flying safer.

Courtesy

As with most issues of courtesy, common sense is key. But what is common? If an activity seems like it may be obnoxious, dangerous, or marginally safe—that's your better judgment whispering: "hmmm, maybe this isn't so bright." Given the observation that it's not so clear-cut, here are some guidelines.

Where to Lay Out

If another pilot already has his wing laid out, avoid setting up in his way. Instead, set up behind or beside him. Even if you think you'll launch first, try to stay clear of his path in case you get delayed. It is bad form to lay your wing out in a way that requires another pilot to steer around it. If you think proximity is an issue, ask the affected pilot if it's OK or just move farther away. By the same token, you'll make no friends by leaving your wing laid out for a long time in a crowded field, taking up valuable space.

Look at where your run will take you and be sure that it's clear. Have a good climbout path that doesn't fly right over any spectators, campers, or other pilots. Being illegal is secondary to being rude and dangerous. An inopportune motor failure would put others in danger.

Even at official gatherings, be mindful of your noise during climbout; change locations, if necessary, to avoid getting too close to people.

While airborne, avoid buzzing about the launch area, especially in light winds. Your wake may linger for several minutes, making it even more difficult for those trying to takeoff. Plus, pilots in challenging conditions may be waiting for just the right puff of breeze and won't appreciate your annoying presence when it comes. Climb up to at least 200 feet AGL after launch or go elsewhere so other pilots get a chance at clean air.

Prop Blast

Be mindful of your prop blast. Don't point it toward other people or their wings. Blowing someone's carefully positioned wing into a tangled mess will quickly sully your reputation. The same thing for fly-bys—be careful about where your prop blast goes. Even if nobody is preparing to launch, don't let wake or prop wash get to any laid-out wings. Flying near enough to roll up someone's wing is a sure sign of industrial grade ignorance.

Keep the plane of the propeller clear so that if a prop were to come apart, the shards would miss anyone nearby.

Risks

We must manage additional collision risks when flying with others. First, be very vigilant about 1) your position, 2) the pattern, and 3) keeping an active scan for other traffic. If you do not know where your flying buddies are, carefully look around, including above and below.

If you suspect there's traffic nearby that you don't see, pick your direction—we'll say right. Look right, beside and behind, look down, then throttle back and smoothly turn right while descending.

In general, do shallow turns to ensure pilots are not cruising directly above and descending towards you. Don't make sudden changes in altitude until you know it is clear in the desired altitude. Don't turn until satisfied there is nobody coming from that direction.

Follow the turning rule without fail: "Look, lean, turn." Besides weight shifting, the lean alerts other pilots of your impending turn. Even better is to **look**, start a **shallow** bank, look **up** and **down** in the turn direction, *then* start your **turn**.

Flying with one or two other pilots adds nearly as much risk as flying with a hundred because we tend to drop our guard. A moment of distraction may be all it takes if your buddy comes up on you unnoticed. Having a launching pilot climb into an already flying pilot is another too-common occurrence.

Collision

One valuable tool on sunny days is your shadow (Fig 14-3). Note where the sun is, then look down at the ground at the same angle. Once you see your shadow, check for other gliders' shadows nearby. **The higher a wing is, the more blurry it is.** So if the shadow you see is blurrier, like in Fig 14-3, carefully (after looking down) descend while looking up towards the sun to find it.

Be cautious with formation flying, especially with strangers, but even with pilots you know (see "Formation" on page 165). Keep a decent distance until it's obvious they know you're there, *then keep tabs on them.*

Most collisions happen between pilots **who know each other,** and frequently are the **only ones flying**. A common situation is when one pilot takes off and climbs into the other. It only takes a few seconds of inattention to lose track of your flying buddy—pay particular attention when flying within a mile of another.

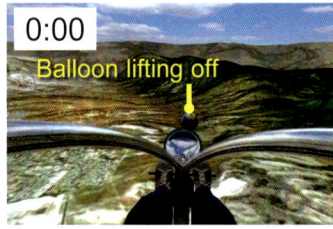
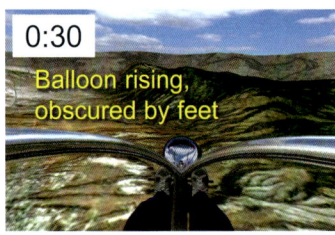
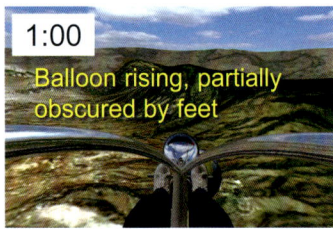

Fig 14-2 Hitting a Balloon

Flying with different types of aircraft adds complexity beyond what's obvious, even if they're slower than you. This animation, done for a real accident, shows how surprisingly insidious a balloon collision could be.

The PPG pilot was keeping track of a group of balloons to his left while a lone balloon, that had been on the ground for a while, launched without notice. Its relatively rapid ascent probably presented little relative motion and may have been partially obscured by the pilot's feet or trike frame.

When flying with others, be vigilant in all directions, including above and below, to track other craft, especially with distractions such as photography.

A periodic turn of a few degrees will dramatically aid seeing another craft, especially one that may be coming from above or below.

Wake

Flying through a paramotor wake can be rough. At best it will be startling; at worst it can fold part of your wing. It's especially dangerous when combined with other factors, like unloading the wing (getting light in your seat). Everything on a paramotor produces turbulence as it parts the air, but wingtip vortices are most worrisome ("Tip Tornadoes" on page 226).

Wing wake settles, spreads out slowly, drifts with the wind, and is worse on heavier craft such as trikes, tandems, and even heavy pilots. The wake of any craft, including your own, is much worse if it's in a steep turn.

The powerful wake of heavier machines, like PPC's, must be given a wide berth, even more so in smooth conditions where it lingers longer.

Treat a wake encounter as you would any other turbulence ("Active Flying in Turbulence" on page 166): basically a bit more brake pressure and throttle for level flight. As always, if you feel the wing fall back, or misbehave, follow the mantra "**reduce power, reduce brakes, then steer.**"

Fly *above* the path of preceding aircraft to avoid their wakes. Flying directly behind and near the same altitude as a preceding wing puts you between the vortices, which is sinking air. As expected, being closer makes it worse.

Rescuing a Pilot

If you fly with others, you may eventually be in a position to help them. Here are some tips. See also "Getting Out of a Tree" on page 200.

What a Drag

Kiting or flying in strong winds makes getting dragged more likely. If you see it happening, don't lunge on the *pilot* (or his motor)—stop the *wing*. A wind-whipped wing can overpower even several burly helpers. Run around behind it so the wing drapes around your legs (see also "Deflating the Wing" on page 26). Grabbing a wingtip and running it towards the pilot is also effective. Whatever you do, don't grab lines—they'll quickly leave painful burns.

Water

One of our biggest fears should be going in the water, more so without an auto-inflating device on the motor ("Flotation" on page 283). Due to extreme exertion, a person can drown in less than a minute. And it doesn't take much water to be deadly, especially if it's moving. One pilot drowned after landing on dry land, but *beside* a culvert with moving water. His wing went in and dragged him under before he could unclip. We're fragile.

If faced with helping a pilot in the water, get flotation. A boat is obviously best, but use whatever else can be found quickly, like a surfboard, inflatable mattress, or life jacket. Jumping in without flotation won't likely help the victim and will probably be *your* demise too. Get something buoyant to the pilot so he can relax for a moment, then carefully unbuckle and get away from his gear.

If he is submersed, your options dwindle. Leaving your own flotation could easily put you in the same tangled dilemma, or drag you down with sinking gear or a panicked flail.

Only go back for gear with a boat or other reliable flotation.

Power Lines

Voltage is to electricity what pressure is to water, and power lines have a *lot* of pressure—enough to push lethal current through paraglider lines. All it takes is for you to make a path to ground—a small one, to be sure, but even residential poles carry

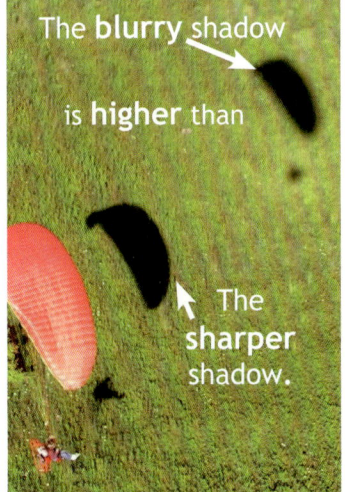

Fig 14-3 Using Shadows
Use this fact to tell the other glider is in front and above.

Fig 14-4 Looking Sketchy
Just because you *can* inflate and run around laid-out wings doesn't mean you should. Others may not know that you have it under control and will, somewhat rightfully, be mad at the attempt. If you're planning something out of the ordinary, even if it just looks that way to others, it's better to talk with them first.

4000+ volts, and high-tension wires go up to half a million. While it may be current that kills, it's voltage that pushes it through our normally-resistant bodies and lines.

So if a pilot lands in power lines and does not fall to the ground, **leave him hanging!** Do not reach up for him—that could complete the circuit that kills you both. Rather contact the power company and wait until they shut the lines down.

Trapped by a Thrusting Motor

It can happen that a pilot's motor goes unexpectedly to full thrust, pinning him in the process. This is risky for pilot *and* rescuer.

Before jumping into the fray, have a plan. Stay clear of the prop *and* make sure the pilot sees you coming so he doesn't swing the revving motor your way. Also, know how you're going to shut it off in case the regular kill switch has failed. Don't think this is so uncommon—a severed throttle cable usually disables the kill switch too.

Alternative shutoff methods are covered in "Motor Stuck at Full or Partial Power" on page 199. They include pulling the choke or covering the air intake. Pulling the spark plug cap off works but be prepared for a startling shock. Shutting off the master switch, if there is one, may not kill the motor—it primarily prevents inadvertent starter activation.

If you're flying with a buddy, know how to shut off each other's motors.

Communications

Flying with others gives added reason to have a radio (see "Radio Compatibility" on page 281), especially if it works through your helmet. Even if it doesn't, carry one so that if you go down, you can work out retrieval plans. Learn the *Bump Scale* (Fig 5-16 on page 61) so you can communicate it to your flying friends.

Formation Flying

Formation flying presents risks beyond just flying with others ("Midair Collision" on page 194) and requires precision handling skills ("Formation" on page 165) in proportion to proximity and complexity. Master precision flying first. Specifically, be able to actively keep the wing where you want it, even in turbulence, without thinking about it. Until that point, stay 5 wing spans away from other pilots and always keep your distance from someone who angles away when approached. They are obviously not comfortable with your closeness.

Never accept a visibly fast closure rate. It could quickly yield a collision or invoke last-minute control inputs that cause a spin or stall. If it looks like you're approaching someone quickly, turn away **NOW**, before it's too late.

Fig 14-5 Loose Formations

Loose formations where pilots follow one another are relatively easy as long as everyone knows how to stay out of the wakes.

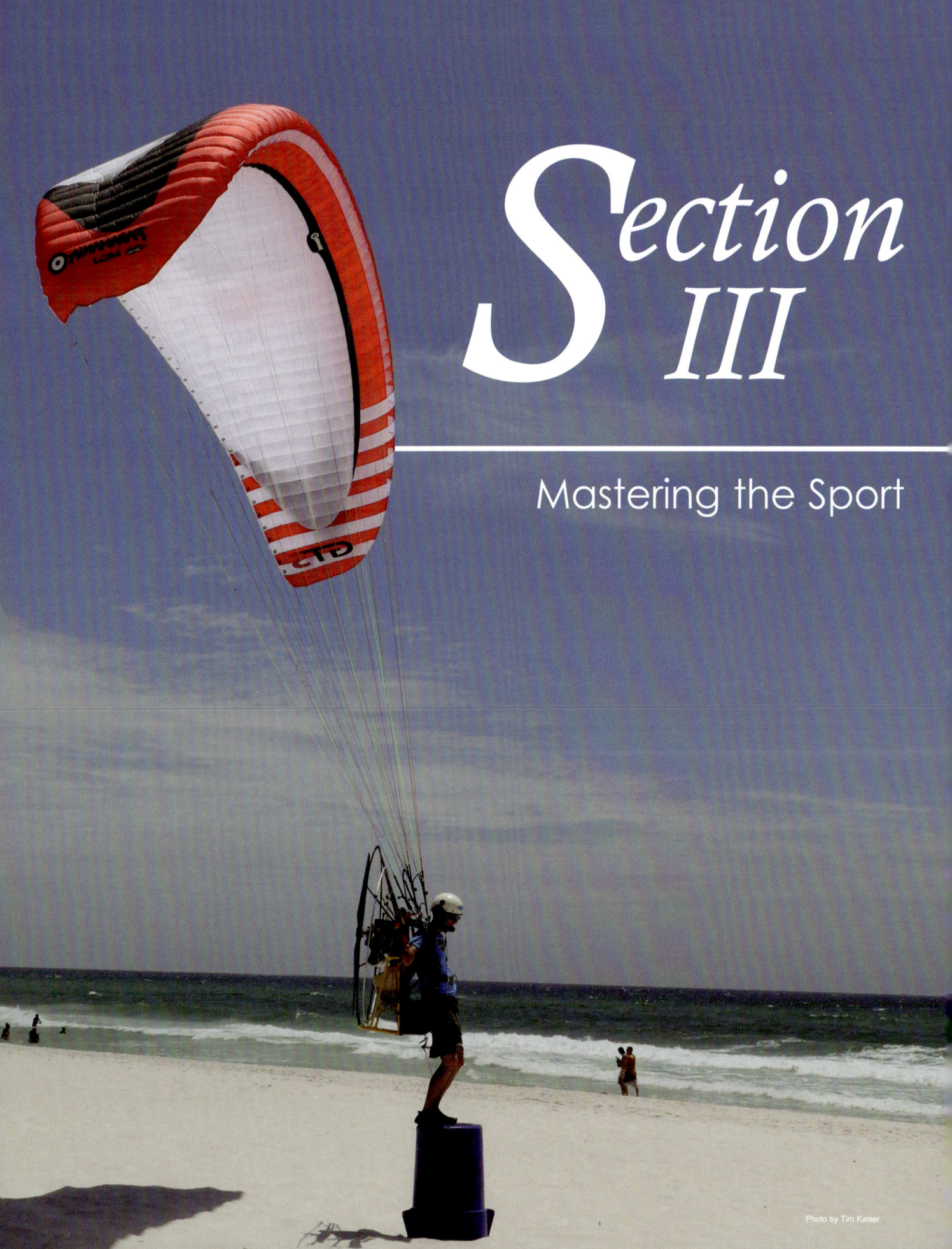

Section III

Mastering the Sport

There's nothing wrong with having merely adequate skill. You can safely enjoy this sport without ever needing to become exceptional. Having basic launch, landing, and flying skills is plenty as long as you stay within your boundaries, fly well-regarded, safe equipment from large fields, and stick to mellow weather. In fact, getting to a high level of mastery involves some extra risk since you must nestle closer to control's edge—exploring the limits of what our craft can do. It can do a *lot*.

We will:

1. Show some of what's possible,
2. Explain some processes to speed up learning,
3. Point out risks, where appropriate, and
4. Show what to practice and how to know if you've actually mastered the techniques involved.

Portions of this will help *any* pilot, while other parts are distinctly for the more risk-tolerant. Find a mentor who also revels in fine control. Besides getting guidance, you may also find a kindred spirit.

You need *some* element of talent—an inherent kinematic sense—but most people have enough. They can become quite accomplished with enough directed practice. That's what we're trying to do here and in the videos described below.

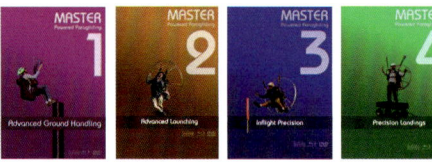

Section III
Mastering the Sport

"It's not how many flights you have; It's what you've done with the flights you've had."

The Master Powered Paragliding video series uses live action, animation, graphics, slow motion, and highly skilled pilots to expose advanced topics clearly. They're intended for use with an experienced coach who will speed the process while reducing risk. The series will help anyone aspiring to mastery.

by Mark MacWhirter

Advanced Ground Handling

CHAPTER 15

It's surprising what can be done with these wings when you know how. It's equally surprising how effortless the experts make it look, and how advancement can be so vexing. Fortunately, most skills can be practiced in the privacy of your own field.

Of course, if you see someone doing something you want to learn, go talk to them about it; they'll almost certainly be happy to share. And the best pilots have the best ground handling skills.

Build slowly! Master steady, moderate winds before taking on anything that could lift you. Work with a coach to hasten the process at lower risk.

Upside Down Kiting to Clean out Cells

All manner of debris gets into a wing, acting like sandpaper, and abrading away the fabric's lift-giving life. It must be removed (see also page 37). You *can*, of course, hold up the trailing edge and shake it out, but that's boring. We'll kite it upside down.

Find a smooth, clean surface (preferably grass) with the wind blowing from 7 to 12 mph. You *can* do this in the sand, but until you're really good, it's tough to avoid re-scooping more sand. Gloves help avoid line burns because you'll be handling lines more than toggles.

Before kiting, shake sand down from the tips down since they don't have cell openings. If you have tip trailing edge openings (Fig 3-26), use them now.

A harness makes it easier, but you *can* use just the risers. Either method takes fine control to prevent the wing from slamming down onto its leading edge—potentially popping out cell stitching (yes, we've seen it happen). Hook into your kiting harness just like you were going to fly, then:

- Get the wing on its back with the leading edge facing up like in Fig 15-1. Either walk it into this position or flip it over while kiting (Fig 15-2).

Fig 15-1 Upside Down Kiting

This is the start position for upside down kiting. Notice he's holding the brake line, not its toggle.

- Once it's on its back, grab the brake line closest to each hand, above (beyond) the pulley as shown in Fig 15-1. Treat the brake lines like the A's in regular kiting. Pull them just enough to get the wing to come up while snatching your body backward. Once it's up enough, pull both brake lines towards you and let up quickly, repeating the action to shake stuff out. A satisfying show of falling debris indicates success. Let the wing down gently on its leading edge.

After dumping debris, and just before the leading edge touches down, lean (or run) towards the wing so that its cell openings lay down, face-up. That avoids scooping up more stuff, especially if you're in sand. Kiting the glider back over like Fig 15-3 takes even more practice to avoid scooping debris back in.

Fig 15-2 Getting The Wing Upside Down

Start from a regular reverse kiting position with the wing overhead. Or, build a wall and pull one tip A line just enough to get it turning over.

Keep pressure on the A line as the wing turns over. Walk with it until it turns, but be prepared to pull on both brakes when it gets upside down.

As it comes over and down, pull on both brakes to cushion the touchdown. Do not let it whack down hard on the leading edge, which can blow out stitching.

With the wing laid out upside down (or towards you, if flat on the ground), grab the brake lines above their pulleys to kite it upside down.

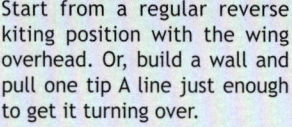

Fig 15-3 Flipping Back

The wing is upside down and you want to flip it back over.

1. Grab the brake line and A riser (outer A if equipped) as shown.

2. Modulate brake line and A line pull to get the wing turning over. Think "cup the wing" then tweak it for motion.

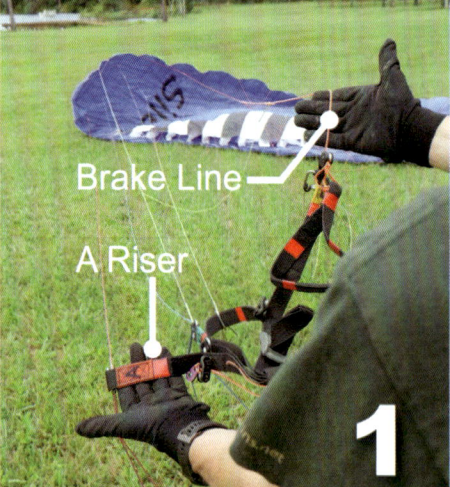

Kiting Without a Harness

There are reasons to learn this (riser kiting) besides it being fun and looking cool:

- it's a great way to get some feel for the air,
- spreads out the wing nicely,
- lets you quickly check for tangles,
- and makes repositioning the wing easy.

Many techniques work and have advantages, but these seem to work especially well. They're all tiring in anything more than about a 7 mph breeze. And it *can* be dangerous if you don't let go upon getting lifted—pilots *have* been injured when they held on too long and dropped too far.

With any method, move with the wing. If it goes left, go with it. In fact, if you *want* it to go left, move right first, let the wing start to fall left, then follow it. To stop a wing that's moving left or right, walk (run) *beyond* it. This works on all the kiting methods. Build finesse so *less* movement is needed in case space is limited.

One Hand per Riser—Good for Higher Winds

By holding a riser in each hand, it spreads out the load, making this the best technique for strong winds. Those who do somersaults while kiting use this method.

Face the wing and hold the risers as shown in Fig 15-4, #3. Inflation may need to be done like in #2.

Modify the grip for your wing so that you can rock its angle, tilting the leading edge up or down. If the wing doesn't want to come up, move your grip so it pulls more A's. If it wants to frontal or overfly, move the grip back so it pulls less A's.

Holding firmly, lurch backward as you would with a harness. When the wing comes overhead, dampen it by decreasing the pull or "rocking" your hands back to pull the rears down. If it tries to overfly you, move backward while rocking your hands back. You have to be quick-footed to stay ahead of it. Primary steering is done by pulling down one riser and letting up on the other. To go left, pull your left hand down and vice-versa with the right hand. To force the wing more overhead, or prevent it from falling back, tilt your hands so the A's are pulled down more.

If the wing is rocketing up during inflation, move *towards* it.

You can re-grip, but that's hard because of the wing's pull. If it's always trying to overfly you, let go of the risers and re-grab them farther back. It's like letting go of a kite briefly while trying to catch its string in a different place.

There are several ways to bring the wing down: 1) walk towards it, steering it to the side so it falls over; 2) let go of one riser (what a mess); 3) briefly letting go to re-grip back near the rear riser; or 4) put both risers in one hand, then with the free hand, reach back to pull the brake lines or rear risers.

A's and Brakes

This offers the best control in light winds and works with or without a harness. Leave the brakes in their holders and grab both A's with your left (or right) hand, and the brake lines (not the toggles) with your other hand as shown in Fig 15-4 #1. Then:

- Inflate by pulling A's *and* brakes with just enough A-pull to keep it coming up. This avoids front tucking the leading edge and inflates quicker. Think of a spinnaker sail cupping the air.

- There is immense control because you can modulate the A's and brakes so widely. If it's jumping up quickly, pull more brakes. If it's sluggish, walk backward faster and let up on the brakes.

- Move left and right as necessary to keep under the wing. Steer with the brake hand, too—moving the hand right makes the wing fall left.

- If the wing wants to fall back, walk backward faster then: 1) pull more A's, and 2) ease both hands downward. When the wind picks back up, let your hands go up. Modulating like this can absorb small changes in wind speed that might otherwise require more moving around.

- If the wind increases and the wing wants to continually overfly you, either pull more brakes or walk downwind to reduce the relative airflow.

Fig 15-4 Risers-Only Kiting

#1 **A's & brakes** works well in light winds. Pull just enough A's and brakes to hasten initial inflation. Get it to billow first then add more A's.

#2 **A's and Rear's** works better in slightly stronger winds because it reduces wing lift vs using brakes.

#3 **One hand per riser** is also good in stronger wind. Play around with the best way to hold the risers, starting with what's shown here. Make sure you can rock your hands back and forth to pull more or less A's.

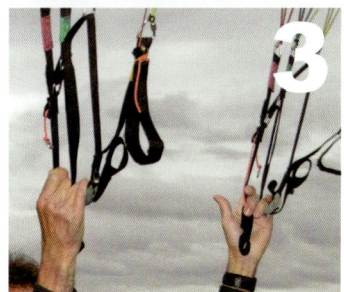

Move around as necessary, but the *goal* is controlling it well enough to stand still. That requires anticipation and finesse born of much practice.

To deflate with this technique in a stronger wind, get the wing overhead—almost front tucking. Then step towards it while aggressively pulling full brakes and letting the A's go loose. It snaps down through the power band (strongest pull) quickly. If you try to bring the wing down while it's hanging back, it pulls much harder.

A's and Rears

Using the A's and rears (Fig 15-4 #2) allows kiting with less lifting. But since the rear risers aren't as effective at steering, it's not as sensitive. Instead of holding the brake lines with your right hand, hold the rear risers. The glider can be steered and slowed this way, like what's described in "Brake Line Failure or Tangle" on page 48.

Loops and Brakes

This is where you hold the risers by the very ends (the loops) with one hand and reach behind to pull on one or both brakes with the other hand. The pilot at left demonstrates steering the wing by pulling the necessary brake line, in this case he's holding both toggles.

To inflate, hold both risers at the loops with your left hand and the A's with your right hand. Pull primarily on the loops, but help it come up by pulling the A's as necessary. Once it nears the top, let go of the A's and be ready to go for one or both brakes with your right hand.

High Wind Techniques

This can hurt—be careful! Don't clip in until you're ready for high forces and have a stout helmet fastened securely.

There must be nothing downwind that would hurt if you got blown into it (or strained through). Start learning these techniques in less than a 15 mph wind and, even then, only with someone who can grab a wingtip and run it to you, or get behind the wing and let it drape around them. They must know not to tackle you—which could get you both dragged. Further, if you get lifted, they must not let themselves get lifted. Helpers have been seriously hurt by doing so.

Be prepared to deflate the wing as covered in "Deflating the Wing" on page 26.

Don't have the motor on—you are vulnerable to *turtling* onto the cage and getting dragged, spewing dollars, until you hit something. About the only way to stop the carnage is unbuckling from the harness (impossible while being dragged), jumping out, and running after the remnants of your bouncing gear. It's much cheaper to master these skills with*out* the motor, and in a harness with back protection.

Laying out & Clipping in

Don't stretch the wing all the way out. Either leave it in a partial ball or lay it out 90° to the wind as described Fig 15-10. In merely moderate wind, spread it out halfway with just the middle exposed.

Don't clip in or pull on the risers until you're ready for action. Initially, lay both risers within 10 feet of the wing's trailing edge. Even a small riser tug can catch air and awaken the monster. It may then spring to life with great vigor, dragging you along for the ride. So clip in close to the wing, risers loose, while getting ready to control it. Walk along with it if it starts drifting downwind.

Consider holding the rear risers while clipping in. If it does come unexpectedly to life, you can pull those risers hard to suck the life out of it.

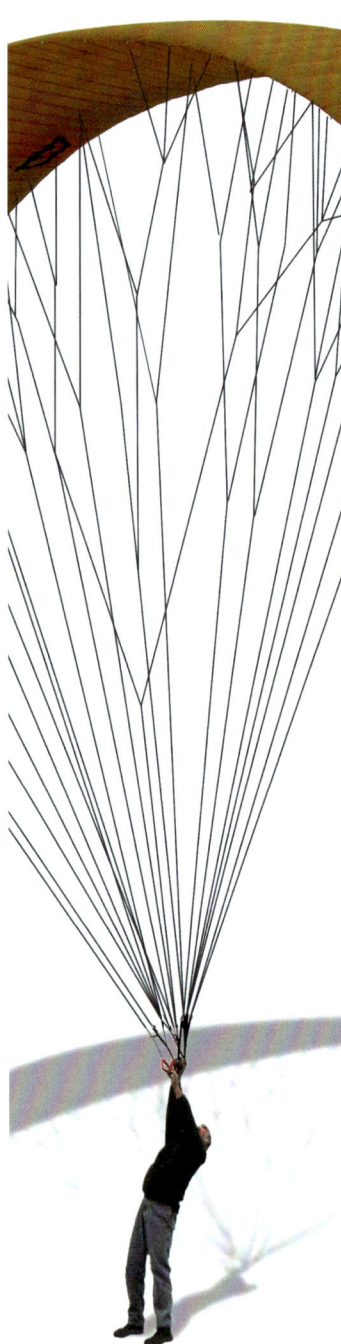

Fig 15-5 Risers and Toggles

In this method, hold the riser loops with one hand and the brake toggles with the other.

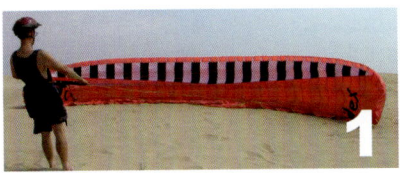
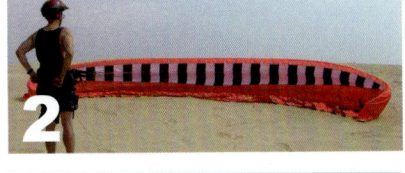

Fig 15-6 The Wall

1. Hold even brakes while pulling your body back against the wall to make it come up higher.

2. Step towards the wall and pull brakes to lower the wing, reducing its tug.

3. Letting the wall down too much can allow wind under the trailing edge which flails upwards. If the tips come up, reach out to the brake lines and pull them in. Keep the wall high enough to prevent this in the first place.

4. By now you probably already know that this pilot needs to step right to bring down the high right side.

Controlling the Wall

Be ready on the brakes when bringing your glider to "attention." Step back (away from the wing) to tension the A's, giving them a small tug if necessary. As soon as it starts to inflate, pull on the brakes *just enough* to hold it down; it may be necessary to pull them *way* back. But if you pull too far, air *can* get under the trailing edge, causing it to snake up out of control. With enough wind you may not need any A-pull at all—just step back and it will lurch to life. Be ready on the brakes to keep it down.

In stronger conditions, pulling brakes alone may not be enough to keep the tips down, especially with longer brake lines. If that's the case, reach to the rear risers and pull them back while keeping hold of the brakes. You can hold both brake lines in one hand, behind your back, to free up the other hand. Be careful wrapping the brake lines around your hand (taking wraps), which could cause line burns and cuts in strong winds. Gloves help.

Once you have a well-formed wall, it may be bucking up and down. As you've already learned, backing away from the wing will raise it while pulling the brakes more, or leaning towards the wall, will lower it. If it gets too high, the pull may be overpowering. If you pull too much brake, the trailing edge may flail up into the breeze; there is a balance.

Done correctly, you'll be standing there with lots of brake pulled, controlling the wall's height by leaning towards or away from it.

If You Get Lifted off Your Feet

If you're hooked in reversed (as you should be) and get airborne, you'll untwist to forward then get deposited downwind somewhere. The *Alan Method*, described shortly, can prevent that—you'll come down while still reversed and under control.

If you *do* get lifted, **don't pull lots of brake!** Don't pull *any* brakes except to keep the wing from front tucking. If you pull lots of brake while facing forward, or with unsure footing, you'll probably lose control—the wing goes back with vigor, first lifting, then straining you through whatever is downwind. Even just tapping the brakes in a strong blow can start this carnage; less brake is best. If it's that strong you should be using the rear risers instead of brakes.

Inflation

On a normal inflation you lean back, away from the wing, and pull just enough A's to help it come up. In high winds that may be difficult—the minute you reach for the A's, you reduce brake pull which may allow the wing to start inflating. Many wings will inflate at the tips, which then come up and inward, leaving a mess. If that wants to happen, here are some techniques to try.

- Pull the tips in. Start with the brake in your right hand, which is going across to the opposite tip—pull it way back. Then reach out with your other hand and

> **Caution!**
>
> High winds can be extremely dangerous. If it's blowing hard enough to use these techniques, then understand the increased risk and be ready to act the minute you clip in. First work with an instructor who is familiar with high winds and can handle getting lifted or dragged himself.

Fig 15-7 Lifted in High Winds

1. Don't take on strong winds until you're ready to get lifted and/or slide. Learn in moderate winds first, where you can run backward and get airborne by pulling some brakes. Practice sliding on your feet during the inflation, too.

2. On higher performance wings, it's difficult to recover a dipping wing with brakes alone, especially if you can't move towards the low side. Try this: Use both hands on the high side—pulling A's and brakes.

3. If you get lifted way up, go hands mostly up initially, then apply some brake pressure as you stop climbing. Look down and flare normally.

pull the tip in farther. Do the same for the other side so both tips are toward you. They may roll up a bit in the wind which is OK. Starting with the wing balled up, or horseshoed slightly can prevent this from happening.

- Inflate the wing without pulling any A's at all. When ready, simultaneously reduce brake pull and step back. The wing will rocket upwards and pull you downwind. Run or slide towards it briefly. It can be tricky—the minute you let go of the brakes it will start coming up, yanking.

There is a balance in how much to resist the wing on its way up and how much to move with it. You must keep *some* resistance or it won't have enough relative wind to work with. And you must have some downwind movement—trying to lock yourself (like with helpers) will make it shoot up and overfly you.

Sliding on your feet during inflation is perfect (and fun), albeit challenging. Done properly, you will slide (or run) 5 to 15 feet then stop as the wing reaches overhead. Applying brakes to stop the wing may lift you—be ready. By walking (or sliding) towards it while it's rising, there will be less chance of getting lifted. Once it stops overhead, you *must* let up on the brakes. Using rear risers instead of brakes reduces this tendency at some cost in controllability.

The Alan Method

One way to kite in high winds is to use the brake lines *above* their pulleys (Fig 15-8). You can also use the rear risers themselves to reduce the likelihood of getting lifted unexpectedly but sacrifice some control. Gloves are helpful since you'll be holding the brake *lines* (not the toggles) that could cause friction burns.

This also gives deep control over the brake pull, and if you get lifted, lets you stay reversed and in control. That's hard to do while holding the brakes by their toggles. Once the risers start to uncross, however, there is not enough leverage to prevent untwisting, so keep yourself a little more twisted than exactly reversed.

1. Hook in reversed like you were going to fly but do not grab the brake toggles.

2. Inflate the wing by stepping back with your body and pulling on the A's as necessary. As the wing nears overhead, let go of the A's, and reach back around the outside of the risers to grab the brakes as shown in Fig 15-8. The challenge is getting to those brake lines quickly.

3. Steering is no longer crossed. Watch the trailing edge to make sense of what's needed and what you're doing. Control fore-aft surges and direction by modulating the brake lines as you would normally.

4. Keep the risers crossed and touching each other. That means you'll be turned slightly beyond 180°. Doing so allows you to remain reversed if you get lifted off your feet.

5. In stronger wind, lean way back to increase rotational inertia. That confers greater resistance to getting swung around if you get lifted off your feet.

Here's the secret sauce: if you do get lifted, keep yourself reversed by opposing the turn with brake lines. For example, if you're untwisting to the left, pull some brake pressure as shown in Fig 15-8 and move both hands left. This only works when using the brakes *above* their pulleys.

It's possible to actually fly this way but is confusing. Pulling more brake with your left hand will slow that side down into a turn—a right turn from the wing's perspective. Watch the trailing edge to visualize what's happening. This needs to be practiced *a lot* before letting yourself get very high.

In light winds, when the wing falls back, you'll need to let go of the brakes, walk

backward, and pull on the A's to help it come back up. Quickly going from brakes to A's is tough. Practice often since you'll need to be fast-acting in stronger winds.

Once mastered, this technique has other benefits. With very light winds, it's a way to quickly go from kiting with the A's to using brakes. That's handy when it's light and switchy.

Kiting Control

Minimize brake pull if you're getting lifted frequently. Use more movement and weight shift—where you dip a hip towards the falling side. Lean way back so that getting lifted upwards a foot or so only angles your body up without losing traction. Keep knees bent to better absorb a gust without getting lifted or knocked off balance. Proper posture (Fig 15-9) really helps.

A good test of skills is to stand there kiting reversed while looking straight ahead at the horizon, past the "V" of your crossed risers. Practice this at first in a steady wind of 8 mph or more. Learn to use risers and feel to know what the wing is doing.

Kiting while facing forward also lets you learn a feel for the wing without looking. There is no magic—you'll feel slight tugs and see slight riser motion in your periphery. Move subtly left/right and forward/backward in response. It's a useful skill.

Assisted Inflation with Motor

In strong winds, helper-assisted motor launches are dangerous, mostly to the assistants, even if they're familiar with flying. Helpers have suffered prop injuries from various causes. If you require assistance, it's probably too strong for your skill. Assistance makes some moves harder while adding risk to you *and* them. It's only a bit safer if you have an electric start, but don't start until they're *well* clear.

Helpers can never be allowed near a spinning prop, which limits assistance to forward inflations if the motor is idling, even with a clutch.

They must move *with you* as the wing comes up, resisting your motion with 30 or so pounds of pull but letting you move downwind. That makes the inflation more manageable. Once your motion stops, then they can try holding you in one place while allowing left/right corrections as necessary. Instruct them that if you get lifted, they should walk downwind while holding you. Emphatically instruct them to let go if they feel themselves start to get lifted (for their safety).

To further reduce risk, have the assistants use short ropes (not long enough to get into the moving bits) tied to a sturdy part of the frame. The assistants pull on those ropes which are easy to let go of (no loops). Assistance is sometimes used when a large wing makes initial inflation difficult.

Fig 15-8 The Alan Method and Flying Backward

Kiting this way offers more control in strong winds. You can oppose the untwisting force and remain facing the wing even after getting lifted.

Steering is easy, look at the trailing edge and imagine how the deflected brake will slow that side down causing a turn.

Preventing untwist: If it's untwisting you left, Pull downward evenly on both brakes while also moving both hands sideways to the left.

The hard part is combining steering and counter-twist inputs. It's a skill that highly experienced paraglider pilots learn for controlling launches in higher wind situations.

Once mastered, you'll also find it helps with kiting up vehicles, poles, etc. just for the fun of it.

Fig 15-9 Posture: Alan Method Kiting

Knees bent, leaned back in proportion to lifting force, with relaxed arms holding brake lines beyond the pulleys.

Fig 15-10 High Wind Tips

1. If you use a helper, he must let you move.

2. Only try this with soft bailouts after mastering it on level ground.

In a strong*ish steady* wind, approach from below the touchdown point, then add some brake, swinging up to it.

Once standing, control via braking, flexing the knees, and directing thrust to oppose unwanted lean. Modulate power and fly the wing while maintaining *some* brake pressure.

3. Sand anchors the upwind tip. Clip in and start pulling the wing into a normal wall, or inflate the downwind tip first, brining it overhead.

Handling smooth surfaces

High winds on smooth surfaces like beaches are tough to manage. The minute you lay the wing out it wants to slide away. The solution is to minimize exposing its cell openings to the wind. Here are some tips.

- If you normally stuff your wing, pull it out in a rosette oriented properly into the wind. It's easier if you always stow it in the same way.

- Lay the wing out parallel with the wind and put something heavy on the upwind tip that won't damage the fabric (Fig 15-10 #3). Sand works, but make sure it won't go in the cells during inflation.

- A slight tug on the downwind "A" will bring the wing to life, yanking it around into position. Use brakes or rear risers immediately to control the wall. You can also pull an A riser and brake on the downwind tip to bring it around (Fig 15-3).

Regardless of the method used, be ready to get dragged or fly (get lifted). Once the wing comes to life, it may be difficult or impossible to unclip. Start with the rear risers pulled in, if possible, to have better control.

A smooth surface will make the wing quicker to "snake" above the ground, so you must hold the wall in a narrow height range. Also, you may need to inflate without any A's if it starts jumping up the moment you let up on the brakes (or rears). In that case, just plan on reducing brake (or rears) to start the inflation—it may need a fast trim setting to come all the way up, though, without A's.

Cart Reverse Launch

It is *possible* to do reverse inflations with a cart but requires high-end kiting skills; moderate, steady winds; and an appropriate cart. And it's still risky. The cart in Fig 15-12 is *not* ideal—bars are in the way, it's too heavy to lift, and its nosewheel doesn't caster. The turn-around must be timed and steered to prevent flipping, which is especially challenging if there's much gusting.

Fig 15-11 Cart Reverse Launch Standing

Fig 15-12 Cart Reverse Launch Seated

Layout like in Fig 15-12 with risers crossed for your turn. Hold yourself solidly by feet or wheel brakes (few have them). Bring the wing up, sliding/rolling towards it as necessary. Steer the wing slightly in the turn direction then use *just* enough power to steer the cart around quickly towards the wing then into the wind. Use minimal brake pressure and don't linger while crosswind—your most vulnerable time.

High Wind Landing

It's safer to leave the motor running when landing in strong wind. You have more options, and are less likely to fall. But if you *do* fall, there's more risk of damage and slightly higher chance for prop-related injury.

Two difficult steps after touchdown are: 1) getting turned around to face the wing, and 2) bringing the wing down. After landing, hold enough thrust to keep the wing overhead while facing forward.

To get turned around, it's helpful to unload the wing. Here's how. Keep enough power to stay in position and hold some brake—as much as you can without getting lifted. When you're ready to turn, let off the brakes and squat down so the wing surges forward. As it unloads, throttle off and turn around while standing up straight.

Now turned around, shut off and bring the wing down (deflate it) using one of the methods described earlier. You can do the unloading trick again, then yank it hard through the power band. As it comes through, expect one brief, powerful yank. Run towards a wingtip and grab fabric.

Light Wind Techniques

Normally, if it's too light to kite the wing overhead, a forward launch is best. But if you're ready to reverse when the wind dies, these tools are handy. It's easier with a clutched machine since there is no idling thrust.

Results can be slightly improved by getting some air flowing over the wing just before inflating. While standing there ready, step towards the wing and turn around to put idle thrust just over the wing. Don't ruffle it, and don't use much thrust since it would blow by the wing too quickly. Then, in one fluid motion, let off the throttle, turn around and inflate. This works for some pilots but not others, and it increases your chance of falling.

Single-Hold Reverse

This is the typical method used for reverse inflations on a motor, but we just take it to the next level by holding the A's longer, extending through the turn. It's described in Fig 15-14.

Fig 15-13 Light Wind Reverse

This page contains video and more details on doing light-wind reverse inflations.

footflyer.com/light-wind-paramotor-reverse

Single-Hold Reverse

Hold both A's in the hand opposite your throttle. You'll turn around in that direction, like the pilot shown below. He has the throttle in his right hand and A's in his left, so he turns to the left.

This allows holding/pulling the A's while turning nearly all the way around, even during initial acceleration. It's good in light winds.

Another help with light wind reverses is to step towards the wing, turn around, and blow air over the wing at just above idle. Watch the lines, though. Throttle off, then *immediately* turn and start the inflation.

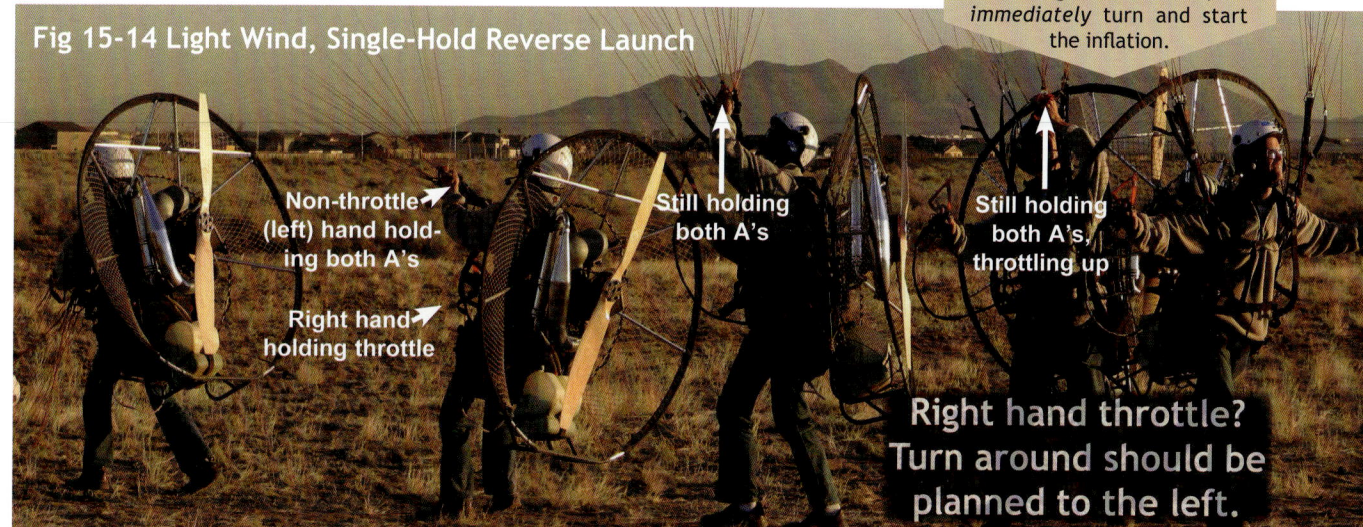

Fig 15-14 Light Wind, Single-Hold Reverse Launch

Cross Arm

Fig 15-15 Cross-Armed Inflation
Don't worry about those crossed brake lines, it will sort itself out when you turn around.

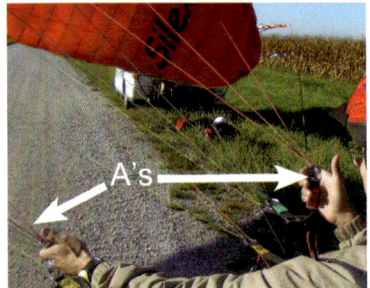

Fig 15-16 Kiting with the A's
Here's inflating and kiting with the A's. Pull more A on the drooping side. If the wind picks up, walk towards the wing as it comes up to mellow the pull.

Fig 15-17 Fixing a Wall
The wing has come down with one side in a heap. Inflate the open side just enough to pressurize the wing and pop out the crumpled side. In this example, your left hand holds the A riser to the open side while your right hand holds *both* brake lines (not the toggles) beyond their pulleys. Pull brakes and A at the same time to cup the air. This fills out the open cells and spreads everything out. Modulate brakes and A-pull to keep it from flopping over or coming overhead.

Cross Armed Reverse

This method works by imparting energy to the wing as you turn around (Fig 15-15). Our description is for a pilot who turns *left* after inflating.

Clip in normally and grab the brakes as usual for a reverse. While holding the toggles, slide your right hand down the right riser to its A as shown in Fig 15-15 #1. Grab that A and continue left and up—that A should have a clear path to the wing. With your left hand, reach *over* the other A and grab it as shown in #2.

Pull your hands back towards your now-crossed arms to see that both A's are clear to the wing. When ready, lunge backward with your body, pulling both A's as necessary. You can help a lagging side by pulling more A on that side. As the wing passes 60° overhead, turn left and throttle up and move forward. Your arms will uncross while imparting some A-pull in the turn.

Kiting with the A's

This technique allows kiting in light to moderate winds while keeping the wing only a few feet above the ground. The skill is fun on its own, but also helps improve nearly all other inflations. It's handy, too, for kiting wars where the goal is to be the last wing up.

Set up for a regular reverse, but do *not* grab the brake toggles. Grab the A risers beyond where they cross like in Fig 15-16.

Inflate the wing by stepping back and helping with the A's as usual. If the left side drops (as you're looking at it), pull more on that A while stepping back. If the right side drops, pull the right A while stepping back. You may have to walk left and right to keep yourself centered as gusts come through.

When the wing is low to the ground your left/right motion is just like when building a wall—step towards the high side. Once the wing arcs above 45°, go back to the normal movement of stepping towards the falling side. As always, strive to do this with*out* having to move, but definitely move when it's necessary.

Inflation Issues

In a perfect world, launch runs are downhill, there's a steady breeze, and the sod farm sign reads "PARAMOTOR PILOTS WELCOME." Right. The following tips will help in *our* world.

Fixing a Wall

An even layout is always best, but sometimes the wing comes down in a heap after an abortive kiting effort. One side sits lifeless while the other has some form. Here's a way to rescue the mess quickly.

As long as some cells can get clear air, hold the A's and brakes like in Fig 15-17. Pull both sharply until they catch air and the wing billows out. *Then* pull more A's. If a whole side is clear, use the riser that goes that side. Be careful when pulling only lines—it's easier to overstress the connection points or get line burns.

Salvaging Bad Inflations

For newer pilots, an inflation that goes this bad (below) has only two outcomes: abort or crash. Aborting is the safest option, but if you are intimately familiar with your wing and don't mind the added risk, you can salvage some launches using the tips below. This *does* tend to feed body parts, lines, etc. to the ever-hungry prop.

- Keep forward motion. Speed is life. Powering up early, at least partially, makes it easier.
- Turn towards the wing and keep pressure on the A's, especially the low side.
- Get some speed. Everything (nearly) is better with more speed.
- Once you've got forward motion, use *just* enough brake pressure on the high side. Too much brake brings the entire wing back down.
- Like all launches, it's an inflation into a controlled run: do not accelerate or accept a liftoff until the wing is fully under control.

If things go south, be lightning fast to kill the motor.

Fig 15-18 Crooked Inflation

This started off poorly, but speed helped salvage the day.

#1 Something snagged the left side.

#2 He looked left to see the wing leaning heavily but kept up some thrust and forward motion.

#3 He turned *slightly* towards it and held enough power to keep moving; you can see prop blast in the wing.

He also kept slight pressure on the low A-riser while adding *slight* brake on the high side and powering up more.

#4 Thankfully, it worked—this time.

Fig 15-19 Crosswind Inflation

Turning slightly like this can counteract a natural tendency. If the wing always seems to come up to your right, angle yourself a bit left.

The same is true for launching in a crosswind. If there is a wind from your right (as pictured), turn slightly left, or take a small step left.

You can also offset yourself from center by a few inches. If the wing always seems to come up and go left, step just to the right of centered.

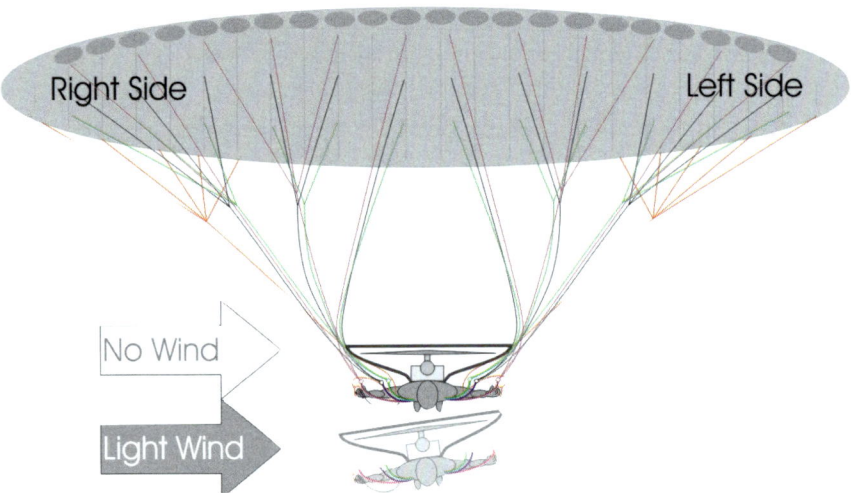

Avoiding Crooked Inflations

Salvaging is good, but prevention is better. Much better.

Out in the snaggly world of less-than-ideal launch surfaces and conditions, give yourself every benefit. Make sure ALL the A lines are clear, the brakes are clear, the grabby ground bits aren't biting lines, and your trimmers are set evenly.

Review "Symptom 1: Wing comes up crooked." on page 58.

Handling Crosswinds

Normally, you always launch into the wind, but at some sites, especially long narrow ones like roads, you may be forced to accept a crosswind. Or the wind may shift after setting up—pretty common when thermals are budding.

The key is to use inflation problems to your advantage. Use them *intentionally* to counter the crosswind effect by running or setting up off-center.

Let's say, for example, that you've set up pointing into a 1-2 mph breeze. But just before launching, the wind starts coming from your right. If you did nothing, the wing would come up and point right. That's just like if you were offset to the right in a calm wind—the wing would come up to the right.

So now, with the wind from your right, either point your launch run 3° to the left or take a half-step to the left. Done correctly, the effects will cancel each other out.

See "Launching in a Crosswind" on page 174 for a "tight sites" twist on this.

On Experience & Skill

Like most of this chapter, we assume your experience is not *just* cruising around, but rather working on *improvement*, challenging yourself, and practicing. This stuff is otherwise a lot riskier, and experience alone is not an indicator of skill.

There's nothing *wrong* with cruising around and flying within your margins—that's safer than pushing it—but it doesn't you prepare for these kinds of challenges. Build up as you would any new skill.

Lastly, here's a well-worn motto that's so true for us: the best pilots use their superior judgment to avoid needing their superior skills.

by Leah Catullo

Precision Flying

CHAPTER 16

Just flying a powered paraglider is all the enjoyment most pilots need. It can be enjoyed safely without ever becoming super precise—just stay within your limits. Being skilled *does* prepare a pilot for the unexpected, but that advantage evaporates if it's spent on more challenging situations. Superior skill is easily overwhelmed by buffoonery.

This chapter is about *mastering* the craft. It's remarkable how much precision is available to those willing to work for it.

Even in moderately bumpy air, a skilled pilot can stay within inches of a desired path. That takes dedicated, directed practice. Pendular weirdness requires anticipation and a sense for how long it takes your body to feel results from control inputs—both vertically and laterally. You must learn the feel of input and consequence. But, oh, how sweet success is.

Foot-dragging is uniquely fun for those who aspire to precision flying. Second only to launch, it expresses our unique ability to interact with Earth in ways formerly known only by birds.

Be careful with water, though. Getting a small wave, or a bit too deep in the shoe, can *rapidly* cause a dunking. Have automatic flotation like she does here.

Brakes—The Feel Position

Much precision flight is done using *just* enough brake pressure to effect minor corrections without giving up speed: the feel position. It's a bit less than the weight of your arms in the toggles, and affords good control feel without sacrificing too much energy (speed). It's what position 1 (Fig 3-3 on page 26) is intended to be. Find the position by pulling pressure without looking at the wing, until you just *start* to notice a course or speed change.

Flying with some pressure is important for high precision, especially next to the ground. You can fly with a lot more brake pressure to go slow, but that requires even more finesse in another area: throttle control.

Brakes should be adjusted for the mission (Fig 12-34 on page 128). Pylon racing (page 206), for example, imposes different requirements than precision flying within a few inches of the ground. Precision flight is easiest when the entire trailing edge deflects with brake pull, not just the tips. But always defer to the wing maker's guidance, if provided.

Fig 16-1 Handling Surges

As soon as the wing *starts* moving forward, pull brakes.

How much depends on how intense the surge is. In worst-case scenarios it could require almost full brake travel. Rapid surge requires a rapid response, which is why flying without holding the brakes is sketchy.

When the wing *starts* coming back, reduce brakes.

Think more in terms of pressure although it may take a lot of travel.

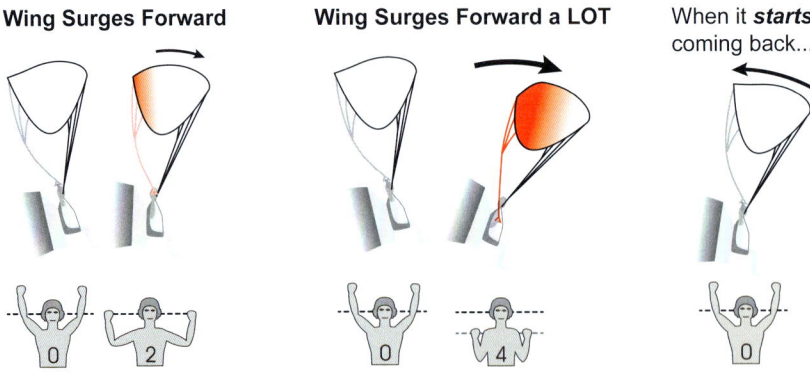

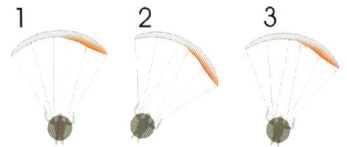

Fig 16-2 Pendular Rate

In a regular turn, you apply brake (1) and hold it. The wing banks out to a maximum (2), then levels back to a lesser amount of bank (3). It stays there as long as you hold the brake. The rate at which it goes out and back is the pendular rate for that motor and wing combination.

Larger wings with their longer lines take longer to swing from side to side.

Fig 16-3 Coordinated Turn

The following will help minimize diving and slipping—where the wing briefly moves sideways through the air. Do these steps about a half second apart until you get a feel for it.

1. Reduce power a bit, especially if turning against the motor's normal torque steer.

2. Weight shift (if able) to start the wing moving.

3. Brake towards the turn then,

4. just after the wing starts responding, prevent a dive by adding a bit of power and/or pulling slight outside brake. The resulting turn is smooth and level.

Bigger wings require slowing down the pace. See also Fig 16-16.

Straight Lines—Pendular Precision

Hanging below the wing means you swing—fore/aft and left/right. Like any pendulum, there is a natural frequency to that swing, its period. Controlling left/right (roll) oscillations is *not* intuitive—in fact, on a small scale, it is backward from what the body feels. The wing goes right and your body goes left. Fore/aft (pitch) motion is easier to learn but has its own quirks.

Precisely controlling oscillations underpins nearly every aspect of mastery—it's what gives us rule over the inches. A telling test of this skill is being able to fly a straight line, within 3 to 6 inches, both vertically and laterally. The only place to even recognize such precision is while flying a few feet above the ground along a line. Corn rows, tracks in the sand, lines in a field, or even gradual curves work.

Crop boundaries are perfect, especially tall corn next to something short like beans. Fly a track just over the corn row. If you hit sink, throttle up and turn towards the beans for an instant escape from corn's tentacles. Only do this into the wind and with heightened vigilance for hazards. Scope out the area first from a safe height, looking for power lines, fences, etc.

Pendular Precision: Roll *Recovery*

You can feel a PPG's pendular action by releasing brake while in a turn. It rolls back and forth in decreasing amounts. You must be able to damp these oscillations.

Refer to the sequence at right. From an established right turn (three 1's), he lets off the right brake, swings back into a left bank, peaking at 4. He immediately pulls left brake and holds for two seconds (5 & 6), easing up just as the wing levels (7).

This works both for preventing oscillations and for damping them once begun. If you have already started a swing, maybe due to turbulence, let it crest, then as soon as your body reverses direction, pull brake in *that* direction.

Timing is crucial—if turbulence induces a left bank (body goes slightly right), let it crest, then pull *left* brake for two seconds and release. It may feel backward at first—your body starts moving left (wing moving right) and you have to pull left brake immediately. Correction should be proportional to the swing's intensity. It's unnatural at first but becomes automatic with practice. And practice you must—before moving on, this *must be* automatic.

The best way to rehearse is with mild wingovers ("Wingovers" on page 186) where you practice returning to level flight with the least amount of oscillation. Fortunately, this skill can be mastered up high.

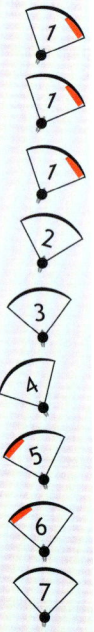

Fig 16-4

Pendular Precision: Roll *Prevention*

Mastery of roll oscillations requires that you learn to arrest it *before* getting swung very far. The previous explanation primarily covered how to stop it after it started—this is how to stop it before it even starts.

You must learn to feel the slight motions and modulate brake pull accordingly—stronger swing, more brake. Your reaction must be quick and short—any delay will only make it worse.

The key to preventing oscillations is braking in the direction of your body's movement, the moment that movement starts. Hold for one second, then let off.

For example, you're flying along a corn row at 3 feet high and feel your body *start* swinging left (body left, wing right). *Immediately* pull left brake, hold it for about a second, then let it up. As long as you catch it before moving more than a few inches, you will dampen the oscillation before it has a chance to get going. If you wait too long, you'll make the swing bigger.

Fore/Aft Pitch Control

The wing is always seeking an equilibrium known as trim speed, 20 mph in the illustration below. If you release brakes from a stable, slower-than-20 condition, you'll dive a bit then accelerate back to trim speed after some pitch oscillations. Pulling trimmers sets a new, slower trim speed equilibrium. Let's see what a gust does.

A headwind gust immediately increases airspeed. You'll swing forward, climb and lose forward momentum (groundspeed) then settle back to 20 mph. You're now moving slower *over the ground* and a few feet higher.

A sudden decrease in headwind (or increase in tailwind) does the opposite: airspeed drops, the wing dives a bit, and you accelerate back to trim speed. So airspeed is

Fig 16-5 Center of Roll
Notice the body goes slightly right when the wing goes left.

Digging Deeper
Pendular damping *seems* backward because we are not *exactly* pendulums.

When the wing goes left, our body goes slightly *right*. Since we control the *wing*, we must translate that kinetic feel into what *it's* doing.

Feel the body go right? *Immediately* add some right brake then let up. When you felt rightward motion, the *wing* was going left and, if you reacted quickly enough, that stopped it.

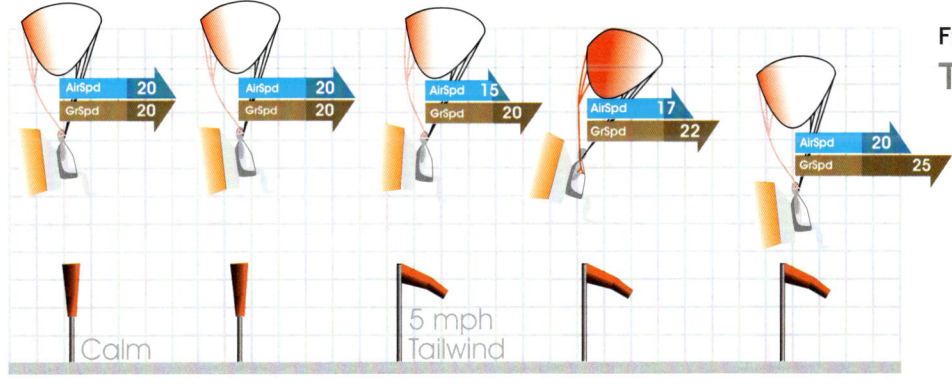

Fig 16-6 Effectively Handling a Tailwind Increase

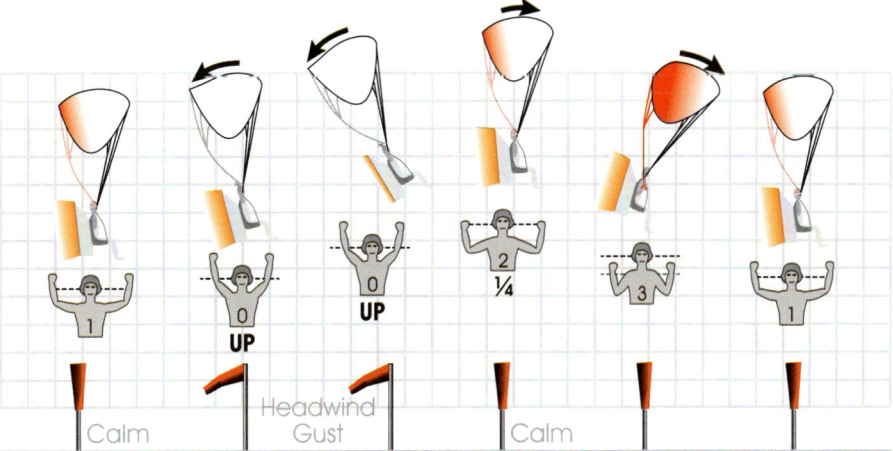

Fig 16-7 Effectively Handling a Headwind Gust

again 20 mph, but you're going faster over the ground and a bit lower.

A brief gust is worse because it's really two changes. In a headwind gust the wing surges back, you climb, and it seeks trim speed. Groundspeed (momentum) decreases too. When the gust subsides, the wing suddenly feels less airflow (less airspeed), and dives to get back to trim speed. It can be dramatic, causing large pitch changes where your body (and wing) angles upward or downward.

This can be minimized by skillful use of brakes and power, keeping the wing mostly overhead—a foundation to safely maintaining altitude within a few inches of the ground. It's part of active flying covered later.

If a gust makes the wing surge forward, you'll dive at the ground. Don't let that happen: immediately pull some brake to stop the surge, then let up the moment it starts coming back.

In turbulence, hold brake pressure 2 to 3 while being mindful of keeping forward speed. Keep enough airspeed so there's brake authority to stop a drop. You'll be modulating thrust, too. So if you get lifted and tilted back: simultaneously reduce brakes and throttle. Then, *as soon* as the wing starts coming forward, add enough throttle and brake to stay level and maintain speed. This requires anticipation.

Build skill through directed practice to really master the necessary reactions. This chapter may explain the principle, but its greatest contribution is describing what to practice and what to expect when you do.

Start off in fairly smooth conditions, flying at 10 feet over landable terrain, looking at or just below the horizon. Sod farms, beaches, or smooth desert floors are perfect. Try to hold altitude precisely. As you improve, go later in the morning or earlier in the evening to master it with mild turbulence. You'll build skill faster that way.

Finessing the Climb

Going from level flight into a climb can be graceful (the pro in Fig 16-8).

Hammering power will swing you out into a brief, steep climb, then settle into a shallower climb after some pitch oscillations. It looks sketchy, and if the motor quits after that first swing out, the forward surge will be dramatic.

Yuck. Let's do it with finesse. From cruise power, throttle to half power. You swing forward, then just before you start swinging back, smoothly add full power. This is similar to how a go-around (aka balked landing) should be done. On most wings it works like this: half power, wait 2 seconds, then ease up to full power.

Fig 16-8 Throttle-Up

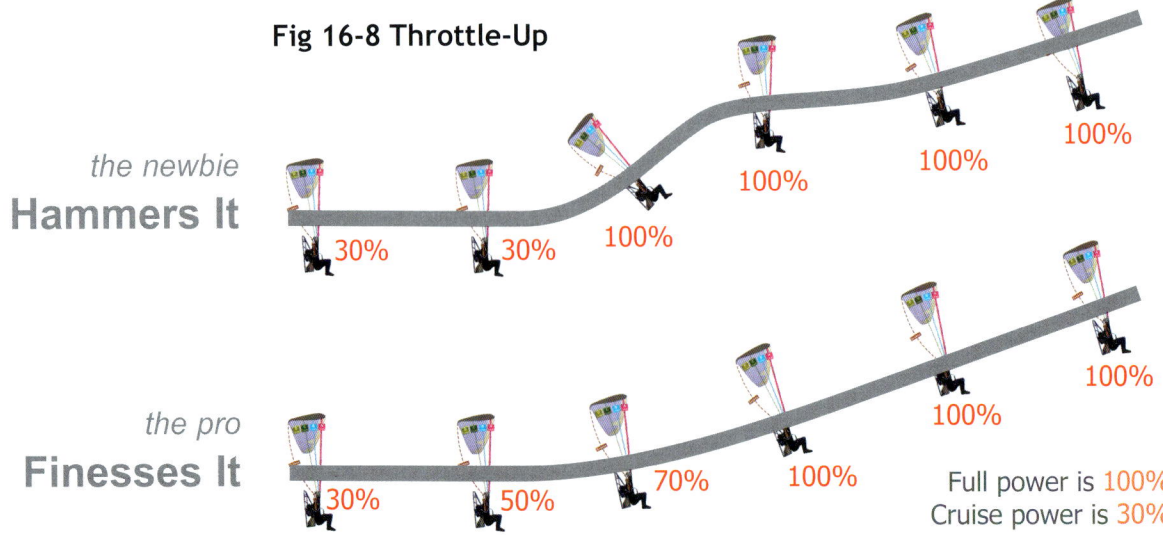

Balance of Power

In normal flight, you've learned that power controls altitude—power up to climb, power back to descend. But throttle changes take a couple seconds to act. For an *immediate* climb or descent use brakes. Its effect is fleeting and limited, but if you're cruising along at a few inches and get dumped, pull brake for an immediate correction, then add power to regain speed.

Energy State

Energy state is a term, fancied by fighter pilots, that describes the trade-off between speed and altitude. You pull brakes and climb a bit while slowing down, trading speed *briefly* for height. Speed is kinetic energy which can be traded for height or potential energy. And just like a roller coaster, friction (drag) makes the cars gradually slow down, losing total energy. Adding power overcomes this loss.

If you're going fast, you have speed energy available to trade for height which is what that quick pull of brake does. Reducing brake pull trades height for increased airspeed. Adding power increases total energy. In level flight, thrust merely overcomes drag.

When flying a few feet above the ground, use minimum brake pressure to leave some brake authority for an immediate climb. If you get dumped, pull brakes to arrest the descent, then add power to regain lost speed (energy). Now if you hit sinking air again, you can again use the brakes.

Slow Flight

First a caution: slow flight gets closer to a stall or spin. If the wing starts to slow or twist unexpectedly, or a brake gets mushy, reduce brake pressure *immediately*.

To get into level slow flight, reduce power then pull enough brakes to stop the drop. You'll almost immediately need to add power in again to hold altitude. As speed slows more, it will take increasing amounts of power to hold altitude. You must know where the wing will stall and what that feels like. Don't go beyond brake position/pressure 4.

In slow flight, the roles of brake and power reverse. Since brakes are already pulled, you must control altitude almost exclusively with power. The good news is that, with so much brake applied, the wing responds quickly to increased power. And since you'll be carrying plenty of power, the motor should respond quickly to throttle changes. Flying at minimum speed requires holding the wing near stall while controlling height with power. Practice this either up very high (and with a reserve) or within a few *inches* of the ground with feet extended in case of touchdown.

The least amount of power is required when flying at the glider's minimum sink configuration: usually slight brake pressure, trimmers slow, and no speedbar.

Turns

Turns require more power to prevent altitude loss since some of the wing's lift is spent on turning. More bank requires more thrust. Competition pilots doing steep low turns are almost always at full power as they swing around pylons and less power as they start to level out (see "Cloverleaf" on page 206). They do use speedbar to convert turn energy into level speed, which lets them keep on some power.

When entering a turn, it can be helpful to reduce power briefly, start the turn, then come back in with power. That slightly reduces Angle of Attack (AoA) and the chance for spinning or stalling, especially if the turn is opposite your motor's natural torque turn direction.

> **Caution!**
>
> Doing steep maneuvers down low is incredibly dangerous. Don't do anything down low that you haven't *mastered* up high, and don't ever let any kind of vertical velocity develop.
>
> Competition pilots minimize their risk because the rules discourage maneuvers with a big vertical component (big dives, for example).
>
> Flying low and downwind sacrifices the inherent slow speed safety advantage of our craft. Higher speed makes it harder to detect/avoid an obstacle while increasing the consequence of a collision.

Fig 16-9 Foot-drag Dump
She got dumped a bit, throttled up and pulled brakes but it wasn't quite enough.

Fig 16-10 Ski Drag
You could call this a version of foot-dragging—the technique is similar but skis are more forgiving of unexpected weight (from lift dumping).

Fig 16-11 Grabbing Balls
This is immense fun, but don't choose objects that can make it into the prop.

Low Flying

For some pilots, low flying is a huge draw—the ability to cruise at any altitude while exploring a three dimensional realm. Unfortunately, it does incur extra risk.

It's harder, but try to stay within reach of a safe landing spot, climbing higher over unsavory terrain. Flying 3 feet over grass has minimal risk; flying 3 feet over wave-ravaged rocks is tempting fate.

Start out by flying relatively high, at least 10 feet, doing gentle maneuvers. Remember that any turn loses altitude, and steep turns lose a lot. Build up to getting lower or to turning steeper. Never let yourself get deep in the brakes—they are your only control, and once pulled, there is nothing left to maneuver with. Like foot-dragging (covered shortly), if you notice that you're pulling high brake pressure, add power and ease your hands up to recover back to cruise speed.

Foot-dragging

It's oddly satisfying to be *flying*, but with a foot sliding on the ground—especially in mildly bumpy air—and in full control.

Start off in mellow air, no more than 2 on the bump scale (page 61). Master precise control of altitude, within a few inches, while also minding power, ground track and speed.

Only fly into the wind at first. In a crosswind, you'd be sliding somewhat sideways and be more susceptible to falling. Going downwind makes face-planting more likely and with uglier consequences.

Have one foot out in front so that you can run if necessary, but don't put much weight on either foot. Its drag can slow you down, causing lost lift, more weight, more lost lift, etc., until you fall. Modulate brakes and power to keep your cage off the ground. On smooth ground you can get away with sliding the cage but it risks damage.

Use brakes to control altitude, and throttle to keep the speed up. If you drop, immediately pull some brake to prevent sinking, then add power to accelerate back to speed. Brakes can arrest a drop far quicker than throttle, but if you're getting heavy in the brakes, airspeed is decaying—throttle up!

Cruise at brake 1 to 2 for best height control. If you get gusted upwards, immediately reduce brake and power to avoid climbing, but be ready to get back on the power.

Picking up Objects

Once you're controlling altitude within a few inches, this is fun. Get down nearly level with the object so you're *not descending on it*. Otherwise, it's easy to hit the ground while concentrating on the object and not powering up in time.

Be flying stable and level, with brake 1 to 2, so that when you close your feet on the object, pulling brake gives an immediate climb. Have a few seconds of level flight to plan the snatch. As you grab for it, whether or not you get it, pull to brake 3 and add power. Then reduce brake pressure during climb as usual.

The best objects for this are medium-sized exercise balls with low pressure or lightweight orange traffic cones. Hard or heavy items are difficult to grasp with your feet. And be careful with anything you're unsure of. One pilot almost broke his foot when the kickball he was nabbing turned out to be a bowling ball. Ouch.

Having a Motor Failure

A motor failure while flying low leaves little time to react. Pull brakes to check a dive and follow the guidance in "Engine Failure" on page 49." Prepare for a firm landing, and try to level out of any turn before flare but always flare.

Catching Suspended Targets

Trying to hit or grab something floating, falling, or flying through the air is a fun challenge. One way to practice is with partially deflated helium balloons since they're neutrally buoyant. Tie it to your front harness webbing for launch. Get to a safe altitude, hold the balloon out to the side, throttle off, then let it go.

As you approach the object, try to put it on the horizon so that it's at your altitude. Head straight for it—if there is no relative motion of the object, then you are dead-on. Make small adjustments as necessary.

Fig 16-13 Paper Airplane Catch
Tucker Gott launched and caught this paper airplane in flight.

Formation

These tips will improve the look and safety of your formation flying.

1. Have radios that can at least let you *hear* instructions from the formation director who is not necessarily the lead pilot and may be on the ground.

2. Avoid having more than one inexperienced pilot in any formation.

3. Build slowly, starting with loose formations, and only tighten up as skill allows.

4. **Never, ever accept a high closure rate!** If one becomes apparent, break it off and re-form. This can happen surprisingly quickly.

5. If you're closing on a pilot who doesn't know you're there, allow room for escape by either pilot. Approach slowly and clearly, staying 5 wingspans away until he's aware of you. If he turns away, leave him be.

6. Keep both hands in the brakes. If taking pictures, be holding the brake that would steer you clear.

7. The lead pilot needs only to fly smoothly without abrupt maneuvering unless it's rehearsed. He can be one of your lesser skilled pilots as long as he reliably follows directions, is predictable, and *smooth*.

The more-skilled flyers should be followers, with the most skilled in the #2 position(s), just behind the lead. They set formation spacing.

Fig 16-12 Formation By Relative Position

Flying a tight formation requires precision and discipline, mostly to maintain long periods of concentration while holding relative position. It's like driving 3 feet behind a truck at highway speed—you gotta pay *close* attention the whole time.

Some positions in a formation are easier than others to make look good. The one illustrated at left is easy by keeping the preceding glider on the horizon and staying behind a particular row of line cascades (red arrow). Most positions can be maintained like this, using two points on the preceding glider. In this example, you'd need to come forward until all the pilots are lined up to provide fore/aft consistency.

Look at the side view. The bottom pilot (Blue) is lead. The **2nd position** is most critical because he sets the shape for everyone else. Numbers 3, 4, and so on can use relative position by looking down a line made by the other pilots (yellow dashed line) but should focus primarily on the preceding glider. You just have to trust whoever is following you. Each pilot should maintain a set, identifiable distance back from their lead. A coach on radio is indispensable for this.

Be aware of wake with its lift and sink (gray arrows) which makes some formations harder.

While making position adjustments, consider your wingman's (following pilot) reaction time.

Head-On Intercepts

Forming up, or *intercepting* another pilot head-on is challenging. The no-cross path is safer. In all cases, the interceptor must start his turn well before passing the interceptee. Starting early is better than starting late since you can just do S-turns to get back in position. If you get behind, it will take time to catch up.

Having the Interceptee fly a steady, shallow turn will let others join up on the inside of the turn.

Consider starting above the interceptee then descending down to his level once you're laterally in position. That way misjudgment doesn't cause a collision *and* it avoids wake. When in position, descend to the desired formation.

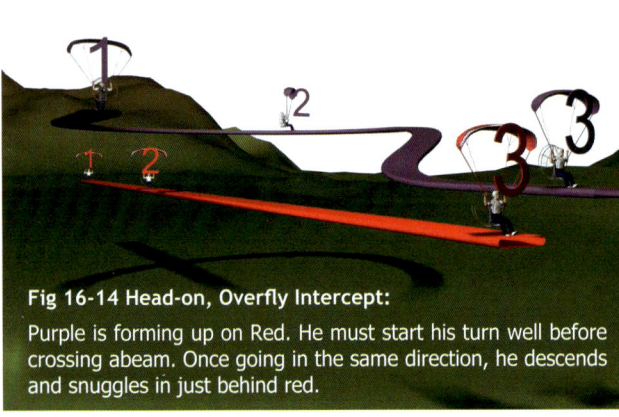

Fig 16-14 Head-on, Overfly Intercept:
Purple is forming up on Red. He must start his turn well before crossing abeam. Once going in the same direction, he descends and snuggles in just behind red.

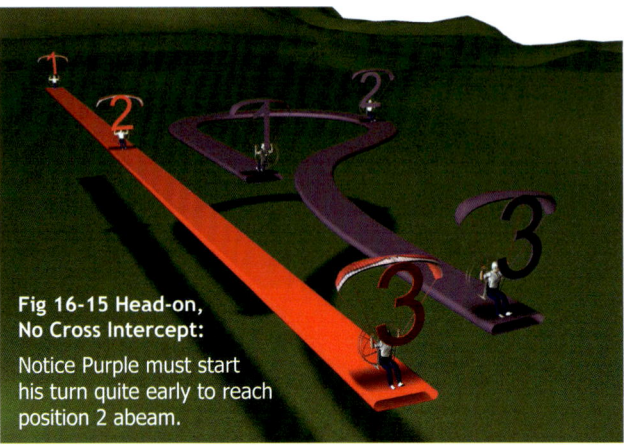

Fig 16-15 Head-on, No Cross Intercept:
Notice Purple must start his turn quite early to reach position 2 abeam.

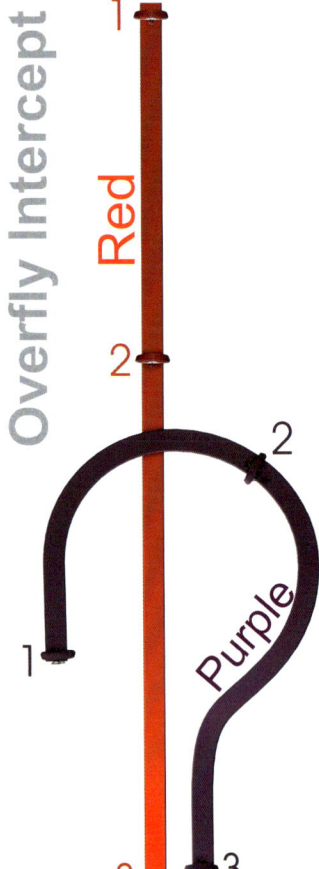

8. Always have an out. Plan an escape in case someone maneuvers unexpectedly, takes a collapse, or has a motor failure.

9. Brief, understand, and fly with an understanding of wake effects (Fig 16-12).

10. Tip-to-tip formations are harder. Like any, each pilot must concentrate on his "leader." If lead is the leftmost glider, then everybody would be focused on the glider immediately to their left.

Intercepting

Joining up to fly alongside another pilot requires care and anticipation since speed is minimally adjustable. The most common error is not leading the intercept enough—turning late then lagging far behind. It's easier to join someone in nearly the same direction rather than head-on. See two methods in Fig 16-14 & Fig 16-15.

Turning

While turning in formation, the outside pilot must go faster than the inside pilot, which may be impossible. A solution is for following pilots to climb up and get just behind and above the inside pilot. When leveling out, move back to the outside. Timed right, it looks good.

Other Considerations

"Walking" on another pilot's wing has ended poorly. The walker can get tangled or disrupt the lower pilot's wing enough to collapse it.

Active Flying in Turbulence

Active flying is using the least amount of control necessary to keep the wing essentially overhead and aligned with the relative wind (slipstream). Passive flying is just holding about pressure 3 while letting the wing move around, or doing whatever the wing maker recommends. It may be to go trims fast and don't do anything (reflex).

The challenge is damping oscillations quickly without overdoing it. If you feel airspeed decay, reduce brakes and power, then power back up as necessary to fly level. Use what's needed—and in a big surge that can be a LOT—but use the least amount required. After a large control input, you'll almost certainly need to let up as soon as the wing starts coming back.

Let the wing wander a bit rather than jabbing at every little twitch. As skill improves, you'll make smaller corrections with better timing. Until then, it's better to let the wing wander within a broader range while mostly holding pressure.

For most gliders, the best turbulence penetration is done with no speedbar, trimmers neutral (slow if there's no neutral), brake pressure 2 or 3, and enough thrust to fly level. Lighter pilots on larger wings must be vigilant about parachutal stall ("Parachutal Stall/Spin" on page 53) and be quick to reduce pressure and power at the first sign of slowing airspeed.

Becoming *effective* at active flying will take at *least* 50 flights, and then only if you really work at it, such as flying exactly straight lines in mildly bumpy air—minimizing the wing's dance. While practicing, keep looking forward; use your kinetic sense to detect motion, then provide control inputs.

If at any time you start to "lose it" (not sure what to do), reduce brake pressure, reduce power for 5 seconds (if altitude allows), let things settle down, then re-engage your corrections.

You must learn to interpret the small angular changes that get transferred to your harness as the wing moves around overhead. That takes practice. You'll apply techniques covered earlier regarding pendular control: if your body swings left, apply left brake as soon as the swing starts, then let up. It's not intuitive—the skill must become automatic to be counted on, which takes repetition.

Don't try damping oscillations for landing until it is automatic since your attention is so focused on the flare that your steering inputs will likely devolve into pilot-induced oscillations (PIO's).

Why Turbulence is so Dangerous

The ability of a paraglider to handle turbulence is tightly connected to pilot skill.

For example, if turbulence causes a dramatic surge that is not checked right away, the wing could go below the horizon, followed by the pilot falling into it. Whereas a pilot with built-up reactions—in the same exact scenario—would react automatically with nearly full brakes for a mere second or two.

The difference between those actions is life and death.

How do you know if you have this automatic response? For one, you must have spent time in turbulence, or in some other situation that requires the response; lots of time. It's all about repetition. If not, taking on bumpy air is gambling with odds that worsen in proportion to the level of turbulence.

Thermal-loving freeflyers deal with this by building slowly, going out in progressively more active conditions. Those that push too fast, then encounter bigger air (highly turbulent), sometimes don't react well and end up on reserve rides or worse.

A reflex glider may make it safer in some ways, but not if you're wearing it.

Slip & Correction

Fig 16-16 Square to the Slipstream

(Left) Sometimes turbulence dumps you into a sideways slip. Pull brake to square up the wing.

Here he has been gusted to the right and reacts by pulling just enough right brake to get "square," making a collapse less likely.

(Right) This pilot is tossed into a dive *and* sideways motion. He pulls both brakes but more on the right to stay square to the slipstream. This is being *coordinated,* which in airplanes, is done with their rudder. See also Fig 16-3.

Slip, Dive & Correction

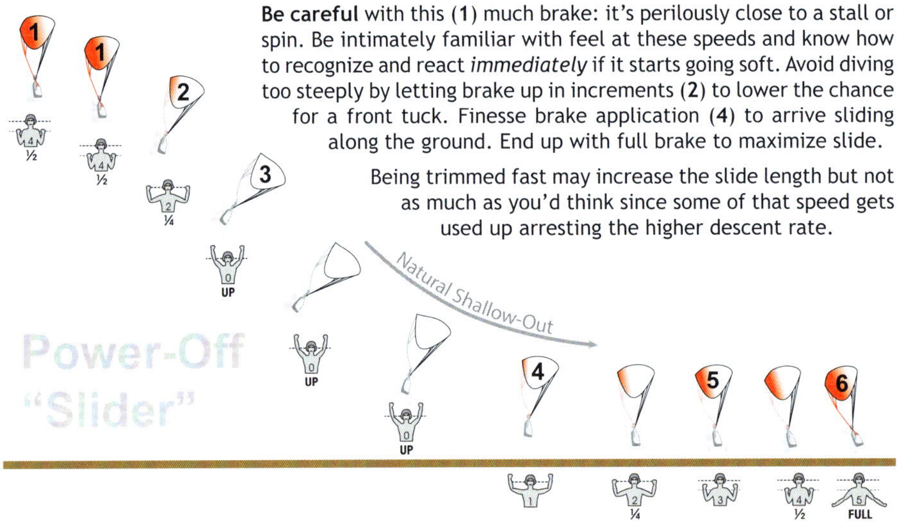

Fig 16-17 Exaggerated Slider or Swoop Landing

This uses the glider's natural tendency to dive then recover after releasing the brakes from a slowed condition. Plan its natural shallow-out to happen as you near the ground.

Beware: mistiming can result in a dangerously hard landing. The key is using the natural swing without overdoing brake pull or starting too low.

This is like "Spot Landing: Last 100 Feet" on page 177 but with more intensity.

Be careful with this (**1**) much brake: it's perilously close to a stall or spin. Be intimately familiar with feel at these speeds and know how to recognize and react *immediately* if it starts going soft. Avoid diving too steeply by letting brake up in increments (**2**) to lower the chance for a front tuck. Finesse brake application (**4**) to arrive sliding along the ground. End up with full brake to maximize slide.

Being trimmed fast may increase the slide length but not as much as you'd think since some of that speed gets used up arresting the higher descent rate.

Fig 16-18 Real Life, Power-off Swoop/Slider
A real-life example of how far you can slide when the glider's energy is maximized. Using a smaller, but still efficient wing, makes for even longer slides.

The Perfect Touchdown

Landing can be remarkably graceful. And consistent. These tips will help achieve finessed touchdowns. The slider is good for fast touchdowns on smooth surfaces, while the one-step helps to minimize run-out when terrain is rough. Getting to the target (spot landing) is covered in "Effect of Brakes on Glide" on page 176.

Sliding In: the Swoop Landing

Sliding in works best on smaller and/or higher performance wings (high glide ratio)—they allow a bigger dive and have lots of flare authority. You have such a wing if, on a power-off landing, you can flare and climb back up a few feet.

For a basic slider (swoop) landing (Fig 16-17), start from a hands-up glide at 50 feet. Reaching about 10 feet, higher on smaller wings, pull enough brakes (position/pressure 1 - 2) to get your body swinging forward, then ease up on the brakes briefly. That initial pull gets your body swinging forward which pitches the wing up, nearly stopping your descent. Time it so the level-off happens right as your feet reach the ground. Practice will reveal how much pull, how high to start, and how long to hold it. As you level off, speed will quickly start bleeding off—apply more brakes to keep weight off your feet as long as possible. Done correctly, you'll skid to a stop with full brakes.

This is useful when groundspeed is high on landing and the surface is smooth. Even if you don't skid to a stop, the slide bleeds off speed that you don't have to run off.

The *exaggerated slider* (Fig 16-17) is a more aggressive swoop that's fun but with little practical value. Practice it up high to get a feel for how much dive you get by first pulling to brake 4, then letting up. If you start it too high on landing, you'll level out too high on the recovery. If you start it too late (low), you'll hit the ground while still diving before it has a chance to recover. Be careful!

Even with high-altitude practice, start it slowly, doing only a small dive at first then increasing it as you gain familiarity.

As mentioned in Fig 16-17, when going into the dive, don't let off the brakes suddenly—take about two seconds to reduce the chance of front tucking.

You can exaggerate the slide even more by doing it from a bank. This dangerous maneuver is hard to judge and has very little margin for error. It's unforgiving, too. Many sky divers have met their demise in an extreme version called the hook turn. Start with shallow banks since risk rises with steepness. Also, rolling out of an excessively steep bank means reaching the ground with too much speed—you'll climb back up then have nothing to flare with. You must bleed off the speed by remaining in a turn (while skimming the ground) then leveling off as speed dissipates.

The One-Step

This may be the most challenging landing to nail and the easiest one to get hurt on.

Everything is normal down to the last 30 feet. Hold minimum brake pressure, making steering inputs as necessary. Then at 4 to 8 feet (depending on wing), pull and hold some brake to start the swing, enough to swing out a bit in front of the glider; climb slightly then drop the last foot or so while pulling more brake. As the swing completes, be adding brake, going to full just before touchdown.

Speed at the start of flare must be such that you only climb up a foot or so. Any more could mean a painful drop. So timing must be right on, too—start the final brake pull so as to exhaust all speed just as you touch down. Some wings (slower) will require starting this from a *no*-brake position, or maybe even swooping a bit.

As much as the exaggerated slider, errors are unforgiving. See also "Power-On Spot Landing over an Obstruction" on page 177.

One-step Power-On Landing

Fig 16-19 One-step with Power

This shows one technique for landing on an elevated spot (motorhome here). Come in slightly below the top, pull some brakes to swing up and touch down, holding until touchdown, then reduce brakes as necessary to keep kiting the wing. Use power to avoid getting pulled back. Not quite one step, but close.

Although power was used, using the swing applies just like it does on any landing, only more.

Before trying this on objects that you can fall from, *master* it on level ground in a moderate, steady wind.

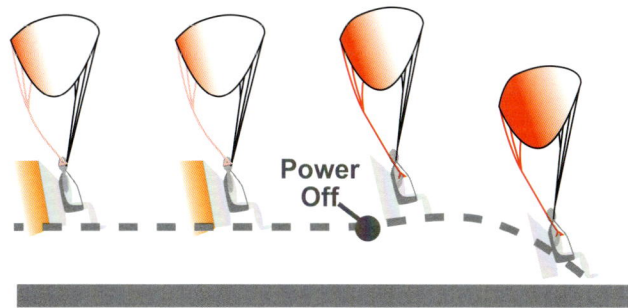

Fig 16-20 One-step with Power—Level

Landing with power can make you look good. Plus, in turbulent conditions, it gives you more options in the event of getting dumped.

One useful technique for power-on landings is to come in like any other approach, but during the last 30 feet or so, throttle up enough to slow the descent rate by half. That enables better timing of the flare since you'll have more time to finesse out any errors.

Another technique that's fun is to turn a foot-drag into a landing. While foot-dragging, be prepared to bear all the weight in case of a gust—otherwise it's easy to fall.

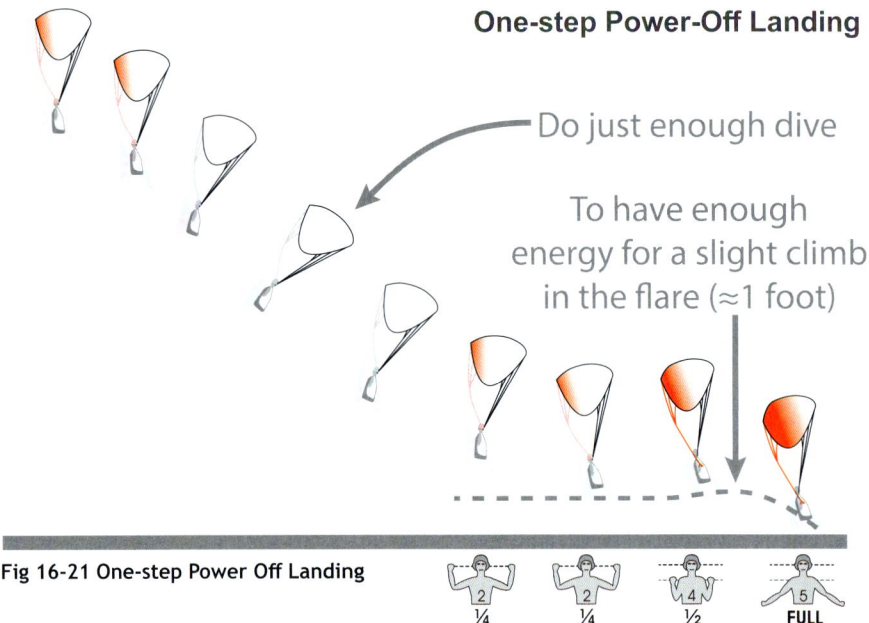

Fig 16-21 One-step Power Off Landing

Surviving Practice

Practicing these types of landings is risky because you're closer to the edges of control *and* near the ground *and* with higher sink rates. There's only so much risk you can mitigate, but these tips will help with *some* of it.

- Insist on a smooth, steady wind of 5 to 10 mph while practicing.
- Favor soft-sand beaches or other forgiving surfaces.
- For "one-step" type landings start by just trying to slow the touchdown speed. Don't try to climb at first, just try to fly level a foot above the ground, which is really a normal landing technique but done very accurately.
- Don't try this until you've mastered precision, low flying in light turbulence.
- On any landing requiring a dive, start by letting up a little first, causing only a slight dive. Take a couple seconds to get zero brake. And avoid other techniques, like banking, until you've mastered the straight-ahead dive.
- Like every other consequential skill, build slowly. Don't try so hard that a crash is likely—save aggressive advancement for things like piano, where failure won't end your chances to walk.

Challenging Sites

CHAPTER 17

The fact that we *can* launch from so many places is awesome, but we need to be smart about it.

Some sites, under some conditions, for some pilots, are *really* dangerous. We must make sure our skills are up to the task. These tools will certainly help in that regard, but more importantly, they will help know when to say no.

The Horror of Hot, High, and Humid

The effect of high Density Altitude on performance is dramatic (see "Density Altitude" on page 78). Gear that blazes at sea level may be blasé at 5000 feet. Marginal gear may not even get you airborne—it takes more thrust to launch than to simply fly.

Everything works against success: thinner air decreases thrust, you get winded quicker, and have to run faster for the same lift. It's especially tricky in still air.

Go to a high-altitude fly-in and witness (or fall victim to) the calamity of the calm—sometimes pilots simply can't get airborne. More thrust helps, but without appropriate skills, it can contribute to plantings of the face. Here are other reasons why we struggle.

1. A slight tailwind may exist up at wing height, maybe enough to prevent getting needed airflow over the wing. Have a super sensitive, highly visible telltale up high to make sure that's not happening, or attempt launching the other direction.

2. A smooth headwind is *extremely* valuable. Each 1 mph of headwind is like reducing density altitude by 2000'. Consider waiting until you have some.

3. The motor won't be putting out full thrust, even at full RPM. But make sure you *are* getting full RPM. It should be close to the sea level value. The chart "Thrust vs Weight" on page 270 equates sea-level thrust with what you'll get at higher density altitudes.

Fig 17-1 Leg Drag
Soft sand contributes to leg drag.
In a dead calm with deep, soft sand, it may be impossible to get enough speed to lift off.

Leg Drag

An insidious cause of launch woe is our landing gear. While carrying all that weight, we can only run a few mph. Legs are great for initial inflation, but beyond about 4 mph, they slow us down—thrust must do the rest. The effect is worsened by:

- High density altitude requires more groundspeed.
- No wind or some tailwind up where the wing is (requires more groundspeed).
- Limited thrust.
- Heavy or awkward gear. Having the motor higher on your back can help. And ensure the seat board goes flat against the frame so it's not hitting your legs.
- Angled-back motor styles. Adjust the motor so that the propeller plane is more vertical in flight rather than leaned-back. If you're leaning back as the wing lifts a bit, you'll actually be pushing slightly *against* your run. Being vertical reduces this. It may not be as comfortable airborne, but at least you'll *get* airborne.
- Rough, soft, or uphill surface.
- Short steps instead of long strides as the wing lifts.

You must accelerate to get lift from the wing, which reduces leg drag. But if you can't accelerate enough to get that lift, takeoff may be impossible. Pulling brakes increases lift, but pulling too much, or too early, can be worse—it's a balance that must be struck *while running*.

Hot and High Solutions

These tips may help with high density altitude launches.

- Start with the smoothest surface available, downhill if possible. Consider launching crosswind from a smooth, firm surface instead of upwind through a soft or rutted surface. For example, soft sand can be impossible to takeoff from in even a 1 mph breeze, whereas the nearby road, even if it's slightly crosswind, might be manageable.
- If you have a choice of wings, pick the slowest one; usually that means the largest size. It must also be easy enough to inflate.
- If you have a choice of motors or propellers, choose pushy.
- If you don't need all the fuel, tools, spare parts, spare oil, bug spray, camera gear, and food, leave them behind. Lighter is better.

And when you're ready to launch:

- Do a power forward if your cage allows. Keep pressure on the A's until the wing is nicely overhead *and* you're moving briskly.
- Once you know the wing won't fall back, concentrate on *running* speed with hands mostly up. Minimize steering inputs—you'll barely feel any feedback.
- Reaching maximum running speed, add enough brake to get the wing lifting to reduce weight on your legs. Don't add too much, and be ready to back off if you slow down.
- Steer to the smoothest, hardest surface possible or into-the-wind direction.

If it works, strides will lengthen, feet will soon be just slapping the ground, then flight will finally win. Once airborne, *ease* up the brakes to avoid settling back down. On most wings, best climb rate will be hands up, slow trim, and brake pressure 1.

If you do settle back down, be prepared to run and start the process again.

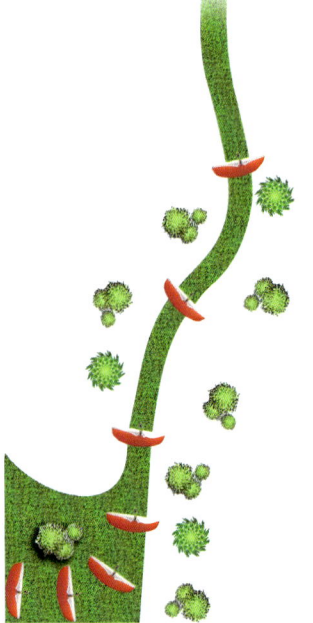

Fig 17-2 Steering Launch
This is a key skill for succeeding in tight launch spaces.

Tight Spaces: Takeoff

Shoehorning into sub-optimal spaces is risky, but with skill, good conditions, and appropriate equipment you can safely fly from surprisingly small areas.

Besides sufficient room for running, a site should provide climbout and departure options so that a motor failure allows either landing safely along the departure path, or circling back to the start (Fig 17-5).

If you can't inflate into the wind, like when launching on a road, consider using what's covered in "Handling Crosswinds" on page 158. Be leery of wind shadows—being surrounded by high obstructions—since it's hard to tell what the winds are doing up higher, and powerful turbulence may lurk.

Steering the Launch

Being able to steer while running or walking with the wing overhead is key to mastering tight locations. It allows launching from places that require a turn before liftoff, like L-shaped or obstructed fields (Fig 17-2). You can also avoid obstacles, like another pilot or their gear, without having to abort. It allows inflating into the wind, then turning to finish the takeoff in a better direction—think crosswind runway.

Steering with the wing overhead is easy to practice. Go out on a mildly breezy day and start to launch, but don't actually take off. Hold just enough thrust while keeping the wing overhead and walking briskly (or slowly in a stronger wind). Learn how to steer the wing without looking up at it. **Get the wing going where you want, then follow it.** In gusty air, walking speed represents a steady wind component so don't dawdle. Need to go left? Get the wing leaning left then follow it.

Remember, the wing has momentum, too. If you and the wing are angling to the right and you stop, the wing will keep going right. You must lead it—while walking right, pull left brake to stop the wing; take a few more steps, then let the wing drift overhead.

While facing forward, learn to *feel* where the wing is without looking. Only look up when necessary, especially while figuring out the feel. Walk forward enough to keep sufficient airspeed—you should feel the lines tugging just a bit. When the glider drifts off to one side, use just enough brake to bring it back overhead.

Tight locations are why we emphasize the ability to kite without moving your body.

Fig 17-3 NM heaven
This beautiful slice of New Mexico is over 6000 feet high, giving these para-campers a challenging launch. Off the road, scrub brush and general roughness made it difficult.
Accepting a small crosswind on the road's smooth surface beat into-the-wind running through rough terrain.

High and Dry

Outside Sky City, NM I was launching my underpowered motor on a rutted surface at 6000' MSL. It was calm. No problem. Or so I thought.

After two tries, getting the wing up and under control, then running at full tilt and not lifting off, I was exhausted. I simply could not generate enough speed in those ruts for the wing to lift the motor so that I could accelerate—leg drag held me back. I waited for a puff of headwind.

Finally, a nearby smoke source exposed the lightest little headwind oozing in, so I stood up and went for it.

The wing came up sluggishly as I lurched over deepish ruts. Running my hardest with hands up and motor screaming, I slowly gathered speed. Finally, it felt fast enough to apply some brakes. Too much, I slowed down. Reducing brakes, I concentrated on speed. Still going full tilt, I reached smoother surface and was able to accelerate. Pulling some brakes added enough lift to unload my legs to accelerate further.

The pace quickened. More lift. More speed. Longer strides. Maximum effort finally yielded to the magic smoothness of flight. Skimming just inches high I *eased* off the brakes, accelerated and settled into a *very* shallow climb. Sweet rise!

More power and a bigger wing would have been easier but the challenge sure made success taste good.

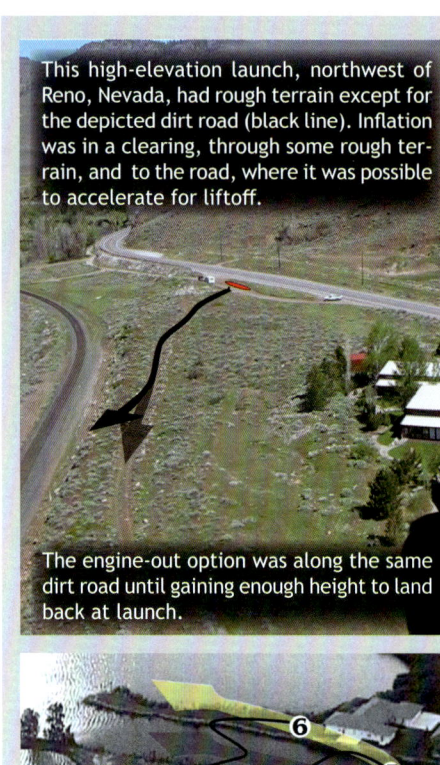

This high-elevation launch, northwest of Reno, Nevada, had rough terrain except for the depicted dirt road (black line). Inflation was in a clearing, through some rough terrain, and to the road, where it was possible to accelerate for liftoff.

The engine-out option was along the same dirt road until gaining enough height to land back at launch.

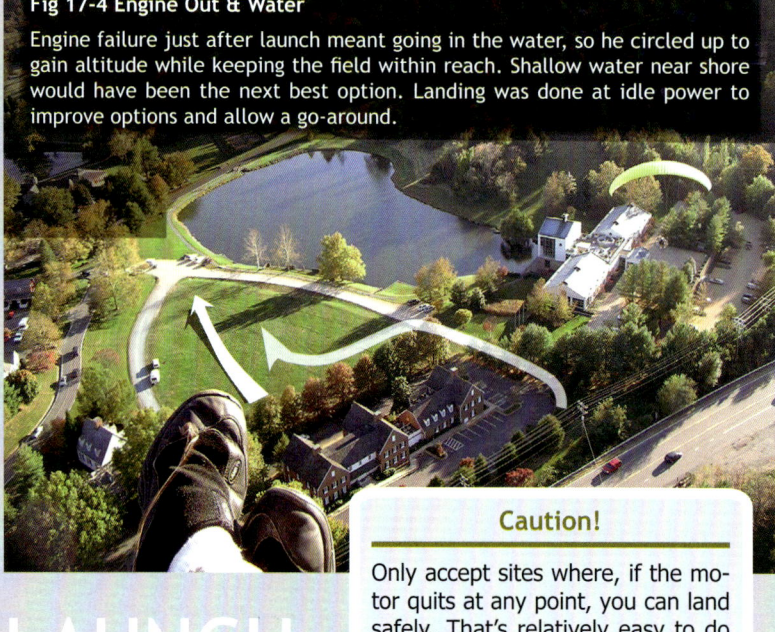

Fig 17-4 Engine Out & Water
Engine failure just after launch meant going in the water, so he circled up to gain altitude while keeping the field within reach. Shallow water near shore would have been the next best option. Landing was done at idle power to improve options and allow a go-around.

Caution!
Only accept sites where, if the motor quits at any point, you can land safely. That's relatively easy to do by circling up.

Fig 17-5 Maintaining Options
Plan every launch to maintain a dry landing option if the engine fails. It's usually easy with a modicum of forethought.

The launch at left shows how he kept his options open. Numbered paths show where he would have gone after an engine-out.

For the first 30 feet, don't accept options that require turning more than 30°, or more than 90° above 60 feet, or more than 180° until above 100 feet.

The goal is to steer primarily with the brakes. Move left or right as needed, of course, (and as space allows) but strive to use only the brakes.

Do practice controlling the wing with only your body (no brakes) to help gain understanding for how the wing reacts. Walk left to get it going right, then follow it. You'll quickly learn to use small motions, and how much to lead the wing with your movements. Having this feel will also help when launching from narrow locations. Taking a step to the left is a great way to get the wing slightly right.

As wind gets lighter, these exercises get harder but are certainly doable. You can even practice in calm wind but that gets tiring fast—it takes a lot of running to keep the wing up with enough feel to be helpful.

Launching in a Crosswind

Start with "Handling Crosswinds" on page 158. Remember that speed is life—a manageable burst of power can improve control enough to succeed. Running left to get the wing moving right is good for slow running speed when brake use may cause the wing to fall back.

If possible, try to lay out at least partially into the wind.

Climbing Out

Try to maintain landing options during climb. If the field is surrounded by obstructions, climb out on the inside edge so that if the motor quits you can turn towards landable surface. Avoid high climb angles for the first 30 feet lest a motor failure swing you into the ground. If possible, plan turns in the motor's normal torque-turn direction. Clutched motors like left turns while others favor right turns.

Landing Pattern

Tight spaces sometimes require different landing patterns. Fly it as standard as possible, knowing that odd field shapes can dictate odd patterns. Mind the landing priorities in "Motor Failure and Landing Priorities" on page 201.

An obstacle-lined field, like in Fig 17-7, will require final descent to follow the contour of obstacles. Descend while just inside the trees, ending with a short final into the wind. Don't get too close—snagging a wingtip is *very* unforgiving.

If you're forced to accept a crosswind, choose a pattern direction where the base leg has some into-the-wind component (Fig 17-6). Slower groundspeed and less turning make it easier to plan (discussion in Fig 10-4).

Dealing with Winds—Using Power

In turbulent conditions it's beneficial to keep the power on. Even if you need to get into a tight space, the value of having thrust available outweighs the chance of breaking a prop on landing. And it's not just to enable a go-around—it can salvage what would otherwise be a hard arrival.

Providing there is room, come up slightly on the power just before touchdown to shallow the descent. In a tight space, wait until you're within 10 feet of the ground or so. This will also "spool up" the motor enough to have quicker throttle response—you'll be better prepared to counter a downward gust.

If everything goes well, and you don't get dumped, then do a normal flare and landing. In strong conditions, be quick to turn around and get the wing down while killing the motor.

This is something to practice long before it's needed. Become adept at making flawless power-on landings during smooth conditions, then practice them when it's a bit rougher.

Without power, a gust that pitches you up (wing goes back) will sap your airspeed followed by a drop and possibly hard landing. As soon as you feel the wing start going back, let up the brakes while preparing to dampen a forward surge. Expect less flare authority, so consider a squirt of power to regain lost speed and preserve brake authority for flare.

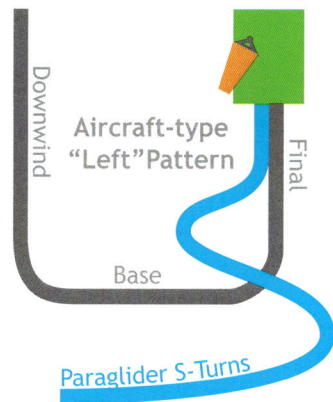

Fig 17-6 Paraglider vs Aircraft-type Patterns

With at least 5 mph wind, the S-turn pattern is a good choice, otherwise, favor aircraft-type patterns with adjustments as shown in Fig 17-10.

Base leg direction is chosen because it's somewhat into the wind.

Tight Spaces: Spot Landing

Next to steering the launch, spot landing skill is what makes tight spaces manageable—consistently touching down within 25 feet of your target. Practice and master it from a large area where there is no consequence of missing. Don't do it for real until you're consistently nailing the spot with and without wind.

There are different kinds of "spots," where you: 1) must come over an obstruction, 2) have minimal ground run, 3) land along a narrow path, and/or 4) have rough surfaces. Each presents its own peculiarities.

Most landings are safer if approach is made at idle but with*out* planning to use power. And don't fly over anything where a power loss would be painful. Use turns if necessary to keep landable terrain available.

Fig 17-7 Tight, Obstructed Landing Site

This tiny, insufficient field would only be considered in an emergency. Plan the touchdown away from rotor-causing obstacles. Hug the edge of the field but don't get too close—hooking a tree up high is worse than rotor down low.

Effect of Brakes on Glide

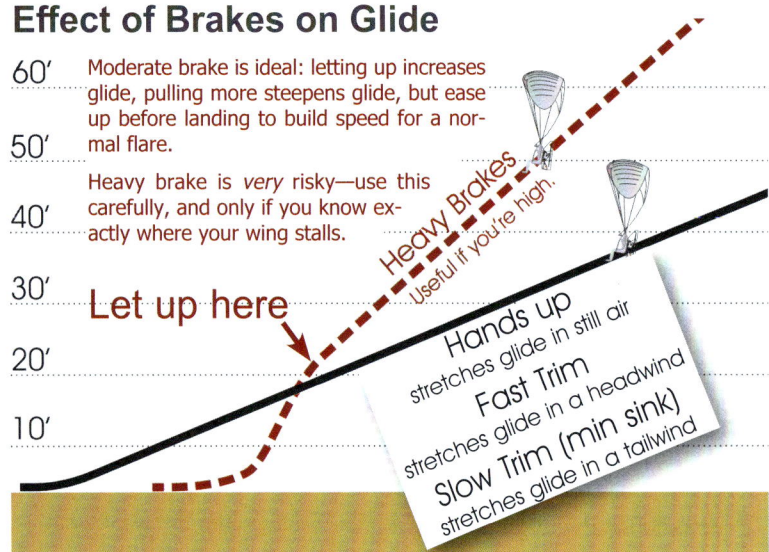

Effect of Wind Gradient on Glide

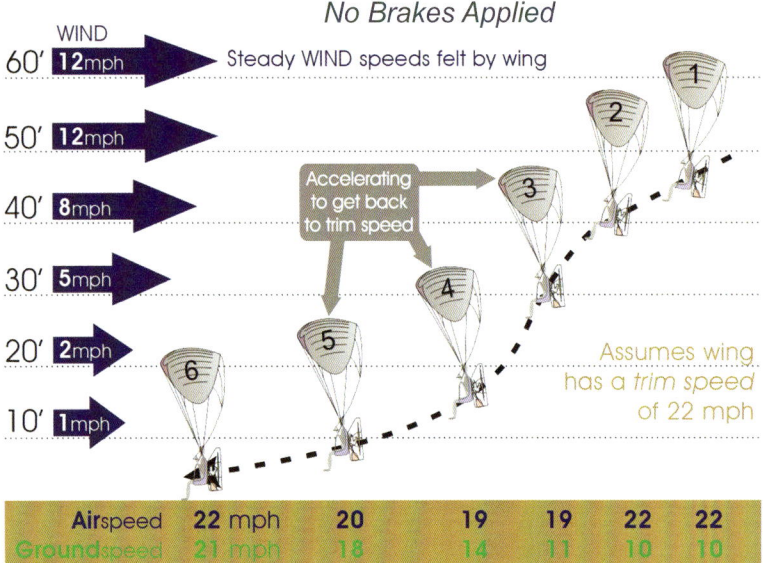

Basic Spot Landing

Fly a normal, but slightly tighter landing pattern to stay oriented and aware of altitudes. Your goal is hitting a 75 to 100 foot final approach where it's easier to judge the crucial final glide. Finish any altitude-losing S-turns by about 50 feet—less as you gain skill.

If the touchdown area is small and obstructed, consider using heavier brake application to slow down and steepen the glide (Fig 17-8). Be careful—you'll be closer to a stall and have minimal maneuvering speed.

Once the wing is slowed there is nothing more you can do with those brakes since more pull risks stall or spin. Practice this at a benign location before depending on it.

Avoid turbulence. Be ready to recover from an incipient (beginning) stall or spin by immediately reducing brakes followed by powering up to half. Recover at the first feel of limp brakes or airspeed decrease.

Judging glide is an essential skill that must be mastered. Practice (or envision) it during your next approach in smooth air. Put a foot up so that it lines up visually with where you think touchdown will be. If your foot starts to pass over the spot—you're high; lift it up a bit to reflect the better glide. If your foot sinks below the spot, you would land short; move it down to reflect the steeper descent. Once the spot is no longer moving up or down, that's your aim line—where you'd hit without flaring if nothing changes (Fig 5-25 on page 67).

With even a light headwind, glide is extended

Fig 17-8 Effect of Brakes on Glide
Pulling brakes can steepen glide if you get too high but don't stall.

Fig 17-9 Effect of Gradient on Glide
Chapter 5 introduced wind gradient effects during landing. To understand them better, this shows what would happen if no brake were applied. You can see why it's even more important to be hands nearly up by 50 feet so you have flare authority.

When dropping into a decreasing headwind, airspeed slows, causing a dive as the wing seeks to regain trim speed. A high (200 foot or more), gradual gradient improves glide, but a small, strong gradient will dump you early, and possibly hard, as the wing dives aggressively.

by letting the brakes up, and steepened by pulling more brakes. More headwind wind requires a steeper approach. In strong headwinds it may even be best to have the trimmers out.

If speedbar is used to overcome a strong headwind, expect to visibly drop initially, then see glide improve. Don't push the bar *while* letting off the brakes—it makes a front tuck more likely.

Only use acceleration if you fully understand the wing's control limitations in that condition. It may only allow tip or rear riser steering.

Follow the guidelines in Fig 17-11, "Spot Landing: Last 100 Feet".

Improving skill will let you concentrate longer (to a lower altitude) on making the spot—staying on the brakes longer when necessary. That sacrifices flare authority and must be timed precisely. Flaring from more than half-brake (pressure 3) is almost useless; you will just whack hard. There must be enough brake authority to cause some forward swing which is what actually slows your descent.

If heavy brakes were applied, ease them up in time to re-build airspeed for flare.

Spot Landing
The Last 100 feet

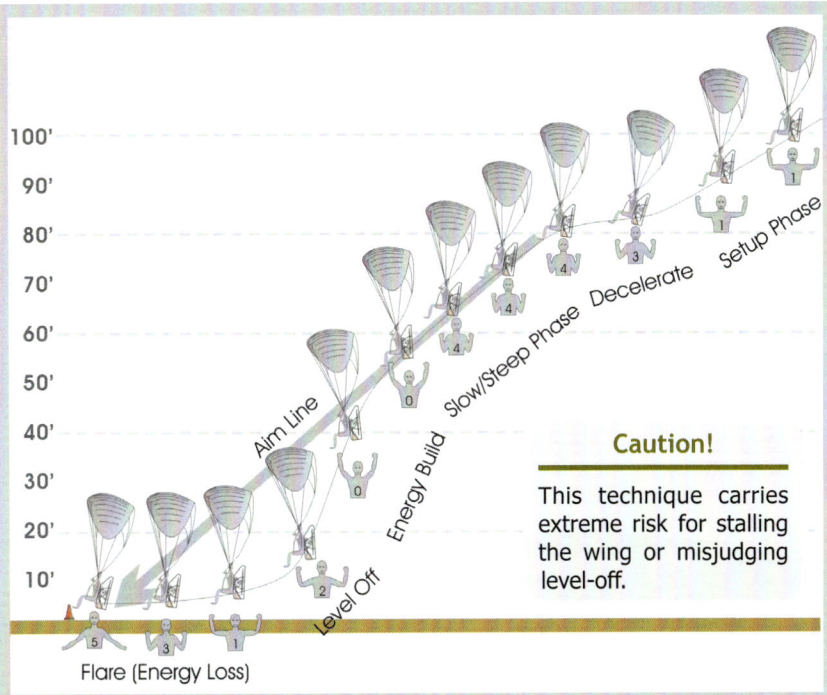

Fig 17-11 Spot Landing: Last 100 Feet

This technique is for hitting an exact spot like a Frisbee—it's *much* riskier than a normal landing, *especially* for less experienced pilots. Allow more room for error and avoid brake extremes. In bumpy conditions, avoid using more than brake pressure 3 which risks hitting sink and not having enough brake authority to arrest the drop. Here are the basic steps.

1. Use a normal power-off landing pattern that is slightly high, adjusting as shown in Fig 17-10.
2. S-Turn on final to bleed off any excess height. If brakes are already pulled, turning can cause an inside spin (in the turn direction). Be ready to immediately let up brake pressure if you sense the first bit of that.
3. Start the final glide with brakes around pressure 3.
4. Hands up to extend the glide, brakes to pressure 4 if you get high.
5. At about 30 feet, forget the spot and reduce brake pressure to near 0 to regain speed for a normal flare and touchdown.

Caution!

This technique carries extreme risk for stalling the wing or misjudging level-off.

Flapping

Flapping is another technique for descending steeply without stalling. The pilot repeatedly snatches heavy brakes, then releases them in a "flapping" motion. It doesn't prevent a stall, it just ensures that the wing sees some time without brake input while creating enormous drag.

Regardless of technique, pulling this much brake adds extra risk for a stall or spin. It would be good to practice during a maneuvers (SIV) clinic.

Power-On Spot Landing over an Obstruction

If you're trying to make it into a really confined area, like the boxing ring below, here's how. Come in with power, be level or slightly below the obstruction (ropes), holding moderate brake pressure (about 3). A second or two before

Fig 17-10 Spot Landing: Pattern

Fly an aircraft-type pattern tighter to reduce the effect of changing winds and thermals.

S-turns are another technique that works. The base and final leg of this pattern is essentially the last S-turn.

Brake to position/pressure 3 after turning base so you can extend glide by reducing brakes. Below 30 feet concentrate *only* on the flare. Land wing-level even if you're not going right into the wind.

As skill builds, this can be flown tighter.

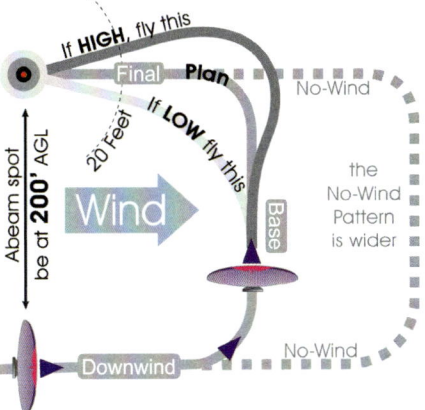

Fig 17-12 Spot Landing: Extending Glide

If forced to land at a spot far away, make your ground track straight towards it. Try to pick a spot where you can arrive with some altitude to spare in case of unplanned headwind or sink. It's useful to inspect and fine tune the landing location.

When it's obvious you've made it, plan at least an abbreviated pattern with base leg and final as shown here. It improves your odds of nailing the spot. Avoid turning completely away from the target.

crossing the obstruction, pull more brake to swing your body forward and slightly up. Coming over the obstruction, throttle off and increase brake pressure to keep the wing behind you as you plunk down onto the target.

The approach is moderately slow, using a combination of power and brakes to hold altitude just a few feet high while keeping some brake authority to stop a drop and flare. The reason for braking just before the obstruction is to swing your body out front, then, after crossing the obstruction, further braking keeps the wing behind you, slowing to touchdown.

Mis-timing this would be painful, so practice with imaginary fences on soft targets like beaches. Be proficient before trying it somewhere hard or important. A motor with rapid response time is helpful since, with all that brake pulled, you'll need throttle to control height.

Choose the slowest wing possible to improve your odds, and be careful!

Fig 17-13 Spot Landing Over Obstacle
Red means more power, white means no power, so pink means some power is being held. Wind helps this effort dramatically as long as it's not too bumpy.

Advanced Maneuvers

CHAPTER 18

Maneuvers serve various purposes: losing altitude, changing flight path, skill enhancement, competition, demonstration, and just plain fun. But danger abounds, especially since lines must always remain loaded.

Before doing anything steep, do a *maneuvers clinic*. You can do this as soon as you're comfortable with basic launching and landing skills, but you'll get more out of it after 50 to 100 flights. Courses teach the latest methods for recovering from unusual situations, and more importantly, let you practice them in a safer, more controlled environment.

Techniques change. What you read here, or even learn in a clinic becomes dated as knowledge and gear improve. Even the experts are always learning better methods to fly and train, especially as gear changes. Ask instructors and respected pilots about the latest wrinkles.

Inducing wing malfunctions outside of a clinic is risky, especially over land. If you do take on the risk, or intentionally fly in turbulence, have a suitable reserve and know how to use it ("Reserve Deployment" on page 52).

Aerobatics such as loops, rolls, helicopters, tumbles, SAT's, "Misty Flips," and such are intended for show. They should only be attempted with the highest level of training—even then be ready for reserve rides. Done wrong, you can get "gift wrapped" in your wing, which rarely ends well.

The more advanced maneuvers should be learned in a free flight harness to reduce the chance of getting tangled in frame parts. Plus, the paramotor's mass and spinning bits could aggravate severe riser twists. If the higher risk of a motor is to be accepted, at least have the propeller stopped before trying anything.

Caution!

The Department of Obvious Risk warns: seek proper guidance from a qualified, experienced instructor before attempting any steep maneuver. The above image is from a maneuvers clinic.

Fig 18-1 Low Hook-In Weight Shifting

This is a typical low hook-in machine with pivoting S-arms. It's in the hips—crossing legs just makes it easier to hold.

Fig 18-2 Anti-Torque Strap
If installed, this strap must be loose to have effective weight shift.

Fig 18-3 High Hook-In Weight Shifting

This is a high hook-in system with fixed underarm bars. These sometimes have anti-torque straps, as shown in yellow.

Weight Shift Turns

This is *not* an advanced maneuver, but we include it here because it's not intuitive on all machines.

Weight shift is really about *riser shift*. You move in the harness so that one riser goes up while the other goes down to start a small turn towards the lowered riser. It makes brake input more effective. Since the goal is *riser* shift, body contorting and leg swinging may look cool, but if the risers don't shift, the wing will *not* be impressed.

Use weight shift to begin a turn, *then* apply brake. As bank increases, pull slight outside brake pressure to reduce diving tendency and prevent collapse of the outside tip. This is part of a *coordinated turn* as described in Fig 16-3 on page 160). Being more efficient makes it valuable for soaring or competing.

More weight shift and less brake reduces the chance of spinning during aggressive maneuvering.

Low Hook-Ins

Typical low hook-in S-arm motors (Fig 18-1), or those with similar geometry, have effective weight shift.

A few models, with even lower hook-ins, get some extra effect from tilting the entire machine, pivoting arms do the rest. On these machines, it's even more in the hips with an action that feels slightly like throwing some weight to one side. That's easier with their low center of gravity being closer to the attachment points.

Machines with low hook-ins but fixed arms will have less weight shift, especially if the center of mass is farther below the hook-in points. Even just a few inches lower sacrifices weight shift ability. Check with the maker or an experienced pilot who knows the model.

Some pilots of low hook-in motors cross their legs (Fig 18-1) when turning, putting the high-side leg over which makes it easier to hold for a longer time, but it doesn't improve the turn. It can also serve as a signal to nearby pilots that you are about to turn, adding value to the "lean" in "look, lean, then turn."

High Hook-Ins

High hook-in models have less weight shift but it can be improved with a moving bar or sliding straps in front of the J-bar. Fixed, over-the-shoulder J-bars—mostly found on legacy machines (right)—have the least amount of weight shift.

Pilot technique varies but the effect must be the same: differential riser shift.

On high hook-in systems, the pilot pushes one leg down to push that side of the seat down which lowers its attached webbing and riser—right leg down to turn right. If it has ground handling shoulder straps (most do), even more weight shift is possible by pushing a shoulder against the strap while pushing down the leg. Experiment to find what works best on your unit.

The harness's chest strap and anti-torque strap (yellow strap in Fig 18-2), if equipped, should be fairly loose for best weight shift. Tighten them back up, as needed, before landing, mostly in case a go-around is needed.

Speedbar Usage

We're not speed demons, but some wings, especially reflex models, have quite the speed range when used properly. There are dark corners, though—follow the wing's manual if it contradicts anything here.

How to Apply

Never apply speedbar if the wing is unloading, as in surging forward. Rather apply it while adding power or passing the bottom of an arc where your body is swinging forward (pitching up).

If combining speedbar with trim; ease out the trimmers first, let the wing surge, *then* add speedbar as it's coming back. Keep your hands up but be *ready* to resume brake use after releasing bar.

It takes significant leg-push to keep the speedbar engaged. That's good on standard gliders because it can be released quickly, restoring normal flight immediately. Trimmers are set once and remain. Trimmer adjustment normally requires releasing brake pressure, too, so consider your situation.

Advanced Wings and Cautions

More advanced wings, usually for competition, may employ a Speedbar/Trimmer Interconnect (STI), as described on page 265. It puts both trimmer *and* speedbar authority at your feet. Use it *very* carefully, especially avoiding any maneuver that involves being even slightly unloaded. These wings will have some kind of tip or stabilo steering. Higher end free flight models have rear riser steering toggles.

Any kind of wing fold is worse when accelerated, especially at higher loadings. Unless you're competing, or the manual says otherwise (some do), avoid speed system use in bumpy air or below about 200 feet AGL (60 m).

On some reflex wings, speedbar should only be used while trimmed fast. On most higher-end wings avoid using main brakes while accelerated—instead favor tip steering or rear riser steering.

Maneuvers Course (SIV)

A well-coached maneuvers clinic, frequently called SIV *(Simulation d'Incident en Vol - simulated incidence in flight)* helps rehearse extreme situations and learn how your wing behaves in them. Flights are usually over water after getting towed 2000' up with a boat. Organizers must be competent since water impact at high speed can still be lethal.

These maneuvers won't make you an expert but will be a good start. Don't get cocky—pilots have died after going home and trying them on their own over land. And mid-day turbulence-induced collapses can be *much* worse than the self-inflicted variety.

Proper and rapid recovery from many maladies requires correct, decisive reactions that, if done at the wrong time, may make matters worse.

If you're using a paramotor, make sure the harness and frame are strong enough with appropriate backups. 200 pounds of body briefly exerts over 600 pounds of force in a typical asymmetric spiral (3 G's).

If you do these courses, or any high G maneuvering a lot, get the glider inspected more frequently.

Fig 18-4 Ideal Speedbar Setup

"Speedbar Setup" on page 117 has the basics. These tips are for those who will be using it a lot.

1. Speedbar in its retracted position and ready.

The green line shows a better pulley position and routing. Line tension should be aligned with the risers as much as possible, not pulling them forward. Route it closer to your hips to avoid squeezing the seat upwards when pushing the speedbar.

2. Fully accelerated. It also shows another possible pulley arrangement that may be more comfortable (green line and pulleys).

3. Pilot's-eye view of extended speedbar.

See also "Speedbar Setup" on page 117.

Have the pulley closer to your hips and secured to the frame for greater comfort

Don't let speedbar line abrade your harness. The pulley positions shown in red are not ideal because the pull force is not in line with the risers.

TWO Pulleys keep pull force more in line with the risers but they will want to squeeze together.

Descent Techniques

This stuff is cool, fun, useful, and dangerous. Learn with a good coach and realize that different wings behave differently so instructions that work well for one glider may be dangerous on another.

Start the following descent methods with trimmers neutral unless told otherwise. Power should be off with the propeller stopped or windmilling. Start out shallow and increase *very* slowly.

Big Ears

Big Ears is a fairly benign technique that roughly doubles your normal descent rate. Combining Big Ears with speedbar (pull ears first, though), adds about 25% to that rate. Steer using weight shift, if available, and avoid adding power or brakes which increase the chance of entering parachutal stall. Stress increases on the center lines, which must support everything once the tips are pulled down. Forward speed stays about the same because, while wing area is reduced, drag is increased.

Descent rate: Up to 800 FPM (4 m/s).

Entry: Reach up with palms facing outward (thumbs down) and pull the outermost A lines or split A down. Twist the hand inward so that your palm faces you.

Recovery: Let go of the A lines and do not pull any brake—see if the tips open on their own. Higher aspect ratio wings tend to recover slower and may even need a brief brake pull to pressure 2.

B-Line Stall

B-Line stalls (Fig 18-9) halt the wing's forward motion while leaving it fully inflated and descending vertically. With the wing creased along its B-lines, air spills equally around the leading and trailing edges. Line attachment points get stressed so use it sparingly, especially if heavily loaded. These are more dramatic than Big Ears, and with more possible complications, especially front horseshoe on exit (Fig 18-11).

Descent rate: Up to 1600 FPM (8 m/s).

Entry: Reach up high on the B-lines (quick links if possible) and pull them down to your shoulders with forearms upright. It will initially take a lot of force which decreases once established. The wing falls back abruptly (you swing forward),

Fig 18-5 Round Spiral Dives

These are one of the more dangerous descent methods. A better choice is the Asymmetric Spiral where you shallow out each revolution.

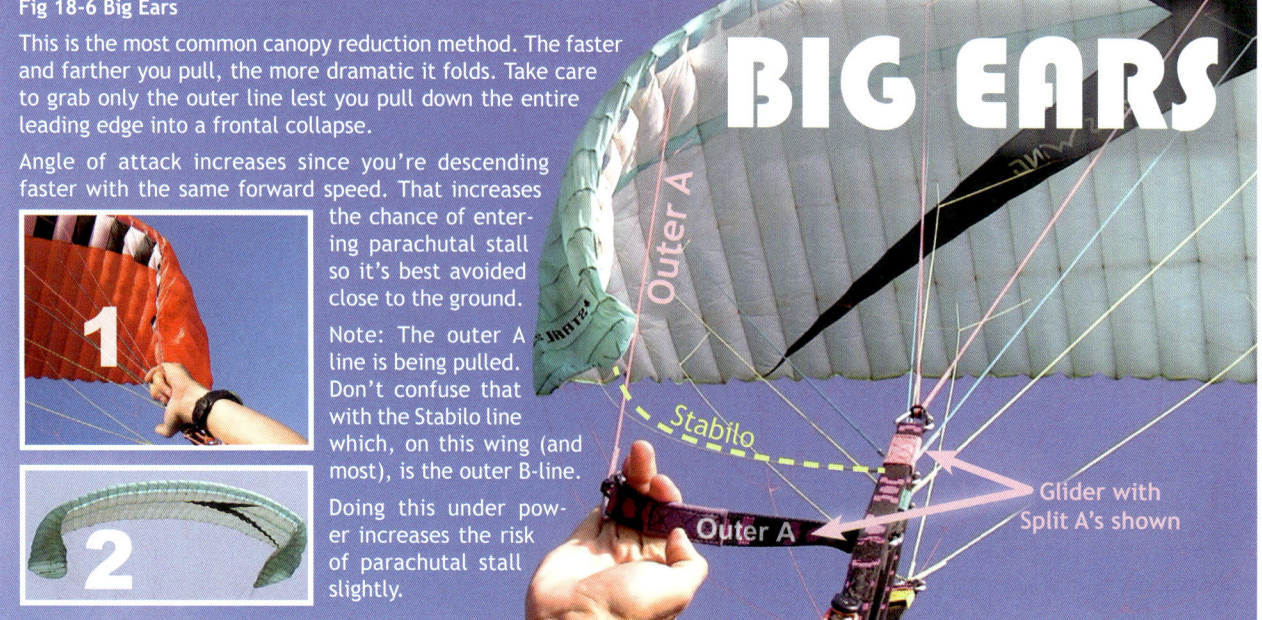

Fig 18-6 Big Ears

This is the most common canopy reduction method. The faster and farther you pull, the more dramatic it folds. Take care to grab only the outer line lest you pull down the entire leading edge into a frontal collapse.

Angle of attack increases since you're descending faster with the same forward speed. That increases the chance of entering parachutal stall so it's best avoided close to the ground.

Note: The outer A line is being pulled. Don't confuse that with the Stabilo line which, on this wing (and most), is the outer B-line.

Doing this under power increases the risk of parachutal stall slightly.

then settles overhead in a vertical descent. How far you pull the B's down depends on the wing and where you grabbed them.

More pull gives more descent but too much pull may cause a front horseshoe (Fig 18-11). If that happens, immediately let your hands up slightly.

Recovery: Let up on the B-lines *quickly* and *evenly,* but don't just let go. Some instructors recommend letting up slowly, but that may cause a parachutal stall, and letting up unevenly may cause a spin. Also, let the wing get fully flying before applying any brakes.

Steep Turns

This works on most gliders. Pull one brake to pressure 2 and hold it. The glider banks some then shallows out a bit, remaining in the turn as long as you hold that pressure. Pull more brake and it does that again—banking more, then mellowing back a bit. At some point, if you pull harder the bank continues to steepen (not coming back towards level). You're entering a steep turn. G-forces build as the bank increases, making you feel pressed into the seat. Brake responsiveness and pressure increase. Don't go steeper than #3 in Fig 18-7).

Small or sporty gliders may keep getting steeper with that amount of brake. Lightly loaded beginner models may not get into a steep turn using this method. They may require getting into it with mild wingovers first.

Any turn increases descent rate (or requires more power). At 60° bank you're pulling 2 G's and probably requiring full power if you were trying to stay level. For most wings, this bank angle is sufficient to maintain a wingtip drag.

Descent rate: up to 1500 FPM (7 m/s), more in nose-over spiral.

Entry: Initiate a turn and hold enough brake so that it gradually steepens to about 60°, then modulate the brakes to hold it there. It looks about like frame 2 at right. Enter into the turn gradually to avoid pulling the wing into a spin.

Recovery: Enormous energy builds up and must be managed. Remove the turn input so that it starts leveling out. Once it *starts* recovering, re-apply some inside brake, slowing the rate to avoid swinging up into a steep climb, possibly followed by the lines going slack.

Spiral Dive (Symmetrical or "Round")

Symmetrical Spiral Dives are steeper turns (more than frame 2 in Fig 18-7) that result in a rapid descent. Beyond a certain point, most wings, including beginner models, will become "locked in" to an essentially vertical ("nose over") spiral. It can take strong opposite brake pressure to start the recovery (possibly two hands).

Once established, the heavily loaded wing is stable but also hyper-sensitive to brake input. Structural failure and blackout is more likely as it quickly exceeds 4 G's. A sadly common cause of fatality is where the pilot blacks out then spirals in. Vertigo, where the pilot gets disoriented, is also a possibility. Think about recovery direction before beginning.

In rare situations, these can become unrecoverable. Besides vertigo, your body is going to the left, while the wing is rocketing right (or vice-versa), further confounding what brake to pull. And high G's can prevent the pilot from getting to his reserve handle in rare cases.

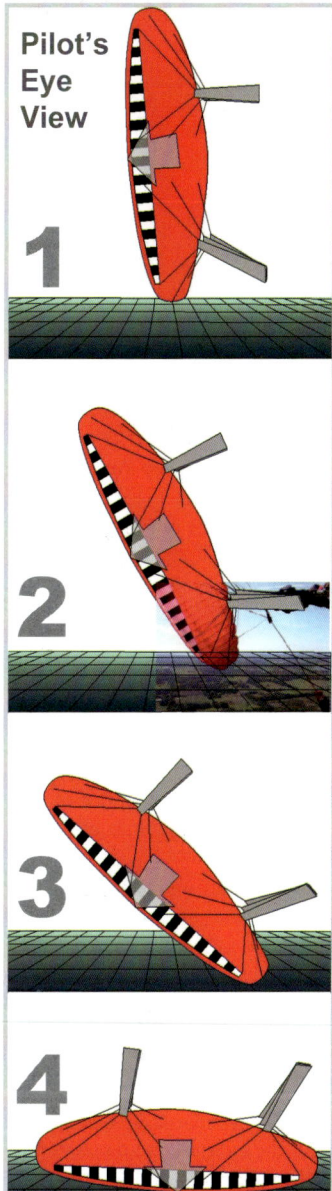

Fig 18-7 Pilot's View Spiral

Banks 1 & 2 are steep turns, 3 is a spiral dive.

#4 is a dangerous "over-the-nose" spiral that may not recover on its own, is disorienting, and can quickly cause blackout.

Caution!

When initiating a turn, if pulling more brake does not cause more turn, don't pull harder! You may spin the glider. Also, once you start coming out of a steep turn, don't try to go back into it; let it fully recover first.

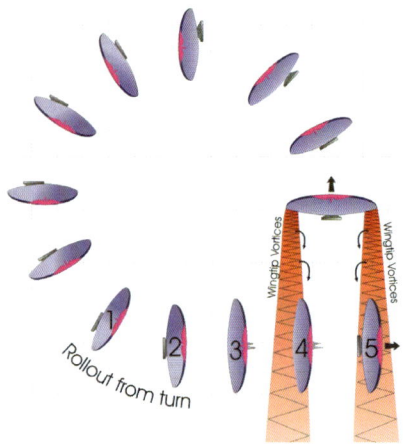

Fig 18-8 Level Steep Turns

Steep, level turns produce powerful wingtip vortices (wake) due to high wing loading. If you roll out just before hitting it, the wing goes back then surges forward, unloading a bit. That's when you're vulnerable to a collapse.

These steps help avoid wake woes.

- Initiate rollout by reducing left brake. Once it starts leveling out, reduce power *some* and reapply some left brake pressure to slow the rollout and climb above the wake turbulence.
- As the wing surges forward, add some brakes and power.
- During the rollout always keep some pressure (2 to 3) on both brakes in anticipation of going through the wake.

Rolling out partially and climbing avoids the wake altogether.

During a symmetrical, steep, level turn, the wing vortices should remain outside your flight path.

Descent rate: Up to 5000 FPM (25 m/s).

Entry: Note the direction. Weight shift (if able), then pull enough brake to keep the bank increasing. You may have to start with a wingover the other way first on lightly loaded and/or beginner models. Build slowly, taking an entire 360° turn to get into the spiral—too much brake can cause a spin.

Recovery: Remove any control input including weight shift. If it doesn't start recovering right away; pull both brakes some then opposite brake. Once it starts recovering, let up. If it's leveling off quickly, ease in some inside brake (in the direction you're turning) to damp recovery. The steepest spirals may require weight shift and heavy opposite brake to start the recovery.

Think about the spiral in advance. With your body whistling earthward at high G's, recovery direction may not be obvious.

In a right spiral, for example, your body is swinging left while the wing races rightward. Remember that you used right brake to enter then needed little or no brake to stay in it, and will need **left** brake to initiate the recovery (if just going hands up doesn't work).

Spiral Dive (Asymmetric)

An *Asymmetric* Spiral is one that's shallowed out a bit on each revolution. It's safer because the chance of "locking in" is *much* less.

G-load decreases in the shallow portion, but high-G's still happen on the steep part so make inputs carefully to avoid slack lines on the shallow part. Solid active flying skills or competent coaching are a must.

Recovery is just like a regular spiral but less extreme. Like all these maneuvers, there's a lot more to it.

Wing Anomalies

Bad stuff happens, especially when pushing the limits of weather, skills, and/or gear. Maneuvers clinics are good, but avoiding nasty conditions is better. Trying this stuff, especially without proper training, has proven fatal.

We cover Parachutal Stall under "Parachutal Stall/Spin" on page 53.

The standard response to unknown *paramotor* situations is: smoothly "**reduce brakes, reduce power, then steer.**" If you're near terrain use *just* enough brake to steer away. Look up at the wing to see what has happened, then look back at the horizon to stay oriented. Motor pilots tend to pull too much brake rather than not enough. Do what it takes, but without over controlling.

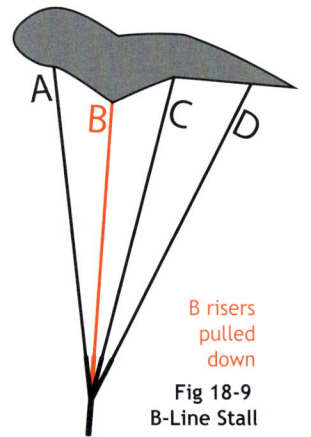

Fig 18-9 B-Line Stall

Fig 18-10 Full Stall

Fig 18-11 Horseshoe

Turbulence can play havoc on recovery, so even if you've practiced, don't expect it to always go the same way in rough air. In any compromised-control descent stay aware of altitude and know where your reserve handle is.

Cravat

Chapter 4 (page 50) covered milder cravats—but larger ones can be far worse. A 60% clean wing fold is manageable, whereas a mere 30% fold that tucks against the lines can quickly cause a radical spiral.

Cravats are frequently complications of collapses from turbulence or botched maneuvers. Once in the spiral, G-forces build rapidly, making recovery difficult or impossible. Tossing the reserve right away, before blacking out, may be all that's left. Otherwise, do what you can to stop the spiral. If you can find the stabilo line, pull it hard, hand over hand if necessary. If you can't find it, use whatever opposite brake it takes.

Spin

Spins are another malady caused by excessive brake pull. If it's uneven pull, especially against the motor's torque, part of the wing stalls while the rest keeps flying. The glider slows then rotates nearly overhead as you descend. A riser twist is possible as the pilot tries to catch up to the spinning wing, potentially locking the brakes in place and preventing recovery.

If you feel any unusual slowing or turning, reduce power and brakes immediately! Most pilots won't detect the spin until it's already spun half way around; that's why prevention is so important.

Descent rate: Around 1200 FPM (6 m/s).

Cause: Uneven heavy braking, especially in turbulence or against the torque. If you're pulling both brakes heavily, like on a spot landing, and let up on *one* brake, it can cause a spin in the other direction since that slows down the other side slightly.

Recovery: Reduce power, reduce brakes immediately, and prepare to dampen the surge. If you get a riser twist, and you're in a low hook-in machine, you may be able to reach above the twist and pull outward to help untwist yourself.

Asymmetric Collapse

What nature doles out can be far worse than what you induce. A big asymmetric collapse may cause a violent bank, dropping you towards the collapsed side and into a diving turn (more collapse, more turn). Don't just start yanking on things, but carefully do what it takes to prevent a spiral.

Frontal Collapse (Tuck)

A frontal, or front tuck, results from the leading edge being forced downward, closing off the cells. You drop and the wing falls back, normally followed by a quick recovery with no pilot input.

Descent rate: Up to 1000 FPM (5 m/s).

Full Stall

Full stalls are violent plummets that start with heavy brake pull. Complications include getting cocooned in your wing.

In most cases, if you merely think you're getting into a stall, reduce brake pressure and power to let the glider fly again. But once you're *in* a stall, recovery is distinctly different.

Entry: Pull the brakes down until your hands are locked below your thighs. The wing slows, then slides aft and starts luffing vertically downward. It initially feels like you're falling on your back.

Hold those brakes until the wing stabilizes overhead. It may be "bucking" about wildly but **hold on for a few seconds!** You'll be dropping at over 2000 FPM (10 m/s).

Recovery: Once the glider is reasonably overhead, reduce brake pull smoothly, evenly, and quickly to about position 4. Hold them for a few seconds. After the glider sorts itself out, let up to pressure 1. Never let up while the **glider is behind!** Don't dampen the surges aggressively, and don't try to control them unless you're certain how.

The only practical value of this maneuver is a last-resort "reset" in seemingly unrecoverable situations. Consider it only if you don't have a reserve, do have lots of altitude, and a crash is otherwise inevitable.

For a pilot who has never done one in a clinic, they have many dangerous possible outcomes.

Fig 18-12 Full Stall

Fig 18-13 Front Collapse (Tuck)
Pulling down all the A's caused these frontals.
A downward gust of wind has the same effect but will be less predictable. On beginner wings recovery is usually quick, even with no pilot input.

Fig 18-14 Induced Collapse (Fold)
Pulling the right A riser down hard caused this 60% collapse. Even with that, it's completely controllable, taking just enough left brake and weight shift to keep it flying straight.

Fig 18-15 Full Stall Into Sand
Entry and recovery vary by wing but it should never be done outside an SIV course or like this, into soft sand that you're willing to fall into. It's apparent why this must not be allowed to fully develop. If the brakes get "mushy," or forward speed deteriorates, *immediately* reduce brake pressure, reduce power, then steer. But if the wing has already fallen back, recover as you've hopefully practiced in a maneuvers clinic.

Causes: Turbulence is the usual culprit, namely a downward gust. But anything that induces a sudden and strong forward surge of the wing will do: 1) bad maneuver recovery, 2) aggressive speedbar application while the wing is already moving forward, or 3) using main brakes while accelerated in reflex mode.

Recovery: Release the speedbar, if engaged, and "tap" the brakes if needed to about pressure 2. Let the glider surge forward to get flying again before adding more brake. Too much brake too soon could cause a parachutal stall (or *constant stall*). If that happens, reduce power, reduce brakes, then steer, and recover as described in Chapter 4.

Pendular Control

Wingovers and surges are foundational maneuvers for staring acro. Start off gently and without power. Rehearse the reserve deployment sequence in your mind just in case things go awry ("Reserve Deployment" on page 52).

Stay up high and never get so steep that the wing unloads (you feel light in the seat). Also, keep some brake pressure on to reduce the likelihood of a front tuck or collapse. Once you've really mastered this level of control, it will help you handle turbulence too. As always, fly by brake pressure, not position. Let the brakes "float" at a given pressure instead of holding them rigidly. Your hands may move a fair amount (lots of brake travel) even though the pressure is relatively low.

Wingovers

Wingovers are sequential coordinated turns (Fig 16-3 on page 160) done in a way that accentuates the glider's natural pendular rates of roll and pitch change.

Start with left turn input (weight shift then brake) and hold for two seconds, then let up. As your body crests and starts coming back, apply right turn input, holding it for three seconds, then release. Repeat back and forth. Smaller wings require less time due to their shorter lines. Adjust the timing for maximum effect.

Like a swing set, you don't need much input if it's done at the right time. Controls are more responsive at the bottom of each swing due to increased G load. At 2 G's, 250 pounds of pilot and motor feels like 500 pounds at the wing.

Use some outside brake at the end of each swing and expect to twist outward slightly (Fig 18-16). This is a great exercise to learn pendular control, but don't let it get too steep, which can happen quickly.

Recover to level by using the opposite actions. As with coming out of a turn, you'll pitch up during rollout. Skill is most evident when you can stop a wingover in only one swing, then control the surge that follows pitch-up. Rollout intensity can be reduced by using some inside brake to absorb energy with bank.

Finesse requires using both brakes at times to prevent the tips from curling up or collapsing. If the tips are folding in periodically, you're probably not using enough outside brake. Always keep some brake pressure throughout, especially on the lightly-loaded high sides. And don't let the glider get too far ahead.

Fore/Aft Pendulums (Surge and Retreats)

Add power and pull brakes to pressure 2 for two seconds then let off. You'll swing out forward as the wing falls back. Then you'll swing back under the wing. When your body starts swinging forward again, gingerly add power and brake for a second, then let off. Like on a swing set, you'll gradually get steeper and steeper. Build slowly! Practice stopping the maneuver quickly. Like the swing, you want to build instinct for how to dampen these pendular actions.

Like any maneuver, as the wing surges farther forward, it gets closer to front tucking, possibly only one side. To reduce this possibility, be mellow and always keep some pressure on the brakes to ensure there is fore/aft tension on the wing fabric.

Also, never get so steep that you feel near weightless in your seat. That's perilously close to unloading the lines and taking a major collapse. Also, avoid using both power and brakes until you're very experienced.

Fig 18-16 Wingover Twist

During bigger wingovers, heading changes continually, requiring fine inputs throughout.

Reaching the steepest point there is a little twist. You turn slower than the wing because of 1) rotational inertia, 2) propeller forces, and 3) being lightly loaded. Heavy motors or carts with higher rotational inertia make this more noticeable.

Fig 18-17 Wingover Illustration

Start with trimmers neutral and build gradually. Risk rises quickly with steepness. Minimize power changes, especially when the lines are lightly loaded which exaggerates torque effects.

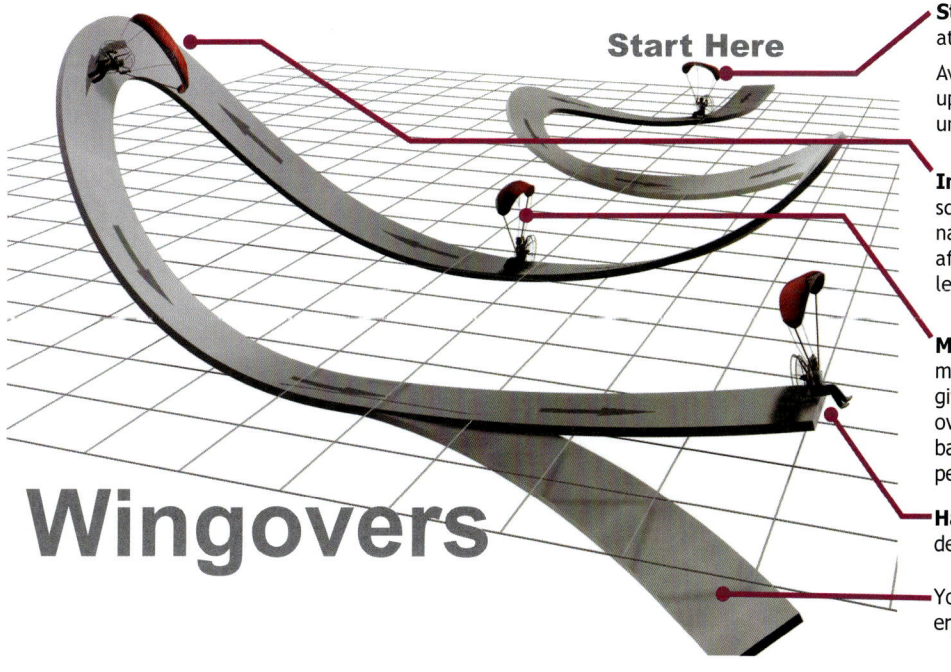

Start Small with little linked turns at the glider's natural swing rate.

Avoid having both hands completely up—especially when lightly loaded—until you're extremely familiar.

Inside Brake here to keep the glider square with the slipstream (coordinated). Otherwise, it slips left just after cresting, possibly curling the left wingtip.

Max G's here, controls are their most responsive. Weight shift left and give left brake *carefully*; it's easy to over-control and end up with more bank than desired. As you gain experience, you can add power here.

Hands up to reduce the climb tendency.

You can also absorb some excess energy **by turning**.

Surge & Retreat Exercise

Fig 18-18 Recover in One Cycle

Start on the right. Set trimmers to neutral or whatever configuration allows normal brake use. The goal is controlling surges so as to recover in just one cycle. This is where real skill comes in. After cresting then bottoming out (5's), add enough power and brake (6), as shown, to finish in level flight by (8).

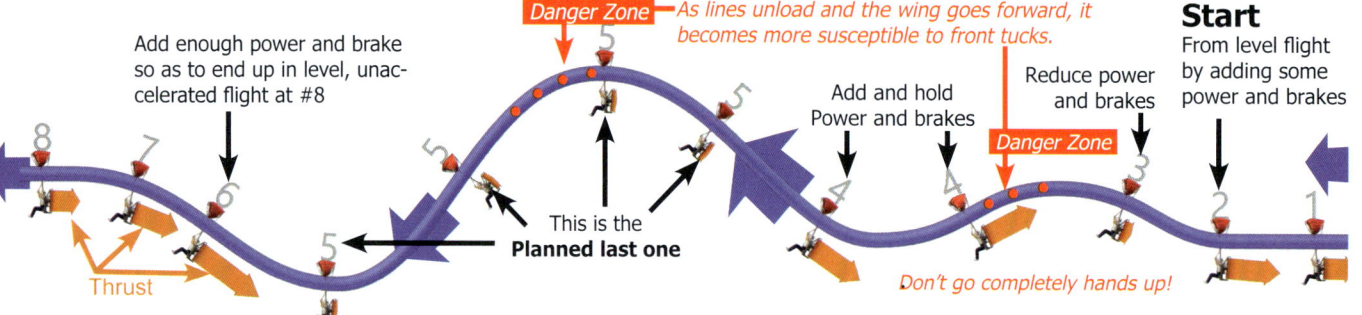

Fig 18-19 Stabilo (Tip) Line

Fig 18-20 Over-the-Top

Tip (Stabilo) Line Pull

Stabilo (Fig 18-19) lines are the outermost B or C lines going to the tip and are often a different color. It's most useful for clearing cravats, discussed earlier, and for efficient but minimally effective steering. Some wings have little balls or toggles that help pull the correct line (Fig 26-21 on page 268).

Pull a big ear and watch what happens with the stabilo line, so you'll know where it is when you need to use it.

Pressure, not Position

During steep maneuvering it's especially important to use brake *pressure*, rather than position. Look at Fig 18-20. He has enough G's to keep the wing loaded and is safely falling through. If he did not start with sufficient energy he may have needed full brake to prevent the wing from front tucking (or worse). There wouldn't be much pressure but you would momentarily be at full arm travel. Turbulence can do that, too.

If holding lots of brakes, as soon as the wing starts loading up, the brakes will want to come back up. Let them! Keep the same *pressure* as your hands return to a nearly full-up position. Holding them against an increasing pressure may lead to a stall or spin. In highly loaded maneuvers, control inputs involve minimal movement—an inch or so—especially on reactive and/or heavily loaded wings.

Risk & Safety

CHAPTER 19

We're fortunate that most mistakes in paramotoring have already been made. And even more fortunate that we know how to prevent them.

The airlines have achieved remarkable safety by analyzing accidents to improve hardware and procedures. They've turned an inherently dangerous operation—flying jets at ridiculous speeds—into the safest form of transportation ever devised. This chapter (and much of the book) aims to use that same type of analysis.

The worn saying, "It's as safe as you make it," *is* true for us since nearly all risk comes from pilot action, not equipment failures or other peoples' actions. Enormous risk can be avoided through behavior changes and an intelligent application of knowledge. Tragedy from ignorance is such a waste.

Low over water, steep and with no helmet? Yup, it's pretty risky. In this case, he built up skill, and is wearing flotation and a reserve.

Some maneuvers are vastly more dangerous than others depending on skill margins. For a new pilot, for example, this would verge on suicidal.

Catastrophic equipment failure, normally very rare, becomes more likely during steep maneuvering.

Probability and Severity

Some behaviors increase the *probability* of mishap while others increase the *severity*. Skipping maintenance, for example, increases the *probability* of a motor failure while flying low over a rocky coastline increases the *severity* if it happens. Each probability has a related severity that changes throughout a flight.

Flying without a helmet is another example. It's like seat belts in a car—they don't prevent accidents, they lessen the consequences.

Some actions do increase both probability and severity: foot drags in water, for example. Water spray increases the *chance* for a power failure, and drowning provides the ultimate severity. Shallow water (less than 6 inches) carries the same increased probability but without the severity.

Energy and Injury

Our sport's overall safety comes mostly from its low speed. Increasing the speed a little increases the injury potential a lot, especially considering how exposed we are. Energy in a collision increases by the *square* of the speed, so doubling the speed quadruples

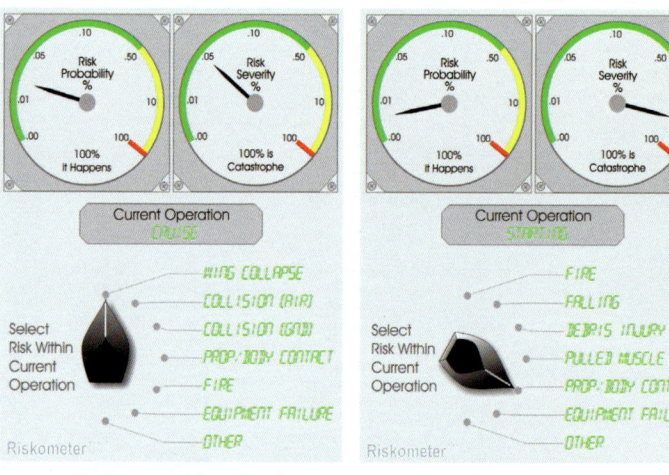

Fig 19-1 Gauging Probability & Severity

If we had risk gages they might look like these—one for probability and another for severity. The system would know your current operation (starting, takeoff, climb, cruise, etc.), then selecting a risk type would display its probability and severity.

For example, the probability of a mishap while cruising along at 500 feet AGL is minuscule. Select FIRE and the probability gauge would be near zero. Severity is high, though, given the longish descent time.

Sitting next to your paramotor during PREFLIGHT, both needles would be 0. After starting, and while standing in front of it, both probability and severity needles go way up since that has proven so risky. Once the motor is on your back, running with throttle in hand, both needles go way down again, it's rare to get hurt at this point.

Doing foot drags is interesting. The pilot doesn't have very far to fall but he has a higher-than-normal chance of it. So, while the probability of a mishap is higher (falling), severity is low as long as the terrain is smooth and flying is into the wind. The probability goes way down for pilots experienced at foot-dragging.

Sometimes needles move in unison. For example, flying downwind, in the mechanical turbulence of large buildings or mountains, both probability and severity increase.

Flying out of a tight field with surrounding corn carries a high probability of hitting the corn, but the severity is low. But flying out of the same field surrounded by razor wire is another story. Flying over water, beyond reach of land, does not increase the probability of an engine failure, but its severity sure goes up, especially without flotation.

One common practice is to keep the severity reading low while letting the probability fluctuate. Maneuvers clinics (SIV courses) are this way. You'll induce serious things (like wing collapses) to learn proper reactions but, through careful preparation (rescue boat, pilot flotation, radio instructions, etc.) organizers keep the severity reasonably low. Frontal collapses, spins, asymmetric collapses and so forth are all induced over water, with a boat and safeguards in place to handle worst case scenarios.

the energy (and injury). So hitting something at 30 mph has four *times* the energy as hitting it at 15 mph. That's potentially lethal. You can see why high-energy (speed), low-level maneuvering is so unforgiving.

Getting Away With It

Personal choice is a valued freedom; our goal is not telling anybody what risk to take, but rather pointing out where the risk is. Standard safety practices—helmets, patterns, safety gear, checklists, etc. are merely layers of protection.

Take helmets. They mitigate impacts from the cage, ground, and exploding props. These events are rare, but far more lethal without head protection. Same with quality footwear which protects feet from rough ground or prop strikes.

This sport is replete with examples of people paying a serious life price for ignoring common safety practices. New people come in, forgo collective wisdom—or never learn it—succeed for a time, and consider the risk acceptable. Then it gets them. It's bad to assume that past success will prevail in spite of bad practices. Accidents are relatively rare, but they happen disproportionately to those taking chances most often. Relish our freedom, but wield it knowingly.

A sad example of "past successes doesn't mean it's safe" is a school that ignored the simple, common practice of requiring helmets for students learning to kite. It worked for several years. Then one day a student lost control, hit his head on a rock and died.

Nobody launches expecting to crash. We have to look at each operation carefully: is it late in the morning? Is there questionable weather? Has someone suggested not flying? Am I going to fly low? Am I medically fit? Am I wearing appropriate safety gear for this flight? And so on.

Where the Risk Is

Here be Dragons. Thankfully we have ways to minimize their fire.

Start by evaluating whether a planned activity is worth the possible consequence. What's the likelihood? How bad would it hurt? And so on.

The top fatality risks happen during: 1) training, 2) steep, low maneuvering, especially spiral dives, speedbar use, and extreme wingovers, 3) ditching (going into water), and 4) flying in sketchy weather. It's not the gear we should fear, it's ourselves.

Starting and Handling the Motor

Propellers are the most injurious part of our sport. Accidents happen predominantly during start and frequently cause life-changing injuries.

They happen, even to highly experienced, conscientious pilots who, in a brief moment of inattentiveness, let the motor get away from them. See "Starting the Motor" on page 45 for more on starting safety. A number of instructors have suffered from these or had *very* close calls.

Training

Training risk is reduced by following the advice in Chapter 1. Poor or careless instruction makes the endeavor particularly perilous, but even with good training, there's significant risk. And previous piloting experience *has no benefit*, either, see "Previous Experience" on page 11).

Do everything you can to be prepared for those first flights. You can only count on reactions that are physically rehearsed.

Intermediate Syndrome

Intermediate Syndrome afflicts the *moderately* experienced. As skills improve, pilots tend to take on challenges beyond their ability. Excelling at *anything* puts your skills to some amount of test, but choose situations where failure isn't catastrophic. For example, only take on higher winds in places where getting dragged won't hurt.

Inappropriate Gear

Inappropriate gear or improper technique for that gear adds risk. Most equipment trade-offs are covered in Section VI but here are some common risks.

- Excessive power for your weight increases the risk of riser twist and, to a lesser degree, makes falling more likely due to weight and torque. It can also increase the chance for a "face-plant."

- Insufficient power increases your risk of 1) tripping due to the extended run, 2) shallow climb ability over surprise obstructions, and 3) vulnerability to even small downdrafts after takeoff.

- Flying an advanced, and/or small wing (highly loaded) without mastery of active piloting increases risk for several accident types, primarily due to overcontrol.

- Using speedbar, especially on more advanced wings, increases risk for those who don't *fully* understand its use and limitations.

- Unduly large, old, out-of-trim, or porous wings increase the chance for parachutal stall, and collapse. Slow speed may prevent penetration into a strong wind.

- Poor motor design (structurally weak, dangerous attributes, etc.) is always risky. Seek out models that embrace safety features over those using older, less-safe technology. It's always a trade-off—sometimes safety features get traded for other attributes. Talk to respected, experienced pilots who are familiar with various models and see "A Better Paramotor" in Chapter 27.

Fig 19-2 Training Aids, Simulator & Reliable Responses

Practice with appropriate training aids, such as this riser-equipped simulator, to prepare for normal flight and unlikely emergencies. In the hands of a good instructor, it's invaluable.

Make sure you can respond to instructions reliably, and know how to avoid roll and pitch oscillations on liftoff. Early flight training risk is *much* higher.

Testing New Gear

Trying new gear *is* riskier but we can make it less so. Start with a hang check while the owner or instructor is present.

1. Note the attachment points. Low hook-ins will have a lower average brake position than higher hook-ins, possibly by a lot. Ask.

2. Find out where the harness adjustments are and how they should be set for takeoff, cruise and landing. Having this wrong could render an otherwise fine machine unsafe.

3. Operate the throttle, starter, and kill switch, especially if the throttle is in a different hand than you're used to. Locate the master switch and think of other ways to shut off the motor.

4. Prepare for the torque effect which may differ in both amount and direction from your usual steed. Belt driven machines twist left, causing a right bank, gear driven machines twist right, causing a left bank.

5. Learn any special instructions for getting into the seat. On some low attachment machines, brake toggles can get in the prop if released, especially while you're still hanging in the harness.

6. Find out what the wing's trimmer settings are for cruising, turbulence, launch and landing. Learn what special handling or procedures apply to the wing, especially if you plan to use the speed system.

Fig 19-3 Motor Starting

Starting is the most likely time to be seriously injured. See Fig 4-12 on page 46. On cart-mounted machines the risk is low.

Comparing The Risk?

PPG is about the same risk as moderately aggressive skiing. You may get a twisted ankle (or equivalent), but probably not a toe tag. Fatality rates are similar to motorcycle riding.

Unlike motorcycles though, we have more control of our risk. Motorcyclists depend significantly on the attentiveness of others.

Steep Maneuvering & Aerobatics

Steep maneuvers, especially with a vertical component (any kind of diving) at low altitude, have proven particularly lethal.

It starts slowly. After gaining some experience pilots get braver, trying maneuvers beyond their skill and without instruction. Little banks graduate to steeper banks that become spiral dives. Little pendulums morph into wingovers, etc. Given the need for our soft wing to always be loaded, these maneuvers can go bad quickly. Plus, when the wing is heavily loaded (as in a steep turn), the controls become *extremely* sensitive, enabling large excursions from small inputs. Steep maneuvering also adds enormous speed and structural load.

Being weightless belongs in outer space—lines can't push. When line tension decreases, a fold becomes more likely. Plus, loose lines find things to wrap around (including pilot parts), only to reload with a bang.

Pilots do this progression naturally, and it's healthy in the right doses, but can quickly go bad. When done without instruction, especially low to the ground, aerobatics are a terrible risk. Low-level shenanigans has been the final ingredient in a dangerous cocktail of risk for pilots who pushed too hard.

Low Flying

You can't hit something if you're above it. Almost all airborne injuries happen while cruising or maneuvering down low. Not only is mechanical turbulence more likely, but it's worse and there's less time to recover. Staying above 200' eliminates most risk.

Simple misjudgments are aggravated down low. The distraction of nearby ground objects contributes, especially with any downwind component.

Wire strikes, even at slow speeds, are a risk, with most injuries coming from the ensuing fall. Electrocution and burns have also happened. In most cases, the pilot was in a familiar area but just forgot about the wires, and didn't see them in time. At some angles they're essentially invisible.

Hitting an obstruction, like a tower or its supporting guy wires, is possible, even up higher. Minimize screen time and other distractions.

If you must fly low, these tips may mitigate some of the risk:

- Avoid flying *downwind* while low. Higher groundspeed makes any miscalculation, unexpected obstruction, motor failure, or collision far worse. There's less time to notice *and* react.

- Fly into new areas above 200' and scout for obstructions. Look for poles or their shadows, and be suspicious of any straight lines (road edges, field edges, etc.).

Fig 19-4 Invisible Wires
Wires don't stand out like they do from the ground where they're contrasted against a plain sky. From above, they can blend completely into the background, especially with a bit of haze. This was taken just before the pilot nearly wrapped himself up in some cleverly hidden wires.
by Travis Burns

Fig 19-5 Crossing Wires
Approach wires at an angle so that you can quickly veer away if the motor quits or you get surprised by sinking air. Fly over the poles since the wires are difficult to judge height over. Be at least twice their height.

As Fig 19-4 shows, this is still no guarantee.

- Stay over landable terrain while respecting power lines and other obstructions. This is even more important down low because you won't have time to maneuver after a power failure. Don't plan a climb over something if a power loss would leave you without options.

Downwind Operations, The "Demon"

To the paraglider itself, flying downwind is no different than flying upwind. The same for turning from upwind to downwind—it's no different. But talk to enough pilots and you'll eventually hear of it: the dreaded "downwind demon." He's a mythical creature, incorrectly suggesting that, when turning downwind, air "hits the back of the wing, causing it to sink."

It simply isn't so. Like a boat in a wide river, our craft operates in a block of fluid (the air) that is moving along over the ground.

To see for yourself, go up high when there's a stiff breeze and do a 360° turn. There is no difference between upwind and downwind. In fact, it's hard to even notice the wind if you're high enough. That boat in the river just did a 360°—the whole wake circle is moving downstream but no part of the turn feels different to the boat driver. And the wake is a nice circle.

There are, however, some **powerful** *illusions*, and one real effect, that happens when turning from upwind to downwind—*they* can easily fool us into pulling too much brake. These are the real "downwind demons," and they only happen while flying down low.

Downwind Demon
Our wing flies in reference to *air*, not ground. "Downwind Demon" illusions happen when pilots look at the ground while maneuvering down low, causing them to pull too much brake in certain situations. Use minimum brake and practice ignoring the illusions.

You can avoid *all* the "downwind demon" risk by climbing up to 200 feet, into the wind, before turning.

Partly this is because pulling brakes causes a fleeting climb, training the subconscious mind—incorrectly—that you "pull brakes to climb."

The Climb Illusion: Take off and climb at 200 fpm into a 10 mph headwind. Climb angle looks impressively steep. Now turn downwind. The *angle* decreases a lot even though the *rate* of climb remains unchanged. Earth is zinging by at 30 mph while you continue climbing at 200 fpm. The subconscious inclination is to pull more brake so that the climb looks the same as before, relative to the ground below.

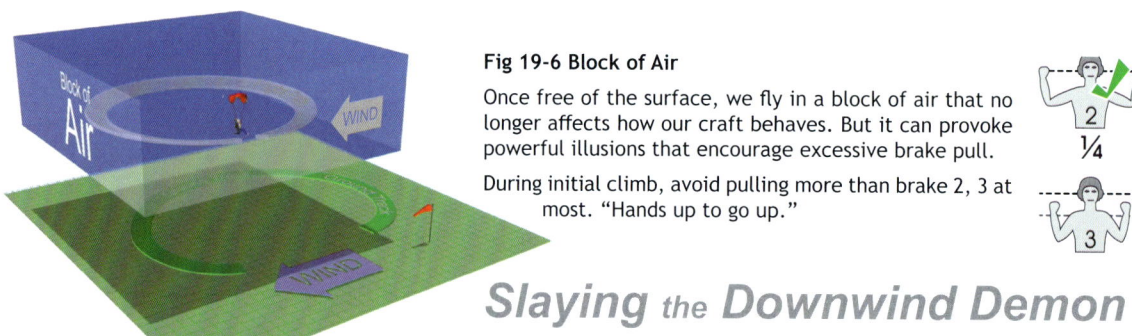

Fig 19-6 Block of Air

Once free of the surface, we fly in a block of air that no longer affects how our craft behaves. But it can provoke powerful illusions that encourage excessive brake pull.

During initial climb, avoid pulling more than brake 2, 3 at most. "Hands up to go up."

Slaying the Downwind Demon

Wind Gradient: This effect is no illusion. If you climb into an increasing headwind (wind gradient), the wing "sees" a bigger headwind and really does climb better as it seeks trim airspeed. Groundspeed is slowing down in the process.

The reverse is true when climbing downwind through that gradient. You'll encounter an increasing tailwind that reduces climb as the wing must accelerate to maintain trim speed. More gradient, more effect, and it's usually most dramatic down low. Climbing upwind for the first 200 feet gets above most sharp gradients.

The Turn Illusion is usually a mild effect that can become overpowering in stronger winds near the ground.

Rate of turn depends only on bank angle and airspeed. If it takes you 2 minutes to turn all the way around when it's calm, it will take 2 minutes when the wind is strong. So turn *rate* is exactly the same whether going upwind or downwind. *However*, when looking at *ground track* the upwind portion describes a tight arc while the downwind portion has a shallow arc (Fig 19-7). Near the ground, that shallow arc can feel like you're hardly turning.

The temptation? Pull more brake to make it feel normal. Bank angle steepens dangerously just before impact which is at higher speed because you're now going downwind.

These effects can **all be avoided** by climbing upwind to 200 feet before turning.

Distractions

Taking pictures, flying formation, fiddling with music, etc. are among the many distractions that increase risk, diverting attention from our primary task of flying.

Stuff hung around your neck can slide back and catch on moving motor parts—not just the propeller. One pilot almost got decapitated when his camera strap went into the pull-start mechanism. Fortunately, the strap broke before his neck did.

Secure anything that moves, especially around body parts.

Midair Collision

Flying with others adds both collision risk and collapse risk from wake turbulence. See Chapter 14, page 144 for more on flying with others, including formation. But note that collisions usually occur with just two or three pilots flying together.

It takes a matter of seconds for someone seemingly far away to suddenly be in your face. The only remedy afterward will likely be a reserve toss..

Fig 19-7 Climb & Turn Illusions

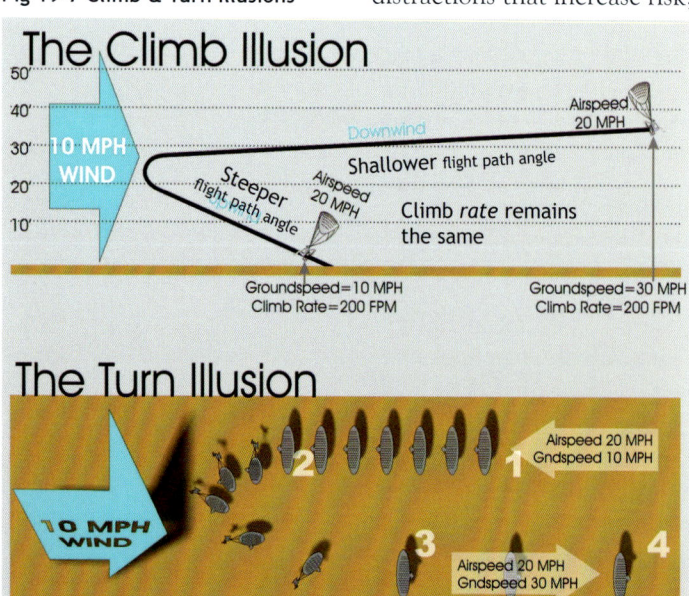

Watch This!

An interesting observation is how many serious accidents happen with spectators present or cameras rolling. The term "Kodak Courage" fits those who push it for glory.

Professional airshow pilots perfect and practice their routines methodically, mostly at relatively high altitudes. Over and over. On performance day they do exactly what was practiced without exceeding their usual limits. "Show-Offs," on the other hand, tend to exceed their limits when being watched. Be like the pros.

Terrain

Flying from flat land, with its more benign weather patterns and forgiving sites, is generally safer than mountain flying. Other risky terrain features include water and congestion.

Local knowledge can be a valuable antidote to the risk imposed by unsavory sites.

Equipment Condition

Wings get porous, lines break, motors wear out, swing arms break, harnesses weaken, carabiners get scratched and other critical components degrade with time and use. These must be maintained properly, inspected regularly, and repaired or replaced when needed if we expect to maintain the same level of safety.

Carabiners are one of few single-point failures that would be catastrophic. They must not be bent, scratched or have malfunctioning gates. Steel is preferred. Some acro pilots replace carabiners annually.

The wing should command most of our attention since its degradation can cause so much grief. Having porous fabric, shortened, or stretched lines makes launching harder and increases the possibility of parachutal stall. Add other factors like being lightly loaded, or flying in turbulence, and a stall may be inevitable.

Don't neglect the motor—some failure modes involve losing a prop and slicing into the fuel tank. Engine failures, while usually benign, can be unsavory depending on where they happen.

Disintegrating props can send shards flying in all directions. Most of the time this happens when a piece of machine vibrates loose and goes through the prop. Anything that can work loose should have lock nuts, safety wire, or other means to prevent ejection. Bad prop repairs, especially on composites, are more susceptible to failure even with no prop strike.

Conventional Wisdom

Conventional wisdom on safety is extremely valuable, and most accidents happen when such guidance is not followed. But it's not everything. You still have to be looking around at what's happening. How could that affect the common guidance? For instance, there are cases where waiting until 3 hours before sunset wasn't enough (Fig 19-8). This is being "situationally aware."

Weather

A large accident category is weather related—pilots ignore weather warnings and fly anyway. It's an easy deception: you get away with something several times and now falsely think that the risk is small.

For example, and this is one of many, most thunderstorms don't actually cause problems until they're fairly close. But

Camera Encounter

An experienced pilot was doing close flybys while an experienced camera man filmed, leaving it up to the experienced pilot to avoid contact. But the pilot wasn't so experienced with higher elevations and misjudged his pull-up, hitting the camera and leaving its operator with a walloping black eye.

YouTube provides a steady diet of reinforcement about this dysfunctional relationship—be vigilant when mixing cameras with flying.

Fig 19-8 Invisible Dust Devil

They were getting ready for what should be an epic evening flight. Winds were light enough that the photographer used bubbles to determine direction.

They wisely decided to skip it.

- 2 hours before sunset, Good?
- But notice the cumulus clouds?

Bubbles for telling wind direction

Dust Devil sucks wing up into a swirl.

by Kevin Hobbs

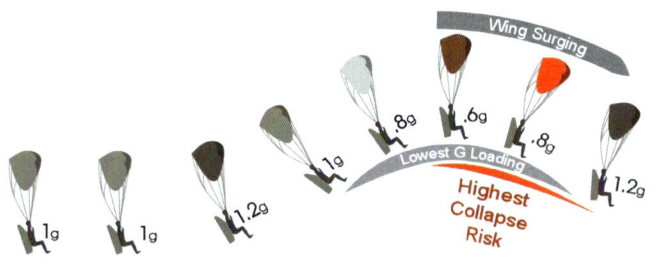

Fig 19-9 Unloading the Wing

The wing has shot back. You went hands up but know that it's about to surge forward. Be prepared for lots of brake, but not yet. It's about to unload and timing is critical.

As the wing *starts* surging—add brakes and power. More surge, more brakes. This will reduce unloading and prevent the wing from getting too far ahead.

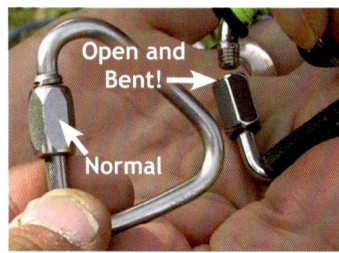

Fig 19-10 Dangerous New Gear

New equipment is normally problem free, but it still deserves a close inspection. The pilot had just landed from a high G flight on this glider's first time out of its bag.

It had arrived from the factory like that—with all the screw gates open, cutting their strength by more than half.

occasionally they reach out and touch from many miles away, causing sudden, horrendous winds. And there's no warning.

Competition

Competition adds risk. It frequently involves low-level maneuvering, high speed, and pushing both pilot and equipment limits. Distracting goals and a willingness to fly in sketchy conditions make matters worse.

Doing tasks over water with rescue equipment mitigates some risk. Keeping pilots from getting high enough to develop dangerous vertical speed helps, but it doesn't take much vertical to get fatal results.

The best way to personally minimize competition's higher risk is to fly within your skill level. If conditions deteriorate too far, man up and decline the task. You may save someone else by your example. Crashing is bad for both body and score.

During practice improve gradually, then don't do anything in competition that you haven't mastered in practice. A middling performer who *finishes* will beat the aggressive superstar who *crashes*.

Unloading The Wing

Minimize low G conditions where the wing gets even partially unloaded (Fig 19-9). It's far more vulnerable to collapse from even small downward gusts, especially if allowed to surge past overhead.

Anything that rocks you back and causes a momentary climb can cause unloading soon after. This happens a lot after steep maneuvers or turbulence. Be on the brakes when the wing is coming forward. It feels like being in a chair that's rocking forward. Have *at least* position/pressure 3 braking as the wing comes overhead, less if it's moving slowly, more if it's moving quickly.

Adding Safety Equipment

Our choice of safety equipment depends on flying style and locale. Fly over forests? Have a tree extraction kit (Fig 28-19). Fly over water? Have flotation (Fig 28-15). Fly remotely? Have a satellite beacon. Always have a cell phone and hook knife.

Some safety gear reduces the *odds* of a mishap while others reduce its *severity*.

Reserve parachutes are severity reducers. They won't decrease the *probability* of a malfunction but sure may improve its outcome. Flying in rowdy air makes a reserve even more beneficial. Make sure it's installed properly (Fig 12-40) and know how to use it ("Reserve Deployment" on page 52). There is some risk of accidental deployment (covered later in this Chapter), and unless the reserve is steerable, you'll have no control of landing.

Gloves are good, especially in windy conditions since ground handling the glider is where you're most likely to get line burns. Boots can prevent ankle injuries and other foot-related maladies like getting a foot in the prop while running or falling.

Helmets are only for those who use their brains. "Helmet up before hooking up."

Combining Risks

Combining risks can increase the chance of a mishap dramatically. Take low, steep maneuvering: both the odds of calamity and its outcome skyrocket.

Look at doing just about anything in rowdy air. The *probability* of an accident increases, especially during takeoff or landing.

Knowing what risk is involved in what operation lets you carefully choose only those operations that are worth it—knowledge that can direct extra attention (skill building or learning) to where it is needed most. This book was largely motivated by a desire to expose where risks are so pilots can make informed choices.

Handling Situational Emergencies

These are situations with time to make choices. They can't be rehearsed in a simulator but rather require a cool, thinking head. Most are highly unlikely, especially during early training where the instructor keeps closer tabs on you.

Situations may have several options, not necessarily covered here, that must be considered with your particular skill set and situation. What's appropriate for one pilot, in one situation, may be disastrous for another.

Be wary of absolutes and analyze your options before acting. Sometimes the first action that pops into your head isn't the best one. Having thought about options in advance (why this is here) can be helpful, but anything that requires a quick response must be rehearsed. Those are in Chapter 4. The airlines have learned that reactionary physical skills, if not rehearsed, cannot be counted on.

Landing In Water (Ditching)

If a water landing is inevitable, your life really does depend on getting this right, especially without flotation. If time permits:

1. Undo your leg, chest, sternum, anti-torque, and reserve straps. That obviously means you can't get out of the seat yet.
2. Don't jump! Pilots have died after misjudging height and jumping early. Telling height over water can be extremely deceptive.
3. Lighten up. Time permitting, dispose of anything attached to your body that could weigh you down (camera, radio, shoes, etc.), and prepare to jump out of the seat **on contact**. Lightening is less important if *you* are wearing a life vest.
4. Grab and extract your hook knife or at least practice reaching for it.

Approach with about brake 2 and don't flare unless you're absolutely certain of your height—it's deceptively difficult to judge. In a light wind, less than about 5 mph, consider landing downwind so the wing goes in leading edge first, trapping air in the cells. In a stronger wind, land into the wind with a firm pull at touchdown to ensure the wing, and its tangly lines, stay well behind. You don't want to get dragged.

Take a full breath of air just before impact. As soon as your feet touch the water, exit and swim away from the gear unless your motor has flotation. Otherwise, the motor, especially carts, may sink quickly once the cavities fill. Also, carts may flip forward, leaving you upside down—this tragedy has happened in shallow water.

Once clear of the gear, ***do not swim back to get it***, especially in moving water. Entanglement is likely. The wing may try to lure you back by floating but the motor will sink. Only go back for your gear with a boat or other really good flotation.

If you start getting entangled in lines, start cutting *immediately*. Lines are cheaper than funerals. Swim away immediately.

Some safety equipment will only help after the fact. See Fig 28-19 for tree self-rescue kits.

Fig 19-11 Surviving Water

If you must tempt Poseidon, these suggestions will help:

1. Use an auto-inflating device which mounts to the paramotor. It inflates upon immersion to keep you and the paramotor afloat.
2. Have personal flotation for the swim to shore. At least one pilot, a strong swimmer, drowned after becoming exhausted while getting away from the motor while fully clothed.

FootFlyer.com has more on water and flotation.

Gusted

After a week of lousy, unflyable weather I was anxious to fly. The receding rumble of thunderstorms had left a quiet calm.

Hmm...maybe?

The mellow sky beckoned and I gathered my gear, heading out to the nicely open field nearby. After getting there, I could see to the horizon and noticed darkness in the distance.

Hmm...

I waited 5 minutes and, sure enough, through the silence of that calm I could make out a muted rumble. More storms growled in the distance. Deciding this wasn't such a good Idea, I packed up and headed home.

Shortly after settling into my project du jour, I heard it. Even before thunder signaled the storm's arrival, there was an unmistakable howl of a gust front. Within minutes, destructive wind blew that would have been disastrous to anyone flying anything, let alone a 15 pound wing.

It was good to be inside.

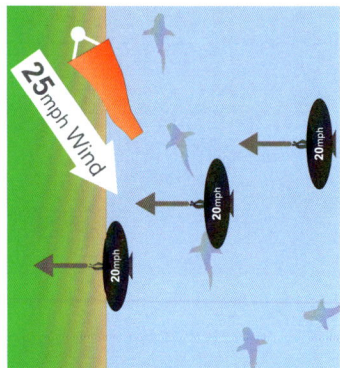

Fig 19-12 Blown Out To Sea
If this happens, head straight towards the beach, flying a heading perpendicular to the shoreline.

If you end up on land but your wing goes into active surf, or a stream, you may only have seconds to escape. It's deceptive—unclip immediately. If a riser is taut, walk briskly toward the wing while concentrating on unclipping quickly with two hands. If pull prevents working the carabiners, start cutting with a hook knife. Seconds matter. Pilots have landed on dry ground then drowned after their wing fell into moving water. It may seem benign, but quickly becomes life threatening.

If landing in very shallow water (less than 3 feet) you obviously don't need, or want, to jump out. Unclip as described above but consider landing seated, with one or both legs forward, especially if there is no wind (high groundspeed). This will prevent you from "face planting" since it is impossible to run out a landing in even a few inches of water.

Getting Blown Out To Sea

You're cruising North, slightly off shore, when the wind turns partially offshore and builds like in Fig 19-12. You turn towards your LZ but are going backward, drifting down the beach and out to sea. The cure is to aim exactly at the beach. You won't make it back to your launch site but walking beats drowning.

Don't angle upwind or downwind at all—head exactly perpendicular to the beach and go as fast as safely possible. That's your best penetration option. It's possible you may have to descend into slower moving air.

This is similar to stretching glide in Fig 19-19. If you were trying to reach an island, fly a heading that *tracks* towards the island.

Gust Front

Gust fronts occur on many scales, the worst being thunderstorms.

Cold air plummets earthward, spreading rapidly at the surface in a deadly cauldron of swirling nastiness. It may be preceded by virga, dust, or debris, but not always. Your first indication may be nasty bumps or negative groundspeed—you are flying into the wind but moving backward over the ground.

If you get caught in that, expect a wild ride with occasional collapses and extreme oscillations. Follow the turbulence penetration advice in "Active Flying in Turbulence" on page 166. Here are some other thoughts:

1. If you can, land before it hits, but only if it won't catch up with you during landing.
2. If you can't land before it reaches you, make a downwind dash to get as far from the source as possible. Even if you can't outrun it, getting farther away may let the front expend itself into a weaker state. Consider going crosswind if that will keep you out of an advancing storm.

If you're *in* a strong wind, consider these options:

1. If you are over a lake consider landing on the downwind shore, even if it's farther than the nearest shore. If you're trying to make shore, follow the advice in Fig 19-12.
2. If you suspect the wind or storm will worsen, power-off and land immediately. Take your lumps, accepting a backward landing even if it means that you may get dragged. Aim for an area offering the most forgiving blowback zone and least mechanical turbulence (it will be wicked). See "Slaying the Downwind Demon" on page 194.
3. Some gust fronts are short lived. If you can safely control the wing, and expect conditions to subside quickly (i.e., it's not part of an approaching thunderstorm) consider waiting it out. Likewise if landing options are bad.

4. Typically, there is a gradient where winds diminish close to the ground. Going lower *may* allow upwind penetration but, be careful, it will also be more turbulent, possibly too much. Don't ever put yourself behind an obstruction that could cause severe rotor. Also consider that gust fronts can be limited, low-level affairs and climbing may help.

Landing Backward

If high winds mean landing backward, be thankful for gloves, and consider these:

1. If it's smooth enough, momentarily let go of a brake or hold both brakes in one hand, then unclip from all but one leg strap to enable a rapid exit after landing. That may avoid getting dragged without being able to exit the harness. Mentally rehearse going for that remaining buckle.

2. Locate your hook knife and be prepared to use it.

3. While still airborne, find the rear risers and prepare to pull them hard at touchdown and hold. Even if you fall, keep pulling until you are able to get up and run around the wing. Unclip as soon as you're able.

4. Kill the wing using one of the methods in "Deflating the Wing" on page 26. If you are getting dragged and risk going through something harmful, use the hook knife to cut through the A risers to depower the wing.

5. Consider finding a site where getting dragged back will be less injurious. Landing in front of a solid tree line, for example, will stop the wing when you get dragged to the trees. Be leery of small ridge-shaped obstructions, though, as the wing can pull you right up over the top, or even back into flight.

Motor Stuck at Full or Partial Power

The most likely cause of this is a throttle cable chopped by the prop.

Pulling Big Ears then going fast (using speedbar/trimmers) or doing asymmetric spirals will help prevent a climb. Don't do B-Line stalls since the recovery may not be possible with the motor at power, and don't do round spirals.

If you decide to reach back and kill the motor, understand the risk—hopefully you've rehearsed it on the ground, preferably in a simulator. On most units, **you *can* get your hand into the prop** so start with the closest options. For example, if the air vent is by your head, plugging it may be safer than reaching farther back for the spark plug.

After making sure you're over landable terrain, here are some ways to shut off the motor. Pick the easiest, most accessible one and mind the prop:

1. If you have an alternate kill switch, relish your forethought and use it.
2. If there's enough of the throttle left, try to work it down to idle. Or if you can safely reach the carburetor throttle arm, move it to idle.
3. If you have a remote choke, or can reach the choke, pull it.
4. If you can reach the fuel line, pinch it hard until it quits (give it 20 seconds).
5. If you can reach the air intake, cover it—takes about 5 seconds. You must plug it completely which can be difficult. Consider stuffing something in it.
6. If you have a primer bulb (or knob), squeeze it to flood out the motor.
7. If you can block the fuel vent, do so. It may take several minutes.
8. If you can reach the spark plug, pull it. Be quick, you may get shocked.
9. If you cannot kill the motor safely, you'll have to run it out of gas.

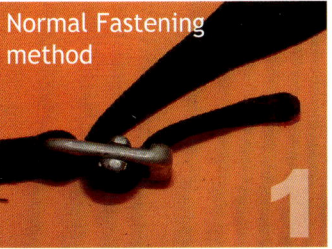

Fig 19-13 Safing Dangerous Buckles
If you encounter this rare, old buckle type, they are nearly impossible to get out of in an emergency (1). To make them better, fasten as shown in picture 2 so that simply pulling on the end will release it immediately.

Fig 19-14 Gusted

#1 After landing in a strong and increasing wind, the pilot got lifted, dragged, and turtled. It took several others to stop the carnage.

Fig 19-15 Throttle Hit By Prop

#2 This throttle got damaged by its prop.

The most common cause of a stuck throttle is a stuck cruise control. Second to that is either debris in the cable or damage when it gets hit by the prop—usually while reaching down to get into the seat.

Fig 19-16 Hanging from Wires

#3 If you wind up in power lines and you survive, there's still another chance for calamity: electrocution or fire.

Landing in a Tree

Trees only look soft from above. If there is no better option, and you're definitely landing in a tree, go for its middle, 10 feet below the top. As always, land into the wind. Do a normal flare but keep your feet together, in front, knees bent, and forearms together in front of your face to deflect branches that may try to skewer or decapitate. Once motion stops, your ride may not be over. Grab a stout branch and hang on.

Getting Out of a Tree

Hopefully you carry a tree rescue kit (page 284) which allows self-rescue. If not, stay put until help arrives. Most injuries come from falling after getting out of the harness. If your perch is precarious, try using harness webbing or wing lines to secure the harness to a solid branch.

If help comes with an adequate rope, lower a line to them. Pull their rope up and loop it over a strong branch. Secure the rope around your waist and have the rescuer wrap the rope around a strong, low branch for friction so he can lower you gently to the ground. If you're 50 feet up, you'll need probably 110 feet of rope.

If you have no rescue kit and time is critical (impending cold, weather, darkness, etc.), *consider* using your reserve or glider lines to help lower yourself.

Getting Out of Power Lines

Paraglider lines can conduct current from even "low" voltage (4000+ volts) power lines. High tension lines are well over 100,000 Volts. Do not allow yourself or rescuers to touch any part of the gear and the ground—they have been electrocuted just by getting close to a hung-up glider. Wait until the power company has removed power. They will also have equipment that can reach up to allow for easy retrieval.

If you're low enough, jumping is an option but it's easy to misjudge height and get hurt. Awaiting rescue is nearly always the best bet.

Cloud Suck

Cumulus clouds over about 500 ft thick can have lift just below the bases. This cloud suck can be dramatic in bigger clouds, with violent updrafts and downdrafts exceeding 3000 feet per minute (fpm). Pilots have died from hypothermia and/or hypoxia after being sucked up by these behemoths.

If you start getting lifted, act quickly, using one of the descent techniques in Chapter 18. Realize that Big Ears, while benign, will not likely be enough.

A quick few asymmetric spirals (page 183) may work unless you become enveloped in cloud—then spirals risk vertigo or blacking out from G-forces. B-line stalls are reasonably effective but can have exit problems. The full stall, which plummets nicely, is even more risky in recovery unless you're experienced with them. Do *not* toss your reserve since that would eliminate all control of descent rate.

Here is where the ounce of prevention is better than many pounds of cure.

Rain

A wet wing is more likely to go parachutal, and may not recover well from collapses. Plus, the extra weight and possible shape changes will degrade climb performance. More wet=more bad. It's generally better to land if possible, especially if you notice water pooling in the trailing edge (rare). That can cause a rapid flapping that adds drag. Avoid using big ears.

As water gathers, consider using a faster trim setting to stave off going parachutal.

Motor Failure and Landing Priorities

If the motor is just running poorly, try to find a throttle range that works ("milking the throttle"). You may be able to hobble home or make it to a better landing site, but unusual vibrations portend parts separation, prop shards through the wing, or other dollar-sucking damage. We'll assume it quit.

For more on spot landings, see "Tight Spaces: Spot Landing" on page 175, and "Engine Failure" on page 49.

When stretching (extending) glide, fly faster upwind for better penetration, and slower downwind to minimize sink rate. Anything over about a 12 mph headwind calls for maximum safe speed on most gliders. Minimum sink speed is usually trimmers slow and brake pressure 1 or 2 but check the manual.

Regardless of wind, minimize drag. Lift your legs and bring your arms in to present the smallest frontal area possible. Turn using weight shift, stabilos, rear risers, or tip steering instead of brakes, if possible.

Landing into the wind is often emphasized, and *is* very important, but it's not *everything*. See Fig 19-17. Priorities change based on circumstance, but only accept an off-wind landing if into-the-wind options are worse. More wind = more reason to land into it.

Once an out-landing is inevitable, use these priorities according to your situation.

1. **Be level and plan to flare!** This reduces both forward speed and vertical speed to the smallest values in a given wind. Only land crosswind or downwind if it's a much better option. Avoiding rocks or power lines, for example, might be such a justification. Try to start the flare from a mostly hands-up condition about 3 seconds before touchdown.

    The only exception to "always flare" is landing in water with a glassy surface. See "Landing In Water (Ditching)" on page 197.

2. Land on a good surface, namely *land*. Landing downwind on shore is *usually* preferable to any landing in water. Another example: landing downwind on a golf green probably beats landing upwind in a boulder field. Landing in water without flotation is frequently called "drowning."

3. Be into the wind by touchdown. The more wind, the more important this is.

4. Favor rotor-free spots with no upslope. Avoid landing in wind shadows or rotor.

5. Scan for wires on the way down. Any straight-line features or poles should raise suspicions that wires may be present. Plan your approach accordingly.

6. Look for animals. A single cow in a field may be a bull.

Fig 19-17 Landing Priorities

This is an example where landing priorities do *not* favor landing into the wind.

He's only about 40 feet high—not enough for the S-turns required to land into the wind on that nice sandy beach. So he must choose between landing into the wind on wave-pounded rocks just ahead, or downwind on smooth beach. It's an easy choice: don't be fish food.

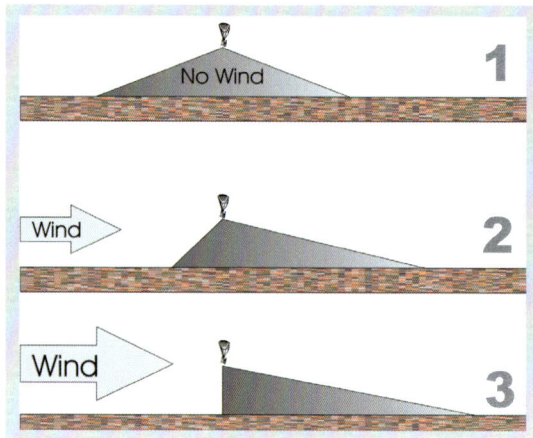

Fig 19-18 Cone of Range

In no wind (1), glide options are the same in all directions. With wind, more are options downwind (2). In a wind blowing as fast as your airspeed (3), upwind groundspeed 0—*all* your options are downwind.

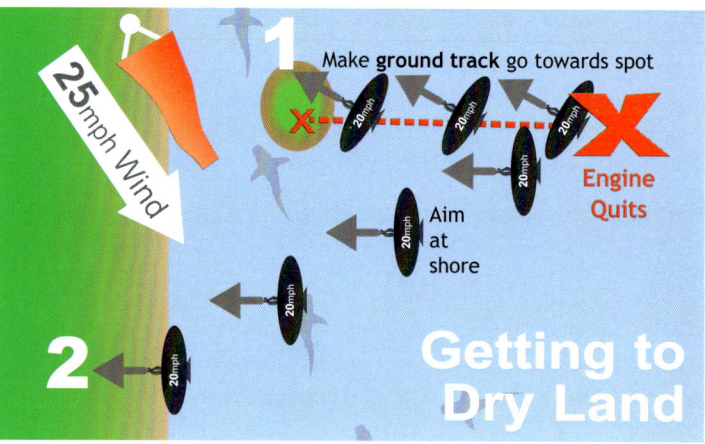

Fig 19-19 Special Cases Stretching Glide

Your best chance of stretching glide to an island (#1, the **x**) is *tracking* to it. Angle upwind enough so that ground track (dashed red line) goes direct. To make a shoreline or road, *head* straight for (point at) it.

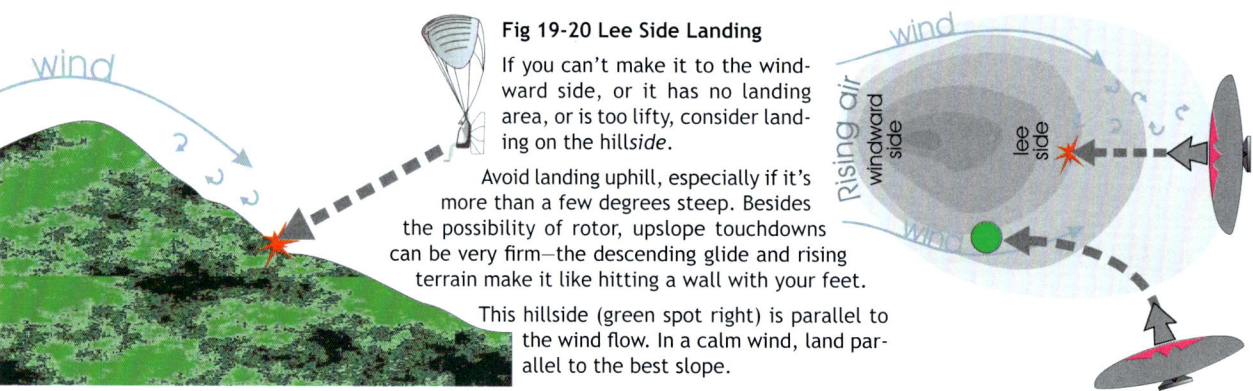

Fig 19-20 Lee Side Landing

If you can't make it to the windward side, or it has no landing area, or is too lifty, consider landing on the hill*side*.

Avoid landing uphill, especially if it's more than a few degrees steep. Besides the possibility of rotor, upslope touchdowns can be very firm—the descending glide and rising terrain make it like hitting a wall with your feet.

This hillside (green spot right) is parallel to the wind flow. In a calm wind, land parallel to the best slope.

7. Consider where the wing will go if landing near water. Avoid moving water, including surf. If a water landing is inevitable, prepare as described on page 197.

8. With lots of *safe* landing options, consider retrieval difficulty. Can they can get to you? Is there a surface feature (mountain range, canal, river, large fence, etc.) blocking the way? Will you have to climb barbed wire fences? Can you re-launch from the site?

Fogged In

Besides being illegal, it's dangerous to fly without ground reference. Even though the craft is stable, fog conceals wires or other surprises. So if you see fog forming or rolling in, land while there is still enough visibility, even if away from your launch site. Failing that, climb up above it, but don't put yourself in busy airspace.

If you can fly to a fog-free location, do so. Here are other considerations.

1. Note or recall the wind direction; you may need that later.

2. Having a GPS in this situation is obviously helpful. Your phone and its map may save the day even if you haven't saved your launch site as a waypoint. In that case, mark your current location and stay nearby. On some units you may be able to follow a plotted ground track back to your site.

3. Consider circling above and waiting if you think the fog may move through or burn off. Use this option only if you're certain that wind drift won't take you somewhere undesirable.

If you must land in fog, consider using the satellite mapping feature of your smartphone. Fly to a huge field then carefully circle down using the Google or Apple Map. Pull no more than pressure 2 for turns.

Use any means available (phone map , compass, GPS, sunlight) to stay pointed into the wind. Consider doing figure eights while descending with all turns into the wind. Keep enough power to reduce descent rate for an easy go-around in case something emerges from the murk. However, there is some benefit to having the prop stopped.

On final descent, go to brake pressure 2 (about ¼ brake) and be ready for impact. Keep your feet angled down and forward, knees together, bent, and ready to absorb the hit, or hopefully to run. Even in thick fog you should have enough visibility to flare—but beware of illusions that could cause a reactionary too-early pull.

Impending Aerial Collision

If you see a threatening aircraft, watch it just long enough to know that it's really on a collision course, then act decisively. If it's stationary relative to you, and just getting bigger, you'll hit. For example, an airplane may be just above you but descending quickly. An aggressive descending spiral could put you in its path whereas doing nothing may let it pass.

If you're sure a collision is imminent, quickly enter as steep a spiral as you're comfortable with. Since you're so slow, this makes you more visible while also getting out of the way quickly. If the other pilot suddenly sees you he will also see your downward motion and should pull up in response. Don't yank the glider into a spin and create another emergency. Exit the spiral *as soon* as the collision risk is over.

Failure of Wing, Lines, Riser, or Connection

Severe structural failures mostly happen during steep maneuvering or recovery from collapses, but there are other possibilities like launching with an open carabiner that fails in flight.

Be thankful for the reserve—this may not be otherwise survivable.

Fig 19-22 Crossing Roads

Don't launch where you'll cross a road (or railroad) unless you have someone looking for traffic. In the heat of launch it would be easy to miss a vehicle from the side—the cause of at least one fatality.

You'll probably be thrust into a spiral with only a few seconds to get the reserve out before rapidly building G-forces prevent it. With no reserve, you'll be riding half the wing down in a high-speed spiral. Pulling brake may only worsen the spiral since most brakes act more towards the tip. The brake on the failed side will probably have ripped out of your hand but, if not, hold onto it as long as you're able.

Quality carabiners and a back-up strap that goes from your harness webbing into the riser loop nearly eliminates the catastrophe of carabiner failure.

Accidental Reserve Deployment

Shut off the motor. Realistically, that's all you'll probably have time for. Grabbing the reserve on its way out is probably only possible if it gets snagged or malfunctions. Even then, having a hand full of reserve lines when its fabric catches air may cause severe line burns as it snaps open.

As long as the reserve comes out properly, ride it down as described in "Reserve Deployment" on page 52. If your main is inflated normally but just downplaning, *and* you're headed for a volcanic cauldron, or some other certain death, consider cutting away the reserve bridles with your hook knife. Think about how you'll hang by that one remaining side before cutting it.

Fire

Fire is extremely rare. Shut off the motor and land immediately. It's so rare that no established procedure has come forward but here are some considerations:

1. Do asymmetric spirals down to minimize time aloft. You may lean forward to

Fig 19-21 Kite Lines

A $4 kite line did this. It was being flown from a beach and was nearly invisible. Much like power lines, your only indication may be the two supports: a kid and his kite. The pilot landed almost normally.

keep your body farther from any fire. Twisting your body may reduce the swirl of wind around your back.

2. If the motor has an ejection feature, use it. Grab those tabs and pull outward like you've rehearsed.

3. Unclip from all but one leg strap and be ready to get away from the machine quickly. Rehearse going for that remaining strap.

4. Consider landing next to, or in, shallow water so you can immerse yourself after getting free of the machine. Only land in water you *know* is less than a foot deep!

5. Roll in dirt, a blanket, tarp, or water as available to put out any remaining fire.

6. Approach the motor with great caution. Although it's unlikely, certain failure modes can allow the tank to burst, spewing flaming fuel.

Impending Loss of Consciousness

A few medical conditions can result in loss of consciousness, and sometimes they give warning.

Avoid spirals since high G's may hasten blackout and leave you in a stable, fatal spiral. Consider instead 1) shutting off or idling the motor, 2) getting on the best heading, 3) putting the wing in its most stable condition (usually trimmers slow), then 4) *letting go* of the brakes so you don't accidentally induce a spiral.

Another approach, if you're over a safe area, is setting one trimmer to slow and the other to neutral to descend in a gentle circle and let go of the brakes. If time allows, call someone, maybe emergency services before passing out. If you do go out, landing will be at about 25 mph forward and 4 mph down.

Launch Risks

All manner of risks lurk in a launch, but these are some of the less common variants.

If launching across roads, railroads or runways, realize how distracted you'll be and get a friend to stand in view while watching for traffic. Or pick a better launch direction.

Holes in fields can break bones. Walk unfamiliar areas and either fill the holes or go elsewhere. Check out the run path carefully, including its immediate climbout. More than one pilot has been hit by cars on roads that crossed their path.

Keep spectators away during runup and launch. Props have come apart even without falling (Fig 19-23).

Risk To Others

Your most important obligation is not risking others on the ground and in the air, including other aviators and their passengers.

Avoid "directing energy" at people. That is, don't allow a situation where loss of control would result in hitting them.

While starting or running up your motor, avoid the scenario where people are within 20 feet or so of the prop plane (Fig 19-23). Metal pieces from the cage of an exploding prop have embedded themselves in the ground over 50 feet away.

It's Not *That* Bad

Reading this chapter is like reading a medical book—lots of maladies, but they're mercifully rare. The sport has proven safer than appearances would indicate but, being aviation, it needs constant vigilance to keep that way.

Fig 19-23 Danger Zone

This shows the highest risk area for hurting someone with prop shards in case of a fall or prop failure. There's risk beyond this, of course, but in decreasing amounts farther away.

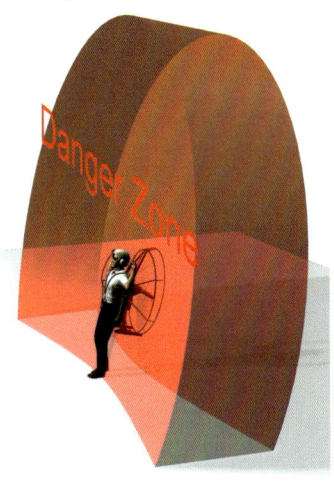

Competition

CHAPTER 20

Weaving the course at a World Pylon Championship in Poland.

It is human nature to see what we're capable of. Like all competition, with the right attitude, it's a healthy motivator to excellence.

To be sure, competing is more risky than just flying around, especially the low-level tasks. It's mitigated somewhat by 1) minimizing tasks where pilots dive towards the ground, 2) minimum experience requirements, and 3) rules that penalize dangerous maneuvers. Still, you're putting a lot on the line.

Those steep and low turns flown by competition pilots are not as dangerous as they seem, at least for the reasons people frequently cite, like engine failure. As long as the pilot knows how to keep his turns level (no diving), even touching the ground doesn't guarantee damage or injury. Of course it does mean zero points. A common question is "what happens if the motor quits during those turns?" Surprisingly, for an experienced pilot, the answer is nothing. There's enough energy for a skilled pilot to level off and land on his feet—it has occurred a number of times.

Rules for competition can be arcane but their goal is to: 1) recognize skill in a fair manner, 2) minimize risk, 3) limit arbitrary factors, and 4) keep the event flowing. Rarely is the simplest solution the most fair. Rules must be understood, too—knowing how a task is scored can be just as important as being talented. More than one loser's last words were "I didn't know you could do that!"

Different sanctioning bodies have different flavors of the same basic tasks, so check the rules closely. The Fédération Aéronautique Internationale (FAI) is the most widely recognized governing body for all aviation competition, and their International Microlight Commission (CIMA) handles microlight activities, including paramotor. Most countries have national organizations that govern national competition and work with the FAI. In the United States, that's USPPA.org through the National Aero Club, NAA.aero.

How Good Do I Need To Be?

Everybody has to start somewhere.

If you have 50+ flights, can reliably launch and land within 50 feet of a target, then you can compete, although organizers frequently impose stricter requirements. Just having the skills as described in Chapter 16 may earn a top 25% ranking. Being *competitive* is another matter, but simply entering these events will improve your skills. And if you've been honing finesse, even just for the fun of it, then you're probably already competitive.

Winning, on the other hand, will obviously require a lot more.

- Precise control, even in level 2 turbulence (see "Balance of Power" on page 163),
- Mastery of pendular weirdness and the ability to be locked under the wing even with bumps.
- Speed control through the wing's entire range. Gaining this skill, because it involves speed system use, may be the most dangerous aspect of gaining a winner's platform. Melding pitch, power and roll into a winning performance will require some raw talent wrung through directed practice—lots of intense, directed practice. Tenacity is probably what wins the day in most cases.

Be mindful of personal limitations; it's easy to get carried away and get hurt. Many pilots have done well by consistently just *finishing* each task, even with middling points. A common pitfall is a good pilot pushing too hard and hitting the ground, zeroing his points for a task, and possibly worse.

Equipment Selection

Low-level precision tasks benefit from powerful motors and small, fast wings while cross country tasks favor efficiency. That's why 4-stroke, and small 2-stroke motors are popular at navigation-heavy competitions. When both types of tasks are flown it's tougher to choose. If you're really good at precision tasks, favor more thrust. If you excel at navigation tasks, lean towards efficiency. Most comps require the same equipment for an entire event so choose wisely.

Wings with a wide speed range (highly reflexed) are best for both cross country and precision tasks. That speed range must be employed carefully—check with the maker about how best to steer in different combinations of speedbar and trimmers.

Ground Precision & Pylon Racing

For many pilots, ground precision—mostly pylon flying—is the fun stuff. It can be intimidating, though. Stay within your ability and build skill slowly. These are normally done over water to reduce the consequence of "pounding in."

Cloverleaf

A Cloverleaf is the mother of all precision flying tasks. It mixes several skills: turning, power management, speed control, spatial orientation, adjusting constantly for the wind, and planning ahead. Don't minimize spatial orientation—it's not as obvious as it seems. When you're down low, cornering hard and looking to the center, telling position can be confusing, leading to wrong turns especially in some wind.

Many pylon races involve the same skills as a Cloverleaf but with different turns and/or pylon layouts. It's hard to get all the turns right; many skilled pilots have lost out after flying super fast runs but in wrong directions.

Pylon races are best limited to lighter winds to avoid fast, downwind ground speeds. Here are some practice tips:

Fig 20-1 Precision Flying Series

Animation extracts used here are from The Master Powered Paragliding Video series. These put precision flying techniques in motion with both live action and animated explanations. They are available at footflyer.com (QR code points there) and other paramotor retailers.

Fig 20-2 Using Wheels

Rodriguez touched his Excitor tire and wingtip while rounding a corner.

1. Be able to kick the center stick (if used) *every time*. You can't win otherwise. Practice on a bush or other safe target, approaching in all directions.

2. At altitude, practice level, steep turns that require modulating power and speedbar as you roll in and out. Pick a distant spot on the horizon and practice rolling out towards it without climbing. Know your wing's brake use limitations instinctively. On most reflex wings, getting this wrong can cause a nearly immediate collapse.

3. Make sure you know the correct pylon/stick order. Fly it first from a couple hundred feet high while looking down on it. Then do it at 50 feet, then at 30 feet, etc. Don't worry about time until direction is nailed.

4. Before starting, mentally go over it. Look at the center, then the left-far stick (1st one), look back to the center, then across to the opposite stick, etc., until visualizing the last stick and finishing kick. Pilots have lost by going the wrong direction or not finishing all four corners.

5. Once these skills are mastered, work on time. Being fast helps, but also minimize *distance*. On some courses, only your *body* must pass the corners. Don't get too close to pylons since a collision can collapse the wing. Plan turns to finish with the least distance to the center *and* next stick.

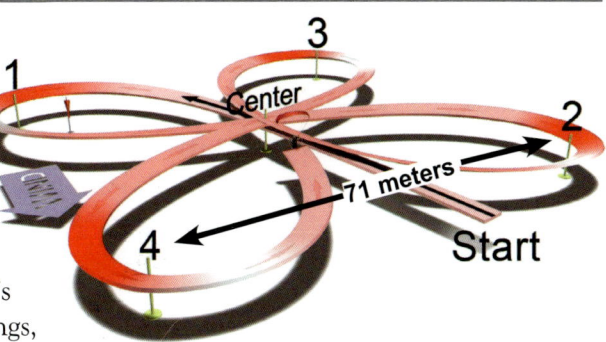

Fig 20-3 Cloverleaf At Home

Make your own course by planting 5 sticks as shown above (1 through 4 and a center kicking stick). The center should be springy enough to not hurt your foot, but also not get in the prop. Use foam, like pool "noodles," on top of the sticks for better visibility, and ribbons for wind direction.

In the above illustration, red is full power and white is no power. As a pilot advances, there is less white because he stays at higher power, absorbing rollout energy with speedbar.

Fig 20-4 Cloverleaf With Wind

In general, if there's some wind, you must move your flight track to be upwind of the sticks likes shown below. More wind, more change.

Steep banks may require full power and benefit from moderate braking. When rolling out of the turn, relax thrust as needed to avoid climbing. Use speedbar to absorb (prevent) the climb and accelerate, applying it as you level out while adding power to keep from settling (red in Fig 20-3). Use tip steering here, as needed, and be thinking about the center stick while on bar. Watch videos of top pilots to get an idea of timing and technique. The best pilots manage energy with speedbar, staying at nearly full power the whole course.

Being fast is good but don't be so heavy (with ballast) as to blow a launch. If the wing has no speedbar/trimmer interconnect (Fig 26-19), set trimmers to fast on windier days. STI really helps because it puts the wing's full speed range at your feet—going slow around the pylons and fast through the center is what pylon racers want.

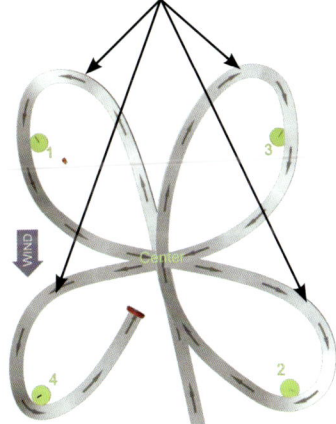

Wind changes how the cloverleaf is flown quite a bit as shown in Fig 20-4. Going upwind of the upwind sticks before turning minimizes turning because you don't get blown. When flying downwind, anticipate the need to start turning earlier. Finish all turns with a crab into the wind to further minimize distance flown.

Collapse risk is high because every trip through the center involves flying through your wake at maximum speed. Know your wing, its steering, its limitations, and handling. Learn these things up high or over water, with flotation, of course. Mishaps while doing these over land has caused many injuries—be careful.

> **Caution!**
>
> Speedbar use increase vulnerability to collapse on most wings, especially while flying through your own wake.

Foot-drag

Once you've mastered foot-dragging ("Foot-dragging" on page 164) then competition just means speeding it up, doing slight turns, and dealing with some crosswind.

You drag at least one foot the whole distance through each of the gates. Faster is better and speed counts heavily. Passing all the gates with a foot on the ground is most important for scoring. Falling scores a 0.

Have one foot out in front of the other to run if necessary. Don't put much

Fig 20-5 Foot-drag

weight on the foot—drag could slow you down into a point-sapping run. Do run, if necessary, to avoid losing so much speed that the wing falls back—another 0.

To be competitive, you'll need to fly with the trimmers out (fast) but only if you're willing to be dumped (downward gust) going fast. Using the speedbar is nearly impossible and, since touching any frame part on the ground zeros all points, may not be worth the risk. Tying off the speed system to its accelerated condition is dangerous.

Slow/Fast

This task is to fly a course, possibly with small turns, as slow as possible, then come around and do it again, in the same direction as fast as possible. To be competitive, though, you must be comfortable trimmed fast and on full speedbar while only a few feet high. In a calm wind, that's fast. Contestants must stay in a lane or kick sticks.

Wings with the largest speed *range* are required to be competitive because it's about speed difference. One common method is using tip steering for directional control and speedbar for height. That's tough, though—if you drop, you must immediately let up on the speedbar then get back on it as you climb, a reaction that must be automatic.

Fig 20-6 Low, Slow & Fast
The slow course requires lots of brakes, power, finesse, and hopefully smooth air. Being too slow means being unable to pop up with the brakes which are already pulled, and adding power may take too much time. Balance.

Going fast makes it hard to stay low enough to kick the sticks since, at speed, it's easy to get popped up.

The slow part requires heavy brake pressure and lots of power. You're vulnerable to getting dumped by sink or lifted too high. Altitude is mostly controlled by power since the brakes are already heavily pulled—pulling more will just stall the wing.

Because this task requires flying at the edges of control, it's not normally run in bumpy conditions. Or at least it shouldn't be because doing so relegates the results to be overly influenced by luck.

Spot Landing

Related tips are found in "Tight Spaces: Spot Landing" on page 175, and "The Perfect Touchdown" on page 168. These are for competition.

After climbing to 300 feet or so, power off, then glide down to land on a Frisbee-sized target and stop. The first point of contact usually counts the most so basically swooping the target and tapping as you fly by is the best technique.

Spot landing is a great task to master given its usefulness elsewhere. But it's risky, especially if you're high and pulling fistfuls of brake to steepen glide. That can easily lead to stalling and falling—a painful, expensive way to score zero points. Some pilots use flapping ("Flapping" on page 177) to steepen their glide, but regardless of technique, allow room to accelerate and flare! A fall is disqualifying at best.

Fig 20-7 Spot Landing
The most points always come from touching the target first but don't crash—that's a 0.

With practice, most pilots can touch the spot nearly every time, but arriving with minimum speed is another matter. A modified version of the task rewards energy management by reducing points for distance traveled after initial touchdown. Its goal: land and stop. Even then, most points are about hitting the target first.

If scoring does *not* incorporate stopping distance then the swoop landing ("Sliding In: the Swoop Landing" on page 168), where you come in fast and just touch the spot, is best.

One way to minimize excessive run-out is to use moderate brakes (pressure 2 - 3) nearly all the way down. Have just enough speed to flare hard and swing forward slightly, stopping just as you touch. This leaves little airspeed for flare, though, risking a point-sapping cage-touch or fall.

Another variation is where there are 5 cones lined up 10 feet apart. Your goal is to kick cone 1, then kick as many of the other cones as you can before touching down. It's tougher because you must land along the cones regardless of wind. Small wings excel. They allow a bigger dive and higher speed during the bottom swoop.

In windy conditions especially, faster trim generally gives better results.

Flight Precision (Navigation)

These tasks require skill at planning, reading maps, pilotage and understanding of your machine's fuel burn characteristics. Scoring involves flying with a sealed GPS that can't be used for navigation.

Competition directors provide maps, pictures (if used) and instructions after which, pilots are given some time to do planning. In most ways this is more relaxed, depending, of course, on your intensity. The most motivated flyers will be constantly looking around to improve their odds—verifying position, studying the map for coming waypoints, determining wind, checking fuel, strategizing, etc.

Finding Points on a Map

One key skill is correlating what's on the map or photograph with what you see on the ground—not necessarily easy to do. Some tasks require familiarity with your machine's fuel burn in various configurations. Be used to flying on speedbar since some of the tasks are almost pure speed. There's no fuel limit but you have limited time to go find as many map points as possible.

Planning

Have some idea of the winds aloft and apply that to planning (see "Navigation" on page 135). Understand the effect of wind gradient and try to maximize it. For example, a headwind at 1000 feet may be a weak tailwind below 300 feet.

Don't count on writing in flight; organize the map and pictures to minimize moving things around. Some contestants have a larger map board that is several pages wide so they don't have to flip pages. Be aware of drag, though.

Fuel Limited Tasks

A variety of fuel-limited tasks require optimization based on conditions. For example, to cover the most ground with the least fuel in still air, fly your glider's most efficient airspeed (best L/D). Fly faster in a headwind and slower in a tailwind but never below minimum sink speed (see "Performance Curves" on page 230).

When flying between thermals, speed up in sink and slow down (or circle) in lift. That maximizes time in lift and minimizes time in sink. Depending on scoring, it may be beneficial to circle in thermals when going downwind and only slow down in them when going upwind. When time matters more, circle less.

Endurance

Endurance, or economy, is a fuel-limited task that rewards those with soaring skills and efficient gear (motor and wing). It would be flown closer to mid-day when thermals are active. On days with little thermal action, it primarily rewards lightweight pilots flying efficient motors on efficient wings.

Some method is used to meter or measure pilots' fuel. They all must launch within a given time window and longer flight times score higher. One fueling option is where pilots are weighed with a highly accurate scale before launch and after landing. Their fuel burn is calculated from the difference and scored by a formula.

One proven method is to climb to a couple hundred feet then throttle back just enough to hold altitude or climb slowly. After finding a thermal, reduce power to about half of what it took to fly level. Circle in the lift, building a mental picture of strength and centering on the best part. If it's strong enough, consider shutting off the motor (providing you can reliably restart it in flight). In weak lift, use some power to help stay in the thermal. Lift intensity is always changing so the mental map must be continually updated.

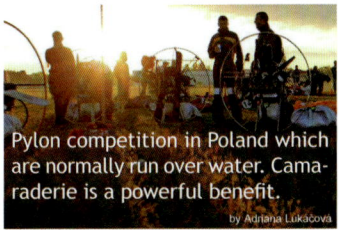

Pylon competition in Poland which are normally run over water. Camaraderie is a powerful benefit.
by Adriana Lukáčová

Fig 20-8 Kneeboard

You don't have to be fancy but being competitive demands having *effective* tools.

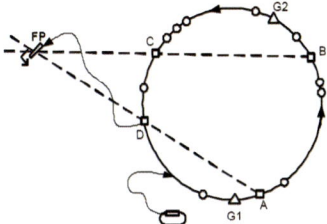

Fig 20-9 Circle & Two Lines

The pilot gets a map with a circle drawn like the one above and a bunch of pictures. His mission is to fly the circle and put a hack mark each time he identifies one of the pictured points.

Once all four marks have been made, the pilot draws two lines that intersect those points. That's the new destination where a judge awaits on the ground.

It's possible to fly the circle and miss only one point, making it impossible to complete the task since all 4 points are needed to find the destination. So an option is provided. Just before takeoff, each pilot is given a sealed envelope with the out-landing site plotted on a map. Of course, opening the envelope entails an enormous penalty but it's still better than not finding the site at all.

Fig 20-10 Unsupported Race
Tucker Gott captured this Canyon scene during his winning run of the Icarus Race, an unsupported 1000 mile run through some gorgeous, but treacherous, U.S. countryside.

Tent

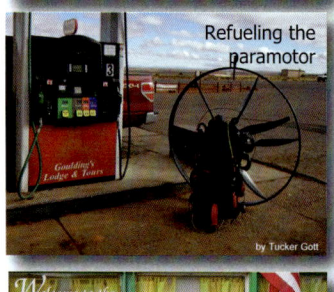

Refueling the paramotor

by Tucker Gott

Refueling Tucker

Kiting War

It starts with pilots arrayed evenly in a field with a clear boundary. When the judge calls "GO," everyone inflates and must not let their wing touch the ground while keeping their body within the boundaries. The last 3 wings up get 1st, 2nd and 3rd.

Pilots try to bring others down by blocking their airflow. Advanced kiting skills are obviously a must. If a couple of wings get upwind of yours, it might be impossible to stay up, especially if your route to clear air is blocked.

In really light winds the challenge is simply keeping the wing up for longer than everyone else while staying in bounds. Kiting without a harness may then be the best strategy if you're comfortable doing so. Some other points of strategy are:

- Pick the right location (if allowed). In a stronger wind, be upwind. In light winds, where simply staying up is hard, start downwind.
- Avoid battles. If one becomes inevitable, try to always stay upwind. You can turn and run forward but mind the boundaries. When you're one of only two remaining, you *must* get in front.
- If your wing gets down low, use the A's to kite it just off the ground.
- If rules allow grabbing other pilots' lines, use that more as a threat since it tends to pull their wing into yours, taking both of you out. That *may* be useful if you're the last two standing.
- In lighter winds consider kiting with A's and brakes (page 149)

As with all tasks, you must use the same wing you started with but are allowed to choose any kiting harness or no harness.

Unsupported Races

A challenging, fun, and rewarding competition is the unsupported race. Pilots fly a long cross country without having anyone to provide transportation, maintenance or fuel. Events allow different levels of support, and may require at least one overnight.

It takes grit. Successful pilots will be able to reliably launch a fast wing while hefting serious kit, possibly including camping supplies and 2-stroke oil. Success requires solid planning, of course, but enough flexibility to benefit from changing situations. Tenacity and a tolerance for discomfort seem to be beneficial, too.

Risk goes up mostly because pilots are motivated to fly in conditions they would normally avoid. But then that's true of all competition.

Demonstration Competitions

A hybrid type of competition is where the organizer chooses sufficiently skilled pilots to fly tasks that are intended for an audience. It's a show. They are indeed competing but, more importantly, they are entertaining. Emphasis is placed on being fun to watch and not having mishaps so pilots don't push quite as hard in the traditional sense.

Tasks and timing are chosen for their crowd appeal and ability to be performed in a small area. Pylons, water slides, balls, and other "toys" add to the effect. Tasks are brief and easy to see when someone is doing well, usually by watching a huge clock with the pilot's time. There is no need for arcane scoring methods.

These are not likely part of the normal sanctioning system because pilot selection is based on criteria other than just ranking.

Free Flight Transition

CHAPTER 21

Free flight paragliding is an adventure worthy of its own pursuit, an enjoyable use of many skills that have already been learned. Both variations deserve respect; adding a powerful motor to the mix, and taking on conditions strong enough to keep you up.

Be ready to learn. Transition is a lot more than just adding another launch skill.

Transition to Thrust: Adding Power

Power expands your opportunities, allowing exploration of new launches, soaring sites, and lift bands that were beyond reach. For example, rising air that coalesces well above its source becomes accessible, offering power-off soaring for hours. Climbing up through the atmosphere helps to better understand it. Partial thrust can let you mimic high performance gliders. But what captivates many motor pilots is the ability to go almost anywhere in the smooth edges of daylight.

When launching a free flight harness, you lean forward with your hands back. When launching with a motor, you *must* stand up straight to let the motor push.

Free flight pilots who get this have less damaged gear than those who try to force free flight techniques on motor launching.

Exploring terrain becomes a purpose unto its own, aided by portability and launch flexibility.

Motors present an entirely different challenge, of course. Where soaring pilots strategize to fleece air of its precious lift, motor pilots can explore precision control of flight path; control that is measured in inches. You don't *have* to go that far, but what's possible is impressive, and the best motor pilots do it effortlessly. You can excel at soaring without needing such precision, just as a skilled motor pilot can be precise without a clue about coring thermals. Fortunately, there's a lot of skill overlap.

If you're an accomplished paraglider pilot who is willing to adapt, then motor flying will come quickly. A very few points must be minded to make the transition painless—most notably, reflex wing differences, and the various demons that lurk in twisty, thrusty motors. They're easy to manage, but *must* be managed.

Seek out an experienced, certified paramotor instructor. His best service will be to set up your equipment, and help you master its nuances, especially launching.

Launch Differences

Hefting the motor is awkward at first. Lightweight gear, adjusted properly, speeds the process.

Reverse Inflation: Getting ready will be quite different. The common free flight turn-round method doesn't work well with a cage, so you'll learn a different technique ("Reverse Inflation: Setup" on page 32). You may find the alternate hook-in method described on page 34 to be easier. It starts with facing forward.

Walking backward is harder, especially if the paramotor cage hits your legs. Avoid doing reverses in winds too light to kite the wing.

Another difference is the riser hold (Fig 21-1). You'll have the correct brake in each hand, as usual, with the risers crossed. But both A's will be in one hand (right hand shown), with the other hand holding a throttle.

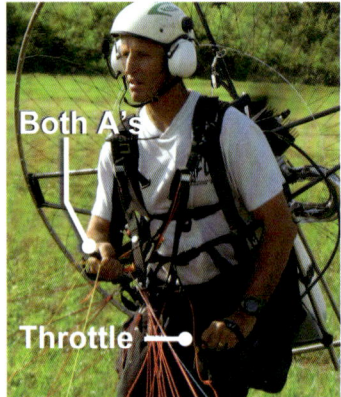

Fig 21-1 Reverse with Power

If the wing comes up crooked such that you would need to pull brake with your A-holding hand, instead, use a finger on your throttle hand to pull the brake above its pulley (Fig 21-2).

Be ready to throttle up the *moment* you turn around, or even *while* turning around. Get moving forward right away with some power, controlling the wing. When everything looks good, add power into a run, check the wing, and go for launch. While learning, it's better to abandon a crooked inflation and try again.

On forward Inflations, you'll hook-in the same, but execution has one glaring difference: when throttling up, you must stand up straight, leaning back against the push. **Don't "torpedo!"** If you do, thrust will push you downward.

Initial inflation is the same. Lean forward as needed, digging into it with your hands back, and pressing upwards on the A's. But once you start applying thrust, stand up straight. Pilots who don't get this difference learn the term "face plant". Remember: **"Stand up at throttle up."**

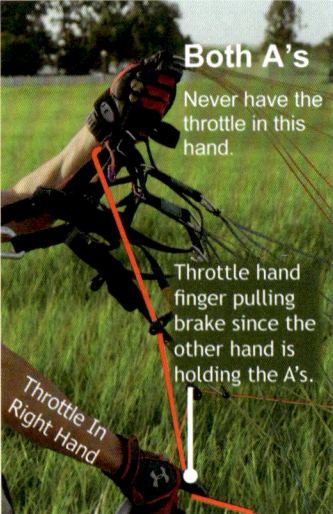

Fig 21-2 Finger Use During Reverse

Hook the brake line as shown in case the wing comes up crooked and you need to slow that side down. The same hand is already holding the other brake.

The partial power forward ("Inflation—Light or Nil Wind" on page 56), where you throttle up some *then* start running, gives the most consistent low-wind success, but starting without power has the least equipment damage. A common cause of failed motor launches by free flight pilots is leaning forward even while adding thrust.

All Launches: learn to be quick on the kill button ("Aborting Launch" on page 48); if a launch goes bad, you must act fast to prevent parablending. If the wing gets nearly all the way up but you need to abort, quickly turn around to face it. Step backward, if needed, to make sure the wing comes down away from the prop.

Some motors make it hard to see the wing because your helmet hits the cage. Get used to looking left or right to tell what the wing is doing.

Be mindful to stay on the power after lifting off—free flyers tend to throttle back and settle to the ground.

Climbout

Torque will be your next surprise: the more power, the more torque—several forces conspire to cause a turn ("Twisting Forces At Work" on page 240). These can be dramatically reduced by proper setup (Chapter 12), which is why a capable motor instructor will quickly earn his keep.

Fig 21-3 Lean Back On Launch

Lean back into the power during launch. Leaning forward (like free flight launches) may cause a faceplant.

Depending on your motor model, the turning tendency can be so powerful that trying to counteract it with brakes alone can cause a spin. If it wants to turn mildly, let it. If it's still turning too much, or in an unwanted direction, ease back on the power then correct the flight path. It is entirely possible for a powerful machine to spin you around into a riser twist. Reduce power smoothly.

Maneuvering Differences

By virtue of adding weight and pushing so far below the wing, motor thrust *slightly* reduces the chance for collapses. And when they do happen they're typically shorter lived. However, it adds the potential to get lines wrapped around prop or other parts in wild air—a good reason to avoid such air while powered. Plus, the motor adds twisting mass and has less weight shift, so wing folds can be more difficult to manage.

Also, be sensitive to the wing falling back. Thrust can hold a glider into parachutal stall which is unlikely in free flight, but more common in motoring. It frequently ends in a spin.

If you do feel the wing go back, or airspeed suddenly slows down, immediately reduce power, reduce brake pull and be prepared to damp the surge. Rehearse that action in normal flight so that it's automatic. Obviously if it feels like a full stall (*very* unlikely unless you were holding heavy brakes), then react accordingly.

Landing

Once you're experienced at power-off landings with the motor, it can be helpful to practice landing power-on. In turbulence, having some thrust reduces descent rate which helps prevent a firm arrival if you hit sink just before touchdown. A quick burst of thrust will regain energy for the flare. If things look really bad, abort the landing. See "Aborting Landing (Go-Around)" on page 48. For the first 10 flights or so, land power-off to reduce the chance of falling due to the motor's extra weight and complexity.

Be ready for the extra weight after landing. Have your knees slightly bent, one foot forward, primed to run heavy-footed. A fast, smooth arrival can be slid out. Most motors will allow sliding on the cage bottom (curved base skids), but that risks damage. It's always best to land on your feet.

Kiting

A good kiter will do well, but there are some differences, especially since you can't lean forward as easily (lines go awkwardly around the cage hoop). The only way to kite safely while facing forward is with the motor pushing you. Trying to forward kite with*out* thrust is ill-advised. A gust is likely to pull you back into the social media position as shown in Fig 21-5.

Reverse kiting is tougher on units with high hook-in points—you use back muscles instead of body weight which is tiring. Plus, if you get lifted in a strong gust, the motor's inertia can make getting turned back forward difficult at best. If that happens, remember to keep flying the wing!

New Capabilities

The motor offers more options—keep them in mind as you fly. Primarily, if the wind picks up you may be able to reach a more favorable landing site, maybe even your original site. Consider going higher or lower to find less wind—normally it's weaker near the ground but expect more mechanical turbulence. At least there's no reason to let yourself get blown into a nasty rotor situation.

Landing in turbulence is easier with a motor. Once you're accustomed to the throttle and how it interacts with surges, you can essentially make every landing far more predictable. However, as mentioned above, it's better to land power off until you gain skill at managing power and the motor's weight.

If you're doing power-off soaring with the ability to restart in the air, you can let yourself get out of gliding distance from launch but always stay in range of a safe landing option. This is a great way to explore an area's thermalscape—you can launch from nearly anywhere and land back there when you're ready.

Fig 21-4 Torque For Free Flyers

Torque and its twisted sisters cause much launch woe. Be prepared to reduce throttle immediately if you feel yourself twisting.

This shows the pilot twisting left, thrust then pushes him left, and the wing goes right. Gear redrives twist the other way.

Tip: Handling The Unknown

If something unusual is happening: **Reduce power, reduce brakes, then steer**. Prepare to dampen a surge if the wing is back. A skilled pilot may get better results by actively controlling the wing, but experience shows that too much brake is more often the culprit rather than not enough. Also, be smooth on power changes—abruptness makes matters worse.

Fig 21-5 Turtle

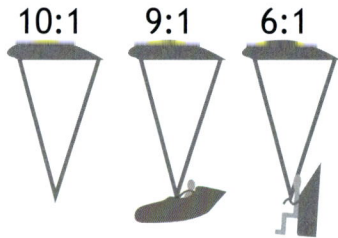

Fig 21-6 Glide Ratios

Paragliders with an advertised glide (Lift/Drag or LD) ratio of 10:1 will be around 9:1 with a good soaring harness and 6:1 with a typical paramotor cage. Cage drag hurts glide ratio even more at higher speeds.

To simulate a favorite glider's performance, throttle up to get the same sink rate as on your free flight harness. Note the RPM and use that value when motor-soaring.

Fig 21-7 Torpedo Launch

Just as motor pilots must **NOT** lean forward, free flyers must. Leaning into the run at about a 45° angle and keeping arms back:

- Balances weight over the carabiners to better load the wing,
- Prevents pulling too much brake while countering the tendency to be forced upright by lift.
- Postures for forward motion which is at least as important when launching on a hill as it is with a motor.

Added Vulnerabilities

It's easy to get complacent about motor failure. Resist. If you fly long enough, it *will* fail. Motor pilots joke that they're really just mechanics who flight test their work. Always be mindful of available options for when it does, especially while climbing right after takeoff.

Be leery of steep climbs, but also avoid the new-motor-pilot tendency to let off the power abruptly just after takeoff. That's followed by swinging into the ground. Hold climb power until you've reached at least 100 feet, then *smoothly* reduce it.

Props mangle. Treat a motor with great respect, especially if it's being hard to start. Pilots reaching back during launch or in flight have also gotten whacked. Bare feet have been sliced. A clutched motor (prop not spinning) at idle is just as dangerous—respect the prop anytime it's powered.

Wires and obstructions become greater risks now that you can spend more time down low. Avoid flying low and downwind since increased groundspeed incurs illusions that cause misjudgments that are not obvious. Plus, escape time plummets, and results worsen due to higher speed.

Soaring

You lose efficiency with the motor, a full point or more off glide ratio, but you can still soar. The windmilling prop of a clutched unit creates more drag than a stopped prop. Prop protection (cages, netting, safety hoops, etc.) is draggy, but less of a drag than missing limbs. Going cageless is nearly suicidal—pilots have been permanently disfigured and nearly beheaded when trying such folly.

Soaring with the motor running at some constant thrust lets you simulate a high performance glider. Just pick a throttle setting that yields some lowered sink rate. Cruise control (throttle lock) may be nice for this but dramatically increases the chance for prop injury—it gets accidentally left at high power before startup.

Noise

Possibly the biggest drawback to motoring is noise. The quickest way to lose sites, or gain the ire of authorities, is to buzz around the same place. If people complain, you will get noticed. People complain the loudest about noise. Altitude is a wonderful buffer and distance is even better, so climb up and get away. Adopt the policy "launch and leave." When returning, do so power off or with minimal power.

Transition to Free Flight: Gone Soaring

Free flight is a quiet realm that's worth preserving. It needs preserving. Sites are limited, with some always teetering on extinction, and they have specific needs regarding winds and slope. Avoid motoring nearby. Respect the local's requests regarding where motoring is OK so everybody wins.

The view alone from many launch sites is stunning; it can be intimidating too. Running into the air from cliffs and mountains can be its own thrill.

High-end wing handling and flying skills, especially in higher winds, will serve you well; a talented motor pilot will do fine flying a paraglider—the challenge will be soaring. Additionally, there are some skills that must be learned to handle potentially perilous sites that are far from flat and grassy. And thermal flying means conquering the turbulent air that stronger conditions beget. First flights should be in relatively still air with less emphasis on soaring vs getting used to the differences in feel and technique.

Free flying adds risk in some areas while reducing it in others; most soaring risk comes from strong conditions and challenging sites. Even ridge soaring, which looks benign, requires significant skills and knowledge to do safely.

Quiet beauty brings many pilots into free flight. It also provides opportunities to match wits with nature, to stay aloft, and even go cross country. For some, lift is merely the means to explore acro.

In this scene from Mexico's west coast of Baja, onshore winds frequently continue well past darkness, allowing all-day flying that continues past sunset. Check local regulations about night flight.

The best money you'll ever spend is to take a course from a free flight instructor that offers transition training. Seek out material on paragliding since what's covered here only scratches the surface.

Free flying in mellow mornings and evenings is not much different than motoring other than the requisite power-off landing. Conversely, flying in air buoyant enough to remain aloft requires far more attention. You must have, or develop, active flying skills ("Active Flying in Turbulence" on page 166) to keep the wing happy without thinking about it. The adage "less brake and let it fly" applies here too. Active flying is a far more important skill than in motoring. If you haven't mastered the wing in rough air, avoid turbulent conditions (thermally or gusty) until experience lays the necessary reactions. Even then, it's still riskier.

An experienced motor pilot should devote from 1 to 3 full days of free flight instruction before going on his own. Plus, many sites require ratings (such as those from the USHPA in the U.S.), and in some countries, licenses, to fly.

Weather at the typical free flight site is often unique; even rated pilots should seek local expertise before flying new sites. Locals will have knowledge gained from sometimes bad experience—it's worth not repeating the experience.

Equipment

You'll love the harness. After being so much more upright, the laid-back position of a soaring rig will feel dreamy. Most harnesses come with a reserve mount, speedbar accommodations, and low hook-in points for comfort and weight shift authority.

They usually have some form of back protection—learn how it works because it may require proper setup. Airbag harnesses, for example, must be zipped a certain way (using the correct compartment) to have any effectiveness. Other styles have their own specifics.

Your motor helmet would work, but since you don't need its ear protection, a lightweight model intended for free flight is more comfortable. Many free flight sites request that pilots use 2-meter radios (in the U.S.) on dedicated frequencies.

Your motoring wing should work just fine as long as you follow the common practice of being heavy on it while motoring. Dedicated motor wings may not be ideal for soaring, though. If it takes a lot of power to fly level, it will take a lot of lift to stay up.

You'll want a reserve parachute even more than with a motor. They have scored many saves for free flyers who ran afoul of mean-spirited air. Good boots (no lace hooks) are helpful, too, especially in the mountains or other challenging terrain.

Fig 21-8 Basic Right-Of-Way

Soaring concentrates traffic in small areas, so a few simple rules help minimize conflict.

First and foremost is "see and avoid" with common sense. For turning, use "Look, lean *then* brake." Look up and down, too.

For thermalling it's pretty easy—if there's already a pilot circling, go in his direction. If another glider is below you, give way to him—he can't see you as well.

On the ridge:

1. Always turn *away* from the ridge. Always. This is a survival rule.

2. Overtake other gliders between them and the ridge. This allows them to turn away from you and be turning away from the ridge.

3. When head-on, the pilot with the ridge to his right has the right of way. If not head-on, give way to whoever is closer to the ridge.

So if you're flying along with the ridge on your left, move away from it to let oncoming traffic pass (the ridge is on their right). Exceptions to 3 are:

a. With the ridge on your left, when you turn around it could be confusing. Do what makes sense.

b. A lower pilot has the right of way—he's probably trying to "scratch" back up and needs to stay close to the ridge.

Ridge on the right, you're alright, stay in tight.

Fig 21-9 Slope Kiting

#1 below: When kiting on a slope the wing wants to overfly and front tuck, or pluck you off the hillside. Consider kiting with the rear risers instead of the brakes, especially while reversed.

Fig 21-10 Never Give Up!

#2 It was blowing hard so he started lower on the hill to take advantage of weaker wind due to compression. He still got lifted and twisted awkwardly but kept working it, garnering enough control to end up triumphantly on top. Never give up.

Fig 21-11 Back Protection

#3 Most free flight harnesses have excellent back protection and some, like this one, are made to reduce wind resistance.

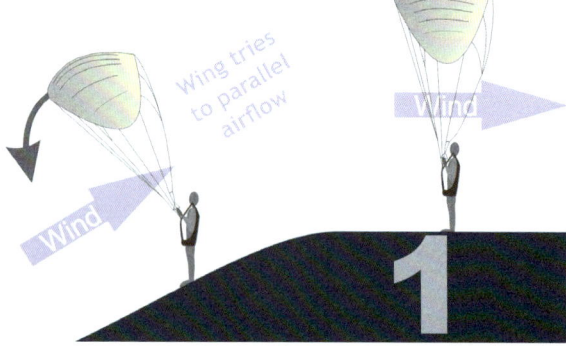

Launch Differences

Being able to deal with rough surfaces and a brisk wind is part and parcel of paragliding. Whether thermals are cranking up the hillside or stiff winds are making a ridge lifty, it is quite common to be launching in winds over 12 mph.

Ingrain the high-wind techniques of Chapter 15 in safe areas. You'll quickly warm up to kiting with a lightweight free flight harness. Since lift is required to stay aloft, pilots frequently seek out wind blowing up hills. Although thermals thrive in low-wind conditions, they get good starts when forced up a mountain or some other land perturbation. Uneven heating on hillsides helps. The vast majority of sites are found atop ridges or mountains, facing the prevailing wind. Expect to deal with small obstructions (plants, rocks, etc.), carefully placed to snag wings and lines.

As for technique, the main difference on launch is that, once committed, you must lean forward to run since there is no motor pushing (Fig 21-7). Whether the initial inflation was reversed or forward, this "Torpedo" stance helps build a good run until you get lifted off the hill.

Doing no-wind forward launches is easier in some ways since the downward slope helps with your run and getting the wing to come overhead. Be ready to brake, though, since it tends to overfly.

One situation that commands particular respect is launching from a cliff. Air carries great momentum, and a vertical cliff will direct it up right in front of launch, leaving you in a difficult rotor. You may have to move back away from the edge just to get your wing in clear enough air.

Be mindful of the preflight check—forgetting to hook up properly is usually fatal when launching from a hill. There *is* a recovery technique; search "Paraglider Harness Leg Strap Recovery." Prevention is better. For starters, never unhook your leg straps without also unhooking the chest strap too. That helps prevent launching without at least one leg strap hooked up. Another technique is to *always* connect its primary straps when first putting the harness on.

Modern harnesses incorporate buckle systems that reduce this possibility—buy one of those, if able.

Maneuvering Differences

The brakes behave the same, of course, but free flight harnesses have better weight-shift capability, which becomes more important for several reasons:

- It's way more effective—the typical harness allows over 8 inches of up and down riser travel for a 16 inch differential.
- It's more efficient than brakes alone. When soaring, the goal is to minimize drag while staying in lift. That means flying near the minimum sink speed of the glider—usually only a few inches of brake pull.
- It enhances recovery from various wing malfunctions or spirals.

Weight shifting is done like most low hook-in motors. It's in the hips—right hip down to turn right. Some pilots cross the high leg over the low one mostly because it's easier to hold the weight shift, but do whatever maximizes riser movement. Use the same technique as described in "Coordinated Turn" on page 160.

Fig 21-12 Hike & Fly
Lightweight gear allows hiking and flying from established or newly found launch sites for highly experienced pilots.

Fig 21-13 Harness Differences
Free flight harnesses have wider attachment points to allow better weightshift while keeping gliders in their certified spread range.

Fig 21-14 Single Surface & Hybrid Gliders
Single surface gliders are the lightest weight choices for hike and fly. Hybrids are double surface from the leading edge to partway back.

Big ears are easier to pull since the risers, and thus their A lines, are easier to reach. Plus, with better weight shift authority you can steer more effectively while holding big ears.

Free flying normally involves finding lifty conditions. But it's entirely possible to get into so much lift (on a mountain or ridge, especially) that you cannot come down at a desired location. Big Ears is the primary way to increase descent, at least for landing in a lifty landing area. But it's marginally effective and reduces control at a critical time.

Most free flying wings don't have trimmers, and they rarely have more than 3 risers. For flying on speedbar (accelerated), they usually recommend using only weight shift and rear riser steering—not brakes—and may provide special toggles for that.

Kiting

There are few differences in kiting. The lack of motor weight and frame makes using body weight more important. Another is that many mountain sites will be steep; bringing a wing up in strong, mountain conditions must only be done if you're fully ready to fly. Becoming proficient at one of the advanced methods mentioned in Chapter 15 will be invaluable since you will stay reversed and maintain better control if you do get lifted.

Slope kiting is different. See Fig 21-9. Steeper slopes, especially, are not the place for kiting practice unless you're OK with getting plucked off the hill.

New Capabilities

The best new capability is to fly soaring locations where motors are not allowed (soaring sites that are sensitive to noise). These treasured spots are gained by, and maintained by dedicated volunteers.

To realize these capabilities, most sites require free flight ratings to ensure some minimum skill level. Working towards these ratings will further advance your skills and will even benefit your motor flying. They're fun too.

Added Vulnerabilities

Without the motor there are some new concerns to deal with. The obvious lack of go-around capability means staying more focused on landing options. Plus, unless you're willing to land away from your landing zone (and the ride home), you must keep getting closer to it as you descend. Pilots do frequently head out on cross-country adventures, but they usually have a ride arranged.

Fig 21-15 Hot Equipment
It's tempting to get equipment that's well beyond our skill level. Especially since higher performance, better gliding, and better thermalling wings make us look better, at least up until the crash. Get evaluated by a competent instructor before moving up.

"Deathblade" by Markus Grundhammer

"Alpine" Harness

Fig 21-16 Motor & Soar
A group of pilots paramotored over to this beach and set up camp. They pulled out alpine soaring harnesses and proceeded to soar all day long. These lightweight harnesses can also just be worn while paramotoring to the site.

Fig 21-17 Free flight Tandem
Tandem paragliding is just as good for free flight training as it is for motoring. For paramotor pilots who already have flying basics down, soaring with a good thermal pilot can reveal secrets of feel and control that are difficult to learn from media, or by flying alone.

You're *far* more likely to need to do a spot landing somewhere strange—make sure your skills are up to par. The experience is surprisingly gratifying but carries risk, especially for mechanical turbulence and wire strikes.

You will be inclined to fly in more turbulent conditions since, by nature, you need thermals or ridge lift to stay up. Most of the increased risk in free flying comes from this fact. Thermal turbulence in some areas, at some times of the day, and some locations can be unmanageable, especially for pilots not adept at active piloting.

The less-loaded wing is slightly more susceptible to collapse, bit should be less violent in the recovery. Default to more brakes in turbulence, about position/pressure 3.

For those who plan on venturing into the "biggest" (most turbulent) air, a maneuvers clinic is highly recommended ("Maneuvers Course (SIV)" on page 181). It will cover descent and recovery techniques that may be extremely beneficial, if not life-saving.

Section IV

Theory & Understanding

Section IV provides a foundation of understanding for the curious, and in some cases, underpins sound decision making. It will also help future designers. The humble paramotor, it turns out, is more involved than its appearance would suggest.

This material is best digested gradually by reading, asking questions, and learning through experience. After gaining some flight time, you'll probably get more out of it. There's nothing like time aloft to grease the gears of understanding.

Aerodynamics & Performance

CHAPTER 22

A fine dance of forces keeps us aloft and in control. We're like airplanes in most respects but with some key differences:

- Thrust, weight, and drag all hang well below the wing. That's great for static stability (more on page 223) but has some side effects, namely, pendular weirdness.

- No tail means very limited control of pitch and yaw (covered later).

- Fabric and lines must always be under tension, so weightlessness, or worse, negative G's, are verboten. Lines can't push (Fig 22-10).

Balance of Forces

You can learn a lot of aerodynamics by sticking your hand out the window of a moving car. Keep it parallel with the air stream (*relative wind*) and it has no lift—but it still gets pushed back a bit: that's drag. Angle it up slightly and it generates lift like "A" (right). Angle it up more (like "B") and it gets more lift while pushing backward more. More lift *and* more drag. Angle it up too much and the lift decreases while drag skyrockets—that's a stall (like "C"). At any given angle, driving faster increases both lift and drag proportionally.

Some of our dynamics can be understood by imagining a small rock tied to string hanging from your finger. Push the rock out with your other hand and let go. That's like goosing the throttle—you swing out then swing back. Turbulence, however, is more like moving your *finger* (the wing) around.

Lift

There is no magic here; we fly by spending money. Aerodynamically, though, it's all about redirecting air downward—like your angled hand out the car window. A wing's curved (*cambered*) surface just does it more efficiently. Motor thrust provides forward speed while the wing redirects air downward. It's a bit of Bernoulli and a lot of Newton: redirect enough air downward and up we go.

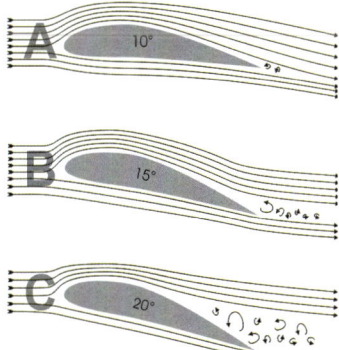

Fig 22-1 Angle of Attack (AoA)

AoA is the angle air hits the wing. Too much angle and airflow separates as shown by the swirls, decreasing lift.

Speedbar and trimmers momentarily affect this, but they primarily change the *Angle of Incidence* (see Fig 22-6).

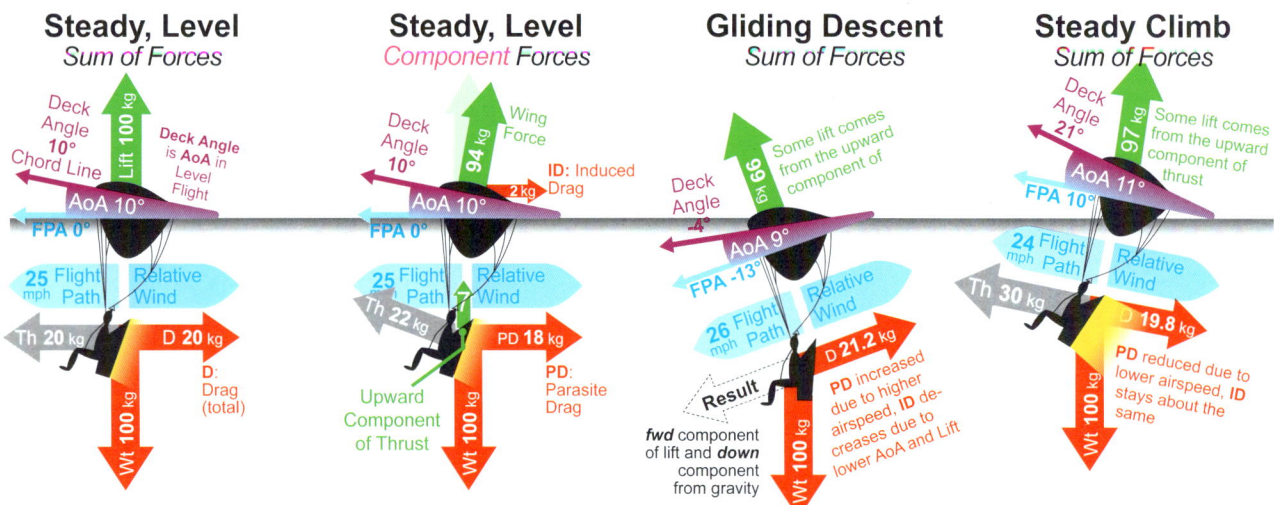

By convention, the four forces are shown like this in level flight. But it's actually kind of messy which is why we show the component forces next.

Having the wing and thrust angled up is what complicates matters most.

Since thrust is angled upwards it contributes to lift, even in level flight.

The wing, too, is necessarily tilted up (10° here) so its force is angled back, directing a portion of lift aft as induced drag. It's added to parasite drag.

At idle, the wing comes forward and flight path angle (FPA) points downward. Gravity is providing "thrust". Without engine push, AoA decreases and airspeed goes up slightly. There's a minor decrease in induced drag due to the decreased AoA & Lift.

In a climb, AoA goes up only slightly, mostly FPA increases. Wing lift *decreases* slightly because thrust is now providing some lift. Airspeed slows down slightly and induced drag may go up a bit. Thrust must now overcome drag *and* gravity.

FPA=Flight Path Angle, **D**=Drag, **Th**=Thrust, **PD**=Parasite Drag, **ID**=Induced Drag, **AoA**=Angle of Attack, **Climb** = thrust in excess of what's required to maintain level flight. Forces are in kg (gravity applied to a mass: kgf)—multiply by 9.8 to get Newtons. Assumes still air.

Fig 22-2 Four Forces & More

Fig 22-3 G Loads

Flying along in level flight is 1 G (force of gravity). In a bank, as you swing around, it forces you against the seat and makes you feel heavier. At 60° bank it feels like you weigh twice your weight—2 G's.

Just like swinging a rock around on a string, the faster you swing it, the higher the G's. Or like a roller coaster where low G's are felt when going over the top of a rise, and high G's at the bottom.

A plywood plank will generate lift. But a curve helps airflow stick to the top which increases efficiency. The plank's sharp angles would make airflow separate quickly into useless, draggy (dirty) eddies, leaving only lift from the bottom, and boatloads of drag from the top. Lift is our superhero; drag is the villain.

Drag

PPG's, with all those lines, frame, and un-aerodynamic pilot, have immense drag. Shape has a lot to do with it—round tubes are terrible while the familiar teardrop shape is pretty clean (less drag). This ⬬ is 5 *times* cleaner than this ⬤.

Drag comes in two forms: *parasite* and *induced*. Parasite drag is basic air resistance (friction) or *form drag*. Induced drag is a result of the wing's lift angling backward ⬈ from the flight path and other by-products of lift like *wingtip vortices*.

Induced drag *decreases* with speed because the angle of attack decreases, whereas parasite drag increases to the square of speed—doubling speed quadruples drag. Thankfully slow speed blunts the effect of our abundant drag.

Put a symmetrical wing ⬬ parallel with the slipstream and it produces no lift, only parasite drag. Angle it up and ⬈ lift starts along with induced drag.

The Center of Drag (Fig 22-5) is where drag appears to act—for our craft, it falls about a third of the way from the pilot to the wing.

Thrust

Thrust overcomes drag. Whenever thrust exceeds drag, pilot and motor swing out in front of the wing and start to climb. Angle of attack increases slightly since thrust imparts a pitch torque on the wing, but mostly flight path angles upward. Thrust is still overcoming drag but also must overcome gravity to keep climbing.

Chapter 22: Aerodynamics & Performance

In level flight these forces are balanced; just enough lift counteracts the total weight, and just enough thrust overcomes the total drag. Climbing flight obviously requires more thrust to overcome gravity and keep the airspeed.

Thrust is vectored—it will always push in the direction it's pointed which is not necessarily the same as the flight path. Serious problems can occur when the thrust line gets too far off kilter. If thrust pushes the pilot left, for example, the wing goes right.

Weight

Weight is what lift overcomes—gravity pulling down on a mass. The center of mass is where an object theoretically balances—for a PPG, near the pilot's upper back since there is so little mass in the wing.

Static and Dynamic Stability

Stability is resistance to upset and the tendency to return to a previous steady state. With center of gravity (CG) so far below the center of lift, our craft is quite stable, like a rock on a string.

Unlike most other aircraft, if the pilot does nothing, paragliders tend to fly straight, holding *trim speed*. Each configuration of speedbar, trimmers, weight, bank, and brake position has a steady-state trim speed.

You'll sometimes hear the term "stability" used to mean collapse resistance ("Stability as Collapse Resistance" on page 264). That's a misnomer—stability is more about the wing's tendency to return to its happy place, generally overhead. *Dynamic stability* means that it does so in fewer oscillations. A more stable wing won't surge as far forward or fall as far back.

Legacy motors that mask wing movements are sometimes called "stable," because they have the *sensation* of stability. Their high, fixed hook-in (pivot) points are well above the pilot/motor CG, so the pilot doesn't move as much. With lower hook-in points, the CG and pivot point are closer together, making the motor respond more to wing motion. It may *feel* less stable but the wing is moving around the same amount.

Glide & Drag

To refresh, glide ratio is how far we travel forward for a given drop at a given airspeed in still air (see "Glide Ratio & Wind" on page 64). It's also the ratio of lift to drag at that airspeed. *Best* glide speed is what yields the best (highest) ratio. Flying faster or slower reduces the ratio according to the glider's *polar curve* (Fig 22-20).

More parasite drag always makes glide worse since the wing planform and shape is fixed. Changes to the wing, such as using brakes, trim-

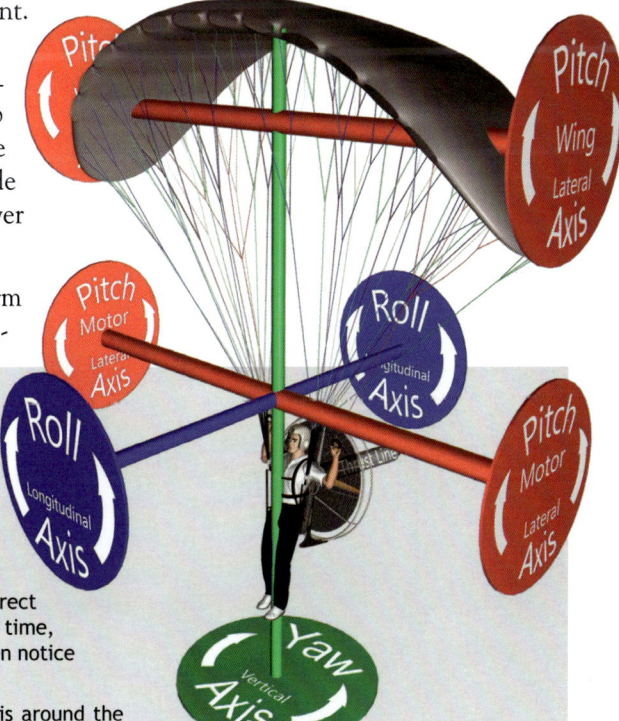

Fig 22-4 Axis of Motion

We introduced the basics in Fig 4-15 on page 49, but the pitch axis is a bit more complicated as shown here.

Pulling brakes makes the wing pitch back around the *motor* lateral axis since the motor keeps moving the same speed (momentarily) as the *wing* angles back. Adding power pitches around the *Wing* lateral axis, for example, because the motor speeds up briefly into a climb.

Pulling one brake imposes drag on one side which causes yaw in the correct direction, but also some roll force in the *opposite* direction. Yaw wins big time, forcing the pilot out and the wing into a bank. On most wings we don't even notice the adverse roll effect.

In standard aviation parlance, roll is around the *Longitudinal* Axis, yaw is around the *Vertical* axis, and pitch is around the *Lateral* axis.

Measuring Glide With GPS & Altimeter

You need to have a GPS and variometer, although an altimeter and watch work in place of the variometer.

Set up the GPS to display speed (it only measures groundspeed). Climb 1000' up into smooth air and align yourself into the wind, watching the ground for left/right drift and correcting until you're flying exactly upwind.

Throttle off. Once in a stable descent, watch the groundspeed while staying into the wind. Note the sink rate (or calculate).

Do that for a half minute; then climb back up to 1000' and turn exactly downwind. Throttle off and again watch the groundspeed and sink rate. Average the two groundspeeds and sink rates. A 10 mph upwind speed and 30 mph downwind speed means your zero-wind groundspeed would be 20 mph. Sink rate should be the same both ways.

Convert sink rate in feet per minute (fpm) to miles per hour (fpm x 0.011). Dividing groundspeed by sink rate gives glide ratio.

Fig 22-5 Center of Lift & Drag

mers, speedbar, or wing deformation (like big ears), also change the ratio.

So an 8 to 1 (8:1) glider goes 8 feet forward for every foot dropped when flown at its best glide speed. For most wings, in no wind, best glide speed is near *trim speed*—usually hands up, no speedbar, and trimmers neutral (as marked). On higher performance soaring models, best glide speed may actually be with some speedbar.

Adding a draggy motor itself mutilates glide ratio by probably 30%. Both the ratio, and speed where it occurs, are lower than with a free flight harness.

Windmilling props worsen glide because airflow "sticks" to the blades. A stopped prop has only the drag of its frontal area. A spinning prop is like a gyrocopter blade, creating "lift" (drag in our case) and reducing glide by 10+%.

Besides reducing parasite drag, glide performance improves with:

- Large span wings. They reduce span-wise airflow around the tips for a given area. That's why soaring wings are long and skinny.
- Fewer and thinner lines to reduce drag. Higher performance models leave off the protective line sheath to reduce line radius. They also have fewer lines by employing more cascades, probably decreasing collapse resistance.
- A flatter profile—longer lines allow a flatter wing which improves efficiency but at the expense of increased line drag and/or collapse resistance.
- More cells or internal bracing to maintain a more precise airfoil shape. Closer spacing prevents each cell from billowing so far out of shape.

Interestingly, increasing weight does *not* change glide performance, rather it increases both the speed at which it occurs (Fig 22-20), and *sink rate*. This fact can be useful. Competition soaring pilots sometimes carry ballast to increase their cross country speeds. For example: A 150 pound pilot on an 8:1 glider may have a best glide speed of 20 mph. With a 200 pound pilot, that same 8:1 glider needs 22 mph (and will sink faster). There is a size advantage, too, related to *Reynolds Number* where bigger gliders perform better than smaller ones.

Wind has a strong effect on glide ratio *over the ground* (Fig 5-20 on page 64). Headwind is bad, tailwind is good.

Center of Lift and Drag

The center of lift is a point on the wing where lift is said to act. The entire wing provides some lift, but it is concentrated in the first 30% of the chord (front to back measurement) and the inside 60% of span. If you could attach a rope to this point the glider/pilot combination would balance from it.

The center of drag is the point where drag is said to act. It will be somewhere between the pilot and wing. If you could attach a towline to the glider/pilot from this point it would have no tendency to pitch or twist due to drag.

Sink Rate

How fast you descend is sink rate, commonly measured in meters per second (m/s) or feet per minute (fpm). Minimum sink rate is the glider's lowest descent rate and it occurs at the *minimum sink speed*. Going faster or slower always increases descent rate. Higher weights *will* increase sink rate.

Wing area affects sink rate. Bigger wings have a lower descent rate that happens at a slower speed. Min sink speed is usually when trimmed slow with brake pressure 2 (Fig 3-3 on page 26). The Polar Curve (Fig 22-20) shows how speed affects sink rate for a particular glider.

Airspeed

More thrust does not add more speed unless you change something on the wing, like trimmers, speedbar or brake pressure. Rather it increases climb rate while slightly *decreasing* speed. If we could have thrust push from up in the lines—closer to the center of drag (Fig 22-5)—then it *would* increase speed. But that's not likely.

Here's how to go faster in our real world of level flight. More thrust *is* always needed to go faster due to pesky parasite drag.

1. Design. Some wings are made for speed. Highly reflexed airfoils, in particular, effectively decrease wing area.

2. Higher wing loading: fly like a Falcon, run like a Gazelle. This is why speed flyers use such tiny excuses for wings and why they require such huge motors to actually fly from level ground.

3. Trimmers typically increase speed by 15% (more on reflex models.)

4. Speedbar typically increases speed by 25%, usually at some increasing probability of frontal collapse due to improper handling. On some models a speedbar/trimmer interconnect (Fig 26-19 on page 267) combines the action of speedbar and trimmers into the speedbar.

5. Angling the thrust line upward (thrust vector downward) is like adding weight and will slightly increase the speed due to increased wing loading.

Efficiency Under Power

Thrust results from the propeller accelerating a mass of air from some speed to some faster speed—pushing us in the opposite direction. How much thrust depends on how much air and how quickly it's accelerated. We can either accelerate a little bit of air a lot, or a lot of air a little.

Jet engines burn copious amounts of fuel to accelerate a little bit of air (relatively) a lot. That's great for going hundreds of mph but not very efficient for going dozens of mph. It's noisy too. For slow craft—and we're about as slow as it gets—higher efficiency comes from accelerating a lot of air a little; i.e. using a big prop. That is, fortunately, also the quietest arrangement.

Efficiency can be spent either on improved fuel consumption or more thrust. In general, the larger the prop, the quieter and more "thrusty" the machine. Even jet engine makers have taken the large mass route, designing high bypass motors with huge fans that are quieter and more powerful.

Wing

The airfoil shape (profile) is chosen by designers to optimize performance. Although, in principle, airfoil design is identical to rigid wings, softness dictates some special requirements. Airfoil shape can change throughout the span.

Size doesn't affect aerodynamic basics, but handling and other characteristics are hugely affected, see "Size (Wing Loading)" on page 262.

Anhedral Curvature

That graceful arc carved by the wing's drooping tips is anhedral curvature, a concession to needing everything in tension and in the right direction. It must keep *perpendicular* pressure on the lines. Without that 90 degree pull angle, the fabric would deform. Higher performance wings minimize the curvature using longer lines at some expense in drag.

Angle of Incidence (AoI)

AoI is what speedbar and trimmers change. On some models they also change the airfoil shape.

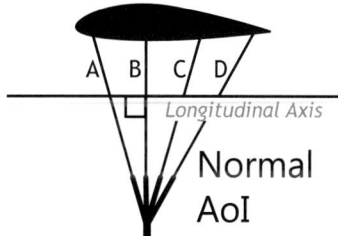

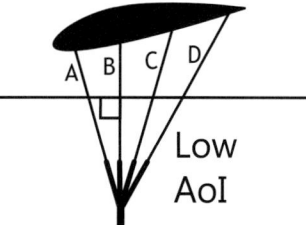

Fig 22-6 Angle of Incidence (AoI)

AoI is the how the wing is "tilted" relative to the riser set. By convention we consider the *longitudinal axis* as being perpendicular to the B-lines.

Speedbar and trimmers change AoI and airfoil shape in varying amounts depending on model.

More detail, including a comparison to airplanes, is in Fig 22-18.

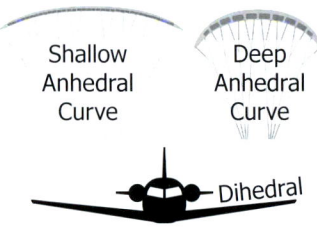

Fig 22-7 Dihedral & Anhedral

Airplane wings use *dihedral* to improve stability whereas paragliders require *anhedral* in order to keep the glider in tension. It doesn't affect stability due to their low CG.

Shallow anhedral is more efficient but sacrifices collapse resistance.

Fig 22-10 Under Tension

Paraglider shape requires every part of the surface to be under tension: everything must be always pulling at the fabric.

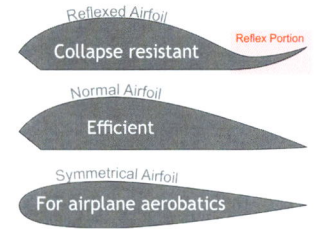

Fig 22-11 Reflex, Normal, & Symmetrical Airfoils

Fig 22-12 Camber Line

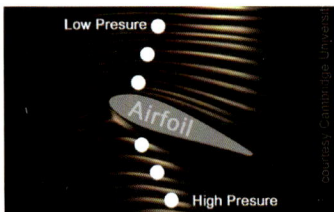

Fig 22-13 Airfoil Air Flow

These pulses of smoke show that no, air doesn't have to move faster on the top to meet the same parcel of air at the trailing edge. They don't meet: the top pulse arrives much quicker.

Fig 22-8 Ground Effect

Ground Effect improves efficiency when flying within a half-wingspan of the ground. Air can't "spill" around the wing.

But paraglider wings are too far above the ground, even during a foot-drag, to benefit much, if any. Plus, a paraglider's anhedral tips reduce lift lost to tip vortices.

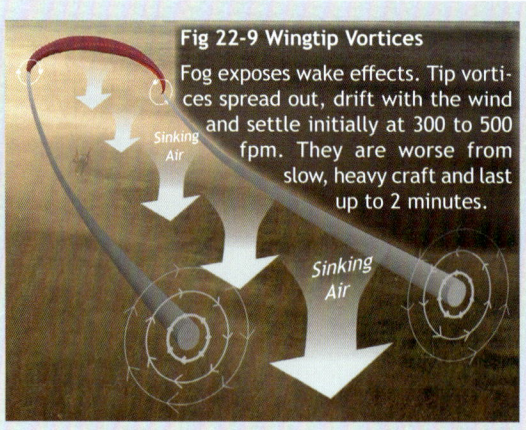

Fig 22-9 Wingtip Vortices

Fog exposes wake effects. Tip vortices spread out, drift with the wind and settle initially at 300 to 500 fpm. They are worse from slow, heavy craft and last up to 2 minutes.

Tip Tornadoes

Tip vortices (Fig 22-9) represent the most dangerous element of wake turbulence left by an aircraft. Prop blast also stirs up the air but it's merely short-lived turbulence like what a boat prop produces. See also Fig 10-14 on page 107.

Heavier craft, including paramotor tandems and powered parachutes, leave vicious wakes that should be avoided for at least 2 minutes.

Tighter turns load the wing more which generates commensurately more powerful wakes. In a 2G turn the craft exerts twice its weight on the air.

Aspect Ratio

Aspect ratio (Fig 22-16) is span / chord of a wing laid out flat (not projected). Without knowing the average chord (or *Mean Aerodynamic Chord*), you can also derive the aspect ratio using $Span^2$ divided by Area.

Long, skinny wings are more efficient (better L/D) than short fat ones because they minimize tip vortices, but there are trade-offs. On a paraglider, the only way to have long, skinny wings is to put them on long lines which increases line drag. Long, skinny wings (high aspect ratio) also tend to have some unsavory behaviors (see Chapter 26), which is why beginner wings have lower aspect ratios.

Airfoil Shape and Bernoulli

A plank will create lift, but an airfoil shape will do so with less drag. Bernoulli's equations, which describe conservation of energy in a fluid medium, help explain how air affects pressure around airfoils while Newton describes what happens when air is directed downward—the ultimate goal of a wing.

Soft wings give up some performance due to their puffed-up cells which builders minimize through line cascades, internal bracing, stiffeners and other tricks, but losses are unavoidable. Higher performance wings reduce the effect by having more cells and fewer lines—lessening the reliance on magic dust.

Shapes have trade-offs too. Some sacrifice stability or collapse resistance for performance and vice-versa.

Airfoil Shape

Reflexed airfoils are more collapse resistant mostly because the center of lift moves forward, loading the A lines more. But there are caveats—see "Reflex" on page 262. A normal paraglider, like nearly every other aircraft, has an airfoil with more curve on top than the bottom, which is more efficient. Symmetrical airfoils, used on acrobatic fixed-wing aircraft, have the same curve on top and bottom as shown in Fig 22-11. *Camber Line* describes the airfoil's average curve (Fig 22-12).

Angle of the Dangle

Air flowing past you is relative wind or *slipstream*. *Angle of attack* (AoA) is the angle between the wing chord line and this relative wind (Fig 22-1). The climb or descent angle is the angle that your flight path makes to the ground. Angle of incidence (AoI) is the angle the chord line makes to the B-lines, or more accurately, a perpendicular line to the B-lines (Fig 22-6).

Deck angle is the angle made between the chord line and Earth.

Increasing the angle of attack increases lift up to a point. That point is called the critical angle of attack beyond which airflow breaks off from the wing's top, causing lift to plummet while drag soars—an aerodynamic stall.

Adding power increases AoA slightly which increases lift, drag, and causes a climb (or decreases descent) with a very slight airspeed decrease. The big angle change we see when someone powers up is flight path which angles upward.

Angle of Incidence (AoI)

AoI is the angle between the longitudinal axis and wing chord line. For our purpose, the longitudinal axis is 90° to the B-Riser as shown in Fig 22-14.

Fig 22-6 shows a simplified view of AoI for paragliders, and Fig 22-18 shows how it relates to an airplane. Our "fuselage" is us, so we use the B-lines as a reference, and by that measure, AoI is *slightly* negative.

Pressing speedbar or letting out the trimmers reduces AoI. Speedbar does it by lowering the leading edge while trimmers raise the trailing edge, but each one may deform the wing also. Trimmers on some reflex wings deform the wing in a way to reduce effective wing area.

Different manufacturers use speedbar and trimmers differently in how much they change the airfoil (profile) as opposed to how much they change the AoI.

Changing Angle of Attack (AoA)

Lift of a given wing varies by speed and Angle of Attack (AoA). More speed, more lift. More AoA, more lift—up to a point. So changing the AoA will have a big effect. Adding or subtracting power imparts a small change to AoA but does a lot to flight path angle—the direction you're actually flying.

Pulling brakes increases the AoA by lowering the trailing edge which immediately tilts the chord line. That also adds drag by making the airfoil shape less efficient.

Reflex Airfoils

Reflex airfoils (Fig 22-11) have been used for many years on tailless aircraft to increase pitch stability. On paragliders they allow greater speed while increasing collapse resistance at that higher speed. See also "Reflex" on page 262.

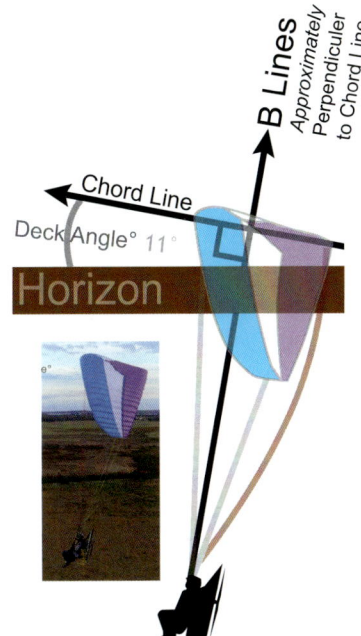

Fig 22-14 Seeing Angles

This helps visualize various angles from an actual photo. Since it was in level flight you can measure Angle of Attack which is the same as Deck Angle.

See Fig 22-2 for more, including what the angles look like in a climb.

Fig 22-15 Flat & Projected Wing Area

Flat Area is what's covered by stretching the wing out flat on the ground.

Projected Area is what's covered by an inflated wing's shadow—usually about 15% less than flat.

Fig 22-16 Aspect Ratio

By convention, aspect ratio is the wing's flat span / average chord.

Since average chord is rarely given, it's also the square of span / wing area.

Technically, the projected numbers are more aerodynamically accurate but flat values are valid for comparison.

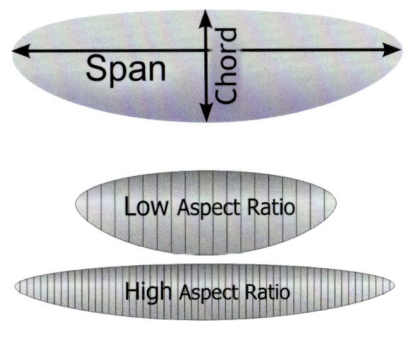

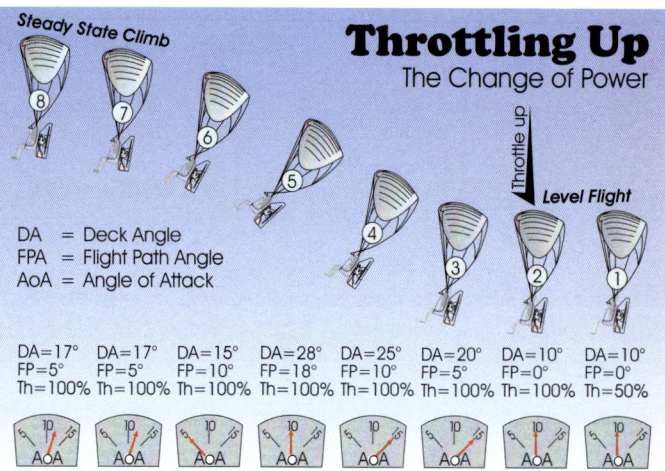

Throttling Up — The Change of Power

Fig 22-17 Aerodynamics of Throttle-Up

A lot happens when you throttle up abruptly. Full power is applied starting at 2; here's the result:

Angle of Attack (AoA) increases as your body swings forward, increasing lift and accelerating you upwards into a steep climb briefly. The AoA peaks (4). Then the wing surges forward, causing AoA to decrease as the wing catches up (6).

After a few oscillations, you settle into a steady state climb (7) with the AoA only slightly higher than when you started. You'll keep this condition as long as the power lasts.

Applied skill can avoid the pendular oscillations by adding power slowly or in two stages. See "Pendular Rate" on page 160.

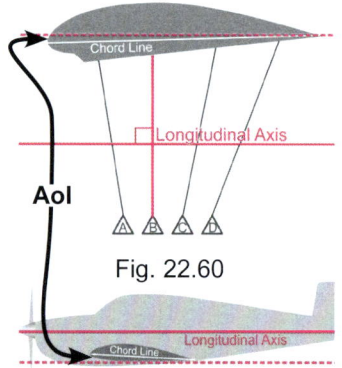

Fig 22-18 Angle of Incidence AoI

This shows how a paraglider's AoI is fixed to the wing lines in the same way an airplane's AoI is fixed to its fuselage (body).

On paragliders we say the longitudinal axis is perpendicular to the B-lines. You could use a line drawn across the quick links, but that varies based on speedbar and trimmer position. A 20 degree angle change at the quick link line would only be a few degrees of the wing's chord line.

Notice on the paraglider that AoI is slightly negative, while on the airplane it's slightly positive. Gravity, and the pilot hanging below, force a paraglider to have some amount of negative AoI.

This frequently gets confused with Angle of Attack (AoA) which is the angle between the wing's chord line and the slipstream (relative wind).

Fig 22-6 shows a simplified version.

Highly reflexed models exhibit a telling behavior while kiting in their reflexed setting: pull down hard on the A lines, getting it to overfly you and see what happens. Where regular gliders front tuck, these tend to maintain their shape. There's some small penalty in efficiency—the more reflex is employed, the less efficient the airfoil is.

Pulling brakes while trimmed fast moves the center of pressure aft and makes the wing more susceptible to front tuck. That's why tip steering is preferred.

Power Up: AoA in crease or Climb Angle Increase?

Confusion exists about what happens to Angle of Attack (AoA) when adding power. Calculations, validated by experiments, show that powering up *mostly* increases flight path angle, and only *slightly* increases AoA.

Turning

When you pull one brake, the trailing edge deflects downward, increasing lift and drag on that side. You might think the wing would bank opposite to brake pull from that lift, but pendular stability overwhelms the effect so drag causes a turn. As the wing changes direction, you swing outward, causing a bank. That bank is what actually does the work by redirecting the wing's overall lift to pull you around the turn.

On many designs, each brake also pulls the wing sideways a bit, which improves handling. Any brake input slows down the overall airspeed, which will either require more power or, if gliding, will worsen glide performance.

A turn always increases sink rate since some of the wing's lift is now being spent pulling you around the turn.

Thrust Vectoring

Ideally thrust is nearly perpendicular to the B or C line of the wing.

If the thrust line is angled upwards (thrust vector pushing you down slightly) then increasing power increases down force on the wing, increasing speed slightly. It's just like adding weight. If the thrust line is pointed downward (motor tilted back) it will have the opposite effect.

If the thrust is offset left or right relative to the risers' center, you'll twist, causing a bank in the opposite direction from re-directed thrust. If the motor pushes your body left, you'll bank right (see "Twisting Forces At Work" on page 240).

On some wings, the motor can interact in a way that causes a "wallowing" action back and forth while under power—wing oscillation. As the wing reaches a bank limit and starts coming back, various forces cause pilot yaw and weight shift to increase roll rate in the other direction. In rare cases it requires significant pilot input to stop, although going to idle also stops it.

How a Wing Collapses

A collapse (deflation) happens when either a downward gust hits part of the wing, or the wing surges too far forward. Small folds usually recover before the pilot even knows it happened. A frontal collapse is where the leading edge tucks under while the rest of the wing remains mostly inflated or forms a "horseshoe" shape. There are two basic causes, atmospheric turbulence and pilot inducement (see Fig 18-14 on page 186).

Turbulence is what most pilots fear—getting swatted out of the sky—but for motor pilots that's surprisingly rare, unless you seek out lively air or are lightly loaded.

Once folded down, slipstream pushes the now-loose fabric (with probably closed cells) back for a few seconds until internal pressure and line geometry sort things out. Pressure to stay inflated (or "open") comes both from the leading edge openings and from the exterior surface tensioning lines.

Turbulence caused fold aggravated by being on speedbar and using main brakes

Turbulence-induced collapses happen mostly from flying into a rapidly changing wind like a thermal, or downwind of obstructions. Horizontal shear can "curl up" a tip as air tries to push the fabric in a different direction. Any maneuver that involves low G's, like wingovers, makes a collapse more likely. Nearing 0.2 G's it's guaranteed.

Stalling: Full & Parachutal

A wing stalls when AoA increases so much that airflow over the top can't "stick" anymore and separates into turbulent, random flow. Drag skyrockets and lift evaporates. Airplane engineers fancy the definition "stall is when the *critical angle of attack (AoA) is exceeded*" with emphasis on how that it can happen at any speed. That *is* true, but if a pilot slows down gradually in level flight, the stall will happen at the same speed for a given configuration. Stall speed increases as wing loading increases.

High AoA can be brought on immediately with heavy brakes, too. If you're already flying slowly, it doesn't take much of a gust to cause a stall. A spin happens when one side of the wing stalls while the other half keeps flying, causing a rotation mostly around the vertical axis. This may seem benign but it sometimes recovers with an aggressive dive.

A paraglider "full stall" (page 185) is more of an aerodynamic aberration than an aerodynamic stall—and far more violent, too. The wing whips through the critical AoA and becomes like a luffing sail—flapping wildly in a hurricane force wind as you fall on your back, going from flying to falling. Raising the brakes lets it re-inflate, returning normal aerodynamics with a barely predictable vengeance.

Parachutal stall (page 53), is where the wing descends vertically while fully inflated. It afflicts powered flyers more because thrust can *keep* a wing stalled where it would otherwise recover.

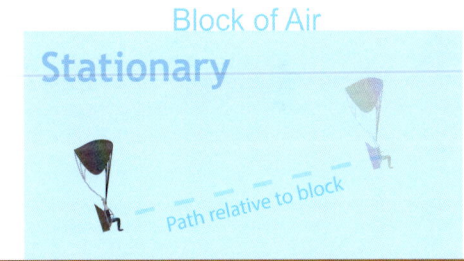

Downwind Flying

An unfortunate myth persists that flying downwind requires more power than flying upwind. This is quickly dispelled by going up high in a strong wind and doing a level 360° turn—it'll take the same power all the way around. Consider being on a cruise ship moving 20 knots. It takes no more effort to walk aft than to walk forward. You don't notice the ship's speed.

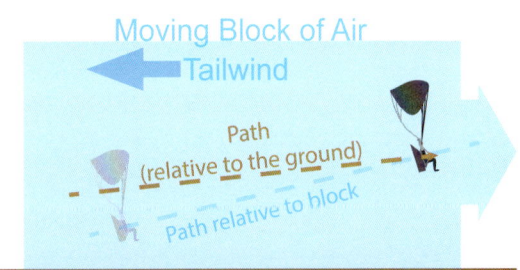

One *tiny* exception occurs in a wind gradient. Say you're cruising a few feet high on a wing whose *air*speed is 20 mph. There's a 5 mph tailwind up at wing height but it's calm at the surface. So your body (and motor) feels an airspeed of 25 mph which does require a bit more RPM.

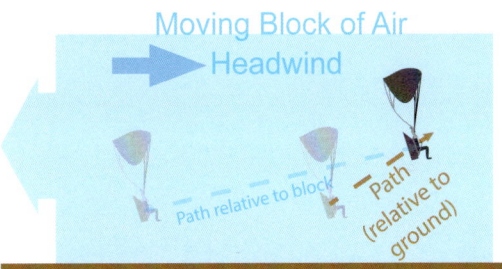

Fig 22-19 Flying Downwind & Upwind

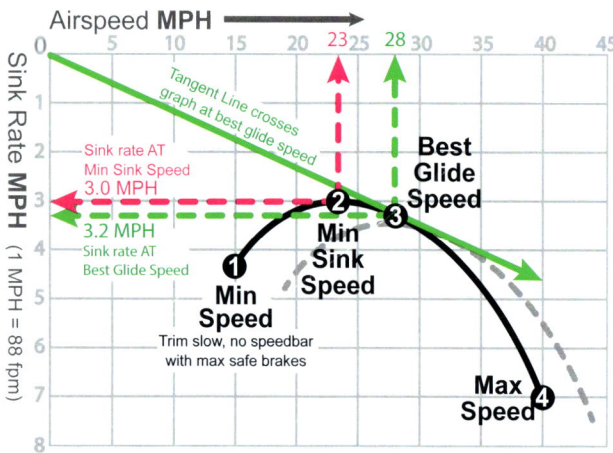

Fig 22-20 Polar Curve

This shows sink rate vs flying speeds, revealing relationships between control settings, speed, sink rate, glide ratio, and endurance.

At the slowest speed, sink rate is high. Speed up and it decreases until reaching the "Min Sink" speed. Then it increases again as speed goes up.

Being *heavy* moves the curve (gray dashed curve) down and right. Glide *ratio* stays the same but it occurs at a faster speed and higher descent rate.

Adding drag (like a big cage) moves the curve vertically down and slightly left.

Fig 22-21 describes the numbered points.

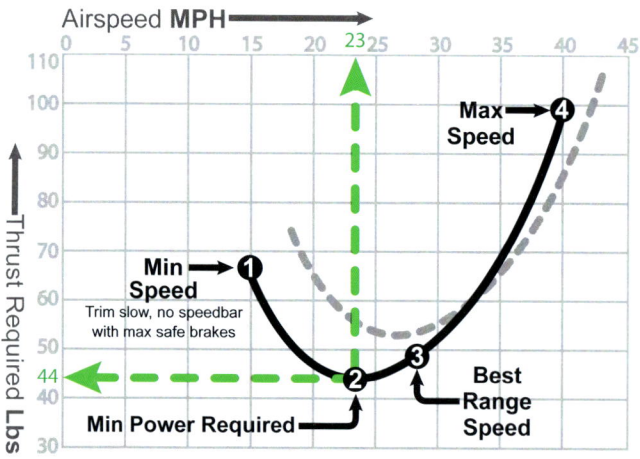

Fig 22-21 Thrust Required for LEVEL flight

This shows how much thrust is required to hold level flight at various airspeeds. The gray dashed line is for a heavier pilot flying the same wing.

Numbered points for both charts are:

1: Slowest safe speed, fairly high thrust required.

2: Minimum thrust required, usually the slowest trimmer setting, no speedbar, and about brake pressure 1.

3: Best range speed, usually trimmers slow (or neutral) and no brakes, provides the most miles per amount of fuel burned. It's usually very close to power-off best glide speed.

4: Maximum speed. Trimmed fast, full speedbar, very high thrust required.

There are some powerful *illusions* related to downwind turns that warrant understanding—see "Downwind Demon" on page 193.

Performance Curves

Airplane and sailplane makers measure their craft's performance in great detail, plotting various parameters at each speed to build a *flight envelope* (allowable range of speeds and weights). One favored type of chart is the Polar Curve (Fig 22-20) which relates airspeed and sink rate.

Glider pilots use it for many things, like calculating speeds to fly between thermals and when to start a final glide to the destination.

For us, a better glide equates to lower fuel burn per *mile* while a lower sink rate equates to lower fuel burn per *time*.

Unfortunately these numbers are rarely provided for paragliders. Mostly because it's hard to know what will be attached to the wing. A sleek torpedo shape will yield a much better glide than a draggy, windmilling paramotor.

It would be easy to build your own polar curve by going up and plotting these values on your own gear. Just record power-off sink rate at speeds from slowest to fastest. Be careful on speedbar, though, and expect sink rates to approach 1000 fpm at the highest speed on faster wings.

Motor & Propeller

CHAPTER 23

Thrust comes from pushing air. Rockets would work, but the fuel is hard to come by and smells bad. Jet engines are thrusty but thirsty, plus they're expensive and loud. Electric motors await improved batteries, and fuel cells await affordability. Four strokes are quiet, clean and efficient but are heavy for their power, at least on backpacks.

That leaves us with the venerable 2-stroke, powerplant of choice for chainsaw men, go-cart racers and nearly all foot-launch powered paraglider pilots. Wheeled craft have more 4-stroke options since wheels carry the weight.

Thrust & Horsepower

The only measure of power that we really care about is thrust—how hard will it push. The industry has never settled on a thrust testing standard, and claims are frequently exaggerated, so independent tests are valuable. Thrust comparisons are most valuable when they come from the same tester, under similar conditions, and with stakeholders mothering over the process. This sometimes happens at fly-ins.

Absolute thrust values will vary based on conditions, but comparisons are valid. Motors should obviously be tested with their harness on (ask—some don't).

Horsepower (HP) is commonly used to measure power, but it's only marginally useful. After all, a 30 HP motor—plenty for our needs—does no good spinning a wood plank. Horsepower only suggests what a motor *can* do given the right prop and reduction ratio. It has value, of course, but thrust is what we're ultimately after.

Expect a lot of variability. One motor that tests at 100 lbs on one day may do 105 lbs on the next day, even using the same tester. Plus, there are surprising variations within brand and propeller. Manufacturing vagaries can incur a 10% difference from the same model of paramotor and prop. Wooden props can account for rpm differences up to 5%. Molded props, usually carbon fiber, are more consistent.

Fig 23-1 Torque & Power

Torque is interesting, but we're more interested in horsepower which is torque applied at RPM. You can have a lot of torque, but if nothing spins, there is no power.

We're even more interested in turning that into thrust with a propeller. More on that later.

This shows the relationship between an engine's torque, RPM, and the resulting hp.

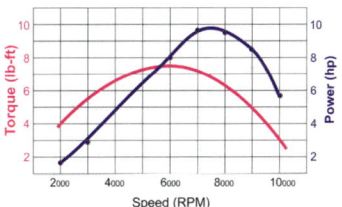

2 And 4-Stroke Motors

"Suck, squeeze, bang, and blow" is the mantra of all internal combustion engines. The term "2-Cycle" (or "2-Stroke") means that a complete cycle of the piston takes only 2 strokes, up and down, firing every time the piston reaches the top. Four-stroke engines fire every *other* time their piston reaches the top. That's why 2-stroke motors get more power per pound and also why they run hotter.

Four-stroke motors have valves and cams so they require better lubrication, ergo crankcase oil, whereas two-stroke engines get lubricated from a gas/oil mix.

Four Strokes

The four-cycle (4-stroke) motor, common in cars, lawnmowers, snow blowers, etc., is more complicated. It has intake and exhaust valves in each cylinder's head (the uppermost part) that open and close in conjunction with the piston's travel. They control fuel/air and exhaust flow in four distinct strokes or cycles.

The valves, piston, camshaft, oil pump and other moving parts add weight and complexity. Some small 4-strokes get by with just splashing the crankcase oil to needy parts.

Understanding the 2-Stroke

These motors maximize power at the expense of efficiency. During one crankshaft revolution, the piston is being pushed down by burning fuel on top while compressing the next fuel/air charge in the crankcase below.

A tuned pipe (or *expansion chamber*), common on modern 2-strokes, optimizes performance but only works through a narrow rpm range: the *power band*. Its improved efficiency can be spent on either reduced fuel consumption or more power. It uses wave action to push some of the fuel/air-containing exhaust discharge back in the cylinder for combustion.

With a two-stroke motor, all the interesting stuff happens during the bottom half of the piston's travel; and there's a lot happening.

1. As the piston rises, it sucks a new fuel/air charge through the carburetor and reed valve, into the crankcase below (**suck**).
2. Above the rising piston, a fuel/air charge is being compressed (**squeeze**).
3. When the piston nears its peak, a spark ignites the mixture, powering the piston downward (**bang**).
4. On its way down, the piston's bottom compresses a new fuel/air charge in the crankcase (**minor squeeze**).
5. About halfway down, the exhaust port is exposed, squirting the burned, high pressure gas out (**blow**). Some of the incoming fuel/air charge can escape out the exhaust, too, but a tuned pipe uses pressure waves to push it back in.
6. As the piston continues down, a transfer port is exposed allowing the newly compressed crankcase fuel/air charge to rush up around the piston and into the cylinder, starting a new cycle.

Besides producing power, the piston doubles as intake and exhaust valves. Having fewer moving parts on a two-cycle makes it lighter and helps reliability. Unfortunately, minimal lubrication and maximum heat (twice as many power strokes) takes its toll on reliability which is why they need more attention than four-strokes. Plus, lubrication relies on the proper type and amount of oil being mixed in with the fuel. Any malady that increases heat, decreases cooling, or decreases lubrication can cause piston seizure, an unwelcome welding of piston to cylinder wall.

Fig 23-2 Horse Power

In the 1800's, James Watt (yes, *that* Watt) was trying to sell his new steam engines but needed a way to compare their output with the standard powerplant of the day: horses.

So he measured how much work a horse could do and deemed that amount to be one horsepower (hp).

Like all measures of power, hp is work per time. All electric, and some gas engine makers measure power in Watts, where 746 Watts=1 Horsepower.

A motor turns torque into propulsion through the prop. In level flight, thrust can itself be measured as horsepower using airspeed where hp = Thrust (lbs) x Airspeed (mph) / 375.

For example, cruising at 30 mph with your motor pushing out 100 pounds of thrust, is 8 HP. The motor is probably putting 14 HP into the prop to achieve that. The difference is due to propeller inefficiency. Normally, cruise thrust is lower but, with the trimmers out and speedbar engaged, it could easily require that much push or more depending pilot weight and wing efficiency.

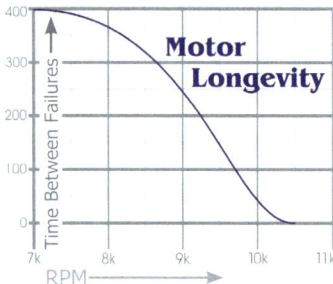

Fig 23-3 Motor Longevity

As you would expect, a good motor motto is: "run hard, fix more."

Amount of wear increases in proportion to heat and high RPM. Operating near a motor's limits can dramatically reduce its lifespan.

Carburetors

Carburetors feed an engine-tasty mix of fuel/air to the motor according to throttle setting. Piston action is always sucking air through the carburetor during intake pulses.

The primary structure of a carburetor is a venturi with throttle valve (Fig 23-14) and fuel outlets. As the throttle valve is opened, more air gets sucked in, which in turn pulls more fuel due to low pressure. Nearly all carbs have adjustments and/or interchangeable parts to optimize operation based on elevation and temperature.

Two carburetor types are common, differing on fuel delivery to the venturi: *float bowls* and *diaphragms*.

Float bowl carbs use a bowl and float like in float bowl toilets. Fuel is delivered into the bowl through a valve. As it fills up, a float inside rises to shut off incoming fuel and maintain a constant level. That provides consistent pressure at the bowl's fuel pickup. A higher float level makes for a slightly richer mixture.

Fuel is sucked up from the bowl's bottom through the main jet (an orifice) into the venturi past a tapered needle. Increasing throttle both opens up the air path while pulling the needle out to allow more fuel. Ergo, more power.

Once properly set up, float bowl carburetors generally provide a somewhat smoother throttle response with fewer adjustments. The drawback is that large changes in mixture require installing different jets (openings). Thankfully that's a painless job. Higher elevations may require smaller jets since less fuel is needed to mix with the

On Mixtures:

As introduced in "Mixtures" on page 42, fuel/air mixture is the ratio of fuel to air. Gas engines burn fuel most completely at 14.7 parts air to 1 part fuel—the *stoichiometric* mixture. Getting that value right is what a carburetor does.

Fuel/oil mixture is the ratio of fuel to oil. A common value is "40 to 1" meaning 40 parts fuel for every part oil. There is a chart in the book's Appendix, and most oil bottles have a chart as well..

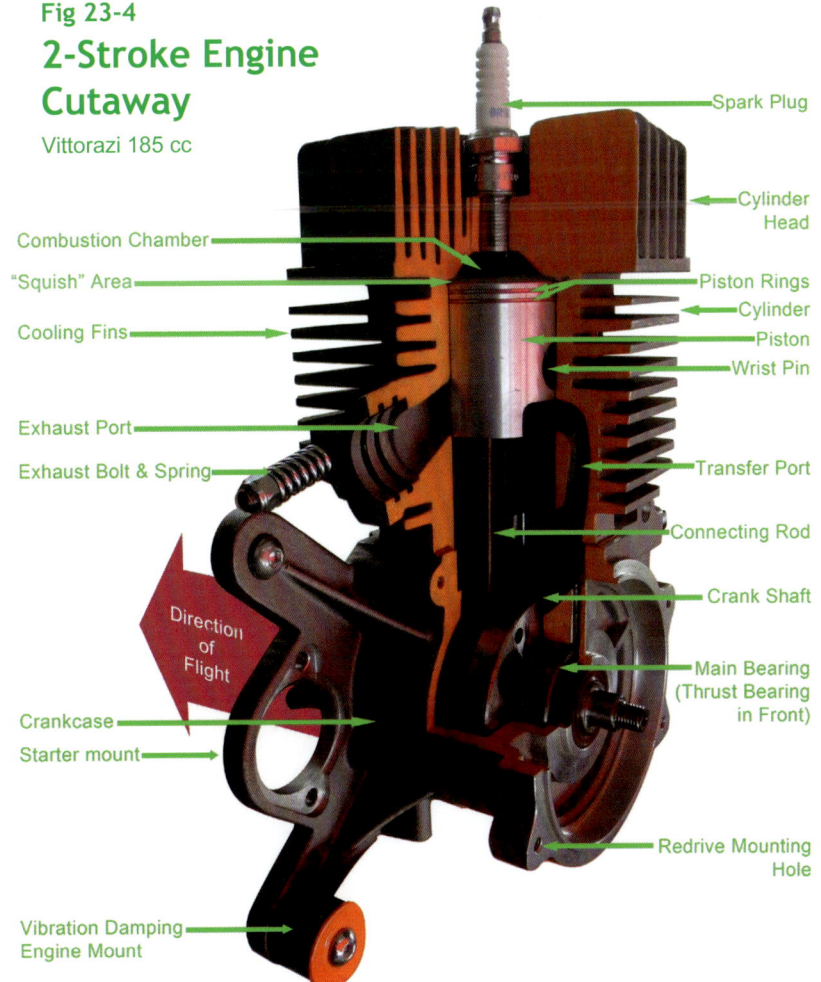

Fig 23-4
2-Stroke Engine Cutaway
Vittorazi 185 cc

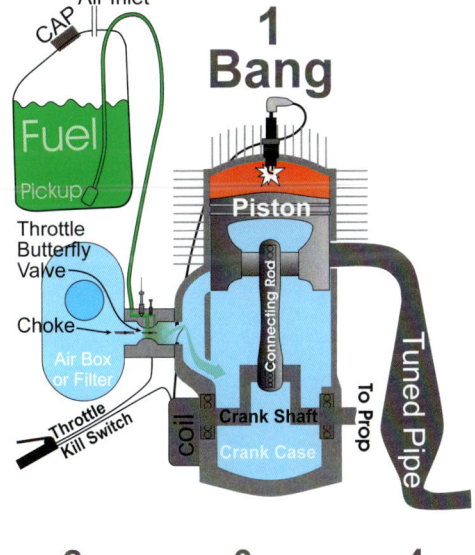

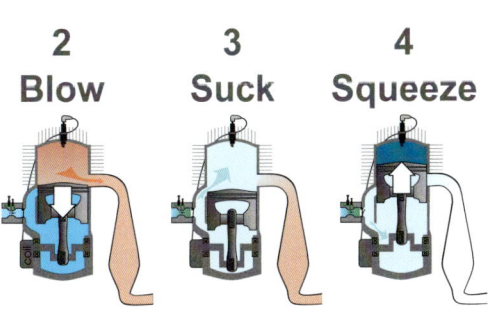

Fig 23-5 Two-Stroke Cycle

"Bang, blow, suck, and squeeze" is the song of a 2-stroke. But as simple as that sounds, there is a lot of devil in the details.

Fig 23-6 Clutched Motor

1: This is a clutched reduction drive engine. The clutch has two or three "shoes" (in red) that expand out as engine rpm increases, contacting the clutch bell which is part of the motor's reduction drive (Fig 23-17).

2: This is a fan-cooled motor with its cooling shroud removed. The visible fan wheel blows air upwards where the cooling shroud redirects it over the motor's cooling fins. If the fan breaks, the motor will overheat in just a few minutes.

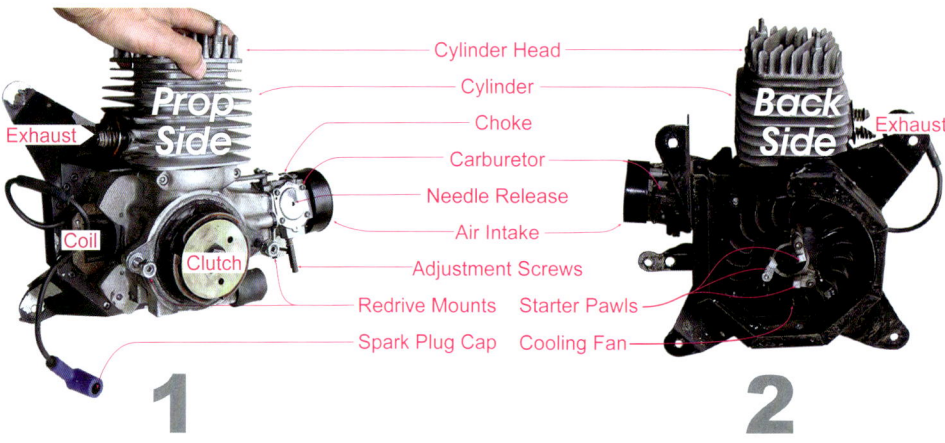

Fig 23-7 Standard Pull Start

This pull starter assembly is what the starter pawls (see motor above) engage when you pull it. Springs hold them against the teeth, then, when it starts, they ride over the back side of the teeth. At idle rpm, centrifugal effect pulls the pawls outward so they don't wear out riding on the teeth.

Fig 23-8 Flash Starters

These make it more practical for larger motors to have clutches.

On belted machines the prop acts as a flywheel, making it easier to get past the compression stroke during start. On clutch units the prop is freewheeling until the clutch engages, so it can't act as a flywheel.

The flash starter loads up the spring as you pull then lets loose when spring tension can get past compression. It keeps applying torque until spring energy is spent.

thinner air. Other minor adjustments may be provided by raising or lowering the needle position or changing fixed air inlets for idle.

Float bowl carbs must be oriented right side up, relative to the frame, and be under positive G-Loading. Paragliders do, too, so that's not a problem.

Diaphragm (also called *Membrane*) carburetors (Fig 23-14) work by filling a small expandable metering chamber with fuel then pulsing it into the venturi. This process uses changing crankcase pressure and one-way valves within the carb. Fuel runs into the chamber when crankcase pressure builds above a certain point, popping a needle valve held closed by spring pressure. See "Pop off Pressure" on page 235.

Membrane carbs were originally intended for gas power tools to work in any orientation. The membrane expands as fuel comes in through the inlet needle so it doesn't matter if the carb is right side up or sideways. They can be finicky, though. Small particles have myriad nooks to lodge in, and the membranes, springs and other small parts can get worn, become brittle, or damaged without looking bad. Degrading fuel line can gum up the works, especially since it's past the fuel filter.

Most of these carbs have various adjustments to fine tune mixture and throttle stop for their respective realm. Be careful, though, some needles adjust fuel flow, and others trim air flow. Getting it wrong can destroy the engine, usually by overheating due to a lean mixture. Consult the engine's manual or a resident expert on it.

Tuning a Membrane Carburetor

A user manual, if available, is your best resource, otherwise this advice may help. If your motor strays too far from the recommended initial settings, it's probably got issues that tuning won't help.

This is primarily for motors with membrane-type carbs having two fuel mixture screws. The high screw primarily affects mixture at high rpm while the low screw primarily affects the mixture at—yup, low rpm. There is some crossover effect.

First, a note about tuning. When a two-stroke motor is rich, it runs rough and sometimes fires every other stroke, that's called 4-cycling. As you lean the mixture, it runs smoother and faster, eventually peaking then decreasing while remaining smooth. Further leaning makes it die. Whenever a needle valve controls fuel (as most do), screwing it in (turning clockwise) makes the fuel/air mixture leaner (less fuel) and unscrewing makes it richer.

Secure the motor—more serious injuries occur from prop strikes than flying. And working on motors is a common time for it to happen because we lose respect for the prop. Start by setting the motor to its initial factory settings.

When cold, motors tend to be lean then get richer during warmup. After a minute

Chapter 23: Motor & Propeller   Page 235

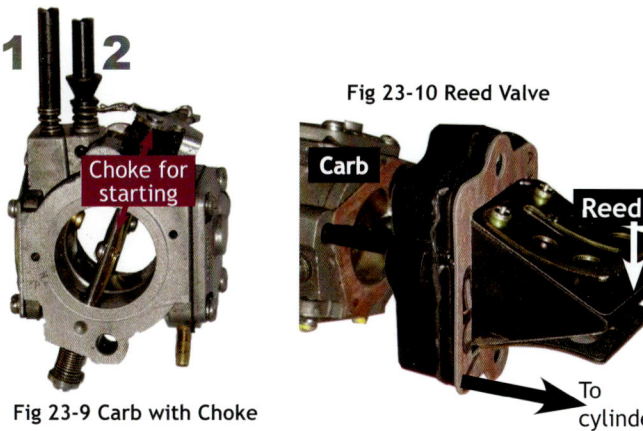

Fig 23-9 Carb with Choke

Fig 23-10 Reed Valve

Fig 23-11 Membrane Carburetor
Besides the main venturi and fuel outlet, most models have two circuits that influence mixture for high and low power. #1 trims idle mixture (screwing in to lean). #2 is the idle throttle stop—screwing it in increases idle rpm.

Fig 23-12 Reed Valve
Reed valves improve efficiency. They are one-way valves that open every time the piston draws in a new fuel/air charge. Like a heart valve, goo squirts through, then it closes so nothing comes back out.

The curved metal parts are strain relief—they make the reeds open around the curve to prevent extra stress at the attachment points.

---

or so, you're ready to begin the adjustments. Use increments of about an 1/8th of a turn when making changes.

Start by adjusting the low screw. Adjust it so the rpm peaks, then unscrew it (richen) slowly until the rpm drops a bit. It should remain smooth. If the motor quits when throttle is applied, richen the low screw further. If it coughs or runs rough when throttle is applied, then lean it a bit.

Now to the high screw. Throttle up to full power. Just like before—you want to adjust the high screw until the rpm peaks, then back off (richen) a bit, about 50 rpm. This makes it slightly "rich of peak," sacrificing higher fuel flow for cooler running—a good trade since a lean mixture frequently overheats and seizes the motor. An excessively rich mixture makes carbon deposits on the cylinder head and spark plug.

With the high screw adjusted, recheck throttle response. Try adding power quickly—if it runs rough, lean the high screw just a bit. If it dies, richen the high screw slightly. You may need to repeat this whole process once or twice.

Higher elevations, above 3000 feet MSL, require leaning the mixtures. Once set, however, you should not have to make adjustments until changing elevations again. Be especially careful to enrichen at *lower* elevations to avoid lean overheating.

When a problem is elusive, consider replacing the whole carburetor. They are inexpensive, install easily, and can save many hours of headache. If that's not the problem, then you've got a spare carburetor on hand.

Pop-off Pressure and Other Membrane Carburetor Issues

The membrane carb's metering chamber is like a float bowl. An inlet needle reacts to incoming fuel pressure and vacuum in the venturi to keep the chamber nearly full of fuel, ready to deliver it to the various throttle circuits. Atmosphere air is on the membrane's other side. When fuel pressure pushes the needle off its seat, fuel flows into the "bowl." That's the Pop off pressure.

If the inlet needle can't unseat easily enough, fuel doesn't fill the chamber and the mixture will be too lean. If the spring is weak and the needle pops off too easily, excess fuel makes the motor run rich. Cutting the inlet needle's spring a bit shorter decreases pop-off pressure and stretching it increases pop-off pressure. Do this only if you know *exactly* what you're doing.

Have a good fuel filter to keep unwanted debris from gumming things up. Carburetor rebuild kits are cheap and relatively easy to install. They usually replace the spring that determines pop-off pressure although that's rarely the problem. They also replace the fuel pump membrane and a miscellany of gaskets and springs.

Fig 23-13 Float Bowl Carb
Float-bowl carburetors don't need much tuning, but when launching from a higher altitude you will benefit from a smaller "jet"—the screw-in orifice that the needle slides into. This reduces fuel flow which leans the overall mixture. The engine would likely *run* at the higher altitude but would be slightly rich.

On this carb, the barrel (inset) slides up and down which also regulates the amount of air that flows through. A tapered needle—attached to the barrel—lets more fuel in as the barrel lets more air through. The only adjustments are for idle—a large screw (1) sets the idle stop up or down and a small screw (2) can change the amount of air let in; screwing it in decreases airflow, making the mixture richer.

Fuel comes up from the bowl that stays about 3/4 full to provide constant pressure to the orifice. A float valve keeps the level just like a float-bowl toilet keeps the tank at a constant level.

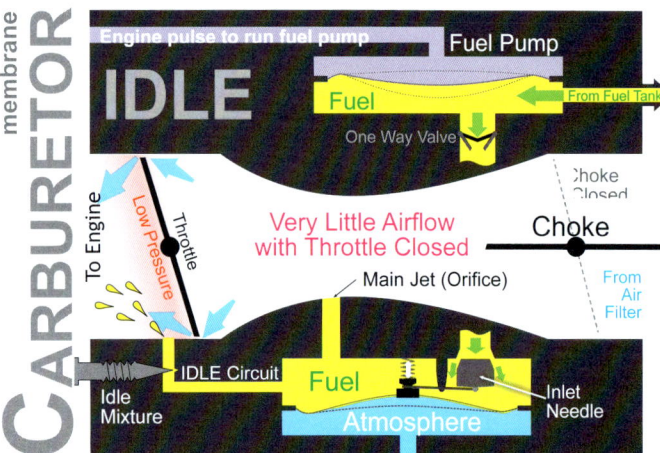

Fig 23-14 Throttle idle (closed) means there's little airflow and low suction through the venturi, so almost no fuel is sucked out of the main jet. Instead, fuel comes through the idle circuit which has very low pressure. The choke stays open except for starting where it's closed to cause vacuum, sucking lots of fuel out of the jets and into the engine. The inlet needle is popped off its seat by fuel pressure ("pop-off" pressure).

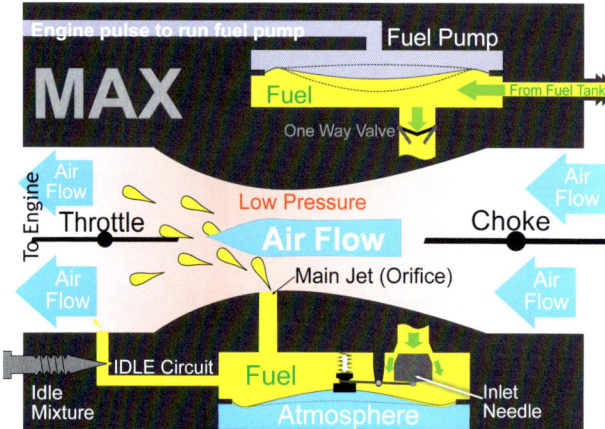

Fig 23-15 Throttle Open allows full airflow which sucks maximum fuel out of the Main Jet and a little bit out of the idle circuit. The inlet needle's purpose is to keep fuel in the chamber and prevent it from leaking out when the engine is off. Remember, these carbs are made for power tools that may get used upside down.

Reed Valves

Most modern two stroke motors employ reed valves (Fig 23-10) to increase efficiency. These stout one-way valves mount between the carburetor and motor. As the piston moves to compress the fuel/air mixture, the reed valve prevents it from going back into the carburetor. They do eventually wear out but are easy to replace.

Compression Release

Some motors may come with a compression release (decompression) valve that makes pull starting easier. It works by venting the cylinder during compression. As soon as the motor fires, the valve closes. Manual versions must be reset after each start but are less prone to sticking open which renders the motor unable to start. Some motors use just a small internal hole that goes from the cylinder head to the crankcase—these must be cleaned out about every 10 to 20 hours of use.

Propeller & Reduction Drives

A propeller is a rotating wing, pitched steeply at the center and flattening out to a skinny tip. Since the tip is moving very fast, it has a shallow angle to the air. Strangely, the most efficient propeller would have only one blade since that blade would have the least amount of interference from the other blade's wake. The extreme imbalance would be a bit problematic.

Propeller choice dramatically affects a motor's performance—it's a case study in compromise. Matching the right prop to a particular motor is critical for harnessing the motor's full potential. Here are some of the trade-offs:

- Long, skinny blades are better for thrust but are harder to make strong. Plus the tips must not get near supersonic due to noise and drag.
- Lighter is better for rpm acceleration but doesn't wear well in the presence of abrasives (beach sand and gravel roadways are good examples).
- Fewer blades are more efficient but more blades allow bigger motors to have a smaller prop diameter.

Tip Speed, Noise and Performance

The only things that move fast on a paramotor are its propeller tips—and they move over 350 mph. That's more than half the speed of sound, or Mach 0.5, where Mach

1.0 is the speed of sound. Any faster and loud, thrust-robbing, neighbor-annoying supersonic shock waves start to form. Above Mach 0.6, (60% the speed of sound), noise and drag increase dramatically with Mach 0.8 being a practical limit.

High prop rpm is particularly harsh due to how we perceive sound. Besides creating stronger sound *waves*, the high pitch is more annoying. Given the same tip speed, a small prop at high rpm will sound louder than a large prop at low rpm.

The quietest combination for any motor is to spin the largest possible diameter prop (45 inches or more) at the slowest possible rpm. The large prop disk helps by having more clean air since it extends outward farther beyond the pilot's body.

Getting the RPM Right

Most two stroke motors get their best power at high rpm, then spin the prop through a reduction drive at a lower rpm. Reduction drives lower output rpm by some ratio. If the input gear has three times as many teeth as the output gear then the ratio is 3:1 (three to one). A motor spinning the small gear at 9000 rpm will drive the propeller at 3000 rpm. The extra weight and complexity of such drives is well worth it.

Direct drive motors, where the prop is bolted to the crankshaft, don't balance the slower rpm needs of the prop with higher rpm needs of the motor. Plus they're noisy.

Since larger pistons typically get their horsepower at lower rpm, larger displacement motors have a better chance of working as direct drives but still give up enormous thrust potential. Larger pistons are heavier, though, so most engines use a small piston and move it really fast (high rpm).

For example, the legacy Solo 210, a relatively large displacement motor (210 cc's), gets its peak HP near 6500 rpm. The Top 80, a small displacement motor (80 cc's), hits peak power over 9500 rpm. The lighter weight Top 80 generates about 90% of the Solo's HP. But the Top 80 could definitely not work as a direct drive.

Even for the slower spinning Solo 210, which was used on direct drive machines, it didn't work well. If a 48 inch prop were attached directly to the Solo, it would need an impossibly fast tip speed of Mach 1.2 to get into the motor's power band. So a smaller prop is used. Even with a tiny 30 inch prop, the motor only achieves 5500 rpm—a noisy Mach .65 (noisy at that high an rpm) and it only gets about 75 pounds of thrust. That same motor, spinning a big prop through a reduction drive, puts out a much-quieter 100+ pounds of thrust.

One major prop maker recommends that wooden PPG propeller tips never exceed Mach 0.75 and should remain under Mach 0.6 for quietness. Mach 0.6 at 3000 rpm will sound quieter than Mach 0.6 at 5000 rpm (smaller prop). And the quietest motors spin large props (48 inches or more) with tip speeds of less than Mach 0.5. On those machines the prop will likely be quieter than the motor, intake, redrive, or exhaust.

Where the Thrust Is

Most thrust comes from the prop's outer third (Fig 23-9) which is faster moving and has the cleanest air. Blades get thinner near their tips which allows forward flexing and some twist. This doesn't affect thrust much but could allow flexing into the cage. A long prop may flex up to 2 inches at full power. Twisting can reduce thrust, and if one blade twists more than the other, will cause vibration since it will be pushing differently than the other blade(s). See "Propeller Imbalance" on page 123.

Pitch – A Bite of Air

A higher (coarser) pitch equates to a higher angle of attack on the blades—a bigger bite of air. It's how far the propeller would travel *forward* during one revolution in a frictionless fluid.

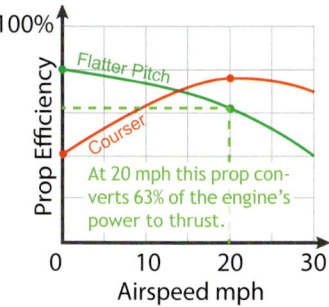

Fig 23-16 Propeller Efficiency

Propeller efficiency is how much of the motor's power gets converted into propulsive thrust.

A flatter pitch prop (green line) tends to be more efficient at 0 airspeed while a higher pitch would be more efficient at flying speed.

Fig 23-17 Redrive Gear Ratio

Reduction drives come in many ratios, usually available in the same housing. Gears bathe continuously in gear oil or grease.

Engine output goes to a small gear that drives the large gear connected to a prop.

Fig 23-18 Calculating Tip Speed

If you're considering a different sized prop, consider the ideal rpm and tip speed with respect to the speed of sound. Besides noise, a lot of power is given up at high tip speeds.

Mach 1 is the speed of sound. It varies only by temperature, being faster in warmer air. At the standard temperature of 15°C (59°F) it is 761 mph.

To calculate tip speed as a mach number, use the following formula:

Tip Speed Mach = Prop rpm x prop diameter (in inches) / 256000. So a 48 inch prop spinning at 3000 rpm would have a tip speed of Mach 0.56 (56% the speed of sound).

The chart at right makes it easy. You want a quiet 45 inch prop, say with a max tip speed of Mach 0.5. What RPM output is needed? Chase the chart around to find it's 2800.

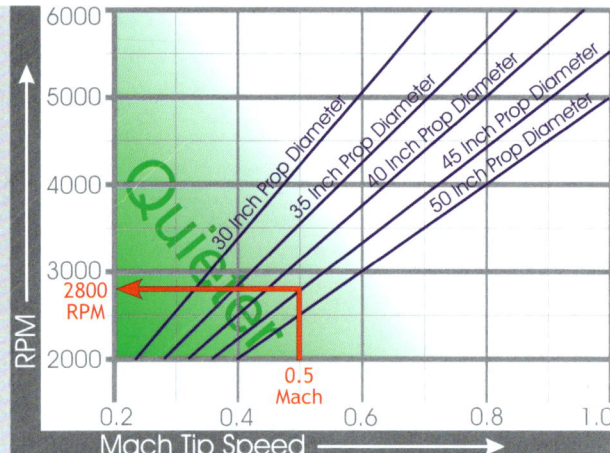

Fig 23-19 Prop Thrust

Most thrust comes from the outer portion of a propeller. Clean airflow around and through the paramotor frame helps maximize efficiency.

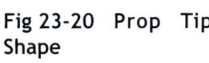

Fig 23-20 Prop Tip Shape

Generally speaking, Rounded ends on props are quieter than flat ends but that's not always true. Makers of higher speed props sometimes angle back (rake) the tips to reduce noise and other methods can work, too.

Fig 23-21 Spinner

A spinner increases thrust up to 5% and coolness by 10%.

There is a small weight penalty and it does sit at the worst place—far back.

Propellers typically give two dimensions—length and pitch. So "48 by 23" is 48 inches long and would travel 23 inches forward in one revolution. Since the outer portions travel a greater distance, blade angle steadily decreases from root to tip. By convention blade *angle* is measured 3/4 of the way to the tip.

Cruise vs Climb Props

Like a wing, more pitch means more lift (thrust) up to a point—at some angle of attack (AoA) airflow separates (bad). But at high forward airspeed, like on a fast airplane, angle of attack *decreases*. That's why some airplanes have higher-pitched "cruise" props. They sacrifice slow speed thrust to get more cruise speed. For us, the difference between 0 and cruise speed is small but it could still matter.

A prop optimized for 30 mph will have more thrust at 30 mph than one optimized for static thrust. In practice our props are designed for static thrust since that's what tests measure and sellers advertise.

Some props have special hubs with pilot-adjustable pitch. They allow finding the best prop pitch for a particular motor and redrive combo. Better ones have internal mechanisms to ensure each blade gets the same angle.

Like wings, long skinny prop blades are more efficient but require more strength. That's why more-expensive composite props enjoy some thrust advantage—they can be made skinnier while maintaining sufficient strength.

Designing For Thrust and Quietness

When designing paramotor propulsion, prop and redrive selection are important to balance noise and power with the available cage space and ground clearance.

Maximum thrust means the most powerful motor you're willing to lift and the largest prop you can fit while keeping the tips below some Mach value. Lets say 0.6—still noisy but with minimal sonic drag. If you have more power than your maximum-radius prop can handle without over revving then you'll need more, or fatter blades. More blades can be quieter since the smaller diameter means lower tip speeds.

For this example, the motor's max hp occurs at 8000 rpm and its cage can fit a 48 inch propeller.

Using Fig 23-18 we see that the prop should spin 3200 rpm to reach Mach 0.6, requiring a reduction ratio of 2.5 (8000 / 3200). Now we need a prop that allows the motor to achieve 8000 RPM.

Having too much pitch, or too much prop area will bog the motor down before hitting 8000—it's *over-propped*. Too little pitch or blade area would make it over-rev, probably causing internal engine damage. Pitches over about 26 inches suggests the need for bigger blades. Two-blade props are more efficient than 3 blades which are more efficient than 4, but more blades are better than having too much pitch.

Fatter, thicker blades can increase the effective push of a prop, and it may be quieter, but there's some cost in efficiency. You can see how this gets complicated.

Materials: Rigidity and Strength

Propellers should be lightweight while being strong enough to handle normal loads. They should be *frangible*—meaning they break easily when striking things like poorly designed cages or careless human parts. That's partly why most PPG props are made of lightweight wood or carbon fiber material that shatters relatively easily. Although damage will still be severe, it will be less than if it were made of strongium.

Being frangible also reduces motor damage from a prop strike by transferring less impact energy to the crankshaft and other rotating parts. In certified aircraft, a prop strike frequently requires an engine teardown, inspection, and consumption of dollars.

Being lightweight also helps the prop spin up faster, especially if weight is concentrated close to the hub. Rotational inertia is based on both weight and its distance from the center. Five pounds, centrally concentrated, will accelerate quicker than the same weight spread out near the tips.

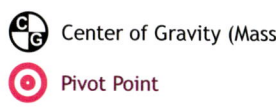

Balance & Paramotor Geometry

Paramotor behavior hinges on geometry—especially pivot points ⊙ relative to thrust line and center of gravity ⊕(CG). Geometry can also eliminate twisting forces (next page). Most fore/aft tilting happens around riser pivot points, even on swing-arm systems (Fig 23-22), *not* frame pivot points. Articulating arms (like S-arms) pivot up and down around the frame pivot points for weight shift.

CG, Hang Point and Thrust Line

The pilot/motor CG is the center of mass (Fig 23-22). It largely determines how far it leans back in level flight. Machines with a heavy engine, set far aft, will have an aft CG that tilts the pilot/motor back. A heavy pilot counters this as does hang point.

Hang point is where the carabiners, or their extensions, connect to the harness or frame. It's also the point around which fore/aft motor swings occur—the Pivot Point. A thrust line above that point will mean that throttling up causes forward tilt. Ideally, thrust will be on or *below* the pivot point. With CG well below the pivot point there will be less swinging around in turbulence. Hang point has no effect on wing stability, it just affects how "busy" the ride feels.

S-Arms

On low hook-in machines with pivoting arms, it's better if the thrust line goes nearly through the riser pivot points. If it pivots too low, the pilot tilts forward at high thrust.

Most modern low hook-in machines avoid that with various methods including a vertical metal piece mounted on the swing arm. But the most common solution is an S-arm that raises the pivot point while providing pilot arm clearance. The S-arm points down at the end to ensure correct seat stowing behavior.

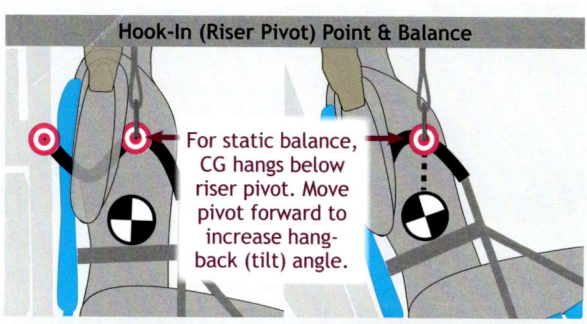

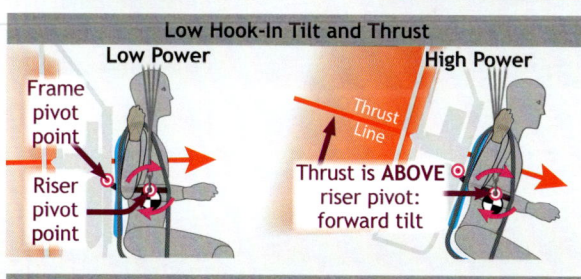

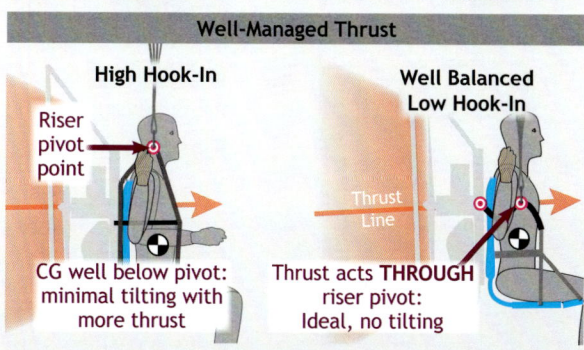

Fig 23-22 Center of Gravity (CG) & Pivot Points

CG is the center of mass for the motor and pilot combined. The motor/pilot pivots around its hang points (riser pivot). If thrust acts above those hang points then you will tilt forward.

Although thrust always acts forward, you'll sometimes hear that "your thrust line is angled down" meaning that the air is blowing downward some amount—you're tilted back (reclining).

Twisting Forces At Work

Prop torque is the biggest villain in a crime gang of twisting forces.

The ones we most care most about express as yaw or roll. To refresh, **Yaw** makes you twist in the risers (Fig 23-24), whereas roll, in *this* context, causes a weight shift effect (Fig 23-23). Yaw is worse because it redirects thrust (Fig 23-25). A full-page summary is on page 242.

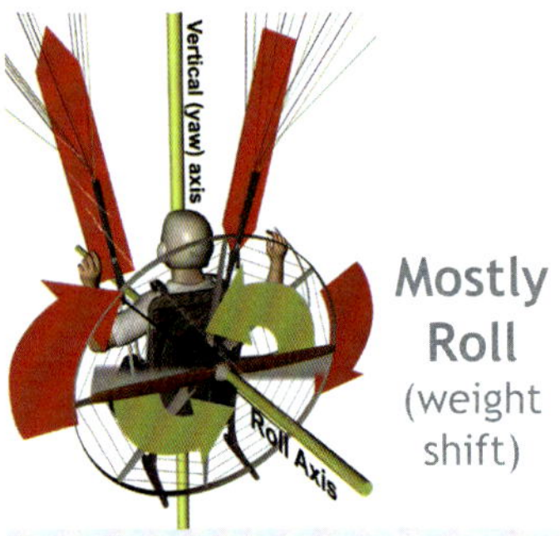

Effects of Torque

Spin a prop one way and the attached motor/pilot tries to spin the other way. Imagine drilling into wood where your hand/drill is the motor and the prop is the bit.

If the propeller plane is vertical, prop torque only imparts a weight shift force, making one riser go down and the other up like in Fig 23-23. But most motors are angled back, so some torque acts in yaw. Imagine leaning back like Fig 23-24—prop action would create immediate and powerful twisting.

This aspect of torque does very little. The most amount of weight shift (riser shift) from this will only be a few inches which is easily countered with brake.

Offset Thrust

Another cause of yaw is *offset thrust*, where it's pushing on a shoulder (Fig 23-27). Lets say thrust is pushing on your right shoulder, causing left twist (yaw). The wing banks right. Besides an unwanted turn, less thrust is going into climbing. Consider if you twisted 90°, there would be **NO** thrust for climb.

The inflight cure is *immediately* reducing thrust, but that can be hard to do at low altitude, especially for those with less experience. Pilots have twisted all the way around while holding full throttle, ending up in an expensive, painful crunch.

Torque-related accidents are common, especially early on or with poorly adjusted machines. Like in the above example, you're facing left but in a right bank (on non-geared machines). That's confusing, especially if you don't *want* to be turning right. Pulling left brake to stop the turn tends to cause a spin since the wing unloads due to thrust direction (Fig 21-4).

More thrust makes matters worse which is why more power is *not* always better, especially for learning.

Gyroscopic Precession

This fleeting, and relatively small force is felt mostly during takeoff or in turbulence at high RPM. Try this sometime: with the motor on your back, run it up while leaned forward then quickly stand up straight (Fig 23-29). On a gear redrive machine you'll feel a momentary right twist. Once erect, the force stops. You can see it in action using any spinning disc (Fig 23-28).

Rotational Mass Acceleration (RMA)

This is another fleeting effect that happens *only* during throttle-up, and vanishes once the motor is at speed. RMA and precession (covered shortly) are the only twisting forces affected by the prop mass.

You may hear that geared reduction drives reduce torque effects because the prop spins opposite to the engine. Not so. However, *during spin-up*, there *is* a tiny difference. Otherwise, torque is identical in strength, and opposite in direction.

Loaded Riser Twist

While running for launch, just before liftoff, the wing goes right a bit. Since you're upright, the left riser is bearing more load. Besides lift, the wing is also exerting some pull backward. If one riser is more heavily loaded, as in this situation, motor thrust will cause a yaw around it. You'll yaw left. See Fig 23-30.

Fig 23-23 Torque Induced Riser Shift

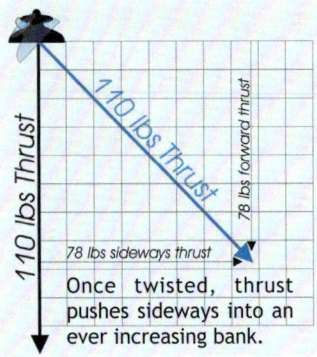

Fig 23-24 Torque Induced Yaw

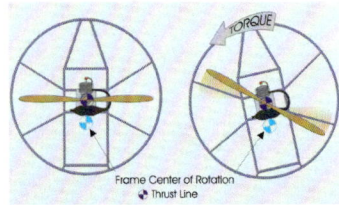

Fig 23-25 Angled Thrust

Fig 23-26 Torque-Induced Offset Thrust

Torque can move the motor into an offset position causing thrust to push more on one shoulder: offset thrust.

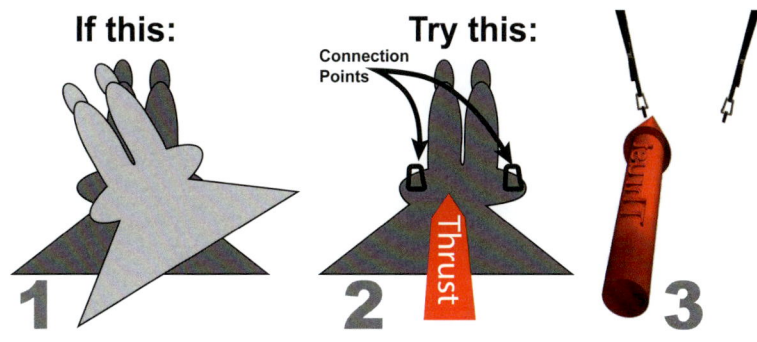

Fig 23-27 Countering Twist

This is the most effective way to counteract twist: offset thrust relative to connection points. It adds no drag like aerodynamic methods (Lamels).

If your motor causes a left twist (1) you'll bank (and turn) *right*. Move your thrust line *left* (2) either by moving the riser connections right or the motor/prop left. Now thrust is trying to twist the other way as shown in (3).

This is what offset riser connection points are doing. With enough offset, turn forces can be zeroed.

If your paramotor uses a geared redrive, it's trying to make you yaw right so these forces tend to cancel. That's a hint. On geared machines, get the wing leaning slightly right just before liftoff (left on non-geared).

Transverse Flow or Angled or Uneven Thrust

Having some airflow blocked by the pilot/motor may induce a slight force left or right at the prop (up or down too but that would be less likely). The farther the prop disk is away from the hang points, the more pronounced the effect.

If the motor hangs off the harness angled left or right then it will push sideways.

Wing Resistance to Riser Twist

Wing shape and lines affect ease of riser twist. While the motor always causes the twisting force, the wing and lines resist it. Just like wide, short lines on a swing make it hard to twist. So do short, wide lines on lower aspect ratio wings. Skinny wings (high aspect ratio) and long lines leave you more susceptible to twisting.

Stopping Torque at the Source: Aerodynamic Airflow Redirection

The prop spins right, the pilot/motor tries to spin left. But what if we could oppose the force at its source? That's what some manufacturers have done, including one who developed an aftermarket torque mitigation using *lamels*—thin plates mounted to the cage's netting (Fig 23-32). In our tests all these methods worked. Thrust loss is kept to a minimum when redirecting elements replace otherwise draggy cage parts.

The best effect is gained when deflection is concentrated nearer the prop tips.

Fig 23-28 Gyroscopic Precession

Fig 23-29 Gyroscopic: Leaning Back

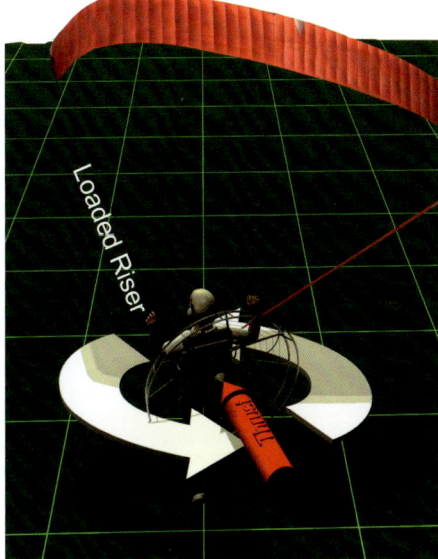

Fig 23-30 Loaded Riser Twist

Twisted

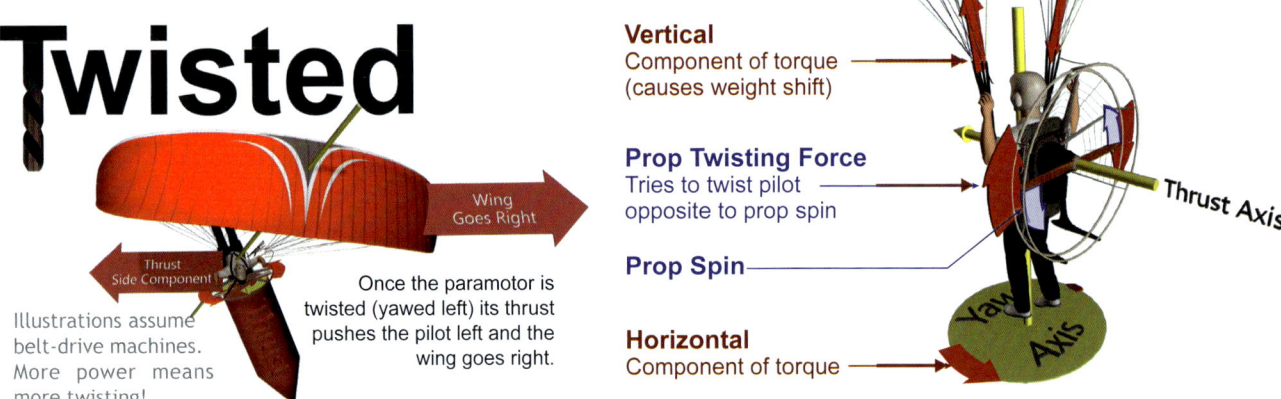

Vertical Component of torque (causes weight shift)

Prop Twisting Force Tries to twist pilot opposite to prop spin

Prop Spin

Horizontal Component of torque

Once the paramotor is twisted (yawed left) its thrust pushes the pilot left and the wing goes right.

Illustrations assume belt-drive machines. More power means more twisting!

Lean Back Twist: The more the paramotor leans back, the bigger the twist around the vertical (yaw) axis.

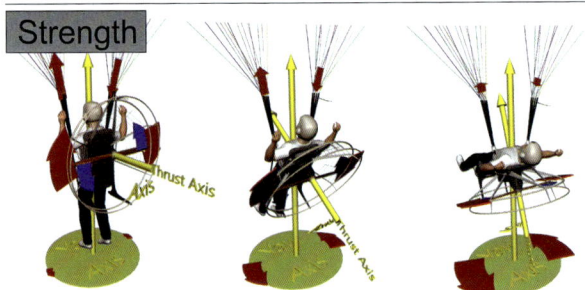

Strength

Effect: Pilot yaws around the vertical axis. On belt drives this left yaw redirects thrust to push the pilot left and the wing right. Also called the horizontal component of torque, it is the most powerful torque effect.

It's more pronounced with the prop plane tilted back. Imagine being tilted all the way back like in the diagram.

Counter: 1) Reduce motor tilt back, 2) On belt drives, move the risers right or the thrust line left, 3) have the right riser clip in forward of the left riser, 4) have cage vanes that redirect airflow to counter prop spin to reduce total torque effect.

Loaded Riser Twist: When the wing goes to one side, the paramotor yaws around the vertical (yaw) axis.

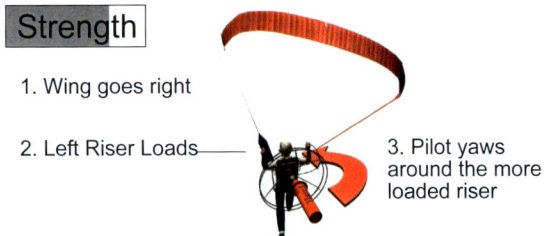

Strength

1. Wing goes right
2. Left Riser Loads
3. Pilot yaws around the more loaded riser

Effect: Pilot yaws around the more loaded riser. When the wing goes right, the pilot yaws left. It's most pronounced at liftoff because the pilot is upright and, when the wing goes right, it loads the left riser and vice versa if the wing goes left. It's also proportional to thrust.

Counter: On belt drive machines, lift off with the wing either directly overhead or slightly left.

Gyroscopic Precession: Yaw & roll force while changing the propeller disk angle.

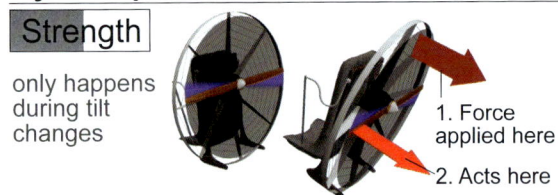

Strength

only happens during tilt changes

1. Force applied here
2. Acts here

Effect: On belt drive units, it yaws the pilot left as he goes from tilted forward to leaning back at liftoff. It aggravates the other left-yawing forces. This fleeting effect only happens during changes in tilt, most notably during takeoff when going from upright to leaning back.

Counter: 1) Less lean back on the motor, 2) lower prop mass, 3) less prop radius, 4) lower RPM.

Riser Shift: Twist along the thrust axis tries to impart a "weight shift" force, lowering one riser.

Strength

Wing banks towards lowered riser

Effect: One riser goes up and the other goes down in opposition to prop spin. On belt drives that means the right riser goes down and the left riser goes up. It slightly aggravates the other twisting forces by making the wing want to bank more. Also called the vertical component of torque. It's slightly more pronounced on low hook-in machines.

Counter: 1) Aerodynamic airflow re-direction (see next page) on cage, 2) Anti-torque strap to reduce riser movement (reduces weight shift). On belt drives, it goes from the harness upper forward left, angling down to the right side. 3) Have more weight (like a reserve) on the raised side.

Thrust Line Offset: Thrust is not centered on the risers' midpoint, causing yaw.

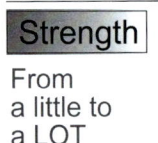

Strength

From a little to a LOT

Riser Midpoint
Offset Thrust

Effect: Thrust pushes left or right of the center causing a yaw, like pushing on your right shoulder. It can be used to counter other yawing forces.

Counter: Ensure the thrust line is centered. Offset thrust to oppose undesirable forces.

Fig 23-31 Top Causes of Twist

Fig 23-32 Aerodynamic Torque Reduction #1 is lamels, #2 & 3 use aerodynamic cage arms.

P-Factor: An Irrelevant Effect

P-Factor, also called Asymmetric Blade Thrust (ABT), is what happens whenever the propeller disk is not hitting the air head-on, like when the pilot is heavily leaned back. It results from one blade having more relative wind than the other. With the motor angled back (as usual), the descending blade has more relative wind so it pulls slightly harder. Picture the prop disc angled flat (Fig 23-33) where the "descending" blade is advancing which means it has a headwind while the retreating blade experiences a tailwind. More airflow at the same angle of attack (AoA) means more lift.

Not only is this effect minor on our craft, but it's in the opposite direction to most other twisting forces. We're just too slow to notice.

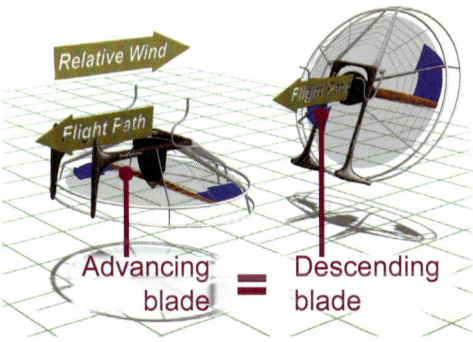

Fig 23-33 P-Factor (ABT)

Electric Propulsion

Electric paramotors are better in nearly every way except for endurance.

The motors themselves are relatively cheap, extremely reliable, quiet, safe, lightweight, require essentially no maintenance, can use renewable energy, don't stink, and can provide instant, programmable throttle response.

Batteries are the bugaboo. They're expensive, add fire risk (like gas but in different ways), degrade in capacity with each charge cycle, can be easily damaged if allowed to overheat, and weigh much more per energy capacity than gas. Thankfully, they are steadily improving.

Terminology of Electrification

We will only scratch the surface on electricity's use as propulsion, but it will cover what's necessary. At this level, a water analogy is pretty good.

Volts are pressure, amps are flow, and watts are work (like horsepower) which can be calculated by multiplying volts and amps. Watt hours (Wh) are an amount of work done for a period of time. Think of watt-hours as capacity—like how full the fuel tank is. A 4000 Watt-hour tank (4 kWh) would empty in an hour by flowing 10 amps at 400 volts or 100 amps at 40 volts.

Fig 23-34 Quad Motor

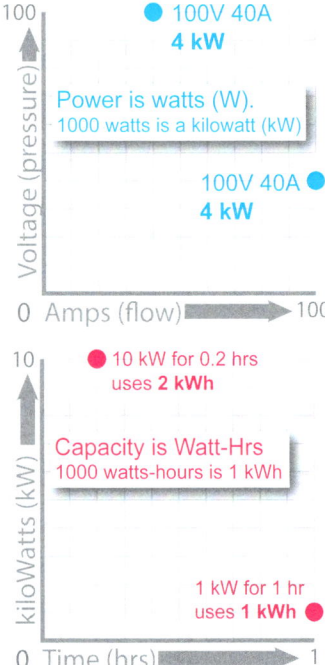

Fig 23-35 Units for Electricity

Now lets say you want to fill the tank, i.e. charge your 4000 kWh battery with the car's 12 volt system. We'll assume it's equipped with unobtanium super-conducting, no-loss charging electronics.

If the car put out 4000 kilowatts for an hour that would do it. But at 12 volts that would be 333 amps! Few automotive alternators can put out more than 200 amps. And even if you could, it would be *really* hard on the batteries being charged. So practically speaking, you're limited to a 120 volt charger that will carefully feed the right amount of current to your expensive batteries for a minimum of 4 hours.

Power Density

Battery capacity weighs about 0.5 kg per minute of flying (200 pound pilot) so 30 minutes would require a battery weighing about 15 kg. Heavier pilots, aggressive flying, and/or less efficient gear will need more.

Sort of an aside is that capacity is frequently given in amp-hours (Ah). But that is only meaningful if you have the battery voltage. Watt-hours (Wh) incorporates voltage. For example, 1 hour of 1 amp at 20 volts is 20 Wh while 1 amp at 40 volts is 40 Wh. Batteries drain at the Wh rate.

Quad Motors: Advantages

Some electric paramotors have four smaller motors arranged like a drone on its side. That has some advantages.

- Torque can be eliminated due to the motors being on fixed arms away from the center and having props spin in different directions.

- Having four points of thrust allows some cool possibilities for vanquishing unwanted motion. Imagine turbulence trying to twist you right. Thrust could be increased on the right and decreased on the left in a way to stop the twist. It's the basic technology that allows non-pilots to fly drones. Inertial sensors detect motion and software uses variable thrust to damp it.

- Four small motors may be cheaper than one big one. Four small, mass produced quadcopter props are a *lot* cheaper than one big one.

- Developers can tap into less-expensive, mass market drone sources for motors, batteries, controllers, etc. Be careful, though, since these things aren't intended for manned flight.

Quad Motors: Drawbacks

It's not all rosy—as usual, there are downsides.

- The smaller props *sound* louder. Mostly it's the high RPM—those little props seem to be screaming even at cruising speed even though they're not actually that loud to a decibel meter. You'll still appreciate ear protection.

- Although having each motor out in the slipstream helps with efficiency, it's not likely enough to overcome the loss from using such small props. All things being equal, a slow speed aircraft like ours benefits from swinging the largest prop it reasonably can. Efficiency is measured in kilowatt-hours used per hour which is like gallons per hour in petrol powered craft.

Battery Care

Some batteries warrant extreme care to prevent damage, degradation, or catching fire. Heat is their mortal enemy with overheating during charging a common threat. At the extremes, it risks thermal runaway where an internal short causes more heat and more current. Heed user manuals, especially regarding charging.

Weather & Wind

CHAPTER 24

You don't have to be a meteorologist to manage a useful understanding of weather. Grasping *micro*meteorology, however, is quite helpful for our uniquely vulnerable craft. We will provide the basics on large scale concepts.

Entire books are devoted to atmospheric lore, a complicated puzzle that academia is still piecing together. We concentrate on what's more useful to paramotor pilots, but for completeness, Dennis Pagen's *Understanding the Sky* covers weather in grand detail.

Most weather predictions revolve around the "big picture," stuff that can be left for the pros—frontal passage, strong winds, precipitation, etc. We're not interested in that kind of violence with our aerial jellyfish. However, on days where basically benign weather is forecast, knowledge of the little stuff helps.

Fig 24-1 Thunderstorms
Yup, that's lighting ahead. It doesn't really look like much, but thunderstorms can hide amidst otherwise normal-looking clouds. And they have proven most unhealthy on our soft-skinned conveyances.

Using Forecasts

Chapter 7 provided the basics on deciding when it's appropriate to fly, let's interpret the details. What happens around this one cumulus cloud? How does air behave in the presence of hills? What happens from the surface up to 100 feet, and so on. Use professional weather people for the big picture, and apply this on the smaller scale.

A forecast can be trusted more if what they expected earlier is becoming reality right now. That shows the weather service grasps what's going on atmospherically. Otherwise, their model is no longer valid—watch out. Did they expect a south wind and it's actually from the northwest? If so, be suspicious of other predictions.

Principles

Peeling back the onion of atmospheric understanding can water the eyes. Deep physics underpin its machinations but these basic rules apply.

1. **Hot air rises, cool air sinks** and then flows downhill to the lowest point, just like how water seeks its lowest point. This is the core of most weather.

2. Air gets thinner with altitude and its pressure drops about 1 inch of mercury

Fig 24-2 Helium Balloon Test

Try this in your car to visualize air's mass in motion. With a helium balloon on a string, drive around and watch how the balloon moves opposite to the air "sloshing" around like water.

What's happening is that acceleration is making a pressure gradient just like gravity does in a vertical direction. Hit the gas and the balloon goes forward as heavier air moves aft.

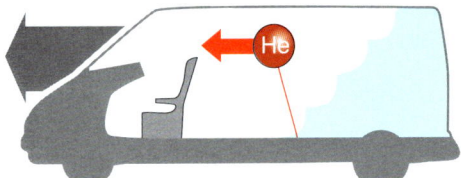

Fig 24-3 Sensing Weather

In an otherwise calm evening where culverts channel cool, descending air, you can feel the effect by flying along where they spill out.

This underpins much of the weather phenomenon we find in mountains, which is significantly based on the simple act of cooler air flowing downhill.

per 1000 feet (Fig 24-6). Sea level is the deepest reach in an ocean of air where, just like in water, pressure is greatest at the bottom.

3. Air gets cooler with altitude at the *Lapse Rate*—about 2°C per 1000 feet.

4. *Radiant cooling* is earth's surface losing heat into space. It's like how a radiant heater can warm your hands without warming the air. The process is always happening, even during the day, but overnight its all cooling.

5. *Conduction* is when terrain warms (or cools) the overlying air and *convection* is when heat is transferred by warm air moving into an area of cold air (or vice versa). Thermals mix up warmer air with colder air aloft through conduction.

6. As covered above, earth is always radiating heat, day and night; more with clear skies since clouds reflect infrared energy back down. During the day, sunlight adds more heat than radiant cooling subtracts, a victory that starts about a 30 minutes after sunrise. Most significantly, sun-facing hills, or dark, dry spots warm up first. These temperature differences underpin thermal formation.

7. In a standard atmosphere (see below), air at higher altitudes is colder than at lower altitudes. The rate that it gets cooler is the *lapse rate*.

8. If you expand a parcel of air (increase its volume), without adding or removing heat, its pressure and temperature drop. That's *adiabatic* cooling because there's no external exchange of heat. The reverse happens when you compress air (i.e. it descends). So, rising air cools at the *Adiabatic Lapse Rate*.

9. Warm air holds more water as invisible water vapor than cool air.

10. When a rising air parcel of air cools enough to become saturated it reaches the dew point and starts condensing out moisture as cloud, a process that releases heat. Now it doesn't cool as fast while its rising, rather it cools at the *Wet Adiabatic Lapse Rate*, its moisture continuing to condense out as cloud. This means it's more likely to be warmer than the surrounding air. See principle #1. This is the stuff of storms.

11. As long as a rising parcel of air remains warmer than the surrounding air, it will keep rising.

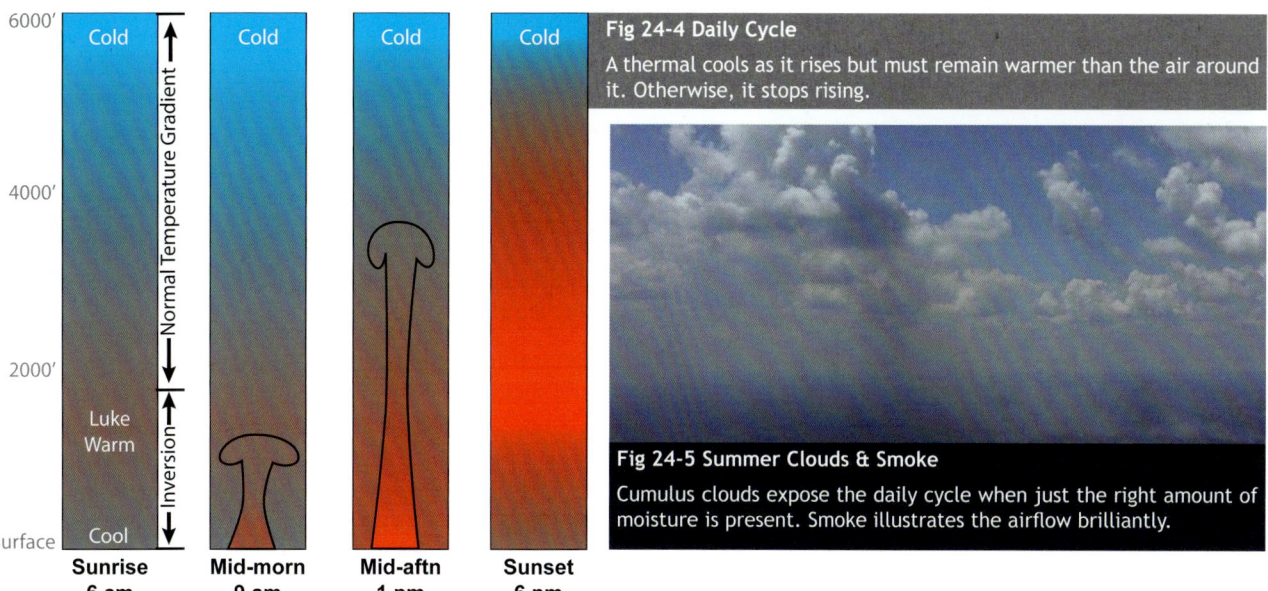

Fig 24-4 Daily Cycle
A thermal cools as it rises but must remain warmer than the air around it. Otherwise, it stops rising.

Fig 24-5 Summer Clouds & Smoke
Cumulus clouds expose the daily cycle when just the right amount of moisture is present. Smoke illustrates the airflow brilliantly.

Standard Atmosphere

A standard atmosphere is meteorology's common point of reference. It is also used by aircraft makers (and others) to base performance numbers on.

The International Standard Atmosphere (ISA) is 0% humidity, 59°F (15°C) and has a pressure of 29.92 inches of mercury (Hg) at sea level. For every 1000 feet of height, the temperature decreases by 3.5°F (2°C) which is the standard lapse rate, and the pressure falls by about 1 inch of mercury (Hg). So at 3000 feet, you would expect the pressure to be 26.92 inches Hg and the temperature to be 10.5°F cooler or 48.5°F. See also "Charting Altitude Feel" on page 78

Daily Cycles

Every location has an underlying daily cycle that represents the norm for that time of year—a cycle that can be as powerful as it is predictable. These frequently yield specific, known places and times when flying is ill advised. That's part of why long-time local pilots can offer such valuable advice.

Since the cycle is driven by sunlight, clouds usually reduce its intensity. But clouds and pressure systems may point to some greater atmospheric change that will overpower the daily cycle—be extra careful.

Radiation Cycle

Overnight, the ground cools, cooling the air just above. That increasingly chilled (and therefore heavier) air tries to sink, finding its way into low spots. The cooling ground is like an ice cube—it just keeps cooling the air nearby. If the air cools enough, some of its water vapor condenses into fog or dew. This is why low spots get foggy first—cool air flows downhill. All this cooling inverts the normal atmospheric temperature gradient. Instead of being cooler aloft, a cooler layer along the ground forms, so by morning the coldest air is at the surface. At some point up higher (maybe only a few hundred feet) there is a significant increase in temperature called an inversion. Above that, the normal temperature gradient of cooling with higher altitude resumes.

A half hour after sunrise this cooling maxes out, leaving a very stable condition, especially in less hilly areas—cool air sits in low places, with nowhere to go. Solar heating overcomes radiant cooling and warming begins. The thermal game is afoot.

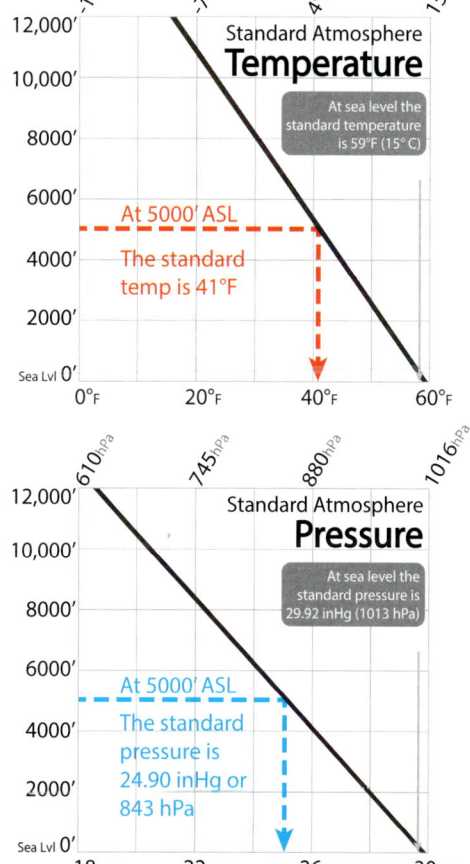

Fig 24-6 Standard Atmosphere

Fig 24-7 Mountains & Water
Mid-day flying in the desert could be treacherous, but the Salton Sea is big enough to make it coastal. If you're careful.

This site is famous for sudden changes when certain pressure conditions exist in those mountains. It frequently goes from coastal to capricious in minutes.

> **Digging Deeper: State Change**
>
> A significant impact on weather is the state change of water—going from ice to liquid to gas. Its lowest energy level is ice.
>
> If you add heat (energy) to ice it will warm up at a constant rate until it gets to the melting point (32°F) where it stays, absorbing heat until changing to the new state, water. Then it continues warming.
>
> For example, put a 10°F block of ice in into a 300°F oven. The ice will warm gradually until it hits 0°C (32°F) where it momentarily stops warming as it changes from ice to water. The difference in energy between the two states is called latent heat.
>
> The water will now continue warming at a steady rate until it reaches the boiling point 100°C (212°F) where it will again stop warming to change state from a liquid to a gas. More latent heat. Then the water vapor will continue warming.
>
> Sublimation is going from ice to water vapor. Evaporation is liquid water going to gas (water vapor), cooling the surface from which it evaporated. The higher the temperatures, the more sublimation or evaporation occurs.
>
> The reverse happens during cooling. As water vapor cools, it does so evenly until becoming saturated. In the process of becoming visible water (clouds) it starts giving up heat, warming the surrounding air, or more accurately, making it chill slower. As it makes the state change, it resists further cooling for a period of time until the state has fully changed. This process continues if the air is lifted until the moisture has nearly all condensed out..
>
> These physics drive the formation of severe weather—giving teeth to a process that would otherwise fizzle, powering thunderstorms and hurricanes.
>
> This phenomenon happens on smaller scales, too. "Cloud suck" is one example, where the cloud formation itself drives lift instead of the original thermal. Air mixing with the cooler surrounding air is what prevents it from shooting out of control.

Dry, dark spots heat up first and the air above them tries to rise. Sun-facing hills heat up even more as the day's nascent thermals begin popping off, increasing in intensity as long as heating continues, mixing and warming the atmosphere.

Rising air expands and cools but the standard atmosphere it's rising through is getting cooler, too, at 2C per 1000 feet. As long as our rising air parcel remains warmer than that, it keeps going. Eventually, though, cooling due to expansion exceeds the atmosphere's normal lapse rate and movement stops. With enough moisture present, clouds will form when cooled to the dew point.

By mid afternoon thermal strength usually peaks although cloud bases keep going up. Solar heating peaked at noon but the ground continues to warm. Late afternoon's decreasing sun angle finally takes its toll and the process wanes. Thermal strength can still be dangerous up to within a couple hours of sunset depending on location and atmospheric conditions.

Flatland

In flat areas the daily cycle and large scale changes prevail. Afternoons can be dangerously turbulent during periods of instability. That's why it's best to favor the first and last few hours of sunlight in the summer.

Typical days start out smooth with nearly calm winds in the morning. These are wonderful times to fly—smooth and pristine. The "dog days of summer" describe a flatlander's heyday, with sultry afternoons of light breezes.

If the wind aloft is very strong, expect it to get bumpy quickly. Wind and thermals don't mix well. You'll know soon after launch what the wind is doing. In fact, it's not difficult to climb up into a perfectly smooth wind that matches or exceeds your airspeed. You end up parked over one location (or moving backward) while facing into the wind. It's strange and can happen pretty low. This is a wind gradient and the smoothness will be short lived once sunlight churns up the air.

Hilly

Surprisingly intense micro meteorology happens when air interacts with hills—even before the sun comes up. That's why flying in mountainous areas warrants so much attention. As air cools it tries to flow downhill, sometimes becoming a torrent. Like an avalanche, it gathers speed, causing rapid wind changes, intensifying in mountain passes or other constrictions. It's just like a wide, mellow river that narrows to rapids in tight places.

Hills also interfere with larger scale movements and mask winds. If the air is forced to go up or around a geographic protrusion you can expect turbulence in the lee (downwind of it). A calm valley with known wind aloft—up near mountain top level—could be hiding a wild ride. And that turbulence can come down well below the peak's height.

Coastal

The beauty of a beach is in its smooth predictability. Usually by 11 AM the warming land is sucking air inland in a steady sea breeze (on shore) that makes launching painless. Free of thermal turbulence, this airflow from the water is usually very smooth, ruffled only by waves. Most of the time the wind continues well past sunset. The cycle reverses at night when the land cools and a land breeze (off-shore) sets in with wind blowing out to sea.

One risk is when a prevailing off-shore wind gets overcome by the sea breeze. A few miles inland the wind is blowing out to sea but on the beach it's coming on shore. Somewhere in the middle, these two airflows meet in a confused convergence zone. Besides turbulence, if you're flying beach side when the prevailing off-shore breeze wins the pushing contest, you could be blown out to sea.

Desert

Deserts are beautiful in their own dry, rugged way. But they spawn the strongest, meanest thermals found anywhere—making for a wild daily cycle that can be much more dramatic than in wetter areas. It happens because the sun's rays don't get used up in evaporation—they go right into heating the ground.

One indicator of thermal strength is the difference in temperature from morning low to afternoon high—something deserts have to an extreme.

These factors combine to make mid-day desert flying a spin of the roulette wheel.

Dust devils are the visible manifestation of a violent cauldron that precedes sometimes huge thermals. These little tornadoes may also be occurring up high but would be invisible.

Flying the desert is beautiful in the mornings and evenings, but deserves great respect during mid-day.

Yearly Cycle

Many yearly cycles are overlaid on daily temperature swings: The monsoons of Tucson and Phoenix, the dry period of Portland, hurricane season, Santa Ana winds, etc. Some of these involve winds erupting with little warning. Long term local knowledge can be a life saver—if you don't know a local pilot, seek one out from the nearest airport or an online forum. Most are happy to answer such questions as "I'm gonna be flying an ultralight in the local area, is there any significant seasonal weather I should know about?"

Fig 24-8 Lava Lamp Thermal
A Lava Lamp demonstrates thermal action nicely.

The most prevalent and relevant cycle, though, is thermal intensity. It follows the length of day where thermals are strongest in summer and weakest in winter. That makes sense—their driving force is sunshine, and summer's mid-day packs many more heating hours, at a more direct angle than winter's.

The difference can be a dramatic. Long hours of direct sunlight heat up the ground, boiling the atmospheric soup into a sporty mix. Winter's few daily hours of low-angle light leave many smooth days to fly even in the desert.

All About Thermals

A lot has been written on this topic but anyone who has watched a 1970's lava lamp (Fig 24-8) knows the process: sun-warmed patches of ground heat the air immediately above, making it want to rise. At some point this warm air blob lets go and punches through the overlying cooler air to begin ascending. Air rushes in below. Free flyers ride these updrafts to sometimes great heights. Most motor pilots avoid them and their turbulence, although a few accept the risk and use them for soaring.

Thriving thermals need the right type of atmosphere. Primarily that means a steady decrease in temperature with altitude (lapse rate), direct sunlight and a heatable surface. An overcast douses the process which is why you can frequently fly all day long on cloudy days (as long as no rain is expected), even in the middle of summer.

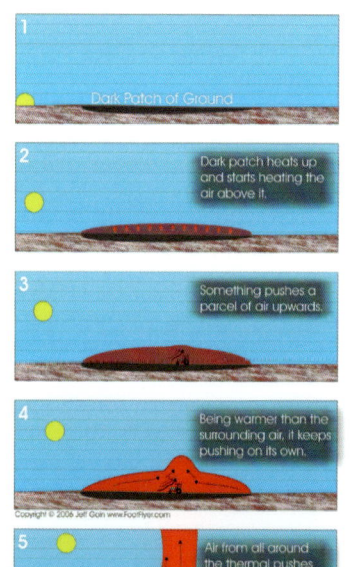

Fig 24-9 Thermal Trigger Theory

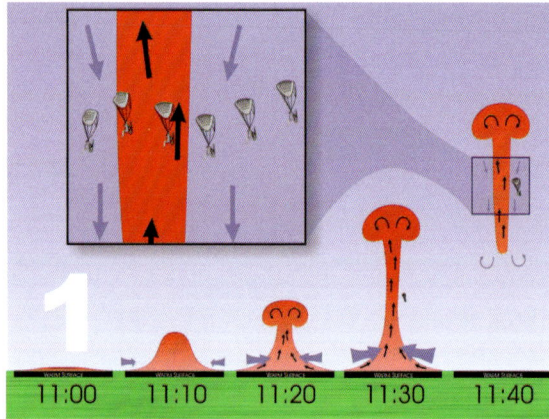

Fig 24-10 Thermal Progression

#1 Here is a fairly typical thermal and what it can do when a paraglider flies through it. As the pilot exits, downward moving air makes him susceptible to a frontal collapse (see Chapter 18).

Fig 24-11 Thermal Strength Distribution

#2 This illustrates the distribution of thermals on a bright, sunny day, especially in the summer. Yellow represents moderate thermals, red represents strong ones, and the skull represents dangerous-to-us versions. How many of these strong thermals exist depends on many factors, but ultimately, missing that killer thermal is a matter of luck on strong days.

Summer afternoon's invisible fury should not be treated lightly.

Telling Thermal Intensity from the Ground

You can predict thermal intensity (turbulence) from wind gusts. Stand in one place or just be observant while setting up. Calm conditions on the ground portend calm air above while gusty conditions suggest lumpy air aloft. Sharp gusts, where the wind speed or direction changes rapidly, indicate sharper, more dangerous thermals.

Flying on a day with rapid gusts from 5-12 mph could be deadly whereas soft changes of the same magnitude might be manageable. Wind direction must be watched too—if it goes from east at 12 mph (wind *from* the east) and suddenly switches to west at 5—that's bad.

Thermals and strong winds don't mix. Gusts from mechanical turbulence add to energetic thermals to make potentially dangerous air.

Dust devils show that, even away from the swirl itself, the atmosphere is particularly turbulent. Any day strong enough to trigger dust devils is going to be ugly.

Where Thermals Thrive

Cross country soaring pilots know where to find the "biggest air"—a description for powerful thermals that can carry pilots skyward at well over 1000 fpm. Associated turbulence can play havoc on a paraglider, causing severe collapses. Every year, it seems, at least one experienced free flyer succumbs to an unpleasant fate in "big air."

Drier air breeds more dramatic thermals. Arid regions consistently give soaring pilots the highest altitude gains and longest soaring flights.

The lifted index is an atmospheric measurement that tells whether a parcel of lifted air will be warmer or colder than its surroundings after reaching a certain height. Negative numbers mean the parcel is warmer—it wants to accelerate upwards. That's unstable. As discussed earlier, if it gets cold quickly as you climb, a lifted parcel of air would tend to remain warmer and therefore keep rising. Lifted index charts can be found on the Internet although you'll want additional study to use them.

Clouds

The highest clouds, cirrus (or cirriform), are wispy affairs comprised of ice crystals. They form above 25,000 feet and can sometimes spread out from jet contrails. Mid-level clouds live between about 8000 and 25,000 feet. They're usually prefaced with the word alto (e.g. altocumulus and altostratus) and mostly only concern our micro view for their value in blocking out thermal-producing sunshine.

Stratiform

Stratus clouds are the flat, boring, frequently drizzly, clouds that form mostly on weekends. Their flat, gray appearance generally indicates stable conditions with little vertical movement. When they drop rain, they're called nimbostratus.

Smooth and frequently layered, stratus clouds are usually associated with fairly benign weather although they can conceal significant ugliness. They are common along fronts and occupy large swaths of low pressure areas. The two worst worries of flying under stratus clouds are rain and embedded thunderstorms. However, if neither is forecast, then all-day flying may be possible. By blocking the sun's most direct heating rays, they block most of the thermal-induced turbulence, leaving good, but bleak, motoring conditions (and lousy soaring conditions).

Stratus clouds must not be ignored when the forecast includes rain *showers*. It's hard to tell where the rain showers are and, with thicker clouds, it's easy to get rained on by surprise. If you see a darkening in the sky, then it's most likely because of embedded cumulus clouds which indicate coming trouble.

Stratus clouds that form around severe weather are particularly dangerous in that they conceal where the really bad weather is. That is why it's important to know the forecast and only fly on forecasted dry days.

Cumuliform

When vertical development gets involved, the term cumulo (having a heaped on appearance) gets appended or prepended to cloud names. Cumulus clouds that form mostly on nice summer afternoons cap thermals and indicate bumpy conditions. Any cloud with more than about 3000 feet of vertical development can produce rain. Once a cloud produces rain it earns the nimbus moniker: Cumulonimbus is the most violent example and is what thunderstorms come from.

The wispy beginnings of cumulus clouds typically form about 3 hours after sunrise and a few thousand feet high. If a steady breeze has picked up within a couple hours of sunrise and cumulus start popping, expect sporty air. Dry air could be just as sporty but without the cumulus clouds.

Pay close attention to cumuliform clouds. What goes up must come down, and big cumulus clouds (aka cumies) can bring air down as strong downdrafts that spread out from where they hit. These are gust fronts (see below). Little ones are felt all the time, both from popping thermals sucking in air, and from sinking air spreading out. But bigger cumulus clouds or, even worse, lines of them, can cause gust fronts tens of miles away. Technically gust fronts are associated with thunderstorms but they happen on all scales.

Be leery of large cumulus clouds. The formation process itself generates extra lift which increases as you near the base. This cloud suck can easily overpower a paraglider pilot's ability to descend. Getting caught in such lift is a chilling experience that some pilots have not survived. Depending on the cloud's size, it can easily take you to heights where temperatures plunge and the air is too thin to stay conscious. But at least it's extremely violent.

Thunderstorms

Nature's fury is unleashed in the majestic and deadly thunderstorm. These mammoth storms, covered in Chapter 7, play havoc with winds over a broad area.

They come in two types: Air mass and frontal. Air mass thunderstorms are usually scattered buildups on otherwise nice but muggy summer afternoons that are not typically as severe. Normally airmass storms germinate in aging high pressure areas with lots of moisture and some instability in the air.

Frontal storms, especially those preceding cold fronts, help fuel the fury. Long before tornadoes threaten they spew windy risk for paramotorists.

When an atmosphere is unstable enough to produce thunderstorms, watch it closely. Don't get suckered by the calm. Wait two hours after a storm passes before considering flying, and make sure there is nothing brewing nearby.

Gust fronts are probably the most dangerous fallout for us. Rain pulls cold air downward until it hits the ground and spreads out in a fast-moving, turbulent boil. Effects can extend many miles from the storm. Obviously tornadoes are their worst feature, but we need to be long gone before it gets to that point. They're more a factor for getting out of the open area we're flying from.

Fig 24-12 Early Cumulus Clouds

In the beginning, they were mere puffs to be toyed with (in G airspace). Later they would become mighty and maleficent, to be revered, respected, and most of all, left alone.

Fig 24-13 Stratiform Clouds

Stratiform clouds usually indicate benign conditions. Be sure you can see everything though, they sometimes hide cumulus clouds.

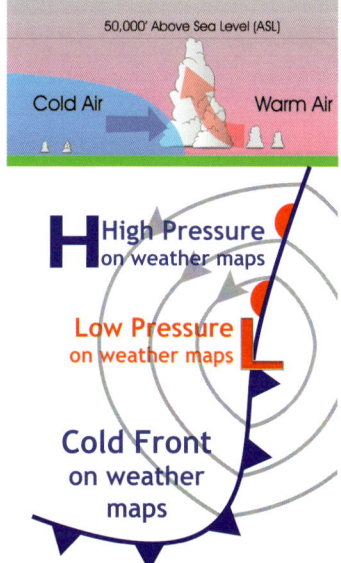

Fig 24-14 Fronts, Highs & Lows

Air flows outward from high pressure areas, and into low pressure areas—turning into increasing counter-clockwise flow due to *Coriolis effect*.

Fig 24-15 Dust Storm

An old but appropriate axiom. In some areas dust storms can build very quickly.

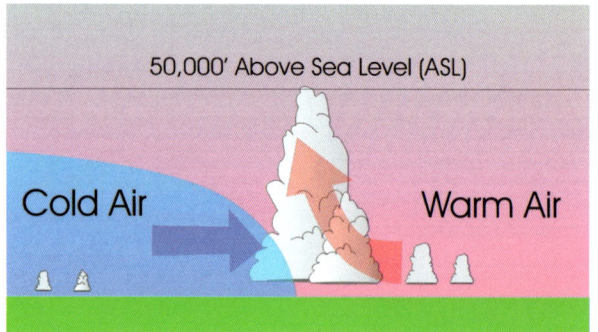

Fig 24-16 Frontal Collision

A cold front spawning thunderstorms. Strong, gusty winds are common after cold fronts pass.

Fronts

Fronts are boundaries between air masses of different temperatures, moved around by high level winds, that frequently swirl around low pressure areas. Low pressure areas arise from many causes, including *jet streams* which can suck air upwards under some conditions. Low-level air tries to flow inward to fill the low pressure and gets turned by Coriolis effect (the result of a spinning world)—thus the low pressure area spins, dragging fronts along with it.

Air masses themselves stir up the pot. A big patch of cold air shoving its way under heavy southern warmth will try to spread out. It gets turned by Mr. Coriolis and can spawn a low pressure area in the process. In the meantime it presses on as a cold front.

Cold fronts are bodies of cooler air pushing under warm air, frequently forming lines of cumulo-nastiness. Fortunately, they are usually fast moving—doing their big blows and moving on. Some of the best flying follows these fronts for days because they tend to be dry and clear albeit a bit bumpy.

Warm fronts ride over retreating cooler air and tend towards being wet and mellow. Be careful, though, they do sometimes harbor thunderstorms in the stratiform mass. Unfortunately, they tend to linger, mucking up the weather for days.

Lots of bad weather happens near fronts. If there is a forecast for frontal passage, even if no rain or clouds are present, be suspicious. Check out the wind forecast—there can easily be a dangerous wind shift in store. If you're at the field, also be suspicious of sudden temperature changes. For example, a day that gets to 80°F by noon but then forecasts a temperature drop to 70°F by afternoon would likely have a wind shift. That is a dry cold front—you would want to avoid flying until after the wind shifts since it could easily be violent.

Highs and Lows

Areas of high and low pressure resemble swells on the ocean but on a very, very large scale, spanning hundreds of miles. The troughs are low pressure and the peaks are high pressure. Air moves, in some ways, like a big Slinky; piling up both vertically and horizontally. For example, it's possible to have air pile up high in the atmosphere. It will, of course, start falling but air has a lot of mass and that will take time.

Other forces act to lift air and pile it up in different ways. For example, the jet stream has influence. It can move in ways that pull air away, creating low pressure areas.

A hurricane is a good example of another force that forms low pressure areas. Warm water feeds a group of thunderstorms that create enormous average lifting force. They're like a bunch of vacuum cleaners, accelerating air upwards and spitting it out the top. Air flows into this continuous low pressure and gets turned by the Coriolis effect (like the marble that you roll inward on a rotating record). Rotation keeps pressure low because air can't fill in the center low. That's why hurricanes cannot form on the equator—there's nothing to force rotation. Low pressure areas form, but air is able to fill them in fairly quickly since it's not deflected into a spin.

Why do lows get the bad rap? Almost by definition, the air in a low is being sucked (or lifted) upwards, frequently by jet stream action. The motion is too slow to feel from the ground or even in flight, but is enough to cool the air which tends to form clouds. Air in a low pressure area gets concentrated since it's flowing inward and upward. Conservation of energy means that when the air is deflected inward, toward the low, it wants to speed up, like a spinning ballerina. But air in a high pressure system is generally descending and heading outward—like a ballerina spreading out and slowing down.

Getting Weather Info

Chapter 7 covers acquiring weather through Flight Service. But a good way to improve your awareness of what's happening aloft is to get the weather at locations around your site, especially upwind of it. It's not foolproof, and it doesn't work as well in mountainous regions, but it's a good start.

Surface wind is not a good indication of where weather is coming from. Look at the clouds and see which way they're moving. Different cloud layers may be moving in completely different directions; you're most interested in the low to mid-level layers (between 3000 and 10,000 feet).

 TV is a reasonable source for weather information but phone apps and the Internet are better; you can customize what you're looking for and get more detail on your particular area. The QR link is a list of useful apps and sites for this purpose and others.

Turbulence from Wind

There are some important differences in what pilots frequently lump into the term *rotor*. Knowing what those differences are could be a life-saver.

Mechanical turbulence is the general bumpiness that extends downwind from anything that sticks up into a wind, up to 20 times the obstacle's height. The resultant eddies drift with the wind and spread upward above the height of the causing obstacle. Turbulence extends further downstream as wind speed picks up. So, too, does intensity and quite dramatically—a 15 mph wind will have over double the intensity of a 10 mph wind.

Rotor itself is a stationary swirl of air that spins immediately downwind of the causing obstruction. It can be very powerful and produce incredibly strong shear since it's so well organized. Rotors don't always form—it depends on the obstruction's shape, wind speed and wind gradients. Soaring pilots who are intimately familar with their

Fig 24-17 Localized Gust Front

This localized gust front near Phoenix, AZ shows how these come in various scales from a few miles to over a hundred miles. They are always dangerous.

Fig 24-18 Small Front with Virga

Another type of localized front that was spawned by a line of cumulus clouds. Virga (rain that evaporates before reaching the ground) was an early indication of dangerous gusts that were soon to hit the ground.

Also, avoid dark bottomed clouds, they indicate there's a lot of vertical development above with potential turbulence.

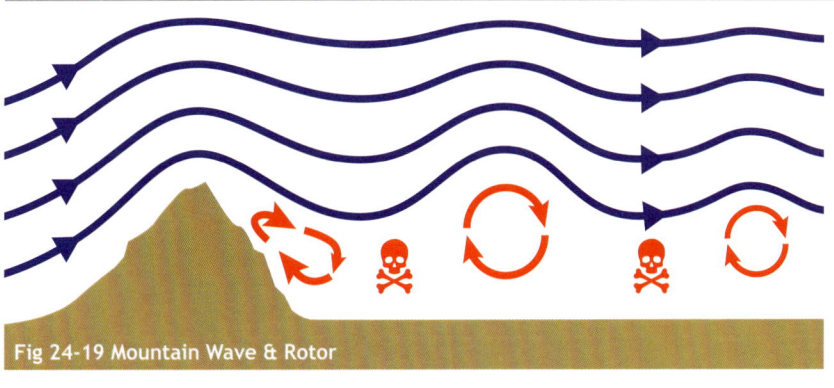
Fig 24-19 Mountain Wave & Rotor

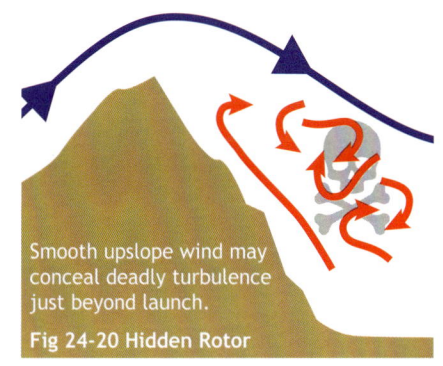
Smooth upslope wind may conceal deadly turbulence just beyond launch.
Fig 24-20 Hidden Rotor

Fig 24-21 Ridge Shape

1. Air has lots of mass. Just like over an airfoil, it won't make sharp bends. So when you envision the airflow past obstructions, expect turbulence and dramatic changes in the area of those bends. This shows that the air cannot stick and creates a standing rotor.

2. The lip of this ridge is sharp enough to create turbulence but not enough to create a standing rotor.

3. This smooth ridge would be perfect for soaring. If you stand near the lip of a sharp edge, you'll feel very little wind on your face. Setting up to launch there would be difficult at best. But on a curvy ridge, like #3, the wind flows steadily along the smoother surface—a much easier launch proposition.

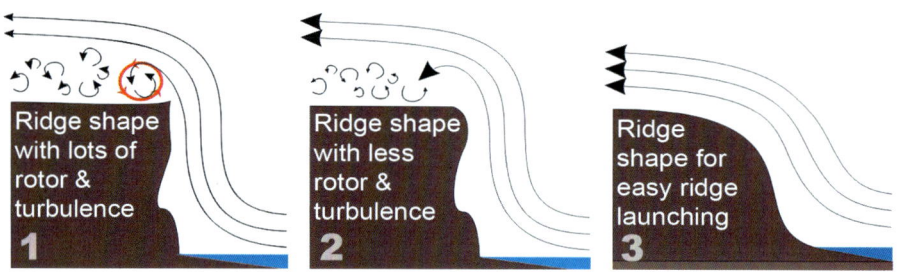

> **Worst Flight. Ever.**
>
> My worst aviation experience ever—in anything—was getting talked into making a flight that I had earlier begged off of. The LZ was in the lee of a "small" mountain.
>
> The local pilot convinced me that this condition was common and wouldn't be a problem. Hmm. It was in another country, on an unfamiliar coast, and I figured he should know, so I went for it. Turns out weather and physics don't care what locals think.
>
> Nearing our destination, downwind of the mountain, it began: extreme turbulence with so much updraft we couldn't get down. Three of us took three different approaches, including one who went well out to sea. It took the last pilot over an hour, in sometimes severe turbulence, to finally land safely. It took luck for all of us to emerge unscathed.
>
> I had seen that wing in places, and in contortions that no wing should be seen. Well beyond any value of understanding weather, this reminds me to heed my inner voice of survival.

mountains will sometimes launch in the updraft of rotor, knowing that they will have to manage strong turbulence shortly after launch. Needless to say, this doesn't always go well.

Wind shadow is the calm that exists just downwind, and usually at the bottom, of an obstruction. It's what you feel when seeking shelter from the wind behind a building (or other obstruction). It extends about to the height of the obstruction. Picture your paraglider moving from that stillness out into the free air stream. That would be bumpy.

In a light wind, less than about 5 mph, mechanical turbulence and rotor are almost nonexistent—flying next to obstructions poses little problem.

Mountain Waves

When strong wind blows perpendicular to a mountain range, there may be mountain waves and severe turbulence downwind of the range. It can extend many thousands of feet above the mountain and create deadly conditions just above the surface. Besides the main rotors, powerful eddies cause turbulence that even sailplanes try to avoid. It's no place for a paraglider. Rotor extends from just below the mountain's crest down to a few hundred feet AGL, sometimes to the surface.

There are also standing mountain waves, with smooth lift and sink, that reach into the stratosphere. Glider pilots use these for record altitude gains.

Terrain and Flow

Whenever air is squeezed between two hills, its speed will pick up just like where a river narrows and the water speeds up. In a craft as slow as ours, that could stop all forward motion. Fortunately for power pilots, we can throttle up and climb away from this venturi effect.

When air is forced up over obstructions it causes lift just upwind of the obstruction. Ridge lift, as it's called, remains fairly smooth as long as there are no thermals in it and the pilot stays upwind or over the causing obstruction. The obstruction's shape determines the strength of the lift—a smooth, steep rise in the face of a steady wind creates the most lift. Terrain can also act like an airfoil where the air goes over the top then back down the back side, sticking to the surface and creating sink. For example, flying just downwind of a tree line can create enough sink to make climbing difficult or impossible.

Roots: Our History

CHAPTER 25

It's a short history. Powered paragliding grew from paragliding which itself started in the early 1980's. Paramotors have several other interesting roots, not all contributing to the same tree, but rather growing in an underbrush of ultralight evolution that prospered simultaneously.

Parasailing

You will soon tire of hearing your sport called parasailing. You *ride* a parasail; you *pilot* a PPG. Parasailing is great fun, to be sure, but is essentially a mindless amusement for riders who hang below a stable parachute with no control. They can whisk unsuspecting tourists up on it—don't try that with a paramotor.

Our sport has no origins in parasailing, a sport that branched off from the round canopies of sport parachuting. They still use modified rounds for stability's sake.

Hang Gliding & Ultralighting

Development of hang gliders started in earnest during the mid-1970's after a few enterprising individuals adopted Francis Rogallo's 1948 design. Rogallo was scheming to safely return spacecraft through the atmosphere. Later on, enterprising earthmen of the 1970's were making bamboo gliders from his designs. Eventually, professional manufacturers entered the fray with real soaring craft.

Efficiency and safety drove improvements into fixed wing variants that eventually included propulsion. Strangely (and fortunately), the FAA did little about any of this since the pilots stayed mostly out of everyone's way and risked only themselves. They remained, literally and figuratively, "below the radar."

The crafts' weight increased, wheels were added, and Ultralighting was born. Flex wing Rogallos got longer, their wings got skinnier, and performance allowed them to become capable soaring craft. The proliferating rigid wing configurations all but took over the powered segment.

Fig 25-1 Early Motor Launch

Frenchman Didier Eymin has done photo work using a paramotor all over the world. He is pictured here taking off with one of his first machines in the early 1990's.

Fig 25-2 Early Hang Glider

Phil Russman flying one of the first Rogallo hang gliders before motors were added. These "weight shift" craft rely completely on pilots moving their body.

Sport Parachuting

Pilots first used cloth to soften their intentional falls in the late 1700's when balloons and buildings were the only way up. But until 1961 there was no control of the canopy—it just broke the fall and sometimes the legs. Then the *Paracommander* came along with holes in the back that offered minimal forward speed. At last the parachutist could influence his destiny. At about the same time, a Rogallo shaped parachute was devised but never really explored.

The big development came in 1964 with the square Ram-Air parachute. This design formed the underpinnings of modern paragliding.

These sport parachutists could fly almost like a glider but with very limited glide performance. French mountain climbers learned to launch their canopies from the slopes, a much quicker way down from the scaled heights. Others saw an opportunity and began to improve the wings, getting the sport well established in Europe by 1986. Modern paragliding came to Joe Public when manufacturers actually started producing wings for the masses by about 1988.

Efficiency gains earned it the name paragliding and enterprising European pilots started adding power. Large motors were required to overcome the draggy early wings. High hang points were needed to balance the heavy motors.

As wings became more efficient, the motors got smaller and lighter, requiring less thrust. By 1989 the Pagojet, using a 3-cylinder radial engine, became the first production unit available to the public. Not that the masses flocked to it, but at least they had the opportunity. By 1991 a number of European manufacturers were building machines and the US market was soon to follow.

Lost Lineage

An evolutionary aside to the paraglider story is that of David Barish—an airline pilot turned aeronautical engineer turned parachute designer. Like Rogallo, he was thinking about space as humans raced moonward in 1965. He and Rogallo only met once at NASA but their re-entry designs both shared some commonality—both sported about a 4 to 1 glide ratio and both were abandoned by the space agency.

But Barish, an avid and accomplished skier, took his single-surface paraglider to the slopes – scooting/flying down the hills at no more than about 30 feet high. He toured the country's finest ski sites in the summer of 1966, demonstrating his newfangled version of "downhill" with an apparently cool reception; it seems the public just wasn't ready yet.

He even tried using a motor with his creation but must not have found an adequate power system that he could lift; there is no record of any motorized flights with his wing. That's not surprising—at least one manufacturer had started producing single surface gliders, but they would have needed lots of thrust.

Powering Up

Englishman Mike Byrne made the first recorded paramotor flight in the fall of 1979 and, by the summer of 1980, was intriguing airshow and television audiences around England. The 95-pound home-built unit used a 3-cylinder Konig motor and hung from his back. It had no seat and probably limited appeal. Flights only lasted about 5 minutes since the motor's weight hung from his back and he hung from the harness. Ouch (think suspension trauma). He was also probably the first to name the craft, along with his brother Johnny, calling it a paramotor.

Fig 25-3 Parascending

This was an English parascending canopy built in about 1987 to carry two people.

Efficiency has come a *long* way. It took Alan 500 feet of altitude loss to do one 360° turn.

The shape was not very distant from its sport parachuting origins although it did have unsheathed lines that are now common on higher performance paragliders. But it had a *lot* of lines, far more than on modern gliders.

Fig 25-4 First Recorded Flights

Mike Byrne about to launch on a 5 minute flight with his home-grown, König-powered early paramotor in 1980. He could only fly for 5 minutes because the 100-pound motor hung from him, not the harness. That got uncomfortable in a hurry!

The rightmost picture was him flying the same wing but with wheels.

It obviously didn't catch on and Mike moved to bigger, faster craft, mostly with wheels or skids (helicopters). No more hanging from a harness: the family jewels could only stand so much.

Barndt Bartig was another pioneer, foot-launching from level ground in 1981. But he kept it secret until the German-built *PagoJet* became the first commercial paramotor for sale in 1987. It too had a 3-cylinder Konig engine.

Right behind him was Jet Pocket (also known as Air Plum), the first French company to manufacture and commercialize a foot-launched paramotor starting in 1988, quickly followed by the Propulsar whose owner then joined up with Guy Leon Dufour of Adventure. There are several pilots in Italy who also started making personal units as early as 1987, including the past owner of Vittorazi and Diego of Miniplane.

The U.S. saw its first paramotor when Patrick Sugrue flew one in 1988. He imported the LaMouette brand and his most notorious customer was James Miller (Fig 25-5) who really brought the sport, if briefly, into American minds.

Fig 25-5 Digging Deeper: Fan Man

James Miller had a passion for both flight and for freedom—paragliding gave his desire wings. He took to it quickly, learning from a friend before instruction was widely available. Residents of Juneau, Alaska spotted him frequently flying from Mt. Roberts near his home. He knew the value of training, though, and sought out advanced instruction in flying and towing from Alan Chuculate, one of the sport's early instructors and certainly one of very few in Alaska.

Alan noted that besides "Having a lot of energy," James was enthusiastic, motivated, and his previous experience made him an easy student. James earned his USHPA (then USHGA) P2 paraglider and tow ratings in the fall of 1990 but he wanted thrust and the freedom it provides. For that he would have to leave Alaska.

James' date with fate and fame was set when he traveled to Las Vegas in 1992. He hooked up with Patrick Sugrue who had recently started importing the LaMouette paramotor. After a few days of instruction he set out on his own flying with power.

Having flown for some time in Alaska, he found the desert conditions quite different. The dry, high-powered thermals caused frequent wing collapses and other maladies. Alan remembers getting a call from James with two questions: "How do I recover from collapses?" and "How do I thermal to stay up?"

The night before his famous flight, James called his brother Eric: "I'm going to do something big tomorrow," he said. Sure enough, on Nov 6, 1993, two minutes into round 7 of the Evander Holyfield-Riddick Bowe heavyweight championship, James Miller landed in the ring, and landed in history. It cost him a beating to unconsciousness by the crowd, 4 days in jail, and a $4000 fine. One year later he made headlines again by landing on the roof of Buckingham Palace, naked.

His irreverence and free spirit bubbled up in English court just before being deported. On hearing that the judge banned him permanently from England, he asked "How about my ashes, can they come back?" She said no.

He eventually gave his life back to the mountains he loved so much. Health problems made the strapping 37 year old James Jarrett Miller unable to care for himself, and in 2002 he took his own life in a wilderness area near his home.

Fig 25-6 Powered Parachute

Fig 25-7 Electric PPG

Electric paramotors will increase in popularity as batteries get better and get cheaper.

See more in "Electric Propulsion" on page 243.

Powered Parachutes

Powered parachutes (PPCs), which came first, represent a common ancestor: skydiving's square parachute.

Early wings were glorified air-plows that required relatively heavy, powerful motors and wheels to heft them. As wings improved, resourceful pilots strapped on relatively tiny engines. The paramotor was born.

The sometimes-blurry difference between PPC's and PPG's is mostly weight and control method. If the engine is commonly used for foot-launching, and the craft uses hand controls, it is more PPG trike than PPC.

Anything over about 120 pounds (trike and motor) was probably designed from the outset to be wheel launched and would be considered a PPC. Most PPC's are way heavier (over 200 lbs) and have proportionally more power.

Performance Improvements Over Time

Most of the technology has matured quite a bit, slowing the rate of improvement in both wings and motors. Gear does get better, knowledge improves, and training availability generally improves—all good progressions.

Advances come in spurts when some new development lifts the entire sector. Hopefully electric motors will be next. Manufacturers employ various innovations and the good ones propagate. Copying is rampant because of the sport's small size which makes patent efforts unduly expensive and difficult to enforce.

Motor technology mostly comes from go-cart racing and motor scooters although purpose built motors have started to evolve. Economies of scale mean that developments in other areas are more likely to drive innovation in our sport. Paramotor production runs are just way too small compared to the thousands built for larger industries. A few manufacturers do specialize in our equipment but improvements are incremental. Power to weight ratio, which measures power per pound, is among the best measures of a new paramotor's capability.

It's hard for a company to invest heavily in an endeavor with so little payoff. Fortunately, enthusiasts come along periodically that pour themselves into a project without need for large profits. We all benefit from their vision.

Our future is bright, with weight coming down, performance improving, and, even more importantly, with knowledge increasing. We have a lot to look forward to.

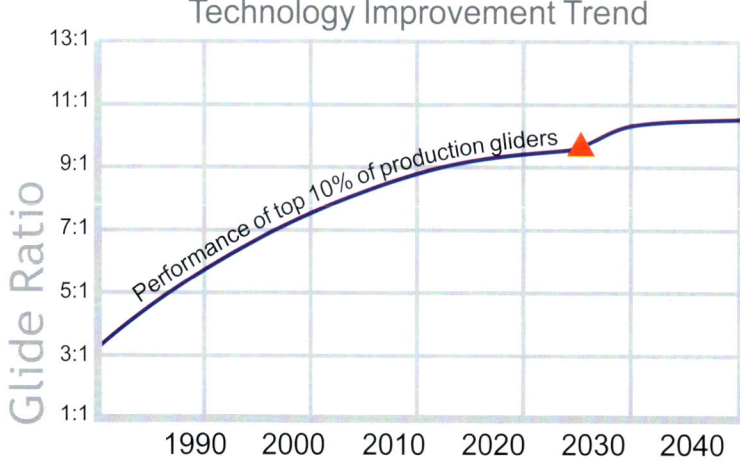

Fig 25-8 Pace of Improvements

As technology matures, the pace of improvements slows. Spurts do happen when something new comes out (red triangle), like a new line material with the same strength at half the diameter. That would incur a big jump in glide ratios until everybody had it, then progress would slow down again.

Section V

Choosing Gear

Section V

Choosing Gear

If you're starting out, review Chapter 1 on choosing an instructor and gear. Use this section to choose gear *after* training.

Who to Talk To

That you're reading this book is a good sign—you want to be informed. Hopefully these words got to you before some shady salesman. The Internet is rife with them.

Your best resource is a trusted, appropriately certified instructor. Absent that, talk to experienced pilots who have nothing to sell, and who have flown a variety of wings and motors. Go to a fly-in to see what's out there. Not only will you see the various offerings, but you'll see what people like and don't like. There will be a broad group of folks to talk with, and pilots love talking about their gear. Visit www.USPPA.org for the events calendar.

Beware the loud mouth. Value seems to be inversely proportional to volume.

Appearances

We all want stuff that looks good, but remember that your life depends on your choice—prioritize accordingly. The best looking gear on the ground pales next to the ugly duckling that will get you airborne. If you can't fly it, looks won't count for much.

Cost

No, it's not cheap. While this is one of the least expensive ways into the air, it's still aviation. Requirements for lightweight reliability drive up the cost as does low sales volume. Sellers and instructors must make profits to keep going—it's good for all of us and for the sport in general.

Cost will certainly be a factor for most people, and you should know what you're getting into. Always price gear with any training packages that might be included.

If avoiding the middleman means skipping the local instructor or school, that's usually a bad trade-off. In the long run, local support can be well worth paying a bit extra through your local dealer.

Realize, too, that costs will continue. Breaking a prop is not terribly uncommon and costs 3% to 6% of your motor's new purchase price. Wings last about 300-500 hours of sun exposure, and motors have a taste for parts.

Test Flying

Be extremely careful when trying out new gear—it can be dangerously different. Have an instructor or experienced pilot who knows the equipment help sort out its idiosyncrasies. If possible, watch a demo flight before buying.

They all have idiosyncrasies. See "Testing New Gear" on page 192 for how to make the process safer.

Other Ultralight Types

Fig 26-1 Weight Shift or Hang Glider Trike

Fig 26-2 Powered Parachute

Fig 26-3 Three-Axis Control

The Wing

CHAPTER 26

Wing choice profoundly affects safety, success, and enjoyment of the sport. Don't skimp or buy on a whim. There is no "best" gear, but rather a range of "fitting your mission." Be leery of loud pitchmen: they are least likely to care about your interests.

Ease of Launch

Paragliders for paramotor have come a long way. Early wings expanded our safe operating range, but had sluggish handling and horrible inflation. No more. Launch characteristics have improved to the point where it's no longer relevant—like how we no longer worry about a car being "hard to start."

Smaller sizes, lighter fabric, thinner lines, reinforcement rods, and better design have made all paragliders better. If a normal sized, modern glider from a reputable builder is hard to launch, there's probably a problem (see "Troubleshooting Forward Launch Problems" on page 58). Any glider that's difficult to launch stands out, which is good since foot-launching in calm air is one of the toughest challenges we face.

Free flight wings are subtly different. The highest performance comes in the skinniest aspect ratios (Fig 22-16), which are more difficult to launch and manage. They also tend to be "slippery" while kiting—once they start sliding off to the side or yawing, it takes more finesse to corral them back without folding a tip. Most motor pilots don't need that last ounce of efficiency, and even free flyers have flocked to more benign, easier kiting wings.

Bigger sizes are a bit more difficult to inflate mostly because it takes more effort to pull, and the wing has farther to travel on the way up.

Single surface gliders and hybrids (Fig 26-5) inflate super easy but don't glide as well, making it a bit trickier to land softly. They're lightweight and pack tightly, so they're ideal for "Hike & Fly" missions (hiking up mountains and flying down).

Age worsens inflation characteristics due to line shrinkage and increasing porosity—a big reason not to go cheap on a wing. Be very careful buying used.

Fig 26-4 Nylon Rods

Manufacturers are always looking for ways to improve efficiency and behavior. Nylon rods improve airfoils and maintain shape. They are used in the leading edges of both wings pictured above.

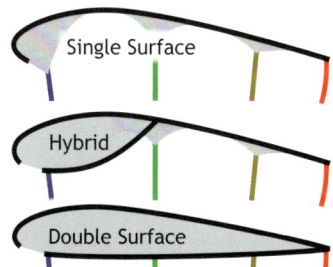

Fig 26-5 Single Surface & Hybrid

Some gliders are made with only a single surface (the top), or a bottom surface partway back (hybrid). Most are double surface.

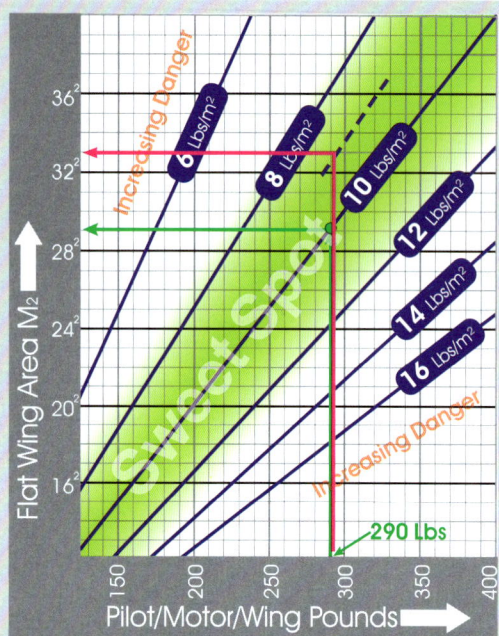

Fig 26-6 Wing Loading: Choosing Size

Wing loading is all-up weight (page 17) divided by flat area. Use this chart to help find an appropriate size glider for your mission.

New pilots should start on school wings (EN-A) in the 8 to 9 pound/m² range while seasoned competition or acro pilots commonly exceed 14. At those higher loadings, roll rate becomes *extremely* high and dive recovery time goes way up.

To find a wing size that puts you in the "sweet spot," start with your all up weight, which includes fueled motor and wing, then go up to the desired angling blue line. Draw left to see what wing size that takes.

Let's say all-up weight is 290 pounds. What's the "sweet spot?" For an experienced pilot (green line) draw up from 290 lbs. to the 10 Lbs/m² line then go left to the size, which is just over 28 m². For a new pilot (magenta line), draw up to the 9 Lbs/m² line then go left. It suggests about 33 m².

Being over Placard

Once a pilot has mastered pendular roll control (50+ flights), going 10% over placarded weight on free flight wings is common. Weights listed for motor wings are frequently already high. They will probably not be certified. Some wings give two weights, one for free flight and higher weights for motoring.

Don't expect any glider placarded over about 10 Lbs/m² to be certified because of aggressive responses to test scenarios. That's telling. Be careful.

Size (Wing Loading)

Wing loading is the weight per flat area (Fig 22-15 on page 227), normally reported as lbs/m² or Kg/m². You could use projected—it's more accurate in some ways—but we standardize on flat area because that's what wing makers typically advertise. At a given clip-in weight, smaller wings are more heavily loaded.

Heavier pilot/motor combinations need bigger wings but size has trended downward thanks to technology and preferences. Wings have a recommended weight range (placard weight) that says a lot about how they're intended to be used.

For example, while a 16 m² race wing may list a max weight of 250 lbs (15 lbs/m² wing loading), a certified standard soaring glider of 25 m² will list closer to 200 lbs (about 8 pounds/m²). That's because soaring pilots need to stay up on thermals and lighter loadings reduce sink rate. Plus, at the higher elevations commonly soared, larger wings are desirable.

Heavier loading (smaller wings) tends to be:

- More dynamic, more responsive to control inputs, have a higher roll rate, and take much longer to level out from a dive.
- Faster, but with a higher sink rate and lower climb rate.
- Easier to inflate but needing a faster run, more takeoff room, and more brake pull to lift off.
- Less likely to enter parachutal stall, and more resistant to collapses, but reacts more violently if either one happens.

Lighter loadings (larger wings) have opposite effects and different risks.

Use Fig 26-6, but rely heavily on your instructor's recommendations since he'll know your skill set and wing model. There's obviously more to it than loading, so resist the urge to go too small. Physics and physiology don't change at the rate of morphing norms.

Reflex

Reflex airfoils allow higher speed with greater safety at those speeds (see also "Reflex Airfoils" on page 227), but with some control caveats. Mostly, it's that pilots must avoid using normal brakes while in reflex mode. Also, it is dangerous to use the speedbar on some reflex models while trimmed slow. Even most free flight wing manuals warn against using *any* brakes while accelerated (on speedbar)—they suggest using weight shift and/or rear riser steering.

Collapses at higher speed will be more dramatic.

Depending on design, speedbar and/or trimmers changes the airfoil shape, taking the wing into reflex mode for higher speed. That's why a wing may have different handling limitations in different configurations. For example, if letting the trimmers out only decreases the wing's angle of incidence (no airfoil shape change), it may not prohibit using brakes. Whereas on speedbar it may go into reflex mode which means don't use brakes. That's why it's so important to follow the manual.

The higher speed range is why essentially all pylon racing and cross country motor wings are reflex.

Fuel burns while reflexed are higher but, since you're going faster, they will be offset somewhat by the higher speed. Fuel burn per mile will only be a bit higher and, in much headwind, could be less. So if you're going cross country, especially with a headwind, reflex wings shine.

Steering Options

Steering choices abound. 2D steering was developed for pylon-type racing, where hard maneuvering and speedbar use require **not** pulling the main trailing edge while accelerated. It could result in *rapid* control loss. Pushing brake toggles outward deflects the main (inner) trailing edge for lift, but without drag from the tips. Methods like tip toggles (Fig 26-12) may be better for cross country.

Standard brake setup (Fig 12-34 on page 128) is fine for most pilots, even those who do acro. More complicated setups require more knowledgeable tweaking—enlist an instructor or experienced pilot who knows the wing. Changing brakes or any line configuration **can render a glider dangerous to fly**.

Tip or rear riser steering is preferred for wings that warn against using main brakes while accelerated. One unique solution, by world Champion Alex Mateos, is to put a hand (toggle) *up* for tip steering in that direction. That way, while flying fully accelerated, he never pulls *down*, since that engages the inner brakes and could cause a collapse. He gets how humans work.

Stabilo steering (Fig 26-13) is *far* less effective but also incurs less drag.

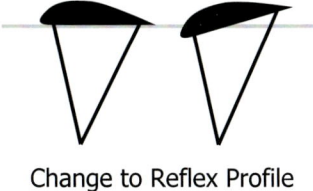

Reduced Angle of Incidence

Change to Reflex Profile

Fig 26-7 Two Ways To Speed Up

Speedbar and/or trimmers employ a combination of these methods to make a glider go faster. See also Angle of Incidence in Fig 22-6.

2D STEERING & Other Options

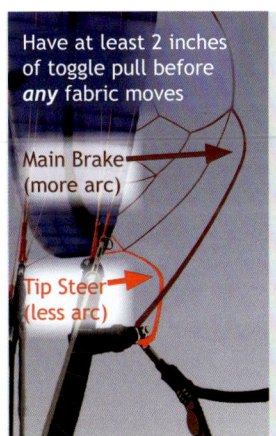

Have at least 2 inches of toggle pull before *any* fabric moves

Main Brake (more arc)

Tip Steer (less arc)

Fig 26-8 Setup 2D Steering

Look at #1 below. See how the brake is above the pulley? That's a conceptual tool because, in flight the lines will all arc back, forcing the toggle to its pulley like at left. Now the tip steer line is tighter (less arc), so pulling the toggle pulls tip fabric *before* main brake. That's what we want.

This can also be achieved with less line drag by modifying upper line geometry. You would lose the ability to activate *only* the center brakes like #4 below.

Pulling only the tips (first part of pull) adds mostly drag.

Fig 26-9 Tip Toggle in Toggle

This method uses two toggles, one inside the other, where the smaller one controls only the tip and the larger one controls both.

A drawback is that this system does not allow pulling ONLY the center (main) brakes. An advantage is less confusion about when main brakes are being pulled.

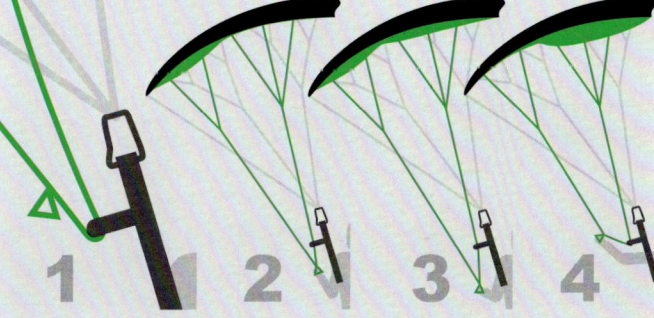

Fig 26-10 Standard Brakes

Most wings use some variation of this.

Fig 26-11 Basic 2D Steering

This is conceptual to help understand: With no input, the brake toggle (1) rides slightly above its pulley so (2) the first few inches of pull is all tip—no main brakes. 3) More pull engages tips *and* main brakes. 4) Pulling directly outward engages only main (inner) brakes.

Fig 26-12 Tip Steering

A separate toggle and line pulls the outer tip.

Fig 26-13 Stabilo Steering

A separate line pulls the Stabilo line.

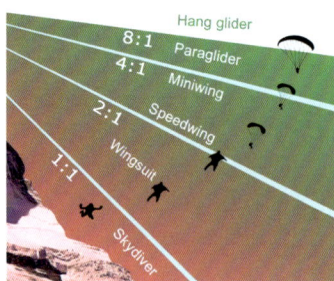

Fig 26-14 Relative Glide Ratio
High end sailplanes glide 50 feet for every foot dropped (50:1). The glide ratio for other pursuits suggest an inverse relationship to adrenalin rush.

Fig 26-15 Center Cell Visibility
It's generally helpful to see the wing's center cell easily—mostly to know that you're centered on it before inflation. It also helps those pilots who look up after inflation to make sure the wing is centered although looking left or right at the tips works better in most cases.

Glide and Sink Rate

The lower the sink rate, the less power you'll need to stay up. The higher (better) the glide ratio, the farther you'll go on a gallon of gas. And because the speed range is so small, wings with a low sink rate will likely also have a good glide ratio.

Overall, wings with a better glide ratio will be easier to land because you'll have more flare authority after the initial pull for landing.

Stability as Collapse Resistance

Stability is frequently used to mean collapse resistance instead of its more technical meaning of resistance to upset ("Static and Dynamic Stability" on page 223).

Beginner-type certified wings are generally more passively collapse resistant and recover more predictably than advanced wings. Of course they must be flown within their placarded weight range to realize that benefit. For new students with uncertain responses, these wings are dramatically safer during training.

Beginner gliders tend to have fewer cells which helps expedite recovery from upsets, and longer brake travel to reduce the likelihood of pilot-induced oscillation.

A high performance glider in experienced hands is no different in collapse resistance than a beginner glider. That's because the pilot will automatically dampen the surges and twists that precede and contribute to most collapses. The higher performance glider is, however, more likely to suffer a complication on recovery.

Handling

Responsiveness to brake input is the foundation of handling. Being heavily loaded on a wing makes it more responsive, along with some other factors.

1. **Brakes**. Toggles should be in a comfortable position and start moving the trailing edge within 3 inches of pull. Besides responsiveness, it ensures full brake travel for landing. When brake application crumples the tip slightly, it confers more responsiveness and dive tendency, which some pilots like.

2. **Linearity**. The response should be incremental throughout the range with no significant dead spots or unexpected reactions. A little pull does a little and more pull does proportionally more.

3. **Dive**. All wings descend faster when banked, but smaller sizes and shorter lines tend to enter a dive easier than others. Nimble handling can be both a fatal flaw for the ham-fisted, or a joy to the master. All wings can "turn flat," but some models require more flying finesse to do so (see "Turns" on page 163 for more about coordinated turns).

4. **Heaviness** is how hard you must pull to achieve the result. Tandem wings flown with two people are going to feel heavy. Small wings will tend to have higher brake pressure but are more responsive, reacting quickly to even short pulls.

Some wings are "twitchy," meaning they move around a lot in turbulence. If you're into active flying this may be okay. These tend to also have sporty handling.

Speed

Advertised speed will be given at the maximum listed weight which is why certified gliders have lower maximum weights—they must pass certification at that weight. Generally speaking, given the same size, highly reflexed wings will be 20% faster.

For wings of about the same efficiency, faster models burn more fuel per *hour* than slow ones, but only a little bit more per *mile*. You'll have less endurance but almost the same range. Of course, it does no good if you're circling around waiting for slower friends.

Speedbar

A speedbar is nearly universal on both motoring and free flight wings even though motor pilots rarely hook it up. Free flight wings need a speed system to cut through sink faster and fight strong winds.

Different arrangements trade foot pressure for travel. Since speedbars pull down the highly loaded A's and B's, most setups use pulleys for mechanical advantage. Having only one pulley means the pilot must push hard for a short distance while having *two* pulleys means more travel but less foot pressure.

Trimmers

You'll want trimmers. Fortunately, most motor wings have them. Trimmer range for the more advanced reflex wings is huge, reflecting their larger speed range. See Fig 26-21.

Speedbar/Trimmer Interconnect (STI)

A feature of some pylon racing wings is the Speedbar/Trimmer Interconnect (STI)—see Fig 26-19. It uses a pulley arrangement so pushing the speedbar also lets the trimmers out (up) at the same time. That puts the glider's entire speed range at your feet.

It's also called a PK System after its innovator Paap Kolar, but manufacturers have their own name.

Mini & Speedflying Wings

Miniwings (Fig 26-16) are essentially smaller versions of regular paragliders whereas Speedflying wings are designed to drop quickly. Pilots relish the ability to follow steep terrain, pulling brake to roll, or fly away at will, sometimes on skis. They especially appreciate being able to stick to the snow, then when ready, pull some brakes and pop up.

For motoring, though, the smaller sizes go from a poor glide to a controlled fall (Fig 26-14), requiring lots of thrust just to fly level, leaving that much less for climb and play.

As usual, a *lot* depends on size (wing loading). Given enough wind and/or big enough size, they *can* be foot-launched, even soared if it's blowing up a decent hill.

One manufacturer wisely recognizes the effect of wing loading in their selection chart (Fig 26-17). It shows that even their "beginner" speedwing, when flown at high weights, should be flown by advanced pilots. That could be applied to every maker's catalog. The regular wing of a lightweight pilot is the miniwing of a heavyweight.

These wings roll more than turn. In fact, *turn* rate is like all other aircraft: more speed at the same bank angle means a lower turn rate. Roll rate makes it seem otherwise.

Handling gets *extremely* responsive as wing area decreases—a little brake does a lot. Get askew of this control input and you'll be upside down before you know it. Experienced pilots do rolls at 50 feet while careening down mountains at 50 mph. Some get maimed or die trying—build up to this slowly!

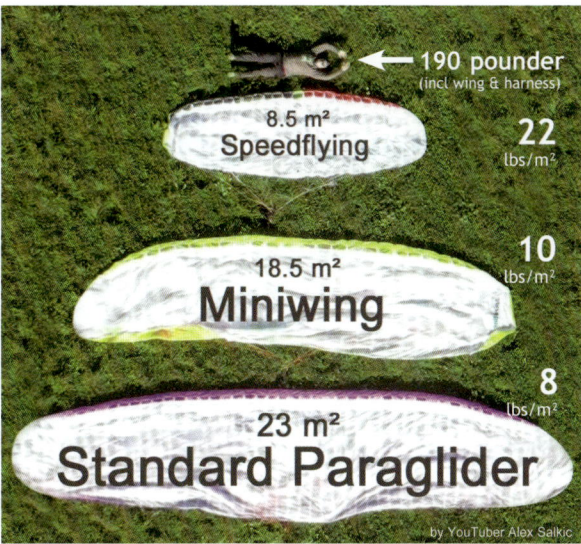

Fig 26-16 Miniwing Comparison

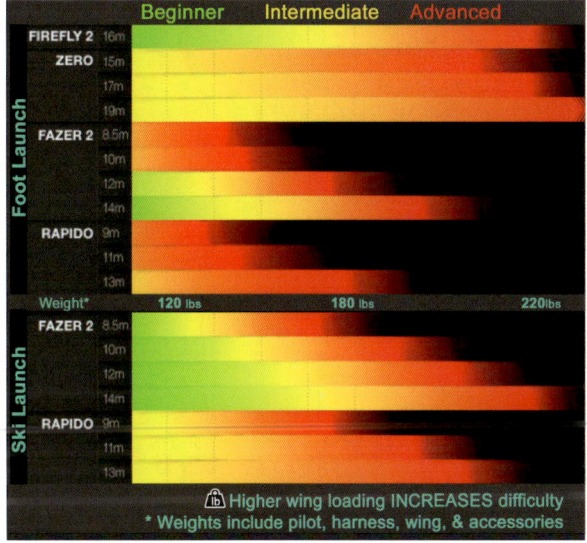

Fig 26-17 Classes of Speedwing

Calling a speedwing a "beginner" glider is like calling a jet trainer a "beginner" airplane. But everyone has to start somewhere. In this use, a "beginner" is an experienced pilot transitioning to speedwings.

The reference to ski launch suggests that those models are too fast to be safely foot-launched. Looking at those sizes, we can't be surprised.

There are *many* variations with overlaps in size, purpose and efficiency. This is just a good starting point.

Fig 26-18 Wing Certification

Above is a chart that shows the relationship between various certifying systems.

The placard above is from an **EN B** category—good for pilots who have gained some experience.

Beginners should start on EN A wings. Some manufacturers have the placards filled in with magic markers at the factory, an unfortunate practice that can be hard to read after a few years.

Some modern "beginner" wings have the same performance as competition wings from 10 years ago but with greater safety.

*DGAC certification is basic self-certification by manufacturers that requires no independent testing.

Certification & Trimmers

It's harder to get a trimmer-equipped glider certified since it must be tested at all its settings. The fast settings don't usually pass.

Those that do get certified typically have a small trimmer range, or the trimmers are locked to slow/neutral. After purchase, the user can then do some simple task to unlock the wing's full speed range. That, of course, takes it out of certification. This is more likely on highly reflexed wings.

Certification

Certification by a recognized body suggests how a wing will behave in certain defined circumstances. Most commonly, flight and strength tests are done to European Normalization (EN) standards that assign a letter, A through D, where A has the most passive safety and D the least. You'll also see DHV and other certifications that use numbers, where 1 has the most passive safety and 3 the least.

Full testing is not done with a motor, but bad behaviors in free flight will be at least as bad with a motor, so it's still quite valuable. That's why new pilots especially should stick with certified wings.

Reflex gliders are usually only tested with trimmers closed (slow) because these gliders concentrate on collapse resistance in their accelerated condition. Small wings (higher wing loadings) are almost never certified because they are too dynamic during deflations. Certification testing is expensive, so it's common that only the popular glider sizes get tested.

A certified wing will have a label stating, among other things, its certification level, make, model, size, and weight range, usually in kilograms. No label means no certification. Avoid uncertified gliders unless you're an expert who can verify their behavior. Labels are usually located near the wingtip or inside a center cell.

Testing involves putting the glider into various maneuvers and collapses, then letting it recover on its own with no pilot input. Time to recover is measured, and fast recoveries get better grades. Those that take a long time, or require pilot input to recover, get lower grades (a higher letter).

Wings with trimmers have special challenges as described in the left sidebar.

Certifications

EN A (DHV 1, AFNOR Standard) gliders are good for new pilots. They're less likely to collapse and generally recover quickly on their own. You can still get into trouble, of course, but it takes more turbulence or pilot buffoonery to do so.

EN B (DHV 1-2, AFNOR Standard) gliders still have good passive safety and are considered suitable for students although they won't recover from collapses quite as quickly as EN A's.

EN C (DHV 2, AFNOR Performance) gliders have moderate passive safety but could be a handful during turbulence, requiring high level active flying skills.

EN D (DHV 3, AFNOR Competition) gliders are for experts who are risk tolerant. They are mostly flown by competition soaring pilots wanting to maximize performance at some increased risk.

Kiting-Only Wing

There are many good deals for new pilots wanting a kiting-only wing. Besides low cost, it spares your main wing all that UV exposure. Older, out-of-date models are good but you'll work harder at inflation. And resist the temptation to fly them.

Smaller, low aspect ratio wings are better because they'll take less effort to kite and can safely handle a higher wind range. Seek ones with easy inflation (they get harder with age) that's not too beat up—you don't want it coming apart if you get lifted in a gust.

Some companies sell wings intended for kiting only which work great but are pricey. They're especially handy in higher winds by virtue of being as small as half the size of a regular wing.

Advanced Risers

Advanced risers like these are more likely found on higher performance models, usually for competition. *Study* the manual—it can be confusing. Hopefully seeing them here in their different configurations will help make sense of all the lines and pulleys.

As covered in Chapter 2, risers set the airfoil shape, tilt (angle of incidence), and anchor the controls. There may be several types of steering available, and different ways of hooking things up.

Fig 26-20 shows some configurations and control combinations on a competition wing. Envision an airfoil attached to their quick links.

Speedbar/Trimmer interconnect (STI) is used on the risers below but not on the next page. It puts full speed control at your feet.

Different manufacturers have different names. Stabilo, for example, may be called "stabilizer." In the case of the glider below, they call it a torque compensator because you can set it and leave it. Of course it also works for slow turning

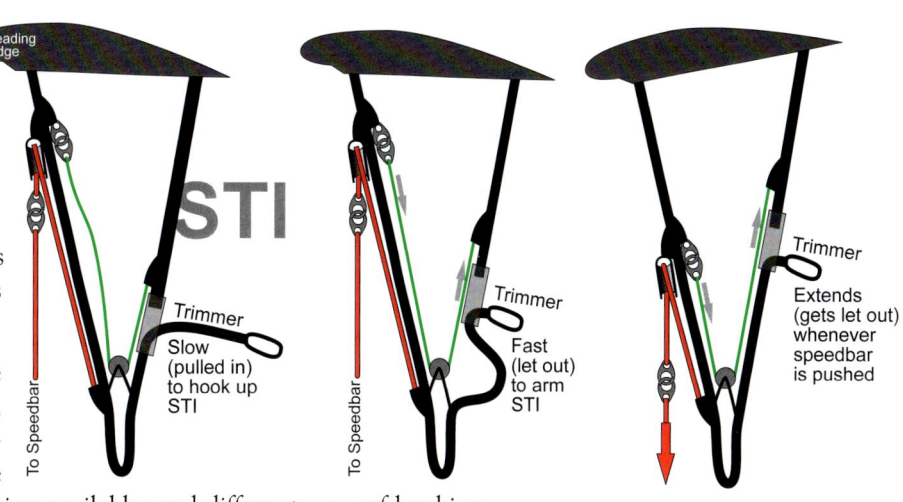

Fig 26-19 Speedbar/Trimmer Interconnect (STI)

When hooked up, the front and back of the glider teeter-totter across the STI pulley. Since there's more load on the A's, with no speedbar pushed, the leading edge is forced up while the trailing edge stays down.

Speedbar action pulls the front down, allowing the rear to go up, and on some models, may change the airfoil shape.

Fig 26-20 Advanced Risers with STI

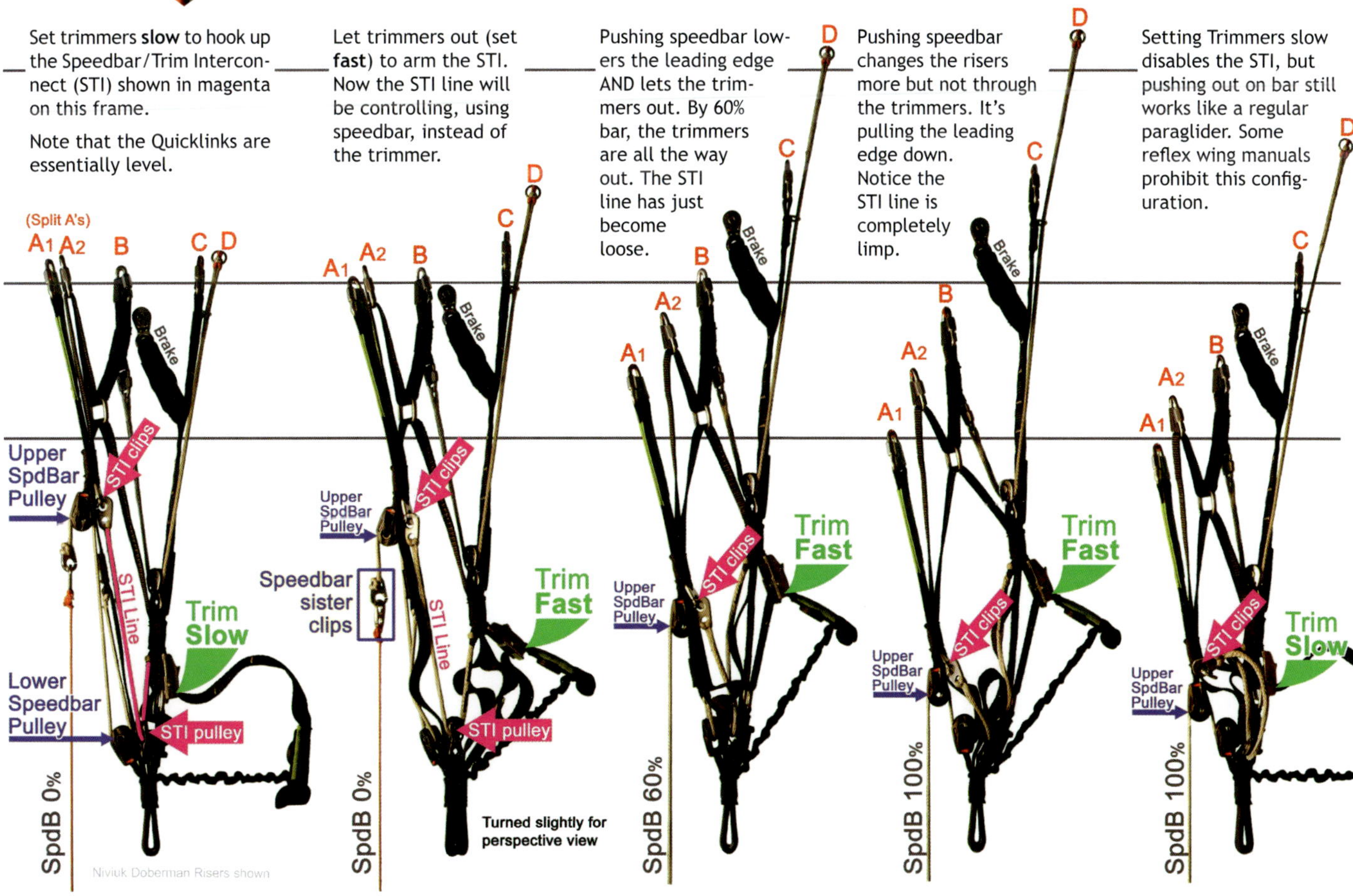

Set trimmers **slow** to hook up the Speedbar/Trim Interconnect (STI) shown in magenta on this frame.

Note that the Quicklinks are essentially level.

Let trimmers out (set **fast**) to arm the STI. Now the STI line will be controlling, using speedbar, instead of the trimmer.

Pushing speedbar lowers the leading edge AND lets the trimmers out. By 60% bar, the trimmers are all the way out. The STI line has just become loose.

Pushing speedbar changes the risers more but not through the trimmers. It's pulling the leading edge down. Notice the STI line is completely limp.

Setting Trimmers slow disables the STI, but pushing out on bar still works like a regular paraglider. Some reflex wing manuals prohibit this configuration.

In Fig 26-21 tip steering lines are in purple, stabilo steering is in blue and main brakes are in red. This glider has multiple pulley positions to accommodate either high or low hook-in machines. Most wings have some option to accomplish that.

The small line diagram (Fig 26-22) shows where on the wing each control goes. Stabilo steering has the least effect on the reflex profile, tip steering has *some* effect in the outer portion, and brakes have a lot. Designers use various means to adjust how much of each control does what. Some wings require ONLY using Stabilo Steering (they'll call it something else) when fully reflexed. Always check the manual.

Some free flight gliders have small toggles on the rear risers meant for steering while accelerated since they don't usually have separate tip-steering lines.

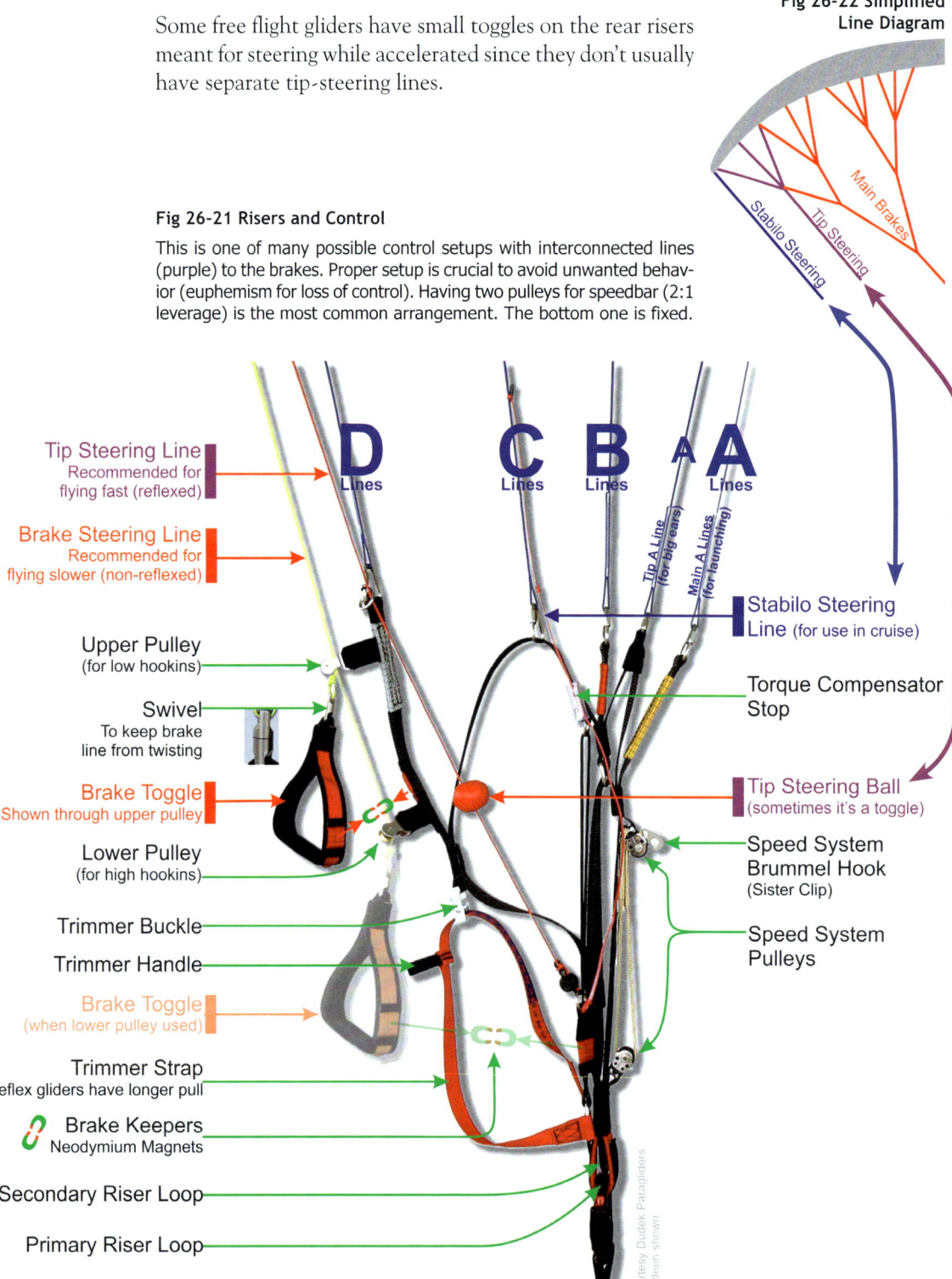

Fig 26-22 Simplified Line Diagram

Fig 26-21 Risers and Control

This is one of many possible control setups with interconnected lines (purple) to the brakes. Proper setup is crucial to avoid unwanted behavior (euphemism for loss of control). Having two pulleys for speedbar (2:1 leverage) is the most common arrangement. The bottom one is fixed.

The Motor Unit

CHAPTER 27

The perfect machine for one person may be another's nightmare. It depends on desires and dimensions. Too big is just as bad as too small. And there is no "best" machine; they are all compromises. Anyone telling you otherwise is selling snake oil.

Trying new gear can be risky, especially for new pilots. Check out "Testing New Gear" on page 192 for tips on minimizing that risk.

Some relics *should* be relegated to leaf blowing, having long been supplanted by better designs, but they're still shamelessly hawked to unwitting marks. Always dig beyond the slick brochures, websites, and loud, fast talkers.

For learning, **don't** buy a powerful machine thinking you'll be taking passengers up. It's *far* more demanding than experienced pilots make it look, and in most countries requires far more certification. Foot-launched tandem requires that you manage a big enough motor and wing for two people. Carts are *much* easier and safer for tandem, but check legalities.

Be suspicious of advertised weights. Some companies don't include the weight of the prop, harness, or other necessary parts and may not say so. It's true that different harnesses and props can be used, but find out how much it *all* weighs.

These considerations are for choosing your *second* motor. Work with your instructor for your first machine unless you have very specific circumstances (like you inherited your mother's motor, for example).

Many design decisions go into each paramotor. This unit uses vanes to redirect some airflow to reduce torque at the source. Plus, the airfoil-shaped supports are less draggy than tubes so thrust loss is likely negligible.

Trade-offs are made, and clever solutions occasionally solve two problems at once, but most improvements come in small increments.

Chapter 6 explores wheeled options and their considerations.

Weight

For foot-launching, lightweight rocks—favor the lighter side of "Thrust vs Weight" on page 270. Electric-start doesn't always add much weight, even with a starter and battery. Thankfully battery weight has dropped a lot for the same energy.

How the machine hangs is another major concern. If it hangs low and cannot

Fig 27-1 Thrust vs Weight

These charts below help determine desirable power and motor weight for your particular situation. "All up" fueled, flyable paramotor and wing.

A powerful motor for its weight has a good "power to weight ratio."

Trike attachments typically add between 30 and 75 pounds. Use dry weight (no fuel) for comparison.

These weights are more for newer pilots where excessive thrust makes a crash more likely.

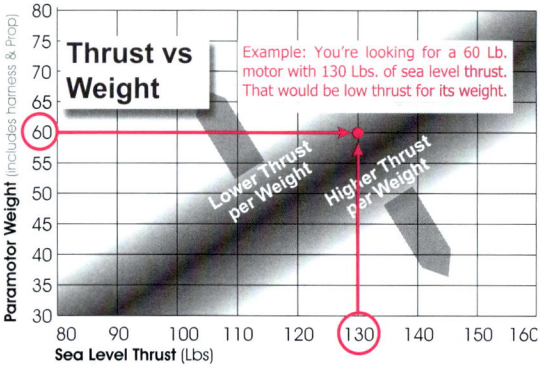

Fig 27-2 Thrust vs Altitude

Thrust decreases with density altitude ("Density Altitude" on page 78). This is a general guide on how much.

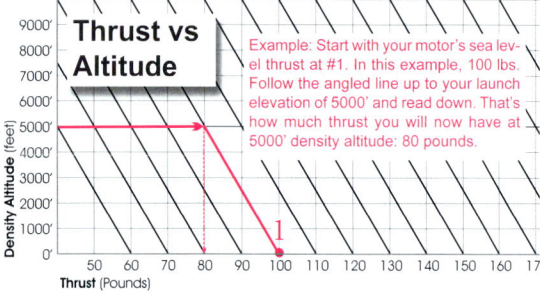

Fig 27-3 Appropriate Thrust

You *can* have too much thrust as well as not enough. This guide intended for new pilots.

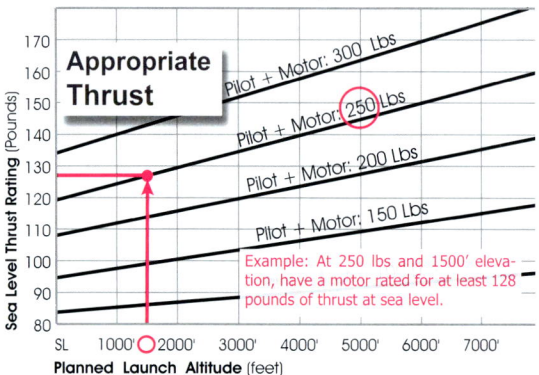

be raised on your back, or if the weight is far from your back, even a lightweight unit can feel awkward and heavy. If wearing the machine strains muscles after only a few minutes, it won't be comfortable on the ground.

Purveyors of heavy, awkward gear will argue that you'll only feel it briefly before launching. That might be true for experienced pilots, but for others it can be miserable. Plus, some pilots enjoy landing, messing around on the ground, and taking off just for the fun of it.

Don't get an underpowered unit, though, in search of lightness. That can be equally frustrating.

Comfort

There are many elements to comfort, both on the ground and in flight. On some physiques, bars or straps may get in the way of either visibility or movement—you have to try it, at least in a simulator. The motor should balance comfortably without pulling you back excessively or interfere with running. Its seatboard should slide all the way back against the frame.

Try to assess comfort only after adjustment by an instructor or another pilot who knows the machine. A motor can be utterly underwhelming until it's adjusted properly.

Can you stand up with it? Do you have to sit on the ground? Does that bother you? Talk to someone—preferably the dealer—about how it's intended to be used. Some motors can seem impossible to maneuver comfortably on the ground until you know the "trick." Very, very few machines are completely horrible.

Thrust

Generally, more thrust is better, up to a point. Beyond that point, too much thrust is dangerous. Thrust helps 1) power through the inflation during a *power forward*, 2) makes launch runs shorter, 3) improves climb, and 4) allows flight at higher elevations. The downside is increased throttle sensitivity and torque, especially for lighter pilots unless they are experienced. A lightweight pilot on a powerful machine can twist all the way around unless the machine is *really* well adjusted.

Fig 27-2 and Fig 27-3 give a good indication of thrust required. All machines will advertise their sea-level thrust. Try to use numbers culled from published tests at fly-ins or by independent organizations. Balance them with advertised numbers, and if there's a big discrepancy, ask why. Some sellers will unscrupulously thrust test without a harness, for example.

Power decreases with height. If you'll be flying in Denver, the sea-level thrust rating must be greater as shown in Fig 27-2.

On carts, more power is almost always better. Add 10%. If you won't be foot-launching, the weight doesn't matter so much. This is why 4-strokes, which are heavier, work pretty well on wheeled machines.

Quality

Like anything built by humans, some machines are better made than others; most call it the "fit and finish."

Quality inhabits many forms. If things don't fit together, that's a sign of sloppy production. Well-made machines will interchange parts easily—the cage frame from one will fit on other like-models as long as neither has been damaged. It is rare, however, that a frame has never been "tweaked" from transportation bumps, being dropped, or small falls.

Welds should look solid and be built to last without being overly heavy. Too much use of wire ties and hardware-store parts may be a bad sign; however field repairability is important. Hardware store parts are OK in places where they're not critical to structural integrity.

Powerplant Considerations

We want smooth, quiet power that's easy to start, has a linear throttle response, sips cheap gas without pollution, and weighs nothing. As long as we're dreaming, it should be maintenance-free, cheap, and provide beer on tap. Or how about electric power? Three hours of flight time on a 10 minute charge would be about right. Waking up, now, we find ourselves in the reality of two-strokeville and its *many* trade-offs.

Electric Start vs Pull Start

Pushing a button to start is nice, and doing so while wearing the motor lessens your exposure to starting injuries, but there are trade-offs.

Most models come with either electric or manual start but not both. Only a few can charge the batteries in flight, and even those will probably require some charging at home to be ready.

Flash starters are manual mechanisms with a second spring that winds up as you pull. It releases its energy at the end of the pull, spinning the motor for start. These are more common on larger, clutched motors since there is no propeller to act as a flywheel, like on non-clutched models. They tend to be needy of maintenance, especially earlier editions that traded away a bit too much strength for weight.

Electric Start Pros: It's convenient, reduces some propeller/body contact risks associated with having to pull start, and enables easy in-flight restarts for soaring or aborting a landing (going around).

Electric Start Cons: Having only electric start means more ways to be grounded. Namely, the battery and starter have to work. They're heavier than pull-starters by a few pounds, cost a bit more, and will likely require extra maintenance—not that pull-starts are maintenance free. There is a *small* increased fire risk, especially with "Lipo" batteries. They also add the risk of injury from an accidental start.

Number of Cylinders & Displacement

Nearly all PPG motors have only one cylinder to minimize weight. Twin or multi-cylinder motors may be smoother but will usually weigh more and offer more opportunity for mechanical problems.

Like motorcycles, displacement is measured in cubic centimeters; it ranges from 80cc up to about 312cc. Beyond that, the human frame starts requiring more maintenance (think "back strain"). Larger sizes typically power tandem units, heavy pilots, trikes, or those flying from high elevations.

Reliability

"Why can't my paramotor be as reliable as my car?" you ask. Good question given how little trouble most cars have in spite of heavier use.

There are three big reasons: weight, production quantity, and vibration.

1. We have to carry it on our back so we demand light weight for the push provided. Parts are built out of lighter material with narrowed strength margins.

2. Even the best-selling motors see fewer than a thousand units per year. They're all essentially hand-built with minimal, if any, automation. That's not enough volume to justify mass production facilities.

3. Even the best balanced motor is imparting a powerful torque pulse with every power stroke. There's no way to eliminate its weld-rending vibration.

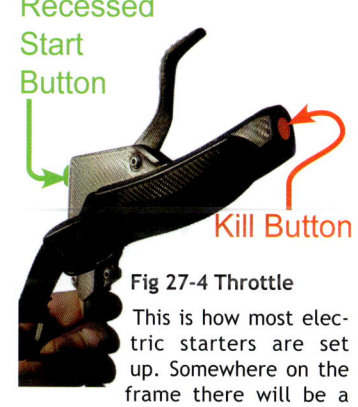

Fig 27-4 Throttle

This is how most electric starters are set up. Somewhere on the frame there will be a master switch to enable the starter system. It usually also serves as an alternative kill switch: turning off the master also shuts off the motor. This arrangement reduces the chance for an accidental start by requiring two actions.

Another approach is using the same button on top for starting and stopping the motor. That makes it quick to restart in the air but easier to start accidentally on the ground.

Longevity & Reliability

Longevity is a measure of overall robustness. How many hours, how many cycles (start, fly, shut off) can you expect of the motor with no problems? It is notoriously difficult to predict.

For one thing, it depends on how hard the motor is run. A small motor, run constantly near its peak, will wear out quicker than a larger one minimally tasked. Aviation is rife with examples of this; motors that run near their peak design limit have shorter recommended times between overhaul (TBO) than derated motors (max power artificially reduced).

Another aspect of longevity is support for the brand after purchase. Obscure motors may be fine as long as everything works, but finding replacement parts could be challenging. It's handy to have a common motor that enjoys good support.

Efficiency

Just like cars, small motors are more miserly. 80cc machines have won competitions where efficiency matters. You don't have to carry as much gas, or you can fly longer on the gas you have.

Efficiency is how much fuel is burned per hour, *at a given thrust*. For example, a big motor may burn 0.7 gallons per hour (gph) to generate 50 pounds of thrust while a small motor may only burn 0.5 gph to generate that same thrust.

Efficiency also depends on the fuel/air mixture: running leaner (less fuel per volume of air) will burn less fuel at the expense of higher temperatures. So any comparison should be done with the same relative fuel/air mixture.

Charging Ability

Some motors output a current for charging batteries. That's nice if you plan to run other 12 volt accessories, such as an aircraft strobe or LED's, but only connect those devices to the battery, *not* the motor's output.

Air Cooled vs Water Cooled

The vast majority of motors are air cooled—it's simpler, lighter, and there's no water to leak out. A very few water-cooled models use convection transfer to eliminate the water pump, but that doesn't cool as well as its more complicated pump-driven brethren. Not surprisingly, pumps are the norm on those very few units using water cooling.

Water Cooling: The ability of a motor to produce power is tied significantly to its ability to dissipate heat, and water does that well. The improved cooling can be used to either increase power or increase longevity by letting it run cooler. That comes at some cost in complexity, weight, and cost.

Air Cooling: Some air-cooled models, especially the smaller ones (80-125cc), use a fan to improve cooling efficiency. If the fan breaks, it's just like losing water: the motor is headed for a meltdown.

Two-Stroke vs Four-Stroke

Simple 2-stroke motors power the bulk of our fleet. They are popular for the same reasons they are used on weed-eaters and such: weight (see Chapter 12 & 23).

Four-stroke motors are quieter, cleaner burning, and more efficient than their two-stroke counterparts. You don't have to mix oil since the motor carries its oil inside, just like a car. But they're heavier for the power and more complicated.

On average, a four-stroke motor will burn between 10 and 15% less fuel than

Fig 27-5 Small Engines (1)
Small engines are lightweight, more efficient, and generally less expensive. They nearly all have clutches. Many moderately bigger machines have clutches, too, and will have either electric or flash starters.

Fig 27-6 Water Cooling (2)
Better cooling can be spent on increasing horsepower or longevity. Note the "or." Watch the temperature, though, a water system failure would soon cook it.

Fig 27-7 Shrouded Cylinder (3)
This optional shroud convinces more air to pass through the motor's cooling fins.

Fig 27-8 Electric Choices
Electric motors are increasingly available for motoring and are especially popular for soaring pilots who just want to get up to altitude. Folding props like this one reduces drag for better glide but the cage still extracts quite a toll. See "Electric Propulsion" on page 243 for more on electrics.

Fig 27-9 Launch Ease
A motor that makes launching hard will cause frustration. For example, lines must slide smoothly up the cage during forward launches. Lightweight cages may not tolerate power forwards with big wings and/or heavy pilots. Choose what makes you look good using *your* preferred techniques.

a two-stroke at the same thrust. The two-stroke is consuming fairly expensive oil with each gallon of gas burned, while the four-stroke uses almost no oil. The four-stroke typically weighs about 15-25% more than a comparably powerful two-stroke but efficiency means you'll require less fuel weight be carried.

Inexpensive four-stroke engines have been successfully employed on carts. They have proven reliable and affordable. Since there is no intent that they be foot-launchable, the carts swing huge props, thus getting plenty of thrust from their lower horsepower.

Ease of Launch

The paramotor design can have a significant effect on how easy it is to launch. A number of factors come into play with varying importance based on your location and experience.

All other things being equal, more thrust will make it easier to launch, up to a point. More thrust also means more torque, which must be managed. Excessive torque effects probably stem from poor adjustments (see Chapter 12), but when actual thrust exceeds about 70% of the pilot's body weight, torque effects become more problematic. Of course the pilot can learn to not use all the power which would eliminate this risk, but that takes practice.

Highly flexible cages can make launch somewhat more difficult if they don't allow power during inflation. You must get the wing nearly overhead by yourself before throttling up. If you don't use power that way, no worry, but for those who do, cage strength is more relevant.

Hang style, covered shortly, is the next element. A motor that sits higher on your back will be easier to manage and be less fatiguing while walking around. Motors that hang low tend to pull your shoulders back.

Fig 27-10 Fuel Tank Styles

Typical - by far the most common arrangement.

Bladder - Lightweight, transportable, no need to vent.

Above Engine - Easy fill, balanced on back, away from prop.

Integral To Frame - Minimal extra weight, stylish.

Metal - Doesn't melt, no discoloring or degrading.

Custom Formed - Max capacity, keeps **fuel away from** prop.

Ease of Maintenance

Complicated or proprietary shapes and pieces make repairs more difficult and expensive. Having pieces that can be readily replaced is handy, too, especially when you're out in the field.

The more parts that can be replaced, or repaired by readily available hardware, or easily stored spares, the better. Consider what "dinging" the cage will entail since it happens occasionally during flying and handling.

Regardless of what shady sellers will hype, any motor will likely be damaged in a fall or even minor crash. So be leery when hearing "you won't need parts because my brand holds up so much better." Nonsense.

Fuel Storage

Almost all fuel tanks (Fig 27-10) are made of a translucent white plastic (polyethylene) that allows easy viewing of the fuel level and easy removal. Aluminum tanks are expensive, require a "sight tube" or quantity indicator, and are more difficult to repair, but they don't melt or discolor.

Fire risk is not affected by whether fuel is stored above or below the engine. In fact, the biggest risk for fire is a prop slicing into the tank from a fall on launch. Thankfully, even though that happens periodically, fire is still rare.

Ideally, fuel tanks will: 1) keep fuel away from the prop and exhaust parts, 2) be forward for balance, 3) hold a lot, 4) be easy to fill, and 5) be lightweight.

Propeller Size and Style

In almost all cases, the largest prop will produce the most thrust with the least noise. But that might not be the most convenient for transport because it requires a proportionally larger cage. For more on prop selection see "Propeller & Reduction Drives" on page 236

A three- or four-bladed prop is normally less efficient than a larger diameter two-blade prop. If the blades themselves are more efficiently shaped they will make more thrust. Carbon fiber or adjustable pitch props will be more expensive but tend to be more consistent. Powerful motors sometimes employ more blades to push out good thrust without needing a mammoth cage.

A few machines can accommodate various prop sizes just by purchasing different cage pieces and reduction drives. You buy the machine with a small prop and cage—maybe for transport—then add the larger one when more thrust is needed.

Fig 27-11 Low Hook-In

This style (Fig 2-21) of low hook-in keeps thrust below the pivot point which allows good weight shift while minimizing fore-aft tilting. It's the most common geometry found on paramotors.

Attachment Points & Spreader Bars

Spreader systems were introduced in "Thrust Spreader" on page 19. To refresh, high hook-in means the attachment point pivots *above* the collar bone. Low hook-in is below, as seen *in flight*.

Pivot point is what the wing and motor moves around (Fig 27-12 and Fig 27-15). Sometimes there is an extension piece that goes up to the carabiner attachment. If that piece can move, then ***it*** is the pivot point.

Low Hook-in

Most motors with low attachments are trying to mimic a free flight harness to some extent, offering closer access to the risers and better weight shift. Soaring (free flight) wings typically have longer risers that work better on these setups.

Motors with the lowest hang points and pivoting bars are able to achieve significant weight shift—allowing differential riser motion of 6-8 inches. Pilots use various combinations of thigh movement, machine tilt, and hip action. See "Brakes—The Feel Position" on page 159 and "Weight Shift Turns" on page 180.

Low attachment machines *without* pivoting bars (Fig 2-25) will have less weight shift, probably trying to minimize the looser feeling it invokes.

High Hook-in

Weight shift, if offered, is usually via pivoting distance bars or a sliding strap arrangement. Pivoting arm units have the front harness segments attached to a free-moving pivot arm. Sliding strap types allow the front harness segments to slide through a cutout as the pilot moves a leg up or down in the seat—it doesn't move quite as freely as a pivot bar, but gives similar weight shift.

Overhead bars dampen out uneven pull from the risers as each side of the wing flies through slightly different air currents. On weight shift units, this uneven pull is transferred to the seat board, which the pilot feels.

If the ground handling straps on pivoting J-bar machines are not properly adjusted, the J-bars can ride uncomfortably on the pilot's shoulders.

The term *mid-attachment* refers to high hang point machines where the carabiner attaches directly to harness webbing. Underarm bars of some sort will be located beneath the pilot's arms. They're called "mid" because of how they look on the ground when hooking up but, in flight, their geometry is that of a high hook-in.

The lowest high hook-in units can be nearly as low as the highest low hook-ins but human geometry means it would likely be uncomfortable.

Hybrid

At least one model (Fig 27-14) starts with high hook-in points during launch, then mechanically moves them down and forward as the pilot pushes out on a bar. It gives a laid-back posture in flight to more closely approximate free flight and improves weight shift at the expense of an increase in complexity and weight.

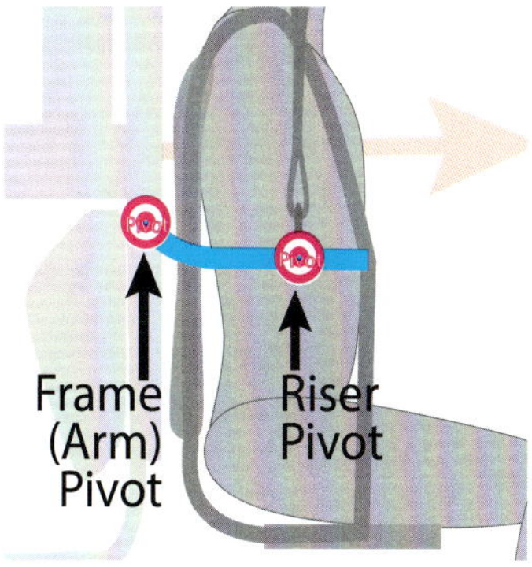

Fig 27-12 Arm & Riser Pivot Points

Swing-arm machines have an *Arm Pivot*, where the arm moves up and down, mostly in response to weight shift, and a Riser Pivot where most of the fore/aft tilt happens around.

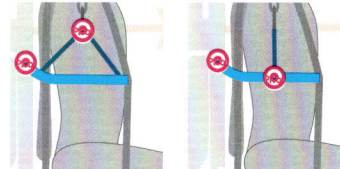

Fig 27-13 Other Pivot Points

Notice the riser pivot is *not* the carabiner's base.

Fig 27-14 Hybrid (1)

Pilot can go from high hook-in during launch to low inflight. This out-of-production model is rare.

Fig 27-15 Weight Shift Pivot (2)

Weight shift happens around this point on most machines with articulating arms.

Fig 27-16 Motor/Riser Pivot (3)

If adding power causes fore/aft tilt, or if the wing moves fore/aft, it will happen around this point.

Gooseneck swing arms raise the pivot point enough to be on the thrust line instead of below, reducing fore-aft tilt during power changes.

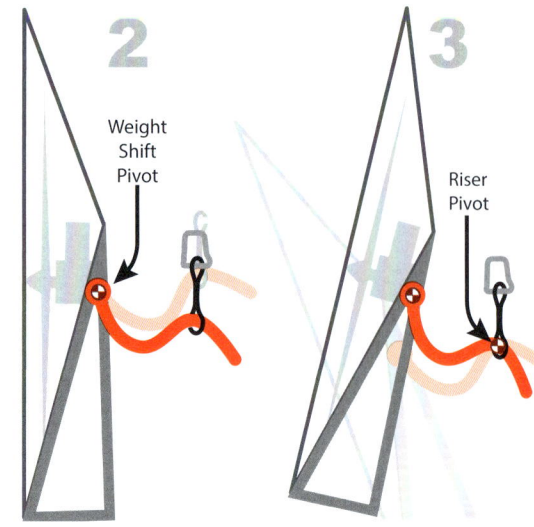

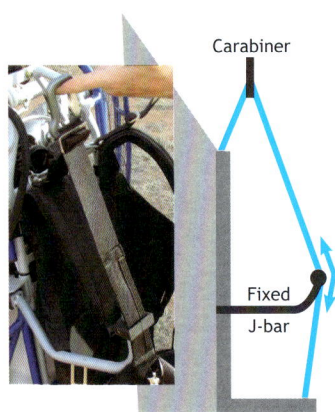

Fig 27-17 Sliding Strap

This legacy design allows weight shift since the forward strap (blue) can slide up and down through a slit or roller.

For weight shift, the pilot puts one leg down, giving about half the travel of S-Arm machines.

Weight Shift

The entire goal of weight shift is moving the risers differentially. There are several ways to do this. Not everybody will like the feel of highly weight-shiftable machines, especially the lowest hook-in styles with their "busier" ride in turbulence. Plus, the fore/aft tilt of some—mostly older—machines can be annoying.

Good weight-shift means over 6 inches of riser travel. Those that aren't designed for it will get less than three inches of travel with a fair amount of effort. Any fixed J-bar system with high hook-ins has an inch or so with great effort. Bigger pilots or more effort will get a bit more.

Sliding strap

This mostly legacy system (Fig 27-17) has fixed J bars with rollers or a slippery plastic slit that forward straps slide through. Being able to weight shift is a by-product of the design's original goal which was to make getting in the seat easier.

Whole-Machine Tilt

On machines with low enough hook-in points, the pilot can tilt the entire machine left and right to get riser movement. Just having low hook-ins is not enough—they must be *very* low. If intended to have weight shift, this arrangement will invariably have pivot bars, even though each bar generally moves only a few inches in flight. These types will get lots of riser travel and are closest to the way freeflyers achieve weight shift.

Having the CG this low tends to make the machine feel "loose" since its pivot point is so close to the center of gravity. They tend to swing around in turbulence both fore/aft and left/right. Pilots acclimate, but it can be disconcerting at first.

If the machine has no pivoting bar, it was probably not intended to have significant weight shift and will only get an inch or two of travel.

Pivoting J-Bars

Machines with high hook-ins can also get weight shift using pivoting arms. Even better action is achieved with a geared arm where, if one arm is pushed down, the other arm is forced up as shown in Fig 27-18. This is rare.

Fig 27-18 Pivoting J-Bars

This is an older-style way to get weight shift with high attachments. This would replace the J-Bars in Fig 27-17

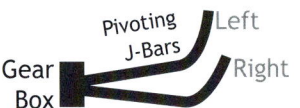

The World's most Portable Aircraft

Transportability

It's an immense appeal but we need to be realistic. See Chapter 31 for more.

Unless you do it all the time, expect to spend a good hour getting your motor down to its smallest size. Some machines that don't break down into small sizes, *do* come apart to useful in-between sizes pretty quickly. For example, if the cage's top half comes off easily, fitting nicely in your SUV, and that's how you travel, then it's perfect for *you*. See Fig 27-21.

Machines made to squeeze into a suitcase will likely be a Rubik's Cube every time you pack them until you know the tricks. What the experienced dealer can do in 5 minutes will take the casual owner 45. And packing *any* machine for shipment, if it doesn't have a dedicated case, will take a good hour regardless of model, until you get it dialed in.

The smallest paramotors are direct drives—legacy machines that are no longer produced because they're too loud and have minimal thrust. Small props and cages allowed carriage in cars (or airplanes or helicopters) without *any* disassembly.

Support—Parts and Expertise

We addressed ease of maintenance, but you must be able to source parts. Even if you're a tinkerer, you'll want support for your particular machine. Cages and frames can usually be fixed by local welding shops, but not the engine itself. The motor and its unique accessories are the important pieces that are not likely to be locally available. Check around to see if other pilots have had good luck getting support for the motor you're considering.

Having a popular engine means having expertise *and* parts availability. If lots of a particular motor are "out there," most of their problems have probably been identified and solutions found. Even if the manufacturer doesn't have the fixes, the pilot community probably will. More people are around to answer questions and there's a bigger market for dealers to profitably stock parts.

If you have a local school or shop that can support what they sell, consider the enormous value of their proximity. It may well be worth several times what you pay for the gear in frustration avoided.

Fig 27-19 Small Aircraft (#1)

If the motor is small enough, it can even fit in a helicopter. You know, as a backup in case the helicopter breaks down.

Fig 27-20 Suitcase Paramotor (#2)

A motor that goes into a suitcase is great if it can be supported and padded sufficiently. History has shown that poorly padded transport attempts are likely to be damaging.

Industrial cases with appropriate internal supports and lots of padding are safer.

Fig 27-21 Vehicle Transport (#3)

The machines' top cage half comes apart quickly, which may be handier than having a style that breaks down more but takes longer.

Paramotor Safety

Hopefully, equipment improvements will someday reduce our sport's biggest risk: the propeller. Many accidents could be prevented with well-designed equipment. Clever designs would impose minimal penalty on performance, price, or weight while adding safety.

It will ultimately be up to consumers to demand sensible safety features. They're expensive. They must be designed, built, tested, adjusted, etc. Then pilots have to buy them. Demand is a powerful driver of innovation.

There is no perfectly safe machine nor will there ever be, but boy is there room for improvement. In the meantime, we must use best practices, and be vigilant when starting or working near running paramotors, and to fly in ways that let us keep flying. More importantly, it's up to us to protect non-participants who may blunder into harm's way.

Fig 27-22 SafeStart

An operating "SafeStart" reduces starting risk. If the motor suddenly goes above a set RPM, SafeStart will shut it off. After 5 seconds or so full RPM is allowed.

Nothing is perfect, but like seat belts in cars, there's enormous safety benefit in trade for minimal hassle.

A safety device like this must be so transparent that pilots actually leave it on and use it. If it shuts off the motor when it shouldn't, or makes starting difficult, pilots will remove or disable it.

This placard should adorn every paramotor since many machines have almost no passive safety built in.

Fig 27-23 A Better Paramotor

Reality is that humans, even conscientious ones, make mistakes. If we learn anything from airline safety, it's that we must **build better machines**. That means accounting for human factors. Footflyer.com's "A Better Paramotor" has more, here are some ideas.

1. The cage, including its lower area (1), should keep an open human hand out of the prop at high thrust. An inner hoop, 1" less than the prop diameter, can be easily added to existing units as shown.

2. Props should be *frangible (*break easily) to lesson injury severity. Most wood and lightweight carbon fiber props are.

3. Pull starter ergonomics should keep hands safe and allow the motor to be well supported if it goes to power. It should also allow starting on the pilot's back.

4. The throttle should not be able to get into the prop and should have an easily accessible kill switch with the throttle hand.

5. An auto-cutoff start system (like SafeStart) should prevent sudden, unexpected thrust within 5 seconds of start. It would be always-on, NOT require pilot intervention, allow air restart, and work as a secondary kill switch. It must operate invisibly without false shut downs or it will not be used.

6. Fuel tanks need clearance from exhaust and prop in case of a crash. Bottom mounted tanks need at least 6 inches of clearance from prop tips, less for short props (under 45").

7. Harness and frame should eliminate most torque twisting effects. That can be done by offsets, weight, hang points, airflow redirection, and other methods.

8. Air bag protection (like on free flight harnesses), frame, or other vertical impact protection.

9. The platform (bottom) should be stable and not tip easily while providing reasonable impact protection. It should not catch on small ground protrusions during the occasional, slide-in landings.

10. The motor, specifically the prop, should be as close to the pilot's back as possible for comfort on the ground and other balance issues.

11. Minimize how far the prop sticks out behind the cage to reduce line snags during aborted launches. This trades off having the prop farther from its cage.

12. If the fuel tank has insufficient prop clearance, it should be reinforced so a prop strike can't breach the tank.

13. Pivot points (colored for clarity) should minimize fore/aft tilt during throttle up and allow for an upright posture on takeoff and landing. Having them in-line with the thrust line or above, helps.

14. Seatboard should fold up completely to allow easy running and getting into the seat without letting go of a brake.

footflyer.com/a-better-paramotor

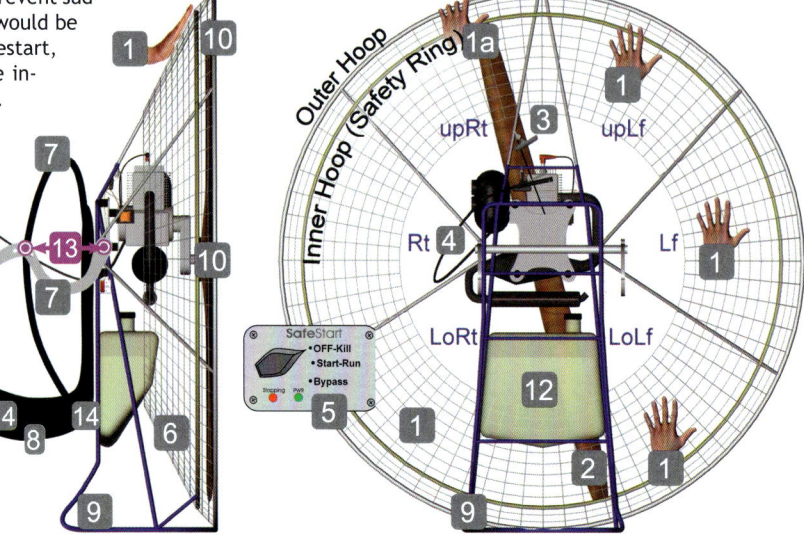

Accessories

CHAPTER 28

This chapter builds on the basics introduced in Chapter 2. It's nice that we *can* accessorize so easily, but be careful—some goodies add more risk than utility depending on how they're attached or carried. Mind the distraction and have a way to avoid the always-hungry propeller: anything that *can* reach it eventually will.

Reserve

There are two basic types of reserve: steerable and non-steerable.

Steerables, which are mostly Rogallo shaped, have an improved descent rate. They weigh slightly more, pack to about the same size, and glide about 2:1 after releasing the brakes. Opening speed and reliability are about the same but packing is more complicated—they warrant help from someone very familiar with your model. Being able to steer will help avoid wires, water and other unwanted spots.

Non steerables have various shapes (Fig 28-2), usually with some form of pulled apex (center portion). They're simpler to install and easier to repack but lack of steering means the landing site is a crap shoot.

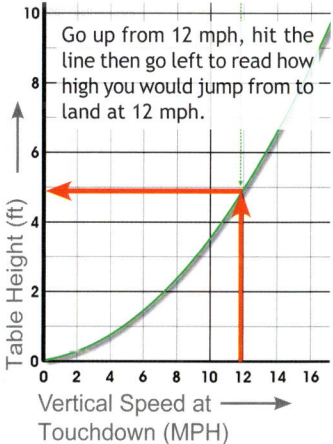

Rapid opening makes paraglider reserves completely unsuitable for free-fall and vice-versa. We can't use sky-diving reserves because they depend on high speed and use a staged opening that would take too long.

Fig 28-2 Non steerables

A huge factor on reserve choice is size which directly affects sink rate: be within the weight range. Unlike paragliders, where pilots frequently fly heavy (small wing), a too-small reserve will not do its job properly. Small reserves are called "meat savers" among pros because you'll *survive* a landing under one, but won't walk away.

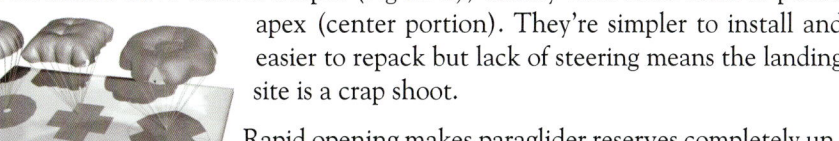

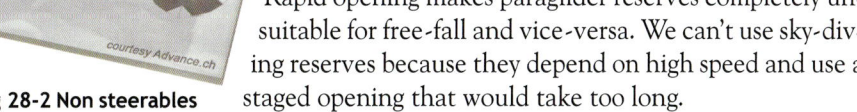

Fig 28-1 Jump Height Equivalent

Buy a big enough reserve so descent rate is < 12 mph. This chart shows how high you would you need to jump from to simulate that.

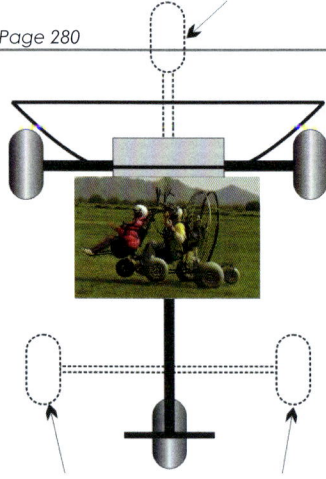

Fig 28-3 Extra Wheels
Extra wheels can enhance stability, reducing the likelihood of either rolling over or flipping back on the cage (turtling). These are primarily used during training on tippy carts.

Fig 28-4 HG / PPG Convertible
The ultimate convertible. This trike accepts either a hang glider or paraglider wing but is powered by a paramotor.

Adding Wheels

Chapter 6, page 69 covered wheeled *flying*, while this looks at a "cart-as-accessory". Ideally it's made for your motor so everything fits. But always do a thorough hang test.

Tire choice depends on where you fly. Balloon tires are great for sand and other soft surfaces but have more rolling drag. Skinnier, larger diameter tires work well on firm surfaces but don't slide well, making them more tippy (grabby). Plus tall wheels add height, which adds even more to "tippiness."

Small wheels won't handle taller grass or rough ground. Having lower hook-in points reduces rollover tendency at the expense of wobbliness in flight.

Strong cages and healthy prop clearance keep lines from flexing the hoop during inflation, possibly hitting the prop. Strength must be in proportion to power.

The simplest add-ons don't have much occupant protection—a safety trade-off. However, if your motor's cage is strong, and the mount stout, it will give some minimal protection. The comfort bars on most paramotors are not designed to support your seated weight during a bumpy roll so the trike should have support under the seat.

On tandem carts (check legalities), look for protection of the front seat occupant. There should be some structure extending beyond the front person's legs so that the frame absorbs a head-on impact, not the passenger.

A functional trike is easy to build, but engineering good handling and crash protection takes thought. As always, there's more than meets the eye.

Stability

Stability, in this context, means resistance to tipping over. In flight it refers to how much the cart moves around in turbulence and power changes. What we want:

- Widely spaced wheels dramatically reduce the tipping tendency. Quads with widely spaced wheels are the most stable, but if they have sled type steering, any bump that hits only one wheel will try to turn the cart in that direction.
- Low center of gravity reduces the tendency to tip over sideways.
- Moderately lower attachment points reduce the tipping tendency but increase the cart's wobbling around during turbulence.
- Mass should be concentrated near the center to reduce rotational inertia which can make for some large swings in turbulence once it gets going.
- The thrust line should be vertically close to, or below, the wing's pivot points so throttling up won't pitch the cart down. Thrust should also angle up enough to keep from ruffling the wing at idle.

Fig 28-5 Wheel Steering

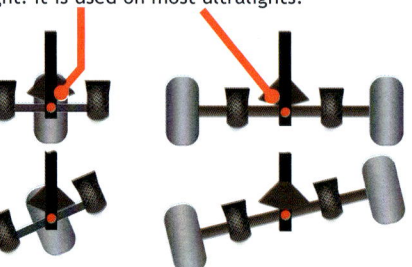

Single Pivot, sled-type steering like these are the norm. But on quads, hitting a bump with one front wheel causes an unwanted turn. This is opposite to how aircraft work since pushing the left pedal turns right. It is used on most ultralights.

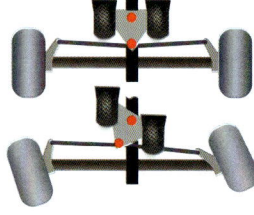

Car-type steering (think more go cart) solves problems but is heavier and more complicated. And very rare. This is how aircraft work: pushing the right pedal steers right.

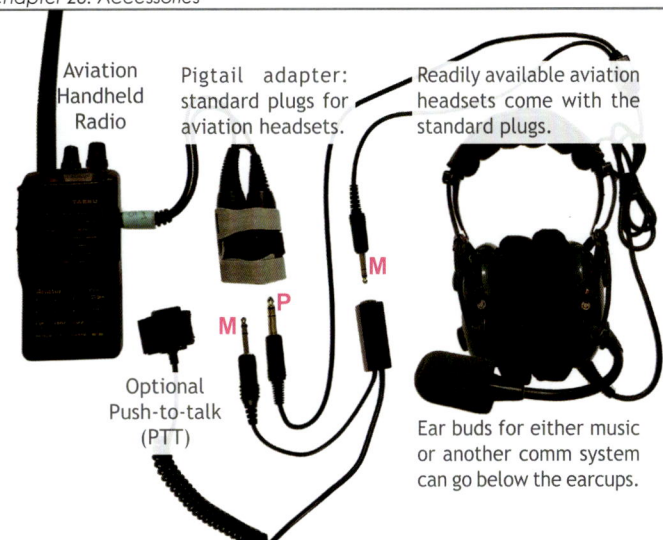

Fig 28-6 Aviation Radio Setup

The most common aviation standard for small aircraft has two sets of plugs: a 1/4 inch "phone" plug (P) and a smaller mic plug (M). These are used by nearly all small aircraft headsets.

A push-to-talk (PTT) add-on goes between the headset and mic plugs. This is great for formation flying or filming where you really want to keep hold of the brakes.

"Jacks" are what "plugs" go into.

Special helmets like this one at right may be available to go over top of aviation headsets. That would allow a standard headset with its standard plugs to be used while still enjoying helmet protection.

Helmet, Hearing & Communications

A helmet should protect both your head and hearing while allowing easy radio communications. If it has no ear protection then use ear plugs with at least 25 dB noise reduction to prevent permanent hearing loss. Even full face motorcycle helmets don't have anything close. Plus, they limit peripheral vision and seeing the wing overhead.

More head and neck coverage is better since it must also protect from propeller shards.

Radio Compatibility

In the U.S., Family Radio Service (FRS) radios are sometimes used and most helmets can be made compatible, but each brand is different. Make sure the helmet and radio play together.

Helmets that work on FRS or 2-meter sets will *not* work on aviation radios. Some models use special "pigtails" where different plugs can be hooked into an in-line connector. But even these can have compatibility issues.

The key to a good-sounding radio for inflight use is its microphone. A high quality dynamic, noise-canceling mic will make a huge difference. Not all microphones work with all radios, though. A dynamic mic requires power and expects the radio to provide it. Some do, some don't—you must check first. 2-meter radios usually do, but they require a HAM license to use, at least in the U.S.

Audio mixers are available that allow music and radio communications to coexist. Music gets turned down when the radio sounds. Ideally this capability is built into the helmet because connections hurt reliability. Another handy, but rare feature is sidetone. You hear your own voice when transmitting which 1) helps keep you from shouting, and 2) lets you know that your microphone is working.

Paramotor ignition circuits generate electronic noise that can interfere with radio and other electronics. It causes static that changes with motor rpm but can be reduced by using a resistor spark plug or cap. Never combine the two—it can degrade motor operation. A braided wrap around the spark plug wire (shield) will also reduce the noise.

Free Flight Radios

U.S. free flight pilots use VHF radios on specially designated channels in the 2-meter band. The Hang Gliding and Paragliding Association (USHPA) manages licensing for the Federal Communications Commission (FCC). These radios are far more reliable, with better range and sound quality, but cost more. The trick will be getting your flying buddies to use them.

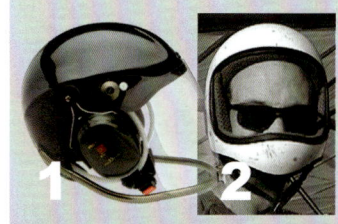

Fig 28-7 Helmet Types

1. Purpose-built paramotor/ultralight helmets elegantly combine head and hearing protection with music, comm, and even cell phone capability.

The pictured model (NAC) includes a chin guard to also get full-face level protection.

2. Motorcycle helmets work but are heavier and usually have minimal noise protection. Some do have voice-activated Bluetooth comms.

Full face motorcycle helmets with tight-sealing chin guard and face shield are good in cold weather. Being full-face, they also help prevent injury in a face plant or head-on mishaps.

Fig 28-8 Engine Instruments

Some engine instrumentation made for model aircraft, scooters, and go carts work.

Fig 28-9 Hunter's Smoke

Hunter's Smoke is a fine powder that shows what the wind is doing in a near calm.

Fig 28-10 Portable Anemometers

Choices abound. The best models work regardless of direction and record peak gusts. Sadly, they're rare.

Some work with compatible phone apps.

Fig 28-11 Multi-Function Meters

Dedicated PPG multifunction meters may include everything from variometers for climb rate info to engine and battery parameters.

This model also provides motor start protection. It can be set to prevent accidental high RPM in the first few seconds after start.

Engine Indicating

Chapter 2 covers the basics for engine RPM (tachometer) and temperature, but there's more.

First, a bit more on tachometers. They nearly all work by counting spark pulses. Given that a 2-stroke fires once per rev, and there's one cylinder, the tach should be set to one pulse per revolution. If it reads half what you expect, or some other multiple, the setting is wrong. Either change the setting or do the math.

Installation is simple, run its detector wire up to the spark plug wire and wrap it according to the instructions. Most tachs work without connecting the ground.

Optical tachometers are handy for working on motors that don't have a tach. You point it at the prop and read its rpm directly. Inexpensive units are available at model airplane (hobby) shops but these need to be held close to the prop. More expensive units, built for airplanes, can be held farther away.

EGT, CHT

This adds to the basics on "CHT, EGT & RPM" on page 22.

There are two types of gauges, digital and analog. No battery is required on analog types since they generate voltage to run the gauge. Anything with an LCD-type display will require batteries. Multipurpose models can come bundled with other indicators that combine temperature, sink rate, rpm and more.

Cylinder Head Temperature (CHT) is far more common since it's easy to install and quite durable. It responds slower to temperature changes because the cylinder head must heat up; that makes it unusable for adjusting the mixture.

Wind Indicators

Simple, purpose built and natural wind indications are in "Telling Wind Direction" on page 82, but we like gadgets, and the choices abound.

Wind speed indicators, or anemometers, have the advantage of quantifying what you feel so you can equate that to values. With practice, you'll be able to estimate the winds within 10% or so. Models for phones work either by sound, having tiny rotating parts, or other more esoteric methods.

A few models may allow mounting on a tripod so they can remain in the field and record maximum gusts. That's handy since higher gust intensity, and sharpness equates directly to stronger turbulence.

Airspeed Indicator

An airspeed indicator tells how fast you're flying through the air. They are rarely found on PPG's because it's difficult to avoid the motor's interfering thrust field. Wind speed indicators (anemometers) can be hand-carried to give an indication, at least while the motor is idling. Some variometers, made for soaring, have an airspeed probe that can be placed on a wing line or hung below the pilot—mind the prop.

Software in at least one phone app made for navigation can derive winds aloft and estimate airspeed.

Multifunction Meters

"Everything *including* the kitchen sink" is what cell phone advancement has given us. We get miniatures for the masses, mostly in sensor technology that allow devices able to provide a wealth of information and capability in one place (Fig 28-11). It's tough for developers to make it worthwhile, though, due to small numbers.

  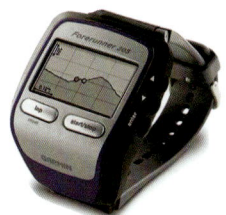 

Fig 28-12 Old-Style GPS units work well enough to give distance and groundspeed.

Fig 28-13 Phone apps provide immense capability, especially with a data plan since you can display aeronautical charts as shown here (Avare). Another app (PPGpS) displays estimated winds aloft while in flight.

Fig 28-14 Wearing GPS nav on your wrist is convenient and accurate. Some also have barometric altimeters.

GPS

Ubiquitous GPS tells us far more than direction and distance to home. Even the most basic devices show groundspeed, ground track, and in some cases, winds aloft. You can use that to tell wind direction at your altitude by doing a 360 turn and noting the slowest groundspeed: that's where the wind is from. The difference between max and min groundspeed, divided by 2, is the wind speed. Some phone apps estimate this pretty well. Other apps use position to show what airspace you're in.

GPS is accurate to within about 10 feet horizontally and 50 vertically—an impressive feat given that its signal comes from space. Find units that display altitude, groundspeed and direction simultaneously. Some include a barometric altimeter but GPS-generated values are usually sufficient unless you're soaring.

Emergency Kit

What you carry depends on where you'll be, but start with a fully charged cell phone, and in more remote areas, a foldable solar charger. Besides basic tools (see "Emergency Tool Kit" on page 129), consider a lighter, regular knife, and bug repellent. For serious cross country flights there's more to consider based on terrain.

Flotation

If you fly beyond reach of shore (See Fig 19-19 on page 202) the whole machine needs flotation to keep it upright after ditching. The best versions use water-triggered CO_2 cartridges that automatically inflate three seconds after submersion. You need

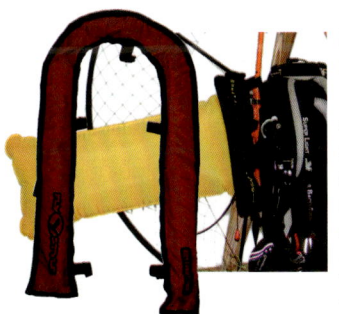

Fig 28-15 Auto-Inflating Device

Ideal auto-inflation devices Velcro to the paramotor frame. Some versions have one per side, meaning two auto-inflater cartridges. Each one has enough buoyancy to float the motor so there is redundancy.

Fig 28-16 Spare Air

For the most serious over-water flyer, this portable tank provides about 30 breaths of air. That will hopefully buy enough time to get out and clear before drowning. It's sold to SCUBA divers as their equivalent of a reserve parachute.

Fig 28-17 Digging Deeper: Altimetry

We live at the bottom of an ocean of air. Pressure is highest down here and decreases as you go up. Pressure is what barometric altimeters measure.

Pilots set current barometric pressure (called altimeter setting in the instrument's *Kollsman Window* (Fig 28-18). It's so you don't have to know your elevation when flying cross country—just set the local pressure and your altimeter displays altitude above sea level.

Fig 28-18 Aircraft Altimeter

At sea level, the standard pressure is 29.92 Hg (inches) of mercury, decreasing one inch for every 1000 ft of altitude increase. So a barometer that was reading 30.00" Hg at sea level would read 29.50 Hg if moved to Atlanta, GA (elevation 500 feet). When meteorologists say the barometric pressure in Atlanta is 29.92, what they mean is that, corrected for elevation, the pressure is 29.92. The actual pressure is 29.42.

If you set an altimeter to the current field elevation and come back a few days later it will have changed. A low pressure area will make it read higher and vice-versa for a high pressure area.

flotation too, of course. A thin life jacket is reliable and requires no action. A CO2 powered vest is more comfortable while flying. Avoid anything that requires pilot action in case you've checked out before hitting the water.

Another option is a small, portable breathing system (Fig 28-16), but it must be within easy reach and requires some practice using, especially if you're not a scuba diver.

Tree Rescue

Possibly the best tree rescue kit is a cell phone. But given how sketchy service can be where we fly, an actual kit is useful in tree-filled landscapes.

There are two approaches. First is to help others get a rope up to you—basically 100 feet of dental floss (or similar) with a metal clasp at the end. Lower the clasp to rescuers so they can tie a *real* rope to. Use as described in "Getting Out of a Tree" on page 200. The floss should be a bit longer than the highest trees in your area.

The next approach incorporates a belay device like in Fig 28-19. It works with 100+ feet of 6mm Perlon rope and a sewn sling, but does requires some minimal practice before being in an actual tree. It'd be a shame to survive crashing into a tree then die after falling out. Don't skimp on rope size—40% of rated strength disappears with the first knot—heat and rough deceleration can eat up any remaining margin.

Fig 28-19 Self Extracting Tree Rescue Kit

Personal Locator

A must-have for flying alone, especially in remote areas, is a personal locator beacon (satellite locator). They can transmit distress signals from anywhere in the world. Press a button to send your location to a satellite rescue network along with the urgency and nature of your emergency.

For a monthly fee, you can add satellite messaging and even voice. Use common sense in equipping yourself for the mission and be prepared to handle being stranded by an engine failure.

Fig 28-20 Personal Locator
An original version of the satellite-based emergency locators.

Cold Weather Gear

Being cold saps the joy of flight right out. Essential accessories include warm inside layers, a windproof outer layer, good gloves, and face protection.

Full face insulated motorcycle helmets with a visor are wonderful, but make sure you can open the visor in flight or otherwise ensure that it can't fog up.

Every part of your body must be covered but no scarves—they're easy prop fodder. Commercially-made flight suits are great as are basic cold-weather overalls or snowmobile suits.

Big gloves are a necessary evil but are a pain to launch with. Some pilots use heated gloves and other garments at some expense in dollars and complexity. Chemical hand warmers, available from department or sports stores, can also work. Moving to warmer climates has proven most effective.

Fig 28-21 Paramotor Lights (LED)
To fly on the dark side of sunrise and sunset, we need enough lighting to be visible from at least 3 miles away. That can be done with a plain strobe, or bathed in color using LED's. These can be configured in many ways, including playing video when used on the prop.

Phone Apps as Accessories

Remote sensors can work with Bluetooth on a phone to give paramotor pilots everything from engine parameters to winds aloft, and a lot in between. Collision avoidance from regular aircraft using ADS-B, FLARM, etc. may even be possible. Limited traffic awareness is possible using flight tracker apps like FlightRadar24 if your device is online while flying.

So yes, there's probably an app for that. Most useful are apps for navigation. Choices change often enough that we've included a page on FootFlyer to suggest some of the best. It's one also referenced on Fig 2-44 but included here for convenience.

Home Building

Fig 29-1 Skybolt

This is Jeff Baumgartner's prototype of a no-weld design that was eventually turned into for-sale plans.

After dozens were sold, and paramotors built, we bought the rights and made them available for free at PPGPlans.com. Pilots must agree to get training to a minimum level.

CHAPTER 29

An entire organization, the Experimental Aircraft Association (EAA), has grown up around regular people building airplanes. There are, in fact, several thousand homebuilt airplanes plying U.S. skies at speeds over of 500 mph. Burt Rutan, pioneer of the first private ride into space, started off as a home builder. So it's a reasonable undertaking for some people.

But it's not for everyone.

There is a whole lot more than meets the eye. For one, there is enormous risk for anyone not taking the project seriously—your life depends on sound design and execution. *Very* few people who set out to build a paramotor from scratch ever actually fly it. However, those who build from respected kits or plans usually *do* succeed in flying them. A useful metric is having plenty of finished units, and a thriving online support group.

PPGPlans.com was set up to provide *reliable* information to help future pilots succeed, and avoid being duped. It's the paramotor pictured above. There is no cost.

Don't build your *first* paramotor. For one thing, you'll be throwing away much of the value of customizing because you won't know what you like. Buy an existing machine, learn on that, *then* build your masterpiece. Better yet, fly different paramotors, with different styles, *then* build your even better masterpiece. It will allow forming ideas of what is safe to change along with what you'd like to change. The information in this book will help you know what not to change.

Build your own paramotor because you like to build, not because you want to save money. Even a well implemented kit will take 50 hours depending on what comes assembled. If it has little or no prefab, expect up to 4 times that much.

If you opt to train on a machine you build, find an instructor that is sufficiently familiar with it and is willing to teach you on it. They must fly it first before training you on it. Most will, provided they feel the machine is reasonably safe and appropriate for your weight. The worst possible combination would be a marginally trained pilot trying to fly an untested, homebuilt motor.

Don't be fooled by build-time estimates. They're only accurate for mythically skilled mechanics who don't re-do parts or need multiple trips to the hardware store.

Non-Welding Choices

Welding aluminum is far more difficult than welding steel and should not be taken lightly. That's why most plans or kit machines do not require any welding. The machine in Fig 29-2 (see PPGPlans.com) uses fittings wherever tubes meet or cross and a very clever key-ring-through-hoop idea to secure the netting. Wheels pop on and off easily for hauling of the machine, wing, helmet etc.

Rivets have been used as fasteners but tend to work loose unless there are lots of them in the right places. Yes, Boeings are built with rivets, but they don't vibrate like a chainsaw, and their riveted material overlap area is huge. On a paramotor, rivets must be employed particularly carefully. The kit in Fig 29-2 used rivets and gussets to fasten pieces together.

Nearly the same technology is used successfully in small aircraft. It will work well if done right, namely with enough of the right type of rivets, in all the right places. Our 2-stroke motors have more vibration than small aircraft, so overbuild accordingly.

Building Your Own Design

There's a lot more to paramotor design than meets the eye. Include an experienced paramotor pilot who understands the constructs, limitations and choices involved. It takes flight experience on different machines to know what ramifications each design feature will have. Experienced builders of other things will still need expert help or extensive paramotor flying experience to sort out paramotor design elements.

Even long time designers get flummoxed when their great ideas don't pan out, so don't be surprised when some super new feature you devised only makes matters worse. Consult "Fig 27-23 A Better Paramotor" on page 278. Pay also close attention to hang points and thrust offset elements covered in "Twisting Forces At Work" on page 240.

If you do have broad paramotor experience, like to build, can work with simple tools and have time on your hands, then building your own design could be quite rewarding. The best approach is to model an existing machine as closely as possible. Find one that you like and learn why it's built that way. Look closely at how the harness attaches to the motor, where it hangs in a simulator and how the motor is mounted. Settle on the same type of motor to keep it balanced and stick with the same geometry. If you innovate, do so with great care.

Surprisingly small changes make big differences. For example, the weight shift bars common on high hook-in machines must be positioned just right. It was found, early on, that positioning the pivot point just 2 inches back (towards the propeller) made them dramatically more effective.

There are *many* factors that likely went into tried and true designs, ones that people are actually flying. Change them at your own peril. In the past, small changes to geometry or function have hobbled a machine to the point of becoming unsafe. Pilots have been injured in such efforts. Be ready to deal with that and do lots of testing in the simulator before taking any new creation aloft.

After settling on a design, the time and tools required to build a machine should be about the same as building from plans.

Fig 29-2 Non-Welding Choices

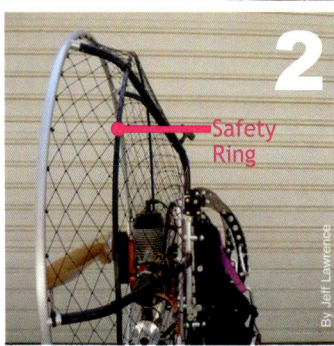

Fig 29-3 Cages and Netting

1. On styles where the net is strung through frame members, it is cumbersome when a line breaks. This ingenious method solves that problem by putting line through riveted loops. Restringing is a piece of cake.

2. Adding the safety ring dramatically reduces prop injury risk.

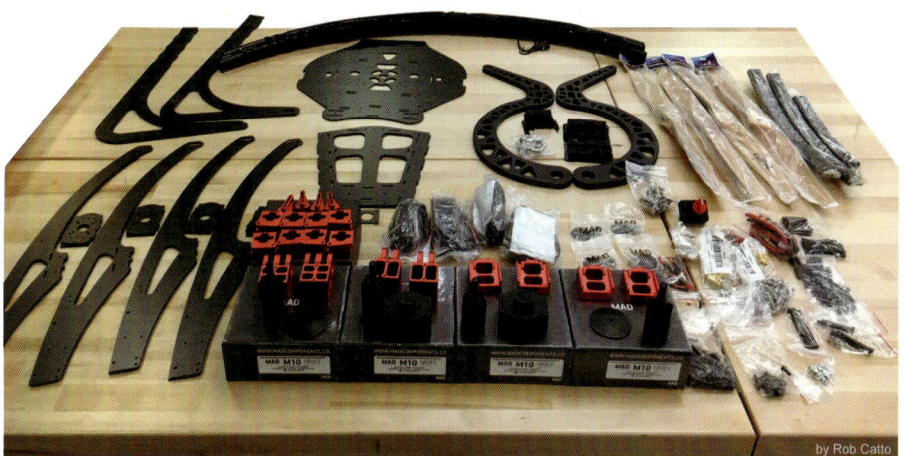

Fig 29-4 Paramotor Kit
This OpenPPG kit comes with almost everything needed to make an electric paramotor except the harness and batteries which can be included. But many pilots want choices there so they're not part of the kit. Like other kits, there is an active group of builders and flyers who contribute to the project in various ways.

Fig 29-5 Paramotor Kit
The finished paramotor before flight. See more under "Electric Propulsion" on page 243.

Building From Plans (Scratch)

If the plans you're considering are for a machine you've never seen fly, be leery. Find plans that have been built and flown!

Buying plans from the back of a magazine or Internet site was a bad idea before today's options existed. It's completely unnecessary now.

One of the biggest challenges will be acquiring all the parts. You'll need a harness, fuel tank, throttle, frame materials, motor mounts, fuel line, motor, netting material, etc. Good plans will have a current and thorough source list.

Tools

What tools are needed depends on the design. The biggie is whether welding is necessary, especially aluminum welding which adds difficulty and expense if you're not already into it.

You can expect to bend tubes, cut thick tubes (fine tooth jigsaw can be used), rivet and/or fabricate various fittings, and drill lots of holes. Anyone considering this should already have a normally equipped shop with the skills to use it. Some reputable plans don't require welding, or you can buy the welded parts separately.

Build Time

Expect to take from 100 – 500 hours total building time from start to first flight—more if the plans don't describe accurately what's needed. Nearly worthless plans have been foisted on unsuspecting buyers for years—buy something that comes recommended.

Building From A Kit

This is, by far, the best approach. Select a proven kit with flying examples flying in the field. Make sure you can watch or talk to pilots who have built it, too. Any reputable seller will offer a list of customers to talk with. Even if they cherry pick the customer list, it would be better than not having the information. Internet groups devoted to the machine provide another valuable resource.

Some kits will provide all the welded bits so the builder is essentially just assembling, riveting, drilling, cutting, and bending.

Kits may use pop rivets. They're cheap and, on a properly designed machine, are plenty strong. The key is to make sure no individual rivet carries much load, and

Fig 29-6 Build it for Safety

Since you build it, you can make it safer. This shows a safety ring added in front of the curved cage spokes, improving cage protection.

Test your creation thoroughly. Do a hang check and get an experienced pilot or instructor to inspect the completed assembly. Make sure you can get in the seat, reach all the controls, etc.

See "Testing New Gear" on page 192.

have a lot of them, spreading out that load. Metal airplanes have been holding together for years this way.

Tools

Generally you will already have what is needed: A drill, small hand tools, and a vice. The process is more assembly than fabrication which is especially good for the critical dimensions regarding motor mounting and frame alignment.

Build Time

Expect to take from 20 – 80 hours total building time from start to flight. These times depend on the kit's level of completion.

Testing & Changes

There's always something. It may seem simple, but strange interactions and problems invariably show up during testing. Some are dangerous. Be ever mindful of the prop while going through the process. Some pilots (or would-be pilots) have been mangled after the briefest moment of inattentiveness. If you're new, have your instructor present when first starting the motor.

Like any new machine, preflight should make sure there's nothing within reach of the prop that could get sucked in. The cage must have good prop clearance and the fuel system should be leak free with a good vent. These cautions go for changes to existing designs, too. Have your instructor or an experienced pilot check it out for you.

Consider what would happen in a crash. Can components skewer the pilot? Will the prop flex down enough to slice through the fuel tank? Spraying fuel could potentially ignite a fireball.

Will the change allow the risers to come together, causing riser twist in flight? Will the cage come forward on the risers and allow the brakes to go through the prop? These things have all happened with horrible consequences, and many other possibilities exist.

Hang the system by its carabiners to make sure you can get in and out of the seat easily. Install a kick-in strap, if necessary, and practice until it's second nature. Have an alternative way, besides the kill switch, to shut off the motor that doesn't involve reaching anywhere near the prop ("Kill Switch or Throttle Failure" on page 51). When everything checks out, run it up on the simulator and see if any problems appear.

Keep those first few flights close to home and check it out after each flight. That's true even on a new commercially-made machine or one that has been worked on. Postflight is a great time to inspect, but even more so on new machines.

Tinkering: Not all bright ideas in paramotoring come from manufacturers; many come from users, especially experienced pilots looking to get the most out of their gear.

Tinkerers have devised both doozies and duds. Wally Hines' counteracting weight shift, where one bar's upward travel pulls the other bar down, was a doozy as an aftermarket for certain brands.

Another creation, pictured right, didn't go so far. While not a complete dud, this retractable foot rest never caught on. It stowed for launch or landing and could be extended whilst cruising. He soon decided that the weight didn't quite justify the benefit. But it sure was comfy once airborne!

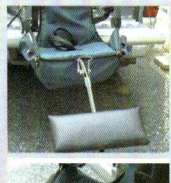

Section VI

Getting the Most out of Powered Paragliding

Photo by Franck Simonnet

Section VI

Getting the Most out of PPG

Now that you're flying an aircraft that can travel with you, the list of possibilities is enormous. Besides a new view of your local slice of heaven, there's a world to explore.

You're suddenly free from the road. Family vacations, for example, can take on a whole new flavor. Business trips can be an excuse to explore from above, and family visits can include "demonstrations." And as you'll see, there are even more ways to enjoy this amazing craft.

Other Uses

CHAPTER 30

Fig 30-1 Water Skiing
It's fun, but have an auto-inflating device. This was done in water shallow enough to stand up in. Launch is made *much* easier with some wind.

It's just one example of the strange, fun variations of flight that have been explored with paramotors.

The many variations of flight provided by a paramotor are surprising. It's certainly more amusing than practical, but who knows—one person's amusement may spawn another person's practical application. Mind the risks, of course, it's still an aircraft with that spinning slicer only inches from precious body parts.

Using PPG for Transportation

Yeah, probably not. Exceptions may indeed allow using a paramotor to get somewhere but fickle weather, limited conditions, less-than-stellar reliability, and slow speed conspire against us. But if you're flexible? On nice days, there is no cooler way to arrive.

Think of actual travel as more of a novelty; a treat.

Ideally, launch is close to home (or better yet, *at* home). Portability means that after you get there it can be folded up for the ride back, especially since one-way trips are better. Like any cross country, you'll be happier on a faster wing.

If you have an airplane (you'd be surprised how many paramotor pilots do), this can be a great way to get back and forth to pick it up from maintenance. The same is true for cars if your shop has a nearby field. You may even need to choose your shop differently now.

Be leery of planning a round trip. If the paramotor is your only ride home it will be tempting to push the limits and fly when you would otherwise pass. "Get-home-itis" has been the fatal flaw in many general aviation flights where pilots took on marginal conditions and lost.

If you have good sites at both ends of a planned trip, plenty of fuel, a legal route (not congested), and have good weather, the PPG is a fun way to get there.

Fig 30-2 Planes, Lanes and Helicopters

Before discovering paramotor, I had a helicopter (Ellie). It required yearly inspections at a shop some 35 miles away—an onerous drive through nasty traffic. Twice. Then along came PPG. Despite living in a suburb, I could thread an uncongested route from my house to the shop which had a helipad (middle picture). It wasn't much, jutting out into a swamp and all, but it would do.

So when the next inspection came due, I loaded my paragear into the helicopter and headed out. Flying there was pretty quick—while helos are slow by aircraft standards, they're greased lightning by paramotor standards. After landing, Darryl Oliver, the shop owner, spirited Ellie into his lair then came out to watch the launch. He thought I was nuts.

With the swamp before me, and the wing laid out behind, I was ready. Nervous, too; if the motor quit, or I couldn't climb well enough, that swamp would be no fun. So I psyched up, powered up, and went for it. The edge came quickly. I lifted off just before water's edge and held my feet up to clear the taller swamp grass. Easing up on the brakes let me accelerate and climb. Whew! That was satisfying. Darryl later admitted that he half expected to fish me out of the muck.

Flying home was almost magical. A couple weeks later I reversed the process—paramotoring up to the helipad and flying everything home. Boy did this beat driving. And landing at the helipad seemed brainless compared to launching there.

Another fun example of usefulness was retrieving a motorcycle after maintenance. How convenient that the shop had a field next door. I'm sure the employees got a kick out of it. And yes, a helmet was worn, both on the road and in the air.

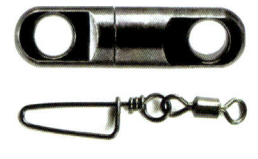

Fig 30-3 Swivels for Banners

Flags & Banners

Flags and banners can be fun to fly but do add some risk. Attaching anything to the wing adds drag which slightly increases the chance for parachutal stall and makes the wing that much more difficult to inflate. Attached stuff may also impede recovery from malfunctions. Risk has proven minimal when flown up high and in good weather. Avoid excessive brake pull and follow the connection guide below.

When connecting a banner or flag: 1) minimize turning tendency, 2) keep it out of the lines and prop, and 3) make sure it flies fully.

There are several ways to attach banners to the wing. Regardless of the method, put it near the center to minimize turning pull, but opposite the side that your motor naturally torque turns. So if the motor makes you turn left, put the flag on the right inside.

Use the most center brake line since that is the most rearward and will minimize turning tendency. You'll feel the flag flapping through your brake handle so some pilots will use a D-line (or C on 3-riser wings) instead.

You will have two lengths of 1/8" nylon strings that are tied to the top and bottom of the banner's leading edge (2 & 3 in Fig 30-4). The top line gets tied to where the brake line connects at the wing (1) and the bottom line connects where the brake line cascades from below (4). The length of each line, plus the flag's height should be slightly longer than the brake line distance between attachment points. This will let the flag "bow" out without crumpling in the middle.

Put fishing clips (snap swivels like in Fig 30-3) on each end to make removal easier.

Before launching, make sure the flag is on the ground and clear of other lines. Generally just making sure it is on the ground and lines are on top of it is enough. After inflating make sure the flag is not hung up on anything before committing to flight—easy to do on a reverse inflation, but more challenging on a forward.

Hanging Banner

Hanging the banner works well if you want to fly somewhere before deploying it, or if no-wind conditions make the inflation difficult.

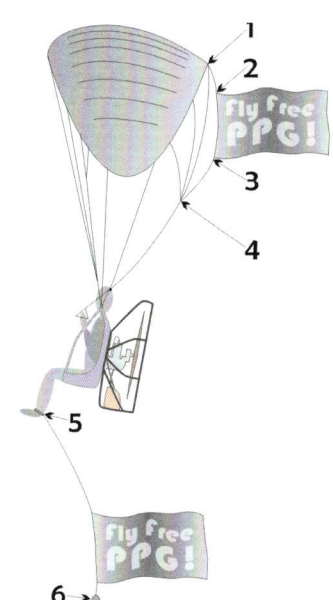

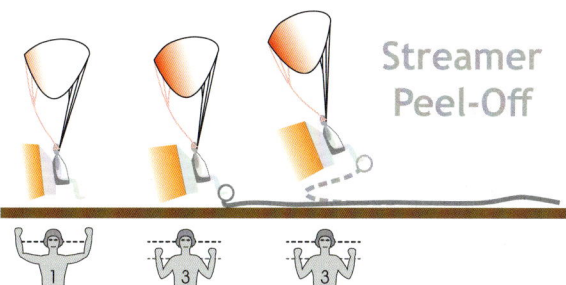

Fig 30-6 Long Banner Pick-Up

When picking up a long banner (or streamer), lay it out with the foot loop downwind so that you're peeling it off the ground after hooking it. Avoid any situation where snagging the banner could pull you into the ground. One way would be to hold it with your foot.

You can also coil the streamer neatly but there's an increased chance it gets a tangle.

The moment it's hooked, pop some brake and go to full power to avoid dragging it along the ground. Then ease off the brake.

Fig 30-4 Banners and Flags   **Fig 30-5 Flag on Trailing Edge**

Tie a weight (3 pounds should suffice, more for a bigger banner) to the banner's leading edge bottom (Fig 30-4 #6) then tie a line to the top and secure that to a Velcro strap. Attach the Velcro to a low-hanging part of the frame or to your foot (5). It should attached so that a snagged banner would only peel the Velcro off.

Launches with the banner stowed then, after reaching a safe altitude, throttle back and drop it. The banner could foul the propeller so have the prop stopped, or at its lowest RPM. Be over landable terrain in case of problems.

With the banner in tow, don't fly near people who could get hurt if it dropped accidentally. Be mindful of how low it hangs and avoid the possibility of snagging on a part of your machine.

Before landing, either drop the banner or stow it back in a bag.

Cattle Herding

Don't laugh, a paramotor "round-up" has been done and the rancher loved it. In fact, he asked the pilots back several times. Of course you can't get paid but you *can* earn another flying site, or at least a welcoming place to fly over.

Coordination is a must to mitigate the higher collision risk and to be effective. Mostly it's a matter of flying in such a way as to keep the cattle moving in a desired direction. Simply going out and finding strays helps a lot, something the PPG can do well thanks to its unrestricted view and slow speed.

Coordination is especially needed when two or more pilots are working one group of cattle and/or with people on the ground.

Be careful since it's easy to get so distracted by the mission that you fly right into wires, fences, another pilot, or the ground. It takes discipline to build a scan that regularly looks where you're going, not getting too focused on the mission target. Being low and distracted commands great care.

Thankfully, grazing land tends to be landable, but not everywhere. Be mindful of engine-out options. It's easy to get caught up in an activity and be unprepared for a motor failure. Surprise is decidedly unhelpful with only a few seconds to touchdown!

Fig 30-7 Cattle Herding

The pilot is working a small band of separated cattle along the Rio Puerco, West of Albuquerque. Legally, this falls under allowed recreational use as long as the purpose of the flight can be called recreational. That precludes getting paid.

Fig 30-8 Finding Lost Models

1 & 2. Looking for lost models can be tedious. There's no guarantee they'll be immediately visible and you must fly a search grid from different altitudes. I spotted this one from 500 feet or so. Notice how very close to the road this model was and how nearly impossible it would have been to see from the ground. From above, though, it was pretty obvious in spite of blending in with other yellow vegetation.

3. On this occasion the model's remote control quit working and the pilotless plane wandered almost a mile away before crashing with little damage. It, too, proved easy to spot from the air while being impossibly hidden from ground searchers.

Search and Rescue

Our high perch is also useful for search and rescue. Yes, cell phones and GPS's reduce our need for such efforts, people still get lost. While we can't do much if they're wandering the woods, we can certainly cover open areas, including difficult to inspect crop lands. This should only be pursued by experienced pilots who generally make launches on their first try.

Contact your state Search and Rescue director (if available) or the local fire and police departments to offer your services. It would be on a volunteer basis and is a great show of community support.

Be up front with them about your capabilities and limitations. The worst thing to do is exaggerate what you can do, and end up needing a rescue yourself. Most important, explain the limited weather window we operate in and time-of-day constraints—don't expect to do this on mid-summer afternoons.

Finding Model Aircraft

A great way to befriend the local Radio Control flying club is offering your search services for their lost airplanes. Give them your telephone number and explain your capability. This is increasingly being done with drones but there's still a place for high-resolution eyeballs.

When those planes go down they can be nearly impossible to find from the ground, and they have quite a range. Tall grass is ideal to find planes by PPG—they're almost impossible to locate from below but frequently pop out from above.

The flying is obviously simple: Pick a pattern and fly it while scanning the ground. Pick different altitudes too. If the airplane is buried in deep grass, you might have to be nearly over it. Going up high puts you farther away but provides the vertical angle that may be necessary.

Once the plane is located, identify nearby landmarks that you can find from the road (or hack a GPS). It's best if you go out personally to get the plane because you know where it is. The nuance of location can get lost in a translation.

Public Relations & Exhibition

Flying in airshows can be difficult. You may need a rating (PPG2 is required for most insurance), approval by airshow management, and must work with the "Air Boss" who's in charge of all flight operations. They have exemptions from certain rules but that means all pilots flying under the exemption must be specially qualified. It's a potentially lengthy process that PPG ratings can smooth out.

At smaller gatherings, or even some airshows, simple demonstrations can showcase the craft, especially if you incorporate information brochures afterwards. Even just static displays are a great way to show off the craft.

Motor Madness

Paramotors have turned up some surprising uses. For one, it is the monster of all leaf blowers. Of course a regular leaf blower won't cut your arm off, but for those willing to try it, there's no better way to move a big volume of air on very little gas. Only do this stuff while wearing the motor on your back, and don't let that cage near anything. Props find bystanders just as tasty as pilots. Be careful!

Traveling with Gear

CHAPTER 31

The ability to travel so readily with our aircraft is unique to powered paragliding. It's not always easy, but it's almost always worth the effort. Free flyers have it even easier, but the motor powers us to the wheres of our wishes. What an extraordinary capability!

Shipping

PPG's can be boxed and shipped around the world using common consumer freight carriers, but there are caveats, requirements and challenges.

First off, if there is obvious gas in the tank or carburetor, it's hazardous materials —it probably won't qualify to even be carried via ground shipping. It must be completely drained, including carburetor bowls or chambers. Removing the gas tank then running the motor until it quits is a good way to do this.

Preparing the Motor

Besides fuel, the machine must be free of fuel odors, and packed well enough to endure rough handling. At least one major carrier requires 3 inches of padding between the box's edge and its contents. Assume that any part touching the package/case sidewall will be damaged.

If they smell fuel, your shipment will be declared hazardous materials ("hazmat"), opening Pandora's Box. You may luck out and not have your motor inspected but, for everybody's sake, don't risk it.

Remove the harness and clean everything. Yes, fuel works well for cleaning, but not now. Use a sweet-smelling degreaser that doesn't harm aluminum. Spray-type carb cleaner gets rid of grime in hard-to-reach areas. Brake cleaner is good on exposed metal surfaces but brutal on paint. It's nice in that it leaves no residue.

If you have an air filter, now is a good time to replace it. Otherwise, double bag it and squeeze out excess air. Clean the air box thoroughly. Wash the tank out with soapy water, then deodorize it with a product like ZorbX (Fig 31-1). If time permits, dry

Fig 31-1 Cleaning for Air Travel
There must be no fuel, fuel vapor, and no odor.

Fig 31-2 Made to Travel

Some machines are made to travel. Key elements are 1) no single piece too long to fit in normal sized checked luggage, 2) it must assemble/disassemble quickly, and 3) the engine must be easy to remove so it can be packed separately.

The machine above has its engine mounted to a piece that's only slightly bigger than the engine itself. Everything else snaps to that—no bolts required.

Other solutions involve an engine that detaches quickly from the frame, which itself breaks down easily. Parts commonality helps by reducing extra things that must be carried for those wanting some backup capability. There's nothing worse than arriving at the world's coolest flying site only to have your pull starter come out in your hands.

Puzzle props, shown above, are used to cut their size nearly in half for better packing.

Be leery of assembly times claimed by sellers. They are frequently based on someone who has done it many times on a perfect machine—one that hasn't been tweaked by rough handling or oopses. Reality reveals that it can easily be three times what the manufacturer says.

---

the fuel tank completely. When there isn't a hint of fuel vapor, it's legal for transport, but airlines may still not take it.

Remove as many attachments as possible—muffler, reduction drive, air filter, carb, etc. If the motor can be removed from the frame easily, do so. Usually only the throttle, fuel line, kill switch and battery line must be disconnected. Having pull-apart electrical connections speeds things up. Being compact is better for motor shipping and probably a lot cheaper. Plus, keeping the motor separate reduces the chance of a careless drop bending the frame.

Packaging

Using just one stout, large case means there's less for the freight company to lose. After all, you need an engine AND frame. If shipped separately, and they lose either one, you're hosed. But if there's only one box, there's only 1 chance. Of course it's super heavy that way.

Pack so the box can survive a drop from several feet high. Moderately firm foam of at least 3 inches, including a softer layer next to the motor, should line the box. Foam can be purchased from fabric shops (and elsewhere) in sheets.

A few models come apart enough to fit in airline-legal hard-sided suitcases, but all airline luggage is now screened in some way. So unless you know the carrier will accept it, have another plan in case it's refused.

Another padding option is forming foam—a material that sprays out from a can and forms to your object (Great Stuff Foam is one brand) then hardens. It can be re-used in new boxes as the old ones wear out. Put your gear in a plastic garbage bag first.

Once the heavy pieces are secure, everything else can be added and packed in bubble wrap. Limit this box to necessary flight gear. Lighter is better. A good idea, for example, is to wrap the muffler, carburetor, and gear box (heavy items) in plastic wrap and put them in with the wing that you will check on the airline. That saves shipping costs, but remember, the fewer boxes you need to have for an airworthy machine at the destination, the better your odds.

Propellers fit nicely in gun cases. Even the cheap cases from discount stores work well and accept two wooden props up to 50 inches long. Puzzle props, those that come apart at the hub (previous page), are great since they fit into your other boxes, negating the need for a separate prop container.

Wings conveniently squish into a sleeping-bag sized, easily checked item. It can be good for packing other things with since the fabric serves as its own protection. Just be sure that nothing sharp protrudes and that no fuel or oil can get on it.

Having more boxes is easier to deal with for one person, but increases the chance of losing a required flight item. Maximum weight limits affect your choice of one big box or several smaller ones. Some shippers may not even take heavy or oversized boxes.

Airlines

Most U.S. airlines prohibit motors by policy, even though there is no regulation that mandates it. And not having crankcase oil (as in 2-strokes) won't help. Motors that have never been run may be allowed which is why cleaning really well is so important. Nearly all carriers follow IATA (International Air Transport Association) guidelines. Include a letter stating that you comply with IATA guidelines (provided you do) and place it in view of those who will invariably inspect your stuff.

Some pilots have succeeded at getting motors on airlines, even regularly, but it's still a gamble. Non-U.S. carriers may be more tolerant. Taking the engine farther apart (exhaust, redrive, cylinder, carb, air box) and calling it "parts" (which it is) may help.

Even if an airline does allow your motor, it probably will be x-rayed and inspected. If they smell any fumes it will not go! Don't think that plastic wrap will solve the problem—officials will probably open that it up too. Consider having a contingency plan. Think about the return trip, too.

For best results, remove the engine and ship it alone in the smallest box possible—it's cheaper, safer for the motor, and doesn't annoy the baggage gorillas as much. Then check everything else on the airline. It'll be a big, but manageable box with the motorless frame, clean gas tank, harness, muffler, prop, redrive, and so on. Expect to pay an oversize or excess baggage fee.

Larger frames with rigid cage pieces are more likely to need 2 boxes and should be lightweight to minimize damage potential.

Freight Carriers

Hazardous material requirements limit what cargo airlines can accept but they're more liberal than passenger lines. The box is still likely to be opened so don't leave fuel in anything. Besides endangering crew members, it's a federal offense. Shippers are obliged to inspect contents, and may even remove gas tank caps.

Each shipping company has its own pricing structure. Some airlines have freight divisions but the cargo usually goes on passenger flights. If it's going to a foreign country, it must clear Customs and may be delayed up to three weeks while incurring steep customs fees (usually refundable once you take the gear back out of the country.) It can be quite the paper chase, too. These are reasons for taking the gear on your

Fig 31-3 Packing Tips

Pet carriers and large plastic storage boxes work well—put a couple of cheap tie-down straps around them for strength.

1. A smaller box for just the engine makes damage and confiscation less likely. It also makes everything easy to carry. Note the strapping tape used to make a carrying handle.

2. Props fit nicely in gun cases.

3. Put the wing in a stout bag before boxing to add protection in case the box gets punctured.

Fig 31-4 Airline Shipping

Packing gear in two hard-sided pieces of luggage makes it easier for airline personnel, but gives you twice the chance of being stranded. If they lose only one piece, you're still out of luck.

Older luggage without the handle and wheels provides more interior room.

1. Expect your bags to be opened by the TSA.

2. Wrap everything, especially if there's a chance for odor.

3. All this went in two bags.

1 by Chris Santacroce

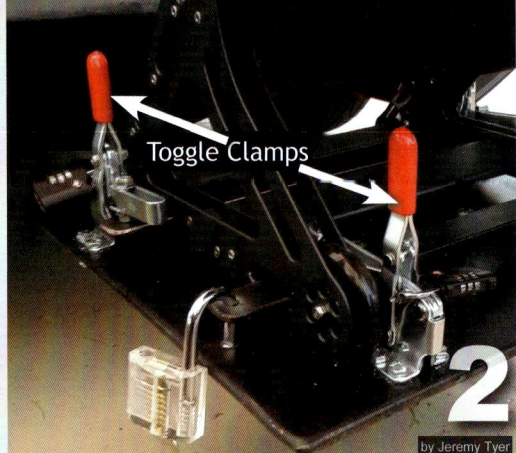
Toggle Clamps
2 by Jeremy Tyer

3

4

5 by Jeff Hamann

TUMBLEWEED
by Martin J. Henderson

6 by Robert Kitilla

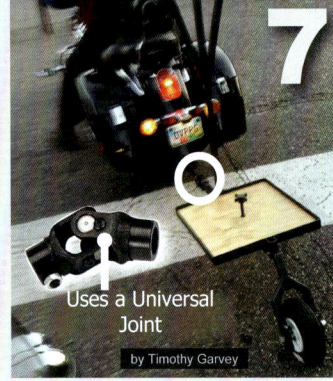
7 Uses a Universal Joint
by Timothy Garvey

8 by John Winkopp

Fig 31-5 Motor Mounting Options

On The Road
A few of the many ideas from some very clever humans

For the latest transport ideas and links to resources, go to the QR link at left. Here are some good ones to start with:

1. This commercially available rack has an option (see inset) to swing out for vehicles with a tailgate. It doubles as a runup rack and place to sit while putting the machine on.

2. Quick release locking clamps work well.

3. Having a trailer to put gear in has all kinds of advantages if you can tow and store the trailer. Having a wagon that allows transporting the motor and accouterments gives even more convenience for some situations like when it's a long walk from the parking lot.

4. A roadable trike negates the need for a platform or trailer.

5. Off the shelf platforms come in many sizes. This one fits two motors; most fit one. There are several sizes of receivers and hitch balls, but since our gear is pretty lightweight, we don't stress even the smallest sizes.

6. Another commercially available solution that uses bicycle mount hardware to make quick work of securing a paramotor. It's available for one or two paramotors.

7. Welders own the world. This custom motorcycle platform is the simplest solution that doesn't involve wearing your machine. It has a universal joint to keep the motor upright while managing dips in the road.

8. Pedal power can be used for short distances as this kayak carrier attests to.

Basic Cautions

All carriers should support the motor near the prop to minimize fore/aft bouncing on bumpy roads. For short trips, it may not matter, but if it's held only by the frame legs, they may crack or bend.

Sun is hard on harness fabric and cage netting. If the motor will be exposed for long it should be covered, ideally with something that goes all around including the bottom. That will minimize dust and road grime.

Paramotors get stolen. Have a good lock attached to a visibly stout cable that's secured to the vehicle.

international passenger flight, if allowed.

Many freight companies offer less-than-truckload (LTL) options. Search "LTL shippers near me." You drop your motor off at their warehouse, they palletize it, ship it; then you pick it up at a warehouse near your destination. It may take 3 weeks, though.

Transporting via Road

Transporting by car is what most of us do, so it ought to be convenient. Plus, breaking it out on long journeys makes for an exhilarating new perspective on travel.

Tall vans are ideal—they keep the paramotor upright and out of bad weather. Trucks are next best but their high beds can make handling awkward. Trailers are great if you have storage space and a tow vehicle, but the most common solution is some kind of platform (Fig 31-5). They work on all vehicles and have many clever implementations.

Using the Platform

A platform lets you carry one or more motors fully assembled outside your vehicle. It usually attaches to a receiver that can be installed at many trailer stores (like U-Haul). Two common sizes are 2 inches for heavier loads, and 1 ¼ inch for lighter ones. Our gear doesn't stress even the smaller one. Trailer lights are not normally required (check your state's laws), but the license place must be visible.

Secure the motor with at least two means in case one lets go. Secure free-spinning props (clutched units) to reduce bearing wear. A bicycle cable and lock provides some security, and if the motor falls off, will drag the remains to your next stop. Try to avoid that. A cover protects from sun, dust, rain, and prying eyes, but road dust gets into anything that's not sealed up, including from the bottom. Large grill covers work, but purpose built paramotor covers are easier to use.

Be careful; gear can easily get damaged in transit for those who travel a lot. Plus, constant bouncing around is hard on everything. If possible, put hard foam on the bottom to absorb some of the jostling.

Making or Selecting the Platform Mount

A paramotor mount must first be strong and durable. But why not also make it convenient? Have everything fit together like a puzzle where the last piece holds it all down with a single toggle clamp, bolt, or other locking device (see Fig 31-5, #2).

This wood and aluminum Rube Goldberg (Fig 31-8) is an example. Numbers indicate how the paramotor is mounted. Do secure its top to prevent fore/aft bouncing with a strap, or some kind of vertical piece. Bicycle mounts can give some ideas. Here is how it fits together.

Fig 31-8 Puzzle Mount

1) Slide the paramotor's bottom, rear crossbar under the angled aluminum and between screwed-down wood strips that keep it from moving around.

2) Slide a pre-drilled 2x4 into the U-bracket (colored cyan for clarity) and the other end over a captured bolt (3).

3) Screw a nut and washer onto the captured bolt to hold everything together. In this case, there is no vertical stand to support the motor from fore/aft motion so a ratcheting strap goes over the frame's top.

Fig 31-6 Prop Cover/Prop Stopper

This clever prop cover primarily protects the prop. But it also prevents spinning during transport *and* provides some start protection (on clutched machines). Check with the maker before assuming it's good for the engine-starting, hand protection mission.

Fig 31-7 Basic Platform Mount

A *trailer hitch receiver* is what the platform slides into. It bolts to your car and can be installed by most car repair shops, trailer suppliers, and others. Two inch size is the most common but 1 1/4 inch is plenty strong for our use. Think bike rack.

courtesy Lowes.com

Platforms are available at many hardware and automotive supply stores. Make sure the tongue size matches your receiver.

Fig 31-9 Minimalist Car Mounts

Vince White has created a minimalist solution for cars with a trunk (or boot) but no hitch. It's similar to some bike mounts which are a great source for paramotor carrier ideas. The PPG's frame legs sit in nylon or plastic holders.

You will need some way to secure the trunk lid while driving.

When not in use, these mounts pull up off the bumper and stow away flat to conserve space.

Gas & Oil

Some travel modes (airlines, freighters) prohibit gas containers that have had fuel in them, ever. So it may be easier just to plan on buying one on arrival and leaving it behind.

Unless you're flying a 4-stroke or electric, you'll need 2-stroke oil. Although it's not considered a hazardous material, most airlines still prohibit it, even in checked baggage. Motorcycle and go-cart racing shops usually have the best selection of oils. Hardware stores frequently carry it for chain saws, and gas stations sometimes stock outboard blends—not ideal, but it works in a pinch. In most cases you'll be OK since your motor is completely emptied on each end of your trip.

See "Oil Selection & Mixing" on page 42.

Bus Lines

Some pilots have had good luck using commercial bus lines. You must drop everything off at the bus terminal and pick it up at a designated spot, but sometimes arrangements can be made for delivery service. Check with the line to see if they'll take your gear.

Customs & Declarations

The problem here isn't fuel, it's taxes and tariffs. Registering your motor with an organization and having the documentation may help to show that it's yours. Some countries (not the US) require registration with the government. The border folks fear that you may be importing the motor for sale so it's more suspicious if you're traveling with more than one. They may also fear some nefarious use so having a picture of it in flight may be helpful. You already look sketchy with all this kit.

If you're traveling with a group, it may be best to have the frame in a box with the prop separated. That attracts less attention.

The most appropriate declaration is "Sporting Equipment" or "Paragliding Equipment" for personal use. It's true, and it's not evoking the horror of something so bold as "aircraft" or even "ultralight."

It can also be helpful if you have a local person there to help deal with issues, especially if you don't speak the language.

In the U.S., anti-terror laws may not allow individuals to ship using airline cargo services—you must go through a freight forwarder who ships using the cheapest means, most likely a freight airline for rapid delivery. Otherwise, you must be certified as a known shipper. Your dealer may have already acquired that status and be able to help.

The large freight companies can be used (FedEx & UPS) but are expensive depending on the destination. They do handle the customs issues but don't be surprised if there is a very large charge at the end. Some countries can be "creative" with charges which is why it's good to enlist the help of a local. Some charges verge on extortion.

In any case, the best advice comes from other pilots who have already traveled to your intended destination. Seek them out and enjoy the immensity of your opportunity.

by Dana Denney

Photography

CHAPTER 32

What an amazing platform for capturing pictures and video. We get perspectives that are difficult or impractical with any other craft, and with immense portability.

Distraction is a concern that requires discipline to address. Remain aware of your surroundings and ensure a clear flight path, especially while flying low or near others. Collisions have happened.

Fig 32-1 Chase Cam

This shows how far sports cameras have come, and what can be done with a well-implemented "Chase Cam." The possibilities are stunning.

Paramotor flying is a harsh environment for camera gear, so pay attention to how it's secured. Use a long enough camera strap to allow movement while making it impossible to get into the spinny bits. Looping the camera strap through a harness piece is better than around a body part. Hanging anything around your neck, for example, could allow it to get caught in the propeller or other moving parts. That has happened. If you do launch with anything around your neck, make sure it is cinched up tight. Once in flight, consider attaching it to a frame part.

Still Photography Basics

Photography merits its own shelf of books, but these tidbits should improve your efforts.

Quality

Regarding gear, there's a lot more to it than pixel count. It's important (see page 306), but so is the lens, sensor, image stabilization, and so on. Other attributes depend on how the camera will be used. Pixel count obviously matters—If your pictures are for print, they need to be at least 300 dots per inch (DPI), whereas most computers display around 96 DPI. Photos from even basic phones meet print needs.

Higher quality gear does better in low light, like sunrise and sunset. For handheld cameras that will be used in the air, favor those with good image stabilization to reduce motion blur. If zoom is used, it's better if it can be operated with one hand.

For most of us, saving pictures as JPEGs using the camera's default settings is good enough. There is some compression loss, but you'd struggle to tell without zooming

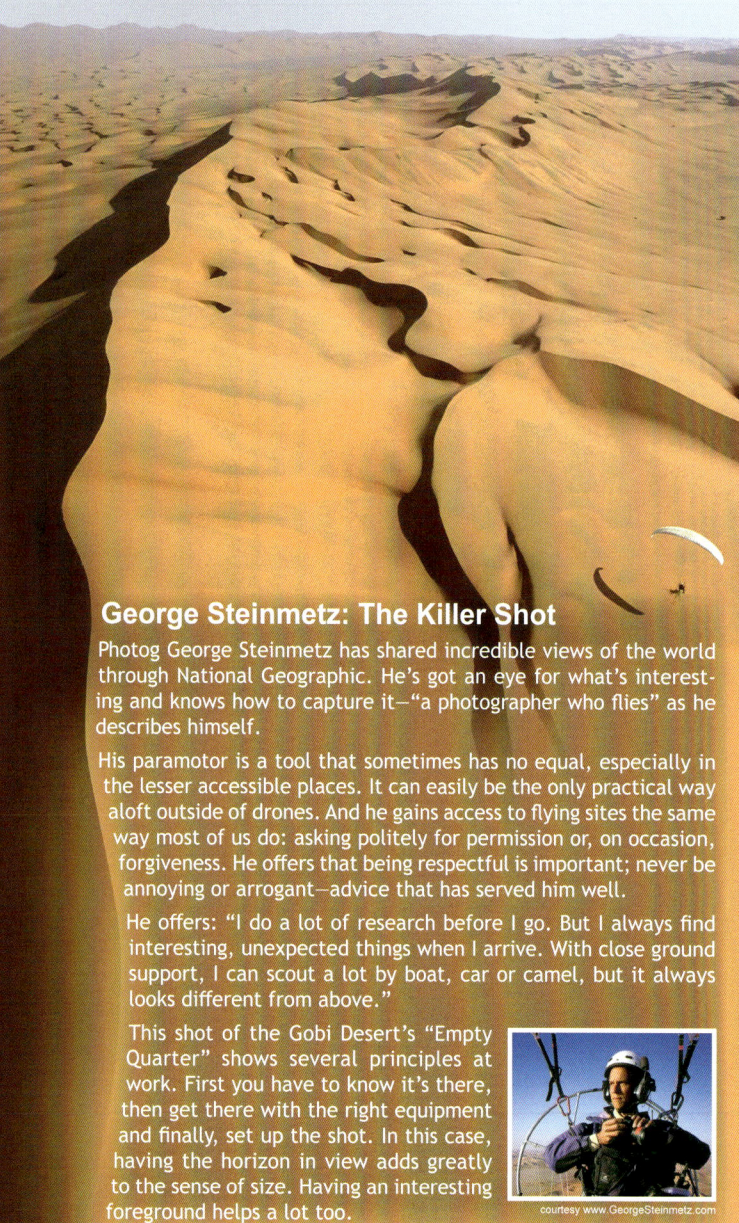

George Steinmetz: The Killer Shot

Photog George Steinmetz has shared incredible views of the world through National Geographic. He's got an eye for what's interesting and knows how to capture it—"a photographer who flies" as he describes himself.

His paramotor is a tool that sometimes has no equal, especially in the lesser accessible places. It can easily be the only practical way aloft outside of drones. And he gains access to flying sites the same way most of us do: asking politely for permission or, on occasion, forgiveness. He offers that being respectful is important; never be annoying or arrogant—advice that has served him well.

He offers: "I do a lot of research before I go. But I always find interesting, unexpected things when I arrive. With close ground support, I can scout a lot by boat, car or camel, but it always looks different from above."

This shot of the Gobi Desert's "Empty Quarter" shows several principles at work. First you have to know it's there, then get there with the right equipment and finally, set up the shot. In this case, having the horizon in view adds greatly to the sense of size. Having an interesting foreground helps a lot too.

in super close.

If you want maximum quality and maximum control, especially in shadows and highlights, select "RAW" which does no compression or processing on the image. Files will be huge and you'll need a RAW editor, but you can extract the most amount of detail from the picture once you learn the software.

The best cameras have removable lenses and fast burst rates with good stabilization. Sensor size is less important in brighter light and the infinity focus settings we tend to use most. Tilting LCD displays let you hold the camera away from your cage while framing.

Phones have better quality imaging than professional cameras of not-so-many years ago, but there's still a place for large lenses and manual control, especially in low light.

Focus

Pictures are worthless if the subject is blurry. Auto-focus is great if it focuses where you want, otherwise, consider using manual focus at infinity.

Set autofocus to "center spot" (if supported) to allow centering on your subject and holding the button halfway down. That way you can focus, reframe how you want, then push the button down all the way.

Most cameras let you touch the desired focus point on a screen which is great if you have an available hand.

In low light situations it gets harder for the camera to focus. On most models, holding the shutter down halfway makes it "calculate" the shot—setting shutter speed, focusing, and other parameters. Then when you press the button fully, it takes the picture right away.

Sharp Subject, Blurry Background

Professional photographers sometimes blur backgrounds to make their subject stand out. There are two primary ways to do this as shown in Fig 32-2.

Depth of field (DoF) is the range of distances from your subject that are in focus. Large (open) aperture settings (small F-Stop numbers) give a narrow depth of field. So a large DoF (small F-Stop) means that most everything, distant and near, is in focus. A small DoF blurs the background (and foreground). Zooming in decreases DoF, making the background more blurry. An open aperture also lets in more light which means that shutter speed will be higher. Longer focal lengths (the MM value on lens) will be better for blurring the background (will have a narrower DoF).

Dof=Depth of Field

f/1.4
Open aperture
Low f-stop
Narrow DoF
Blurs background

f/5.6
Small aperture
High f-stop
Wide DoF

Other Settings & Tidbits

Auto settings are *normally* good enough, and they leave you free to fly and frame. There are no hard and fast rules, but these guidelines are a good start.

- Only use manual settings if you *really* know what you're doing and the camera allows for quick adjustments. Two exceptions might be setting focus to infinity unless you're doing *very* close work, and using manual exposure when shooting both above and below the horizon.

- Have sufficient light. Once the sun gets too low you must be very steady for pictures to be sharp. Or consider a higher *ISO* number which increases sensitivity but adds *noise*—the grainy distortion that's visible when zoomed in.

- Unless scenery is the star, make your subject at least 50% of the shot. Sometimes, though, having a tiny paraglider for scale adds to the landscape's appeal.

- Be leery of zoom. Autofocus gets easily confused and even slight camera movement blurs the shot. *Do* use zoom when appropriate—it's better to zoom optically than to crop digitally. Take multiple shots at different zooms if possible. Never bother with *digital zoom* where the camera essentially just makes the pixels bigger. Cropping later does the same thing but gives you more control. When capturing another pilot, being close (carefully) almost always looks better than zooming in.

- Wide angle lenses are great for shots that include you or your aircraft.

- Higher resolution gives better frame grabs (video) and the ability to zoom in on an area afterwards.

Fig 32-2 Background Blur

1. **Depth of field** blur. A big sensor, some zoom and an open aperture.

2. **Motion Blur.** Zoom a bit, slow down the shutter speed, then follow the subject.

3. **Control.** For most cameras, controlling shutter speed and aperture require being in "Program" (P).

Digging Deeper: Exposure, the Right Light

Exposure tells a lot about a picture. Underexposed is dark, and over exposed is too light. Anytime you must correct something later, information is lost—try to have the best settings. Three notable attributes affecting exposure:

ISO is the camera's sensitivity to light. A lower ISO number means less sensitivity. A high ISO, say 3200, is very sensitive, meaning it can take pictures with very little light. At the higher end of any sensor's ISO range is more noise—images are splotchy or grainy when enlarged. As technology improves, so does the quality of low light capture.

Shutter speed is how long the shutter stays open. Longer times mean more light. So 1/60th of a second gathers more light than 1/250th but the faster shutter speed will have less motion blur. Really fast shutter speeds can "stop the action." For stationary shooting, a good rule for the slowest shutter speed is to use the lens's focal length in MM as the shutter speed fraction. So a 50 MM lens would be 1/50th of a second. Double that to 1/100th of a second or more if there's much motion.

Aperture is how big the opening is where light comes through and is expressed as *f-stop* or *f-number*, where larger numbers mean a smaller opening. So an f-stop of f1.8 is wide open (many cameras can't open that wide) and f5.6 is a smaller opening. The bigger the aperture (lower number), the more light can pass, which is better for lower light and faster shutter speeds.

Most cameras automatically choose aperture and f-stop based on lighting when you press the shutter button down halfway. Nearly all models also let you change one setting while it adjusts the other. For example, if you want to stop the action in a shot, set a faster shutter speed and let the camera choose an optimum aperture. Auto logic may also adjust the ISO depending on camera setup.

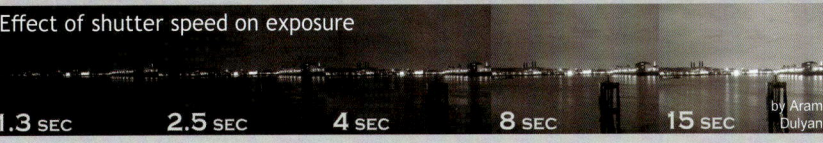

Effect of shutter speed on exposure — 1.3 sec, 2.5 sec, 4 sec, 8 sec, 15 sec — by Aram Dulyan

- Be close and get your subject to do banks and dives for added interest. Of course you must keep flying *your* craft! Look around frequently while flying.

- Generally, try keeping your subject down sun. But sometimes cool effects are had by shooting *into* the sun, especially when it's low, in hazy conditions, or with clouds.

- Try to get the pilot's face, especially if he's looking at you. There are exceptions, of course, and experimenting is half the fun.

- Unless you have specific scenery in mind, try to get a human subject in the shot, especially another PPGer.

- Have something or someone of prominence in the foreground to add interest and scale.

Video

For inflight video, smooth is king and framing is queen. Use the camera's highest resolution. The most amazing shots still come from a talented helmet cam flyer framing artfully, but a well-implemented chase-cam can catch short clips of coolness on ever-cheaper gear. The chapter image (page 301) was from a sports cam.

For stills, consider setting the camera (if supported) to capture at once per half-second or so. Stills usually have higher resolution.

Helmet Cam

You must be able to see what you're framing (Fig 32-8) unless you're using a 360° camera (Fig 32-3). 360 cams are great in that you're shooting everything then framing later, but there's a seam, and resolution goes way down when rendering normal views.

A helmet with sighting viewfinder, either mechanical or electronic, is invaluable. Besides freeing your hands up to fly, it yields better shots since you can see what you're framing. Mounting a wide-angle action cam works without a sight but you'll still want to adjust it to get close. The aimer can be as simple as bending a coat hangar for the sight. **External helmet attachments add risk of line snag.**

Mounted Cams

Some great clips have come from either frame-mounted or line-mounted (chase cam) setups. Given the motion inherent in chase cams, clips will typically be short. Setup is tricky, see Fig 32-7, #4 for some ideas that have proven effective.

Fig 32-3: 360° "Action" Camera

Several cameras record front and back highly-stabilized video to produce a 360° spherical image. They can be used for virtual reality headsets or with special editing tools to produce stunning results.

Many models allow you to pan, tilt and rotate *after* recording. Resolution is lost because you're taking just a piece of what it recorded.

Fig 32-4 Including Frame Part **Fig 32-5 "Hairy Leg Cam."** **Fig 32-6 Drones**

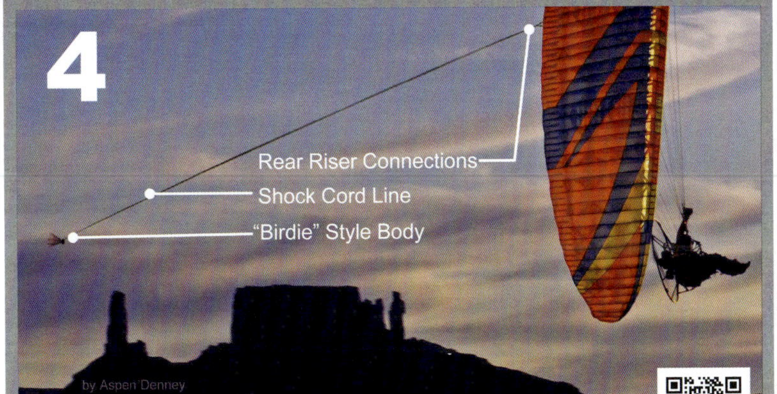

Chapter 32: Photography

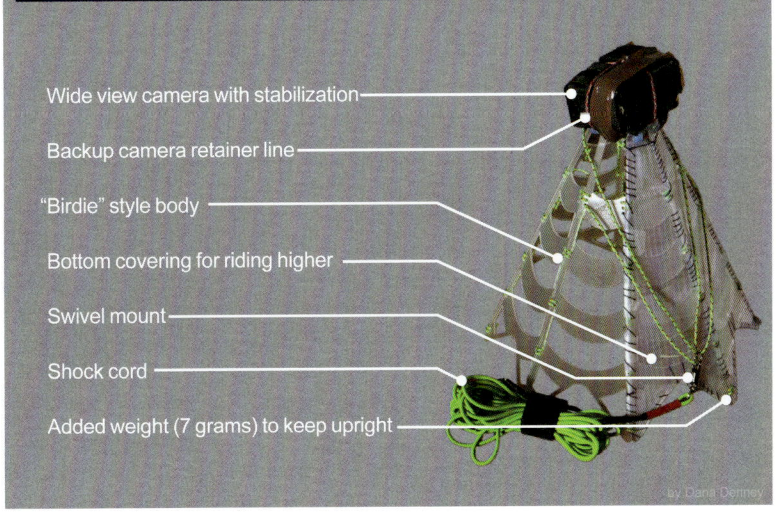

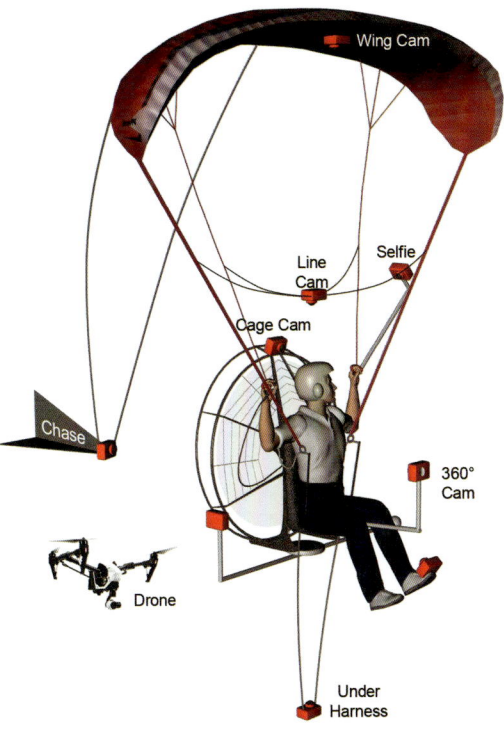

Fig 32-7 Camera Mounting Locations

When connecting *anything* to the frame or wing, consider the affect on flight behavior and other risks, including what could happen in an accident.

A wing cam can be mounted using neodymium magnets on 2 pieces of Coroplast. One piece goes in the wing's cell, the one holding the camera sticks to it from below. Tie a back-up string on the camera.

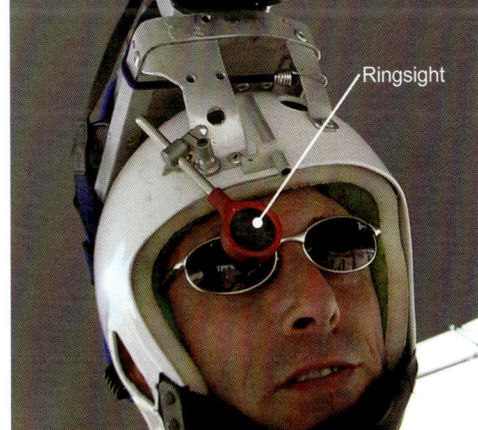

Fig 32-8 Helmet Cam & Sight

Helmet mounts allow regular video cameras which offer more options but require more skill and gear. *Ringsights* show the camera's aim point even if the flyer's eye moves a bit. GoPro-type mounts are much easier, and alignment is not as critical.

Alignment is done by having someone zoom the helmet-mounted camera in on a distant object while you're wearing it. You then adjust the ring sight to be looking at that object. Use your phone if the camera can transmit its image.

Digging Deeper: Pixels and Pictures

Pixels are the colored dots recorded by cameras and displayed on monitors or printed pages. Resolution is the number of pixels horizontally and vertically. More is better up to the point where our eye cannot detect the difference. That's when "more" becomes "marketing." There is some value in more resolution because it allows zooming in after an image or video is recorded.

A one megapixel image has a resolution of 1200 by 800 (1200 dots across by 800 dots down). That looks OK on a monitor, which uses 72 dots per inch (DPI) but is only 4 inches wide in print which uses 300 DPI.

Cameras and monitors use 3 colors per pixel—the same colors our eyes have receptors for: red, green, and blue. An eye's resolution is equivalent to a 25 megapixel camera.

The physics of *print* means that it uses somewhat different colors (Cyan, Magenta, Yellow, and Black). Mostly because these choices allow lighter colors to be printed more accurately.

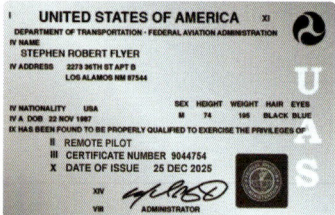

Fig 32-9 Drone License

Drones

Now that first person view (FPV) drones are ubiquitous, there are some cool video opportunities. The person flying the drone can follow you from any position, or maintain slow motion as you fly by. The coolest part is that the drone can capture from in *front* of the paramotor pilot.

Needless to say, with bigger drones the collision risk must be controlled. Hitting a 30 mph drone head on at 30 mph won't do either of you any good, even without the churning props. Have a plan, and only trust experienced drone pilots *or* limit what they do.

In many countries, including the U.S., a drone license (Fig 32-9) is required for any commercial operation, and registration of the drone is required for any flying, private or commercial, if it weighs over a certain amount. These laws change frequently so check the Footflyer.com link from the QR code.

General Tips

A camera *can* be handheld but only do so if it has *really* good stabilization. Weight shift steering is a plus here.

Consider mixing lenses to add interest and capability if possible. The wide angle of action cameras require being very close to subjects other than landscapes.

Hanging small cameras from your wing or other locations can add interest. Be careful launching—making sure you're balanced and the camera stays put.

Formation flying on others while getting stills or video requires extreme vigilance, not only to avoid collisions, but to avoid wake turbulence and ground protrusions.

The following will improve your in-flight video recording:

- Rule #1: Be smooth. If it wiggles, it won't likely make the cut. Great stabilization is essential, but smooth air and smooth camera work really help.
- Be leery of zoom. It often causes violation of Rule #1. Only zoom when you can hold it steady. Even then be ready for throw-away footage.
- Use the widest angle you can get if you're close enough to the subject.
- Frame your subject close. Little gliders, far away, are rarely interesting unless the landscape is compelling. In that regard, gliders can give scale to a scene for added interest.
- Vary the shot. Vary the angle, the zoom, the background, the subject, bank angles, etc. Edited shots rarely exceed 5 seconds without compelling narration.
- Have something in the shot moving relative to the rest of the scene. For example, occasionally having the subject flying by from right to left may be more interesting than following him. Point the camera so that he flies into and out of frame where the background is stationary or slides by slowly.
- Have interesting audio, preferably well-paced narration, and *minimal* motor noise.

Some of the best PPG video is shot on the ground. It's not as much fun to shoot, but does capture the frequently-entertaining launches and landings. Getting experienced pilots to play around on objects also makes for fun video.

Have someone record your own flights for later review and critique. It's an invaluable tool for learning.

Go out and capture the coolest form of flight ever devised. Enjoy!

Appendix - Checklists & Usage

Checklists are on the inside back cover of for quick reference, or for cutting out and using in the field. Paper checklists aren't practical for much of the training environment so don't expect to use them. Your instructor will have some routine to memorize that should include these elements while adding in what's appropriate.

The gold standard of checklists, used by airlines, is *"challenge-response,"* where one pilot reads (challenges) and the other responds as he checks each item. The reader checks, too. So have your copilot read the checklist... oh wait, nevermind. While that obviously won't work for us, you get the idea—be vigilant. The sport is replete with stories of how a simple missed checklist item had severe consequences. And it's easy to forget the whole checklist—build good habit patterns.

Another technique, also used by airlines and many air sports, is to have a flow, where you go from top to bottom, or bottom to top, saying *and checking* each item as you go. Airlines layer a challenge-response on top of flows. Given that we don't have that layer, more vigilance is required.

Pre-Launch and Pre-Landing Checklist

Use the pre-launch checklist (see inside back cover) like this: once you're standing there, ready to launch, but before you've grabbed the A's, run through it by memory. When you get to "brakes and biners," hold out the brakes to see that they're clear to the pulleys and nothing is wrapped up in anything or looks unusual. After doing it by memory, look at the list to see that you've covered everything. Soon you will not need to keep referring to the paper.

The Pre-Launch and Pre-Landing checklists have been designed with a "memory aid," sing-song cadence to improve recall. Try to do it by memory; then refer back to the checklist to see if you've missed anything. It's worth practicing at home once you've had enough training to know what's being checked. Stand there imagining being ready for takeoff and going through the motions. "Leg, leg chest and chin," for example, starts the pre-launch checklist.

Make it Your Own

If you make your own checklist, it should be compact and easy to remember or else it will eventually be discarded. That means **it must be brief**—covering only what's important and rolling easily off the tongue. It's useless if it's not used.

Items may be different based on your machine but these checklists give a good basic plan. If you do not recognize a part name then it probably doesn't apply to you. For preflight checking the motor, start with your carabiners and proceed around. Look for the most obvious items: loose, missing or damaged parts, broken safety wire, etc. If a machine has just been assembled, do a post-assembly inspection as well as a good once-over before flying. A paramotor preflight takes only a minute, and you'll be surprised at what gets uncovered every now and then. Don't skimp on inspections when borrowing gear, either—it's a useful minute.

After flying, clean the machine so you can see cracks or leaks early on. Do a thorough postflight inspection to find problems *now* so they can be fixed before your next session.

These checklists will help know what to look for. Once you're familiar with the flow then the paper checklist becomes optional.

Checklists on inside back cover

Appendix - Resources

Fuel/Oil Mix Chart

Consult your engine maker for recommended types of gas, two-stroke oil, and desired mixes. There are different requirements for breaking in a motor (seating the rings properly) which is normally considered the first 5 hours. This table shows how to mix some common fuel/oil ratios (32:1, 40:1 and 50:1) using the markings on many oil and fuel containers. This may be helpful when the gas and oil container markings are not uniform.

For this quantity of fuel	Add this many **ounces** of oil:			Add this many **milliliters** of oil:		
Ratio →	at 32:1	at 40:1	at 50:1	at 32:1	at 40:1	at 50:1
1 gal.	4.0	3.2	2.6	118	95	76
2 gal.	8.0	6.4	5.1	237	189	151
5 gal.	20.0	16.0	12.8	591	473	379
1 ltr.	1.1	0.8	0.7	31	25	20
2 ltr.	2.1	1.7	1.4	63	50	40
5 ltr.	5.3	4.2	3.4	156	125	100
10 ltr.	10.6	8.5	6.8	313	250	200

Note the crazy English volume units: 1 US Gal = 4 quarts = 8 pints = 128 ounces = 3.785412 liters = 0.832 UK gallons

Metric units: 1 Liter = 1000 milliliters = 0.2641721 US gallon

Repair

The best resource for replacement or repair is the dealer where you bought the gear. It's likely that they know where to look, or what can be substituted. They will also know best whether replacement is necessary. Visit www.FootFlyer.com for updates to resources along with other new information relating to powered paragliding.

Instruction

A valuable resource is www.USPPA.org which lists certified paramotor instructors, including those who are actively giving ratings. That's desirable. In the USA, solo pilot certification programs are run by the U.S. Powered Paragliding Association (USPPA) and U.S. Ultralight Association (USUA). Tandem exemption programs may be run by the USPPA or other organizations but check out their website. FootFlyer.com maintains a section on the current status of training exemptions under Educational, Chapter 1. Check with the organization for your country to find a certified instructor for solo or tandem training.

Welding

Aluminum welding is very specialized and not all shops do it. Even fewer will do it if they know it's for a flying machine. Look in the yellow pages under welding—even if they don't do aluminum, they should know who to call.

When you do find someone to weld, avoid describing its primary function unless it comes up. Some pilots have tried calling it by one of its auxiliary uses such a glorified leaf blower, ski & skate power for the vertically challenged, etc.

Glossary

2-Stroke—A valveless motor with a power stroke every time the piston goes down.

4-Stroke—A valved motor with a power stroke every other time the piston goes down.

A Lines—The first row of paraglider lines; they go from the A riser to the leading edge of the wing.

Absolute Altitude—height above the terrain if you could measure it with a long tape measure.

Accelerator—System used to accelerate the wing using a foot bar connected to the risers, through the harness. The pilot activates it by pushing the bar out with both feet. Also called Speedbar.

Active Flying—The fine control inputs required to keep the wing exactly overhead in turbulence or maneuvering, damping both left/right oscillations and fore/aft surges.

A/FD—Airport Facility Directory. On internet: "digital A/FD"

AGL—Above Ground Level.

ACPUL—Association des Constructeurs de Parapente Ultra Legers. European association that developed test standards for paragliders later adopted by AFNOR.

AFNOR—Association Française de Normalisation, French organization that does certification of paragliders (among many other things).

ASL—Above Sea Level.

ATC—Air Traffic Control, which consists of Approach Controls, Control Towers and Air Route Traffic Control Centers (just called "Center").

Airspeed—Speed through the air. A GPS reads groundspeed; the pilot feels airspeed.

Aspect Ratio—Ratio of the wingspan (projected) to the average chord.

Asymmetrical Collapse—When one side of the wing deflates and not the other. It is the most common paraglider malady that results from turbulence.

Asymmetric Blade Thrust—see P-Factor.

Asymmetric Spiral—A spiral dive where the bank on one side of the circle is shallower than the other.

B-lines—The second row of paraglider lines; they go from the B riser to the wing.

B-line Stall—A condition where the wing is stalled by virtue of the pilot pulling the B-lines down to his chest. Descent rate is usually about 4 times normal.

Big Ears—A maneuver where the pilot pulls the outer A lines such that the tips of the wing fold downward to increase descent rate.

Brake Lines—Lines that go from the brake toggles, through a pulley or loop on the rear riser, and up to the trailing edge of the wing.

Brake Toggles—The handles used by the pilot to control the craft. They attach to the brake lines.

C Lines—The third row of lines; goes from the C riser to the wing.

Canopy—Another name for the wing.

Carabiners—Metal fasteners that attach the wing, through its riser loops, to the harness.

Cart—Wheeled assembly that allows for a rolling launch.

Cascade—The split in a wing's lines where it spreads from one line to several as it goes up to the wing. This design feature reduces the total line count and resulting drag.

Cells—A single sewn section of a wing containing air that makes up the airfoil shape.

CEN—Comitee of the European standards organization that set certification standards for paragliders (among other things).

CHT—Cylinder Head Temperature.

Check the Wing—Apply brakes to stop it's forward motion, usually to prevent it from overflying and front-tucking..

CIMA—International Microlight Commission of FAI.

Clip-In Weight—The pilot weight plus motor, fuel, and any accessories necessary to fly. Aka hook-in weight.

Chord—The distance from the leading edge to trailing edge at any point along the span.

Collapse—What happens when part or all of the wing deforms (aka fold or deflation) due to turbulence or pilot input.

Constant Stall—see Parachutal Stall.

Crab—Heading some amount into the wind to maintain a desired ground track.

Damping/Dampen—Control input required to reduce roll or pitch oscillation.

Deck Angle—see Pitch.

Deflation—see Collapse.

Density Altitude—Altitude adjusted for pressure, temperature, and humidity. Hot, humid air hurts aircraft performance—it is said to be at a higher density altitude. Aircraft performance is based on density altitude, not the actual altitude as read on an altimeter.

DHV—German Hanggliding and Paragliding Federation "Deutcher Hangeleiter Verband." They certify free flight paragliders, harnesses and related equipment in Germany. This is the most common service used to certify paragliders.

DULV—German Ultralight Flight organization that certifies paramotors and paramotor wings designed for paramotoring.

Downwind Demon—Series of illusions that frequently lead to a pilot pulling too much brake when low to the ground and turning downwind.

EN—European Standards organization. See also CEN.

FAI—Fédération Aéronautique International. The world's Air Sports Federation. See also CIMA.

FAR—Federal Aviation Regulations; governing law for paramotor pilots in the USA.

Float Bowl Carburetor—A type of carburetor that uses a float to regulate fuel level in the bowl.

Fold—See collapse.

FPM—Feet Per Minute. A measure of climb or descent rate.

Full Stall—An extreme maneuver where the pilot pulls enough brake to deform the wing so much that slows dramatically and deforms the glider and is characterized with a very high descent rate.

Forward Inflation—Any inflation done while facing away from the wing and into the wind; usually done in light winds.

Front Tuck—see frontal.

Frontal—A wing deformation where the leading edge folds downward. Maintained in this state, the wing will descend about 3 times the normal rate.

Free Flyer—One who flies without a motor; a paraglider pilot. They generally seek out natural lift sources and launch from high places or get towed in aloft.

GA—General Aviation; all aviation that is not military, governmental, or scheduled airlines.

Gyroscopic Precession—The characteristic of any rotating mass whereby a force acting perpendicular to the direction of rotation will cause the reaction 90 degrees in the direction of rotation.

Harness—The combination of fabric and straps that holds the pilot up in flight through an attachment to the wing and also what the motor is attached to.

Glossary

Helicopter—One of several aerobatic maneuvers where the pilot is spinning around an axis other than the center of the wing.

Latitudinal (Lateral) Axis—An imaginary left/right line around which the PPG pitches up or down. The extended arms of a seated pilot represent the lateral axis direction, but the axis itself is between the pilot and wing.

Leading Edge—Front of the wing where the cell openings are.

Longitudinal Axis—An imaginary front-to-back line around which the PPG rolls (banks).

Horseshoe—When referring to a paraglider, the wing deformation where the wingtips come forward and may touch each other. Descent rate is usually about 4 times normal.

Loop—A high energy aerobatic maneuver where the pilot uses speed from a steep spiral to fly over the top of the glider.

Maillon—see quick link.

Membrane Carburetor—A type of carburetor that uses a membrane to regulate fuel flow.

Mechanical Turbulence—Random swirls of air downwind of a solid object (building, hill, mountain, etc.).

MSL—Mean Sea Level. Usually is used in reference to altitudes above sea level (ASL).

NOTAM—Notice To Airmen.

Outlanding—Landing somewhere other than intended, usually after an engine failure.

Over-The-Nose Spiral—A spiral dive where the wing is pointed nearly straight down. Recovery can be problematic.

P-Factor—Asymmetric force caused by a prop that is not acting perpendicular to the relative wind.

PK System—see STI (speedbar/trimmer interconnect).

Parablend—An expensive Nylon/Kevlar cocktail that is stirred via propeller. Frequently served after an aborted launch.

Parachutage—see Parachutal Stall.

Parachutal Stall—A stall where the fully-formed wing stops flying forward and descends like an old round parachute.

Parasite—Location where powered paragliding takes place.

Pendulum—The left right swinging action that occurs whenever the glider is upset laterally.

Pitch—Motion around the PPG's latitudinal axis. The pilot is said to Pitch up when power is added.

PLF—Parachute Landing Fall.

PPG—Powered Paraglider

Pressure Altitude—Pressure represented as an altitude, assuming a standard atmosphere. It is also the altitude indicated on your altimeter when set to 29.92 in Hg. See also Density Altitude.

Propeller—The long skinny blade that provides propulsion.

Quick Link—The steel ring that connect the wing's A, B, C, or D lines to their respective riser. The usually use screw-together gates.

Rear Riser—The aftmost riser. On 3-riser wings, it is the C riser. On 4-riser wings it is the D riser.

Reverse Inflation—Any inflation started while facing the wing instead of the wind. Usually done in stronger wind.

Riser Loops—The loops at the very bottom of each riser where the carabiner goes through.

Riser Set—The combination of individual A, B, C and D risers and their corresponding loop for each side of the wing that connect to the harness through a carabiner and lines through quick links.

Roll—Motion around the PPG's longitudinal axis.

Rotor—The swirling air that results from wind blowing around an obstacle.

S.A.T.—"Safety Acrobatic Team" maneuver where the glider and pilot appear to be rotating around each other.

SHV—Swiss paraglider certifying agency of the Swiss Hang gliding Association.

STI—Speedbar/Trimmer Interconnect, aka PK System.

Speedbar—see Accelerator.

Spiral Dive—An extreme banked turn where the wing is angled towards the ground. See also "Over-The-Nose" spiral dive.

Stall—see Full Stall.

Surge—The characteristic of the wing to overfly the pilot under some conditions. It can be induced by pilot action or turbulence.

Stabilo Line—Line that goes to the wing's tip, usually a B-line.

Tell Tale—A small wind indicator, usually a streamer of some sort.

Torque—The property of a motor/propeller that makes the motor, and its harnessed occupant, want to twist in the opposite direction of propeller spin.

Torque Induced Lockout—A condition where angled thrust pushes the pilot sideways, and into a bank the other way. Lockout is reached when brake pressure alone cannot compensate for the resulting turn.

Trailing Edge—The rearmost part of the wing when in flight.

Trimmers—Mechanism of some risers (usually on motoring wings) that allows changing the rear risers to increase speed. The pilot pulls a "Trim Tab" to effect the change.

Trim Speed—The speed that results when flying with no brakes applied, trimmers in their cruise setting, and no speedbar.

True Airspeed—Actual speed through the air as opposed to what it feels like to the pilot. At high elevations, the pilot must move faster through the air to get the same feel as at lower elevations.

True Altitude—Altitude above sea level if you could measure it with a long ruler. see also absolute altitude.

Turtle—The occurrence when a pilot falls backward such that he is lying on top of the motor, unable to move until un-clipping from the unit.

Vertical Axis—an imaginary top-to-bottom line around which the PPG yaws (twists left or right).

Virga—Precipitation that evaporates before reaching the ground.

VOR—Very High Frequency (VHF) Omni Directional Range used for navigation or reference points by airplane pilots.

Waypoint—point on the surface used for navigation.

Windmilling—The spinning of a prop due solely to the relative wind blowing through it.

Wind Shadow—A calm that exists downwind of obstructions.

Wing—The means to our magic.

Wing Fold—see Collapse.

Wing Over—A series of turns in concert with the natural pendular bank rate of the glider.

Yaw—Motion around the PPG's vertical axis. If the PPG rotates to the left without banking it is said to yaw to the left.

Index

2D steering 263
2-stage
flare 67
speedbar 118
throttle change 62
turn 62
2-stroke motor 232
3-axis control 260
3-line glider 17
3-wheel 69
4-line glider 17
4-stroke motor 232
4-wheel 69
100LL 42

A

A-assists 69, 70, 71
abort 52
launch 48, 56, 59, 60, 72
AC 90-66 105
accelerated 181
accessories 23
accordion fold 39
active piloting 162, 167, 184, 191, 215, 218, 264, 266
description 166
adiabatic lapse rate 246
ADIZ 95
aerobatics 179
aerodynamic airflow redirection 241. See also lamels
aerodynamics 221–230
aeronautical charts. See sectional charts
AFNOR 266
Agonic line 137
A-helpers 71. See A-assists
Air Defense Identification Zones 95
airfoil 13, 16, 227
airlines 9
airport
flying at 104
patterns 105
airspace 91–100
airspace classes 92
airspeed 225
indicator 282
trim speed 161
all-up weight 17, 262
altimeter 22, 113, 224, 283
watch 139
altimetry 283
altitude
cruising 64
pattern 64
anemometer 282
angle of attack. See AoA
angle of incidence. See AoI
anhedral curvature 225
anti-torque strap 18, 116, 117, 180, 197
AoA 182, 221, 227, 228. See angle of attack
AoI 225, 227, 228, 267
Aramid 16, 17. See also Kevlar
articulating bars. See swing arm
A's and Brakes
kiting 149

A's and Rears
kiting 149
aspect ratio 182, 226, 227, 241, 266
A's, split 29
asymmetric blade thrust 243
asymmetric spiral dive 184
asymmetric wing fold 50
athletic. See physical
ATIS 110
avgas 42
axis of motion
basic 49
complete 223

B

balked landing. See go-around
band, power 155, 232
banners 292
batteries
Lip 271
belt drive 121
belt tightening 121
Bernoulli 221, 226
big air 50, 167, 250
big ears 182
B-line
for AoI 225, 227, 228
stall 182, 184, 199, 200
boat
for transporting 68
for wind direction 65
towing 6
bolt
grades 123
tightening 120, 124
braiding fold 40
brake
position 26, 163, 188, 192, 223
position illustration 26
brake lines 8, 16, 28, 127, 128, 148, 149, 150, 151, 156
Brummel Hooks 16. See sister clips
buckles 20
bump scale
graphic 61
use 144, 164

C

calm 27, 31, 44, 56, 57, 58, 65, 67, 74, 78, 79, 80, 81, 82, 102, 103, 173, 248, 250, 254
inflation 27
camber 221
camber line 226
camera
action 302
follow-me 300
camping 140
carabiners 17, 21, 22, 23, 32, 43, 115, 116, 118, 130, 131
carbon build up 46
carburetor 233–244
diaphram. See carburetor, membrane
float bowl 43, 235
membrane 234
tuning 234–244
carry strap 117
cart 18, 69, 71, 72, 74, 154
flipping 69

catching suspended targets 165
cattle herding 293
center cell visibility 264
center of drag 222
center of gravity. See CG
certification
DGAC 266
instructor 3, 5, 89
pilot 2, 12, 304
tandem 4, 269
wing 115, 127, 262, 264, 266
CG 69, 72, 239
hang point & thrust line 239
challenge-response 303
charts. See aeronautical charts
chart supplements. See airport/facility directory, AFD
checklist 55, 303
chicken strap. See sternum strap
children 3
choke 235
chord line 227
CHT 22, 282
cleaning 68
for air travel 295
wing 37
climb 61, 174
angle 103
best rate 172
for free flyers 212
illusion 193
clip-in weight 17, 262. See also weight range
clouds 250
cumulus 79
cloud suck 200
cloverleaf 206–208
clubs 109
clutch 122, 234
CNC 13
collapse 13, 181, 229, 262
asymmetric 185
while accelerated 51
comfort bar 19
communications 24, 144
competition 181, 205–210
demonstration 210
compression release 236
concertina Bag 39
cone of glide range 202
constant stall. See parachutal stall
control
basic 62
control tower 110
control, two stage 63
convergence zone 81
coordinated turn 160, 167, 180, 186
cost 13
cravat 50, 51, 185
clearing 188
critical angle of attack 229
crooked inflation 157, 158
cross armed reverse 156
crosswind 65, 73, 158
for base leg 66
inflation 158
launching 174

cruise control 21, 46, 200
cuise control 43
customs 300
cylinder head temperature. See CHT

D

DAGC certification 266
daisy chain folding 40
Deathblade 218
default emergency reaction 54
deflating 26, 37, 150
density altitude 72, 78, 171, 172, 270
depower wing 155. See also deflating
descent techniques 182–188
designing for thrust 238
DHV 1 - 3 266
diaper buckle 20
diaper (reserve). See deployment bag
diaphragm carburetor 233
difficult sites 171
direct drive 20, 237
ditching 191, 197
downplaning 53
downwind demon 193
drag 17, 222, 223–230
drowning 143

E

efficiency 13, 70, 206, 214, 222, 224, 228
under power 225
EGT 22, 282
electric propulsion 243
electric start 271
emergencies 47–54
radio failure 48
situational 197
EN A - D 266
endurance
competition 209
energy state 163
engine
failure 50, 61, 141, 166, 173, 174, 189, 192, 201, 214, 293
starting 46
engine instruments 282
equipment
choosing 9
ethanol in fuel 42
events, sporting 95
exercise 10
exhaust gas temperature. See EGT
expansion chamber. See tuned pipe
expensive 13
experience and skill 158
experience, previous 11

F

FAA
AC for frequencies 24
advisory circulars 88
certified pilots 77
governing airspace 85
inspectors 89
on congested 87, 88

on trespass 87
on violations 90
fabric
   wing 13
face plant 191, 212
FAI 205
failure 49
Fan Man 257
FCC 281
feel position 63
first flight 11
flags 292
flapping, spot landing 177
flare 67
flash starter 121, 234, 271
flight service (FSS) 83, 84, 95, 106, 109, 134, 253
flipping (cart) 69
float bowl carburetor 233
flotation
   inflatable 197
Fly Henry Meter 282
folding 39
fontal collapse 185
foot-drag 105, 159, 164, 169, 226
   description 164
   risk 190
   water 189
footwear 24
force, bolt tightening 120
forces in flight 221–230
formation flying 141, 142, 144, 165, 165–170, 194
   radio 281
   video 302
form drag 222
forward
   inflation 27, 28
   launch no power 57
   launch partial power 56
   launch troubleshooting 58, 59
   partial power 57
frangible propeller 239
free flight 13, 17
   transition 211
frontal collapse 176, 182, 185
fronts (weather) 251
front tuck. See frontal collapse
frustration 11
FSS 83
fuel
   fill pump 42
   storage 274
fueling 42
   at gas station 210
fuel line 121
   securing 121
full stall 229

G

gas
   shipping 300
gauges
   multifunction 282
geared 240
gear oil 237
gear ratio 237
gear reduction 122
geometry of paramotor 239
G-force 52, 183
glide 223–230
   cone of range 202
   controlling 67
   ratio 64

stretching 201, 202
glider. See wing
glide ratio
   in wind 64
glide ratios 214
gloves 152
go-around 48, 66, 162, 174, 180, 203, 217
go around (verb) 48, 174
gooseneck. See s-arm
GPS 22, 87, 90, 99, 108, 133, 134, 139, 140, 283
grant assurances 99, 105
grease 237
ground handling. See kiting
ground handling straps 19, 117, 180, 275
groundspeed 194
ground track 64, 65, 194, 202
gunslinger A Grab 29
gust front 198
gyroscopic precession 241

H

HAM license 281
handling 264
hands up to go up 58, 61, 194
hand towing 7
hang angle 70, 116
hang check 41, 70
hang glider trike 260
hanging from leg straps 46
harness 18, 19, 20, 22, 41, 115, 116, 130, 148
   buckles 20
   ground handling 19
Harness Hang Syndrome. See Suspension Trauma
hazmat 295
hearing protection 24
helicopter (maneuver) 179
helicopter pilot 11
helmet 24, 27, 144
helmet cam 300, 301
high density altitude 104, 171–178
high hook-in 19, 116, 275
high wind
   landing 155
   reverse 59
hike & fly wings 261
hill 8
hook-in
   adjustment 116
   attachment low 116
   bar attachment 116
   hard point 118
   reversed 33
   reversed alternate 34
hook knife 24
horsepower 232
hot and high 172
hunter's smoke 282
hybrid glider (surfaces) 261
hybrid wing 261

I

IATA 297
illusions
   climb 193
imbalance, prop 123
incidence, angle of 267
inflation 57, 65
   assisted motor 153

crooked 31, 158
cross-arm 156
crosswind 158
forward 26, 30
forward light wind 56
reverse 32, 35, 37
reverse high winds 59
riser only 35
salvaging 157
inflation type chart 58
in-flight weight 17
inglefield clips 16. See sister clips
inner bag. See deployment bag
instructing 5
instructor
   finding 3
   score sheet 12
instruments
   engine 22
insurance 2
intercepting 166
intermediate syndrome 191
isogonic line 137

J

J bars 18, 19, 20, 22, 41, 115, 116, 130, 148
jiggle pump 42
judgment 158
jump height (reserve) 279

K

Kevlar 16, 17, 44, 128. See also Aramid
kick-in bar 117
kill button 271
   failure 51
kiting 10, 11, 12, 147, 196
   A's & Brakes 149
   competition 210
   forward 33
   harness 22
   higher wind 5
   rear riser 152
   reverse 35
   reversed - straight risers 36
   riser only 35
   upside down 147
   war 25
   wing 266
   with the A's 156
Kollsman Window 283

L

lamel 118, 241, 243
landing
   high wind 155, 199
   in a tree 200
   lee side 202
   one-step 169
   pattern 66, 175
   power-off 170
   power-off one-step 170
   power-off swoop 168
   power-on 169
   priorities 201
   problems 65
   slider 168
   spot 175, 176
   swoop 168
   turbulence 175
lapse rate 246
launch 55–68
   crosswind 174
   differences 212
   engine-out 174

high elevation 174
steering during run 173
wheel 71
leading edge 13
LED lighting 284
lee side landing 202
leg drag 172
leg loops - forgetting 51
license 3
lift
   orographic 83
   ridge 83
liftweb 115
light wind 27. See also calm
   inflations 155
line
   break 17
   unsheathed 17
lines 14
loaded riser twist 60, 240
locator, satellite 284
locking in, spiral 184
lockout 7
   motor-induced 51, 61
longitudinal axis 225, 228
look, lean, turn 142
low hook-in 275
   adjustment 116

M

maillons 17. See also quick links
maintenance
   ease of 274
maneuvers
   advanced 179–188
maneuvers clinic 177, 179
maneuvers course 181–188, 190
marginal gear 171
materials for props 239
Mean Aerodynamic Chord 226
mechanical turbulence 103, 253
membrane carburetor 235
microbursts 80
midair collision 52, 66, 194
   avoidance 66, 142
   impending 203
   risk 142
mid-day 181
Mike Byrne 256
military airspace 95
minimum sink 163, 224
miniwing 265
mirror 22, 63, 72, 134
misty flips 179
mixture
   fuel 233
   fuel/air/oil 42
model aircraft finding 294
motor 9, 164
   2-stroke 232–244
   4-stroke 232
   adjustment 41
   features 13
   longevity 232
motor failure. See engine failure
motor-induced lockout 51
mountain 254
   waves 254
mountainous 5
mountain waves 254
muffler 43
multifunction meters 282
Multimedia 9

trim 161
speedbar 16, 17, 28, 44, 51, 54, 63, 65, 117, 130, 163, 167, 176, 181, 182, 186, 225, 227, 265
  in competition 207
  ladder type 118
  pulleys & leverage 268
  setup 117, 181
  two-stage 118
  usage 181
speedbar/trimmer interconnect 44, 181, 265, 267
speed control 63
speedflying wing 265
spin 61, 185
spinner, prop 238
spiral dive 183, 192
  as risk 191
  asymmetric 184
  caution 50
  reserve deployment 52
  round 183
  round (illustration) 182
split A's 17, 30
sporting equipment 300
spot landing 175, 176, 185, 218
  competition 208
  extending glide 177
  landing priorities 201
  over obstruction 177
  touchdown 168
spreader
  thrust 19
stabilo 267
  accidental pull 182
  pull for cravat 185
  pull in cravat 50
  steering 181, 188, 263, 268
stall 229
  full 229
  parachutal 182, 186, 229
stamina 10
start button 271
starter
  flash 271
starting the motor 46, 191
steep turn
  level 184
steerable reserve 23, 132, 279
steering, rear riser 181
steering the launch 173
sternum strap 19, 116, 117, 197
STI. See speedbar/trimmer interconnect
streamer 293
stretching glide 67, 201, 202
strobe for visibility 284
suitcases 296
surges 160
suspension 18
suspension lines 14
suspension trauma 61
swing arm
  setup 115
switch, kill 9
swoop landing 168
syllabus 4, 8
symmetrical airfoil 222

T

tachometer 22
tailwind 171
takeoff 173–178
  distance 103

tandem 2, 3, 4, 5, 7, 8, 12, 69
  cart 74
  exemption 74
  free flight 218
  introductory flight 4
  wheel 4, 5
target fixation 65
TBO 272
temporary flight restriction. See TFR
tension 226
tension on lines 221
terminal forecasts 83
testing
  paramotor 288
TFR 83, 91, 95, 96, 97, 134. See Temporary Flight Restriction
thermalling 213, 214, 215
thermals 56, 79, 167, 209, 246, 247, 248, 249, 250
  illustration 247
  telling intensity 250
  trigger theory 249
throttle
  cable caught 48
  check 43
  failure (rescue) 144
  milking 201
  overview 21
  simulator 8, 11, 12, 27, 30, 32, 34, 56
thrust
  offset 240, 241
  vectoring 228
thrust spreader 19
thunderstorm 245, 251
tilt. See AoI
tip speed
  prop 238
tip steering 16, 18, 63, 65
tip vortices. See wingtip vortices
torque
  bolt tightening 120
  forces 240
  loaded riser twist 240
  reduction 118
  twist on launch 213
tower airport talk 110
towing 6, 7
towing banners 292
tracking 124
training
  duration 10
  process 3
  towing 6
training risk 191
transition area 100
transportation
  as 291
transporting gear 68
trapped
  thrusting motor 144
trauma, suspension 256
travel
  via road 298
  with gear 295–300
traveling
  bus lines 300
tree
  landing 200
  rescue 200, 284
trimmers 15, 16, 17, 31, 44, 65, 225, 227, 265
  adjusting brakes 127, 128
  avoiding parachutal 54

crooked inflations 158
exaggerated slider 168
  for descent 182
  for forward 58
  for glide 67
  for hot and high 172
  for landing 65
  for min sink 163
  for surge exercise 188
  for takeoff 57
  for trim speed 161
  for wingovers 187
  preflight check 44
  reflex wing 65
  replaced risers 126
  set for turbulence 49, 166–167
  spot landing 176
  usage 63
  with speedbar 181
trim speed 161, 194, 223, 224
troubleshooting 120
  forward launch 144
  landing problems 65
true airspeed 140
true north 137
tuned pipe 119, 232
turbulence 7, 49, 64, 79, 80, 81, 103, 107, 166, 185, 188, 253, 254
  handling 186
  mechanical 253
  precision flying 162
  thermal 218
  wind turbine 80
turn 64, 228
  coordinated 180
  for wingovers 186
  hook 169
  illusion 194
  in formation 166
  look lean turn 142
  two-stage 62
  weight shift 180–188
turn-around direction 33
turn-around pulley 6, 7
twist, loaded riser 58
twist, riser 185
two-seater. See tandem

U

underarm bars 19
unload (wing) 155, 181, 184, 186, 187, 188, 196
  speedbar 181
unsheathed lines. See line, unsheathed
unsupported Races 210
untangling 27
USHPA.org 24
USPPA 3, 4, 5, 6, 12, 74, 76, 89, 205, 260, 304
UV exposure 13, 68, 266

V

valves 232
variation (magnetic) 137
variometer 23
vehicle 86
vibration 201
viewfinder
  ringsight 300
virga 198, 253
Virtual FootFlyer 9
V layout 28
V of crossed risers 153
VOR 83, 97
vortices (tip)

wingtip 107, 184

W

wake turbulence 64, 107, 143, 184
wall (kiting) 33, 59, 157
water
  landing 197
  rescuing from 143
  salt 38
  skiing 291
weather forecast 83, 245
  for aviation 83
webbing 13
weighted frame 9
weightlessness 221
weight range
  paraglider 262
  terms 17
weight shift 63, 182
  free flight 216
  turn 180–188
wet adiabatic lapse rate 246
wet wing 200
wheel brakes 69
wheel launch. See cart
wheels 8, 18, 69. See also carts
wilderness area 95
winch 6
wind
  gradient 194
  indicators 282
  light 37
  shadow 254
winds aloft 83
wind shear 82
wind turbine turbulence 80
wing 13, 225–230, 261–268
  anomalies 184
  beginner 264
  depower 155
  durability 13
  folding 39
  folding - daisy chain 40
  folding - halves 40
  for training 9
  loading 229, 262–268
  longevity 13
  maintenance 126
  older 30
  oscillation 228
  overview 13
  size 262
  speed 264
  storing 38
wingover 160, 183, 184, 186, 191, 192, 229
  illustration 187
  twisting 187
wingtip drag 183
wingtip vortices 222
wires
  obstruction 102, 103, 104, 133, 144
  rescue 143, 200

Z

zip ties 121
zone, shear 82
ZorbX 295

music 281

N
NAA.aero 205
naked pilot weight 17
navigation 24, 135
Newton 221
noise 214
noise abatement 86
nosewheel 70
nylon, ripstop 13
nylon rods 261

O
obstructions 103, 174
oil 119
  for redrives 121
  selection & mixing 42
  shipping 300
optical tachometer 282
orographic lift 83
oscillation
  damping 166
  in turbulence 167
  landing 65
  roll 61
  roll - cart 74
overcontrol 47
over-propped 238

P
Paap Kolar 265
packaging
  paramotor 296
Pagen, Dennis 54
parachutal 191, 229
parachute landing fall 54
paraglider. See wing
paramotor
  general description 13
parawaiting 5
partial power
  launch 56
pattern
  aircraft-style 66
  aircraft vs paraglider 175
  airport 105, 106, 110
  altitude 64
  choosing direction 103
  landing 46, 103, 175
pendular control 186–188
pendular period 62
pendular precision 160
pendulum 62
penetrating airspace 201
performance 221–230
period of swing 62
permission 86, 87, 91, 101, 104
  controller 92, 100, 109, 110
  legal 85
  vs forgiveness 298
personal locator beacon 284
P-factor 243
physical requirements 2
pilot-induced oscillations.
    See PIO
PIO 51, 62, 167. See
    also oscillations
piston 232
pitch
  control 161
  of prop 22
  prop 237
pivoting S-arms. See s-arm
pixels 302

PK System. See speedbar/trimmer interconnect
placard weight 262
plastic rods. See nylon rods
platforms for carrying 298
PLF 54
polar curve 230
pop-off pressure 235
porosity 13, 37
postflight 68
posture 50, 153
  for landing 67
  inflight 63
  kiting 35, 153
  launch 56
power band
  motor 237
  wing 26, 35, 150
powered parachute 69, 70, 89, 110, 226, 258, 260
  wings 70
power lines. See wires
PPC. See powered parachute
practice throttle 27, 28, 32, 34, 59
preflight inspection 43
pre-launch checklist 303
previous experience 11
probability 189
  risk 190
profile, airfoil. See airfoil shape
projected wing area 227
prop case 296, 297
propeller 236
  balance - aerodynamic 123
  balancing 123
  blast 142
  bolts 123
  efficiency 237
  imbalance 236
  maintenance 122–132
  noise 236
  puzzle 296
  repair 125
  spinner 238
  tape 124, 125
  tip speed 238
  tracking 124
prop stopper 45, 299
PTT 24
pull start 119, 234, 236, 271, 278, 296
  flash 122
  problems 119
  surviving 46
push-to-talk. See PTT
puzzle props 296
pylon race 159, 163, 206, 210
  wings 263, 265

Q
quick links 17, 128

R
race (pylon). See pylon race
race (unsupported) 210
radio 9
  aircraft 93, 98, 107, 109, 114
  at SIV clinic 190
  commands 47
  compatibility 281
  failure 46, 48
  for formation 141, 144, 165
  free flight 281
  helmet compatibility 281

instructions by 8, 47, 63
rain 200
rating. See also certification
  instructor 5, 12
  pilot 4, 294
rear riser 17
  deflation 26
  kiting 152
  steering 48
reduce power, reduce brakes... 47, 48, 50, 51, 52, 54, 143, 184, 185, 186, 213
reduction drive 43, 121, 236, 237
  belt 121
  gear 122
  gear ratio 237
reed valve 235, 236
reflex 13, 17, 181, 262
  cross section 16
reflex airfoils 227
reflex wing 65
reliability 271
rescue parachute. See reserve
reserve
  care 131, 132
  clinic 53
  deployment 52
  jump height equivalant 279
  mounting 23, 131
  mounting examples 131
  mounting & mx 130–132
  practice 47, 53
  preflight 44
  repacking 131
  Rogallo-style 23
  round 23
  steerable 23, 279
  types 279
  under seat 131
reverse
  carts 154
  cross-armed 156
  high wind 59
  hook-in 33
  inflation 59
  light wind 155
  single-hold 155
  troubleshooting 59
reversing pulley. See turnaround pulley
Reynolds Number 224
ridge
  lift 83
  rules 215
  shape 254
right-of-way
  freeflight 215
ringsight 301
ripstop fabric 14
riser attachment. See hook-in
riser kiting 33, 35, 148
riser-only inflation 35
risers 15, 17, 268
  replacing 126
riser spread 115–132
riser twist 51, 52, 60, 179
risk 191–204
  cart vs footlaunch 74
  probability & severity 190
  propeller 191
  training 191
Risk & Reward 10
roll oscillation prevention 161
roll oscillation recovery 160
rollover 73, 74, 280

rollover (cart) 70, 72
roll recovery 160
rope trick 45
rosette 38, 40, 67, 154
  illustration 39
rotational mass acceleration 240
rotor 83
rotor turbulence 253
round spiral dive 182, 183
runup 45, 46, 204
runup rack 298
runways
  airport 106

S
SafeStart 43, 278
safety ring 45
sailplane 264
s-arm 13, 19, 180. See
    also swing arm
  failure 115
  strap 116
SAT 179
Saucisse bag 39
school 4, 5, 7, 8, 23, 24, 33, 76, 99, 108
  choosing 3, 4
score sheet - instructor 12
SCUBA 283
sea breeze 10, 79, 81, 248, 249
seatboard
  mechanics 60
seated
  getting 61
sectional charts 91, 97–100, 137
security airspace 95
severity 189
shackle
  soft 21
shadow for collision risk 142
Shatner, William 10
shipping 295
  as freight 300
  packaging 296
simulator 8, 9, 41
  throttle 8, 56
single surface glider 261
sink rate 224
siphoning fuel 42
sister clip 15, 16
site
  challenging 171
  launch choices 102
situational awareness 195
SIV 177, 181. See maneuvers cource
skill & experience 158
skydiver 11
skyvector.com 91
slider landing 168
slipstream 167, 227
soaring 7, 84
  motor 271
  transition from motors 214
soaring pilots 83, 211
soft shackle 21
Solo 210 237
Spare Air 283
speed
  of wings 264
  system 17